NOVEL & SHORT STORY WRITER'S MARKET

2017

includes a one-year online subscription to **Novel & Short Story Writer's Market** on

THE ULTIMATE MARKET RESEARCH TOOL FOR WRITERS

To register your *Novel & Short Story Writer's Market 2017* book and **start your one-year online genre-only subscription**, scratch off the block below to reveal your activation code, then go to www.WritersMarket.com. Find the box that says "Purchased a Deluxe Edition?" then click on "Activate Your Account" and enter the activation code. It's that easy!

UPDATED MARKET LISTINGS FOR YOUR INTEREST AREA

EASY-TO-USE SEARCHABLE DATABASE • RECORD-KEEPING TOOLS

PROFESSIONAL TIPS & ADVICE • INDUSTRY NEWS

Your purchase of *Novel & Short Story Writer's Market* gives you access to updated listings related to this genre of writing (valid through 12/31/17). For just $9.99, you can upgrade your subscription and get access to listings from all of our best-selling Market Books. Visit **www.WritersMarket.com** for more information.

36TH ANNUAL EDITION

NOVEL & SHORT STORY WRITER'S MARKET

2017

Rachel Randall, Editor

WRITER'S DIGEST
BOOKS
WritersDigest.*com*
Cincinnati, Ohio

Publisher: Phil Sexton

Writer's Market website: www.writersmarket.com
Writer's Digest website: www.writersdigest.com

Distributed in Canada by Fraser Direct
100 Armstrong Avenue
Georgetown, Ontario, Canada L7G 5S4
Tel: (905) 877-4411

Distributed in the U.K. and Europe by F&W Media International
Brunel House, Newton Abbot, Devon, TQ12 4PU, England
Tel: (+44) 1626-323200, Fax: (+44) 1626-323319
E-mail: postmaster@davidandcharles.co.uk

ISSN: 0897-9812
ISBN-13: 978-1-4403-4775-7
ISBN-10: 1-4403-4775-1

Attention Booksellers: This is an annual directory of F + W Media, Inc.
Return deadline for this edition is December 31, 2017.

Edited by: Rachel Randall
Designed by: Alexis Estoye
Production coordinated by: Debbie Thomas

CONTENTS

MARKETS

RESOURCES

INDEXES

FROM THE EDITOR

PHOTO: STACEY DOWNEY

"Oh, I'm a terrible public speaker."

I was sitting in the hotel lobby after a long day of working at our annual conference. Phil Sexton, the publisher of Writer's Digest—and my boss—had just asked me if I'd ever consider speaking at one of our events.

The thought of standing at a podium and addressing an audience nearly made me hyperventilate. I had no desire to explore the realm of public speaking in any capacity.

Sometimes it takes a catalyst to shake us of our insecurities. Other times, a quiet nudge will do. A year later, Phil asked me if I'd like to attend the San Francisco Writers' Conference, and I quickly said yes. But I soon discovered that the invitation came with a caveat: I'd have to speak on a few panels.

I was filled with absolute terror. But what could I do? So I brushed up on my publishing knowledge, practiced speaking slowly and calmly in front of a mirror, and read every article I could find about overcoming stage fright. Then I went to the conference, and I spoke.

To my astonishment, the audience listened intently and without judgment. I realized I'd been telling myself a story about my speaking skills, one that was born of fear. Fear that I'd sound stupid. Fear that I'd make some unforgivable mistake.

That fear can be paralyzing. It can limit us in ways we don't even realize.

Maybe you've dreamed of submitting your first novel or getting published in a revered literary magazine, but you're imprisoned by fear. *My work isn't good enough*, you tell yourself. *No one will ever take me seriously as an author.*

Rubbish, I say. Look your fear in the eye, name it, and tell it to go to hell.

And as you do, know that *Novel & Short Story Writer's Market* can make the process easier. Check out the listings sections to find markets for your fiction, literary agents to represent your work, and contests and conferences that will motivate and inspire you. Then peruse the articles to discover new outlining methods, creative cures for writer's block, ways to develop authentic characters, and much more. And finally, access the exclusive webinar from award-winning author Jane K. Cleland to learn how to crank up the tension in your stories and keep readers on the edge of their seats. (Go to www.writersmarket.com/nsswm17-webinar.)

This fall, I presented my first solo session at the Writer's Digest Annual Conference. My fear of public speaking hasn't dissipated, but I no longer let it hold me back. Don't let your fear hold you back either. Don't let it limit you or your fiction. Believe me: If I can stand in front of a group of people and speak clearly and calmly, you can overcome your fear—of the blank page, of rejection, of the submission process—and make this your best writing year yet.

Rachel Randall
Editorial Director, Writer's Market

HOW TO USE *NSSWM*

To make the most of *Novel & Short Story Writer's Market*, you need to know how to use it. And with more than five hundred pages of fiction publishing markets and resources, a writer could easily get lost amid the information. This quick-start guide will help you navigate through the pages of *Novel & Short Story Writer's Market*—as well as the fiction-publishing process—and accomplish your dream of seeing your work in print.

1. READ, READ, READ. Read numerous magazines, fiction collections, and novels to determine if your fiction compares favorably with work currently being published. If your fiction is at least the same caliber as what you're reading, then move on to step two. If not, postpone submitting your work and spend your time polishing your fiction. Reading the work of others is one of the best ways to improve your craft.

You'll find advice and inspiration from best-selling authors and seasoned writers in the articles found in the first few sections of this book (**Craft & Technique**, **Interviews**, and **The Business of Fiction Writing**). *Novel & Short Story Writer's Market* also includes listings for **Literary Agents** who accept fiction submissions, **Book Publishers** and **Magazines** that publish fiction in a variety of genres, **Contests & Awards** to enter, and **Conferences & Workshops** where you can meet fellow writers and attend instructive sessions to hone your skills.

2. ANALYZE YOUR FICTION. Determine the type of fiction you write to target markets most suitable for your work. Do you write literary, genre, mainstream, or one of many other categories of fiction? For definitions and explanations of genres and subgenres, check out the **Glossary** and the **Genre Glossary** in the **Resources** section of the book. Many magazines and presses are currently seeking specialized work in each of these areas as well as numerous others.

For editors and publishers with specialized interests, see the **Category Index** in the back of the book.

3. LEARN ABOUT THE MARKET. Read *Writer's Digest* magazine; *Publishers Weekly*, the trade magazine of the publishing industry; and *Independent Publisher*, which contains information about small- to medium-size independent presses. And don't forget the Internet. The number of sites for writers seems to grow daily, and among them you'll find www.writersmarket.com and www.writersdigest.com.

4. FIND MARKETS FOR YOUR WORK. There are a variety of ways to locate markets for fiction. The periodical section in bookstores and libraries is a great place to discover new journals and magazines that might be open to your type of short stories. Read writing-related magazines and newsletters for information about new markets and publications seeking fiction submissions. Also, frequently browse bookstore shelves to see what novels and short story collections are being published and by whom. Check acknowledgment pages for names of editors and agents, too. Online journals often have links to the websites of other journals that may publish fiction. And last, but certainly not least, read the listings found here in *Novel & Short Story Writer's Market.*

5. SEND FOR GUIDELINES. In the listings in this book, we try to include as much submission information as we can get from editors and publishers. Over the course of the year, however, editors' expectations and needs may change. Therefore, it is best to obtain a copy of the submission guidelines. You can check each magazine's and press's website—they usually contain a page with guideline information. Or you can do it the old-fashioned way and send a self-addressed, stamped envelope (SASE) with a request for them.

6. BEGIN YOUR PUBLISHING EFFORTS WITH JOURNALS AND CONTESTS OPEN TO BEGINNERS. If this is your first attempt at publishing your work, your best bet is to begin with local publications or those you

KEY TO ICONS & ABBREVIATIONS

- Ⓐ market accepts agented submissions only
- ⊘ market does not accept unsolicited submissions
- award-winning market
- Canadian market
- market located outside of the U.S. and Canada
- $ market pays (in magazine sections)
- comment from the editor of *Novel & Short Story Writer's Market*
- ○ actively seeking new writers
- ◐ seeks both new and established writers
- ● prefers working with established writers, mostly referrals
- ◎ market has a specialized focus
- imprint, subsidiary, or division of larger book publishing house (in book publishers section)
- publisher of graphic novels or comics

know are open to beginning writers. After you have built a publication history, you can try submitting to the more prestigious and nationally distributed magazines. For markets most open to beginners, look for the ○ symbol preceding listing titles. Also look for the ◐ symbol, which identifies markets open to exceptional work from beginners as well as work from experienced, previously published writers.

7. SUBMIT YOUR FICTION IN A PROFESSIONAL MANNER. Take the time to show editors that you care about your work and are serious about publishing. By following a publication's or book publisher's submission guidelines and practicing standard submission etiquette, you can increase your chances that an editor will want to take the time to read your work and consider it for publication. Remember: First impressions matter. A carelessly assembled submission packet can jeopardize your chances before your story or novel manuscript has had a chance to speak for itself.

8. KEEP TRACK OF YOUR SUBMISSIONS. Know when and where you have sent fiction and how long you need to wait before expecting a reply. If an editor does not respond in the time indicated in his or her market listing or guidelines, wait a few more weeks before following up with an e-mail or letter (with SASE) asking when the editor anticipates making a decision. If you do not receive a reply from the editor within a month or two, send a letter withdrawing your work from consideration and move on to the next market on your list.

9. LEARN FROM REJECTION. Rejection is the hardest part of the publication process. Unfortunately rejection happens to every writer, and every writer needs to learn to deal with the negativity involved. Believe it or not, rejection can be valuable when used as a teaching tool rather than a reason to doubt yourself and your work. If an editor offers suggestions with his or her rejection slip, take those comments into consideration. You don't have to agree with an editor's opinion of your work. It may be that the editor has a different perspective on the piece than you do. Or you may find that the editor's suggestions give you new insight into your work and help you improve your craft.

10. DON'T GIVE UP. The best advice we can offer you as you try to get published is to be persistent and to always believe in yourself and your work. By continually reading other writers' work, constantly working on the craft of fiction writing, and relentlessly submitting your work, you will eventually find that magazine or book publisher that's the perfect match for your fiction. *Novel & Short Story Writer's Market* will be here to help you every step of the way.

GUIDE TO LISTING FEATURES

Below is an example of the market listings contained in *Novel & Short Story Writer's Market*, with callouts identifying the various format features of the listings. (For an explanation of the icons used, see the sidebar on page 3.)

THE SOUTHERN REVIEW

Old President's House, Louisiana State University, Baton Rouge, LA 70803-5001. (225)578-5108. Fax: (225)578-5098. E-mail: southernreview@lsu.edu. **Website:** www.lsu.edu/thesouthernreview.

Contact Cara Blue Adams, editor. Magazine: 6¼ × 10; 240 pages; 50 lb. Glatfelter paper; 65 lb. #1 grade cover stock. Quarterly. Circ. 3,000.

- Several stories published in *The Southern Review* were Pushcart Prize selections.

NEEDS Literary. "We select fiction that conveys a unique and compelling voice and vision." Receives approximately 300 unsolicited mss/month. Accepts 4-6 mss/issue. Reading period: September-June. Publishes ms 6 months after acceptance. Agented fiction 1%. Publishes 10-12 new writers/year. Recently published work by Jack Driscoll, Don Lee, Peter Levine, and Debbie Urbanski. Also publishes literary essays, literary criticism, poetry, and book reviews.

HOW TO CONTACT Mail hard copy of ms with cover letter and SASE. No queries. ("Prefer brief letters giving author's professional information, including recent or notable publications. Biographical info not necessary." Responds in 10 weeks to mss. Sample copy for $8. Writer's guidelines online. Reviews fiction, poetry.

PAYMENT/TERMS Pays $30/page. Pays on publication for first North American serial rights. Sends page proof to author via e-mail. Sponsors awards/contests.

TIPS "Careful attention to craftsmanship and technique combined with a developed sense of the creation of story will always make us pay attention."

AT-A-GLANCE REFERENCE ICONS

E-MAIL AND WEBSITE INFORMATION

SPECIFIC CONTACT NAMES

DETAILED SUBMISSION GUIDELINES

TIPS FOR SUBMISSION

OUTLINE YOUR STORY LIKE A SUBWAY MAP

Gabriela Pereira

The writing sphere has entertained a long-standing debate between "plotters" and "pantsers"—the one concerning whether or not you should outline a novel. Plotters fervently believe in outlines. They plan their books down to the smallest detail so that when they finally sit down to write, the manuscript pours out of them like water from a faucet. Pantsers, on the other hand, prefer to write by the seat of their pants, following the story wherever it leads and letting it grow organically. Personally, I think this plotter-versus-pantser dichotomy is a myth, and it exists because most self-declared pantsers haven't yet found an outline technique to suit their style.

For a long time I struggled with outlines myself. As a former product designer and someone obsessed with visual arts, I found the typical "1. A, 2. B" outline method confining and confusing. I understood what the numbers and letters meant *in theory*, but I couldn't "see" the story in my head. At the same time, the thought of writing without a plan scared me senseless. I needed a way to organize my ideas that didn't feel like a set of shackles. I also needed a solution to help me visualize how different components of my story worked together. This is why I developed the subway map outline method, or what I call story mapping.

THE INSPIRATION

As a New Yorker born and raised, I have been riding the subway for about as long as I've been able to walk. If you've ever visited the Big Apple, you know that the subway system is the heart and soul of the city, similar to the way that the freeway system is the lifeblood of Los Angeles. For New Yorkers, knowing the subway system inside and out is a badge of honor, and die-hard city dwellers often get into heated discussions over the perfect route to travel from one borough or neighborhood to another.

The subway has also been a tremendous source of inspiration to me—as well as a geeky obsession. Unlike the more sterile and streamlined rail systems in other American cities, the New York City subway is among the oldest systems in the country, and if you take time to explore it, you'll discover several interwoven layers of history. Many of the original mosaics on the station walls have been preserved, and several newer stations have adopted similar styling. The subway has also been a place where I sneak in moments of writing: When I attended an MFA program a few years ago, I wrote many assignments in a pocket notebook while riding the subway to and from class.

The inspiration for story mapping came to me when I was outlining a term paper that would later become the literature component of my master's thesis. I had spent weeks trying to sort out my thoughts but couldn't seem to bring my ideas together in a cohesive fashion. Then, while switching subways on one of my many jaunts around the city, I remembered the advice an English professor gave me in college: "As a writer, you must take your reader by the hand and lead him through the landscape of your story."

In my New Yorker brain, it all suddenly made sense. My outline was nothing more than a series of directions, a sequence of subway switch overs that would get my reader from the beginning of my essay's argument to the end. That night I sat down and drew a subway map of my term paper. After that, the project practically wrote itself. From that moment on, I stopped using traditional outlining methods and shifted to using a story map for all my writing projects. Here's how to apply this technique to your own novel or short story.

THE METHOD

Story mapping works by helping you track different plot threads, characters, or themes in your story so you can see how they relate to each other. If the subway imagery doesn't work for you, feel free to adjust the metaphor to suit your experience. For instance, if a road map resonates more, think of the subway lines as highways and the subway stops as exits or interchanges between the roads.

In your story map, each subway line represents a different story thread (e.g., plotline, character arc, or sequence of imagery). The dots (subway stops) represent the scenes in your story. Solid dots (local stops) are scenes that exist only on one story thread, while the white dots (interchanges) indicate scenes where two or more story threads intersect.

When you outline your book using the story map method, you can tease apart the various threads and examine both how they operate individually and how they intertwine to make up the whole story. It can be difficult to juggle multiple plotlines, points of view, imagery, or themes, but with a story map, you can isolate one of those threads and examine it apart from the other threads in your story.

This step-by-step guide will help you put together a story map for your own writing. Keep in mind that while you can use story maps with nonfiction as well as fiction, this method is best suited for writing projects with a narrative arc.

Step 1: Create a Scene-by-Scene Outline

Begin by listing all the scenes in your story or novel. I like to use index cards for this step, because it allows me to move scenes around and also to look at individual scenes apart from the rest of the story. I give each scene a title and then list the major characters who appear and the actions that occur. Finally, I'll make a note to myself about why the scene is important to the story overall. This last detail is a litmus test—if I can't think of a compelling reason for why that scene exists, then it's likely dispensable, and I consider cutting it.

Step 2: Decide Which Elements to Track, and Mark Scenes Accordingly

You can track just about any aspect of your novel or story with the story mapping technique: multiple plotlines, different points of view, and recurring images or thematic elements. You can even use a story map to keep track of your supporting cast and which characters appear in which scenes. To prevent your map from sprawling out of control, I recommend focusing on one of three types of maps: (1) a plot-centered map, (2) a character-centered map, or (3) an imagery or theme-centered map. If you want to examine both the plot development and your character arcs, I recommend creating two separate maps.

Plot-Centered Map

A plot-centered map focuses on your novel or short story's main plot and subplots. When creating this type of map, you must first determine the dramatic question that relates to each of those threads. In order for a work of fiction to have a narrative arc, it must have at least one plot thread; this is the main plot of your story. Novels and longer short stories might also include subplots, while very short pieces will have only one central plot. The major dramatic question (MDQ) is the question that drives the main plot in a story. For example, in *The Hunger Games* the MDQ is "Will Katniss survive the Games?"

More complex works of fiction will often have various subplots as well as the main plotline. Driving these subplots are lesser dramatic questions (LDQs) that sum up the conflict or problem behind each subplot. For instance, in *The Hunger Games* one of the big subplots is the budding romance between Peeta and Katniss. In this case, the LDQ is "Will Peeta win Katniss's affections?" Notice that while the MDQ of the novel or story must center around the protagonist, an LDQ might actually center around one of the supporting characters. For example, while the above LDQ still involves Katniss, the protagonist, Peeta is the character driving this subplot—so naturally the LDQ centers around him and his motivations.

Once you have decided on the main plot and the subplots you want to track along with their respective dramatic questions, mark each scene to indicate which plot thread it contributes to. (I like to draw different-colored dots on each card with a marker.) Keep in mind that some scenes might contribute to more than one plot thread, and that's okay. If a particular scene doesn't apply to *any* plot thread, note that as well. You will need to take a closer at that scene and decide if it belongs in your story.

Character-Centered Map

A character-centered map is useful if you need to keep track of an extensive supporting cast or multiple points of view. To create this type of story map, select a color for each character whose arc or POV you want to track, and color-code each scene accordingly. Remember that if more than one viewpoint character appears in a particular scene, you'll also need to note whose point of view that scene is in.

For the character-driven story map, instead of worrying about MDQs for the different plot threads, you will need to think of a dramatic question specific to each character you are tracking. This question usually centers around that particular character's biggest desire. Use this formula as a starting point: "Will [character name] [get what he or she wants]?" For example, the dramatic question for Dorothy in the movie *The Wizard of Oz* is: "Will she ever get back to Kansas?" The Scarecrow's dramatic question is: "Will he finally get a brain?"

Imagery or Theme-Centered Map

If you already have a good sense of your plot or your characters, you might want to track certain imagery or thematic elements throughout your story. This is where an imagery or theme-centered story map is useful, because it allows you to better understand key images and details, and see where they appear throughout your story. You can track just about anything with this map—music, color, art, weather, nature, etc.—but it's best used for elements that relate to the emotions you want your to readers feel. This type of story map is extremely powerful because it allows you to tap into how your readers might experience your book and further shape that experience depending on what you discover.

A great study of imagery or thematic elements in action is in the movie *The Sixth Sense*. The color red, as well as the drops in temperature in several scenes, are often linked to significant events in the story or are used to foreshadow terrifying moments. These images don't necessarily drive plot or character development, but instead drive the emotional roller coaster the audience experiences. As with the previous two types of maps, you can create this story map by assigning a color to each image or thematic element you want to track, and then marking your scenes accordingly.

Step 3: Create Your Map

Once you have created your scene-by-scene outline and labeled each scene according to the various threads or elements you want to track, the only task that remains is to draw the actual map. Start by plotting the scenes where two or more threads intercept (the express stops), and then fill in the other scenes (local stops) around those pivotal moments.

Below is an example of the story map in action. (To download a full-color version of this map, go to DIYMFA.com/storymap and sign up with your e-mail.)

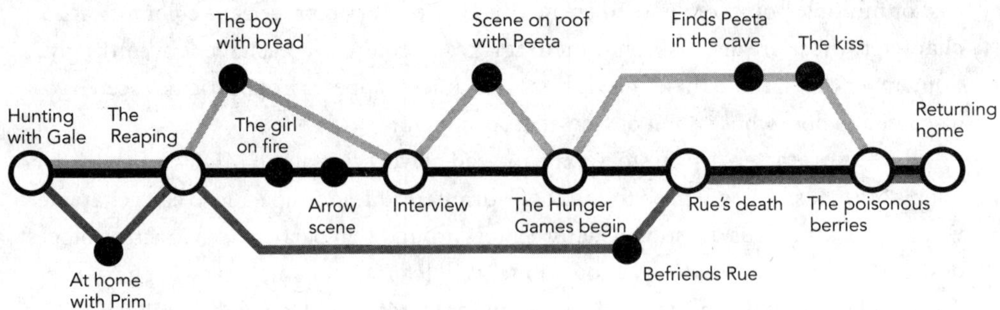

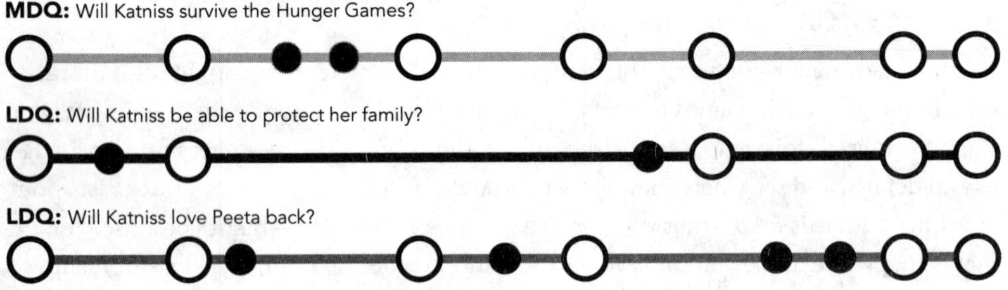

***The Hunger Games* Story Map (Plot)**

WHY IT WORKS

The first and most obvious benefit of story mapping is that it allows you to tease apart different aspects of your narrative and see if they hold up on their own, as well as within the overall story. I have tried many other outline methods, including lists, spreadsheets, mind maps, and so on, but none of them give me the same degree of flexibility.

But there is more to story mapping than just a pretty diagram. Unlike other outlining methods that hop from story event to story event, this technique places the conflict and emotion front and center. To create a plot-centered story map, you must determine the MDQ and LDQs, which in turn requires you to boil down each plotline of your story into one central question or problem that your character faces. In order to do that, you must identify the problem (i.e., conflict) before moving on. Similarly, with a character-centered story map, you must have a sense of what each character wants, again putting conflict at the center of your outline. Finally, with a map that focuses on imagery or themes, the entire map centers around the emotion created by these elements. In each scenario, this mapping technique asks you to focus on the most important aspects of your novel or short story.

Finally, story mapping is a visual tool that allows you to see your entire story at a glance and to understand how all the plotlines, characters, or thematic elements fit together. For writers like me, who are more visually oriented than verbal, this type of outline can make more sense than a traditional list approach. Keep in mind that from a story map outline, you can also easily extract a traditional outline or spreadsheet, and you can adapt this technique to use in concert with other types of outlines as well. The most important step is to find an outline technique that works best for you.

Gabriela Pereira is the founder of DIYMFA.com, the do-it-yourself alternative to a masters degree in writing. She teaches writing at conferences, workshops, and online. She also hosts the podcast *DIY MFA Radio*. Her book, *DIY MFA: Write with Focus, Read with Purpose, Build Your Community*, was released in July 2016 from Writer's Digest Books. For a full-color download of the story map in this article, go to DIYMFA.com/storymap and sign up with your e-mail address.

CREATIVE CURES FOR WRITER'S BLOCK

Jennifer D. Foster

Rod Serling, creator of the cult classic television show *The Twilight Zone*, believed that good ideas "come from every human experience that you've either witnessed or have heard about, translated into your brain in your own sense of dialogue, in your own language form. Ideas are born from what is smelled, heard, seen, experienced, felt, emotionalized. Ideas are probably in the air, like little tiny items of ozone." He proclaimed that ideas are omnipresent, just waiting to be plucked and translated onto the page.

But as most writers know, it's hardly ever that simple. For some, writer's block is so insidious that it causes them to blame themselves, question their credibility, and consider switching careers.

Regardless of what you call it—creative drought, blank-page syndrome, brain blockage, a dry spell, a crippling loss for words—writer's block is an unwelcomed guest, creating an often-debilitating cessation in the writing process. It usually arrives unannounced; doesn't discriminate with hosts; can last for days, weeks, months, or even years; and then can slip away quietly, sometimes leaving devastation in its path. Sounds akin to a disease, doesn't it? So before we look at some cures, let's look at the symptoms (what a block can feel like) and the causes (why a block can happen).

SYMPTOMS OF WRITER'S BLOCK

Jess Keating, a middle-grade and picture-book author in Toronto, Ontario, says writer's block "feels a lot like treading water—like I'm trying to get somewhere, but I can't seem to find an island to land on. It's very uncomfortable." When Newfoundland-based Charis Cotter, award-winning children's author of *The Swallow: A Ghost Story*, experiences it, she feels helpless and frustrated, and her self-worth takes a beating. "I feel like I've been fooling everyone and I'm not really a writer at all, but a fake. I start attacking myself." And frustration reigns supreme. Children's author Tekeyla Friday of Swift Current,

Saskatchewan, points to frustration as the chief symptom of her block: "I know the ideas are there; I just cannot access them. It's like trying to remember someone's name. You can see them clearly in your mind, but the name just won't come."

Robin Black, Philadelphia-based author of the novel *Life Drawing* and *Crash Course: Essays from Where Writing and Life Collide*, says she feels anxious. "When I was unable to write a novel for which I was under contract, I most keenly felt anxiety about disappointing other people—which took me so far from anything to do with creativity that it was an incredibly unhelpful response."

In addition to feeling frustrated, Tanya Geisler, certified leadership coach and writer in Toronto, Ontario, says she feels "impatient and annoyed. I recognize in that moment that it is my perfectionism creeping in. I want whatever I'm writing to be the most brilliant piece of prose ever penned—by anyone."

Toronto, Ontario-based Tish Cohen, who wrote the best-selling novels *The Search Angel* and *The Truth About Delilah Blue*, experiences guilt: "I love to be on fire with my writing. To be so excited about what I'm creating that I'm nearly lifting off my chair. It's my happy place, and when I'm not there I feel guilty. I know I'm meant to be writing and creating, and when I'm not, I'm cheating myself." Washington State and Arizona-based J.A. Jance, *New York Times* best-selling author of more than fifty books, says she "mostly feels sleepless, because I spend a lot of time tossing and turning overnight, trying to see my way through the story. I refer to this as 'wrestling with the Devil,' and that's exactly how it feels."

> "When we write, we put a little of ourselves out there, and we're judged on it. It's tough. It takes courage." **—MARY LOU GEORGE**

PROBABLE CAUSES

Admitting the presence of a problem is the first step toward recovery. So now that we've acknowledged its lowly existence and identified its main symptoms, let's uncover some of the common reasons behind writer's block.

Sam Hiyate, president of The Rights Factory in Toronto, Ontario, and founder/editor of the online magazine *Don't Talk to Me About Love* (www.donttalktomeaboutlove.com), thinks the most common cause "is the overwhelming nature of the endeavor of being a writer—being alone and having to confront characters in your imagination. It has to be one of the most difficult artistic undertakings."

American prizewinning author Elizabeth Sims believes the block may have multiple roots. "Sometimes I just get fatigued, or I feel boring and dull. Sometimes I think that's because I haven't done anything new lately; haven't read something really stimulating or gone after a new experience; haven't given myself time to reflect on ideas and the life experience I've gained already."

Black feels writers may also become blocked when their aims and aptitudes aren't in sync. "That happens when my ambitions or my hunches about what a story might do outstrip my current ability to pull off what I envision. Sometimes the result of that standoff is that I can't write for a while."

Kevin Smokler, a San Francisco-based writer, cultural critic, and author of *Practical Classics: 50 Reasons to Reread 50 Books You Haven't Touched Since High School*, says the cause of being blocked is "the unwillingness to be terrible." He says he has good days and then bad, when he can't verbalize his thoughts or overjudges his ideas. But, he stresses, "as long as you write [the ideas] down, even the terrible ones, you aren't blocked."

Anna Boyar, managing editor of Freehand Books in Calgary, Alberta, contends that "focusing too much on small details and trying to perfect something before it even takes shape" can cause writer's block. Toronto, Ontario, author and freelance editor Ali MacGee feels the same, saying that "stupid, idiotic perfectionism" is a common cause. She often bolsters herself by saying, "There, there. It doesn't have to be perfect. Just play with it."

Many writers, consciously or not, sabotage their own process. Sarah Selecky of Prince Edward County, Ontario, is the author of the Giller-nominated short story collection *This Cake Is for the Party.* She says, "There is no block, really, other than myself. I get in my own way … usually because I've stopped feeling curious about my work. I've decided my writing is supposed to *be* something … good or smart or worthy. That doesn't sound like it would be so harmful to the creative process, but it is. Because without curiosity and permission to make something bad or stupid or ugly … I stop creating."

Sharon Crawford, editor, writing instructor, author of the Beyond mystery series, and founder of the East End Writers' Group in Toronto, Ontario, believes that often the cause is fear. "If we write, we may write something awful, or if we write something good, it could be published, and some writers can't deal with the afterward of getting published," she says. "So subconsciously their mind is saying, 'If I don't write, I won't have to face the consequences.'" Selecky agrees. "My own criticism is more harsh than any external one. I think what all writers grapple with, in one form or another, is fear. Fear can shut us down." Nina Munteanu, a Canadian novelist and writing instructor at the University of Toronto in Toronto, Ontario, holds a similar perspective: "If you're emotionally or psychologically not ready for the consequences of getting published, then you will falter, procrastinate, forever fuss over your creation, and convince yourself that it isn't ready. In truth, it's *you* who isn't ready to shine."

Toronto, Ontario, romance novelist Mary Lou George also thinks writer's block stems from fear. "We wonder: 'What if I exhausted all my ideas with my last book?' 'What if I can't do it again?' 'What if they don't like me?' When we write, we put a little of ourselves out there, and we're judged on it. It's tough. It takes courage."

CREATIVE CURES

When you're face-to-face with a blank page and thinking, *An idea. My kingdom for an idea!,* keep in mind these tried-and-true strategies to stimulate creativity, squelch writer's block, and inspire imagination.

Write Yourself Past the Block

"The key is simply putting your butt in the chair and staying there," says Terence M. Green, two-time World Fantasy Award finalist for best novel and creative writing lecturer at Western University in London, Ontario. "As a writing instructor, I stress routine and self-discipline, not waiting for the muse, and getting something down on paper—almost anything. Nearly all inspiration happens while one is in that chair, involved in the writing process. … The hardest draft to write is the first one—filling up those blank sheets of paper. But once that first draft is there, the road widens and things become easier, because one has something to work with and to work from."

Lynn Wiese Sneyd, owner of LWS Literary Services in Tucson, Arizona, says, "I think writers who believe in writer's block are inclined to stop writing. … They want to work out the issue prior to writing it, but I think if you keep writing, even if you have to delete 80 percent of what you've written, you find your way. If you keep writing, you become 'unblocked.' You don't have to know where things are going in advance." She trusts the story to "find its way."

Don't Force a Flow

Martha Webb, a literary agent and partner with McDermid Agency Inc., in Toronto, Ontario, has a different take. "Just *keeping on keeping on* in a halfhearted way is not the way to go," she says. Cotter shares Webb's belief. "The least effective technique is to sweat it out and force the words to come. This is painful and frustrating, and really part of being stuck, not getting free."

Black offers what she calls a slightly counterintuitive solution: "If you can't write at all, then write for five minutes and only five minutes a day. Don't allow yourself to do more than that. Eventually—sometimes quite soon—you'll begin wanting more and more time. So instead of forcing yourself to the keyboard, you're having to force yourself to leave it."

Turn Your Attention Elsewhere

In her conversations with authors, Webb has found that "it seems to be less a matter of being blocked generally and more about hitting a wall with a given project." Her remedy?

"Often putting it aside for a bit and working on something else, either a short story or an essay or something very different from the current project, can help." Webb says many of the writers she works with have several projects in the works simultaneously. Munteanu uses a similar strategy. "I drop the troublesome piece like a hot potato and go to something else. I let it come back to me on its own. This is why I can say that I don't suffer from writer's block—yet I'm dealing with it all the time. I just don't feel its debilitating effects because I work—and write—around it."

Black also feels the need to switch writing gears. "When I feel blocked with prose, I sometimes write (very bad) poetry. It's a way of abandoning expectation and of detaching my relationship with words from any ambitions or professional concerns. … [This] allows me to get back in touch with the more playful elements of writing, which are very often lost in the anxiety about not doing what I feel I should be doing."

Like Black, Cotter tackles another writing project, but on a more personal level. "I write about what it feels like, and what emotions are going through me, as I feel blocked. It also helps just to write about anything at all other than the thing that I'm supposed to be writing about." For example, she finds it "very helpful to write a diary entry for one of the characters. Or I can describe something, a room or a landscape. All that matters is that I pick something where the words flow freely. It's like I'm walking around the block, instead of going through it."

Come at Your Project from the Side

Selecky uses words to "override the impulse to shut down," complete with her own specific technique. "I like to write a list of unconnected words or unconnected sentences. That way I'm working with language, but with no expectations of story or meaning or caliber … and that *feels* like writing. Which is a start—usually that's enough to reassure me." And speaking of writing words, Anita Purcell, executive director of the Canadian Authors Association in Orillia, Ontario, turns to a search engine for help. "I Google phrases somewhat but not completely related to my project, just to get my brain moving in another direction." She also revisits and possibly reworks her outline.

Friday also finds an outline "sketch" to be a helpful trigger. She fleshes out the story with bold plot points in order to see what the story should look like. She also finds that "people watching and making up stories about the people you see is a great way to stimulate ideas. I think this one is born in writers."

Ignore Your Impulse to Edit

Purcell believes that many writers experience writer's block because they "tend to be perfectionistic as they write—wearing the editor's hat rather than the creator's hat—[which is] a surefire way of driving your muse to sit with a more welcoming client." Kathryn

Mockler, editor, publisher, and creative writing instructor at Western University, agrees: "Focusing on the final product or the outcome of your efforts while you are in process can be debilitating. Avoid thinking about how the work will be received or where you'd like to publish it until it's ready to send out."

"If you can't write at all, then write for five minutes and only five minutes a day. Don't allow yourself to do more than that. Eventually—sometimes quite soon—you'll begin wanting more and more time."
—ROBIN BLACK

Take a Kindergarten Approach

Sims advises, "[I write] almost everything in longhand first, using the process of typing it into my computer as a first line edit. I like to change up my pens and papers, which seems, on a kindergarten-type level, to keep the physical act of writing interesting and even exciting."

Tish Cohen takes this ritual a step further. "If my focus is shattered because I'm looking for an answer for a particular plot or character problem, my favorite thing to do is get down on the floor with a pen and a pad of paper." Her rationale? "It's an instant way to reconnect with 'Little Tish.' That child was always on the floor. It's where the great ideas live." So, recommends Cohen, "Lie down on your belly and swing your feet in the air behind you, pen poised. I guarantee the ideas will come scampering out from beneath the sofa and land on your page. In extreme cases, add candy to the above [exercise]."

Like Cohen, Keating finds helpful what she calls "the old-fashioned tools of the trade: plain old pen and paper." She lets herself "write *anything*, just to get the ball rolling again. I think writing by hand activates your creativity much more than a computer, especially if you're blocked. Sometimes little snippets of plot or dialogue will peek out, and that's usually enough to spark what comes next in the story."

Take a Time Out

A huge fan of quiet time, Keating says, "Many ideas whisper rather than yell, so I like to allow a few moments of real quiet every day, without the usual background noise of the Internet, e-mail, and television." Dawn Green, Victoria, British Columbia, author of *When Kacey Left* and *In the Swish*, is also a fan of quiet time, but with this caveat: "I try to rest my brain, calm myself, and be confident that when I am ready to write, I will.

But I think setting a time limit on that is a good thing, too, because not writing can become a habit."

Hiyate believes in making time for exercise—a walk, a gym visit, or a yoga class. "It tends to restore some of the artistic expression that might become dormant—or spent—over time." Selecky agrees wholeheartedly. "If it's really going terribly, and even reading feels hard, then start exercising more. Take up running, dancing, rock climbing. Work your body hard—make yourself sweat until you stop thinking. Don't forget you're a body/mind, not just a mind. Your thoughts are holding you back, so outsmart your thoughts with your physical body." Munteanu concurs. "Walks, particularly in the natural environment—devoid of human-made distractions—unclutters the mind and soul. It grounds you back to the simplicity of life and connects you back to your intuitive soul." She also finds traveling revitalizing for the creative muscle. "Traveling helps me focus outward; I forget myself and embrace my wonder for the world. My mind opens to adventure. Road trips are metaphoric journeys of the soul."

Find Inspiration in Other Forms

Jack David is the co-publisher of ECW Press in Toronto, Ontario. His approach to tackling writer's block echoes the themes of restoration and quiet reflection: "If I have a block in creativity, the best answer is to do nothing—to waste a day or two by reading some unrelated, unusual material and let the answer I'm hoping for creep into my brain. Wait patiently for the inspiration to return and keep a notepad close at hand, day and night. Something will happen, but you won't predict when." Boyar agrees with David. "If you can't write, then read. Read widely. Be inspired by what you are reading. Don't stop reading until you can write again." MacGee subscribes to the same train of thought. With reading, she always comes across something that sets off a lightbulb in her head, especially while reading a favorite author's work. "A sentence or a paragraph often sets off inspiration. What I end up writing usually bears no resemblance whatsoever to the inspiration. It just sends a ball down my bowling alley toward a strike."

Susannah Coneybeare, professional organizer and owner of officize inc., in Toronto, Ontario, indulges in music as her personal "brand of creative inspiration." She chooses "a partner during the writing journey … a singer whose music is going to stay with me through the whole process, or a writer whose work I can turn to. They motivate in many ways. I feel if they can create, I can create, too. And their message is important to me how they are saying it affects me and puts me in a certain mood or frame of mind. They inspire me, even though I don't know them." Muntenau's a big fan of the power of music, too. "I use music like a soundtrack in my novel writing. Just hearing a piece that I associate with a character or scene sets the tone and mood for me to write. This can serve as a powerful trigger to work through the block." Her reasoning? "I think it's because the music allows you to approach your work in a more oblique way, like metaphor in a story. The music unleashes the emotional subtext you need to connect with the story elements that require solving."

Toronto, Ontario–based Trevor Cole, award-winning author of *Practical Jean* and three other novels, says he gives himself over to the work of other artists by attending art galleries or plays, or by reading books by authors he admires "for as long as it takes. The blocked creative mind is like a planted field gone dry. Consuming and immersing yourself in the work of other artists brings the rain."

> "I try to rest my brain, calm myself, and be confident that when I am ready to write, I will. But I think setting a time limit on that is a good thing, too, because not writing can become a habit."
> **—DAWN GREEN**

Stick to a Schedule

Crawford suggests carving out scheduled writing time to help with momentum and inspiration. Set ground rules, hire a sitter, or get help from a partner if need be. And if you can't write each day, then aim for five days a week or during weekends. "This way, if you have other responsibilities, like family and work, you don't have to take yourself on a guilt trip."

Journey Prize–nominated short story writer and freelance editor Marnie Lamb, of Toronto, Ontario, says routine is crucial to the writing process. "Writing when the mood strikes or when you have time rarely results in a high-quality or -quantity output. The key is discipline. The more disciplined I am about sticking to a regular schedule of writing, the more I'm in the mood to write, the more easily stories slip from me, and the less writer's block I experience."

Coneybeare is in agreement with Crawford and Lamb. "Stop multitasking, and compartmentalize. Schedule writing. Block time in your weekly or monthly calendar to write, in whatever increments of time work for you, and do nothing else during that time." And if writer's block is an ongoing issue, Crawford suggests "free-fall writing." Set a timer for, say, twenty minutes, "then pick a word, a subject, a few phrases, and start writing. Your subconscious is at work. If you're angry or afraid of something, even if you haven't decided to write about it, that subject or situation can pop up. Keep writing—go where the fear or anger takes you. The purpose is to loosen up your creativity."

THE LAST WORD

Like many authors, Cotter believes that writer's block is entrenched in the creative process. "Writing is an emotional journey for me. It's very influenced by where I am in my life. When things are going well, and I'm completely absorbed in the world of my novel, I couldn't be happier. But the other side of that positive experience is struggle and hard work. I believe it's part of the balance between light and dark." Lamb views it this way: "I even see the block as healthy in that it's evidence of a meticulous and discerning mind, one that's not willing to write just anything—although writing something, however poor, can be one of the ways of handling the block—but rather a mind that wants to wait until it can produce quality work."

Dawn Green sees it this way: "I think writers build up their own walls that block them, and the only ones who can knock them down, who know where the cracks are, are the writers themselves. Writers are the architects of their own *block*ades and, because of that, they have to be the demolition crew, too." Maybe that's precisely why writer's block can feel so all-consuming and daunting when you're in the thick of it.

But chances are, the block will pass. So when you're feeling immobilized, stuck in the deepest of creative quagmires, unable to break through that seemingly impenetrable barrier, take comfort in knowing that you're not alone. Most writers experience this malady at some point along their creative journey. When the going gets unbearably tough, keep these motivational words in mind from literary icon Mark Twain: "The secret of getting ahead is getting started. The secret of getting started is breaking your complex, overwhelming tasks into small, manageable tasks and then starting on the first one."

Jennifer D. Foster is a Toronto, Canada-based freelance writer, editor, and content strategist, and her company is Planet Word. Her clients are from the book and custom publishing, magazine, and marketing and communications fields. When she's not busy spilling ink for her first novel, she carves out time to be a mentor to novice editors and writers, as well as a board member of a monthly reading series in Toronto. Find her online at lifeonplanetword.wordpress.com.

EXPLORING EXPOSITION & SUMMARY

Jack Smith

Fiction depends largely on strong scenes and heightened dramatic moments, but it also requires solid narrative summary as well as exposition. Narrative summary telescopes time. Exposition—and by this I mean *expository prose,* not the first part of a five-stage story structure—is used, among other things, to delve into characters' feelings, thoughts, and reflections. The risk with either of these modes—narrative summary or exposition—is that the writing can become very dull. How do you prevent that? How do you craft strong exposition and summary that keeps readers engaged?

HANDLING EXPOSITION WITH DRAMATIC APPEAL

Let's begin with exposition, one of the toughest fictional modes to handle well. To energize your expository prose, start by finding ways to create vivid imagery. Christine Sneed, author of the novel *Paris, He Said,* states, "I try to do a kind of literary braiding in expository passages—that is, along with hinting at or saying outright what a character's emotional state is, I bring in visual or other sensory details so that readers can clearly picture the character and/or the setting." She does as much as she can to represent "both the interior and exterior lives" of characters. Note, for example, the following excerpt from Sneed's "The Virginity of Famous Men," the title story of her recently published collection:

> The eighth arrondissement apartment Will and his girlfriend Jorie moved into, a three-bedroom on the fourth floor of a Haussmann-era building, overlooked the effusively floral Square Marcel Pagnol. Their place was advertised as a luxury property and the owner charged an exorbitant rent; Will paid for three months up front in order to beat out two other applicants for the same apartment. Jorie assumed from the beginning that this prepayment was a greedy landlord's ruse, and Will did now too: as often as not, the elevator was out of order, and their unit had leaky windows.

Look at the precise detail here. First, we know the apartment is in the eighth arrondissement of Paris. We know its size—a three-bedroom flat—and, more to the point, we know its style—a Haussmann-era building. In a nice little detail, we learn that it overlooks the "effusively floral Square Marcel Pagnol." No need to draw a map for the reader; anyone can search online for Paris and find the location of Square Marcel Pagnol, but stating a particular location fuels interest. More interesting details follow: The characters paid three months' rent up front for a place with an out-of-order elevator and leaky windows. See how much detail is packed in such a short paragraph? This passage isn't just cerebral or abstract; the descriptions conjure pictures in our minds. Concreteness is vital in pulling readers in, says Sneed, but she cautions against overdoing it. "No word should be superfluous."

External concreteness can function not only to develop the interiority and exteriority of characters but also to create a rich, interesting voice. For Lori Ostlund, author of *After the Parade*, your voice will fall flat if you "over-report." She states: "The more that readers are *told* that a character is sad and is crying, the less sad they tend to feel." Instead you must get *inside* your characters, not view them from the outside. To do this, to reveal what Ostlund calls your "character's internal landscape," she suggests "transferring the emotion to something external." As we've seen in the Sneed passage, this means an objective referent that subjective feelings and emotions can be attached to. According to Ostlund, "What a character is observing and how he or she chooses to interact with the environment can help to keep the exposition interesting." With this idea in mind, consider the following short excerpt from Ostlund's novel *After the Parade*:

> He went into the bedroom and turned on the corner lamp. The room looked strange without his belongings. Gone were the rows of books and the gifts from his students, as well as the Indonesian night table that Winnie had given him when he and Walter moved from Minnesota to New Mexico. It was made from recycled wood, old teak that had come from a barn or railroad tracks or a chest for storing rice—Winnie was not sure what exactly.

This point-of-view character's sense of loss isn't stated explicitly but instead is suggested by his noticing the absence of his personal things in the room: remembered books, gifts from students, the Indonesian night table and the teak it was made from. The lamp illuminates the sheer lack of these things. As Ostlund points out, it is much less effective to dwell on a character's emotional state—here, a sense of loss—than it is to focus on specific things linked to this state. The external associations help the reader feel the emotion more intensely.

Another hallmark of strong exposition is an interesting pacing or tempo. Award-winning author Robert Garner McBrearty cautions against the use of prose that monotonously plods along, prose "which makes readers feel like they're wading through weedy passages to get back to a more interesting scene." McBrearty's recommendation is either to speed up the prose or to vary its rhythm "so that the exposition is just as lively and intense as the scenes." Consider making your prose lyrical, says McBrearty, "creating a kind of music that carries the reader along." If the writing is lyrical enough, it will pull readers in so that they can hardly stop reading, "one line pouring effortlessly into the next as the music builds to a crescendo." And here, at this heightened emotional moment, says McBrearty, the surprise suddenly comes: "Exposition reveals something unexpected before we drop into the next scene, a little breathless now, and eager for more." With the right pacing, as with other well-handled techniques, exposition can be a great benefit, not a burden.

But now for an important process question, perhaps one you hadn't imagined. Should you limit exposition as much as possible in early drafts? Is there a disadvantage in opting for exposition at critical junctures of your preliminary drafting? For Angela Pneuman, author of *Lay It on My Heart,* there can be. In her own fiction, says Pneuman, if she depends very much on exposition in the formative stages of her story or novel, she will find herself "trying to figure things out too quickly—steering the story towards meaning too early." Instead, states Pneuman, "What I really need to be doing is watching, listening, and trying things out." Once she understands her characters' motivations, she feels "more sure-handed with interior exposition, more sure about where it belongs."

Good exposition is critical, but Pneuman has taken us beyond the question of how to create strong exposition. To avoid authorial shaping and engineering, should we avoid it in early drafts and save it for later? Writers have to decide this issue on their own, but Pneuman has raised a significant question related to the early stages of the drafting process.

HANDLING NARRATIVE SUMMARY

First, let's distinguish between scene and summary. With scene, you focus on one event, achieving as much dramatic intensity as possible; with summary, you cover more than one event, or perhaps several, over time. "As writers," says McBrearty, "we don't want to, or shouldn't, dramatize each passing moment or day, so we give just a sense of what is occurring." Yet McBrearty reminds us that, fundamentally, all writing must be dramatic, and narrative summary is no exception.

The question is, how do you invigorate your narrative summary?

One way, says McBrearty, is to include "a conflict of interest" between your characters. This conflict can certainly be backward-looking at times, but mostly it should be forward-looking. Above all, says McBrearty, we need "to care about what's in store for them in the future." Note how the following excerpt from McBrearty's novel *The Western Lonesome Society* provides compelling historical context but also creates dramatic expectation:

> The years go by and they live as wild Indians. Tom fights it inside, clings to the pictures of home, but Will's letting it go. What good is the past to him now? What good are his parents? They never came for him. He cannot even see their faces anymore. They are part of an old dream, and soon he will lose even the dream. Tom fights for him, reminds him of the old days, but

> Will runs from him and covers his ears. He does not even like the old language anymore. He refuses to understand it. But inside Tom has not forgotten his promise. He will take Will home.

The opening line establishes this passage as summary. Notice how the brothers Tom and Will view their captivity differently and how McBrearty embeds conflict in the likelihood of Tom's eventual attempt to escape and return home. Strong summary, like strong exposition, pulls us inside characters, enabling us to sense their emotional lives. Notice the sadness and longing in Tom's mounting sense of loss, his two poignant questions, followed by an even more poignant realization, wired with fine dramatic tension: "They are part of an old dream, and soon he will lose even the dream."

"I believe to embrace the 'whole truth' in fictional narrative art is to create a character who *yearns*. It is simply not enough to narrate the troubles one is confronting. It's getting inside the ineluctable heart of a character that causes a story to resonate in a reader's mind." **—DENNIS MUST**

For Dennis Must, author of two collections and two novels, drama is as important in summary as it is in scene. To achieve rich, dramatic power in his own fiction, Must draws on years of writing and directing plays. In addition he depends on the quality of his creative imagination. "It's how close I have gotten to the pulse of the vision and/or recall that is occurring in my consciousness," he says. This vision is informed principally by his growing up in the Rust Belt in the 1950s. According to Must, "Having grown up in the industrial belt and worked in a steel mill and on the railroad, these images are as familiar as family voices." He finds the need to "conjure them awake in the imagination." As Must emphasizes, "I must be inside the experience of my characters if the narrative is to come to life for the reader."

Notice how a mix of narrative scene and summary from Must's novel *Hush Now, Don't Explain* places the reader there:

> With the lights of the city beyond, we sought sleeping quarters outside a furnace room where men wrestled fiery ingots to a cooling platform. The workers appeared miniature, as if to betray how their aspirations had conspired to dominate them.
>
> The locomotives, skyscrapers with their steel beams and trusses, open-hearth furnaces aproning the mighty river, coal rising on small handcars from deep beneath the earth, ore-laden barges, industry on the backside of the cities—it all transcended anything Billy, Mr. Willard, or I

> had ever imagined. Yet we saw hundreds of men working through the night, tending the maw of these leviathans of commerce. The bells of industry, metal clanging against metal, never ceased …

Here, with great force, Must captures the characters' arrival at this industrial leviathan as well as their long, dark, clamorous night. The language is specific and concrete, not vague and general. The narrator's amazement in the face of such mammoth machinery, such alien forces, makes this more than a dull recounting but instead a passage that is experimentally alive.

Summary, then, collapses time, whether it's several years or a single night. The best summary is energetic and vivid. It burrows into character, just as scene does. For Pneuman, it's this character function which summary must absolutely satisfy. For her, good summary creates the most "scenic points of entry" as possible. "Usually," she says, "I keep narrative summary close to a character. I admire writers who navigate a greater distance, but in my own work, summary feels like it's in a character's head. So it becomes a matter of characterization and voice." We certainly see this in the following excerpt from Pneuman's *Lay It on My Heart:*

> As the years spread out and my father goes off his medication—once, twice, again, each time a little worse—the halfway houses won't hold him, and it's Phoebe, of course, who takes him back. First with hope, as a husband. Then with resignation, and perhaps true Christianity. This goes on long after she's had to sell the house in town. After she's put in a phone line at the river and found full-time teaching. After Daze recovers for what she calls her "third act," the shortest one yet. After I've left East Winder.

Observe how closely we are drawn to Pneuman's characters, how much real-life experience is represented here: the medication, the halfway houses, Phoebe's progressive attempts to help her husband—at first with hope, then resignation, then with true Christian spirit. Note how effective the repetition of the word *after* is. In loading this passage with so much felt life, Pneuman provides inroads into her characters. This isn't scene, but it packs plenty of energy, and as a result, it grabs the reader.

SCENE OR SUMMARY?

You can know the difference between scene and summary and still wonder: When it comes to the actual writing, which portions of your story or novel need scene, and which require summary? Ostlund has discovered that her creative writing students often choose summary when they really should choose scene: "It's hard to build tension with summary; key moments, especially at the end of a story, shouldn't be summarized. I also think of scenes, particularly the accretion of scenes, as the primary way that we have to show changes in characters. Scenes allow us both to see what caused a change and also what the change is (the effects on the character)." But summary *is* needed at times, says Ostlund, as a way of moving certain necessary events along quickly—and quite often at section or chapter beginnings. When it is needed, the writer has to know how *much* summary to use because, as Ostlund points out, "too much summary or unclearly sequenced summary can weigh down the beginning."

TIPS FROM THE PROFESSIONALS

No one can tell you everything about writing good exposition and summary. But certainly the professionals can give you some useful tips on handling exposition-related issues.

- **THE MERELY FACTUAL:** Must has come to embrace this passage by Boris Pasternak: "What is laid down, ordered, factual is never enough to embrace the whole truth: life always spills over the rim of every cup." For Must, regardless of fictional mode—scene, summary, exposition—the burden of the writer is to create a character whose life spills over beyond the mere facts of daily existence. What we need, according to Must, is a character who desperately *needs* and *wants*. As Must says, "I believe to embrace the 'whole truth' in fictional narrative art is to create a character who *yearns*. It is simply not enough to narrate the troubles one is confronting. It's getting inside the ineluctable heart of a character that causes a story to resonate in a reader's mind."
- **INTERIORITY OF CHARACTERS:** Exposition can be used to capture the interior lives of characters. But when, and how much? How about in scenes? In her creative writing classroom, Pneuman helps her students learn to judge the impact of interiority in scene writing by doing a three-part exercise. First they write "entirely in scene, with dialogue, gestures, little descriptions if necessary, but no interior." Then she invites them to include "all interior—memories, evaluations, private thoughts, impressions." In the third exercise, they play around with both the external (actions, speech) and internal (thinking, memory). "There's no right or wrong," says Pneuman, "just degrees of the effect the writer wants to produce. It can be a great joy to tinker in this way, trying out different things."
- **MOOD AND TONE:** "Consider the mood you're trying to set," says Garner McBrearty. "Is it funny? Sad? Ironic? Foreboding?" Too often, he says, writers tend to equate exposition and summary with "providing necessary information," but, he points out, that shouldn't be the only goal, or even the primary goal of these two fictional modes—the goal should be to keep readers enthralled. You can accomplish this feat by developing a compelling mood and tone. McBrearty offers a few interesting scenarios: "Maybe your main character says cheerful things in a crowd but secretly views the world through a dark inner lens. Or maybe the seemingly cynical person is filled with hopeful inner longing."

- **BACKSTORY:** Backstory, which may call for exposition, is often essential for context, as Sneed points out, because you can't rely only on the present time frame of your story. But be sure to prune what *isn't* necessary and to be fairly ruthless about it. "You have to be pretty unsentimental when you're editing backstory, exposition, or narrative summary," says Sneed. Knowing what to prune, and what not to, comes in time, she says. It's a matter of learning "the right balance between backstory and the story's present, but eventually I think it becomes easier."
- **THE "THESIS-STATEMENT SYNDROME":** Exposition can be a real spoiler, says Ostlund, when a writer sums up everything that's about to happen in a scene. Her example: "He then told her about the time that his best friend pulled a gun on him, destroying his faith in friendship." This kind of exposition, says Ostlund, will kill any tension—and reading pleasure—in the scene because "the reader already knows about the gun and has also been instructed how to interpret this scene." Ostlund does grant that this syndrome can be useful as a story planning technique, but she suggests that if you want to make your writing vibrant, you must delete expository spoilers as you revise.

SUMMING UP

Exposition and narrative summary are difficult to write, but if you find ways to make these prose modes dramatic, they can benefit your storytelling. Don't laboriously tell. Do find ways to create vivid imagery for your readers and enter the minds and hearts of your characters. Be careful to choose the right places for exposition as well as narrative summary. Probably the best way to learn how to handle these modes well, and when to use them, is to find good models from the professionals. See the craft in action.

Jack Smith has published three novels: *Being* (2016), *Icon* (2014), and *Hog to Hog*, which won the 2007 George Garrett Fiction Prize and was published by Texas Review Press in 2008. He has published stories in a number of literary magazines, including *Southern Review, North American Review, Texas Review, Xconnect, In Posse Review,* and *Night Train*. His reviews have appeared widely in such publications as *Ploughshares, Georgia Review, American Book Review, Prairie Schooner, Mid-American Review, Pleiades,* the *Missouri Review, Xconnect,* and *Environment* magazine. He has published a few dozen articles in both *Novel & Short Story Writer's Market* and *The Writer* magazine. His creative writing book, *Write and Revise for Publication: A Six-Month Plan for Crafting an Exceptional Novel and Other Works of Fiction*, was published in 2013 by Writer's Digest Books. His co-authored nonfiction environmental book titled *Killing Me Softly* was published by Monthly Review Press in 2002. Besides his writing, Smith was fiction editor of *The Green Hills Literary Lantern*, an online literary magazine published by Truman State University, for 25 years.

FROM FIRST DRAFT TO FINAL

Navigating the Stages of Manuscript Drafting

Leslie Lee Sanders

If you're like most writers, you will need to write numerous drafts before you can consider your manuscript complete. Drafting a novel is a process made up of several stages: the rough draft, the rewrite drafts, and the final draft. Each stage is essential to help you *write*, *clarify*, and then *polish* your story.

Drafting allows you to divide your revisions into segments so you can focus on one component at a time. Attempting to write and edit simultaneously can slow or stall your progress. Instead the goal of the first draft should be to get the story on paper. Then you can rewrite for clarity in the second draft, and polish the writing quality in the third. You can also use subsequent drafts to enhance the reader's experience, apply feedback from beta readers or critique partners, and tighten up your prose.

THE ROUGH DRAFT

It's no secret that the first draft of anything is often terrible. However, writing a bad first draft is necessary for two reasons. First, it eases the crippling effect of perfectionism, which can slow your progress or prevent you from reaching the end. Second, it allows you to devote your initial efforts to larger concerns—like the structure of your story—and leave smaller tasks like grammar and punctuation for later.

Sometimes writers have the tendency to be perfectionists, but trying to write the perfect story in the first draft will set you up for delay—or worse, writer's block. Just keep in mind that every first draft will benefit from a fresh perspective, clarification, or revision of some sort, but you needn't address every major issue at once. At this stage, it's more important to *just write.*

To complete your first draft quickly and effectively, follow these strategies:

- **SET AND HIT A DAILY WORD COUNT GOAL.** This method of writing is a tried-and-true favorite because it forces you to put aside disruptions and put words onto paper, moving you closer to the finish line with each sentence.
- **CREATE AN OUTLINE.** Plotting your story before writing the opening line helps you envision your scenes to better steer your plot. Many writers find that an outline—even a loose one—helps their words flow more easily, since they know ahead of time how to navigate their scenes.
- **WRITE TERRIBLY.** As you write your first draft, resist the temptation to correct misspellings, write more eloquent sentences, or add that perfect line of dialogue. Save those changes for the rewrite, and give yourself permission to write terribly—for now, at least.

  If you do come up with a good line of dialogue or a particularly well-written description that you simply *must* include, make a note in brackets to insert it in a later draft. Whatever you do, continue writing.
- **DON'T REREAD WHAT YOU'VE WRITTEN.** When you return to your draft after taking a break, don't reread what you've already written. If you have to familiarize yourself with a preceding scene before writing the next one, read no more than a few paragraphs. This will prevent you from falling into the trap of self-editing before the story is finished.

Attempting to write and edit simultaneously can slow or stall your progress. Instead, the goal of the first draft should be to get the story down on paper. Then you can rewrite for clarity in the second draft, and polish the writing quality in the third.

THE REWRITE DRAFT

After celebrating the completion of your rough draft, you'll probably look it over and realize that you still have a lot of work to do. This is where the real writing begins. You have to tunnel through the rewrite to unearth the hidden gems beneath.

During the rewrite, you will evaluate the quality of your *storytelling.* This differs from fixing the quality of your writing, which is a concern for the final draft. Use the second stage of drafting to address issues with larger elements of your novel, such as the plot, setting, and theme; character development; worldbuilding; and overall clarity. Since you'll be altering, adding, and removing large chunks of text during this round, don't get bogged down with minor grammar, spelling, and mechanical concerns. To do so is time-consuming, because you'll end up utilizing more than one draft to edit minor grammatical mistakes.

Here are some elements to address during the rewrite phase:

- **ADDRESS PLOT HOLES, CONTINUITY PROBLEMS, EXCESSIVE DESCRIPTION, ETC.** Your primary goal with the rewrite is to clean up the issues and errors that get in the way of good storytelling. Make sure your novel is solid from beginning to end before stressing over trivial errors, like misspelled words.
- **ENRICH YOUR CHARACTERS.** Characters are one of the most important elements of storytelling. It's through your characters that readers experience your fictional world. So make sure your characters are three-dimensional, emotional, and relatable. Emphasize their importance to the story. Tweak their dialogue and physical descriptions.
- **ATTEND TO WORLDBUILDING.** Your story's world should be just as visible in your readers' minds as it is in yours. Color your settings with vibrant description and distinct details, establish your story world's rules, and bring the environment to life.
- **REINFORCE YOUR STYLE AND VOICE, AND ESTABLISH TONE AND MOOD.** Make sure the tone of your novel—lighthearted and breezy, or dark and cynical—is prevalent throughout. Lock in the mood of the novel at both the beginning and the end, and make sure your voice and style are consistent. For example, an analogy that references famous cartoon characters might not be appropriate when describing your story's serial killer. Pinpoint incongruities like these and find appropriate alternatives.
- **EXAMINE YOUR STORY'S STRUCTURE.** Make sure you have successfully set up the most significant parts of your story. Polish the hook, make your inciting incident stand out, and be sure that the events in your story build to a gripping climax. Tweak your twists, surprises, and reveals so that they pack a punch. Your ending should leave a lasting impression on readers.

SUBSEQUENT DRAFTS

You may find that you need to write more than three drafts before you can consider your manuscript finished. Here are some reasons to write more drafts:

- **TO FOCUS ON SPECIFIC ISSUES.** Use a draft to zero in on one issue throughout the entire piece before moving on to the next. For example, you can use a draft to enrich your characters' development, and then another draft to enhance your story's setting.

- **TO APPLY BETA READER FEEDBACK.** At some point in the drafting process, you may receive input from critique partners, members of your writing group, or even an editor you've hired to look at an early draft. You could use a subsequent draft to apply changes suggested by these readers. Some of the suggestions might involve removing or restructuring plot points, or focusing on specific issues related to characterization, theme, dialogue, and so on. For instance, after a critique you may decide that your story would benefit from adding, eliminating, or combining characters with similar roles.
- **TO SET UP YOUR STORY FOR A SEQUEL OR BOOK SERIES.** While working on Book One of a new series, use a draft to specifically identify areas where you can set up events in Book Two. Check for continuity of the main theme, premise, and key factors of the series.
- **TO DO ADDITIONAL FACT-CHECKING AND RESEARCH.** One of the last drafts you write should be used to fact-check and apply the information you've discovered while researching certain elements of your story. For instance, if your character is a gun-wielding soldier, review gun mechanics and details of military rank to avoid making mistakes that savvy readers will pick up on.

THE FINAL DRAFT

Now that you've reached the final rewrite, your focus should switch from evaluating the quality of your *storytelling* to assessing the quality of your *writing*. Here is where you correct errors in spelling, grammar, punctuation, sentence structure, and so on.

In the final draft, go over your manuscript carefully and immerse yourself in the nitty-gritty details of the project. This is the last draft you will complete before you move to the next phase in the life of your novel, be it submission to an agent or editor, entry in a writing competition, or self-publication.

A famous adage says that novelists never finish a book; they merely abandon it to the public. Because of the need to perfect a novel, many writers have the tendency to keep editing. But remember that there is such a thing as over-editing. You have to know when to quit, otherwise your story will never see the light of day. You need to identify the moment when you can no longer improve your manuscript. Upon completion of the final draft, you have arrived at that moment.

To determine whether your manuscript is complete, try these techniques:

- **GET SOME DISTANCE.** Take a step back from writing, reading, and thinking about your story for a few days or weeks, and then reread your manuscript with a fresh perspective. Only then will you have the ability to decipher whether the story would benefit from another draft.

- **START A NEW PROJECT.** It's usually after starting a new writing project that you realize that the previous project is indeed finished.
- **DEFINE YOUR GOAL.** Remember the reasons you needed to write the story? Maybe you had something you needed to say, an opinion you needed to express, or a view of the world you needed to share. If you feel certain that your story effectively spreads your message, your work is done.

When it comes to producing a publishable novel, expect a long rewriting phase or several drafts. You'll either rewrite and spend a considerable amount of time on the manuscript to polish it to perfection, or use several drafts for the same effect. Either way, writing at least three drafts is ideal. Your efforts won't be for nothing—in the end, you'll have a final draft you'll be eager to share with the world.

Leslie Lee Sanders is the published author of the post-apocalyptic and dystopian Refuge Inc. series, with more than ten years of fiction-writing and book-publishing experience. She teaches the art and craft of blogging, writing, and publishing on her blog at leslieleesanders.com. Her work has been included in the following Writer's Market books: *Writer's Market 2016*, *Novel & Short Story Writer's Market 2016*, and the 2014 and 2015 editions of *Guide to Self-Publishing*.

INJECTING AUTHENTICITY INTO A STORY

Fred White

Despite the obvious distinction between fiction and nonfiction, the similarities outweigh the differences. A good story is brought to life by authenticity—the authentic depictions of setting, character behavior, and situation. This holds true for all story genres, not just historical or biographical fiction. That's because all good fiction, by dramatizing a hypothetical reality, captures what is essential about the human and natural world. People read fiction for the pleasure of becoming part of the story's invented world. But a crucial contributor to that experience, whether readers realize it consciously or not, is the implicit learning that takes place: learning how a private investigator searches for clues, interrogates suspects, and connects with police to solve a crime; or learning how a Florida amusement park performer like Ava Bigtree, Karen Russell's protagonist in her novel *Swamplandia!* (Vintage, 2011), raises and wrestles alligators.

So how does a fiction writer seamlessly meld narrative with information? I suggest following this three-step process:

1. Lay the groundwork for your story.
2. Search for behind-the-scenes information.
3. Integrate factual details into your narrative.

1. LAY THE GROUNDWORK

Some writers worry that pre-planning will interfere with creative spontaneity. Well, it's possible that *obsessive* planning can interfere with the insights that can spring from spontaneity. But laying the groundwork by outlining, storyboarding, and creating profiles of the principal characters and the settings is necessary and can be just as creative and spontaneous as drafting—*if* you allow for flexibility. Keep in mind that your characters will likely take on a life of their own when the situations you put them in demand that they behave in ways you never anticipated. And that's a good thing. As in real life, a certain degree of unpredictability will enhance the authenticity of your fiction.

Prepare Profiles of Your Characters

To create characters that ring true, it helps to write out detailed profiles of them before you start drafting. Doing so will make them seem like real persons to you and thus help you to present them realistically in your story.

For each character, prepare a profile page. I recommend using filler paper—this makes it easier to add details and to store in a three-ring binder. Of course, you can also maintain these profiles on your computer; my personal preference just happens to be for hard copy.

Be copious with specific details. You want your characters to emerge as distinctive individuals both physically and behaviorally. For example, here is the profile page for the central character in my short story "Ramón," about a Mexican-American teenager who, tormented by his father's tragic death, is driven to perform dangerous stunts:

RAMÓN GUTIERREZ
(Age 17)

ETHNICITY: Mexican-American

PARENTS: Felicia (a seamstress); Luis (a professional race car driver, deceased)

PHYSICAL ATTRIBUTES: tall (6'), athletic, agile, jet-black hair, scars from street-fighting (including one on his abdomen from a fight with broken bottles)

BEHAVIORAL/PSYCHOLOGICAL ATTRIBUTES: aggressive (but intolerant of bullies), a risk taker (loves performing dangerous stunts), intolerant of cowardice, driven to exhibit courage by the death of his father during a racing event, can be intimidating, taunts protagonist out of his introverted tendencies

SPECIAL SKILLS: juggling, bicycle acrobatics

Profile pages enable you to work out important contrasts between your characters. For example, in my short story, Ramón's improbable new friend, Gerald (the story's narrator), is his polar opposite in temperament: Gerald hates daredevilry yet secretly envies Ramón for his ability to perform dangerous stunts—so much so that he lets Ramón try to teach him some of them, with nearly disastrous consequences.

Fiction writers should be students of human behavior, and the lessons should derive, ideally, from extensive interaction with and observation of people, along with a general knowledge of psychology. Such grounding will help you convey your characters' actions, feelings, aspirations, obsessions, and aberrations realistically.

For instance, if your protagonist is a private detective, you'll want to do plenty of background reading in criminal investigation. Start with overviews on the Internet, such as the online version of Encyclopedia Britannica, or Wikipedia—but don't stop there. Also study a good introductory text, such as *The Everything Private Investigation Book* by Sheila L. Stephens (Adams Media, 2008) or (for gaining a broad overview of the full spectrum of police work) *Criminal Investigation*, 10th Edition by Charles R. Swanson et al. (McGraw-Hill, 2009). No matter how much background reading you do, though, nothing beats having an extended conversation with actual criminal investigators. You'll likely discover that their experiences are not quite like those of their fictional counterparts.

> One of the pleasures of researching comes from unexpected discoveries you make along the way toward locating the material you intended to find. Unexpected findings have a way of adding unanticipated insights into your pre-planned story.

Prepare Descriptions of the Settings

Readers want to be transported to intriguing places. As Emily Dickinson put it, "There is no frigate like a book / To take us lands away." Your story's settings—exterior and interior—need to be conveyed vividly enough for readers to feel transported, to experience your fictional world vicariously. You accomplish this with imagery and vivid, concrete, sensory details. As you did with character rap sheets, prepare setting sheets. Don't hold anything back for these sheets; you most likely will use only a handful of details in the final story, but you want a full palette of choices to start with. You might also want to supplement your setting sheets with photographs.

Description of a setting can play an important role in establishing the tone or mood of an entire short story or novel. In *The Scarlet Letter* (1850) Nathaniel Hawthorne's portrayal of Puritan society in seventeenth-century Salem, Massachusetts, comes to life through Hester Prynne's ordeal as a woman shamed and punished for having a child out of wedlock. Here is how Hawthorne sets the scene—and the mood—in the opening paragraph of the first chapter, "The Prison-House":

> A throng of bearded men, in sad-colored garments and gray, steeple-crowned hats, intermixed with women, some wearing hoods, and others bare-headed, was assembled in front of a wooden edifice, the door of which was heavily timbered with oak, and studded with iron spikes.

Note how Hawthorne, in his description of the prison-house entrance, conjures up sharp images with just a few words like "steeple-crowned hats" and the door studded with "iron spikes" to give readers the sense of the setting. Note also how the modifiers "sad-colored" and "gray" establish a somber mood that is sustained for the entire novel.

Let's look at a modern example. Here is a list I made of John Updike's description of a barn in his short story, "Pigeon Feathers," about a young man's nostalgic return to his parents' Pennsylvania farm:

DAVID'S PARENTS' BARN

barn interior like a small night
splinters of light
dry shingles
high roof
rafters, crossbeams
built-in ladders: like tree branches
smell of old straw
empty bins, gaping like caves
coils of baling wire
spare tines for a harrow
handleless shovel

In some novels, setting and situation become intertwined. For example, in his thriller, *The Burning Wire* (Simon & Schuster, 2010), in which a killer sabotages the New York City power grid, Jeffrey Deaver takes time to explain some of the inner workings of the grid in a way that is both informative and provocative:

> In the suburbs and countryside the grid is clearly visible—those bare overhead high-tension wires and power poles and service lines running into your house. When a line goes down there's little difficulty finding and fixing the problem. In many cities though, like NewYork, the electricity flows underground, in insulated cables. Because the insulation degrades after time and suffers groundwater damage, resulting in shorts and loss of service, power companies rely on double or even triple redundancy in the grid.

Such expository prose might seem tedious out of context, but in this case it informs the plot, and—most important—it comes after we learn that one segment of the grid is experiencing "critical failure."

Fiction Writing as Worldbuilding

If your fiction genre of choice is science fiction or fantasy, you are faced with the challenge of worldbuilding, whereby you not only convey particular alien or magical settings but an entire world. Creating strangeness may seem antithetical to creating authenticity, but it isn't. Science fiction and fantasy readers love oddities and peculiar details, but no matter how weird a landscape, it has to contain elements with which readers can identify. Purple, sentient trees must still share some of the properties of ordinary earthly trees. The same holds true with alien life forms or mythical monsters. The strangest creatures in Greek mythology—centaurs, griffins, harpies, and the like—are amalgams of terrestrial animals and humans.

In one of my favorite fantasy novels, *A Voyage to Arcturus* (Ballantine, 1920), David Lindsay evokes a world so alien as to defy comparison with our own—but the similarities, however faint, are just enough to lend authenticity to the tale. On a quest to understand the enigmas of existence, the protagonist, Maskull, treks through some of the most bizarre terrain ever conceived:

> The sea was unlike any sea on Earth. It resembled an immense liquid opal. On a body color of rich, magnificent emerald-green, bright flashes of red, yellow, and blue were everywhere shooting up and vanishing. … Pinnacles of water were slowly formed until they attained a height of perhaps ten or twenty feet when they would suddenly sink downward and outward, creating in their descent a series of concentric rings for long distances around them.

2. SEARCH FOR BEHIND-THE-SCENES INFORMATION

After you've profiled the characters and settings for your short story or novel, take the time to search for information—not just overviews about places, events, or pursuits, but nitty-gritty stuff that calls attention to the human element or the unusual. If you want to write a story about hot air ballooning, for example, search for testimonials from balloon racers (if you don't have the opportunity to interview them) or information on how to operate a hot air balloon. Resist the temptation to draft too soon. Instead, spend time absorbing the subject matter of your story to better capture authenticity.

By "behind-the-scenes" I refer to factual details derived from firsthand experience *or* from talking to or shadowing experts in the same or similar line of work, or at least doing a lot of in-depth reading. Often it's the overlooked details of a setting—the smells and sounds of an infirmary; the riot of half-empty oil-paint tubes and unfinished canvasses in an artist's studio— that can add realism and emotional power to a story. Relying on superficial knowledge or inventing things outright won't do the trick; your story quite likely will not ring true.

By the way, did you notice that I used the word *search* instead of *research*? To *search* connotes an unknown factor in the process: There is more to find than you think! *Search* also connotes adventure in the act of digging for material, not unlike an archaeologist's search for a lost Egyptian tomb. The point here is to have faith in serendipity. In her essay "Under No Certain Terms," published in the *New York Times Book Review* in January 2016, the historian and author of *Daughters of the Samurai* (Norton, 2015) Janice P. Nimura wittily points out that the problem with researching using Google is that "you find exactly what you're looking for, and nothing you're not." In other words, one of the pleasures of researching comes from unexpected discoveries you make along the way toward locating the material you intended to find. Unexpected findings have a way of adding unanticipated insights into your pre-planned story.

Drawing from Firsthand Experience

Don't rely on mere recollections during the drafting stage. Take "mental inventories"; writing stuff down beforehand, over several days, will provide you with the palette of details from which to choose as the particular story moment warrants. Your inventory sheets should include meticulous physical and behavioral details of your characters, painterly descriptions of the places where the events are going to unfold, and accurate depictions of the events themselves.

Even if you're inventing your story content from whole cloth, you will want to allot extra time to research relevant material.

There are two kinds of research—secondary and primary—and fiction writers ought to engage in both. Let's say that one of your characters suffers from obsessive-compulsive disorder. You would conduct *secondary* research into the affliction by reading books and articles about OCD—its causes, symptoms, and methods of treatment. You would conduct *primary* research by interviewing health professionals dealing with OCD patients and with the patients themselves. Primary research is invaluable for getting "inside" your subject to ensure authenticity.

3. INTEGRATE

If only writing fiction were as simple as following a kitchen recipe in which you add all the ingredients into a bowl, mix thoroughly, and … voilà! Integrated!

Alas, it's never that simple. However, it isn't difficult either.

The trick is to weave in factual details without disrupting story flow. Review the setting sheet I produced in step one, based on John Updike's description of the barn in his short story "Pigeon Feathers." Now look at how Updike weaves those details into his narrative:

> A barn, in day, is a small night. The splinters of light between the dry shingles pierce the high roof like stars, and the rafters and crossbeams and built-in ladders seem, until your eyes adjust, as mysterious as the branches of a haunted forest. David entered silently, the gun in his hand. … The smell of old straw scratched his sinuses. … The mouths of empty bins gaped like caves.

In her novel *Swamplandia!*, Karen Russell enriches her story's milieu by having her protagonist describe real estate developers' efforts to drain the swamps by importing an Australian tree, *Melaleuca quinquenervia*, to absorb the water. Alas, the tree proved to be an invasive species that destroyed all the other trees and proliferated uncontrollably. Note how Russell integrates this information into her protagonist's narrative:

> If you were a swamp kid, you were weaned on the story of the Four Pilots of the Apocalypse, these men who had flown over the swamp in tiny Cessnas and sprinkled melaleuca seeds out of restaurant salt and pepper shakers. Exotic invasives, the "strangler species" threatened our family long before the World of Darkness [a competing amusement park]. … The dikes and levees that the Army Corps had recommended for flood control had turned the last virgin mahogany stands into dust bowls; in other places, wildfire burned the peat beds down to witchy fingers of lime.

A final suggestion to help you with integrating your researched material into your narrative: Don't "copy and paste." Instead, review the material enough times for you to absorb the essentials into your subconscious, and then plunge into the narrative. Likelier than not, the factual stuff will surface when you want it to … and provide plenty of surprises to boot.

Fred White's fiction and essays have appeared in many periodicals, including *Atticus Review, The Chronicle of Higher Education, College Literature, Confrontation, Pleiades, Rathalla Review, Southwest Review, Writer's Digest, Limestone*, and, most recently, *Praxis Literary Journal*. His most recent books are *The Writer's Idea Thesaurus* and *Where Do You Get Your Ideas?: A Writer's Guide to Transforming Notions into Narratives* (both published by Writer's Digest Books). His article "Post-Production" appears in *Novel &Short Story Writer's Market 2016*. A professor of English Emeritus (Santa Clara University), Fred lives with his wife, Therese, an attorney, near Sacramento, California.

THE ART OF DISTRACTION

Master the Use of Red Herrings

Jane K. Cleland

The first novel I wrote didn't sell. I worked on it for three years, and it didn't sell. Then I learned about red herrings, integrated them into my next novel, and it sold in a week as part of a three-book deal. Red herrings lead to suspenseful moments, the pulse of storytelling. Without them, your story will invariably be overly linear and pedestrian. With them, you'll keep your readers on the edge of their seats.

> "You add the ground mustard at the end," my mother told me as she poured in the milk. "After the vanilla."
>
> I was twenty and trying to learn how to make crepes the way she did, light and rich and not too sweet.
>
> "At the end? How come?"
>
> She nodded toward a yellowed index card that lay on the counter, far from my reach, guarded, sacred. "My mother was precise."
>
> "What was Grandma like?" I asked. "I don't remember her at all."
>
> "She was a liar."

If you're like most people, you want to know more. What's going on between this mother and daughter? Is the cooking lesson the point? Or is it a red herring?

Red herrings are intentional misdirections that work to add real-world intricacy to narrative nonfiction, children's literature, plays, and all types of fiction (not just mysteries).

Writers use red herrings in much the same way thieves use diversions. If I can get you looking over here, you may not notice what I'm doing over there. For instance, if a woman yells, "Help! He stole my purse!" and points into a teeming crowd, anyone within earshot will follow her gaze and the line of her trembling arm. They won't notice her partner jimmying his way into the jewelry store behind them.

When integrated seamlessly, red herrings are invisible. Readers believe the words on the page, whether those words include lies, or seemingly irrelevant facts that turn out to have import, or ostensibly important facts that turn out to be inconsequential, or what an expert tells them is true. Specifically, red herrings fall into three broad categories:

1. characters' motivations and habits
2. characters' capability and expertise
3. empirical evidence

CHARACTERS' MOTIVATIONS AND HABITS

Psychologist Edward L. Thorndike coined the term "halo effect" in the early twentieth century. He observed that if you perceive someone as physically attractive, you are likely to assume he is also kind and pleasant, an overall good person. Likewise, if someone does something altruistic, such as volunteer at a pediatric ward in a hospital, readers will assume this person is good through and through. The "reverse halo effect," also known as the "devil effect," says that readers assign evil attributes to a person if she is ugly or if she does one bad thing. Allowing your readers to be swept along with these preconceptions is an effective way to use red herrings. When you finally spring the truth on them, they'll experience a delicious moment of surprise.

In Paula Hawkins's 2015 breakout novel, *The Girl on the Train*, the protagonist, Rachel, is a falling-down drunk. She lost her job, is obsessed with her ex-husband, and can't manage even the smallest, most mundane task without screwing up. With evidence of these character flaws, it's easy to impute other negative qualities to her, too—to assume she's lazy or uncaring, maybe even capable of stalking or other criminal acts. That's the devil effect at work.

> "What did Grandma lie about?" I asked, half-convinced I misheard.
>
> "Her husband."
>
> "Your father?"
>
> She tilted the frying pan, swirling the butter to cover the bottom. The batter was resting. "Sam wasn't my father."
>
> I blinked, momentarily speechless.
>
> "I understand why she did it," Ma added. "Back then, there was a stigma."
>
> "Who's your dad?"
>
> "I don't know and I don't care. Don't trust anyone. That's the lesson here."
>
> "How did you find out?"
>
> "Sam needed a transfusion. They tested us. I just got the call."
>
> "Grandma was trying to protect you. That isn't a lie."
>
> She placed the frying pan on a cool burner and walked out of the room.

This short memoir has become more complicated. What might be a red herring?

CHARACTERS' CAPABILITY AND EXPERTISE

Capability and expertise come up in my Josie Prescott Antiques mysteries all the time. Josie, an antiques appraiser, is an expert in a broad range of antiques and collectibles. She's also as honest as they come—but not all experts are, and you can use that fact to distract your readers from the main event.

Rex Stout, a Mystery Writers of America Grand Master, applied this technique in multiple ways in his novella *The Gun with Wings*. In the story, genius detective Nero Wolfe investigates what appears to be the suicide of an eminent opera singer. The singer had seriously injured his larynx in a fistfight, and everyone assumes that he shot himself out of despair that he might not regain his voice. His doctor, a world-renowned surgeon, can't understand it. The operation was a success, and the singer's throat was healing nicely. When physical evidence proves that the singer's death was a homicide, not a suicide, the chief suspects include the man who hit him, the singer's wife, and the man she's fallen in love with ... all your basic red herrings. But the killer turns out to be—wait for it—the doctor. He'd messed up the operation and couldn't bear the thought that his mistakes would come to light. Now that's a masterful use of a red herring!

In Stout's story, the doctor's profession distracts us from suspicion. Think about it: When a doctor tells you to open wide and say, "Aaahh," what do you do? You tilt your head back, open your mouth, stick out your tongue, and stare at the ceiling. You expect to feel a bit of pressure as the doctor uses the tongue depressor to gain a better view. In *The Gun with Wings*, that opera singer believed that his doctor had his best interests at heart. He never saw the gun the doctor slid into his mouth.

Think of all the experts in your life. If the people you're writing about interact with doctors, lawyers, accountants, interior designers, scientists, or anyone else with specialized expertise, you can use that to layer in complexity. Words to live by: Be careful whom you trust.

Then again, expertise—or lack of it—doesn't have to be specialized. It can simply be unique to a certain situation. For example, in Newbery Medal–winner Avi's *Nothing but the Truth: A Documentary Novel*, the narrator, Philip, lies to cover up his lack of capability. Philip becomes a cause célèbre in a national tug-of-war between proponents of free expression and those who value patriotism above all else. When Philip insists on humming (not singing) the national anthem, his teacher takes it as a sign of disrespect. The flap over free expression is a red herring; the truth is that Philip didn't know the words, so he hummed.

RED HERRINGS: WHAT'S IN A NAME?

Brewer's Dictionary of Phrase and Fable and Merriam-Webster, among other sources, have consistently attributed the term *red herring* to a centuries-old dog training technique. Hunting dogs need to be able to follow an underlying scent. This is true whether the dogs are hunting for foxes, criminals, cadavers, or drugs. They must be able to keep their noses on the job and avoid being distracted by tempting, but irrelevant, aromas. By dragging a smoked fish—a red herring—across the track, the trainer could assess a dog's readiness for work. If the dog followed the strong—and wrong—scent of a red herring, he wasn't properly trained. If, however, he didn't follow the false trail, pursuing the underlying scent instead, he was ready for action.

The *Oxford English Dictionary* now disputes that history, instead attributing the phrase to nineteenth-century journalist William Cobbett. A piece he wrote in 1807 for England's weekly *Political Register* detailed how, as a boy, he'd used a red herring to distract hunting dogs from their jobs. The parable, evidently a fictional account, was intended to communicate Cobbett's disdain toward members of the press for allowing themselves to be distracted from crucial domestic issues by the government's report that Napoleon had been defeated.

Whichever is correct, the meaning of the term is unchanged: A red herring is an intentional misdirection.

EMPIRICAL EVIDENCE

The array of details we see, hear, touch, taste, and smell each day is astonishing. Some things capture your attention because they stand out as unusual or unexpected; others you don't notice at all because they're so familiar you no longer register their presence or because they're merely one element in a cluttered world. What your characters observe—or don't—can be effective red herrings.

German psychologist Hermann Ebbinghaus described the "serial position effect": People are more likely to recall information that is recent and first in a list. If I list items, the third of which is relevant to the story, on page 1, but don't refer to it again until page 200, you are likely to have forgotten it. If I list five objects, you're much more likely to remember the first one than the third.

Consider this list of objects on a man's desk: an airline ticket from his home city of Dallas to Belize City; a "Make it legal—do it with a lawyer" coffee mug; a gilt-framed photo of the man, a pretty auburn-haired woman, and a teenage boy; a throwaway pen from Texas North Community Bank squared up on a yellow legal pad; a laptop computer; a telephone; and a bank statement from Campbell Bank.

When the man is accused of embezzlement, readers may recall the ticket to Belize and wonder if he may be stashing money in an offshore account. The ticket, though, is a red herring. He's going to Belize with his wife and son on a diving vacation. What your readers will probably forget, if they even noticed it in the first place, is the pen from the community bank. If the man has an account at Campbell, why does he have a pen from another bank? There could be countless reasons, of course, including that one of his clients left it behind, but it also could be a clue—or a red herring. Perhaps he rented a safety deposit box at this out-of-the-way bank to hide the money he's embezzled from his partner. Or maybe he rented that safety deposit box for an innocuous reason that will become apparent later in the book. For instance, maybe he plans on terminating his partnership to open his own practice. To that end, he's building a relationship with a new bank.

It's also worth noting that sometimes the most telling detail is the one you don't mention. In Sir Arthur Conan Doyle's 1892 short story "Silver Blaze," for instance, Sherlock Holmes solves a crime because a dog *didn't* bark.

Even the savviest readers won't know if a particular detail is a red herring or whether it's central to the story.

> I found my mother in the den, at her desk, typing away. The rule was never to disturb her while she was writing. She was working on a romance novel, her second.
>
> "I don't know what to do," I said.
>
> She swiveled toward me. Her eyes were narrowed and cold, her lips pursed. I didn't understand why she was mad. I didn't know if she was mad at me or her father or her mother or Sam.
>
> "Should I put the batter in the fridge?" I asked.
>
> "Yes." She spun back to her computer.
>
> After I placed the bowl in the refrigerator, I picked up the yellowed recipe card from the counter, the first one of my grandmother's I'd ever seen close up. My mother never shared recipes, not even with me. She stored the cards in a turquoise metal box in a locked drawer in her desk as if they were gold. I recognized Grandma's spidery handwriting. Flour, salt, eggs, milk, butter. Four simple steps. Mix the flour, salt, and eggs. Slowly add the milk and melted butter. Swirl ¼ cup batter around a lightly oiled frying pan and cook the crepe for two minutes a side over medium heat. Ground mustard? Vanilla? Butter in the pan? I understood now. This wasn't about Sam or lies my grandmother told. This was about my mother, who, for some reason known only to her, wanted me to fail.
>
> I centered the bottle of vanilla extract and the small jar of ground mustard on top of the recipe card. It felt important—though even at twenty, I knew it probably wasn't—that my mother realize I wasn't stupid, that she could dress up the truth in any guise she chose, and I'd still see that she was the only one among us who lied.

At the start of the story, did you notice that my mom said to add vanilla and ground mustard to the batter and that she was coating the pan with butter? Maybe it registered as a bit odd, but most people would have been so startled by my mother's revelation about Sam that they wouldn't give it a second thought. Misdirection adds complexity every time. This kind of multifaceted plotting and characterization is at the heart of storytelling. Red herrings help create the kind of blazing suspense that readers can't resist. They burn to know what happens. These are the stories that win reader loyalty. These are the stories that sell.

Jane K. Cleland (janecleland.com) is the award-winning author of the Josie Prescott Antiques Mystery series. Her book *Mastering Suspense, Structure & Plot: How to Write Gripping Stories That Keep Readers on the Edge of Their Seats* (Writer's Digest Books) was released in April 2016.

KATHRYN CRAFT

How Structure Supports Meaning

Janice Gable Bashman

In *The Far End of Happy*, Kathryn Craft novelizes her first husband's suicide standoff with the police by confining the story to its true twelve-hour time frame. Adding a ticking clock is a well-known way to inject edge-of-the-seat tension into thrillers and suspense novels, but Kathryn co-opted the technique for her women's fiction. The novel's one-hour blocks add a sense of weight to each unfolding moment of that fateful day. While Kathryn expands the frame of the story with pertinent events that brought the characters to this moment in time, and suggests the ramifications for their futures should they not be able to face their issues, the reader senses the dividing line: Because of this day, where one man's life hangs in the balance, these characters' lives will never be the same. She further divides each hour between three points of view that show the impact of the standoff on the wife, the wife's mother, and the despondent man's mother, as each woman sifts through her memory for clues as to "how the heck she got there this day."

Kathryn's interest in weaving backstory threads into the ongoing narrative reveals her fascination with why people do the things they do, placing her firmly in the psychological subgenre of women's fiction. She had already experimented with such techniques in her first novel, *The Art of Falling.*

In addition to her two novels from Sourcebooks, Kathryn is a contributor to the book *Author in Progress,* a no-holds-barred look at what it takes to get published, authored by the blogging team at the online writing community Writer Unboxed (www.writerunboxed.com). Her decade of work as a freelance developmental editor at writing-partner.com follows a nineteen-year career as a dance critic. A longtime leader in the southeastern Pennsylvania writing scene, she has served on boards for the Greater Lehigh Valley Writers Group, their annual Write Stuff conference, the Philadelphia Writers' Conference, and in several volunteer capacities for the Women's Fiction Writers Association. She hosts lakeside writing retreats for women in northern New York State, leads writing workshops, and is a member of the Tall Poppy Writers.

Here Craft shares her insights on structuring a novel, using backstory to fuel readers' engagement, and developing rich character arcs within a short time line.

The word *structure* can mean different things when referring to novel writing. How do you define it?

I see it two different ways. The most crucial decisions an author makes are in terms of storytelling structure, which really isn't about "telling" at all. It's about how you will raise questions in the reader's mind about whether your character can achieve her story goal. Storytelling structure fuels the novel with backstory motivation that creates a deep desire for the protagonist, suggests the stakes should the character not succeed, and creates a yardstick by which to assess the protagonist's progress ("Yes, this is just what he needed," or "Oh no, things aren't looking so good for him just now!"). With the right kind of overarching span and page-by-page tension, the desire to answer the story question will pull the reader all the way to the end of a book.

While wrestling down the myriad decisions of storytelling structure, though, we writers sometimes forget to tend to the way the larger structures of a book—what I call "macrostructures," ([or] how it's divided into chapters and sections and perspectives)—can contribute meaning. One of my favorite examples is the novel *The Secret Life of Bees,* in which Sue Monk Kidd begins each chapter with a nonfiction epigraph about bees. As the novel progresses, the astute reader can't help but seek parallels in human and insect behavior.

How did the craft of communicating through structure first occur to you?

As with many discoveries, it happened by mistake. In early drafts, *The Art of Falling* opened with Penelope Sparrow's moment-by-moment actions as she parted from a high-rise balcony and landed on a bakery truck fourteen stories below. The chapter's tension and drama earned the chapter an award in a statewide contest, but it couldn't fool my advance readers, who could not engage with Penelope. I finally figured out why: The question raised by this opening is "Oh my gosh, will she survive?" Well, guess what happens when the reader turns the page and sees Penelope waking in a hospital room? When the story question is answered, the story is over. I needed a structure that would raise book-length questions, not answer them.

So was that complicated to set up?

In a word, yes. I needed to create an inciting incident—that incident that changes everything in my protagonist's life and incites her to set a story goal—that would raise questions about both the ongoing and backstory threads. I found my solution in creating a slight disconnect in perception among my characters as to what that incident really was. My secondary cast—new friends outside the dance world, the local dance critic, and Penelope's doctors—helped me raise the first question, since they all perceive the inciting incident as being the fall. They ask Penelope outright: What happened out on that ledge? By this point the reader wants to know as well.

Penelope's ongoing inner conflict causes her to see things differently. While her body brings her life joy and meaning, she blames its imperfections for the loss of her dream career. Now the strength and resiliency of that same body has caused her to survive what should have been a deadly fall. The aforementioned disconnect is revealed: For Penelope, the inciting incident is not the fall. If she had died, her soul would have been released from the burden of her imperfect body and free to dance with the gods. No, for Penelope, the inciting incident was surviving the fall.

The two story questions are now opened: (1) What put Penelope on the penthouse balcony, at the height of what [appeared to be] her dream career, and (2) How can she remobilize her life in a more meaningful way now that she's hit ground zero? Those questions drive both the backstory and present storylines, which intertwine until we get the missing piece at the end. The piece Penelope's traumatized brain has been unwilling to face, and the piece I had mistakenly, at first, opened with what happened between the balcony and the ground. By making a personal mystery of it, and waiting until Penelope had learned some important lessons before showing what happened, I was able to sustain reader interest all the way until the end.

You use similar backstory interweaving in your second novel as well. Did you employ the same process?

In a way, but in *The Far End of Happy* there is no misperception about the inciting incident, which is painfully clear. In the opening my protagonist is sitting on the guest room bed, writing in her journal. Here, she presses her pen "to a cool, fresh page" and writes:

> *Today Jeff is moving out.*
>
> She would not have predicted this day in her marriage. Its impact was impossible to fathom. How could she write beyond such words? Ronnie shut her journal. Only one sentence, but it was a good one. Full of hope but also one of the saddest she's ever written. She'd have to sort her feelings tomorrow. Today was a day for moving forward. She capped the pen and placed the notebook on the growing pile of journals beneath the bed.

When instead of moving out Jeff shows up drunk and armed, and holes up in a building on the property, the story question is set: Will Ronnie be able to move forward if her husband is determined to stand off?

Again, I used secondary characters to open the backstory thread. Since the police are coming to the situation cold and seeking context, they ask, What happened? How

"The most crucial decisions an author makes are in terms of storytelling structure, which really isn't about 'telling' at all. It's about how you will raise questions in the reader's mind about whether your character can achieve her story goal."

was your husband this morning? Has he exhibited signs of depression recently? Each of the questions leads the reader back in time, until she too wants to know how a life that once held such promise has come to this.

Other writers might have examined the protagonist's life both before and after the suicide standoff, or started the story earlier in the marriage and ended on the day of the standoff. Why did you choose to start and end the novel on the day of the standoff and keep it confined to its one-hour blocks?

Since the novel is based on true events, I originally drafted this story as a memoir that explored how such a happy marriage had devolved, over fifteen years, into my need to divorce and my husband's threats of suicide. Frankly, I needed that story. But the knowledge of what was to come colored everything. As I sorted through my journals in search of the most relevant scenes from my marriage, my thoughts kept snapping back to the suicide: Had my husband been in a bad mood that day, or was this a clue? Had this been manipulation, or love? I realized the daylong standoff was the perfect metaphor for exploring one partner's deep need to keep things the same even as the other must honor her deep need for change. What better way to highlight how these twelve hours changed this family's life forever than to devote the whole novel to it? This was easier done in fiction than in memoir, since I'd have to compress the time line of actual events to complete my protagonist's arc in just twelve hours. But the high stakes, tough choices, and nagging shameful secrets would now be palpable in every single minute.

You further divide the one-hour blocks into chapters, each limited to one of three points of view. What difficulties did you face when structuring the novel like this, and how did you manage to make it all come together in one cohesive story that keeps the pages turning?

The multiple points of view were key to my decision to novelize. A memoir would throw the spotlight on what happened to *me* and what I learned. I wanted to suggest the widespread impact of suicide. I gained this meaning through the perspectives of the mother who has to watch her daughter pay such a high price for love and the mother who must face that she cannot save her son.

As to how it all came together, well, ahem, that took several rounds of trial and error. At one point I had chapters sitting all over my floor with character codes and key words scrawled at the top, arranged in twelve fanned stacks like a giant game of solitaire, so I could see how best to balance perspectives and backstory within each one-hour block.

How did you manipulate the novel's structure so that the backstory threads, which are told in three points of view, wouldn't pull the reader out of the story tension and make her want to set your novel down?

The secret here is to raise a question about the backstory for which the reader desires an answer. For me this often comes in the form of a little question bomb at the end of a chapter—a reveal about the past that makes the reader sit up and say, "Wait, *what*?" Then I'd break away for another bit of forward-moving story, ending only when a new question was raised. The reader doesn't want to stop reading then, either, but she still wants to know the answer to that backstory question, so she'll gladly delay moving on to circle back for more complete knowledge.

I used those same techniques in *The Art of Falling*, but in that book, it helped that there was a troubled romance in the backstory thread. Readers rarely mind cutting away for romance.

Giving three point-of-view characters a growth arc over a twelve-hour period sounds challenging. How did you create believable growth arcs for these women?

One way I met this challenge was to firmly root each character's desire in the backstory and then allow the inciting incident—the start of the standoff—to intensify that desire, allowing for a longer arc. An example is the backstory of my protagonist's mother. Beverly has unresolved issues involving suicide that she's hidden from her daughter, Ronnie. The tension she feels in watching her daughter go through this standoff is palpable—Beverly knows the stakes all too well. This long backstory tail [makes] Beverly's arc the most profound, because it gives us some sense of what will be needed for Ronnie to heal. It sets up the possibility for hope.

Not all arcs are equal, though. Jeff's mother has allowed denial to define her relationship with her son for his entire life, so one small step in the right direction by day's end will be huge for her. These backstories suggest the stakes: If these women can't support one another in facing this [crisis] head-on, this suicide will cripple Ronnie for the rest of her life. Completing the arc in twelve hours didn't leave me much time for a resolution, so I allowed symbolic actions to do much of the work.

What advice do you have for authors who might want to use a macrostructure to support meaning in their novels?

I suggest you pull way back and think about what you are trying to accomplish. An accurate synopsis will help you see the story all at once. In *The Art of Falling*, I wanted to show that Penelope's whole life, like modern dance itself, is about effort and surrender (gravity provides the metaphor). To support this meaning I divided the novel into four sections—Fall, Recovery, Contraction, and Release—based on the philosophies of early American model dance pioneers. [I used] as epigraphs quotes from both dancers (to represent body experience) and critics (to represent societal judgment). In this way I tied the healing journey she undertakes to the source of her conflict. Dance critic John Martin's quote for "recovery" is a metaphor for storytelling structure itself: "All movement can be considered to be a series of falls and recoveries; that is, a deliberate unbalance in order to progress, and a restoration of equilibrium for self-protection."

Ask yourself: What is this story's organizing principle (also known as theme, premise, or what choreographer Twyla Tharp, in her book *The Creative Habit*, calls a spine)? Is there a way you could reinforce it through the way you name your chapters or sections? No one who has read Mark Haddon's *The Curious Incident of the Dog in the Night-time* will forget that his novel begins with "Chapter 2" because his protagonist prefers prime numbers. Such structural considerations can help your project stand out in a crowded market.

Janice Gable Bashman is the Bram Stoker–nominated author of *Predator* and *Wanted Undead or Alive*. She is the publisher of *The Big Thrill*, the International Thriller Writers' magazine. Visit Janice at janicegablebashman.com.

GARTH STEIN

Illuminated

Jessica Strawser

Garth Stein has never been a stranger to small audiences. He's stage managed "theater at sea" on cruise ships. He's written stage plays produced by community theaters. He's made documentary films. He's written well-reviewed novels published by independent presses. Put it all together, and he's done the very thing so many people aspire to do but so few accomplish: simply make a living by making art.

And then, he did what some might imagine to be the equivalent of literary suicide: He wrote a book from the point of view of a dog.

It was called *The Art of Racing in the Rain*. And the unique perspective of its canine narrator, Enzo, who longs to be a human race car driver, had so much heart that its 2008 release did find a *slightly* bigger audience—to the tune of more than *4 million copies* sold and over *three years* on *The New York Times* bestsellers list.

Where do you go from there?

Well, if you're Garth Stein, you buckle in for the ride of your life. You go on tour. You sell movie rights. You create a special edition for teen readers (*Racing in the Rain: My Life as a Dog*) and a picture book adaptation (*Enzo Races in the Rain!*). You pay it forward, joining forces with other published writers to create a successful and growing nonprofit,

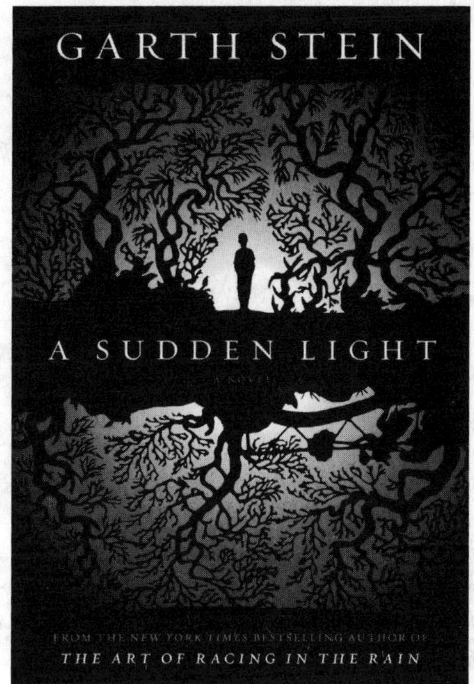

Seattle7Writers. ("We should be marshaling our energy for the greater good," Stein told me, describing the organization as a "win-win-win" for author-members, local bookstores and libraries, and the reading and writing public.)

And eventually, of course, you write something new.

A Sudden Light, centered on the descendants of lumber barons and the fate of their crumbling mansion, is part coming-of-age story, part ghost story, part reminder of the price nature has paid for man-made fortunes. In October, a few weeks after its hardcover release, it made a brief appearance on *The New York Times* bestsellers list. And then …

Well, the next chapter has yet to be written. Can lightning strike twice for the same author? Stein spoke with us about what it takes to write a book you truly believe in.

If *The Art of Racing in the Rain* had been narrated by any other character, it would have been a very different book. And while *A Sudden Light* evolved from your play "Brother Jones," that title character is not the narrator of the novel. So how do you choose a narrator?

Well, with *The Art of Racing in the Rain*, I knew from the very beginning the only way that story could be told was from the dog's point of view. Otherwise it would just be a family drama that's been done before. [But] with *A Sudden Light*, it took me a long

"I'm a big fan of telling young writers to take all the detours they possibly can, both in life and in writing. Those detours are going to lead you to where you need to be."

time to find the narrative voice because it was a much larger novel in terms of spanning multiple generations, and I like having a first-person [POV].

I spent quite a long time—years—writing five generations of the Riddell family history. I thought that was my novel. I wrote 100,000 words of the family from 1890 through 1990, and I thought it was good, but then I stepped back and looked at it and said, "Oh, this isn't my novel. This is research I've been doing in *preparation* to write my novel."

So then it became: I wanted to write the present-day story of the family, and the idea of redemption and how this family resolves its issues over generations, but do it from the contemporary vantage point. Who can narrate *this novel?*

Like you said, Brother Jones was the protagonist—and I have to say, that's one of the flaws of the play. He's too—well, his son calls him a "waffle." He's a little too waffle-y. To be a good protagonist you have to have a clear and substantial goal. Whether or not you achieve that or that's *really* what you want, it gives momentum to propel the story forward.

So that's where Trevor [Jones's son, and the narrator of the novel] came from. Jones did not have a son in the play. And so I brought the son in because he is untainted by the dark history of the Riddell family. He knows nothing about it, in fact—his father has never spoken about it. So [when his parents separate and his father takes him to the Riddell house], he comes in completely clean and has a simple, clean, objective goal, which is, *I want my parents to stay together. How am I going to achieve that?* Now, the path of that goes many directions, and as the Rolling Stones say, you can't always get what you want, but if you try, you'll get what you need—and I think that's a good protagonist, right?

Then there came this problem with having Trevor as the protagonist: He would have to learn everything [about the family's history] through discovery, and that becomes very awkward. That's when I put the lens in of the story being told by thirty-eight-year-old Trevor to his children and his wife, who he's returned to the estate with, to tell them what happened to him when he was fourteen years old.

That lens gives perspective from a more mature voice as someone who has been able to process everything that's gone on and so can add some clarity to what happened. It [also] allowed me to set it in 1990, a really innocent time, pre-digital. I wanted young Trevor to be isolated in a strange world. He leaves The North Estate [only] twice in the book—I wanted him to have that sense of isolation. His mother, who he loves and is depending on, is some distant voice [on the phone from her own family's house in] England; his father is reticent at best; his grandfather may or may not have dementia; and his aunt is always playing a game—he can't get a straight answer out of her. The only person he can come to depend on is the ghost of Benjamin Riddell. So that's how the whole scheme came together.

As you alluded to, you're not afraid to end a story in a way where readers don't get everything they've been hoping for. Do you know the end before you start? I suppose not, if you threw out 100,000 words. ...

That was just my self-deception. You know, when you work on something like that, you're not going to sit down and say, "You know what I'm going to do? I'm going to sit down and spend two-and-a-half years writing character sketches!" That would be demoralizing. You just wouldn't do it. So you say, "Oh no, my book isn't *this* now; there's going to be a Part One and a Part Two"—that's how I convinced myself. The Part One is the history, and the Part Two is the contemporary story. You know, that's just self-delusion. We *have* to do that as writers, though. We're building mountains, not molehills, and it takes a long time to do it, and I find that most writers—when I teach a writing workshop—think their book is done and it's just not. You've got to get it [written], and then have smart people give you feedback, and then spend another year or so working on it, and then you've gotta do that again. And again. And it's just not done yet. But we want it to be done so badly, we convince ourselves it must be.

I do know *an* ending, always. I feel you have to write *to* something—you have to aim for something or you're not going to get anywhere. You're just going to be wandering around the countryside. The ending, though, has to be true to the drama, and so therefore the ending may change. You may have *an* ending, but it's not the right ending.

I went to film school, so I have a pretty strong background in dramatic structure. I do a whole outline, and as I work it gets progressively more detailed. But if something happens in those spontaneous moments of writing that's different than my outline, I go with the spontaneity and change the outline to suit it.

Because the spontaneity, that's the *art*. My intentions are the *craft*, right? That's what I'm *trying* to do. But what is *being done* is where the magic is. I like to say that the first draft of anything I write is about me: It's about, *I have an idea and I'm trying to write a story*. Every subsequent draft is all about the characters and the story, and it's my job to shepherd the story. It's fiction, but it has to have a dramatic truth that people will believe. So then it's not about the writer anymore, then it's about the work.

The writer has to step aside and acknowledge that, because otherwise that's where the contrivance happens. Everyone's read those books. You're like, "I was really into it until this happened, and I just don't buy it." Because the writer has tried to do something that is contrary to the true nature of his story or his characters. And you *cannot* do that. If you want something to happen, you've got to set it up. If you want something to happen on page 180, you better fix it back on page 17 so that the character takes the reader where you want the reader to go.

How else does your background as a filmmaker influence the way you approach a novel?

I wanted to be a writer, but when I was going through college it was pretty irresponsible to say, "I'm going to be a novelist!" So I got my MFA in film. But I hated screenwriting, just hated it—I had kind of an allergic reaction. I was really lucky that I got the attention of a documentary filmmaker who was teaching at Columbia: Geof Bartz. He saw that I was struggling and was like, "Let's go into the editing room," and he showed me how to tell a story using found objects, which is what documentary filmmaking is. It's nonfiction, but it's still got to have a story. It's still got to have a protagonist or an issue people care about; there has to be some obstacle involved; there has to be a crisis, a climax, a resolution; it has to follow dramatic structure. And I *loved* editing films. I went into making documentaries and worked for nearly ten years doing different aspects of filmmaking, making my own films as well, and that gave me a lot of time to develop as a person and as a storyteller. …

I'm a big fan of telling young writers to take all the detours they possibly can, both in life and in writing. Those detours are going to lead you to where you need to be. If someone says, "How would you like to spend two years working in the Czech Republic for the state department?," you should do that. You can always get back to your novel. You need to have as many experiences as possible.

It's the same in writing a book. If a new character walks in or your character does something unexpected, you have to go with that. If it's a dead end, you can always get back to your map. But chances are, it's happening for a reason.

The craft is something we can teach. The art is the inspiration that we can't teach. We want the art, that's what we're aiming for. We're aiming to suppress our cautious editor who always tells us what to do. I think one of the big writers said, "Write drunk, edit sober." I say: *Write fat, edit lean.* In that first draft, put all the extra stuff in, anything that comes into your head. What happens is we self-edit as we're writing—*Oh, that's not going to make it in the final.* Don't worry about that. Put it in. It's going to add flavor, and it's going to inform the text. Once you're done with that, *then* go through and put it on a diet. You know, we *want* a fat baby. They've got the chubby cheeks, the chubby arms, the chubby fingers—we love that! That's good. When the baby grows up, *then* we want the lean muscle.

I've interviewed other authors who were releasing new books years after a mega-hit, and they all acknowledged the pressure that can come with that. How do you think that has affected you?

Uh, gray hair? My son says I have "vintage" hair. [Laughs.] It's very difficult, because there *are* expectations, and there's, *What did I do, and how do I do it again?*

I've never worked under contract before, and I don't like it—I feel guilty, because it took me longer to write the book than I expected—but I told them right on, turning out books in a similar vein, I can't do that. All the books I've written [are] similar thematically. But I invented a rule, by the Writers Guild of the Universe: One dog book per writer per lifetime, and that's it. So I kind of had to hold firm to that.

Did you any get pushback?

I didn't. … But in terms of the pressure, the thing is, I'm not going to put out a book until it's the best book I possibly could've written. It's just not fair to do anything other than that. So if it takes twenty years, it's going to take twenty years.

Writers and readers have a trust. You give me your time, and I'm going to give you a really good story that's provocative and it's going to make you think and it's going to make you close the book and have that feeling of catharsis: *I wish I could spend more time with these characters.* And if you're not there yet, *don't* put your book out there; it's a betrayal of the trust. So in that sense, if you adhere to that, like I've tried to, the pressure is in just getting the book to that level.

Sometimes, though, you do have to say, "Okay, this book isn't going to get to that level," and then you have to set it aside. But we can't be depressed about that, we just have to say, "Well, I was learning about my craft and learning about myself as a writer and I was practicing—that's good time."

What's it like now, being on such an extensive book tour?

I'm doing *such* a long tour. It's really important that I get this book out there and stand behind the book. To *me* it's important. Because everyone expects me to fail. In general, [for other recent authors who've had a runaway hit] the follow-up hasn't done as well. Will I succeed? I don't know. I'll try it. If I have to go put the book in every person's hand and start reading with them, like I do with my seven-year-old, then I'll do that, because I do believe in this book.

There's a *Racing in the Rain* movie in development. Are you involved with that at all?

Not at all. … You know what was great? It was done as a play by Book-It Repertory Theatre in Seattle, and there was an actor playing Enzo. I remember sitting next to this guy, and he was having none of it, and clearly his wife had cajoled him into coming. And I leaned over finally and said, "It sounds ridiculous, I know. But stick with it. Because by the end of the play, you're going to believe that actor is the dog." And at the end I looked over at him and he had tears coming down his cheeks. If the film could get some of that magic, it would be amazing. So I have my fingers crossed.

Jessica Strawser is the editor of *Writer's Digest* magazine.

PATRICK ROTHFUSS

Worldbuilder

Rich Shivener

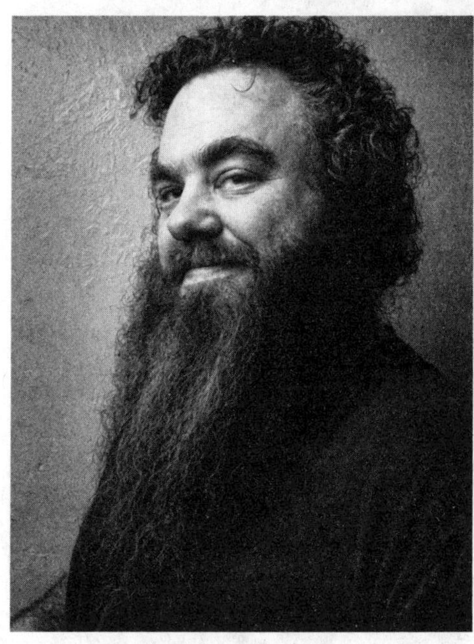

In less than a decade, Patrick Rothfuss, forty-two, has risen to the ranks of the most celebrated authors in the fantasy genre. The Kingkiller Chronicle trilogy, following the adventures of young actor/musician-cum-legendary-wizard Kvothe in the Four Corners of Civilization, launched in 2007 with his debut novel, *The Name of the Wind*. The book was named to numerous high-profile "best of" lists, slowly but surely became a *New York Times* bestseller, and inspired a cultlike following among fantasy enthusiasts. Book Two, *The Wise Man's Fear*, which picks up with Kvothe at "The University," followed in 2011 and topped the *Times*' hardcover fiction list, garnering praise from genre giant George R.R. Martin and a television option for the series by 20th Century Fox and New Regency Productions. While a release date has yet to be announced for the third Kingkiller novel, *The Doors of Stone*, fans speculate tirelessly on Rothfuss's popular blog and Twitter feed.

That's a lot of pressure for an author new to the scene, but Rothfuss still finds time to pay that positive energy forward. In 2008, he founded Worldbuilders Inc., a nonprofit that has raised more than $3 million for Heifer International to help fight poverty and hunger. Worldbuilders hosts auctions and campaigns offering all sorts of ephemera for fantasy diehards—from signed books to posters to comics.

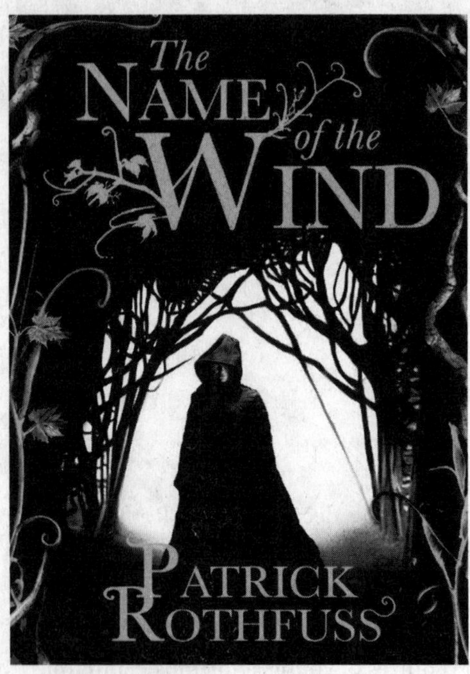

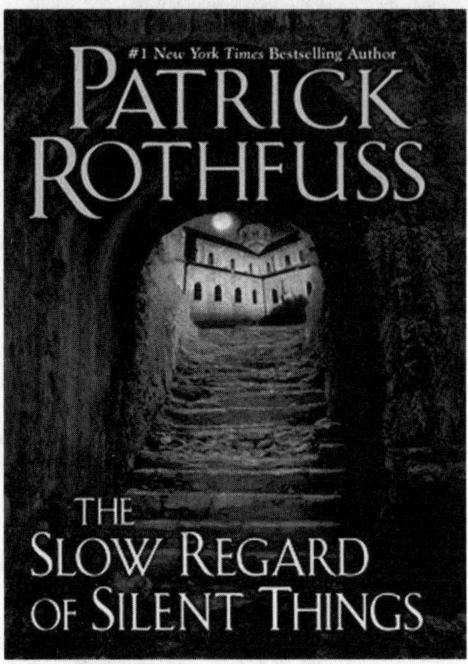

We caught up with Rothfuss by phone from his home in Wisconsin, poised to return to his writing and excited to spend time with his wife and two young sons after an intense tour that included dates in Germany.

Your Kingkiller series has required substantial worldbuilding and mapping. What does it take to construct an entirely new world—especially in the fantasy genre?

There's no simple answer. A lot of people follow [J.R.R.] Tolkien's lead, because he was one of the first people to make his splash with this elaborate secondary world. A lot of people followed very closely in his footsteps, and it led to a lot of uninspired worldbuilding, in my opinion. What made Tolkien's Middle-earth so wonderful—what made it feel so rich and full—is the fact that it was informed by the things that Tolkien was passionate about. He was a linguist, he loved mythology and history. He was a geek for them, in the truest sense of the word. When you're a geek for something, it means you love it beyond all sense. I always encourage people when they are attempting to do worldbuilding to focus on their passions. I'm really interested in economy, psychology, sociology, religion, anthropology, and currency systems, and that's why my world is very different from Tolkien's. I come from a strong science background, and you see that in my world. There's a strong element of technology in my world that is only very vaguely defined in Tolkien's. It's the same thing with economy. People didn't use money in Middle-earth. I have a ridiculously elaborate series

"What do you do when you finish the first draft? That's pretty easy. You should set it down, you should get up from the table, and you should have a party. Call your friends, tell your mom, have a drink, celebrate a little bit, because getting to the end of that draft is an important thing."

of currency systems that I developed and then, by and large, left out of the story. It's there if people want to peek at it in the story.

Could you talk more about your science background?

In college, my plan was to become a chemical engineer. I'm a scientist at heart. That doesn't mean that I don't also love stories and words and literature, but I've always enjoyed the hard sciences. And that isn't unique by any means, but I think that is a little more of the exception to the rule for fantasy authors.

Your first book hit *The New York Times* bestsellers list. So many writers dream of that happening. Did the experience live up to the hype? Was there anything about it that surprised you?

I don't know. ... Hype implies an artificially created, usually monetary-based ploy, and if you know anything about publishing, you know that they don't have the money to throw at new authors like me.

My book came out, and they were hoping that it would take off—no. 1 in the *Times*, movie deal—but it didn't. It came out, and it had a very respectable opening. But then it didn't tail off quickly. Books tend to do the same thing movies do—they have a strong opening weekend and then quickly drop off. My book was odd in that respect because it came out, people were excited, and it sold consistently well. And that's because people were giving a copy to a friend and saying, "Have you read this book? Have you heard about this?"

Your fans are awaiting the final book of the series now, and fantasy readers in particular are known for being ardent and, some might say, *impatient*. Does that inherent pressure affect your work at all?

It definitely affects me as a person. It's harder to do anything when somebody is looking over your shoulder, and it's exponentially harder when there are several million people looking over your shoulder. It's taken a lot of time for me to get my head in a place where I can put all of that out of my mind and not have it interfere with me.

Does some of that interference come from your presence on Twitter and your blog? You have a very public persona in addition to your novel writing.

It doesn't come from my presence there. The pressure comes from people, and being available only means there are more ways that the info can come at you.

How do you prefer to interact with your fans?

In some ways, I prefer to meet them in person. I preferred to do a lot of signing. People would come, I'd meet them, we'd talk, and that worked really well when thirty to forty people would show up. But then three hundred people would show up, and if you gave everyone a minute, you would be there for five hours. I went to Madrid, and two thousand people showed up.

I've been trying to find a way that I can interact with my readers in a way that makes them happy and gives them the content that we both enjoy but doesn't devour my life. It's something that I'm still struggling with. The blog, in some ways, is very efficient. I get to share things, answer questions, and discuss writing, and twenty thousand people stop by and read it.

How *do* you balance your reader outreach, your promotional efforts, your novel writing, your home life?

It's hard. If I'm spending time writing, I feel bad because I'm neglecting my sons, and if I'm spending time with my family, I feel bad because I'm not writing, and if I do a third thing, I feel bad because I'm not working on the book and I'm not spending time with my family.

Honestly, it's the hardest part of my life right now. It's not something I'm on top of. It does not seem like there is a way that I can comfortably fulfill all of the obligations and still maintain a certain level of happiness that I would like to have in my life. And so for years now I've been putting off things, such as having friends and doing social activities. I don't teach fencing anymore. I trimmed all of those things out of my life to make time for the book, my work, and it's not sustainable in the same way that running a strip mine isn't sustainable. I'm trying to fix that now.

What does your typical day of writing look like?

There is no typical day. Some people say, "I get up, I take my daughter to school, I go to the gym, and I write in the afternoon." I don't have that. Today I spent all day trying to catch up on e-mail, and tomorrow I'll write something for a website. Some days I have to answer forty questions on my translator forum. Some days I travel, and then I talk at a radio station, then I do a panel, then a book signing. Some days I spend sixteen hours on copy edits. There is no schedule.

When you have a completed draft, what's the next step for you?

It depends on what sort of draft it is. What do you do when you finish the first draft? That's pretty easy. You should set it down, you should get up from the table, and you should have a party. Call your friends, tell your mom, have a drink, celebrate a little bit, because getting to the end of that draft is an important thing.

And honestly, step away from the project for a while, because to get to the end of that draft, you've had to become extraordinarily tangled up in your writing. Emotionally, you're way too close to the project, and you need to get a little space from it, because the next thing that is required is editing. In some ways, you can only truly edit and revise something after it reaches a complete draft stage.

You get emotional distance in a couple of different ways. You let it sit for a month. Sometimes you can give it to someone else, and they read it, and since they cannot be close to it, you can feel that person's emotional distance from your story. That's why beta readers are so important; that's why editors are so important.

You edit, you edit, you edit. … Still, to judge whether it is effective, you have to have some distance. Sometimes even just the thought of, *In a week I'm going to mail this to my editor*, makes your brain process the story in a different way.

What are your strategies for sustaining a series character such as Kvothe over thousands of pages?

That's not something I worry about any more than I worry about sustaining language use, or sustaining a consistent presentation of the world, or sustaining pacing and tension. All of those are equally important. Those go back to revision. The more you write, the better you get at judging these things, but invariably, you will be too close to catch the missteps. That's why I employ a host of beta readers who read my early draft, my middle draft, and my late drafts. I do hundreds of drafts, and then if they say, "This seems really out of character," or, "Did you say the eyes were blue?" they help keep me on track. They help keep me aware of what a reader is doing.

Hundreds of drafts? Wow.

I probably run through more drafts than any living writer, and I don't say that glibly. I've asked around, and a lot of very good authors write three drafts. They write the first draft, revise it, give it to their editors, make revisions, and they're done. But I'm really, really obsessive.

You did university course work for nearly a decade, and taught writing classes. How was that academic experience an asset to you in launching a writing career?

It has virtually nothing to do with my writing career. I didn't get an MFA, and I didn't study writing intensively [in school]. Some of the tricks that I learned as a teacher make me a good public speaker—or, rather, the fact that I'm a good public speaker makes me a good teacher and entertaining author when I'm in front of the crowd—but that's not really what you're asking.

How did those experiences affect your writings about The University setting in your books?

A lot of people assume that I went to college for nine years and [*then*] wrote a book about a kid who goes to college. [But] I was writing that when I was in school, back in 1994 and 1995. It's a great example of how a lot of people can make reasonable conclusions that "this thing happened in the author's life, and it obviously led to him to writing this," and it's just wrong. I always think looking too much into a writer's life and assuming it gives you some insight into the writing itself—it's a fun game, but it's viewed in the same light as reading tea leaves. You should not assume that it teaches you anything meaningful.

I can see how if you've been asked that question a lot, it could be annoying.

Oh, not annoying. I'm using that as an example to kind of reveal the underlying ridiculousness of trying to unpack a work through the understanding of an author's life. The artist and the art occupy entirely separate spaces. I've had people say, "Oh, thank God, a musician is finally writing about music," and I say, "No, sorry, [I'm] not a musician, don't play an instrument, can't read music." … I like to underscore that when I can. You're interpreting and building stories [about the author] out of these elements that you see, but that does not make it the truth.

What would you most like people to know about your Worldbuilders nonprofit?

Worldbuilders: I view it as a place where readers and writers and publishers and gamers and people who love comics—pretty much geeks of all creeds and nations—are coming together to make the world a better place.

Why was it important for you to use your power for good, so to speak?

What happened was, I was writing my blog and one day I said, "Let's have a photo contest," just goofing off. Hundreds of people sent in photos, and I had no idea people were that excited. And I think when you realize that enthusiasm about your work, I think you can use it in a masturbatory way and pat yourself on the back, or you can try to do something worthwhile in the world. *How about we do something that maybe channels all of this excitement into something productive? Let's do some good stuff while we're at it—let's start a charity and see if people get on board.* And people were even more enthusiastic. The community continues to delight me with this desire to make a positive change in the world.

What's next for you, after the series concludes?

I'll have a long nap. I'll stay home for a while, I'll play with my children, and I will hopefully get better at having my life be a sensible thing—a sensible, long-term sustainable endeavor, where I'm healthy and happy and I produce books that people enjoy, and I run a charity which makes the world a better place.

Rich Shivener has interviewed a variety of fiction and comics writers.

BUSINESS BASICS

Successfully Submit Your Novels & Short Stories

It's true there are no substitutes for talent and hard work. A writer's first concern must always be attention to craft. No matter how well presented, a poorly written story or novel has little chance of being published. On the other hand, a well-written piece may be equally hard to sell in today's competitive publishing market. Talent alone is just not enough.

To be successful, writers need to study the field and pay careful attention to finding the right market. While the hours spent perfecting your writing are usually hours spent alone, you're not alone when it comes to developing your marketing plan. *Novel & Short Story Writer's Market* provides you with detailed listings containing the essential information you'll need to locate and contact the markets most suitable for your work.

Once you've determined where to send your work, you must turn your attention to presentation. We can help here, too. We've included the basics of manuscript preparation, along with information on submission procedures and how to approach markets. We also include tips on promoting your work. No matter where you're from or what level of experience you have, you'll find useful information here on everything from presentation to mailing to selling rights to promoting your work—the "business" of fiction.

APPROACHING MAGAZINE MARKETS

A query letter by itself is usually not required by most magazine fiction editors. If you are approaching a magazine to find out if fiction is accepted, a query is fine, but editors looking for short fiction want to see the actual piece. A cover letter can be useful as a letter of introduction, but the key here is brevity. A successful cover letter is no more than one page (20-lb. bond paper). It should be single-spaced with a double space between paragraphs, proofread carefully, and neatly typed in a standard typeface (not script or italic). The writer's name, address, phone number, and e-mail address must appear at the top, and the letter should be addressed, ideally, to a specific editor. (If the editor's name is unavailable, use "Fiction Editor.")

The body of a successful cover letter contains the name and word count of the story, a brief list of previous publications, if you have any, and the reason you are submitting to this particular publication. Mention that you have enclosed a self-addressed, stamped envelope for reply. Also, let the editor know if you are sending a disposable manuscript (not to be returned; more and more editors prefer disposable manuscripts that save them time and save you postage). Finally, don't forget to thank the editor for considering your story.

Note that more and more publications prefer to receive electronic submissions, both as e-mail attachments and through online submission forms. See individual listings for specific information on electronic submission requirements, and always visit magazines' websites for up-to-date guidelines.

APPROACHING BOOK PUBLISHERS

Some book publishers ask for queries first, but most want a query plus sample chapters or an outline or, occasionally, the complete manuscript. Again, make your letter brief. Include the essentials about yourself: name, address, phone number, e-mail address, and publishing experience. Include a three- or four-sentence "pitch" and only the personal information related to your story. Show that you have researched the market with a few sentences about why you chose this publisher.

BOOK PROPOSALS

A book proposal is a package sent to a publisher that includes a cover letter and one or more of the following: sample chapters, outline, synopsis, author bio, publications list. When asked to send sample chapters, send up to three consecutive chapters. An outline covers the highlights of your book chapter by chapter. Be sure to include details on main characters, the plot, and subplots. Outlines can run up to thirty pages, depending on the length of your novel. The object is to tell what happens in a concise but clear manner. A synopsis is a shorter summary of your novel, written in a way that expresses the emotion of the story in addition to just explaining the essential points. Evan Marshall, literary agent and author of *The Marshall Plan for Getting Your Novel Published* (Writer's Digest Books), suggests you aim for a page of synopsis for every twenty-five pages of manuscript. Marshall also advises you write the synopsis as one unified narrative, without section heads, subheads, or chapters to break up the text. The terms *synopsis* and *outline* are sometimes used interchangeably, so be sure to find out exactly what each publisher wants.

ABOUT OUR POLICIES

We occasionally receive letters asking why a certain magazine, publisher, or contest is not in the book. Sometimes when we contact listings, the editors do not want to be listed because they:

- do not use very much fiction.
- are overwhelmed with submissions.
- are having financial difficulty or have been recently sold.
- use only solicited material.
- accept work from a select group of writers only.
- do not have the staff or time for the many unsolicited submissions a listing may bring.

Some of the listings do not appear because we have chosen not to list them. We investigate complaints of unprofessional conduct in editors' dealings with writers and misrepresentation of information provided to us by editors and publishers. If we find these reports to be true after a thorough investigation, we will delete the listing from future editions.

There is no charge to the companies that list in this book. Listings appearing in *Novel & Short Story Writer's Market* are compiled from detailed questionnaires, phone interviews, and information provided by editors, publishers, and directors of awards and conferences. The publishing industry is volatile, and changes of address, editor, policies, and needs happen frequently. To keep up with the changes between editions of the book, we suggest you check the market information on the Writer's Market website at www.writersmarket.com. Many magazine and book publishers offer updated information for writers on their websites. Check individual listings for those website addresses.

Organization newsletters and small magazines devoted to helping writers also list market information. Several offer online bulletin boards, message centers, and chat lines with up-to-the-minute changes and happenings in the writing community.

We rely on our readers, as well, for new markets and information about market conditions. E-mail us if you have any new information or if you have suggestions on how to improve our listings to better suit your writing needs.

A FEW WORDS ABOUT AGENTS

Agents are not usually needed for short fiction and most do not handle it unless they already have a working relationship with you. For novels, you may want to consider working with an agent, especially if you intend to market your book to publishers who do not look at unsolicited submissions. For more on approaching agents and to read listings of agents willing to work with beginning and established writers, see our **Literary Agents** section. You can also refer to this year's edition of *Guide to Literary Agents*, edited by Chuck Sambuchino.

MANUSCRIPT MECHANICS

A professionally presented manuscript will not guarantee publication. But a sloppy, hard-to-read manuscript will not be read—publishers simply do not have the time. Here's a list of suggested submission techniques for polished manuscript presentation:

- For a short story manuscript, your first page should include your name, address, phone number, and e-mail address (single spaced) in the upper left corner. In the upper right, indicate an approximate word count. Center the name of your story about one-third of the way down the page, skip a line, and center your byline (the byline is optional). Skip four lines and begin your story. On subsequent pages, put your last name and page number in the upper right corner.
- For book manuscripts, use a separate title page. Put your name, address, phone number, and e-mail address in the lower right corner and word count in the upper right. If you have representation, list your agent's name and address in the lower right. (This bumps your name and contact information to the upper left corner.) Center your title and byline about halfway down the page. Start your first chapter on the next page. Center the chapter number and title (if there is one) one-third of the way down the page. Include your last name and the novel's title in all caps in the upper left header, and put the page number in the upper right header of this page and each page to follow. Start each chapter with a new page.
- Proofread carefully. Keep a dictionary, thesaurus, and stylebook handy and use the spell-check function on your computer.
- Include a word count. Your word processing program can likely give you a word count.
- Suggest art where applicable. Most publishers do not expect you to provide artwork and some insist on selecting their own illustrators, but if you have suggestions, let them know. Magazine publishers work in a very visual field and are usually open to ideas.
- Keep accurate records. This can be done in a number of ways, but be sure to keep track of where your stories are and when you sent them out. Write down submission dates. If you do not hear about your submission for a long time—about one to two months longer than the reporting time stated in the listing—you may want to contact the publisher. When you do, you will need an accurate record for reference.

Electronic Submissions

- If sending electronic submissions via e-mail or online submission form, check the publisher's website first for specific information and follow the directions carefully.

Hard-Copy Submissions

- Many publications no longer accept hard-copy submissions. Make sure to read the submission guidelines carefully.
- Use white 8½" × 11" bond paper, preferably 16- or 20-lb. weight. The paper must be heavy enough not to show pages underneath and strong enough to take handling by several people.
- Type your manuscript on a computer and print it out using a laser or ink-jet printer (or, if you must, use a typewriter with a new ribbon).
- An occasional spot of white-out is okay, but don't send a marked-up manuscript with many typos.
- Always double-space and leave a 1" margin on all sides of the page.
- Don't forget word count. If you are using a typewriter, there are several ways to count the number of words in your piece. One way is to count the words in five lines and divide that number by five to find an average. Then count the number of lines and multiply to find the total words. For long pieces, you may want to count the words in the first three pages, divide by three, and multiply by the number of pages you have.
- Always keep a copy. Manuscripts do get lost. To avoid expensive mailing costs, send only what is required. If you are including artwork or photos but you are not positive they will be used, send photocopies. Artwork is hard to replace.
- Enclose a self-addressed, stamped envelope (SASE) if you want a reply or if you want your manuscript returned. For most letters, a business-size (#10) envelope will do. Avoid using any envelope too small for an 8½" × 11" sheet of paper. For manuscripts, be sure to include enough postage and an envelope large enough to contain it. If you are requesting a sample copy of a magazine or a book publisher's catalog, send an appropriately sized envelope.
- Consider sending a disposable manuscript that saves editors time (this will also save you money).

RIGHTS

The Copyright Law states that writers are selling one-time rights (in almost all cases) unless they and the publisher have agreed otherwise. A list of various rights follows. Be sure you know exactly what rights you are selling before you agree to the sale.

Copyright is the legal right to exclusive publication, sale, or distribution of a literary work. As the writer or creator of a written work, you need simply to include your name and the date on your piece in order to copyright it. Be aware, however, that most editors today consider placing the copyright symbol on your work the sign of an amateur and many are even offended by it.

To get specific answers to questions about copyright (but not legal advice), you can call the Copyright Public Information Office at (202)707-3000 weekdays between 8:30 A.M. and 5 P.M. EST. Publications listed in *Novel & Short Story Writer's Market* are copyrighted unless otherwise stated. In the case of magazines that are not copyrighted, be sure to keep a copy of your manuscript with your notice printed on it. For more information on copyrighting your work, see *The Copyright Handbook: What Every Writer Needs to Know, 11th edition*, by Stephen Fishman (Nolo Press, 2011).

Some people are under the mistaken impression that copyright is something they have to send away for and that their writing is not properly protected until they have "received" their copyright from the government. The fact is, you don't have to register your work with the Copyright Office in order for your work to be copyrighted; all writing is copyrighted the moment it is put to paper.

Although it is generally unnecessary, registration is a matter of filling out an application form (for writers, that's Form TX). The Copyright Office now recommends filing an online claim at www.copyright.gov/forms. The online service carries a basic claim fee of $35. If you opt for snail mail, send the completed form, a nonreturnable copy of the work in question, and a check for $65 to the Library of Congress, Copyright Office-TX, 101 Independence Ave. SE, Washington, DC 20559-6000. If the thought of paying $35 each to register every piece you write does not appeal to you, you can cut costs by registering a group of your works with one form, under one title, for one $65 fee.

Most magazines are registered with the Copyright Office as single collective entities themselves; that is, the individual works that make up the magazine are not copyrighted individually in the names of the authors. You'll need to register your article yourself if you wish to have the additional protection of copyright registration.

For more information, visit the U.S. Copyright Office online at www.copyright.gov.

First Serial Rights

This means the writer offers a newspaper or magazine the right to publish the article, story, or poem for the first time in a particular periodical. All other rights to the material remain with the writer. The qualifier "North American" is often added to this phrase to specify a geographical limit to the license.

When material is excerpted from a book scheduled to be published and it appears in a magazine or newspaper prior to book publication, this is also called first serial rights.

One-Time Rights

A periodical that licenses one-time rights to a work (also known as simultaneous rights) buys the nonexclusive right to publish the work once. That is, there is nothing to stop the author from selling the work to other publications at the same time. Simultaneous sales would typically be to periodicals with different audiences.

Second Serial (Reprint) Rights

This gives a newspaper or magazine the opportunity to print an article, poem, or story after it has already appeared in another newspaper or magazine. Second serial rights are nonexclusive; that is, they can be licensed to more than one market.

All Rights

This is just what it sounds like. All rights means a publisher may use the manuscript anywhere and in any form, including movie and book club sales, without further payment to the writer (although such a transfer, or assignment, of rights will terminate after thirty-five years). If you think you'll want to use the material more than once, you must avoid submitting to such markets or refuse payment and withdraw your material. Ask the editor whether he is willing to buy first rights instead of all rights before you agree to an assignment or sale. Some editors will reassign rights to a writer after a given period, such as one year. It's worth an inquiry in writing.

Subsidiary Rights

These are the rights, other than book publication rights, that should be covered in a book contract. These may include various serial rights; movie, television, audiotape, and other electronic rights; translation rights, etc. The book contract should specify who controls these rights (author or publisher) and what percentage of sales from the licensing of these subrights goes to the author.

Dramatic, Television, and Motion Picture Rights

This means the writer is selling his material for use on the stage, in television, or in the movies. Often a one-year option to buy such rights is offered (generally for 10 percent of the total price). The interested party then tries to sell the idea to actors, directors, studios, or television networks. Some properties are optioned over and over again, but most fail to become dramatic productions. In such cases, the writer can sell his rights again and again—as long as there is interest in the material.

Electronic Rights

These rights cover usage in a broad range of electronic media, from online magazines and databases to interactive games. The editor should state in writing the specific electronic rights he is requesting. The presumption is that the writer keeps unspecified rights.

Compensation for electronic rights is a major source of conflict between writers and publishers, as many book publishers seek control of them and many magazines routinely include electronic rights in the purchase of print rights, often with no additional payment. Writers can suggest an alternative way of handling this issue by asking for an additional

15 percent to purchase first rights and a royalty system based on the number of times an article is accessed from an electronic database.

MARKETING AND PROMOTION

Everyone agrees writing is hard work whether you are published or not. Yet once you achieve publication, the work changes. Now not only do you continue writing and revising your next project, you must also concern yourself with getting your book into the hands of readers. It's time to switch hats from artist to salesperson.

While even best-selling authors whose publishers have committed big bucks to marketing are asked to help promote their books, new authors may have to take it upon themselves to plan and initiate some of their own promotion, usually dipping into their own pockets. While this does not mean that every author is expected to go on tour, sometimes at their own expense, it does mean authors should be prepared to offer suggestions for promoting their books.

Depending on the time, money, and personal preferences of the author and publisher, a promotional campaign could mean anything from mailing out press releases to setting up book signings to hitting the talk-show circuit. Most writers can contribute to their own promotion by providing contact names—reviewers, hometown newspapers, civic groups, organizations—that might have a special interest in the book or the writer.

Above all, when it comes to promotion, be creative. What is your book about? Try to capitalize on it. Focus on your potential audiences and how you can help them connect with your book.

IMPORTANT LISTING INFORMATION

- Listings are not advertisements. Although the information here is as accurate as possible, the listings are not endorsed or guaranteed by the editors of *Novel & Short Story Writer's Market*.
- *Novel & Short Story Writer's Market* reserves the right to exclude any listing that does not meet its requirements.

PUBLISHING, DECODED

Become Your Book's Best Advocate

Phil Sexton

Every writer who secures a publishing contract desires the same thing: a successful book. The exact definition of "success" varies from author to author, but as you might expect, it is most commonly measured by positive critical and commercial performance. (That's certainly how publishers measure it.)

I'm not here to help you earn rave reviews. There are better, more experienced advisors for that. But as a book publisher with thirty years of prior industry experience—including roles as a bookseller, merchandiser, marketing manager, and sales director—my goal is to help you understand what happens behind the scenes at a publishing house and make you aware of the questions you should be asking in order to help ensure that the people handling your book—from design to sales to marketing—give it the best possible treatment.

Publishing has many moving parts—which means that you'll find plenty of opportunities for errors to be made. Fortunately, arming yourself with basic insights into how the business works can help mitigate those mistakes and give your book the best chance of success.

WHY YOU NEED TO KNOW WHAT YOU NEED TO KNOW

Let me start with four key things you must understand in order to maximize your success while working with a traditional publisher. They are:

1. You are your own best advocate.
2. You have the right to ask questions.
3. You have the right to get answers.
4. You have the right to dislike the answers.

This important stuff sounds simple, and perhaps obvious, but the breadth of responsibility it puts in your court is surprisingly large and varied.

First, let's talk about why all of this is necessary. Publishers and editors aren't withholding information from you because they're underhanded or foolish. They want your book to succeed. To a degree, their jobs depend on it. They are, however, likely overworked, overburdened, and left with little time, if any, to proactively teach you the ins and outs of the publishing business. Likewise, some topics are likely to spur uncomfortable conversations—so if you aren't pushing to discuss those topics, your editor isn't likely to bring them up.

I've heard numerous writers (and even some publishing professionals) suggest that editors no longer edit, and that it's all up to authors and their agents to perfect their books before even submitting. I've never found this to be the case. The editors I know still edit as much as they ever did. Unfortunately, though, many of them are now also charged with creating presentation materials for the sales and marketing teams, writing jacket copy, managing their own editorial marketing (yes, many editors now sell as well), styling manuscripts in page templates, and more. They are not simply "editors"—in an age where publishing has expanded into the digital realm and publishers have tightened their purse strings to adapt, they are now "managers of content." Their jobs have become much bigger than "just" editing. But they still do that, too.

Let's jump back to the first item on our list: *You are your own best advocate.* Which is to say that the responsibility falls to you to ensure that your book gets the best possible treatment from the publisher.

When I give this speech at writing conferences, inevitably someone in the audience raises a hand and says, "But isn't that what your agent does?" To a degree, that's true. Your agent will negotiate the best possible contract on your behalf. She'll represent your concerns if you don't like your cover or title (yes, it's likely your title will be changed from the one you proposed). And some agents do even more. But the questions I suggest you ask are things that few, if any, authors or agents broach until it's too late. It's not your agent but *you* who's going to have regular correspondence with the editor, so *you* are the one who must be prepared to inquire about certain things at various stages of the publishing process, from before you sign a contract to after your book goes on sale.

When I say *you have the right to get answers,* I don't mean to imply that editors or publishers won't provide them. What I mean is that they may not provide you with *all* the relevant information—purely due to the type of question you've asked. Few of today's overextended editors have the time to elaborate on an issue that you've not specifically called out.

Finally, *you have the right to dislike the answers.* Some writers are so grateful and relieved to finally secure a book deal that they give up their willingness to push for the best possible treatment for their book, or they simply don't know any better. I'm not suggesting you antagonize your publisher—far from it. But I am suggesting that you consider yourself a business partner and someone whom the publisher should treat as such. Don't let yourself and your work be treated as if this were a work-for-hire arrangement in which you were paid a fee by the publisher and agreed to a contract that gives you no say in what happens to your book.

The key to getting good answers (and by that I mean truly valuable and detailed information rather than vague generalizations) is to ask *specific* questions. For example, if you ask, "Is the sales team behind my book?" the answer will be, "Oh, absolutely." If, however, you ask if there's co-op reserved for your book, or how your book is positioned on the publisher's list, or if you can review the metadata for your book, the answers will be much more illuminating.

Keep in mind that these kinds of questions are not ones publishers are used to getting from most authors, so you might get the impression that they're annoyed by your asking. So be it. Your writing career is at stake here.

By asking all of these questions, it may sound like you're interviewing the publisher. Guess what? That's exactly what you're doing. You need to make sure your prospective business partner is the right one for your book.

QUESTIONS TO ASK *BEFORE* SIGNING A CONTRACT

1. Where do you expect my book to rank on your list?

This is important to know, because rank = treatment. Is your book an "A" title (also called a "lead title")? If not, then what are their expectations? Discuss this with your agent and ask, *Can we do better?* It's not just about the size of your advance—it's about a publisher's commitment to your work.

This is not the only question you'll be asking that relates to how your book will be sold. Believe it or not, what happens during a sales call can almost singularly determine whether or not your book succeeds.

Let's look at a single major account to see why this is so important. We'll use Barnes & Noble as an example. Here's how it works:

Six months prior to the publication of your book, your publisher's sales representative sets an appointment with the B&N book buyer. Buyers require reps to present at least five books in order to get a face-to-face meeting (something to be aware of if you're publishing with a small press that isn't releasing as many as five per season). The rule of thumb is that five books will secure the rep a fifteen-minute meeting during which he can pitch those titles. Ten books will get him a half-hour. Fifteen books will earn forty-five minutes. You get the idea.

Let's break down a typical fifteen-minute sales call, then, to see what that looks like:

The first five minutes are chitchat, discussion of the business in general, and a review of the successes or failures of any recent promos that took place since the last sales call. The next three to five minutes are spent on the title that the rep deems most important for that sales call. (This title typically demands more attention because the publisher has paid more money to acquire it or feels that it has the most sales potential if it gets enough support from various retail accounts. It's the aforementioned "A" title.) So figure eight to ten minutes have been burned up and only one title has been sold to the buyer. That leaves five to seven minutes, total, for the other four books, or an average of ninety seconds per book. Years of work, and your book might be "sold" for all of a minute and a half.

And *that* is why it's important to ask these questions: They could ultimately get your book more time in front of buyers, a higher profile on the publisher's list, and the best possible treatment in the lead-up to publication.

2. Can you show me a standard marketing plan for a similarly ranked book?

You may find that they have no intention to market your book or that their plan consists of a limited review copy mailing with a press release. Don't let yourself be surprised by this revelation *after* you've signed a contract. Ask for the details in advance. If they aren't what you'd like them to be, that should be a point of negotiation, particularly if you are agreeing to a smaller advance. You might think that this is one of those questions that your agent will ask, but I can tell you from personal experience that in my years of acquiring hundreds of books, I've had only *two* agents ask about marketing prior to signing a contract.

3. Will you be nominating my book for display and, if so, at what accounts?

Getting a book on display at bookstores (as in, not spine-out on the shelf, but with prime placement) costs the publisher serious money (referred to as "co-op"). Knowing if a publisher is committed to spending co-op on your book tells you a couple of things. One, its team believes that getting your book on display will enable it to sell at a velocity high enough to warrant the expense. And, two, it will give the book enough visibility to break out and sell at a higher level than it would otherwise, even after it's taken off display.

Some writers are so grateful and relieved to finally secure a book deal that they give up their willingness to push for the best possible treatment for their book.

4. How big is your list each season, particularly in my category or genre?

Finding this out will give you an indication of how big a presence your publisher has in your particular category—and how many other books you'll be competing with on the publisher's list. That's right—you'll have competition from *inside* the publisher, as well as from other publishers. For example, Writer's Digest Books publishes sixteen titles on writing instruction each year. We're careful to make sure that each of those books is distinct, in order to ensure that none of them are in direct competition with any other out the gate. If we're publishing a book on plot in 2016, then that author can be assured that it's the only book we've committed to on that topic for that year (though, of course, we do have plenty of others on our backlist). Ask what other books your publisher has planned during the season in which your book is to be published, and if anything concerns you, speak up.

5. How many sales people do you have, and what accounts do they cover?

How does the company handle library, academic, and specialty market sales? Do they have co-op reserved for your book in each of those markets? If, for example, you believe that your book has big potential in the academic market, but it turns out the publisher doesn't have a system in place for aggressively pursuing academic sales, it may not be the right publisher for your book. This applies to any other nontraditional-bookstore market as well (Walmart, Target, specialty shops, etc.).

By asking all of these questions, it may sound like you're interviewing the publisher. Guess what? That's exactly what you're doing. Again, this is a business relationship and you need to make sure your prospective business partner is the right one for your book.

Once the contract is signed and you've determined that you and your publisher are on the same proverbial page, it's time to relax, yes? Unfortunately, no. This is when mistakes start to occur.

QUESTIONS TO ASK *AFTER* SIGNING A CONTRACT

6. Will you please keep me apprised of important in-house dates regarding my book?

As you work your way through the publishing process, you want to rely on your editor to share with you when the catalog will be created, when the book will be presented to bookstore chain buyers, when the cover will be designed, etc. If you don't ask to be looped in, you might not be. (Again, this is not your publisher being malicious. Some authors are all too content to stay out of that part of the process. But they shouldn't be.)

7. Can I see my book's catalog listing in advance?

If you haven't yet seen one of your publisher's catalogs, it's likely available online. Download a copy (or ask to be sent one) so that you can see how different books are treated. Then, follow up to ask: How much space is my book getting? A full page? A half-page? A quarter-page? If it's a quarter-page, that may be another indication that the publisher doesn't expect much from your book. Ask what it would take to ensure that your book gets more real estate.

Ask to see the catalog copy when the time comes. Are there marketing bullets? If not, ask why. If you negotiated for a marketing plan, why isn't it in the copy? Marketing plans (good ones, anyway) can influence how many copies of your book an account will buy.

8. What does my book's metadata look like?

In its most basic form, metadata is all of the information about your book that publishers share with the accounts that will be selling it. Metadata includes things like title and subtitle, author name, page count, trim size, category, and more. Robust and *accurate* metadata helps improve the ease with which buyers and consumers can find your book in search results within an account's online store (Amazon, for example), as well as more generally online. The publisher can upload reams of metadata to various accounts, but if it's not accurate, it's next to useless.

9. How soon can I see my cover design?

When a book is being designed, it often happens that a designer will select an unusual typeface for the title—one that might be difficult to read. The problem is that the people working on the book, from the editor to the sales reps to the publicist, don't always recognize that there's an issue with legibility. They know full well what the title of the book is, so looking at a typeface and divorcing oneself from an awareness of the title can be difficult to do. They have to look at it with the eyes of a customer who has never heard of the book before. It's harder than it sounds. Look for yourself. Is the title legible from a distance, at a glance, and at the size of a postage stamp (the way it will appear online)? If you have concerns, raise them.

Also, ask to see the spine of your book jacket. Yes, the spine. Most authors and agents will request to see the cover in advance and request revisions as they see fit (assuming they have consultation rights in the contract). But no one *ever* asks to see the spine. And yet, in a brick-and-mortar environment, the spine is some of the most important real estate your book has, because most books are turned spine out. As a rule of thumb, designers will apply the font used on the front cover to the spine. While this makes sense from the perspective of unifying a product's design, it's also true that some fonts are not easily read sideways. Check to make sure yours is, and if it isn't, request that it be changed.

WHERE TO GO FROM HERE

When I've shared these suggestions in other forums, some have suggested that getting results is easier said than done. That may be true. After all, there's nothing that *requires* a publisher or editor to provide you with the information I'm suggesting you ask for. But sensible publishers will recognize the value such questions bring to a project and welcome them. No one wants the publishing process to be a disappointing one. Knowing how to advocate for the best possible treatment for your book is one way to help ensure that it's not. That brings us back to our original set of assertions, with one important addition.

You are your own best advocate.

You have the right to ask questions.

You have the right to get answers.

You have the right to dislike the answers.

You have the power to change the answers.

Phil Sexton is the publisher of Writer's Digest Books in addition to his role overseeing *Writer's Digest* magazine, events, online education, and more.

8 ELEMENTS TO AMPLIFY YOUR AUTHOR BRAND

Mary Buckham

What makes a reader choose to buy one book over another? Is it randomness? Fate? Its position on *The New York Times* bestseller list? More important, do you, as an author, have any control over that buying decision?

If you want to learn the answer to this last question, keep reading, because you—whether you're not yet published, a debut author, or a writer seeking to sell more books—can absolutely impact your visibility in a crowded marketplace, and even sway your readers to buy books.

In today's publishing climate, most writers (or at least those who want to get published) have heard of author branding. Branding, at it's most basic level, is what readers think and feel when they hear or read your name on a book. To improve their authorial presence, writers are instructed to build a website, get a Facebook page, learn to tweet, use Instagram, and become visible on a myriad of social media platforms.

But writers aren't told about the all-important underlying elements of branding that are essential for reaching both potential and existing readers. Without these elements, we risk adding to the increasing noise of those writers who clamor for attention without aim or intent.

Not every book is meant for every reader. That sounds simplistic, but it is a powerful and freeing mantra when you start to consider who *your* readers are. There are enough readers to keep you gainfully employed and very successful—*if* you are able to identify them. You accomplish this by knowing precisely what you offer to readers and conveying that message effectively so they have no doubt about what they are purchasing.

You must go deeper than the name of your latest book, or the series you're writing, to implement the eight elements of strong brand identification. The more elements you have in place, the stronger your brand will become, and the stronger your brand becomes, the easier it will be for your readers to discover and trust you.

The eight elements of author branding are as follows:

1. The Origin Story
2. The Promise
3. Beloved Images
4. Communication Style and Delivery
5. The Opposite
6. Sacred Words
7. You, the Author
8. Action

The goal of understanding and using these elements is to create a message that is strong enough to excite and resonate with readers. The stronger your brand, the stronger the sense of community, of belonging, you've created for readers. From this point forward, we're stepping away from the premise that all we need to do is write good books—that's a given. Instead we must start thinking in terms of the emotional connection we want to create with our readers. The more attention you devote to your author brand, the stronger and easier it will be to make that connection.

The great news about understanding and creating an author's brand is that, at its heart, it's about storytelling. When strands of the story are missing, the author and her work become forgettable. Don't let that happen to you.

1. THE ORIGIN STORY

At its core, this element of branding is a story about a writer who did something, tried something, thought something, or felt a certain way about something. In many cases this element is a consistent, oft-repeated story about why a writer started writing.

There's an innate human need to understand where we came from, what created our need to write, or from where our characters sprang. If you read interviews with well-known authors, you'll note that the question of their origins is consistently asked and answered. The difference between authors with an effective brand and authors without one is the consistency and the emotion behind that origin story.

This story is the crucial first step in providing answers to why people should care about you or your books. Make it interesting, and be consistent in how you communicate it.

Think of writers with strong origin stories. Nora Roberts started writing when she was stuck at home with two small boys during a snowy winter in Maryland. Sherrilyn Kenyon was close to abandoning her writing career—even though she'd already been published—but instead borrowed a postage stamp from a neighbor to send one last proposal to an editor. Suzanne Brockmann wanted to write screenplays but couldn't break in—and then she discovered romance. John Grisham wrote every day on the Chicago subway as he rode to work.

Determination, frustration, and hope are only a few of the emotions that drive a writer to write. Do any others come to mind for your own origin story?

2. THE PROMISE

The promise defines and communicates what you want your audience to believe about you and your books. It is a simple, concise statement that embodies hugely bold ideas. In the corporate world the creed can be a mission statement, but in the world of authors and stories, this promise defines *you*: It sets you and your writing apart from other writers and stories in the same genre.

The promise originates in what you believe in and how you communicate that via your stories. Do you believe in hope, or magic, or the power of good over evil, or the danger of too much power, or unfettered passions, or antipathy? What core principles drive you to write the stories you write? Do you believe in happy-ever-afters? Maybe your thing is a fear of the dark or a need to observe and comment on the damage humans can inflict on one another?

These are examples of basic beliefs and emotions that drive us, but they are not the same for everyone. Dig down to determine what drives you to write.

What makes you keep writing in spite of the challenges of publication and rejection? Why must *your* stories be heard? That's your promise to the reader, regardless of the type of story you are writing.

3. BELOVED IMAGES

The images created within our stories, as well as in our communications to our readers, can impart subtle meaning. These images resonate and reconfirm your promise to the reader. They can include a color, a shape, a texture, a taste, a sound, or a smell. Think about your cover images, your website color choices, and your author photo. Think of the messages imparted by these elements.

Here are a few examples of beloved images associated with authors or stories. See if you can determine the author based on the image alone:

- a deerstalker cap
- the running of the bulls
- a lightsaber
- the Nimbus 2000

If you associated the deerstalker cap with Sherlock Holmes, the running of the bulls with Ernest Hemingway, the lightsaber with the *Star Wars* universe, and the Nimbus 2000 with the Harry Potter series, you've witnessed firsthand the power of imagery in branding.

Images that communicate emotion or a connection to either you or your stories can create the sense of unity and community that comprises your author brand.

4. COMMUNICATION STYLE AND DELIVERY

Have you attended a book signing or an author reading? Have you spotted a notice on social media about an author's new release or upcoming event? Branded communication includes the repeated interactions readers have with an author or a product. Think about the release events for the Harry Potter books or Twilight novels. Think about the author who barely glances up when she signs your book versus the one who takes the time to engage with you. Do you hear from an author only when he has a new book coming out, or is he visible all the time?

Look not only to the big-name authors for how they communicate with readers but also to newer authors whom you feel you know without ever having met them. How do these authors interact on social media? How do they consistently present themselves?

Keep in mind that the style and delivery of your interactions are active engagements that can be imbued with either positive or negative meaning.

5. THE OPPOSITE

Characterizing who you are *not* as a writer is important in defining who you are, what you believe, and what resonates with you.

For instance, consider the following:

- Do you write beach reads or book club reads?
- Would your books be categorized as erotica or inspirational?
- Is your mystery filled with cutting-edge tension, or would it be more fittingly described as "cozy"?
- Do you drop F-bombs or favor the Queen's English?
- Is your YA novel more Harry Potter or Hunger Games?
- Are your children's books more akin to the work of Dr. Seuss or Beatrix Potter?

Embracing the differences between you and another author creates a shorthand message to your reader. Of course, readers can like more than one author and more than one type of book, but letting them know clearly what you are offering makes it easier for them to set the right expectations.

Not every book is meant for every reader. That sounds simplistic, but it is a powerful and freeing mantra when you start to consider who *your* readers are.

Many writers start with a tagline that encompasses what their work is about and what readers can expect. Learn from the consistent, continuous messages you see from branded authors to determine how to create and communicate your beliefs and define who you are—and who you are not.

6. SACRED WORDS

All belief systems come with a set of specialized words or cues that must be learned in order for its members to belong. Remember that branding is partially about defining who your reader is and who belongs to *your* readership group. You will want to provide unique words, phrases, and acronyms that your readers will easily identify with you and your stories. Here are some examples of sacred words written by famous authors:

- "One ring to rule them all" (J.R.R. Tolkien)
- "Elementary." (Sir Arthur Conan Doyle)
- "May the odds be ever in your favor." (Suzanne Collins)
- "I do not like green eggs and ham." (Dr. Seuss)
- "It was the best of times, it was the worst of times. …" (Charles Dickens)
- "My name is Inigo Montoya. You killed my father. Prepare to die." (William Goldman)

Fans of these authors or their stories can quickly identify with the above sacred words. Nothing else is needed to create a quick, clear image of the source of these phrases.

7. YOU, THE AUTHOR

This can be a tricky concept, because writers often forget that they are a large part of their brand. Some authors prefer to let a character act as a *visual* stand-in—think Sherlock Holmes for Arthur Conan Doyle, Bella Swan for Stephenie Meyer, or Gandalf or Bilbo Baggins for J.R.R. Tolkien.

But remember that *you* embody the mythos behind your creation legend. Vision is the sign of a great leader. A leader gives meaning to the brand and symbolizes what it stands for.

When your audience questions whether they're getting the straight story about who you are and what you intend to share, your brand suffers. Determining who you are and making it clear to readers weaves the threads of your brand into a tighter, more compelling and consistent message.

8. ACTION

This last element is key. Creating a brand does not happen overnight. It takes thought, self-awareness, and the willingness to study and learn from others while still being true to yourself. Brands are built a layer at a time, which is where this last stage comes into play.

Studying the brands of others is very different than implementing your own. Allow yourself to learn by trial and error. Brand building is a process and not a one-time, one-shot, check-it-off-the-list event.

Be consistent. Be true. Be real. Communicate who you are and what you write in all of your interactions with your readers.

Mary Buckham is a *USA Today* best-selling author of urban fantasy, young adult, and romantic suspense novels, as well as nonfiction writing craft books. Her latest book for writers, *A Writer's Guide to Active Setting*, was published in January 2016 by Writer's Digest Books. When she isn't writing fiction touted for its unique voice, high action, and rich emotion, Mary travels around the country and works with writers of all genres to craft stronger stories and understand the constantly evolving publishing landscape. She has been an article writer, a regional magazine editor, the co-founder of an online writing venue, and a sought-after writing instructor.

CROWD WISDOM

Could You—and Should You—Crowdfund Your Novel?

Diane Shipley

Asking family, friends, and even strangers for money doesn't carry the stigma it used to. In the last few years, crowdfunding sites—where people collect donations to cover the cost of everything from essential surgery to wearable technology—have become a legitimate option for writers who want to self-publish without plunging into debt.

Novelists are using crowdfunding to bring passion projects to life, communicate with fans, and connect with Hollywood producers. In some cases, they're even garnering critical respect. Paul Kingsnorth's crowdfunded postapocalyptic novel, *The Wake*, won The Bookseller Industry Book of the Year Award 2015, was long-listed for the Man Booker Prize, and received a favorable review from *The New York Times*.

On Kickstarter, the biggest and best-known crowdfunding site, donors gave more than $23 million to publishing projects in 2015 alone. But only 40 percent of projects ever reach their funding goal. So how can you ensure success? In a word, *planning*.

DEFINE YOUR CROWDFUNDING STRATEGY

Kickstarter's publishing outreach lead, Maris Kreizman, says that authors need to do their research before deciding how much to ask for. That means getting quotes for services like editing, cover design, and printing. Plus you need to factor in site fees (Kickstarter and its main competitor, Indiegogo, take a 5 percent cut of the earnings for successful projects, plus 3 to 5 percent for processing payments), and the cost of shipping and rewards.

A key part of crowdfunding campaigns is offering backers something for their money at different donation levels: For example, a donation of $10 awards an e-book, and a pledge of $20 awards a print copy. Sometimes authors create merchandise, which Kreizman says is a nice idea but an unnecessary expense. "You can still do exclusive rewards, but it doesn't have to be a physical object. A phone call or recommended reading list can be just as meaningful." While crowdfunding campaigns that rake in millions hit the headlines, it's more realistic to aim for an amount that covers your costs. "We recommend [trying to raise] the bare minimum to make the book you want to make," Kreizman says.

Whichever site you choose, you'll need to make your project page as attractive as possible in order to appeal to potential backers, which means explaining what your book's about and what it means to you. Break up any large blocks of text with bullet points, links to other writing samples, and relevant images (as long as you own the rights to them). According to Indiegogo, campaigns with videos raise 114 percent more money than the average campaign, but a video doesn't have to be professional quality. Keep it short (under two minutes), sincere, and free of background noise.

SPREAD THE WORD

Once you're happy with the look of your project page, it's time to launch your campaign. Kelly Thompson, who has used Kickstarter to fund two novels, says that a social media presence is crucial. "You need to be on Twitter or Tumblr or Facebook or a blog, or all of the above," she says. "You can't expect to go to Kickstarter and find an audience there. You have to have a preexisting audience, even if it's a small one."

Publishing consultant Jane Friedman says that before launching a crowdfunding campaign, you should make a spreadsheet of your contacts and estimate how much you can reasonably expect them to donate. "I recommend with social media that people consider 1 percent of their total following to be potential donors. If you have three thousand [followers], that's at most thirty [donors], and even that [number] feels optimistic."

Ideally, you'll know a handful of people who will be willing to put up the initial 10 to 20 percent in order to build momentum for the campaign. Friedman recommends that authors send an e-mail to their contacts at the start of a campaign asking for support—but know who it's appropriate to approach. Because Friedman has a lot of Twitter followers (215,000 at last count), strangers frequently ask her to tweet about their campaigns. "They've asked me to support their project because they know it can be helpful to have someone with a following mention them. But that doesn't work; you need to have had some sort of interaction."

Liz Hennessy, who writes as E.A Hennessy, used Indiegogo to raise money for her first novel, *Grigory's Gadget*, a steampunk adventure story. She was keen to self-publish so she could keep creative control, and she looked to crowdfunding when she realized how costly that route would be. She found asking for donations difficult and says that if she were to crowdfund again, she'd assemble a team of ambassadors to help promote her campaign. "I'm a shy, introverted person, so it was difficult for me to approach even friends and family. You know they care, but it's hard to reach out and say, 'This is how you can help me.'" In the end, she raised $2,021 of her $4,000 goal, and as she'd chosen Indiegogo's flexible funding option (as opposed to fixed funding, which requires the campaign to be fully funded to pay out), she got to keep the money she raised. That gave her enough to cover editing. By using personal savings to cover smaller publishing expenses, she was still able to self-publish *Grigory's Gadget.*

WHICH SITE IS RIGHT FOR YOU?

Weigh the pros and cons of the different options before making your choice.

- **KICKSTARTER (KICKSTARTER.COM):** The biggest and best-known crowdfunding site, and the one with the strictest guidelines. Every project must be well-defined and have a clear end goal and delivery date. Fixed funding only.
- **INDIEGOGO (INDIEGOGO.COM):** This site doesn't have the reach or cachet of Kickstarter, but it allows you to choose between fixed or flexible funding, where you can keep every cent you raise (minus fees).
- **UNBOUND (UNBOUND.CO.UK):** This U.K.-based crowdfunding publisher is favored by literary authors and celebrities. It encourages authors to pitch their book before they've started writing and to update their backers regularly.
- **INKSHARES (INKSHARES.COM):** This crowdfunding publisher allows authors to upload drafts of their projects to receive feedback and build a following before their campaign. It offers the option of a 250-book print run for niche projects.
- **PUBLISHIZER (PUBLISHIZER.COM):** A crowdfunding site/matchmaker. For every presales goal met (from 250 to 1000 copies), an author's book proposal is shared with a bigger group of publishers. It offers flexible funding, but fees start at 15 percent.

WEIGH THE PROS AND CONS

The upside of being your own publisher is that you're in control of everything—but that's also the downside. Administrative tasks can be more stressful, time-consuming, and costly than authors anticipate. Kelly Thompson says that these tasks have eaten up a fair amount of her time, meaning that she is currently writing a book every two years rather than every year, as she had originally planned. She asked for $8,000 on Kickstarter in 2012 for her first novel, *The Girl Who Would Be King,* the story of two young women with extraordinary powers. Although she raised $26,478, she ended up paying $5,000 out of pocket and going into credit card debt in order to fulfil her orders, mostly because she underestimated shipping costs. She also had to make multiple trips to the post office and says that parcels took over her fourth-flight New York walk up. In 2014 she raised $57,918 for her second book, *Story Killer,* and moved temporarily to her parents' house in Utah so she could ship books more easily. "We had 709 backers for the first one and almost double that for the second—there is no way I could have done that [from my apartment in] New

York." Because she was more organized and had better calculated her costs, *Story Killer* was profitable from the start.

However, it hasn't generated as much buzz as *The Girl Who Would Be King*. In early 2013, a writer for influential science and culture site io9 gave the book a glowing review, which sparked renewed interest in the book. It's since become an Amazon bestseller and been optioned twice, most recently for television. Thompson had originally tried to get the novel traditionally published, and even came close with one of the big five, but kept getting feedback that it was too dark, not YA enough, and didn't fit neatly into a particular genre. She now thinks those are the elements that have made it a success. "I found it interesting that *Story Killer* didn't find the same success when *The Girl Who Would Be King* seemed like a much riskier model. But I think it goes to show that people want something different, and when they see it, they respond to it." She understands why publishers are cautious about acquiring this type of book, but she thinks they're missing an opportunity by not looking to crowdfunding success stories for new talent with a built-in audience.

CROWDFUNDING SUCCESS STORIES

- ***TO BE OR NOT TO BE: THAT IS THE ADVENTURE:*** Ryan North's choose-your-own-adventure version of *Hamlet* raked in a jaw-dropping $580,905 on Kickstarter.
- ***HELLO RUBY:*** This children's book by Linda Liukas that uses storytelling to teach the principles of computer coding, raised $380,747 and was republished by the Macmillan imprint Feiwel & Friends.
- ***THE SERENDIPITY FOUNDATION:*** Sam Smit's debut, a thriller about 'terrorism with a social conscience,' is the most-funded novel on Unbound, raising 132 percent of its goal.
- ***MAGPIES:*** Sara Lando raised $30,566 on Indiegogo for this beautifully rendered graphic novel about love and loss.
- ***ABOMINATION:*** *After Earth* screenwriter Gary Whitta used Inkshares to sell 9,198 copies of his historical fantasy set in England during the reign of Alfred the Great.
- ***WOLLSTONECRAFT:*** This adventure story by Jordan Stratford, about the adolescent versions of real-life feminist heroes Ada Lovelace and Mary Shelley, raised $91,751 on Kickstarter.

CONSIDER HYBRID CROWDFUNDING OPTIONS

You don't necessarily have to choose between traditional publishing and going it alone. Hybrid publishers are filling a gap for authors who are happy to self-promote but don't want to handle the production and distribution process. Filip Syta's novel *The Show* is a dark satire about the seedy underbelly of a huge tech company. Instead of using a crowdfunding platform, he turned to Inkshares, a publisher that uses crowdfunding to pay for the books it publishes. Authors upload projects to the site for sixty days, during which time at least 750 people have to preorder a copy. For copies sold beyond this initial amount, authors receive 50 percent of paperback and 70 percent of e-book sales. Kingsnorth's publisher, Unbound, works in a similar way but doesn't disclose how many books an author needs to presell and only reveals what percentage of the goal has been reached.

Although you don't earn any money up front, you also don't have to go into your own pockets. And because Inkshares and Unbound function as publishers, they are able to get books into stores like Barnes & Noble and to be considered for review by major publications. Syta sold 1,001 preorders and says that knowing people were waiting to read his book spurred him to keep writing.

As well as posting about *The Show* on Facebook and Twitter, and writing guest posts for blogs, Syta connected with potential readers in real life, a tactic he recommends to other authors. "Go to events that have something to do with the subject of your book or where there's a crowd you think would be interested. Define your audience and where they are, and then go to those places." Once you're there, emphasize what people will get from the book rather than why you want them to buy it. For *The Show*, that pitch would be something like: "It's a book to help people realize it's never too late to follow their dreams." Syta thinks that hybrid crowdfunding will become increasingly common. "There's a lot of talent out there, but to score a traditional publisher is time-consuming and extremely difficult. [Novels published through crowdfunding go] straight to the reader without asking an agent or someone at a publishing house for permission."

Jane Friedman says that working with a hybrid crowdfunding publisher is ideal for authors who enjoy collaboration, but that they should be realistic about how much their book will benefit. "Just because you work with one of these companies doesn't automatically mean you're going to see more sales or a better marketing campaign; a lot of the responsibility is still on your shoulders."

Whichever crowdfunding site you choose, if you have a plan of attack, some loyal supporters, and an indefatigable spirit, it could make your publication dreams a reality. And your first crowdfunded novel doesn't have to be a one-off. "We've seen a bunch of repeat creators," says Maris Kreizman. "As long as you have fans who want to be a part of it, you can have unlimited success."

TOP TIPS FOR CROWDFUNDING SUCCESS

- **READ THE CROWDFUNDING BIBLE(S).** The Kickstarter Creator Handbook (kickstarter.com/help/handbook) and the Indiegogo help section (support.indiegogo.com/hc/en-us) will guide you through every step of a campaign.
- **TIME YOUR CAMPAIGN WISELY.** Avoid the holidays—people are too preoccupied (and broke) to donate. You can usually choose how long your project runs, but Wharton researchers recommend thirty days for best results.
- **BE TAX SMART.** Any profit you make above the cost of making and shipping your book is treated as income by the IRS, so keep detailed records and start and finish your campaign in the same tax year to avoid complications. (Consult an accountant to be on the safe side.)
- **BE AVAILABLE.** Most crowdfunding sites allow potential backers to ask you questions. Answer as promptly as possible, so they're confident in your ability to deliver.
- **DON'T STRETCH OUT.** When a project funds quickly, some creators add "stretch goals," extra rewards for additional funding targets. This can incentivize donors, but usually involves more work for creators, so remember they're not compulsory.

Diane Shipley is a freelance journalist who writes about books, pop culture, technology, and psychology—or any combination of the above. Her bylines include *The Guardian*, *The Los Angeles Times*, *Writer's Digest*, and *Mental Health Today*. She's also a frequent contributor to Twitter (@dianeshipley).

SHORT & STRATEGIC

How to Self-Publish Short Fiction Singles

James Scott Bell

The new world of self-publishing options for short fiction calls to mind the golden age of the pulp magazines. During that era, roughly 1920–1950, writers could earn decent money pounding out stories and novellas for a penny a word.

Later, the 1950s boom in mass-market paperbacks provided another source of lettuce for the enterprising author. Production and quality were key. If you could deliver the goods on a regular basis, you could actually make a go of the uncertain and unpredictable writer's life.

Those times are back.

Thousands of writers are now realizing substantial self-publishing income. Many have quit their day jobs. A few have even reached megastar level. How? By following the pattern of the pulp writers. They keep the words coming, and they know their craft.

Many use short-form fiction as a strategic component of building a lasting readership. With tablets and even smartphones increasingly used as reading devices, short fiction is once again in demand, as evidenced by new, popular venues for the form, such as Amazon's Kindle Singles.

THE POTENTIAL

Hugh Howey, the self-publishing superstar who shot to fame with his Wool series of science fiction, had no idea what was going to happen when he published the first installment—at the time, a 12,000-word novelette—on the Kindle platform. "That was it," Howey says. "There was no more story. I made the work available and did zero promotion for it. I thought it was the least commercial of my works, being short and very inexpensive."

But soon *Wool* was outselling all his previous works combined. One thousand copies in a month, three thousand the next, and ten thousand the month after that.

As the great pulp writer Edgar Rice Burroughs once put it, "If you write one story, it may be bad; if you write a hundred, you have the odds in your favor."

Howey knew he had a hit. "I heeded the flood of e-mails and reviews," he says, "and started writing the next part."

The rest is well-known in the indie world. The film rights for the Wool series were sold to 20th Century Fox, and the stories were gathered together in a single volume. A pioneer six-figure print-only deal with Simon & Schuster followed. Howey retained the right to publish the e-books on his own.

There is always the chance that a good series of short fiction will catch on and become a solid income stream. But that's not the only reason to pursue short-form work.

Prolific writer Kristine Kathryn Rusch, who makes good money from short stories, also uses them to help enhance her full-length fiction. "I explore the worlds of my novels," she says. "If I introduce a major new character, I write a short story to figure out who that character is."

Rusch also uses her short work to find new readers. She'll take a story that is normally for sale online and make it free for a week. "I put up a free short story every Monday, and take that story down the following Monday. Free, one week only. And boy, has that grown my blog's readership, and my own."

THE FORMS

Short-form fiction is anything less than a novel. The minimum word count for a novel varies, depending on genre, audience, and (as with many things in publishing today) whom you ask, but is usually tagged at 50,000. Below that you have the following:

Novella

Between 20,000 and 50,000 words, the novella was a popular form in the age of the pulps because it could take up most of a magazine and leave readers feeling like they got a good story for their money.

But when the pulps dried up, so did novellas. Although a title occasionally broke through (e.g., *The Bridges of Madison County*) or was included in a collection of short fiction by a single author, most traditional publishers did not find novellas cost-effective to produce.

Now the novella is back, and self-publishers—who don't need to worry about things like print runs and page signatures where e-books are concerned—are releasing them in droves.

A novella works best when it has one main character and one main plot. An example is James M. Cain's crime classic *The Postman Always Rings Twice*. Coming in at about 35,000 words, it's a love-triangle-leads-to-murder story. It has the famous opening line: "They threw me off the hay truck about noon." The story is told in first-person narration by Frank Chambers. But novellas work equally well in third-person point of view.

Other famous novellas include:

- The Pearl by John Steinbeck
- *The Old Man and the Sea* by Ernest Hemingway
- *A Christmas Carol* by Charles Dickens
- *The Escape Route* by Rod Serling
- *A River Runs Through It* by Norman Maclean

Novelette

Not quite as well known is the novelette. At between 7,000 and 20,000 words, it allows for a little more breathing space than a short story without requiring the fuller complexity of a novel.

A novelette, like its beefier cousin the novella, is most effective when it's about one main character and story. Novelettes are perhaps best known in the science fiction world. Howey's original *Wool*, for example, was novelette length. The Science Fiction and Fantasy Writers of America give an annual Nebula Award in this category. Here's a list of some famous winners:

- Philip K. Dick for "Faith of Our Fathers"
- Harlan Ellison for "Basilisk"
- Orson Scott Card for "Ender's Game" (later expanded into a novel)
- Isaac Asimov for "The Bicentennial Man"

Short Story

An enduring and popular form, the short story can pack an emotional punch as powerful as a novel. At 1,000 to 7,000 words in length, the best stories usually revolve around *one shattering moment.*

The shattering moment can come at the beginning of the story, with the consequences played out to a resolution (e.g., "A Candle for the Bag Lady" by Lawrence Block), or it can come at the end, usually as part of an intriguing plot that has a surprise ending. A master of this form is Jeffery Deaver (see his collections *Twisted* and *More Twisted*).

And, yes, the shattering moment can be in the middle, as in Raymond Carver's classic "Will You Please Be Quiet, Please?"

THE STRATEGIES

Short-form fiction published as independent, stand-alone works should not be viewed (at least initially) as a source of major self-publishing profits. That's because to remain competitive on Amazon, BN.com, Kobo, and other retailers, you have to price them at the lower end—usually ninety-nine cents or even, for periods of time, free. Pricing is not a science, so you should experiment. A novella might support a price of $2.99 or more on occasion. It takes several months to a year of conducting pricing and promotional experiments and collecting data to figure out what works best for you.

Here are some other strategic uses for short stories:

Use them in the Kindle Select program.

Kindle Select is a promotional program Amazon offers under the Kindle Direct Publishing umbrella. Through the program, by giving Amazon exclusive distribution rights in ninety-day increments, you can offer a work for free for five days. Those days can be spaced apart or used all at once. On the other days in this period, your story is priced as usual.

My preference is to use all five "free" days in a row and get the word out on social media. The goal is to get eyeballs on the story and reach new readers who will then want to seek out your full-length books. If you're just starting out and don't yet have full-length books, the free looks can begin to build your readership for the future.

Use them as giveaways when people sign up for your e-newsletter.

Successful indie writers know that the two best marketing tools are word of mouth and an e-mail list of readers. To start building that list, many authors offer on their blog or website a sign-up form which gives out a free story or book in return for your e-mail address.

I recommend using at least a novelette-length story for this—and make it a good one. You don't just want those sign-ups; you want readers who will become fans.

Use them as serials.

Many writers are now serializing their novels, using another model from the good old days. They'll publish in installments, with a low price. Some authors refer to this as episodic fiction, likening it to a television series such as *Lost* or *True Detective.*

Later, as Howey did with *Wool*, you can gather the series into one volume. But also listen to Howey's counsel: "I think it's a bad idea to simply chop up a novel into shorter pieces. Each work needs to satisfy on its own."

Howey emphasizes that each piece "should have its own beginning, middle, and end. Cliff-hangers only work if the protagonists have overcome some other obstacle along the way. Don't string your readers along; invite them back for more."

Use them to promote a new novel.

A few years ago the big publishing houses started getting in on the game by commissioning short works from their A-list authors. Lee Child, Michael Connelly, and Janet Evanovich—just to name a few—now put out shorts featuring their popular series characters. This not only helps promote the next novel but keeps their readers engaged during that in-between period.

Use them to keep your joy alive.

Sometimes you need to write something just for the fun of it. This keeps your writing chops sharp and your writer's soul soaring. That's how it was with my short story "Golden." It's not my usual thriller or noir beat, but it was a story I needed to write. It makes me happy that it's out there—and that readers have found it.

"If you like to read short stories, write them," Rusch says. "It's that simple. Write what you love. That's really the most important thing—and, believe it or not, the most important thing to making a living."

Use them to increase your chances of success.

If there's one consistent drumbeat from successful indie authors, it's that production is key, not unlike the writer's life in that pulp era we discussed earlier. As the great pulp writer Edgar Rice Burroughs once put it, "If you write one story, it may be bad; if you write a hundred, you have the odds in your favor."

James Scott Bell (jamesscottbell.com) has written fiction in every form and in multiple genres. His novella *One More Lie* was the first self-published work to be nominated for an International Thriller Writers Award.

LITERARY AGENTS

Many publishers are willing to look at unsolicited submissions, but most feel having an agent is in the writer's best interest. In this section we include agents who specialize in or represent fiction.

The commercial fiction field is intensely competitive. Many publishers have small staffs and little time. For that reason, many book publishers rely on agents for new talent. Some publishers even rely on agents as "first readers" who must wade through the deluge of submissions from writers to find the very best. For writers a good agent can be a foot in the door—someone willing to do the necessary work to put your ms in the right editor's hands.

It would seem today that finding a good agent is as hard as finding a good publisher. Yet writers who have agents say they are invaluable. Not only can an agent help you make your work more marketable, an agent also acts as your business manager and adviser, protecting your interests during and after contract negotiations.

Still, finding an agent can be very difficult for a new writer. If you are already published in magazines, you have a better chance than someone with no publishing credits. (Some agents read periodicals searching for new writers.) Although many agents do read queries and mss from unpublished authors without introduction, referrals from their writer clients can be a big help. If you don't know any published authors with agents, attending a conference is a good way to meet agents. Some agents even set aside time at conferences to meet new writers.

Almost all the agents listed here have said they are open to working with new, previously unpublished writers as well as published writers. They do not charge a fee to cover the time and effort involved in reviewing a manuscript or a synopsis and chapters, but their time is still extremely valuable. Send an agent your work only when you feel it is as complete and polished as possible.

USING THE LISTINGS

It is especially important that you read individual listings carefully before contacting these busy agents. The first information after the company name includes the address and phone, fax, e-mail address (when available), and website. **Member Agents** gives the names of individual agents working at that company. (Specific types of fiction an agent handles are indicated in parentheses after that agent's name). The **Represents** section lists the types of fiction the agency works with. Reading the **Recent Sales** gives you the names of writers an agent is currently working with and, very important, publishers the agent has placed mss with. **Tips** presents advice directly from the agent to authors.

Also, look closely at the openness to submissions icon that precedes most listings. It indicates how willing an agency is to take on new writers.

THE AHEARN AGENCY, INC.

2021 Pine St., New Orleans LA 70118. (504)861-8395. **Fax:** (504)866-6434. **E-mail:** pahearn@aol.com. **Website:** www.ahearnagency.com. **Contact:** Pamela G. Ahearn. Member of MWA, RWA, ITW. Represents 35 clients.

Prior to opening her agency, Ms. Ahearn was an agent for 8 years and an editor with Bantam Books.

REPRESENTS Fiction. **Considers these fiction areas:** romance, suspense, thriller, women's.

Handles general adult fiction, specializing in women's fiction and suspense. Does not deal with any nonfiction, poetry, juvenile material or science fiction.

HOW TO CONTACT Query with SASE or via e-mail. Please send a one-page query letter stating the type of book you're writing, word length, where you feel your book fits into the current market, and any writing credentials you may possess. Please do not send ms pages or synopses if they haven't been previously requested. If you're querying via e-mail, send no attachments unless requested. Accepts simultaneous submissions. Responds in 2-3 months to queries and submissions. Obtains most new clients through recommendations from others, solicitations, conferences.

TERMS Agent receives 15% commission on domestic sales; 20% commission on foreign sales. Offers written contract, binding for 1 year; renewable by mutual consent.

RECENT SALES *Black-Eyed Susans* by Julia Heaberlin, *The Art of Sinning* by Sabrina Jeffries, *The Comfort of Black* by Carter Wilson, *Flirting with Felicity* by Gerri Russell, *The Iris Fan* by Laura Joh Rowland, *The Loner* by Kate Moore, *Can't Find My Way Home* by Carlene Thompson.

TIPS "Be professional! Always send exactly what an agent or editor asks for—no more, no less. Keep query letters brief and to the point, giving your writing credentials and a very brief summary of your book. If an agent rejects you, keep trying—there are a lot of us out there!"

BETSY AMSTER LITERARY ENTERPRISES

6312 SW Capitol Hwy., #503, Portland OR 97239. **E-mail:** b.amster.assistant@gmail.com (for adult titles); b.amster.kidsbooks@gmail.com (for children's and young adult). **Website:** www.amsterlit.com. **Contact:** Betsy Amster (adult); Mary Cummings (children's and young adult). Estab. 1992. Member of AAR. Represents more than 65 clients.

Prior to opening her agency, Ms. Amster was an editor at Pantheon and Vintage for 10 years and served as editorial director for the Globe Pequot Press for 2 years.

REPRESENTS Nonfiction, fiction, juvenile books. **Considers these fiction areas:** crime, detective, juvenile, literary, middle-grade, multicultural, mystery, picture books, police, women's, young adult.

"Actively seeking strong narrative nonfiction, particularly by journalists; outstanding literary fiction (the next Jennifer Haigh or Jess Walter); witty, intelligent, commercial women's fiction (the next Elinor Lipman); mysteries that open new worlds to us; and high-profile self-help and psychology, preferably research-based." Does not want to receive poetry, children's books, romances, western, science fiction, action/adventure, screenplays, fantasy, techno thrillers, spy capers, apocalyptic scenarios, or political or religious arguments.

HOW TO CONTACT See submission requirements online at website. For adult titles: b.amster.assistant@gmail.com. "For fiction or memoirs, please embed the first 3 pages in the body of your e-mail. For nonfiction, please embed your proposal." For children's and young adult: b.amster.kidsbooks@gmail.com. "For picture books, please embed the entire text in the body of your e-mail. For novels, please embed the first 3 pages." Accepts simultaneous submissions. Responds in 1 month to queries; in 2 months to mss. Obtains most new clients through recommendations from others, solicitations, conferences.

TERMS Agent receives 15% commission on domestic sales; 20% commission on foreign sales. Offers written contract, binding for 1 year; three-month notice must be given to terminate contract. Charges for photocopying, postage, messengers, galleys/books used in submissions to foreign and film agents and to magazines for first serial rights. (Please note that it is rare to incur much in the way of expenses now that most submissions are made by e-mail.)

ANDERSON LITERARY MANAGEMENT, LLC

244 Fifth Avenue, Floor 11, New York NY 10001. (212)645-6045. **Fax:** (212)741-1936. **E-mail:** info@andersonliterary.com; kathleen@andersonliterary.com; adam@andersonliterary.com; jessie@andersonliter-

ary.com; tess@andersonliterary.com. **Website:** www.andersonliterary.com. **Contact:** Kathleen Anderson. Estab. 2006. Member of AAR. Represents 100+ clients.

MEMBER AGENTS Kathleen Anderson, Adam Friedstein, Tess Taylor.

REPRESENTS Nonfiction, fiction. **Considers these fiction areas:** ethnic, historical, humor, literary, middle-grade, multicultural, suspense, thriller, women's, young adult, contemporary, international.

"We do not represent plays or screenplays, science fiction, cookbooks, gardening, craft books, or children's picture books. While we love literature in translation, we cannot accept samples of work written in languages other than English."

HOW TO CONTACT Query with SASE. Submit synopsis, first 3 sample chapters, proposal (for nonfiction). Snail mail queries only. Accepts simultaneous submissions. Responds in 6 weeks to queries.

APONTE LITERARY AGENCY

E-mail: agents@aponteliterary.com. **Website:** aponteliterary.com. **Contact:** Natalia Aponte. Member of AAR. Signatory of WGA.

MEMBER AGENTS Natalia Aponte (any genre of mainstream fiction and nonfiction, but especially seeking women's novels, historical novels, supernatural and paranormal fiction, fantasy novels, political and science thrillers); **Victoria Lea** (any category, but especially interested in women's fiction, science fiction and speculative fiction).

REPRESENTS Nonfiction, fiction. **Considers these fiction areas:** fantasy, historical, paranormal, science fiction, supernatural, thriller, women's.

Actively seeking women's novels, historical novels, supernatural and paranormal fiction, fantasy novels, political and science thrillers, science fiction, and speculative fiction. In nonfiction, will look at any genre with commercial potential.

HOW TO CONTACT E-query. Accepts simultaneous submissions. Responds in 6 weeks if interested.

RECENT SALES *The Nightingale Bones* by Ariel Swan, *An Irish Doctor in Peace and At War* by Patrick Taylor, *Siren's Treasure* by Debbie Herbert.

THE AXELROD AGENCY

55 Main St., P.O. Box 357, Chatham NY 12037. (518)392-2100. **E-mail:** steve@axelrodagency.com. **Website:** www.axelrodagency.com. **Contact:** Steven Axelrod. Member of AAR. Represents 15-20 clients.

Prior to becoming an agent, Mr. Axelrod was a book club editor.

REPRESENTS Fiction. **Considers these fiction areas:** crime, mystery, new adult, romance, women's.

This agency specializes in women's fiction and romance.

HOW TO CONTACT Query via e-mail. Accepts simultaneous submissions. Obtains most new clients through recommendations from others.

TERMS Agent receives 15% commission on domestic sales; 20% commission on foreign sales. No written contract.

WRITERS CONFERENCES RWA National Conference.

AZANTIAN LITERARY AGENCY

E-mail: queries@azantianlitagency.com. **Website:** www.azantianlitagency.com. **Contact:** Jennifer Azantian. Estab. 2014. Member of AAR. Signatory of WGA.

Prior to her current position, Ms. Azantian was with Sandra Dijkstra Literary Agency.

REPRESENTS Fiction. **Considers these fiction areas:** fantasy, horror, middle-grade, science fiction, young adult.

Actively seeking fantasy, science fiction, and psychological horror for adult, young adult, and middle-grade readers. Does not want to receive nonfiction or picture books.

HOW TO CONTACT To submit, send your query letter, one- to two-page synopsis, and first 10-15 pages, all pasted in an e-mail (no attachments) to queries@azantianlitagency.com. Please note in the e-mail subject line if your work was requested at a conference, is an exclusive submission, or was referred by a current client. Accepts simultaneous submissions. Responds in 6 weeks. Check the website before submitting to make sure Jennifer is currently open to queries.

BARONE LITERARY AGENCY

385 North St., Batavia OH 45103. (513)732-6740. **Fax:** (513)297-7208. **E-mail:** baroneliteraryagency@roadrunner.com. **Website:** www.baroneliteraryagency.com. **Contact:** Denise Barone. Estab. 2010. Member of AAR, RWA. Signatory of WGA. Represents 10 clients.

REPRESENTS Fiction. **Considers these fiction areas:** action, adventure, cartoon, comic books, commercial, confession, contemporary issues, crime, detective, erotica, ethnic, experimental, family saga, fantasy, feminist, frontier, gay, glitz, hi-lo, historical, horror, humor, inspirational, juvenile, lesbian, literary, mainstream, metaphysical, military, multicultural, multimedia, mystery, new adult, New Age, occult, paranormal, plays, police, psychic, regional, religious, romance, satire, science fiction, sports, supernatural, suspense, thriller, urban fantasy, war, westerns, women's, young adult.

Actively seeking adult contemporary romance. Does not want textbooks.

HOW TO CONTACT "We are no longer accepting snail mail submissions; send a query letter via e-mail instead. If I like your query letter, I will ask for the first 3 chapters and a synopsis as attachments." Accepts simultaneous submissions. Obtains new clients by queries/submissions via e-mail only.

TERMS Agent receives 15% commission on domestic sales; 20% on foreign sales. Offers written contract.

RECENT SALES *All The Glittering Bones* by Anna Snow (Entangled Publishing), *Melody Massacre to the Rescue* by Anna Snow (Entangled Publishing), *Devon's Choice* by Cathy Bennett (Clean Reads), *Molly's Folly* by Denise Gwen (Clean Reads), *In Deep* by Laurie Albano (Solstice Publishing).

WRITERS CONFERENCES Willamette Writers Conference.

TIPS "The best writing advice I ever got came from a fellow writer, who wrote, *Learn how to edit yourself*, when signing her book to me."

BAROR INTERNATIONAL, INC.

P.O. Box 868, Armonk NY 10504. **E-mail:** heather@barorint.com. **Website:** www.barorint.com. **Contact:** Danny Baror; Heather Baror-Shapiro. Represents 300 clients.

MEMBER AGENTS Danny Baror; Heather Baror-Shapiro.

REPRESENTS Fiction. **Considers these fiction areas:** fantasy, literary, science fiction, young adult, adult fiction, commerical.

This agency represents authors and publishers in the international market. Currently representing commercial fiction, literary titles, science fiction, young adult, and more.

HOW TO CONTACT Submit by e-mail or mail (with SASE); include a cover letter and a few sample chapters. Accepts simultaneous submissions.

BARRON'S LITERARY MANAGEMENT

4615 Rockland Dr., Arlington TX 76016. **E-mail:** baronsliterary@sbcglobal.net. **Contact:** Adele Brooks, president.

REPRESENTS Nonfiction, fiction. **Considers these fiction areas:** legal, crime, techno or medical thrillers, all romance.

HOW TO CONTACT Contact by e-mail initially. Send bio and a brief synopsis of story (fiction) or a nonfiction book proposal. Accepts simultaneous submissions. Obtains most new clients through e-mail submissions.

TIPS "Have your book tightly edited, polished, and ready to be seen before contacting agents. I respond quickly, and if interested I may request an electronic or hard-copy mailing."

THE BENT AGENCY

E-mail: info@thebentagency.com. **Website:** www.thebentagency.com. **Contact:** Jenny Bent, Susan Hawk, Molly Ker Hawn, Gemma Cooper, Louise Fury, Brooks Sherman, Beth Phelan, Victoria Lowes, Heather Flaherty. Estab. 2009. Member of AAR.

Prior to forming her own agency, Ms. Bent was an agent and vice president at Trident Media.

MEMBER AGENTS **Jenny Bent**, queries@thebentagency.com (adult fiction, including women's fiction, romance, and crime/suspense; she particularly likes novels with magical or fantasy elements that fall outside genre fiction; young adult and middle-grade fiction; memoir; humor); **Susan Hawk**, kidsqueries@thebentagency.com (young adult, middle-grade, picture books; within the realm of kids stories, she likes contemporary, mystery, fantasy, science fiction, and historical fiction); **Molly Ker Hawn**, hawnqueries@thebentagency.com (young adult and middle-grade books, including contemporary, historical, fantasy, science fiction, thrillers, mystery); **Gemma Cooper**, cooperqueries@thebentagency.com (all ages of children's and young adult books, including picture books; likes historical, contemporary, thrillers, mystery, humor, and science fiction); **Louise Fury**, furyqueries@thebentagency.com (picture books, literary middle-grade, all young adult, speculative fiction, suspense/thriller, commercial fiction, all subgenres of romance [including erotic], cookbooks, pop culture); **Brooks Sherman**, shermanqueries@thebentagency.com (speculative and literary adult fiction; select narrative nonfiction; all ages of children's and young adult books, including picture books; likes historical, contemporary, thrillers, humor, fantasy, and horror); **Beth Phelan**; phelanagencies@thebentagency.com (young adult, thrillers, suspense and mystery, romance and women's fiction, literary and general fiction, cookbooks, lifestyle, pets/animals); **Victoria Lowes**, lowesqueries@thebentagency.com (romance and women's fiction, thrillers and mystery, young adult); **Heather Flaherty**, flahertyqueries@thebentagency.com (young adult and middle-grade fiction in all genres; select adult fiction, including upmarket, women's, and female-centric thrillers; select nonfiction, including pop culture, humorous, and social media-based projects, as well as teen memoir).

REPRESENTS Nonfiction, fiction, short story collections, juvenile books. **Considers these fiction areas:** commercial, crime, erotica, fantasy, feminist, historical, horror, juvenile, literary, mainstream, middle-grade, multicultural, mystery, picture books, romance, suspense, thriller, women's, young adult.

HOW TO CONTACT "Tell us briefly who you are, what your book is, and why you're the one to write it. Then include the first 10 pages of your material in the body of your e-mail. We respond to all queries; please resend your query if you haven't had a response in 4 weeks." Accepts simultaneous submissions.

RECENT SALES *Caraval* by Stephanie Garber (Flatiron), *The Smell of Other People's Houses* by Bonnie-Sue Hitchcock (Wendy Lamb Books/Random House), *My Perfect Me* by J.M.M. Nuanez (Kathy Dawson Books/Penguin BFYR), *The Square Root of Summer* by Harriet Reuter Hapgood (Roaring Brook/Macmillan), *Dirty Money* by Lisa Renee Jones (Simon & Schuster), *True North* by Liora Blake (Pocket Star),

VICKY BIJUR LITERARY AGENCY

27 W. 20th Street, Ste. 1003, New York NY 10011. **E-mail:** queries@vickybijuragency.com. **Website:** www.vickybijuragency.com. Estab. 1988. Member of AAR.

Vicky Bijur worked at Oxford University Press and with the Charlotte Sheedy Literary Agency. Books she represents have appeared on *The New York Times* Bestseller List, in *The New York Times* Notable Books of the Year, *Los Angeles Times* Best Fiction of the Year, *Washington Post* Book World Rave Reviews of the Year.

MEMBER AGENTS Vicky Bijur, Alexandra Franklin.

REPRESENTS Nonfiction, fiction. **Considers these fiction areas:** commercial, literary, mystery, new adult, thriller, women's, young adult, campus novels, coming-of-age.

"We are not the right agency for screenplays, picture books, poetry, self-help, science fiction, fantasy, horror, or romance."

HOW TO CONTACT "Please send a query letter of no more than 3 paragraphs on what makes your book special and unique, a very brief synopsis, its length and genre, and your biographical information, along with the first 10 pages of your ms. Please let us know in your query letter if it is a multiple submission, and kindly keep us informed of other agents' interest and offers of representation. If sending electronically, paste the pages in an e-mail as we don't open attachments from unfamiliar senders. If sending by hard copy, please include an SASE for our response. If you want your material returned, include an SASE large enough to contain pages and enough postage to send back to you." Include a cover letter with a proposal and the first 10 pages for nonfiction projects. Accepts simultaneous submissions. "We generally respond to all queries within 8 weeks of receipt."

RECENT SALES *That Darkness* by Lisa Black, *Long Upon the Land* by Margaret Maron, *Daughter of Ashes* by Marcia Talley.

DAVID BLACK LITERARY AGENCY

335 Adams St., Ste. 2707, Brooklyn NY 11201. (718)852-5500. **Fax:** (718)852-5539. **Website:** www.davidblackagency.com. **Contact:** David Black, owner. Member of AAR. Represents 150 clients.

MEMBER AGENTS **David Black; Jenny Herrera; Gary Morris; Joy E. Tutela** (narrative nonfiction, memoir, history, politics, self-help, investment, business, science, women's issues, LGBTQ issues, parenting, health and fitness, humor, craft, cooking and wine, lifestyle and entertainment, commercial fiction, literary fiction, middle-grade, young adult); **Susan Raihofer** (commercial fiction and nonfiction, memoir, pop culture, music, inspirational, thrillers, literary fiction); **Sarah Smith** (memoir, biography, food, music, narrative history, social studies, literary fiction).

REPRESENTS Nonfiction, fiction. **Considers these fiction areas:** commercial, literary, middle-grade, thriller, young adult.

HOW TO CONTACT "To query an agent, please follow the specific query guidelines outlined in the agent's profile on our website. Not all agents are currently accepting unsolicited queries. To query the agency, please send a one- to two-page query letter describing your book, and include information about any previously published works, your audience, and your platform." Do not e-mail your query unless an agent specifically asks for an e-mail. Accepts simultaneous submissions. Responds in 2 months to queries.

RECENT SALES Some of the agency's best-selling authors include Erik Larson, Stuart Scott, Jeff Hobbs, Mitch Albom, Gregg Olsen, Jim Abbott, and John Bacon.

BOOK CENTS LITERARY AGENCY, LLC

364 Patteson Dr., #228, Morgantown WV 26505. **E-mail:** cw@bookcentsliteraryagency.com. **Website:** www.bookcentsliteraryagency.com. **Contact:** Christine Witthohn. Estab. 2005. Member of AAR, RWA, MWA, SinC, KOD.

MEMBER AGENTS Christine Witthohn.

REPRESENTS Considers these fiction areas: commercial, literary, mainstream, multicultural, mystery, new adult, paranormal, romance, suspense, thriller, urban fantasy, women's, young adult.

- Actively seeking upmarket fiction, commercial fiction (particularly if it has crossover appeal), women's fiction (emotional and layered), romance (single title or category), mainstream mystery/suspense, thrillers (particularly psychological), and young adult. For a detailed list of what this agency is currently searching for, visit the agency website. Does *not* want to receive third-party submissions, previously published titles, short stories/novellas, erotica, inspirational, historical, science fiction/fantasy, horror/pulp/slasher thrillers, middle-grade, children's picture books, poetry, screenplays, or stories with priests/nuns, religion, rape, serial killers, or abuse of children/animals/the elderly.

HOW TO CONTACT Accepts e-submissions only from agency's website via an online form. Accepts simultaneous submissions.

TIPS Sponsors International Women's Fiction Festival in Matera, Italy. See www.womensfictionfestival.com for more information. Christine is also the U.S. rights and licensing agent for leading French publisher Bragelonne, German publisher Egmont, and Spanish publisher Edebe. For a list of upcoming publications, leading clients, and sales visit www.publishersmarketplace.com/members/bookcents.

THE BOOK GROUP

20 W. 20th St., Ste. 601, New York NY 10011. (212)803-3360. **E-mail:** submissions@thebookgroup.com. **Website:** www.thebookgroup.com. Estab. 2015. Member of AAR. Signatory of WGA.

MEMBER AGENTS **Julie Barer**; **Faye Bender**; **Brettne Bloom** (fiction: literary and commercial, select young adult; nonfiction: cookbooks, lifestyle, investigative journalism, history, biography, memoir, psychology); **Elisabeth Weed** (upmarket fiction, especially plot-driven novels with a sense of place); **Rebecca Stead** (innovative forms, diverse voices, and open-hearted fiction for children, young adults, and adults); **Dana Murphy** (story-driven fiction with a strong sense of place, narrative nonfiction/essays with a pop-culture lean, and young adult with an honest voice).

REPRESENTS Considers these fiction areas: commercial, literary, mainstream, women's, young adult.

- Please do not send poetry or screenplays.

HOW TO CONTACT Send a query letter and 10 sample pages to submissions@thebookgroup.com, with the first and last name of the agent you are querying in the subject line. All material must be in the body of the e-mail, as the agents do not open attachments. "If we are interested in reading more, we will get in touch with you as soon as possible." Accepts simultaneous submissions.

RECENT SALES *The Family Fang* by Kevin Wilson, *The Violets of March* by Sarah Jio, *The Husband's Secret* by Liane Moriarty.

BOOKS & SUCH LITERARY MANAGEMENT

52 Mission Circle, Ste. 122, PMB 170, Santa Rosa CA 95409-5370. **E-mail:** representation@booksandsuch.com. **Website:** www.booksandsuch.com. **Contact:** Janet Kobobel Grant, Wendy Lawton, Rachel Kent, Mary Keeley, Rachelle Gardner. Estab. 1996. Member of CBA (associate), American Christian Fiction Writers. Represents 250 clients.

- Prior to becoming an agent, Ms. Grant was an editor for Zondervan and managing editor for Focus on the Family before founding the agency. Ms. Lawton was an author, sculptor, and designer of porcelain dolls and became an agent in 2005. Ms. Keeley previously was an acquisitions editor for Tyndale. Ms. Kent has worked as an agent for 9 years and is a graduate of UC Davis, majoring in English. Ms. Gardner worked as an editor at NavPress, at General Publishing Group in rights and marketing, and at Fox Broadcasting Company as special programming coordinator before becoming an agent in 2007.

REPRESENTS Nonfiction, fiction, novellas, juvenile books. **Considers these fiction areas:** action, adventure, commercial, crime, family saga, frontier, historical, inspirational, juvenile, literary, mainstream, middle-grade, mystery, new adult, religious, romance, spiritual, suspense, women's, young adult.

This agency specializes in general and inspirational fiction and nonfiction, and in the Christian booksellers market. Actively seeking well-crafted material that presents Judeo-Christian values, if only subtly.

HOW TO CONTACT Query via e-mail only; no attachments. Accepts simultaneous submissions. Responds in 1 month to queries. "If you don't hear from us asking to see more of your writing within 30 days after you have sent your e-mail, please know that we have read and considered your submission but determined that it would not be a good fit for us." Obtains most new clients through recommendations from others, conferences.

TERMS Agent receives 15% commission on domestic sales; 20% commission on foreign sales. Offers written contract; two-month notice must be given to terminate contract. No additional charges.

RECENT SALES A full list of this agency's clients (and the awards they have won) is on the agency website.

WRITERS CONFERENCES Mount Hermon Christian Writers Conference, American Christian Fiction Writers Conference, San Francisco Writers Conference.

TIPS "Our agency highlights personal attention to individual clients that includes coaching on how to thrive in a rapidly changing publishing climate, grow a career, and get the best publishing offers possible."

BRADFORD LITERARY AGENCY

5694 Mission Center Rd., #347, San Diego CA 92108. (619)521-1201. **E-mail:** queries@bradfordlit.com. **Website:** www.bradfordlit.com. **Contact:** Laura Bradford, Natalie Lakosil, Sarah LaPolla, Monica Odom. Estab. 2001. Member of AAR. RWA, SCBWI, ALA Represents 130 clients.

MEMBER AGENTS **Laura Bradford**, queries@bradfordlit.com (romance [historical, romantic suspense, paranormal, category, contemporary, erotic], mystery, women's fiction, thrillers/suspense, young adult); **Natalie Lakosil**, queries@bradfordlit.com (children's literature [picture books, teen, new adult], romance [contemporary and historical], cozy mystery/crime, upmarket women's/general fiction and select children's nonfiction); **Sarah LaPolla**, sarah@bradfordlit.com (young adult, middle-grade, literary fiction, science fiction, magical realism, dark/psychological mystery, literary horror, upmarket contemporary fiction); **Monica Odom**, monica@bradfordlit.com (nonfiction by authors with demonstrable platforms in the areas of pop culture, illustrated/graphic design, food and cooking, humor, history, and social issues; narrative nonfiction; memoir; literary fiction; upmarket commercial fiction; compelling speculative fiction and magic realism; historical fiction; alternative histories; dark and edgy fiction; literary psychological thrillers; illustrated/picture books).

REPRESENTS Nonfiction, fiction, juvenile books. **Considers these fiction areas:** erotica, juvenile, middle-grade, multicultural, mystery, new adult, paranormal, picture books, romance, science fiction, thriller, women's, young adult.

Laura Bradford does not want to receive poetry, screenplays, short stories, westerns, horror, New Age, religion, crafts, cookbooks, gift books. Natalie Lakosil does not want to receive inspirational novels, memoir, romantic suspense, adult thrillers, poetry, screenplays. Sarah LaPolla does not want to receive nonfiction, picture books, inspirational/spiritual novels, romance, or erotica. Monica Odom does not want to receive genre romance, erotica, military, poetry, or inspirational/spiritual works.

HOW TO CONTACT Accepts e-mail queries only. The entire submission must appear in the body of the e-mail and not as an attachment. The subject line should begin as follows: "QUERY: [the title of the ms or any short message that is important should follow]." For fiction, e-mail a query letter along with the first chapter of ms and a synopsis. Include the genre and word count in your query letter. For nonfiction, e-mail full nonfiction proposal, including a query letter and a sample chapter. Accepts simultaneous submissions. Responds in 2-4 weeks to queries; in 10 weeks to mss. Obtains most new clients through queries.

TERMS Agent receives 15% commission on domestic sales; 25% commission on foreign sales. Offers written contract. Charges for extra copies of books for foreign submissions.

RECENT SALES Sold 115 titles in the last year, including *Skinny Dipping with Murder* by Auralee Wallace (St. Martin's), *All the Secrets We Keep* by Megan Hart (Montlake), *Magnate* by Joanna Shupe (Kensington), *Always and Forever* by Soraya Lane (Amazon), *Billionaire After Dark* by Katie Lane (Grand Central), *Coming Back* by Lauren Dane (Grand Central), *Finding Fraser* by kc dyer (Berkley), *Under the Wire* by HelenKay Dimon (Avon), *Tailored for Trouble* by Mimi Jean Pamfiloff (Ballantine), *Dinosaur Boy Saves Mars* by Cory Putman Oakes (Sourcebooks).

WRITERS CONFERENCES RWA National Conference, Romantic Times Booklovers Convention.

BRANDT & HOCHMAN LITERARY AGENTS, INC.

1501 Broadway, Ste. 2310, New York NY 10036. (212)840-5760. **Fax:** (212)840-5776. **Website:** brandthochman.com. **Contact:** Gail Hochman. Member of AAR. Represents 200 clients.

MEMBER AGENTS **Gail Hochman** (literary fiction, idea-driven nonfiction, literary memoir, children's books); **Marianne Merola** (fiction, nonfiction, and children's books with strong and unique narrative voices); **Bill Contardi** (voice-driven young adult and middle-grade fiction, commercial thrillers, psychological suspense, quirky mysteries, high fantasy, commercial fiction, memoir); **Emily Forland** (voice-driven literary fiction and nonfiction, memoir, narrative nonfiction, history, biography, food writing, cultural criticism, graphic novels, young adult fiction); **Emma Patterson** (fiction from dark, literary novels to upmarket women's and historical fiction; narrative nonfiction that includes memoir, investigative journalism, and popular history; young adult fiction); **Jody Kahn** (literary and upmarket fiction; narrative nonfiction, particularly books related to sports, food, history, science, and pop culture; cookbooks; literary memoir and journalism); **Henry Thayer** (nonfiction on a wide variety of subjects and fiction that inclines toward the literary). The e-mail addresses and specific likes of each agent are listed on the agency website.

REPRESENTS Nonfiction, fiction. **Considers these fiction areas:** fantasy, historical, literary, middle-grade, mystery, suspense, thriller, women's, young adult.

No screenplays or textbooks.

HOW TO CONTACT "We accept queries by e-mail and regular mail; however, we cannot guarantee a response to e-mailed queries. For queries via regular mail, be sure to include an SASE for our reply. Query letters should be no more than 2 pages and should include a convincing overview of the book project and information about the author and his or her writing credits. Address queries to the specific Brandt & Hochman agent whom you would like to consider your work. Accepts simultaneous submissions. Obtains most new clients through recommendations from others.

TERMS Agent receives 15% commission on domestic sales; 20% commission on foreign sales.

RECENT SALES This agency sells 40-60 new titles each year. A full list of its clients is on the agency website.

TIPS "Write a letter that will give the agent a sense of you as a professional writer—your long-term interests as well as a short description of the work at hand."

THE BRATTLE AGENCY

P.O. Box 380537, Cambridge MA 02238. (617)721-5375. **E-mail:** christopher.vyce@thebrattleagency.com; submissions@thebrattleagency.com. **Website:** thebrattleagency.com. **Contact:** Christopher Vyce. Member of AAR. Signatory of WGA.

Prior to being an agent, Mr. Vyce worked for the Beacon Press in Boston as an acquisitions editor.

MEMBER AGENTS Christopher Vyce.

REPRESENTS Nonfiction, fiction. **Considers these fiction areas:** literary, graphic novels.

HOW TO CONTACT Query by e-mail. Include cover letter, brief synopsis, brief CV. Accepts simultaneous submissions. Responds to queries in 72 hours; to approved submissions in 6-8 weeks.

BARBARA BRAUN ASSOCIATES, INC.

7 E. 14th St., #19F, New York NY 10003. **Fax:** (212)604-9023. **E-mail:** bbasubmissions@gmail.com. **Website:** www.barbarabraunagency.com. **Contact:** Barbara Braun. Member of AAR, Authors Guild, PEN Center USA.

MEMBER AGENTS Barbara Braun.

REPRESENTS Nonfiction, fiction. **Considers these fiction areas:** commercial, historical, literary, multicultural, mystery, thriller, women's, young adult, art-related fiction.

"Our fiction is strong on stories for women, art-related fiction, historical and multicultural stories, and to a lesser extent mysteries and thrillers. We are interested in narrative nonfiction and current affairs books by journalists, as well as young adult literature. We do not represent poetry, science fiction, fantasy, horror, or screenplays."

HOW TO CONTACT "We no longer accept submissions by regular mail. Please send all queries via e-mail, marked 'Query' in the subject line. Your query should include a brief summary of your book, word count, genre, any relevant publishing experience, and the first 5 pages of your ms pasted into the body of the e-mail. (NO attachments—we will not open these.)" Accepts simultaneous submissions.

TERMS Agent receives 15% commission on domestic sales; 20% commission on foreign sales. No reading fees.

TIPS "Our clients' books are represented throughout Europe, Asia, and Latin America by various subagents. We are also active in selling motion picture rights to the books we represent, and work with various Hollywood agencies."

CURTIS BROWN, LTD.

10 Astor Place, New York NY 10003-6935. (212)473-5400. **Website:** www.curtisbrown.com. **Contact:** Ginger Knowlton. Member of AAR. Signatory of WGA.

MEMBER AGENTS **Noah Ballard** (literary debuts, upmarket thrillers, and narrative nonfiction; he is always on the lookout for honest and provocative new writers); **Ginger Clark** (science fiction, fantasy, paranormal romance, literary horror, young adult, middle-grade); **Kerry D'Agostino** (a wide range of literary and commercial fiction, as well as narrative nonfiction and memoir); **Katherine Fausset** (literary fiction, upmarket commercial fiction, journalism, memoir, popular science, and narrative nonfiction); **Holly Frederick; Peter Ginsberg**, president; **Elizabeth Harding**, vice president (juvenile, middle-grade, young adult); Steve Kasdin (commercial fiction, including mysteries/thrillers, romantic suspense—emphasis on the suspense—and historical fiction; narrative nonfiction, including biography, history, and current affairs; and young adult fiction, particularly if it has adult crossover appeal; NOT interested in science fiction, fantasy, memoirs, vampires, and writers trying to capitalize on trends); **Ginger Knowlton**, executive vice president (authors and illustrators of children's books in all genres); **Timothy Knowlton**, chief executive officer; **Jonathan Lyons** (biographies, history, science, pop culture, sports, general narrative nonfiction, mysteries, thrillers, science fiction and fantasy, young adult fiction); **Laura Blake Peterson**, vice president (memoir and biography, natural history, literary fiction, mystery, suspense, women's fiction, health and fitness, children's and young adult, faith issues, popular culture); **Maureen Walters**, senior vice president (women's fiction and nonfiction projects on subjects as eclectic as parenting and child care, popular psychology, inspirational/motivational volumes, and medical/nutritional books); **Mitchell Waters** (literary and commercial fiction and nonfiction, including mystery, history, biography, memoir, young adult, cookbooks, self-help, and popular culture).

REPRESENTS Nonfiction, fiction. **Considers these fiction areas:** fantasy, horror, humor, juvenile, literary, mainstream, middle-grade, mystery, paranormal, picture books, religious, romance, spiritual, sports, suspense, thriller, women's, young adult.

HOW TO CONTACT Please refer to the "Agents" page on the website for each agent's submission guidelines. Accepts simultaneous submissions. Responds in 3 weeks to queries; in 5 weeks to mss. Obtains most new clients through recommendations from others, solicitations, conferences.

TERMS Agent receives 15% commission on domestic sales; 20% on foreign sales. Offers written contract; 75-day notice must be given to terminate contract. Charges for some postage (overseas, etc.).

RECENT SALES This agency prefers not to share information on specific sales.

MARIE BROWN ASSOCIATES, INC.

412 W. 154th St., New York NY 10032-6302. (212)939-9725 for Marie Brown; (678)515-7907 for Janell Walden Agyeman. **Fax:** (212)939-9728. **E-mail:** info@janellwaldenagyeman.com. **Website:** www.janellwaldenagyeman.com. **Contact:** Marie Brown, Janell Walden Agyeman. Estab. 1984. Member of Author's Guild, Independent Book Publishers Association, SCBWI.

MEMBER AGENTS Marie Brown, Janell Walden Agyeman.

REPRESENTS Nonfiction, fiction, juvenile books. **Considers these fiction areas:** contemporary issues, ethnic, hi-lo, historical, juvenile, literary, mainstream, middle-grade, multicultural, new adult, paranormal, picture books, supernatural, urban fantasy, women's, young adult. "We welcome debut fiction for adults (literary and popular) and for young readers."

Does not want to receive genre fiction, true crime, high fantasy, or poetry.

HOW TO CONTACT **Marie Brown**: "Query first via snail mail. With fiction, you may include your first 20-25 pages; with nonfiction, include annotated table of contents." **Janell Walden Agyeman**: "E-submissions only. Queries should include a brief synopsis, no more than 150 words. For fiction submissions you may also attach to the e-mail a Word document containing the first 20-25 pages. For nonfiction attach the completed proposal." Responds within 12 weeks. Obtains most new clients through recommendations from others, conferences.

TERMS Agent receives 15% commission on domestic sales; 20% commission on foreign sales. Offers written contract.

RECENT SALES *The Man in 3B* by Carl Weber, *Pushout* by Monique Morris, *Born Bright* by C. Nicole Mason, *Degree Zombie Zone* by Patrik Henry Bass, *Harlem Renaissance Party* by Faith Ringgold, *Stella by Starlight* by Sharon M. Draper, *Grant Park* by Leonard H. Pitts, Jr., *Delta Jewels: In Search of My Grandmother's Wisdom* by Alysia Burton Steele, *My Sweet Vidalia* by Deborah Mantella, *Deadly Satisfactions* by Trice Hickman.

TIPS "Have your project professionally edited and/or critiqued before submitting; show us your very best work."

KIMBERLEY CAMERON & ASSOCIATES

1550 Tiburon Blvd., #704, Tiburon CA 94920. (415)789-9191. **Website:** www.kimberleycameron.com. **Contact:** Kimberley Cameron. Member of AAR. Signatory of WGA.

Kimberley Cameron & Associates (formerly The Reece Halsey Agency) has had an illustrious client list of established writers, including Aldous Huxley, Upton Sinclair, William Faulkner, and Henry Miller.

MEMBER AGENTS **Kimberley Cameron**; **Elizabeth Kracht**, liz@kimberleycameron.com (literary, commercial, women's, thrillers, mysteries, historical, young adult with crossover appeal, health, science, environment, prescriptive, investigative, true crime, memoir, sexuality, spirituality, animal/pet stories); **Pooja Menon**, pooja@kimberleycameron.com (currently closed to unsolicited submissions); **Amy Cloughley**, amyc@kimberleycameron.com (literary and upmarket fiction, women's, historical, narrative nonfiction, travel or adventure memoir); **Mary C. Moore** (currently closed to submissions); **Lisa Abellera**, lisa@kimberlycameron.com (currently closed to unsolicited submissions); **Douglas Lee**, douglas@kimberlycameron.com (looking for science fiction and fantasy mss that utilize the craft elements of literary fiction and the best parts of these imaginative genres; open to all subgenres of science fiction and fantasy; has a soft spot for cyberpunk, weird fiction in the flavor of China Mieville, steampunk, and noir-influenced voices; welcomes LGBTQ mss).

REPRESENTS **Considers these fiction areas:** commercial, fantasy, historical, literary, mystery, romance, science fiction, thriller, women's, young adult, LGBTQ.

"We are looking for a unique and heartfelt voice that conveys a universal truth."

HOW TO CONTACT Prefers e-mail queries. Only query 1 agent at a time. For fiction, fill out the correct submissions form for the individual agent and attach the first 50 pages and a synopsis (if requested) as a Word doc or PDF. For nonfiction, fill out the correct submission form of the individual agent and attach a full book proposal and sample chapters (includes the first chapter and no more than 50 pages) as a Word doc or PDF. Accepts simultaneous submissions. Obtains new clients through recommendations from others, solicitations.

CYNTHIA CANNELL LITERARY AGENCY

54 W. 40th Street, New York NY 10018. (212)396-9595. **Website:** www.cannellagency.com. **Contact:** Cynthia Cannell. Estab. 1997. Member of AAR. Women's Media Group, Authors Guild.

Prior to forming the Cynthia Cannell Literary Agency, Ms. Cannell was the vice president of Janklow & Nesbit Associates for 12 years.

REPRESENTS Nonfiction, fiction.

Does not represent screenplays, children's books, illustrated books, cookbooks, romance, category mystery, or science fiction.

HOW TO CONTACT "Please query us with an e-mail or letter. If querying by e-mail, send a brief description of your project with relevant biographical information, including publishing credits (if any), to info@cannellagency.com. Do not send attachments. If querying by conventional mail, enclose an SASE." Responds if interested. Accepts simultaneous submissions.

RECENT SALES Check the website for an updated list of authors and sales.

CAPITAL TALENT AGENCY

1330 Connecticut Ave. NW, Ste. 271, Washington DC 20036. (202)429-4785. **Fax:** (202)429-4786. **E-mail:** literary.submissions@capitaltalentagency.com. **Website:** capitaltalentagency.com/html/literary.shtml. **Contact:** Cynthia Kane. Estab. 2014. Member of AAR. Signatory of WGA.

Prior to joining CTA, Ms. Kane was involved in the publishing industry for more than 10 years. She has worked as a development editor for different publishing houses and individual authors and has seen more than 100 titles to market.

MEMBER AGENTS Cynthia Kane.

REPRESENTS Nonfiction, fiction, movie scripts, stage plays.

HOW TO CONTACT "We accept submissions only by e-mail. We do not accept queries via postal mail or fax. For fiction and nonfiction submissions, send a query letter in the body of your e-mail. Please note that while we consider each query seriously, we are unable to respond to all of them. We endeavor to respond within 6 weeks to projects that interest us." Accepts simultaneous submissions.

MARIA CARVAINIS AGENCY, INC.

Rockefeller Center, 1270 Avenue of the Americas, Ste. 2320, New York NY 10020. (212)245-6365. **Fax:** (212)245-7196. **E-mail:** mca@mariacarvainisagency.com. **Website:** mariacarvainisagency.com. Estab. 1977. Member of AAR. Signatory of WGA. Other memberships include Authors Guild, Women's Media Group, ABA, MWA, RWA. Represents 75 clients.

Prior to opening her agency, Ms. Carvainis spent more than 10 years in the publishing industry as a senior editor with Macmillan Publishing, Basic Books, Avon Books, and Crown Publishers. Ms. Carvainis has served as a member of the AAR Board of Directors and AAR Treasurer, as well as the chair of the AAR Contracts Committee. She presently serves on the AAR Royalty Committee.

MEMBER AGENTS **Maria Carvainis**, president/literary agent; **Elizabeth Copps**, associate agent.

REPRESENTS Fiction. **Considers these fiction areas:** action, adventure, commercial, contemporary issues, crime, historical, horror, humor, juvenile, literary, mainstream, middle-grade, multicultural, mystery, romance, suspense, thriller, women's, young adult.

The agency does not represent screenplays, children's picture books, science fiction, or poetry.

HOW TO CONTACT If you would like to query the agency, please send a query letter, a synopsis of the work, first 5-10 pages, and note of any writing credentials. Please e-mail queries to mca@mariacarvainisagency.com. All attachments must be either Word documents or PDF files. We also accept queries by mail: Maria Carvainis Agency, Inc., Attention: Query Department, 1270 Avenue of the Americas, Ste. 2320, New York, NY 10020. If you want the materials returned to you, please enclose an SASE. Otherwise, please be sure to include your e-mail address. We typically respond to queries within 1 month, if not earlier." No reading fee. Accepts simultaneous submissions. Obtains most new clients through recommendations from others, conferences, query letters.

TERMS Agent receives 15% commission on domestic sales; 20% commission on foreign sales. Offers written contract. Charges clients for foreign postage and bulk copying.

RECENT SALES *Only Beloved* by Mary Balogh (Signet), *Friction* by Sandra Brown (Grand Central), *Enraptured* by Candace Camp (Pocket Books), *The Infinite* by Nicholas Mainieri (Harper Perennial), *If You Only Knew* by Kristan Higgins (HQN Books), *Anatomy of Evil* by Will Thomas (Minotaur Books).

CASTIGLIA LITERARY AGENCY

P.O. Box 1094, Sumerland CA 93067. **E-mail:** castigliaagency-query@yahoo.com. Member of AAR. Other memberships include PEN. Represents 65 clients.

MEMBER AGENTS Julie Castiglia (not accepting queries at this time); Win Golden (fiction: thrillers, mystery, crime, science fiction, young adult, commercial/literary fiction; nonfiction: narrative nonfiction, current events, science, journalism).

REPRESENTS Fiction. **Considers these fiction areas:** commercial, crime, literary, mystery, science fiction, thriller, young adult.

"We'd particularly like to hear from you if you are a journalist or published writer in magazines." Does not want to receive horror, screenplays, poetry, or academic nonfiction.

HOW TO CONTACT Query via e-mail to castigliaagency-query@yahoo.com. For first contact, send no materials besides a one-page query. No snail mail submissions accepted. Accepts simultaneous submissions. Obtains most new clients through recommendations from others, solicitations, conferences.

TERMS Agent receives 15% commission on domestic sales; 25% commission on foreign sales. Offers written contract; six-week notice must be given to terminate contract.

WRITERS CONFERENCES Santa Barbara Writers Conference, Southern California Writers Conference, Surrey International Writers Conference, San Diego State University Writers Conference, Willamette Writers Conference.

TIPS "Be professional with submissions. Attend workshops and conferences before you approach an agent."

CHALBERG & SUSSMAN

115 W. 29th St, Third Floor, New York NY 10001. (917)261-7550. **Website:** www.chalbergsussman.com. Member of AAR. Signatory of WGA.

Prior to her current position, Ms. Chalberg held a variety of editorial positions and was an agent with The Susan Golomb Literary Agency. Ms. Sussman was an agent with Zachary Shuster Harmsworth. Ms. James was with The Aaron Priest Literary Agency.

MEMBER AGENTS **Terra Chalberg**; **Rachel Sussman** (narrative journalism, memoir, psychology, history, humor, pop culture, literary fiction); **Nicole James** (plot-driven fiction, psychological suspense, uplifting female-driven memoir, upmarket self-help, lifestyle books); **Lana Popovic** (young adult, middle-grade, contemporary realism, speculative fiction, fantasy, horror, sophisticated erotica, romance, select nonfiction, international stories).

REPRESENTS Nonfiction, fiction. **Considers these fiction areas:** erotica, fantasy, horror, literary, middle-grade, romance, science fiction, suspense, young adult, contemporary realism, speculative fiction.

HOW TO CONTACT To query by e-mail, please contact 1 agent: terra@chalbergsussman.com, rachel@chalbergsussman.com, nicole@chalbergsussman.com, lana@chalbergsussman.com. To query by regular mail, please address your letter to 1 agent and include an SASE. Accepts simultaneous submissions.

RECENT SALES The agents' sales and clients are listed on their website.

CHASE LITERARY AGENCY

242 W. 38th St., Second Floor, New York NY 10018. (212)477-5100. **E-mail:** farley@chaseliterary.com. **Website:** www.chaseliterary.com. **Contact:** Farley Chase.

MEMBER AGENTS Farley Chase.

REPRESENTS Nonfiction, fiction. **Considers these fiction areas:** commercial, historical, literary, mystery.

No romance, science fiction, or young adult.

HOW TO CONTACT E-query. If submitting fiction, please include the first few pages of the ms with the query. "I do not respond to queries not addressed to me by name." Accepts simultaneous submissions.

RECENT SALES *And Every Day Was Overcast* by Paul Kwiatowski (Black Balloon), *The Badlands Saloon* by Jonathan Twingley (Scribner).

ELYSE CHENEY LITERARY ASSOCIATES, LLC

78 Fifth Ave., Third Floor, New York NY 10011. (212)277-8007. **Fax:** (212)614-0728. **E-mail:** submissions@cheneyliterary.com. **Website:** www.cheneyliterary.com. **Contact:** Elyse Cheney, Adam Eaglin, Alex Jacobs.

Prior to her current position, Ms. Cheney was an agent with Sanford J. Greenburger Associates.

MEMBER AGENTS **Elyse Cheney**; **Adam Eaglin** (literary fiction and nonfiction, including history, politics, current events, narrative reportage, biography, memoir, and popular science); **Alexander Jacobs** (narrative nonfiction [particularly in the areas of history, science, politics, and culture], literary fiction, crime, memoir); **Sam Freilich** (literary fiction, crime, biography, narrative nonfiction, anything about Los Angeles).

REPRESENTS Nonfiction, fiction. **Considers these fiction areas:** commercial, crime, family saga, historical, literary, short story collections, suspense, women's.

HOW TO CONTACT Query by e-mail or snail mail. For a snail mail response, include an SASE. Include up to 3 chapters of sample material. Do not query more than 1 agent. Accepts simultaneous submissions.

RECENT SALES *The Love Affairs of Nathaniel P.* by Adelle Waldman (Henry Holt & Co.), *This Town* by Mark Leibovich (Blue Rider Press), *Thunder & Lightning* by Lauren Redniss (Random House).

WM CLARK ASSOCIATES

186 Fifth Ave., Second Floor, New York NY 10010. (212)675-2784. **E-mail:** general@wmclark.com. **Website:** www.wmclark.com. Estab. 1997. Member of AAR.

Prior to opening WCA, Mr. Clark was an agent at the William Morris Agency.

REPRESENTS Nonfiction, fiction. **Considers these fiction areas:** contemporary issues, ethnic, historical, literary, mainstream, young adult.

"It is advised that before querying you become familiar with the kinds of books we handle by browsing our Book List, which is available on our website."

HOW TO CONTACT Accepts queries via online form only. "We will endeavor to respond as soon as possible as to whether or not we'd like to see a proposal or sample chapters from your ms." Responds in 1-2 months to queries.

TERMS Agent receives 15% commission on domestic sales; 20% commission on foreign sales. Offers written contract.

TIPS "WCA works on a reciprocal basis with Ed Victor Ltd. (U.K.) in representing select properties to the U.S. market and vice versa. Translation rights are sold directly in the German, Italian, Spanish, Portuguese, Latin American, French, Dutch, and Scandinavian territories in association with Andrew Nurnberg Associates Ltd. (U.K.); through offices in China, Bulgaria, Czech Republic, Latvia, Poland, Hungary, and Russia; and through corresponding agents in Japan, Greece, Israel, Turkey, Korea, Taiwan, and Thailand."

RECENT SALES This agency represents many bestselling clients such as David Sedaris and Kathryn Stockett.

CONNOR LITERARY AGENCY

Website: www.connorliteraryagency.webs.com. **Contact:** Marlene Connor Lynch, Deborah Connor Coker.

Prior to opening her agency, Ms. Connor served at the Literary Guild of America, Simon & Schuster, and Random House. She is author of *Welcome to the Family: Memories of the Past for a Bright Future* (Broadway Books) and *What Is Cool: Understanding Black Manhood in America* (Crown).

MEMBER AGENTS **Marlene Connor Lynch**; **Deborah Coker** (young adult and mainstream fiction and nonfiction, suspense, historical fiction, humor, illustrated books, children's books).

REPRESENTS Nonfiction, fiction. **Considers these fiction areas:** historical, literary, mainstream, picture books, suspense, young adult.

HOW TO CONTACT Inquire via form on website. "Please include information about your writing experience and your general bio with your inquiry. Whenever submitting sample material, remember to add headers or footers that identify you and the name of your material." Accepts simultaneous submissions.

JILL CORCORAN LITERARY AGENCY

P.O. Box 4116, Palos Verdes Peninsula CA 90274. **E-mail:** query@jillcorcoranliteraryagency.com. **Website:** jillcorcoranliteraryagency.com; jillcorcoran.blogspot.com. **Contact:** Jill Corcoran. Estab. 2013. Member of AAR. Signatory of WGA.

REPRESENTS **Considers these fiction areas:** juvenile, middle-grade, picture books, romance, young adult.

HOW TO CONTACT Send queries and first 10 pages of your ms embedded into your e-mail, plus a link to your portfolio (illustrators), to query@jillcorcoranliteraryagency.com. Accepts simultaneous submissions.

RECENT SALES *Guy-Write: What Every Guy Writer Needs to Know* by Ralph Fletcher; *Kiss, Kiss Good Night* by Kenn Nesbitt; *The Plot Whisperer: Secrets of Story Structure Any Writer Can Master* by Martha Alderson; *Blind Spot* by Laura Ellen; *How I Lost You* by Janet Gurtler.

CORNERSTONE LITERARY, INC.

4525 Wilshire Blvd., Ste. 208, Los Angeles CA 90010. (323)930-6039. **Fax:** (323)930-0407. **E-mail:** info@cornerstoneliterary.com. **Website:** www.cornerstoneliterary.com. **Contact:** Helen Breitwieser. Member of AAR.

REPRESENTS Nonfiction, fiction, short story collections. **Considers these fiction areas:** commercial, literary.

"We do not consider business, how-to, photography books, poetry, screenplays, self-help or westerns."

HOW TO CONTACT "Submissions should consist of a one-page query letter detailing the book as well as the qualifications of the author. For fiction, submissions may also include the first 10 pages of the novel pasted in the e-mail or 1 short story from a collection. We receive hundreds of queries each month and make every effort to give each one careful consideration. We appreciate your patience in waiting 6-8 weeks for a response before contacting us with a gentle reminder. We cannot guarantee a response to queries submitted electronically due to the volume of queries received." Accepts simultaneous submissions.

CORVISIERO LITERARY AGENCY

275 Madison Ave., at 40th, 14th Floor, New York NY 10016. **E-mail:** query@corvisieroagency.com. **Website:** www.corvisieroagency.com. **Contact:** Marisa A. Corvisiero, senior agent and literary attorney. Member of AAR. Signatory of WGA.

MEMBER AGENTS **Marisa A. Corvisiero**, senior agent and literary attorney (contemporary romance, thrillers, adventure, paranormal, urban fantasy, science fiction, middle-grade, young adult, picture books, Christmas themes, time travel, space science fiction, self-help, science business); **Saritza Hernandez**, senior agent (all kinds of romance, LGBTQ, young adult, erotica); **Sarah Negovetich** (young adult); **Doreen McDonald** (do not query); **Cate Hart** (young adult, fantasy, magical realism, middle-grade, mystery, fantasy, adventure, historical romance, LGBTQ, erotic, history, biography); **Samantha Bremekamp** (children's, middle-grade, young adult, new adult; closed to blind queries); **Veronica Park** (dark or edgy young adult/new adult, commercial adult, adult romance and romantic suspense, and funny, current, and/or controversial nonfiction); **Vanessa Robins** (new adult, human, young adult, thrillers, romance, science fiction, sports-centric plots, memoirs, cultural, ethnic, sexuality, humor, medical narratives); **Kelly Peterson** (middle-grade: fantasy, paranormal, science fiction; young adult: steampunk, historical, dystopian, sword and sorcery; new adult: romance, historical romance; adult: fantasy, romance).

REPRESENTS Nonfiction, fiction. **Considers these fiction areas:** adventure, erotica, fantasy, gay, historical, lesbian, middle-grade, mystery, paranormal, picture books, romance, science fiction, suspense, thriller, urban fantasy, young adult, magical realism, steampunk, dystopian, sword and sorcery.

HOW TO CONTACT Accepts submissions via e-mail only. Include 5 pages of complete and polished ms pasted into the body of an e-mail, and a one- to two-page synopsis. For nonfiction, include a proposal instead of the synopsis. Put "Query for [Agent]" in the e-mail subject line. Accepts simultaneous submissions.

CREATIVE MEDIA AGENCY, INC.

1745 Broadway, 17th Floor, New York NY 10019. (212)812-1494. **E-mail:** paige@cmalit.com. **Website:** www.cmalit.com. **Contact:** Paige Wheeler. Member of AAR, WMG, RWA, MWA, Authors Guild. Represents over 30 clients.

After starting as an editor for Harlequin Books in New York and Euromoney Publications in London, Paige repped writers, producers, and celebrities as an agent with Artists Agency until she formed Creative Media Agency in 1997. In 2006 she co-created Folio Literary Management and successfully grew that company for 8 years into a successful mid-size agency. In 2014 she decided to once again pursue a boutique approach and relaunched CMA.

REPRESENTS Nonfiction, fiction. **Considers these fiction areas:** commercial, crime, detective, historical, inspirational, mainstream, middle-grade, mystery, new adult, police, romance, suspense, thriller, women's, young adult.

Fiction: All commercial and upscale (think book club) fiction, as well as women's fiction, romance (all types), mystery, thrillers, inspirational/Christian and psychological suspense. "I enjoy both historical fiction as well as contemporary fiction, so do keep that in mind. I seem to be especially drawn to a story if it has a high concept and a fresh, unique voice." Does not want to receive children's books, science fiction, fantasy, or academic nonfiction.

HOW TO CONTACT E-query. Write "query" in your e-mail subject line. For fiction, paste the first 5 pages of the ms after the query. For nonfiction, paste in an extended author bio as well as the marketing section of your book proposal after the query. Accepts simultaneous submissions.

D4EO LITERARY AGENCY

7 Indian Valley Rd., Weston CT 06883. (203)544-7180. **Fax:** (203)544-7160. **Website:** www.d4eoliteraryagency.com. **Contact:** Bob Diforio. Estab. 1990.

Prior to opening his agency, Mr. Diforio was a publisher.

MEMBER AGENTS **Bob Diforio** (prefers to see recommendations from clients and writers with previously published works); **Joyce Holland**; **Pam Howell** (genre fiction, middle-grade, young adult, new adult).

REPRESENTS Nonfiction, fiction. **Considers these fiction areas:** adventure, detective, erotica, juvenile, literary, mainstream, middle-grade, mystery, new adult, romance, sports, thriller, young adult.

HOW TO CONTACT Each agent has a different submission e-mail and different tastes regarding how he or she reviews material. See the individual agent pages on the website. Responds in 1 week to queries if interested. Obtains most new clients through recommendations from others.

TERMS Offers written contract, binding for 2 years; automatic renewal unless 60 days notice given prior to renewal date. Charges for photocopying and submission postage.

LAURA DAIL LITERARY AGENCY, INC.

350 Seventh Ave., Ste. 2003, New York NY 10001. (212)239-7477. **E-mail:** ldail@ldlainc.com. **E-mail:** queries@ldlainc.com. **Website:** www.ldlainc.com. Member of AAR.

MEMBER AGENTS Laura Dail, Tamar Rydzinski.

REPRESENTS Nonfiction, fiction, juvenile books. **Considers these fiction areas:** commercial, crime, detective, fantasy, feminist, historical, juvenile, mainstream, middle-grade, multicultural, mystery, thriller, women's, young adult.

Specializes in women's fiction, literary fiction, young adult fiction, as well as both practical and idea-driven nonfiction. Tamar is not interested in prescriptive or practical nonfiction, humor, coffee table books, or children's books (meaning anything younger than middle-grade). She is interested in everything else that is well-written and has great characters, including graphic novels. Due to the volume of queries and mss received, we apologize for not answering every e-mail and letter." Does not want children's picture books or chapter books, New Age, screenplays, or poetry."

HOW TO CONTACT "If you would like, you may include a synopsis and no more than 10 pages. If you are mailing your query, please be sure to include an SASE; without it, you may not hear back from us. To save money, time, and trees, we prefer queries by e-mail to queries@ldlainc.com. We get a lot of spam and are wary of computer viruses, so please use the word 'Query' in the subject line and include your detailed materials in the body of your message, not as an attachment." Accepts simultaneous submissions.

DARHANSOFF & VERRILL LITERARY AGENTS

133 W. 72nd St., Room 304, New York NY 10023. (917)305-1300. **E-mail:** submissions@dvagency.com. **Website:** www.dvagency.com. Member of AAR.

MEMBER AGENTS Liz Darhansoff, Chuck Verrill, Michele Mortimer, Eric Amling.

REPRESENTS Nonfiction, fictions. **Considers these fiction areas:** literary, middle-grade, suspense, young adult.

HOW TO CONTACT Send queries via e-mail. Accepts simultaneous submissions.

RECENT SALES A full list of clients is available on their website.

LIZA DAWSON ASSOCIATES

350 Seventh Ave., Ste. 2003, New York NY 10001. (212)465-9071. **Website:** www.lizadawsonassociates.com. **Contact:** Caitie Flum. Member of AAR. Other memberships include MWA, Women's Media Group. Represents 50+ clients.

Prior to becoming an agent, Ms. Dawson was an editor for 20 years, spending 11 years at William Morrow as vice president and 2 years at Putnam as executive editor. Ms. Blasdell was a senior editor at HarperCollins and Avon.

MEMBER AGENTS **Liza Dawson**, queryliza@lizadawsonassociates.com (plot-driven literary and popular fiction, historicals, thrillers, suspense, history, psychology [both popular and clinical], politics, narrative nonfiction, memoirs); **Caitlin Blasdell**, querycaitlin@lizadawsonassociates.com (science fiction, fantasy [both adult and young adult], parenting, business, thrillers, women's fiction; **Hannah Bowman**, queryhannah@lizadawsonassociates.com (commercial fiction, especially science fiction and fantasy, young adult; nonfiction in the areas of mathematics, science, and spirituality); **Jennifer Johnson-Blalock**, queryjennifer@lizadawsonassociates.com (nonfiction, particularly current events, social sciences, women's issues, law, business, history, the arts and pop culture, lifestyle, sports, and food; and commercial and upmarket fiction, especially thrillers/mysteries, women's fiction, contemporary romance, young adult, and middle-grade); **Caitie Flum**, querycaitie@lizadawsonassociates.com (commercial fiction, especially historical, women's fiction, mysteries, young adult, and middle-grade; middle-grade, young adult, and crossover fantasy; nonfiction in the areas of theater, memoir, current affairs, and pop culture).

REPRESENTS **Considers these fiction areas:** action, adventure, commercial, contemporary issues, crime, detective, ethnic, family saga, fantasy, feminist, gay, historical, horror, humor, juvenile, lesbian, mainstream, middle-grade, multicultural, mystery, new adult, police, romance, science fiction, supernatural, suspense, thriller, urban fantasy, women's, young adult.

This agency specializes in readable literary fiction, thrillers, mainstream historicals, women's fiction, young adult, middle-grade, academics, historians, journalists, and psychology.

HOW TO CONTACT Query by e-mail only. No phone calls. Each agent has her own specific submission requirements, which you can find on the website. Accepts simultaneous submissions. Responds in 6 weeks to queries; in 8 weeks to mss. Obtains most new clients through recommendations from others, conferences, queries.

TERMS Agent receives 15% commission on domestic sales; 20% commission on foreign sales. Offers written contract.

THE JENNIFER DECHIARA LITERARY AGENCY

31 E. 32nd St., Ste. 300, New York NY 10016. (212)481-8484. **Fax:** (212)481-9582. **Website:** www.jdlit.com. **Contact:** Jennifer DeChiara. Estab. 2001.

MEMBER AGENTS **Jennifer DeChiara**, jenndec@aol.com (literary, commercial, women's fiction [no bodice rippers, please], chick-lit, mysteries, suspense, thrillers, funny/quirky picture books, middle-grade and young adult; for nonfiction: celebrity memoirs and biographies, LGBTQ, memoirs, books about the arts and performing arts, behind-the-scenes-type books, and books about popular culture); **Stephen Fraser**, fraserstephena@gmail.com (one-of-a-kind picture books; strong chapter book series; whimsical, dramatic, or humorous middle-grade; dramatic or high-concept young adult; powerful and unusual nonfiction; nonfiction with a broad audience on topics as far reaching as art history, theater, film, literature, and travel); **Marie Lamba**, marie.jdlit@gmail.com (young adult and middle-grade fiction, along with general and women's fiction and some memoir; interested in established illustrators and picture book authors); **Roseanne Wells**, queryroseanne@gmail.com (literary fiction, young adult, middle-grade, narrative nonfiction, select memoir, science [popular or trade, not academic], history, religion [not inspirational], travel, humor, food/cooking, and similar subjects); **Victoria Selvaggio**, vselvaggio@windstream.net (lyrical picture books, middle-grade and young adult fiction, mysteries, suspense, thrillers, paranormal, fantasy, narrative nonfiction).

REPRESENTS Nonfiction, fiction, juvenile books. **Considers these fiction areas:** commercial, contemporary issues, crime, ethnic, family saga, fantasy, feminist, gay, historical, horror, humor, inspirational, juvenile, lesbian, literary, mainstream, middle-grade, multicultural, mystery, new adult, New Age, paranormal, picture books, suspense, thriller, urban fantasy, women's, young adult.

HOW TO CONTACT Each agent has a specific e-mail submission address and submission instructions; check the website for the current updates, as policies do change. Accepts simultaneous submissions. Obtains most new clients through recommendations from others, conferences, query letters.

TERMS Agent receives 15% commission on domestic sales; 20% commission on foreign sales. Offers written contract.

DEFIORE & CO. LITERARY MANAGEMENT, INC.

47 E. 19th St., 3rd Floor, New York NY 10003. (212)925-7744. **Fax:** (212)925-9803. **E-mail:** info@defliterary.com; submissions@defliterary.com. **Website:** www.defliterary.com. Member of AAR. Signatory of WGA.

Prior to becoming an agent, Mr. DeFiore was publisher of Villard Books (1997-1998), editor-in-chief of Hyperion (1992-1997), editorial director of Delacorte Press (1988-1992), and an editor at St. Martin's Press (1984-88).

MEMBER AGENTS **Brian DeFiore** (popular nonfiction, business, pop culture, parenting, commercial fiction); **Laurie Abkemeier** (memoir, parenting, business, how-to/self-help, popular science); **Matthew Elblonk** (young adult, popular culture, narrative nonfiction); **Caryn Karmatz-Rudy** (popular fiction, self-help, narrative nonfiction); **Adam Schear** (commercial fiction, humor, young adult, smart thrillers, historical fiction, quirky debut literary novels, popular science, politics, popular culture, current events); **Meredith Kaffel Simonoff** (smart upmarket women's fiction, literary fiction [especially debut], literary thrillers, narrative nonfiction, nonfiction about science and tech, sophisticated pop culture/humor books); **Rebecca Strauss** (literary and commercial fiction, women's fiction, urban fantasy, romance, mystery, young adult, memoir, pop culture, select nonfiction); **Lisa Gallagher** (fiction and nonfiction); **Nicole Tourtelot** (narrative and prescriptive nonfiction, food, lifestyle, wellness, pop culture, history, humor, memoir, select young adult and adult fiction); **Ashely Collum** (women's fiction, kids and teens, psychological thrillers, memoir, politics, photography, cooking, narrative nonfiction, LGBTQ+ issues, feminism, the occult); **Colin Farstad** (literary fiction, upmarket fiction, young adult, narrative nonfiction, graphic novels, science fiction and fantasy); **Miriam Altshuler** (adult literary and commercial fiction, narrative nonfiction, middle-grade, young adult, memoir, narrative nonfiction, self-help, family sagas, historical novels); **Reiko Davis** (adult literary and upmarket fiction, narrative nonfiction, young adult, middle-grade, memoir).

REPRESENTS Nonfiction, fiction, short story collections. **Considers these fiction areas:** commercial, ethnic, literary, mainstream, middle-grade, mystery, paranormal, picture books, romance, short story collections, suspense, thriller, urban fantasy, women's, young adult.

"Please be advised that we are not considering poetry, adult science fiction and fantasy, or dramatic projects at this time."

HOW TO CONTACT Query with SASE or e-mail to submissions@defliterary.com. "Please include the word 'Query' in the subject line. All attachments will be deleted; please insert all text in the body of the e-mail. For more information about our agents, their individual interests, and their query guidelines, please visit our 'About Us' page on our website." Accepts simultaneous submissions. Obtains most new clients through recommendations from others.

TERMS Agent receives 15% commission on domestic sales; 20% commission on foreign sales. Offers written contract; 10-day notice must be given to terminate contract. Charges clients for photocopying and overnight delivery (deducted only after a sale is made).

DEFIORE AND COMPANY

47 E. 19th Street, Third Floor, New York NY 10003. (212)925-7744. **E-mail:** miriam@defliterary.com. **E-mail:** querymiriam@defliterary.com. **Website:** www.defliterary.com. **Contact:** Miriam Altshuler. Member of AAR. Represents 40 clients.

Ms. Altshuler has been an agent since 1982.

MEMBER AGENTS **Miriam Altshuler** (literary and commercial fiction, nonfiction, children's books); **Reiko Davis** (literary fiction, well-told commercial fiction, narrative nonfiction, young adult).

REPRESENTS Nonfiction, fiction, short story collections. **Considers these fiction areas:** commercial, family saga, historical, literary, middle-grade, short story collections, women's, young adult.

Seeking adult literary and commercial fiction and general nonfiction, young adult, and middle-grade fiction. Does not want adult mystery, romance, horror, science fiction or fantasy, poetry, screenplays, westerns.

HOW TO CONTACT Please send an e-mail to querymiriam@defliterary.com. Miriam only accepts e-mail queries. Include the following: A brief description of your book; a brief, relevant bio; the first chapter pasted in the body of your e-mail. Attachments will not be opened. "I also really want to know what you feel the heart of your book is, in 1-2 sentences." Accepts simultaneous submissions. Obtains most new clients through recommendations from others.

TERMS Agent receives 15% commission on domestic sales; 20% commission on foreign sales. Charges clients for overseas mailing, photocopies, overnight mail when requested by author.

WRITERS CONFERENCES Bread Loaf Writers Conference, Muse and the Marketplace, Squaw Valley, SCBWI.

JOELLE DELBOURGO ASSOCIATES, INC.

101 Park St., Montclair NJ 07042 USA. (973)773-0836. **Fax:** (973)783-6802. **E-mail:** joelle@delbourgo.com. **E-mail:** submissions@delbourgo.com. **Website:** www.delbourgo.com. Member of AAR. Represents more than 500 clients.

Prior to becoming an agent, Ms. Delbourgo was an editor and senior publishing executive at HarperCollins and Random House. She began her editorial career at Bantam Books, where she discovered the Choose Your Own

Adventure series. Jacqueline Flynn was executive editor at Amacom for more than 15 years.

MEMBER AGENTS Joelle Delbourgo, Jacqueline Flynn.

REPRESENTS Fiction. **Considers these fiction areas:** adventure, commercial, contemporary issues, crime, detective, fantasy, feminist, juvenile, literary, mainstream, middle-grade, military, mystery, new adult, New Age, romance, science fiction, thriller, urban fantasy, women's, young adult.

"We are former publishers and editors with deep knowledge and an insider perspective. We have a reputation for individualized attention to clients, strategic management of authors' careers, and creating strong partnerships with publishers for our clients."

HOW TO CONTACT It's preferable if you submit via e-mail to a specific agent. Query 1 agent only. No attachments. Put the word "Query" in the subject line. "While we do our best to respond to each query, if you have not received a response in 60 days, you may consider that a pass. Please do not send us copies of self-published books unless requested. Let us know if you are sending your query to us exclusively or if this is a multiple submission. For nonfiction, let us know if a proposal and sample chapters are available. If not, you should probably wait to send your query when you have a completed proposal. For fiction and memoir, embed the *first* 10 pages of ms into the e-mail ,after your query letter. Please no attachments. If we like your first pages, we may ask to see your synopsis and more ms. Please do not call us or make a follow-up call unless we call you." Accepts simultaneous submissions.

TERMS Agent receives 15% commission on domestic sales; 20% commission on foreign sales. Offers written contract. Charges clients for postage and photocopying.

RECENT SALES *Searching for Sappho* by Philip Freeman (Norton), *UnSelfie: The Habits of Empathy* by Dr. Michele Borba (Touchstone/Simon & Schuster), *Underground Airlines* by Ben H. Winters (Mulholland/Little Brown).

TIPS "Do your homework. Read and follow submission guidelines before contacting us. Do not call to find out if we received your material. No e-mail queries. Treat agents with respect, as you would any other professional, such as a doctor, lawyer, or financial advisor."

SANDRA DIJKSTRA LITERARY AGENCY

1155 Camino del Mar, PMB 515, Del Mar CA 92014 USA. **E-mail:** elise@dijkstraagency.com. **E-mail:** queries@dijkstraagency.com. **Website:** www.dijkstraagency.com. Member of AAR, Authors Guild, Organization of American Historians, RWA. Represents 100+ clients.

MEMBER AGENTS **Sandra Dijkstra** president (adult only). Acquiring associate agents: **Elise Capron** (adult only); **Jill Marr** (adult only); **Thao Le** (adult and young adult); **Roz Foster** (adult and young adult); **Jessica Watterson** (subgenres of adult and new adult romance, and women's fiction).

REPRESENTS Nonfiction, fiction, short story collections, juvenile books, scholarly books. **Considers these fiction areas:** commercial, horror, literary, middle-grade, new adult, romance, science fiction, suspense, thriller, women's, young adult.

HOW TO CONTACT "Please see guidelines on our website. Please note that we only accept e-mail submissions. Due to the large number of unsolicited submissions we receive, we are only able to respond those submissions in which we are interested." Accepts simultaneous submissions. Responds to queries of interest within 6 weeks.

TERMS Works in conjunction with foreign and film agents. Agent receives 15% commission on domestic sales and 20% commission on foreign sales. Offers written contract. No reading fee.

TIPS "Remember that publishing is a business. Do your research and present your project in as professional a way as possible. Only submit your work when you are confident that it is polished and ready for prime-time. Make yourself a part of the active writing community by getting stories and articles published, networking with other writers, and getting a good sense of where your work fits in the market."

⊙ DONADIO & OLSON, INC.

40 W. 27th St., Fifth Floor, New York NY 10001. (212)691-8077. **Fax:** (212)633-2837. **E-mail:** neil@donadio.com. **E-mail:** mail@donadio.com. **Website:** donadio.com. **Contact:** Neil Olson. Member of AAR.

MEMBER AGENTS **Neil Olson** (no queries); **Edward Hibbert** (no queries); **Carrie Howland** , carrie@donadio.com (adult literary fiction and narrative nonfiction as well as young adult, middle-grade, and picture books.

REPRESENTS Nonfiction, fiction. **Considers these fiction areas:** literary, middle-grade, picture books, young adult.

This agency represents mostly fiction and is very selective.

HOW TO CONTACT "Please send a query letter and the first 3 chapters or first 25 pages of the ms to mail@donadio.com. Please allow a minimum of 1 month for a reply. Accepts simultaneous submissions.

DONAGHY LITERARY GROUP

6-14845 Yonge Street, Ste. # 123, Aurora, ON, L4G 6H8, Canada, (647)527-4353. **E-mail:** stacey@donaghyliterary.com. **E-mail:** query@donaghyliterary.com. **Website:** www.donaghyliterary.com. **Contact:** Stacey Donaghy.

Prior to opening her agency, Ms. Donaghy served as an agent at the Corvisiero Literary Agency. Before this, she acquired and edited academic materials for publication and training. Ms. Noble interned for Jessica Sinsheimer of Sarah Jane Freymann Literary Agency. Ms. Miller previously worked in children's publishing with Scholastic Canada and also interned with Bree Ogden during her time at the D4EO Agency.

MEMBER AGENTS **Stacey Donaghy** (romantic suspense, LGBTQ, thriller, mystery, contemporary romance, erotic romance, young adult, quirky middle-grade); **Valerie Noble** (historical, science fiction and fantasy [think Kristin Cashore and Suzanne Collins] for young adults and adults); **Sue Miller** (young adult, urban fantasy, contemporary romance).

REPRESENTS **Considers these fiction areas:** commercial, erotica, ethnic, fantasy, gay, juvenile, lesbian, mainstream, multicultural, mystery, new adult, police, psychic, romance, science fiction, sports, suspense, thriller, urban fantasy, young adult.

HOW TO CONTACT Query via e-mail; no attachments. Visit agency website for submission guidelines and agent bios. Do not e-mail agents directly. Accepts simultaneous submissions. Responds in 6-8 weeks to queries; in 8-12 weeks to mss. Time may vary during holidays and closures.

TERMS Agent receives 15% commission on domestic sales; 20% commission on foreign sales. Offers written contract, 30-day notice must be given to terminate contract.

WRITERS CONFERENCES Romantic Times Booklovers Convention, Windsor International Writers Conference, OWC Ontario Writers Conference.

TIPS "Only submit to 1 DLG agent at a time. We work collaboratively and often share projects that may be better suited to another agent at the agency."

JIM DONOVAN LITERARY

5635 SMU Blvd., Ste. 201, Dallas TX 75206. **E-mail:** jdliterary@sbcglobal.net. **Contact:** Melissa Shultz, agent. Estab. 1993.

MEMBER AGENTS **Jim Donovan** (history [particularly American, military, and Western]; biography; sports; popular reference; popular culture; literary fiction; thrillers; mystery); **Melissa Shultz** (all subjects listed above, along with parenting and women's issues).

REPRESENTS Nonfiction, fiction. **Considers these fiction areas:** action, adventure, commercial, crime, detective, frontier, historical, mainstream, multicultural, mystery, police, suspense, thriller, war, westerns.

This agency specializes in commercial fiction and nonfiction. "Does not want to receive poetry, children's, science fiction, fantasy, short stories, memoir, inspirational, or anything else not listed above."

HOW TO CONTACT "For nonfiction, I need a well thought-out query letter telling me about the book: what it does, how it does it, why it's needed now, why it's better or different than what's out there on the subject, and why the author is the perfect writer for it. For fiction, the novel has to be finished, of course. A short, two- to five-page synopsis—not a teaser, but a summary of all the action, from first page to last—and the first 30-50 pages is enough. This material should be polished to as close to perfection as possible." Accepts simultaneous submissions. Responds in 2 weeks to queries; in 1 month to mss. Obtains most new clients through recommendations from others.

TERMS Agent receives 15% commission on domestic sales; 20% commission on foreign sales. Offers written contract, binding for 1 year; 30-day notice must be given to terminate contract. Charges for overnight delivery and ms copying. Charges are discussed beforehand.

RECENT SALES *Manson* by Jeff Guinn (S&S), *The Last Outlaws* by Thom Hatch (NAL), *Rough Riders* by Mark Lee Gardner (Morrow), *James Monroe* by Tim McGrath (NAL), *What Lurks Beneath* by Ryan

Lockwood (Kensington), *Battle for Hell's Island* by Stephen Moore (NAL), *Powerless* by Tim Washburn (Kensington).

TIPS "Get published in short form (magazine reviews, journals, etc.) first. This will increase your credibility considerably and make it much easier to sell a full-length book."

DUNHAM LITERARY, INC.

110 William St., Ste. 2202, New York NY 10038. (212)929-0994. **E-mail:** query@dunhamlit.com. **Website:** www.dunhamlit.com. **Contact:** Jennie Dunham. Estab. 2000. Member of AAR. SCBWI Represents 50 clients.

Prior to opening her agency, Ms. Dunham worked as a literary agent for Russell & Volkening. The Rhoda Weyr Agency is now a division of Dunham Literary, Inc.

MEMBER AGENTS Jennie Dunham, Bridget Smith.

REPRESENTS Nonfiction, fiction, juvenile books. **Considers these fiction areas:** fantasy, historical, humor, juvenile, literary, mainstream, middle-grade, multicultural, mystery, picture books, science fiction, women's, young adult.

HOW TO CONTACT E-mail queries preferred, with all materials pasted in the body of the e-mail. Attachments will not be opened. Paper queries are also accepted. Please include an SASE for response and return of materials. If submitting to Bridget Smith, please include the first 5 pages with the query. Accepts simultaneous submissions. Responds in 4 weeks to queries; in 2 months to mss. Obtains most new clients through recommendations from others, solicitations.

TERMS Agent receives 15% commission on domestic sales; 20% commission on foreign sales.

RECENT SALES The Bad Kitty Series by Nick Bruel (Macmillan), *The White House* by Robert Sabuda (Simon & Schuster), *The Gollywhopper Games* and sequels by Jody Feldman (HarperCollins), *First & Then* by Emma Mills (Macmillan), *Learning Not to Drown* by Anna Shinoda (Simon & Schuster), *Gangsterland* by Tod Goldberg (Counterpoint), *A Shadow All of Light* by Fred Chappell (Tor), *Forward From Here* by Reeve Lindbergh (Simon & Schuster).

DUNOW, CARLSON, & LERNER AGENCY

27 W. 20th St., Ste. 1107, New York NY 10011. (212)645-7606. **E-mail:** mail@dclagency.com. **E-mail:** mail@dclagency.com. **Website:** www.dclagency.com. Member of AAR.

MEMBER AGENTS **Jennifer Carlson** (narrative nonfiction covering current events and ideas and cultural history, as well as literary and upmarket commercial fiction); **Henry Dunow** (quality fiction—literary, historical, strongly written commercial—and voice-driven nonfiction across a range of areas—narrative history, biography, memoir, current affairs, cultural trends and criticism, science, sports); **Erin Hosier** (popular culture, music, sociology and memoir); **Betsy Lerner** (nonfiction: psychology, history, cultural studies, biography, current events, business; fiction: literary, dark, funny, voice driven); **Yishai Seidman** (broad range of fiction: literary, postmodern, thrillers; nonfiction: sports, music, pop culture); **Amy Hughes** (nonfiction: history, cultural studies, memoir, current events, wellness, health, food, pop culture, biography; literary fiction); **Eleanor Jackson** (literary, commercial, memoir, art, food, science, history); **Julia Kenny** (fiction: adult, middle-grade, and young adult; especially interested in dark, literary thrillers, and suspense); **Edward Necarsulmer IV** (strong new voices in teen and middle-grade as well as picture books); **Stacia Decker**; **Arielle Datz** (fiction: adult, young adult, middle-grade, both literary and commercial; nonfiction: essays, unconventional memoir, pop culture, sociology).

REPRESENTS Nonfiction, fiction, short story collections. **Considers these fiction areas:** commercial, literary, mainstream, middle-grade, mystery, picture books, thriller, young adult.

HOW TO CONTACT Query via snail mail with SASE, or by e-mail. E-mail preferred; paste 10 sample pages below query letter. No attachments. Will respond in 4-6 weeks only if interested. Accepts simultaneous submissions.

RECENT SALES A full list of agency clients is on the website.

DYSTEL & GODERICH LITERARY MANAGEMENT

1 Union Square W., Ste. 904, New York NY 10003. (212)627-9100. **Fax:** (212)627-9313. **Website:** www.dystel.com. Estab. 1994. Member of AAR, SCBWI. Represents 600+ clients.

MEMBER AGENTS **Jane Dystel**; **Miriam Goderich**, miriam@dystel.com (literary and commercial fiction as well as some genre fiction, narrative nonfiction, pop culture, psychology, history, science, art, business books, and biography/memoir); **Stacey Kendall**

Glick, sglick@dystel.com (adult narrative nonfiction, memoir, parenting, cooking and food, psychology, science, health and wellness, lifestyle, current events, pop culture, young adult, middle-grade, children's nonfiction, select adult contemporary fiction); **Michael Bourret**, mbourret@dystel.com (middle-grade and young adult fiction, commercial adult fiction, and all sorts of nonfiction, from practical to narrative; especially interested in food- and cocktail-related books, memoir, popular history, politics, religion [though not spirituality], popular science, and current events); **Jim McCarthy**, jmccarthy@dystel.com (literary women's fiction, underrepresented voices, mysteries, romance, paranormal fiction, narrative nonfiction, memoir, and paranormal nonfiction); **Jessica Papin**, jpapin@dystel.com (plot-driven literary and smart commercial fiction, and narrative nonfiction across a range of subjects, including history, medicine, science, economics and women's issues); **Lauren E. Abramo**, labramo@dystel.com (humorous middle-grade and contemporary young adult on the children's side, and upmarket commercial fiction and well-paced literary fiction on the adult side; also interested in adult narrative nonfiction, especially pop culture, psychology, pop science, reportage, media, and contemporary culture; in nonfiction she has a strong preference for interdisciplinary approaches, and in all categories she's especially interested in underrepresented voices); **John Rudolph**, jrudolph@dystel.com (picture book author/illustrators, middle-grade, young adult, select commercial fiction, and narrative nonfiction [especially music, sports, history, popular science, "big think," performing arts, health, business, memoir, military history, and humor]); **Sharon Pelletier**, spelletier@dystel.com (smart commercial fiction, from upmarket women's fiction to domestic suspense to literary thrillers; strong contemporary romance novels; compelling nonfiction projects, especially feminism and religion); **Michael Hoogland**, mhoogland@dystel.com (thriller, science fiction/fantasy, young adult, upmarket women's fiction, narrative nonfiction); **Erin Young**, eyoung@dystel.com (young adult, middle-grade, literary and intellectual commercial thrillers, memoirs, biographies, sports and science narratives); **Amy Bishop**, abishop@dystel.com (commercial and literary women's fiction, fiction from diverse authors, historical fiction, young adult, personal narratives, and biographies); **Kemi Faderin**, kfaderin@dystel.com (smart, plot-driven young adult, historical fiction and nonfiction, contemporary women's fiction, literary fiction); **Eric Myers**, emyers@dystel.com (young adult and middle-grade fiction, adult nonfiction [especially history, biography, psychology, health and wellness, mind/body/spirit, pop culture, thriller, and memoir]).

REPRESENTS **Considers these fiction areas:** commercial, ethnic, gay, lesbian, literary, mainstream, middle-grade, mystery, paranormal, romance, suspense, thriller, women's, young adult.

⊶ "We are actively seeking fiction for all ages, in all genres." No plays, screenplays, or poetry.

HOW TO CONTACT Query via e-mail and put "Query" in the subject line. "Synopses, outlines, or sample chapters (1 chapter or the first 25 pages of your ms) should either be included below the cover letter or attached as a separate document. We won't open attachments if they come with a blank e-mail." Accepts simultaneous submissions. Responds in 6-8 weeks to queries; in 8 weeks to mss. Obtains most new clients through recommendations from others, solicitations, conferences.

TERMS Agent receives 15% commission on domestic sales; 19% commission on foreign sales. Offers written contract.

WRITERS CONFERENCES Backspace Writers Conference, Pacific Northwest Writers' Association, Pike's Peak Writers Conference, Writers League of Texas, Love Is Murder, Surrey International Writers Conference, Society of Children's Book Writers and Illustrators, International Thriller Writers, Willamette Writers Conference, The South Carolina Writers Workshop Conference, Las Vegas Writers Conference, Writer's Digest, Seton Hill Popular Fiction, Romance Writers of America, Geneva Writers Conference.

TIPS "DGLM prides itself on being a full-service agency. We're involved in every stage of the publishing process, from offering substantial editing on mss and proposals to coming up with book ideas for authors looking for their next project, negotiating contracts, and collecting monies for our clients. We follow a book from its inception through its sale to a publisher, its publication, and beyond. Our commitment to our writers does not, by any means, end when we have collected our commission. This is one of the many things that makes us unique in a very competitive business."

EDEN STREET LITERARY

P.O. Box 30, Billings NY 12510. **E-mail:** info@edenstreetlit.com. **E-mail:** submissions@edenstreetlit.com. **Website:** www.edenstreetlit.com. **Contact:** Liza Voges. Member of AAR. Signatory of WGA. Represents over 40 clients.

REPRESENTS Nonfiction, fiction, juvenile books. **Considers these fiction areas:** juvenile, middle-grade, picture books, young adult.

HOW TO CONTACT Check the website before submitting, as the agency will close itself off to submissions sometimes. When open, contact submissions@edenstreetlit.com. Accepts simultaneous submissions. Responds only to submissions of interest.

RECENT SALES *Dream Dog* by Lou Berger, *Biscuit Loves the Library* by Alyssa Capucilli, *The Scraps Book* by Lois Ehlert, *Two Bunny Buddies* by Kathryn O. Galbraith, *Between Two Worlds* by Katherine Kirkpatrick.

JUDITH EHRLICH LITERARY MANAGEMENT, LLC

146 Central Park W., 20E, New York NY 10023. (646)505-1570. **Fax:** (646)505-1570. **E-mail:** jehrlich@judithehrlichliterary.com. **Website:** www.judithehrlichliterary.com. Estab. 2002. Member of the Author's Guild and the American Society of Journalists and Authors.

Prior to her current position, Ms. Ehrlich was a senior associate at the Linda Chester Agency and is an award-winning journalist; she is the co-author of *The New Crowd: The Changing of the Jewish Guard on Wall Street* (Little, Brown).

MEMBER AGENTS **Judith Ehrlich** jehrlich@judithehrlichliterary.com (fiction: upmarket, literary, and quality commercial; nonfiction: narrative, women's, business, prescriptive, medical and health-related topics, history, current events); **Sophia Seidner** sseidner@judithehrlichliterary.com (upmarket fiction and nonfiction, including prescriptive, narrative nonfiction, memoir, and biography; areas of special interest include medical and health-related topics, science [popular, political, and social], animal welfare, current events, politics, law, history, ethics, parody and humor, sports, and business self-help).

REPRESENTS Nonfiction, fiction, short story collections, juvenile books. **Considers these fiction areas:** adventure, commercial, contemporary issues, crime, detective, family saga, historical, humor, juvenile, literary, middle-grade, mystery, picture books, short story collections, suspense, thriller, women's, young adult.

Does not want to receive novellas, poetry, textbooks, plays, or screenplays.

HOW TO CONTACT E-query, with a synopsis and some sample pages. The agency responds only if interested. Accepts simultaneous submissions.

RECENT SALES Fiction: *The Bicycle Spy* by Yona Zeldis McDonough (Scholastic), *The House on Primrose Pond* by Yona McDonough (NAL/Penguin), *You Were Meant for Me* by Yona McDonough (NAL/Penguin), *Echoes of Us: The Hybrid Chronicles* Book Three by Kat Zhang (HarperCollins), *Once We Were: The Hybrid Chronicles* Book Two by Kat Zhang (HarperCollins).

EINSTEIN LITERARY MANAGEMENT

27 West 20th St., 1003, New York NY 10011. **E-mail:** submissions@einsteinliterary.com.. **Website:** einsteinliterary.com. **Contact:** Susanna Einstein. Estab. 2015. Member of AAR. Signatory of WGA.

Prior to her current position, Ms. Einstein was with LJK Literary Management and the Einstein Thompson Agency.

MEMBER AGENTS Susanna Einstein.

REPRESENTS Nonfiction, fiction. **Considers these fiction areas:** commercial, crime, historical, literary, romance, women's.

"We represent a broad range of literary and commercial fiction, including upmarket women's fiction, crime fiction, historical fiction, romance, and books for middle-grade children and young adults. We also handle nonfiction, including cookbooks, memoir and narrative, and blog-to-book projects." Does not want picture books, poetry, textbooks, or screenplays.

HOW TO CONTACT Please submit a query letter and the first 10 double-spaced pages of your ms in the body of the e-mail (no attachments). Does not respond to mail or telephone queries or queries that are not specifically addressed to this agency. Accepts simultaneous submissions. Responds in 6 weeks if interested.

ETHAN ELLENBERG LITERARY AGENCY

155 Suffolk St., 2R, New York NY 10002. (212)431-4554. **E-mail:** agent@ethanellenberg.com. **Website:** ethanellenberg.com. **Contact:** Ethan Ellenberg. Estab. 1984. Member of AAR, Science Fiction and Fantasy Writers of America, SCBWI, RWA, MWA.

MEMBER AGENTS **Ethan Ellenberg**, president; **Evan Gregory**, senior agent; **Bibi Lewis**, associate agent (young adult and women's fiction).

REPRESENTS Nonfiction, fiction. **Considers these fiction areas:** commercial, ethnic, fantasy, literary, middle-grade, mystery, picture books, romance, science fiction, thriller, women's, young adult, general.

"We specialize in commercial fiction and children's books. In commercial fiction we want to see science fiction, fantasy, romance, mystery, thriller, women's fiction; all genres welcome. In children's books, we want to see everything: picture books, early reader, middle-grade, and young adult. We do some nonfiction: history, biography, military, popular science, and cutting-edge books about any subject." Does not want to receive poetry, short stories, or screenplays.

HOW TO CONTACT Query by e-mail. Paste all material in the order listed: for fiction, query letter, synopsis, first 50 pages; for nonfiction, query letter, book proposal; for picture books, query letter, complete ms, 4-5 sample illustrations; for illustrators, query letter, 4-5 sample illustrations, link to online portfolio. Will not respond unless interested. Accepts simultaneous submissions. Responds in 2 weeks.

FELICIA ETH LITERARY REPRESENTATION

555 Bryant St., Ste. 350, Palo Alto CA 94301-1700. **E-mail:** feliciaeth.literary@gmail.com. **Website:** eth-literary.com. **Contact:** Felicia Eth. Member of AAR.

REPRESENTS Fiction. **Considers these fiction areas:** historical, literary, mainstream, suspense.

This agency specializes in high-quality fiction (preferably mainstream/contemporary) and provocative, intelligent, and thoughtful nonfiction on a wide array of commercial subjects. "The agency does not represent genre fiction, including romance novels, science fiction and fantasy, westerns, anime and graphic novels, or mysteries."

HOW TO CONTACT For fiction: Please write a query letter introducing yourself, your book, and your writing background. Don't forget to include degrees you may have, publishing credits, awards, and endorsements. Please wait for a response before including sample pages. "We only consider material where the ms for which you are querying is complete, unless you have previously published." For nonfiction: A query letter is best, introducing the idea and what you have written already (proposal or ms?). "For writerly nonfiction (narratives, biography, memoir) please let us know if you have a finished ms. Also, it's important to include information about yourself, your background and expertise, and your platform and notoriety, if any. We do not ask for exclusivity in most instances but do ask that you inform us if other agents are considering the same material." Accepts simultaneous submissions.

TERMS Agent receives 15% commission on domestic sales; 20% commission on foreign sales; 20% commission on film sales. Charges clients for photocopying and express mail service.

RECENT SALES *Bumper Sticker Philosophy* by Jack Bowen (Random House), *Boys Adrift* by Leonard Sax (Basic Books), *The Memory Thief* by Emily Colin (Ballantine Books), *The World Is a Carpet* by Anna Badkhen (Riverhead).

WRITERS CONFERENCES "We attend a wide array—from Squaw Valley to Mills College."

● FAIRBANK LITERARY REPRESENTATION

P.O. Box 6, Hudson NY 12534-0006. (617)576-0030. **Fax:** (617)576-0030. **E-mail:** queries@fairbankliterary.com. **Website:** www.fairbankliterary.com. **Contact:** Sorche Fairbank. Member of AAR.

MEMBER AGENTS **Sorche Fairbank** (narrative nonfiction, commercial and literary fiction, memoir, food and wine); **Matthew Frederick**, matt@fairbankliterary.com (scout for sports nonfiction, architecture, design).

REPRESENTS Nonfiction, fiction, short story collections. **Considers these fiction areas:** action, adventure, feminist, gay, lesbian, literary, mainstream, mystery, sports, suspense, thriller, women's, Southern voices.

"I tend to gravitate toward literary fiction and narrative nonfiction, with a strong interest in women's issues and women's voices, international voices, class and race issues, and projects that simply teach me something new about the greater world and society around us. We have a good reputation for working closely and developmentally with our authors and love what we do." Actively seeking literary fiction, international and culturally diverse voices, narrative nonfiction, topical subjects (politics, current affairs), history, sports, architecture/design and pop culture. Does not want to receive romance, poetry, science fiction, pirates, vampires, young adult, or children's works.

HOW TO CONTACT Query with SASE. Submit author bio. Accepts simultaneous submissions. Obtains most new clients through recommendations from others, solicitations, conferences, ideas generated in-house.

TERMS Agent receives 15% commission on domestic sales; 20% commission on foreign sales. Offers written contract, binding for 12 months; 45-day notice must be given to terminate contract.

RECENT SALES *When Clowns Attack* by Chuck Sambuchino (Running Press), 101 Things I Learned in School series by Matthew Fredericks. All recent sales available on website.

TIPS "Be professional from the very first contact. There shouldn't be a single typo or grammatical flub in your query. Have a reason for contacting me about your project other than I was the next name listed on some website. Please do not use form query software! Believe me, we can get a dozen or so queries a day that look identical—we know when you are using a form. Show me that you know your audience—and your competition. Have the writing and/or proposal at the very, very best it can be before starting the querying process. Don't assume that if someone likes it enough they'll 'fix' it. The biggest mistake new writers make is starting the querying process before they—and the work—are ready. Take your time and do it right."

DIANA FINCH LITERARY AGENCY

116 W. 23rd St., Ste. 500, New York NY 10011. (917)544-4470. **E-mail:** diana.finch@verizon.net. **Website:** dianafinchliteraryagency.blogspot.com. **Contact:** Diana Finch. Estab. 2003. Member of AAR. Represents 40 clients.

Seeking to represent books that change lives. Prior to opening her agency in 2003, Ms. Finch worked at Ellen Levine Literary Agency for 18 years.

REPRESENTS Nonfiction, fiction. **Considers these fiction areas:** action, adventure, contemporary issues, crime, detective, ethnic, historical, literary, mainstream, police, sports, thriller, young adult.

"Does not want romance, mysteries, or children's picture books."

HOW TO CONTACT This agency prefers submissions via its online form: dianafinchliteraryagency.submittable.com/submit. Accepts simultaneous submissions. Obtains most new clients through recommendations from others.

TERMS Agent receives 15% commission on domestic sales; 20% commission on foreign sales. Offers written contract. "I charge for overseas postage, galleys, and books purchased, and try to recoup these costs from earnings received for a client rather than charging outright."

TIPS "Do as much research as you can on agents before you query. Have someone critique your query letter before you send it. It should be only 1 page and describe your book clearly—and why you are writing it—but also demonstrate creativity and a sense of your writing style."

FINEPRINT LITERARY MANAGEMENT

115 W. 29th, Third Floor, New York NY 10001. (212)279-1282. **Website:** www.fineprintlit.com. Member of AAR.

MEMBER AGENTS **Peter Rubie**, CEO, peter@fineprintlit.com (nonfiction: narrative nonfiction, popular science, spirituality, history, biography, pop culture, business, technology, parenting, health, self help, music, and food; fiction: literate thrillers, crime fiction, science fiction and fantasy, military fiction and literary fiction, middle-grade and boy-oriented young adult fiction); **Stephany Evans**, stephany@fineprintlit.com (nonfiction: health and wellness, spirituality, lifestyle [including home renovating, decorating, food and drink, and sustainability], running and fitness, memoir, and narrative nonfiction; fiction interests include women's fiction from literary to romance, including mystery, historical, and romantic suspense); **Janet Reid**, janet@fineprintlit.com (crime fiction and narrative nonfiction); **Laura Wood**, laura@fineprintlit.com (serious nonfiction, especially in the areas of science and nature, along with substantial titles in business, history, religion, and other areas by academics, experienced professionals, and journalists; select genre fiction only [no poetry, literary fiction, or memoir] in the categories of science fiction and fantasy and mystery); **June Clark**, june@fineprintlit.com (nonfiction: entertainment, self-help, parenting, reference/how-to, food and wine, style/beauty, prescriptive business); **Penny Moore**, penny@fineprintlit.com (all genres of middle-grade and young adult fiction; adult fiction, specifically upmarket, speculative fiction, science fiction, fantasy, psychological thrillers, and select romance; nonfiction projects in the realm of pop culture, humor, travel, food, and pets); **Jacqueline Murphy**, jacqueline@fineprintlit.com.

REPRESENTS **Considers these fiction areas:** commercial, crime, fantasy, historical, middle-grade, mystery, romance, science fiction, suspense, thriller, women's, young adult.

HOW TO CONTACT E-query. For fiction, send a query, synopsis, bio, and 30 pages pasted into the e-mail. No attachments. For nonfiction, send a query only; proposal requested later if the agent is interested. Accepts simultaneous submissions. Obtains most new clients through recommendations from others, solicitations.

TERMS Agent receives 15% commission on domestic sales; 20% commission on foreign sales.

FLETCHER & COMPANY

E-mail: info@fletcherandco.com. **Website:** www.fletcherandco.com. **Contact:** Christy Fletcher. Estab. 2003. Member of AAR.

MEMBER AGENTS **Christy Fletcher** (referrals only); **Melissa Chinchillo** (select list of her own authors); **Rebecca Gradinger** (literary fiction, upmarket commercial fiction, narrative nonfiction, self-help, memoir, women's studies, humor, pop culture); **Gráinne Fox** (literary fiction and quality commercial authors, award-winning journalists and food writers, American voices, international, literary crime, upmarket fiction, narrative nonfiction); **Lisa Grubka** (fiction: literary, upmarket women's, young adult; nonfiction: narrative, food, science, and more); **Sylvie Greenberg** (literary fiction, business, sports, science, memoir and history); **Donald Lamm** (history, biography, investigative journalism, politics, current affairs, business); **Todd Sattersten** (business).

REPRESENTS Nonfiction, fiction. **Considers these fiction areas:** commercial, crime, literary, women's, young adult.

HOW TO CONTACT Send queries to info@fletcherandco.com. Please do not include e-mail attachments with your initial query, as they will be deleted. Address your query to a specific agent. No snail mail queries. Accepts simultaneous submissions.

FOLIO LITERARY MANAGEMENT, LLC

The Film Center Building, 630 Ninth Ave., Ste. 1101, New York NY 10036. (212)400-1494. **Fax:** (212)967-0977. **Website:** www.foliolit.com. Member of AAR. Represents 100+ clients.

Prior to creating Folio Literary Management, Mr. Hoffman worked for several years at another agency. Mr. Kleinman was an agent at Graybill & English.

MEMBER AGENTS **Claudia Cross** (romance novels, commercial women's fiction, cooking and food writing, serious nonfiction on religious and spiritual topics); **Scott Hoffman** (literary and commercial fiction, journalistic or academic nonfiction, narrative nonfiction, pop culture, business, history, politics, spiritual or religious-themed fiction and nonfiction, science fiction/fantasy literary fiction, heartbreaking memoirs, humorous nonfiction); **Jeff Kleinman** (book club fiction [not genre commercial, like mysteries or romances], literary fiction, thrillers and suspense novels, narrative nonfiction, memoir); **Dado Derviskadic** (nonfiction: cultural history, biography, memoir, pop science, motivational self-help, health/nutrition, pop culture, cookbooks; fiction that's gritty, introspective, or serious); **Frank Weimann** (biography, business/investing/finance, history, religious, mind/body/spirit, health, lifestyle, cookbooks, sports, African-American, science, memoir, special forces/CIA/FBI/mafia, military, prescriptive nonfiction, humor, celebrity, adult and children's fiction); **Michael Harriot** (commercial nonfiction [both narrative and prescriptive], fantasy/science fiction); **Erin Harris** (book club, historical fiction, literary, narrative nonfiction, psychological suspense, young adult), **Molly Jaffa** (middle-grade, young adult, select nonfiction), **Katherine Latshaw** (blog-to-book, food/cooking, middle-grade, narrative and prescriptive nonfiction); **Annie Hwang** (literary and upmarket fiction with commercial appeal; select nonfiction: popular science, diet/health/fitness, lifestyle, narrative nonfiction, pop culture, humor); **Erin Niumata** (fiction: commercial women's fiction, romance, historical fiction, mysteries, psychological thrillers, suspense, humor; nonfiction: self-help, women's issues, pop culture and humor, pet care/pets, memoirs, anything blogger); **Ruth Pomerance** (narrative nonfiction and commercial fiction); **Marcy Posner** (adult: commercial women's fiction, historical fiction, mystery, biography, history, health, and lifestyle, commercial novels, thrillers, narrative nonfiction; children's: contemporary young adult and middle-grade novels, mystery series for boys, select historical fiction and fantasy); **Jeff Silberman** (nonfiction: narrative nonfiction, biography, history, politics, current affairs, health, lifestyle, humor, food/cookbook, memoir, pop culture, sports, science, technology; fiction: commercial, literary, book club fiction); **Steve Troha**; **Emily van Beek** (young adult, middle-grade, picture books), **Melissa White** (general nonfiction, literary and commercial fiction, middle-grade, young adult); **John Cusick** (middle-grade, picture books, young adult).

REPRESENTS Nonfiction, fiction. **Considers these fiction areas:** commercial, fantasy, horror, literary, middle-grade, mystery, picture books, religious, romance, thriller, women's, young adult.

No poetry, stage plays, or screenplays.

HOW TO CONTACT Query via e-mail only (no attachments). Read agent bios online for specific submission guidelines and e-mail addresses, and to check if someone is closed to queries. "All agents respond to queries as soon as possible, whether interested or not. If you haven't heard back from the individual agent within the time period that they specify on their bio page, it's possible that something has gone wrong, and your query has been lost. In that case, please e-mail a follow-up."

TIPS "Please do not submit simultaneously to more than 1 agent at Folio. If you're not sure which of us is exactly right for your book, don't worry. We work closely as a team, and if 1 of our agents gets a query that might be more appropriate for someone else, we'll always pass it along. It's important that you check each agent's bio page for clear directions as to how to submit, as well as when to expect feedback."

FOUNDRY LITERARY + MEDIA

33 W. 17th St., PH, New York NY 10011. (212)929-5064. **Fax:** (212)929-5471. **Website:** www.foundrymedia.com.

MEMBER AGENTS **Peter McGuigan**, pmsubmissions@foundrymedia.com (smart, offbeat voices in all genres of fiction and nonfiction); **Yfat Reiss Gendell**, yrgsubmissions@foundrymedia.com (practical nonfiction: health and wellness, diet, lifestyle, how-to, and parenting; narrative nonfiction: humor, memoir, history, science, pop culture, psychology, adventure/travel stories; unique commercial fiction, including young adult fiction, that touch on her nonfiction interests, including speculative fiction, thrillers, and historical fiction); **Chris Park**, cpsubmissions@foundrymedia.com (memoirs, narrative nonfiction, sports books, Christian nonfiction, character-driven fiction); **Hannah Brown Gordon**, hbgsubmissions@foundrymedia.com (stories and narratives that blend genres, including thriller, suspense, historical, literary, speculative, memoir, pop science, psychology, humor, pop culture); **Brandi Bowles**, bbsubmissions@foundrymedia.com (nonfiction: cookbooks, prescriptive books, science, pop culture, real-life inspirational stories; high-concept novels that feature strong female bonds and psychological or scientific themes); **Kirsten Neuhaus**, knsubmissions@foundrymedia.com (platform-driven narrative nonfiction: memoir, business, lifestyle [beauty/fashion/relationships], current events, history and stories with strong female voices; smart fiction that appeals to a wide market); **Jessica Regel**, jrsubmissions@foundrymedia.com (young adult and middle-grade books, as well as a select list of adult general fiction, women's fiction, and adult nonfiction); **Anthony Mattero**, amsubmissions@foundrymedia.com (smart, platform-driven nonfiction, particularly pop culture, humor, music, sports, and pop business); **Peter Steinberg**, pssubmissions@foundrymedia.com (narrative nonfiction, commercial and literary fiction, memoir, health, history, lifestyle, humor, sports, young adult); **Roger Freet**, rfsubmissions@foundrymedia.com (narrative and idea-driven nonfiction: religion, spirituality, memoir, and cultural issues by leading scholars, pastors, historians, activists, musicians); **Adriann Ranta** arsubmissions@foundrymedia.com (accepts all genres and age groups and loves gritty, realistic, true-to-life narratives; women's fiction and nonfiction; accessible, pop nonfiction in science, history, and craft; and smart, fresh, genre-bending works for children).

REPRESENTS **Considers these fiction areas:** commercial, historical, humor, literary, middle-grade, suspense, thriller, women's, young adult.

HOW TO CONTACT Target 1 agent only. Send queries to the specific submission e-mail of the agent. For fiction, send query, synopsis, author bio, and first 3 chapters pasted in the e-mail. For nonfiction, send query, sample chapters, table of contents, and author bio pasted in the e-mail. "We regret that we cannot guarantee a response to every submission we receive. If you do not receive a response in 8 weeks, your submission is not right for our lists at this time." Accepts simultaneous submissions.

RECENT SALES *The Last September* by Nina de Gramont, *The Hired Girl* by Laura Amy Schlitz.

TIPS "Consult website for each agent's submission instructions."

FOX LITERARY

110 W. 40th St., Ste. 2305, New York NY 10018. **E-mail:** submissions@foxliterary.com. **Website:** www.publishersmarketplace.com/members/fox.

MEMBER AGENTS Diana Fox.

REPRESENTS Nonfiction, fiction, graphic novels. **Considers these fiction areas:** fantasy, historical, romance, science fiction, thriller, young adult, general.

HOW TO CONTACT E-mail query and first 5 pages in body of e-mail. E-mail queries preferred. For snail mail queries, must include an e-mail address for response, and no response means NO. Do not send SASE. No e-mail attachments. Accepts simultaneous submissions.

RECENT SALES *Black Ships* by Jo Graham (Orbit), Evernight series by Claudia Gray (HarperCollins), October Daye series by Seanan McGuire (DAW), *Salt and Silver* by Anna Katherine (Tor), *Alcestis* by Katharine Beutner (Soho Press), *Shadows Cast by Stars* by Catherine Knutsson (Atheneum), *Saving June* and *Speechless* by Hannah Harrington (Harlequin Teen), Spellcaster trilogy by Claudia Gray (HarperCollins).

SARAH JANE FREYMANN LITERARY AGENCY

(212)362-9277. **E-mail:** sarah@sarahjanefreymann.com;. **E-mail:** submissions@sarahjanefreymann.com. **Website:** www.sarahjanefreymann.com. **Contact:** Sarah Jane Freymann, Steve Schwartz.

MEMBER AGENTS **Sarah Jane Freymann** (nonfiction: spiritual, psychology, self-help, women/men's issues, books by health experts [conventional and alternative], cookbooks, narrative nonfiction, natural science, nature, memoirs, cutting-edge journalism, travel, multicultural issues, parenting, lifestyle; fiction: literary, mainstream young adult); **Jessica Sinsheimer**, jessica@sarahjanefreymann.com; **Steven Schwartz**, steve@sarahjanefreymann.com (popular fiction [crime, thrillers, and historical novels], world and national affairs, business books, self-help, psychology, humor, sports, travel).

REPRESENTS Nonfiction, fiction. **Considers these fiction areas:** crime, historical, literary, mainstream, thriller, young adult, popular fiction.

HOW TO CONTACT Query via e-mail. No attachments. Below the query, please paste the first 10 pages of your work. Accepts simultaneous submissions.

TERMS Charges clients for long distance, overseas postage, photocopying; 100% of business is derived from commissions on ms sales.

FREDRICA S. FRIEDMAN AND CO., INC.

857 Fifth Ave., New York NY 10065. (212)829-9600. **Fax:** (212)829-9669. **E-mail:** submissions@fredricafriedman.com. **Website:** www.fredricafriedman.com. **Contact:** Ms. Chandler Smith.

Prior to establishing her own literary management firm, Ms. Friedman was the editorial director, associate publisher, and vice president of Little, Brown & Co., a division of Time Warner, and the first woman to hold those positions.

REPRESENTS Nonfiction, fiction.

Does not want poetry, plays, screenplays, children's picture books, science fiction/fantasy, or horror.

HOW TO CONTACT Submit e-query, synopsis; be concise, and include any pertinent author information, including relevant writing history. If you are a fiction writer, submit the first 10 pages of your ms. Keep all material in the body of the e-mail. Accepts simultaneous submissions. Responds in 6 weeks.

REBECCA FRIEDMAN LITERARY AGENCY

E-mail: abby@rfliterary.com. **Website:** www.rfliterary.com. Estab. 2013. Member of AAR. Signatory of WGA.

Prior to opening her own agency in 2013, Ms. Friedman was with Sterling Lord Literistic (2006-2011), then with Hill Nadell Agency.

MEMBER AGENTS **Rebecca Friedman**, brandie@rfliterary.com (commercial and literary fiction with a focus on literary novels of suspense, women's fiction, contemporary romance, and young adult, as well as journalistic nonfiction and memoir); **Kimberly Brower**, kimberly@rfliterary.com (commercial and literary fiction, with an emphasis on contemporary romance, women's fiction, mysteries/thrillers, and young adult); **Rachel Marks,** rachel@rfliterary.com (young adult, fantasy, science fiction, new adult, romance).

REPRESENTS Nonfiction, fiction. **Considers these fiction areas:** commercial, fantasy, literary, mystery, new adult, romance, science fiction, suspense, women's, young adult.

HOW TO CONTACT Please submit your query letter and first chapter (no more than 15 pages double-spaced). If querying Kimberly, paste a full synopsis into the e-mail submission. No attachments. Accepts simultaneous submissions. Tries to respond in 6-8 weeks.

RECENT SALES A complete list of agency authors is available online.

THE FRIEDRICH AGENCY

19 W. 21st St., Ste. 201, New York NY 10010. (212)317-8810. **E-mail:** mfriedrich@friedrichagency.com; lcarson@friedrichagency.com; kwolf@friedrichagency.com. **Website:** www.friedrichagency.com. **Contact:** Molly Friedrich, Lucy Carson, Kent D. Wolf. Estab. 2006. Member of AAR. Signatory of WGA. Represents 50+ clients.

Prior to her current position, Ms. Friedrich was an agent at the Aaron Priest Literary Agency.

MEMBER AGENTS **Molly Friedrich**, founder and agent (open to queries); **Lucy Carson**, TV/film rights director and agent (open to queries); **Kent D. Wolf**, foreign rights director and agent (open to queries).

REPRESENTS Nonfiction, fiction, short story collections. **Considers these fiction areas:** commercial, literary.

HOW TO CONTACT Query by e-mail only. Please query only 1 agent at this agency. Accepts simultaneous submissions.

RECENT SALES *W Is For Wasted* by Sue Grafton, *Olive Kitteridge* by Elizabeth Strout. Other clients include Frank McCourt, Jane Smiley, Esmeralda Santiago, Terry McMillan, Cathy Schine, Ruth Ozeki, Karen Joy Fowler, and more.

FULL CIRCLE LITERARY, LLC

Website: www.fullcircleliterary.com. **Contact:** Stefanie Von Borstel. Estab. 2005. Member of AAR, SCBWI, Authors Guild. Represents 100+ clients.

"Please read the 'Our Agents' pages on our website and determine the Full Circle Literary agent that is the best fit for your work."

MEMBER AGENTS **Stefanie Von Borstel**, **Adriana Dominguez**, **Taylor Martindale** (multicultural voices), **Lilly Ghahremani**.

REPRESENTS **Considers these fiction areas:** literary, middle-grade, multicultural, picture books, women's, young adult.

Actively seeking nonfiction by authors with a unique voice and strong platform, projects that offer new and diverse viewpoints, and literature with a global or multicultural perspective. We are particularly interested in books with a Latino or Middle Eastern angle.

HOW TO CONTACT Online submissions only via submissions form at www.fullcircleliterary.com. Please complete the form and submit cover letter, author information and sample writing. For fiction, please include the first 10 ms pages. For nonfiction, include a proposal with 1 sample chapter. Accepts simultaneous submissions. "Due to the high volume of submissions, please keep in mind we are no longer able to personally respond to every submission. However, we read every submission with care and often share for a second read within the office. If we are interested, we will contact you by e-mail to request additional materials (such as a complete ms or additional mss). Please keep us updated if there is a change in the status of your project, such as an offer of representation or book contract. If you have not heard from us in 6-8 weeks, your project is not right for our agency at the current time and we wish you all the best with your writing. Thank you for considering Full Circle Literary, we look forward to reading!" Obtains most new clients through recommendations from others, conferences.

TERMS Agent receives 15% commission on domestic sales; 25% commission on foreign sales. Offers written contract which outlines responsibilities of the author and the agent.

RECENT SALES "Please visit our website to learn about our latest deals and book news. Follow our agency on Twitter: @fullcirclelit."

FUSE LITERARY

Website: www.fuseliterary.com. Member of AAR. Signatory of WGA.

MEMBER AGENTS **Laurie McLean** (only accepting referral inquiries and submissions requested at conferences or online events, with the exception of unsolicited adult and children's science fiction); **Gordon Warnock**, querygordon@fuseliterary.com (fiction: high-concept commercial fiction, literary fiction [adults through young adult], graphic novels [adults through middle-grade]; nonfiction: memoir [adult, young adult, new adult, graphic], cookbooks/food narrative/food studies, illustrated/art/photography [especially graphic nonfiction], political and current events, pop science, pop culture [especially punk culture and geek culture], self-help, how-to, humor, pets, business and career); **Connor Goldsmith**, queryconnor@fuseliterary.com (fiction: science fiction, fantasy, horror, thrillers, upmarket commercial fiction with a unique and memorable hook; books by and about people from marginalized perspectives, such as LGBTQ people and/or racial minorities; nonfiction from recognized experts with established platforms: history [particularly of the ancient world], theater, cinema, music, television, mass media, popular culture, feminism and gender studies, LGBTQ issues, race relations, the sex industry); **Sara Sciuto**, querysara@fuseliterary.com (middle-grade, young adult, standout picture books); **Michelle Richter**, querymichelle@fuseliterary.com (fiction: book club reads, literary fiction, mystery/suspense/thrillers; nonfiction: fashion, pop culture, science/medicine, sociology/social trends, economics); **Emily S. Keyes**, queryemily@fuseliterary.com (young adult, middle-grade, select commercial fiction, [including fantasy and science fiction, women's fiction, new adult fiction], pop culture, humor); **Tricia Skinner**, querytricia@fuseliterary.com (romance: science fiction, futuristic, fantasy, military/special ops, medieval historical; brand-new relationships; diversity); **Jennifer Chen Tran**, queryjennifer@fuseliterary.com (literary fiction, commercial fiction, women's fiction, upmarket fiction, contemporary romance, mature young adult, new adult, suspense/thriller, select graphic novels [adult, young adult, middle-grade]; memoir, narrative nonfiction in the areas of adventure, biography, business, current affairs, medical, history, how-to, pop-culture, psychology, social entrepreneurism, social justice, travel, and lifestyle books [home, design, fashion, food]).

HOW TO CONTACT E-query an individual agent. Check the website to see if an agent is closed to submissions, as well as each agent's submission preferences. Accepts simultaneous submissions.

WRITERS CONFERENCES Agents from this agency attend many conferences. A full list of their appearances is available on the website.

GLASS LITERARY MANAGEMENT

138 W. 25th St., 10th Floor, New York NY 10001. (646)237-4881. **E-mail:** submissions@glassliterary.com. **Website:** www.glassliterary.com. **Contact:** Alex Glass. Estab. 2014. Member of AAR. Signatory of WGA.

REPRESENTS Nonfiction, fiction.

- Represents general fiction, mystery, suspense/thriller, juvenile fiction, biography, history, mind/body/spirit, health, lifestyle, cookbooks, sports, literary fiction, memoir, narrative nonfiction, pop culture. "We do not represent picture books for children."

HOW TO CONTACT "Please send your query letter in the body of an e-mail. If we are interested, we will respond and ask for the complete ms or proposal. No attachments." Accepts simultaneous submissions.

IRENE GOODMAN LITERARY AGENCY

27 W. 24th St., Ste. 700B, New York NY 10010. **Website:** www.irenegoodman.com. Member of AAR.

MEMBER AGENTS Irene Goodman, Miriam Kriss, Barbara Poelle, Rachel Ekstrom, Beth Vesel, Kim Perel, Anne Baltazar, Brita Lundberg.

REPRESENTS Nonfiction, fiction, juvenile books. **Considers these fiction areas:** crime, detective, historical, mystery, romance, thriller, women's, young adult.

- Commercial and literary fiction and nonfiction. No children's picture books, screenplays, poetry, or inspirational fiction.

HOW TO CONTACT Query. Submit synopsis, first 10 pages pasted into the body of the e-mail. E-mail queries only! See the website submission page. No e-mail attachments. Query 1 agent only. Accepts simultaneous submissions. Responds in 2 months to queries. Consult website for each agent's submission guidelines.

TIPS "We are receiving an unprecedented amount of e-mail queries. If you find that the mailbox is full, please try again in 2 weeks. E-mail queries to our personal addresses will not be answered. E-mails to our personal in-boxes will be deleted."

SANFORD J. GREENBURGER ASSOCIATES, INC.

55 Fifth Ave., New York NY 10003. (212)206-5600. **Fax:** (212)463-8718. **Website:** www.greenburger.com. Member of AAR. Represents 500 clients.

MEMBER AGENTS **Matt Bialer**, lribar@sjga.com (fantasy, science fiction, thrillers, and mysteries, as well as a select group of literary writers; also loves smart narrative nonfiction, including books about current events, popular culture, biography, history, music, race, and sports); **Brenda Bowen**, querybb@sjga.com (literary fiction, picture books, chapter books, middle-grade and teen fiction); **Faith Hamlin**, fhamlin@sjga.com (receives submissions by referral); **Heide Lange**, queryhl@sjga.com (receives submissions by referral); **Daniel Mandel**, querydm@sjga.com (literary and commercial fiction, as well as memoirs and nonfiction about business, art, history, politics, sports, and popular culture); **Courtney Miller-Callihan**, cmiller@sjga.com (young adult, middle-grade, women's fiction, romance, historical novels, as well as nonfiction projects on unusual topics, humor, pop culture, lifestyle books); **Nicholas Ellison**, nellison@sjga.com; **Chelsea Lindman**, clindman@sjga.com (playful literary fiction, upmarket crime fiction, forward-thinking or boundary-pushing nonfiction); **Rachael Dillon Fried**, rfried@sjga.com (both fiction and nonfiction authors, with a keen interest in unique literary voices, women's fiction, narrative nonfiction, memoir, and comedy); **Lindsay Ribar**, co-agents with Matt Bialer (young adult and middle-grade fiction); **Bethany Buck** querybbuck@sjga.com (middle-grade fiction and chapter books, teen fiction, and a select list of picture book authors and illustrators); **Stephanie Delman** sdelman@sjga.com (literary/upmarket contemporary fiction, psychological thrillers/suspense, atmospheric, near-historical fiction); **Ed Maxwell** emaxwell@sjga.com (narrative nonfiction, expert nonfiction, fiction, graphic novels, children's picture books).

REPRESENTS Nonfiction, fiction, novels, juvenile books. **Considers these fiction areas:** commercial, crime, family saga, fantasy, feminist, historical, literary, middle-grade, multicultural, mystery, picture books, romance, science fiction, thriller, women's, young adult.

⊶ No screenplays.

HOW TO CONTACT E-query. "Please look at each agent's profile page for current information about what each agent is looking for and for the correct e-mail address to use for queries to that agent." Agents may not respond to all queries; will respond within 6-8 weeks if interested. Obtains most new clients through recommendations from others.

TERMS Agent receives 15% commission on domestic sales; 20% commission on foreign sales. Charges for photocopying and books for foreign and subsidiary rights submissions.

RECENT SALES *Inferno* by Dan Brown, *Sweet Pea and Friends: A Sheepover* by John Churchman and Jennifer Churchman, *Code of Conduct* by Brad Thor.

GREYHAUS LITERARY

3021 20th St. Pl. SW, Puyallup WA 98373. **E-mail:** scott@greyhausagency.com. **E-mail:** submissions@greyhausagency.com. **Website:** www.greyhausagency.com. **Contact:** Scott Eagan, member RWA. Estab. 2003. Member of AAR. Signatory of WGA.

REPRESENTS Fiction. **Considers these fiction areas:** romance, women's.

⊶ Greyhaus only focuses on romance and women's fiction. Please review submission information found on the website to know exactly what Greyhaus is looking for. Stories should be 75,000-120,000 words in length or meet the word count requirements for Harlequin found on its website. Does not want fantasy, single-title inspirational, young adult or middle-grade, picture books, memoirs, biographies, erotica, urban fantasy, science fiction, screenplays, poetry, or authors interested in only e-publishing or self-publishing.

HOW TO CONTACT Submissions to Greyhaus can be done in one of these ways: (1) Send a standard query letter via e-mail. If using this method, do not attach documents or send anything else other than a query letter. (2) Use the submission form found on the website on the Contact page. (3) Send a query, the first 3 pages, and a synopsis of no more than 5 pages (and an SASE) by snail mail. Accepts simultaneous submissions.

JILL GRINBERG LITERARY MANAGEMENT

392 Vanderbilt Avenue, Brooklyn NY 11238. (212)620-5883. **E-mail:** info@jillgrinbergliterary.com. **Website:** www.jillgrinbergliterary.com. Estab. 1999.

Prior to her current position, Ms. Grinberg was at Anderson Grinberg Literary Management.

MEMBER AGENTS **Jill Grinberg**; **Cheryl Pientka**, cheryl@jillgrinbergliterary.com; **Katelyn Detweiler**, katelyn@jillgrinbergliterary.com.

REPRESENTS Nonfiction, fiction. **Considers these fiction areas:** fantasy, juvenile, literary, mainstream, middle-grade, romance, science fiction, young adult.

HOW TO CONTACT Please send your query letter to info@jillgrinbergliterary.com and attach the first 50 pages (fiction) or proposal (nonfiction) as a Word doc file. All submissions will be read, but e-mail is preferred. Accepts simultaneous submissions.

RECENT SALES *Cinder* by Marissa Meyer, *The Hero's Guide to Saving Your Kingdom* by Christopher Healy, *Kiss and Make Up* by Katie Anderson, *Eon* and *Eona* by Alison Goodman, *American Nations* by Colin Woodard, HALO Trilogy by Alexandra Adornetto, *Babymouse* by Jennifer and Matthew Holm, Uglies/Leviathan Trilogy by Scott Westerfeld, *Liar* by Justine Larbalestier, *Turtle in Paradise* by Jennifer Holm, *Wisdom's Kiss* and *Dairy Queen* by Catherine Gilbert Murdock.

TIPS "We prefer submissions by e-mail."

JILL GROSJEAN LITERARY AGENCY

1390 Millstone Rd., Sag Harbor NY 11963. (631)725-7419. **E-mail:** JillLit310@aol.com. **Contact:** Jill Grosjean. Estab. 1999.

Prior to becoming an agent, Ms. Grosjean managed an independent bookstore. She also worked in publishing and advertising.

REPRESENTS Fiction. **Considers these fiction areas:** historical, literary, mainstream, mystery, thriller, women's.

Actively seeking literary novels and mysteries.

HOW TO CONTACT E-mail queries preferred; no attachments. No cold calls, please. Accepts simultaneous submissions, though when ms requested, requires exclusive reading time. Accepts simultaneous submissions. Responds in 1 week to queries; month to mss. Obtains most new clients through recommendations and solicitations.

TERMS Agent receives 15% commission on domestic sales; 20% commission on foreign and film sales.

RECENT SALES *The Edison Effect* by Bernadette Pajer (Poison Pen Press), *Neutral Ground* by Greg Garrett (Bondfire Books), *Threading the Needle* by Marie Bostwick (Kensington Publishing), *Tim Cratchit's Christmas Carol: A Novel of Scrooge's Legacy* by Jim Piecuch (Simon & Schuster), *A Murder in Time* by Julie McElwain (Pegasus Books).

WRITERS CONFERENCES Thrillerfest, Texas Writer's League, Book Passage Mystery Writers Conference.

HARTLINE LITERARY AGENCY

123 Queenston Dr., Pittsburgh PA 15235-5429. (412)829-2483. **E-mail:** joyce@hartlineliterary.com. **Website:** www.hartlineliterary.com. **Contact:** Joyce A. Hart. Member of ACFW. Represents 200 clients.

MEMBER AGENTS **Joyce A. Hart**, principal agent (no unsolicited queries); **Jim Hart**, jim@hartlineliterary.com; **Diana Flegal**, diana@hartlineliterary.com; **Linda Glaz**, linda@hartlineliterary.com; **Andy Scheer**, andy@hartlineliterary.com; **Cyle Young**, Cyle@hartlineliterary.com.

REPRESENTS Nonfiction, fiction, novellas, juvenile books, scholarly books. **Considers these fiction areas:** contemporary issues, family saga, humor, inspirational, new adult, religious, romance, suspense, women's, young adult.

"This agency specializes in the Christian bookseller market." Actively seeking adult fiction, self-help, nutritional books, Christian living, devotional, and business. Does not want to receive erotica, gay/lesbian, fantasy, or horror.

HOW TO CONTACT E-query preferred; USPS to the Pittsburgh office. Target 1 agent only. "All e-mail submissions sent to Hartline Agents should be sent as a Microsoft Word doc (or in RTF file format from another word processing program) attached to an e-mail with 'Submission: [title, author's name, and word count]' in the subject line. A proposal is a single document, not a collection of files. Place the query letter in the e-mail itself. Do not send the entire proposal in the body of the e-mail or send PDF files." See further guidelines online. Accepts simultaneous submissions. Responds in 2 months to queries; in 3 months to mss. Obtains most new clients through recommendations from others, conferences.

TERMS Agent receives 15% commission on domestic sales. Offers written contract.

JOHN HAWKINS & ASSOCIATES, INC.

80 Maiden Lane, Ste. 1503, New York NY 10038. (212)807-7040. **E-mail:** jha@jhalit.com. **Website:** www.jhalit.com. **Contact:** Moses Cardona (rights and translations); Liz Free (permissions); William Reiss, literary agent; Warren Frazier, literary agent; Anne Hawkins, literary agent. Member of AAR. Represents 100+ clients.

MEMBER AGENTS **William Reiss**, reiss@jhalit.com (historical narratives, biography, slightly off-beat fiction and nonfiction, children's books, nature writing); **Moses Cardona**, moses@jhalit.com (commercial fiction, suspense, business, science, multicultural fiction); **Warren Frazier**, frazier@jhalit.com (fiction; nonfiction: technology, history, world affairs and foreign policy); **Anne Hawkins** ahawkins@jhalit.com (thrillers, literary fiction, serious nonfiction; interested in science, history, public policy, medicine, and women's issues).

REPRESENTS Nonfiction, fiction. **Considers these fiction areas:** commercial, historical, literary, multicultural, suspense, thriller.

HOW TO CONTACT Query. Include the word "Query" in the subject line. For fiction, include 1-3 chapters of your book as a single Word attachment. For nonfiction, include your proposal as a single attachment. E-mail a particular agent directly if you are targeting one. Accepts simultaneous submissions. Responds in 1 month to queries. Obtains most new clients through recommendations from others.

TERMS Agent receives 15% commission on domestic sales; 20% commission on foreign sales. Charges clients for photocopying.

RECENT SALES *Forty Rooms* by Olga Grushin, *The Man Without a Shadow* by Joyce Carol Oates, *After Alice* by Gregory Maguire, *The Adventuress* by Tasha Alexander, *Harbour Street* by Ann Cleeves, *What Philosophy Can Do* by Gary Gutting.

HELEN HELLER AGENCY INC.

4-216 Heath Street W., Toronto Ontario M5P 1N7 Canada. (416)489-0396. **E-mail:** info@helenhelleragency.com. **Website:** www.helenhelleragency.com. **Contact:** Helen Heller. Represents 30+ clients.

Prior to her current position, Ms. Heller worked for Cassell & Co. (England), was an editor for Harlequin Books, a senior editor for Avon Books, and editor in chief for Fitzhenry & Whiteside.

MEMBER AGENTS **Helen Heller**, helen@helenhelleragency.com (thrillers and front-list general fiction); **Sarah Heller**, sarah@helenhelleragency.com (front-list commercial young adult and adult fiction, with a particular interest in high-concept historical fiction); **Barbara Berson**, barbara@helenhelleragency.com (literary fiction, nonfiction, young adult).

REPRESENTS Nonfiction, fiction. **Considers these fiction areas:** commercial, crime, historical, literary, mainstream, thriller, young adult.

HOW TO CONTACT E-mail info@helenhelleragency.com. Submit a brief synopsis, publishing history, author bio, and writing sample, pasted in the body of the e-mail. No attachments with e-queries. Accepts simultaneous submissions. Responds within 3 months if interested. Accepts simultaneous submissions. Obtains most new clients through recommendations from others, solicitations.

RECENT SALES *Broken Promise* by Linwood Barclay, *When the Moon Is Low* by Nadia Hashimi, *Fear the Darkness* by Becky Masterman. A full list of deals is available online.

TIPS "Whether you are an author searching for an agent, or whether an agent has approached you, it is in your best interest to first find out who the agent represents, what publishing houses the agent has sold to recently, and what foreign sales the agent has made. You should be able to go to the bookstore, or search online, and find the books the agent refers to. Many authors acknowledge their agents in the front or back or their books."

RICHARD HENSHAW GROUP

145 W. 28th St., 12th Floor, New York NY 10001. (212)414-1172. **E-mail:** submissions@henshaw.com. **Website:** www.richardhenshawgroup.com. **Contact:** Rich Henshaw. Member of AAR.

Prior to opening his agency, Mr. Henshaw served as an agent with Richard Curtis Associates, Inc.

REPRESENTS Fiction. **Considers these fiction areas:** fantasy, historical, horror, literary, mainstream, mystery, police, romance, science fiction, thriller, young adult.

"We specialize in popular fiction and nonfiction and are affiliated with a variety of writers' organizations. Our clients include *New York Times* bestsellers and recipients of major awards in fiction and nonfiction. We only consider works between 65,000-150,000 words. We do not represent children's books, screenplays, short fiction, poetry, textbooks, scholarly works or coffee-table books."

HOW TO CONTACT "Please feel free to submit a query letter in the form of an e-mail of fewer than 250 words to submissions@henshaw.com." No snail mail queries. Accepts simultaneous submissions. Obtains most new clients through recommendations from others, solicitations, conferences.

TERMS Agent receives 15% commission on domestic sales; 20% commission on foreign sales. No written contract. Charges clients for photocopying and book orders.

TIPS "While we do not have any reason to believe that our submission guidelines will change in the near future, writers can find up-to-date submission policy information on our website. Always include an SASE with correct return postage."

HILL NADELL LITERARY AGENCY

6442 Santa Monica Blvd., Ste. 201, Los Angeles CA 90038. (310)860-9605. **E-mail:** queries.hillnadell@gmail.com. **Website:** www.hillnadell.com. Represents 100 clients.

MEMBER AGENTS **Bonnie Nadell** (nonfiction: current affairs, food, memoirs, narrative nonfiction; fiction: thrillers, upmarket women's, literary fiction); **Dara Hyde** (literary and genre fiction, narrative nonfiction, graphic novels, memoir, the occasional young adult novel).

REPRESENTS Nonfiction, fiction. **Considers these fiction areas:** literary, mainstream, thriller, women's, young adult.

HOW TO CONTACT Send a query and SASE. If you would like your materials returned, please include adequate postage. To submit electronically, send your query letter and the first chapter (no more than 15 pages double-spaced) to queries@hillnadell.com. No attachments. Due to the high volume of submissions the agency receives, it cannot guarantee a response to all e-mailed queries. Accepts simultaneous submissions.

TERMS Agent receives 15% commission on domestic sales; 20% commission on foreign sales; 15% commission on film sales. Charges clients for photocopying and foreign mailings.

RECENT SALES *S Street Rising* by Ruben Castaneda, *Spare Parts* by Joshua Davis, *Men Explain Things to Me* by Rebecca Solnit, *Bellweather Rhapsody* by Kate Racculia.

O HOLLOWAY LITERARY

Raleigh NC **E-mail:** submissions@hollowayliteraryagency.com. **Website:** hollowayliteraryagency.com. **Contact:** Nikki Terpilowski. Estab. 2011. Member of AAR, ITW, RWA. Signatory of WGA.

MEMBER AGENTS **Nikki Terpilowski** (romance, women's fiction, Southern fiction, historical fiction, cozy mysteries); **Rachel Burkot** (young adult contemporary, women's fiction, upmarket/book club fiction, contemporary romance, Southern fiction, urban fiction, literary fiction).

REPRESENTS Fiction. **Considers these fiction areas:** erotica, ethnic, fantasy, glitz, historical, literary, mainstream, middle-grade, multicultural, regional, romance, thriller, women's, young adult.

"Note to self-published authors: While we are happy to receive submissions from authors who have previously self-published novels, we do not represent self-published works. Send us your unpublished mss only." Does not want horror, true crime or novellas.

HOW TO CONTACT "Send your query and the first 15 pages of your ms pasted into the body of your e-mail to submissions @ hollowayliteraryagency.com. In the subject header write: Nikki/[Title]/[Genre]. You can expect a response in 4-6 weeks. If Nikki is interested, she'll respond with a request for more material. If she's not interested in your query but thinks it will be a good fit for others at the agency, she'll share your submission. Due to the number of emails we receive, Nikki will only respond if she's interested." Accepts simultaneous submissions.

RECENT SALES A list of agency clients is available on the website.

HSG AGENCY

37 W. 28th St, Eighth Floor, New York NY 10001. **E-mail:** channigan@hsgagency.com; jsalky@hsgagency.com; jgetzler@hsgagency.com; dburby@hsgagency.com; tprasanna@hsgagency.com; leigh@hsgagency.com. **Website:** hsgagency.com. **Contact:** Carrie Hannigan, Jesseca Salky, Josh Getzler, Danielle Burby, Tanusri Prasanna, Leigh Eisenman. Estab. 2011. Member of AAR. Signatory of WGA.

Prior to opening HSG Agency, Ms. Hannigan, Ms. Salky. and Mr. Getzler were agents at Russell & Volkening.

MEMBER AGENTS **Carrie Hannigan**; **Jesseca Salky** (literary and mainstream fiction); **Josh Getzler** (foreign fiction, women's fiction, straight-ahead historical fiction, thrillers, mysteries); **Danielle Burby** (young adult, women's fiction, mysteries, fantasy); **Tanusri Prasanna** (associate assisting current kidlit agents); **Leigh Eisenman** (literary and commercial fiction, foodie/cookbooks, health and fitness, lifestyle, select narrative nonfiction).

REPRESENTS Nonfiction, fiction, novels, juvenile books. **Considers these fiction areas:** adventure, commercial, contemporary issues, crime, detective, ethnic, family saga, historical, juvenile, literary, mainstream, middle-grade, multicultural, mystery, picture books, thriller, translation, women's, young adult.

HOW TO CONTACT Electronic submissions only. Send query letter and first 5 pages of ms pasted into e-mail, and send to appropriate agent. Avoid submitting to multiple agents within the agency. For picture books, include entire ms. Accepts simultaneous submissions. Responds in 4-6 weeks.

RECENT SALES *The Beginner's Goodbye* by Anne Tyler (Knopf), *Blue Sea Burning* by Geoff Rodkey (Putnam), *The Partner Track* by Helen Wan (St. Martin's Press), *The Thrill of the Haunt* by E.J. Copperman (Berkley), *Aces Wild* by Erica Perl (Knopf Books for Young Readers), *Steve & Wessley: The Sea Monster* by Jennifer Morris (Scholastic), *Infinite Worlds* by Michael Soluri (Simon & Schuster).

INKLINGS LITERARY AGENCY

3419 Virginia Beach Blvd #183, Virginia Beach VA 23452. (757)340-1070. **Fax:** (904)758-5440. **E-mail:** michelle@inklingsliterary.com. **E-mail:** query@inklingsliterary.com. **Website:** www.inklingsliterary.com. Estab. 2013. Member of RWA, SinC, HRW.

"We offer our clients interactive representation for their work, as well as developmental guidance for their author platforms, working with them as they grow. With backgrounds in book selling, business, marketing, publicity, contract negotiation, editing, writing, and script work, we work closely with our clients to build their brands and their careers." The face of publishing is ever-changing, and bending and shifting with the times and staying ahead of the curve are key for Michelle and her agency. The agents of Inklings Literary Agency strictly adhere to the AAR's code of ethics.

MEMBER AGENTS **Michelle Johnson**, michelle@inklingsliterary.com (adult and young adult fiction, contemporary, suspense, thriller, mystery, horror, fantasy [including paranormal and supernatural elements within those genres], romance of every level, nonfiction in the areas of memoir and true crime); **Dr. Jamie Bodnar Drowley**, jamie@inklingsliterary.com (new adult fiction in the areas of romance [all subgenres], fantasy [urban fantasy, light science fiction, steampunk], mystery and thrillers, young adult [all subgenres], middle-grade); **Margaret Bail**, margaret@inklingsliterary.com (romance, science fiction, mystery, thrillers, action adventure, historical fiction, western, some fantasy, memoir, cookbooks, true crime); **Naomi Davis**, naomi@inklingsliterary.com (romance of any variety [including paranormal, fresh urban fantasy, general fantasy, new adult, and light science fiction]; young adult in any of those same genres; memoirs about living with disabilities, facing criticism, and mental illness); **Whitley Abell**, whitley@inklingsliterary.com (young adult, middle-grade, and select upmarket women's fiction); **Alex Barba**, alex@inklingsliterary.com (young adult fiction).

REPRESENTS Nonfiction, fiction, juvenile books. **Considers these fiction areas:** action, adventure, commercial, contemporary issues, crime, detective, erotica, ethnic, fantasy, feminist, gay, historical, horror, juvenile, lesbian, mainstream, metaphysical, middle-grade, military, multicultural, multimedia, mystery, new adult, New Age, occult, paranormal, police, psychic, regional, romance, science fiction, spiritual, sports, supernatural, suspense, thriller, urban fantasy, war, women's, young adult.

HOW TO CONTACT E-queries only. To query, type "Query (Agent Name)" plus the title of your novel in the subject line. Send your query letter, short synopsis, and first 10 pages pasted into the body of the e-mail to query@inklingsliterary.com. Check the agency website to make sure that your targeted agent is currently open to submissions. Accepts simultaneous submissions. For queries, no response in 3 months is considered a rejection.

TERMS Agent receives 15% commission on domestic sales; 20% on subsidiary sales.

INKWELL MANAGEMENT, LLC

521 Fifth Ave., 26th Floor, New York NY 10175. (212)922-3500. **Fax:** (212)922-0535. **E-mail:** submissions@inkwellmanagement.com. **Website:** www.inkwellmanagement.com. Represents 500 clients.

MEMBER AGENTS **Stephen Barbara** (select adult fiction and nonfiction); **William Callahan** (nonfiction of all stripes, especially American history and memoir, pop culture, and illustrated books, as well as voice-driven fiction that stands out from the crowd); **Michael V. Carlisle**; **Catherine Drayton** (best-selling authors of books for children, young adults, and women readers); **David Forrer** (literary, commercial, historical, crime, suspense/thriller, humorous nonfiction, popular history); **Alexis Hurley** (literary and commercial fiction, memoir, narrative nonfiction, and more); **Nathaniel Jacks** (memoir, narrative nonfiction, social sciences, health, current affairs, business, religion, popular history, literary and commercial fiction, women's, young adult, historical, short stories, among others); **Jacqueline Murphy** (fiction, children's books, graphic novels and illustrated works, compelling narrative nonfiction); **Richard Pine; Eliza Rothstein** (literary and commercial fiction, narrative nonfiction, memoir, popular science, and food writing); **Emma Schlee** (literary fiction, the occasional thriller, travel and adventure, popular culture, philosophy); **Hannah Schwartz; David Hale Smith; Lauren Smythe** (smart narrative nonfiction [narrative journalism, modern history, biography, cultural criticism, personal essay, humor], personality-driven practical nonfiction [cookbooks, fashion and style], contemporary literary fiction); **Kimberly Witherspoon; Monika Woods** (literary and commercial fiction, young adult, memoir, and compelling nonfiction in popular culture, science, current affairs); **Lena Yarbrough** (literary fiction, upmarket commercial fiction, memoir, narrative nonfiction, history, investigative journalism, cultural criticism); **Jenny Witherell; Charlie Olson; Liz Parker** (commercial and upmarket women's fiction and narrative, practical, platform-driven nonfiction); **George Lucas; Alyssa diPierro.**

REPRESENTS Nonfiction, fiction. **Considers these fiction areas:** commercial, crime, historical, literary, middle-grade, picture books, romance, short story collections, suspense, thriller, women's, young adult.

HOW TO CONTACT "In the body of your e-mail, please include a query letter and a short writing sample (1-2 chapters). We currently accept submissions in all genres except screenplays. Due to the volume of queries we receive, our response time may take up to 2 months. Feel free to put 'Query for [Agent Name]: [Your Book Title]' in the e-mail subject line." Accepts simultaneous submissions. Obtains most new clients through recommendations from others.

TERMS Agent receives 15% commission on domestic sales; 20% commission on foreign sales. Offers written contract.

TIPS "We will not read mss before receiving a letter of inquiry."

INTERNATIONAL TRANSACTIONS, INC.

P.O. Box 97, Gila NM 88038-0097. (845)373-9696. **Fax:** (480)393-5162. **E-mail:** submission-nonfiction@intltrans.com; submission-fiction@intltrans.com. **Website:** www.intltrans.com. **Contact:** Peter Riva.

MEMBER AGENTS Peter Riva (nonfiction, fiction, illustrated; television and movie rights placement); **Sandra Riva** (fiction, juvenile, biographies); **JoAnn Collins** (fiction, women's fiction, medical fiction).

REPRESENTS Nonfiction, fiction, short story collections, juvenile books, illustrated books, anthologies. **Considers these fiction areas:** action, adventure, commercial, crime, detective, erotica, experimental, family saga, feminist, gay, historical, humor, inspirational, lesbian, literary, mainstream, middle-grade, military, multicultural, mystery, new adult, police, satire, science fiction, spiritual, sports, suspense, thriller, translation, war, westerns, women's, young adult, chick lit.

"We specialize in large and small projects, helping qualified authors perfect material for publication." Always actively seeking intelligent, well-written, innovative material that breaks new ground. Does not want to receive material influenced by TV (too much dialogue),; a rehash of previous successful novels' themes, or poorly prepared material.

HOW TO CONTACT E-query with an outline or synopsis. E-queries only. Put "Query: [Title]" in the e-mail subject line. Responds in 3 weeks to queries; in 5 weeks to mss. Obtains most new clients through recommendations from others, solicitations.

TERMS Agent receives 15% (25% on illustrated books) commission on domestic sales. Agent receives 20% commission on foreign sales and media rights. Offers written contract; 120-day notice must be given to terminate contract. No additional fees, ever.

RECENT SALES Averages 20+ book placements per year.

JANKLOW & NESBIT ASSOCIATES

445 Park Ave., New York NY 10022. (212)421-1700. **Fax:** (212)980-3671. **E-mail:** submissions@janklow.com. **Website:** www.janklowandnesbit.com. Estab. 1989.

MEMBER AGENTS Morton L. Janklow; Anne Sibbald; Lynn Nesbit; Luke Janklow; Cullen Stanley; PJ Mark (interests are eclectic, including short stories and literary novels; his nonfiction interests include journalism, popular culture, memoir/narrative, essays, and cultural criticism); **Richard Morris** (books that challenge our common assumptions, be it in the fields of cultural history, business, food, sports, science, or faith); **Paul Lucas** (literary and commercial fiction, focusing on literary thrillers, science fiction, and fantasy; also seeks narrative histories of ideas and objects, as well as biographies and popular science); **Emma Parry** (nonfiction by experts, but will consider outstanding literary fiction and upmarket commercial fiction; not looking for children's books, middle-grade, or fantasy); **Alexandra Machinist; Kirby Kim** (formerly of WME).

REPRESENTS Nonfiction, fiction.

HOW TO CONTACT Query via snail mail or e-mail. Include a cover letter, synopsis, and the first 10 pages if sending fiction (no attachments). For nonfiction, send a query and full outline. Address your submission to an individual agent. Accepts simultaneous submissions. Responds in 8 weeks to queries/mss. Obtains most new clients through recommendations from others.

TIPS "Please send a short query with first 10 pages or artwork."

J DE S ASSOCIATES, INC.

9 Shagbark Road, Wilson Point, South Norwalk CT 06854. (203)838-7571. **E-mail:** jdespoel@aol.com. **Website:** www.jdesassociates.com. **Contact:** Jacques de Spoelberch.

Prior to opening his agency, Mr. de Spoelberch was an editor with Houghton Mifflin.

REPRESENTS Fiction. **Considers these fiction areas:** crime, detective, frontier, historical, juvenile, literary, mainstream, mystery, New Age, police, suspense, westerns, young adult.

HOW TO CONTACT "Brief queries by regular mail and e-mail are welcome for fiction and nonfiction, but kindly do not include sample proposals or other material unless specifically requested to do so." Accepts simultaneous submissions. Responds in 2 months to queries. Obtains most new clients through recommendations from authors and other clients.

TERMS Agent receives 15% commission on domestic sales; 20% commission on foreign sales. Charges clients for foreign postage and photocopying.

RECENT SALES *A Grown-Up Kind of Pretty* by Joshilyn Jackson (Grand Central), *Elizabeth I* by Margaret George (Penguin), *A Vine in the Blood* by Leighton Gage (Soho), *Under the Same Sky* by Genevieve Graham (Berkley Sensation), *The Galahad Legacy* by Dom Testa (Tor).

THE CAROLYN JENKS AGENCY

30 Cambridge Park Dr., #3150, Cambridge MA 02140. (617)354-5099. **E-mail:** queries@carolynjenksagency.com. **Website:** www.carolynjenksagency.com. **Contact:** Carolyn Jenks. Estab. 1987. Member of AAR. Signatory of WGA.

MEMBER AGENTS Carolyn Jenks, Eric Wing. See agency website for current member preferences as well as a list of junior agents.

REPRESENTS Considers these fiction areas: action, adventure, ethnic, experimental, family saga, fantasy, feminist, frontier, gay, historical, horror, humor, inspirational, juvenile, lesbian, literary, mainstream, mystery, psychic, regional, religious, science fiction, supernatural, thriller, westerns, women's, young adult.

HOW TO CONTACT Please submit a one-page query, including a brief bio, via the form on the agency website. "Due to the high volume of queries we receive, we are unable to respond to everyone. Queries are reviewed on a rolling basis, and we will follow up directly with the author if there is interest in a full ms. Queries should not be addressed to specific agents. All queries go directly to the director for distribution." Accepts simultaneous submissions. Obtains new clients by recommendations from others, queries/submissions, agency outreach.

TERMS Offers written contract, 1-3 years depending on the project. Requires 60-day notice before terminating contract.

TIPS "Do not make cold calls to the agency. E-mail contact only. Do not query for more than 1 property at a time. If possible, have a professional photograph of yourself ready to submit with your query, as it is important to be media-genic in today's marketplace. Be ready to discuss platform."

JET LITERARY ASSOCIATES

941 Calle Mejia, #507, Santa Fe NM 87501. (505)780-0721. **E-mail:** etp@jetliterary.com. **Website:** www.jetliterary.wordpress.com. **Contact:** Liz Trupin-Pulli. Estab. 1975.

MEMBER AGENTS **Liz Trupin-Pulli** (adult fiction/nonfiction, romance, mysteries, parenting); **Jim Trupin** (adult fiction/nonfiction, military history, pop culture).

REPRESENTS Nonfiction, fiction, short story collections.

"JET was founded in New York in 1975, so we bring a wealth of knowledge and contacts, as well as quite a bit of expertise, to our representation of writers." JET represents the full range of adult fiction and nonfiction, including humor and cookbooks. Does not want to receive young adult, science fiction, fantasy, horror, poetry, children's, how-to, or religious books.

HOW TO CONTACT Only an e-query should be sent at first. Accepts simultaneous submissions. Responds in 1 week to queries; in 8-12 weeks to mss. Obtains most new clients through recommendations from others, solicitations, conferences.

TERMS Agent receives 15% commission on domestic sales; 10% commission on foreign sales, while foreign agent receives 10%. Offers written agency contract, binding for 3 years. This agency charges for reimbursement of mailing and any photocopying.

TIPS "Do not write cute queries; stick to a straightforward message that includes the title and what your book is about, why you are suited to write this particular book, and what you have written in the past (if anything), along with a brief bio."

KELLER MEDIA INC.

578 Washington Blvd., No. 745, Marina del Rey CA 90292. (800)278-8706. **Website:** www.KellerMedia.com. **Contact:** Wendy Keller, senior agent (nonfiction only); Megan Close Zavala, associate agent (nonfiction and fiction); Elise Howard, query manager. Estab. 1989. Member of the National Speakers Association.

Prior to becoming an agent, Ms. Keller was an award-winning journalist and worked for PR Newswire. Prior to her agenting career, Ms. Close Zavala read, reviewed, edited, rejected, and selected thousands of book and script projects for agencies, film companies, and publishing companies. She uses her background in entertainment and legal affairs in negotiating the best deals for her clients and in helping them think outside the box.

REPRESENTS Nonfiction, fiction. **Considers these fiction areas:** action, adventure, commercial, family saga, historical, literary, multicultural, mystery, new adult, police, regional, romance, suspense, thriller, women's.

"All of our authors are highly credible experts who have or want to create a significant platform in media, academia, politics, paid professional speaking, syndicated columns, and/or regular appearances on radio/TV. For fiction submissions, we are interested in working with authors who have strong, fresh voices and who have unique stories (especially in the mystery/thriller/suspense and literary fiction genres!)." Does not want (and absolutely will not respond to) scripts, teleplays, poetry, juvenile, anything religious or overtly political, picture books, illustrated books, young adult, science fiction, fantasy, or first-person stories of mental or physical illness, wrongful incarceration, abduction by aliens, books channeled by aliens, demons, or dead celebrities ("We wish we were kidding!").

HOW TO CONTACT To query, go to www.kellermedia.com/query and fill in the simple form; it takes 1 minute or less. You'll get a fast, courteous response. "Please do not mail us anything unless requested to do so by a staff member." Accepts simultaneous submissions. Responds in 7 days or less. Obtains most new clients through referrals.

TERMS Agent receives 15% commission on domestic sales; 20% commission on foreign, dramatic, sponsorship, appearance fees, audio, and merchandising deals; 30% on speaking engagements booked for the author.

RECENT SALES "For our latest sales, please go to www.kellermedia.com/sold-list."

TIPS "If you are submitting fiction to us, please make sure that the story hasn't been told 1,000 times over and that your unique voice shines through!"

VIRGINIA KIDDLITERARY AGENCY, INC.

P.O. Box 278, Milford PA 18337. (570)296-6205. **Fax:** (570)296-7266. **E-mail:** subs@vk-agency.com. **Website:** www.vk-agency.com. Member of include SFWA, SFRA. Represents 80 clients.

REPRESENTS Fiction. **Considers these fiction areas:** fantasy, science fiction, speculative.

This agency specializes in science fiction and fantasy. "The Virginia Kidd Literary Agency is one of the longest-established, science fiction-specialized literary agencies in the world—with almost half a century of rich experience in the science fiction and fantasy genres. Our client list reads like a top notch 'who's-who' of science fiction: Beth Bernobich, Gene Wolfe, Anne McCaffrey, Ted Chiang, Alan Dean Foster, and others set the bar very high indeed. Our authors have won the following awards and honors: Hugo, Nebula, World Fantasy, Tiptree, National Book Award, PEN Malamud, SFWA Grandmaster, Gandalf, Locus Award, Margaret Edwards Award, IAMTW Lifetime

Achievement Award (Grand Master), Rhysling Award, Author Emeritus SFWA, BSFA Award—and more. The point is, we represent the best of the best.We welcome queries from prospective and published authors."

HOW TO CONTACT Snail mail queries only. Accepts simultaneous submissions.

TERMS Agent receives 15% commission on domestic sales; 20-25% commission on foreign sales; 20% commission on film sales. Offers written contract; two-month notice must be given to terminate contract. Charges clients occasionally for extraordinary expenses.

RECENT SALES *Sagramanda* by Alan Dean Foster (Pyr), *Incredible Good Fortune* by Ursula K. Le Guin (Shambhala), *The Wizard and Soldier of Sidon* by Gene Wolfe (Tor), *Voices and Powers* by Ursula K. Le Guin (Harcourt), *Galileo's Children* by Gardner Dozois (Pyr), *The Light Years Beneath My Feet* and *Running from the Deity* by Alan Dean Foster (Del Ray), *Chasing Fire* by Michelle Welch. Other clients include Eleanor Arnason, Ted Chiang, Jack Skillingstead, Daryl Gregory, Patricia Briggs, and the estates for James Tiptree, Jr., Murray Leinster, E.E. "Doc" Smith, R.A. Lafferty.

TIPS "If you have a completed novel that is of extraordinary quality, please send us a query."

HARVEY KLINGER, INC.

300 W. 55th St., Ste. 11V, New York NY 10019. (212)581-7068. **E-mail:** queries@harveyklinger.com. **Website:** www.harveyklinger.com. **Contact:** Harvey Klinger. Member of AAR. Represents 100 clients.

MEMBER AGENTS **Harvey Klinger**; **David Dunton** (popular culture, music-related books, literary fiction, young adult, fiction, memoirs); **Sara Crowe** (children's and young adult authors, adult fiction and nonfiction, foreign rights sales); **Andrea Somberg** (literary fiction, commercial fiction, romance, science fiction/fantasy, mysteries/thrillers, young adult, middle-grade, quality narrative nonfiction, popular culture, how-to, self-help, humor, interior design, cookbooks, health/fitness); **Wendy Levinson** (literary and commercial fiction, occasional children's young adult or middle-grade, wide variety of nonfiction).

REPRESENTS Nonfiction, fiction, juvenile books. **Considers these fiction areas:** action, adventure, commercial, crime, detective, erotica, family saga, fantasy, gay, glitz, historical, horror, juvenile, lesbian, literary, mainstream, middle-grade, mystery, police, suspense, thriller, women's, young adult.

This agency specializes in big, mainstream, contemporary fiction and nonfiction.

HOW TO CONTACT Use online e-mail submission form on the website, or query with SASE via snail mail. No phone or fax queries. Don't send unsolicited mss or e-mail attachments. Make submission letter to the point and as brief as possible. Accepts simultaneous submissions. Responds in 2-4 weeks to queries, if interested. Obtains most new clients through recommendations from others.

TERMS Agent receives 15% commission on domestic sales; 25% commission on foreign sales. Offers written contract. Charges for photocopying mss and overseas postage for mss.

RECENT SALES *Land of the Afternoon Sun* by Barbara Wood; *I Am Not a Serial Killer* by Dan Wells; *Me, Myself and Us* by Brian Little; *The Secret of Magic* by Deborah Johnson; *Children of the Mist* by Paula Quinn. Other clients include George Taber, Terry Kay, Scott Mebus, Jacqueline Kolosov, Jonathan Maberry, Tara Altebrando, Alex McAuley, Eva Nagorski, Greg Kot, Justine Musk, Michael Northrup, Nina LaCour, Ashley Kahn, Barbara De Angelis, Robert Patton.

KNEERIM & WILLIAMS

90 Canal St., Boston MA 02114. **Website:** www.kwblit.com. Also located in New York and Washington D.C. Estab. 1990.

Prior to becoming an agent, Mr. Williams was a lawyer. Ms. Kneerim was a publisher and editor. Mr. Wasserman was an editor and journalist. Ms. Bloom worked in magazines. Ms. Flynn worked in academia.

MEMBER AGENTS **Katherine Flynn**, flynn@kwblit.com (nonfiction: history, biography, politics, current affairs, adventure, nature, pop culture, science, psychology; particularly loves exciting narrative nonfiction; crime novels; literary and commercial fiction with urban or foreign locales, insight into women's lives, biting wit, and historical settings); **Jill Kneerim**, jill@kwblit.com (narrative history, sociology, psychology and anthropology, biography, women's issues, good writing); **Ike Williams**, jtwilliams@kwblit.com (biography, history, politics, natural science, anthropology); **Carol Franco**, carolfranco@comcast.net (business, nonfiction, distinguished self-help/how-to); **Gerald Gross**, ggreens336@comcast.net (array of nonfiction, serious history, memoir).

- Actively seeking distinguished authors, experts, professionals, intellectuals, and serious writers.

HOW TO CONTACT E-query an individual agent. Send no attachments. Put "Query" in the subject line. Accepts simultaneous submissions. Obtains most new clients through recommendations from others.

STUART KRICHEVSKY LITERARY AGENCY, INC.

6 E. 39th Street, Ste. 500, New York NY 10016. (212)725-5288. **Fax:** (212)725-5275. **Website:** www.skagency.com. Member of AAR.

MEMBER AGENTS **Stuart Krichevsky**, query@skagency.com (emphasis on narrative nonfiction, literary journalism and literary and commercial fiction); **Allison Hunter**, ahquery@skagency.com (literary and commercial fiction, memoir, narrative nonfiction, cultural studies and pop culture; always looking for funny female writers, great love stories, family epics, and nonfiction projects that speak to the current cultural climate); **Ross Harris**, rhquery@skagency.com (voice-driven humor and memoir, books on popular culture and our society, narrative nonfiction and literary fiction); **David Patterson**, dp@skagency.com (writers of upmarket narrative nonfiction and literary fiction, historians, journalists and thought leaders).

REPRESENTS Nonfiction, fiction. **Considers these fiction areas:** commercial, contemporary issues, literary.

HOW TO CONTACT Please send a query letter and up to 10 pages of your ms or proposal in the body of an e-mail (not an attachment) to 1 of the e-mail addresses. No attachments. Responds if interested. Accepts simultaneous submissions. Obtains most new clients through recommendations from others, solicitations.

THE LA LITERARY AGENCY

P.O. Box 46370, Los Angeles CA 90046. (323)654-5288. **E-mail:** ann@laliteraryagency.com; mail@laliteraryagency.com. **E-mail:** ann@laliteraryagency.com; mail@laliteraryagency.com. **Website:** www.laliteraryagency.com. **Contact:** Ann Cashman.

- Prior to becoming an agent, Eric Lasher worked in broadcasting and publishing in New York and Los Angeles. Prior to opening the agency, Maureen Lasher worked in New York at Prentice-Hall, Liveright, and Random House. Please visit the agency website for more information.

MEMBER AGENTS Ann Cashman, Eric Lasher, Maureen Lasher.

REPRESENTS Nonfiction, fiction. **Considers these fiction areas:** action, adventure, commercial, contemporary issues, crime, detective, family saga, feminist, historical, literary, mainstream, mystery, suspense, thriller, women's.

HOW TO CONTACT For nonfiction, send query letter and book proposal. For fiction, send query letter and full ms as an attachment. Accepts simultaneous submissions.

PETER LAMPACK AGENCY, INC.

The Empire State Building, 350 Fifth Ave., Ste. 5300, New York NY 10118. (212)687-9106. **Fax:** (212)687-9109. **E-mail:** andrew@peterlampackagency.com. **Website:** www.peterlampackagency.com. **Contact:** Andrew Lampack.

REPRESENTS Nonfiction, fiction. **Considers these fiction areas:** action, adventure, commercial, crime, detective, family saga, literary, mainstream, mystery, police, suspense, thriller.

- "This agency specializes in commercial fiction, and nonfiction by recognized experts." Actively seeking literary and commercial fiction in the following categories: adventure, action, thrillers, mysteries, suspense, and psychological thrillers. Does not want to receive horror, romance, science fiction, westerns, historical literary fiction, or academic material.

HOW TO CONTACT The Peter Lampack Agency no longer accepts material through conventional mail. E-queries only. When submitting, you should include a cover letter, author biography, and a one- or two-page synopsis. Please do not send more than one sample chapter of your ms at a time. "Due to the extremely high volume of submissions, we ask that you allow 4-6 weeks for a response." Accepts simultaneous submissions. Obtains most new clients through referrals made by clients.

TERMS Agent receives 15% commission on domestic sales; 20% commission on foreign sales.

RECENT SALES *The Assassin* by Clive Cussler and Justin Scott, *The Solomon Curse* by Clive Cussler and Russell Blake, *Patriot* by Ted Bell, *The Good Story* by J.M. Coetzee and Arabella Kurtz.

WRITERS CONFERENCES BookExpo America, Mystery Writers of America.

TIPS "Submit only your best work for consideration. Have a very specific agenda of goals you wish your prospective agent to accomplish for you. Provide the agent with a comprehensive statement of your credentials—educational and professional accomplishments."

LAURA LANGLIE, LITERARY AGENT

147-149 Green St., Hudson NY 12534. (518)828-4708. **Fax:** (518)828-4787. **E-mail:** laura@lauralanglie.com. **Contact:** Laura Langlie. Represents 25 clients.

Prior to opening her agency, Ms. Langlie worked in publishing for 7 years and as an agent at Kidde, Hoyt & Picard for 6 years.

REPRESENTS Considers these fiction areas: commercial, crime, detective, ethnic, feminist, gay, historical, humor, juvenile, lesbian, literary, mainstream, multicultural, mystery, police, romance, suspense, thriller, young adult, mainstream.

"I'm very involved with and committed to my clients. Most of my clients come to me via recommendations from other agents, clients, and editors. I've met very few at conferences. I've often sought out writers for projects, and I still find new clients via the traditional query letter." Does not want to receive how-to, children's picture books, hardcore science fiction, poetry, men's adventure, or erotica.

HOW TO CONTACT Query with SASE. Accepts queries via fax. Accepts simultaneous submissions. Responds in 1 week to queries; in 1 month to mss. Obtains most new clients through recommendations, submissions.

TERMS Agent receives 15% commission on domestic sales; 20% commission on foreign and dramatic sales. No written contract.

RECENT SALES *The Evening Spider* by Emily Arsenault (William Morrow), *The Swans of 5th Avenue* by Melanie Benjamin (Delacorte Press). Sold 15 titles in the last year.

TIPS "Be complete, forthright, and clear in your communications. Do your research as to what a particular agent represents."

THE STEVE LAUBE AGENCY

24 W. Camelback Road, A-635, Phoenix AZ 85013. (602)336-8910. **Website:** www.stevelaube.com. Member of CBA, RWA, Author's Guild. Represents 250+ clients.

Prior to becoming an agent, Mr. Laube worked over a decade as a Christian bookseller (named bookstore of the year in 1989) and 11 years as editorial director of nonfiction with Bethany House Publishers (named editor of the year by AWSA). Mrs. Murray was an accomplished novelist and agent for 15 years. Mrs. Ball was an executive editor with Tyndale, Multnomah, Zondervan, and B&H Publishing. Mr. Balow was marketing director for the Left Behind series at Tyndale.

MEMBER AGENTS Steve Laube (president), Tamela Hancock Murray, Karen Ball, Dan Balow.

REPRESENTS Nonfiction, fiction. **Considers these fiction areas:** fantasy, inspirational, religious, science fiction.

Primarily serves the Christian market (CBA). Actively seeking Christian fiction and Christian nonfiction. Does not want to receive children's picture books, poetry, or cookbooks.

HOW TO CONTACT Submit proposal package, outline, 3 sample chapters, SASE. For e-mail submissions, attach as Word doc or PDF. Consult website for guidelines, because queries are sent to assistants, and the assistants' e-mail addresses may change. Accepts simultaneous submissions. Responds in 6-8 weeks to queries. Obtains most new clients through recommendations from others, solicitations, conferences.

TERMS Agent receives 15% commission on domestic sales; 20% commission on foreign sales. Offers written contract; 30-day notice must be given to terminate contract.

RECENT SALES Closes on a new book deal an average of every 2 business days, often for multiple titles in a contract. Clients include Cindy Woodsmall, Susan May Warren, Lisa Bergren, Lynette Eason, Deborah Raney, Allison Bottke, H. Norman Wright, Ellie Kay, Karol Ladd, Stephen M. Miller, Judith Pella, Nancy Pearcey, William Lane Craig, Elizabeth Goddard, Pamela Tracy, Kim Vogel Sawyer, Mesu Andrews, Mary Hunt, Hugh Ross, Roseanna White, Bill and Pam Farrel, Ronie Kendig.

WRITERS CONFERENCES Mount Hermon Christian Writers Conference, American Christian Fiction Writers Conference.

LAUNCHBOOKS LITERARY AGENCY

E-mail: david@launchbooks.com. **Website:** www.launchbooks.com. **Contact:** David Fugate. Represents 45 clients.

David Fugate has been an agent for more than 20 years and has successfully represented more than 1,000 book titles. He left another agency to found LaunchBooks in 2005.

REPRESENTS Nonfiction, fiction. **Considers these fiction areas:** action, adventure, crime, fantasy, horror, mainstream, military, satire, science fiction, suspense, thriller, urban fantasy, war, westerns, young adult.

"We're looking for genre-breaking fiction. Do you have the next *The Martian*? Or maybe the next *Red Rising, Ready Player One, Ancillary Sword*, or *The Bone Clocks*? We're on the lookout for fun, engaging, contemporary novels that appeal to a broad audience. In nonfiction, we're interested in a broad range of topics. Check www.launchbooks.com/submissions for a complete list."

HOW TO CONTACT Query via e-mail. Accepts simultaneous submissions. Responds in 1 week to queries; in 4 weeks to mss. Obtains most new clients through recommendations from others, solicitations.

TERMS Agent receives 15% commission on domestic sales; 25% commission on foreign sales. Offers written contract; 30-day notice to terminate contract. This agency's agreement limits any charges to $50 unless the author gives a written consent.

RECENT SALES *The Martian* by Andy Weir (Random House); *The Remaining: Allegiance* by DJ Molles (Orbit); *The Fold* by Peter Clines (Crown); *Faster, Higher, Stronger* by Mark McClusky (Hudson Street Press); *Fluent in Three Months* by Benny Lewis (HarperOne); *The Science of People* by Vanessa Van Edwards (Portfolio); *Born for This* by Chris Guillebeau (Crown); *The Art of Invisibility* by Kevin Mitnick (Little, Brown); *Hell Divers* by Nicholas Smith (Blackstone); *A History of the United States in Five Crashes* by Scott Nations (William Morrow); *Level Up Your Life* by Steve Kamb (Rodale).

LEVINE GREENBERG ROSTAN LITERARY AGENCY, INC.

307 Seventh Ave., Ste. 2407, New York NY 10001. (212)337-0934. **Fax:** (212)337-0948. **E-mail:** submit@lgrliterary.com. **Website:** www.lgrliterary.com. Member of AAR. Represents 250 clients.

Prior to opening his agency, Mr. Levine served as vice president of the Bank Street College of Education.

MEMBER AGENTS **Jim Levine** (nonfiction: business, science, narrative nonfiction, social and political issues, psychology, health, spirituality, parenting); **Stephanie Rostan** (adult and young adult fiction; nonfiction: parenting, health and wellness, sports, memoir); **Melissa Rowland**; **Daniel Greenberg** (nonfiction: popular culture, narrative nonfiction, memoir, and humor; literary fiction); **Victoria Skurnick**; **Danielle Svetcov** (nonfiction); **Lindsay Edgecombe** (narrative nonfiction, memoir, lifestyle and health, illustrated books, literary fiction); **Monika Verma** (nonfiction: humor, pop culture, memoir, narrative nonfiction, style and fashion; some young adult fiction: paranormal, historical, contemporary); **Kerry Sparks** (young adult and middle-grade; select adult fiction and occasional nonfiction); **Tim Wojcik** (nonfiction: food narratives, humor, pop culture, popular history, science; literary fiction); **Arielle Eckstut** (no queries).

REPRESENTS Nonfiction, fiction. **Considers these fiction areas:** literary, mainstream, middle-grade, young adult.

HOW TO CONTACT E-query to submit@lgrliterary.com or via online submission form. "If you would like to direct your query to a specific agent, please feel free to include the agent's name in the online form or in the e-mail you send." Cannot respond to submissions by mail. Do not attach more than 50 pages. "Due to the volume of submissions we receive, we are unable to respond to each individually. If we would like more information about your project, we'll contact you within 3 weeks (though we do get backed up on occasion!)." Accepts simultaneous submissions. Obtains most new clients through recommendations from others.

TERMS Agent receives 15% commission on domestic sales; 20% commission on foreign sales. Offers written contract. Charges clients for out-of-pocket expenses—telephone, fax, postage, photocopying—directly connected to the project.

RECENT SALES *Notorious RBG* by Irin Carmon and Shana Knizhnik, *Pogue's Basics: Life* by David

Pogue, *Invisible City* by Julia Dahl, *Gumption* by Nick Offerman, *All the Bright Places* by Jennifer Niven.

WRITERS CONFERENCES ASJA Writers Conference.

TIPS "We focus on editorial development, business representation, and publicity and marketing strategy."

LIPPINCOTT MASSIE MCQUILKIN

27 W. 20th Street, Ste. 305, New York NY 10011. **E-mail:** info@lmqlit.com. **Website:** www.lmqlit.com.

MEMBER AGENTS **Laney Katz Becker**, laney@lmqlit.com (book club fiction, upmarket women's fiction, suspense, thrillers, memoir); **Ethan Bassoff**, ethan@lmqlit.com (literary fiction; crime fiction; narrative nonfiction in the areas of history, sports writing, journalism, science writing, pop culture, humor, and food writing); **Jason Anthony**, jason@lmqlit.com (commercial fiction of all types, including young adult, and nonfiction in the areas of memoir, pop culture, true crime, and general psychology and sociology); **Will Lippincott**, will@lmqlit.com (narrative nonfiction and nonfiction in the areas of politics, history, biography, foreign affairs, and health); **Rob McQuilkin**, rob@lmqlit.com (literary fiction; narrative nonfiction and nonfiction in the areas of memoir, history, biography, art history, cultural criticism, and popular sociology and psychology); **Rayhane Sanders**, rayhane@lmqlit.com (literary fiction, historical fiction, upmarket commercial fiction [including select young adult], narrative nonfiction [including essays], and select memoir); **Stephanie Abou** (literary and upmarket commercial fiction (including select young adult and middle-grade), crime fiction, memoir, and narrative nonfiction).

REPRESENTS Nonfiction, fiction. **Considers these fiction areas:** commercial, crime, literary, mainstream, middle-grade, suspense, thriller, women's.

"Lippincott Massie McQuilkin is a full-service literary agency that focuses on bringing fiction and nonfiction of quality to the largest possible audience."

HOW TO CONTACT E-query preferred. Include the word "Query" in the subject line of your e-mail. Review the agency's online page of agent bios (lmqlit.com/contact.html), as some agents want sample pages with their submissions and some do not. If you have not heard back from the agency in 4 weeks, assume they are not interested in seeing more. Accepts simultaneous submissions. Obtains most new clients through recommendations from others, solicitations, conferences.

TERMS Agent receives 15% commission on domestic sales; 20% commission on foreign sales. Offers written contract; 30-day notice must be given to terminate contract. Only charges for reasonable business expenses upon successful sale.

RECENT SALES Clients include Peter Ho Davies, Kim Addonizio, Natasha Trethewey, David Sirota, Katie Crouch, Uwen Akpan, Lydia Millet, Tom Perrotta, Jonathan Lopez, Chris Hayes, Caroline Weber.

LIVING WORD LITERARY AGENCY

P.O. Box 40974, Eugene OR 97414. **E-mail:** livingwordliterary@gmail.com. **Website:** livingwordliterary.wordpress.com. **Contact:** Kimberly Shumate, agent. Estab. 2009. Member of AAR. Signatory of WGA. Member Evangelical Christian Publishers Association

Kimberly began her employment with Harvest House Publishers as the assistant to the national sales manager and the international sales director, and continued into the editorial department.

REPRESENTS **Considers these fiction areas:** inspirational, adult fiction, Christian living.

Does not want to receive young adult fiction, cookbooks, children's books, science fiction or fantasy, memoirs, screenplays, or poetry.

HOW TO CONTACT Submit a query with short synopsis and first chapter via Word document. Agency only responds if interested.

STERLING LORD LITERISTIC, INC.

65 Bleecker St., New York NY 10012. **Fax:** (212)780-6095. **E-mail:** info@sll.com. **Website:** www.sll.com. Estab. 1987. Member of AAR. Signatory of WGA.

MEMBER AGENTS **Philippa Brophy** (represents journalists, nonfiction writers and novelists, and is most interested in current events, memoir, science, politics, biography, and women's issues); **Laurie Liss** (represents authors of commercial and literary fiction and nonfiction whose perspectives are well developed and unique); **Sterling Lord**; **Peter Matson** (abiding interest in storytelling, whether in the service of history, fiction, or the sciences); **Douglas Stewart** (primarily fiction for all ages, from the innovatively literary to the unabashedly commercial); **Neeti Madan** (memoir, journalism, popular culture, lifestyle, women's issues, multicultural books, and virtually any intelligent writing on intriguing topics); **Robert Guinsler** (literary and commercial fiction [including young adult], journalism, narrative nonfiction with an emphasis on pop culture, science and current events, memoirs, and biographies); **Jim Rutman; Celeste Fine** (expert, celebrity, and corporate clients with strong national and international platforms, particularly in the health, science, self-help, food, business, and lifestyle fields); **Erica Rand Silverman** (children's: picture books through young adult novels, both fiction and nonfiction; adult: nonfiction, predominantly in the areas of parenting and humor); **Martha Millard** (fiction and nonfiction, including well-written science fiction and young adult); **Mary Krienke** (literary fiction, memoir, and narrative nonfiction, including psychology, popular science, and cultural commentary); **Jenny Stephens** (nonfiction: cookbooks, practical lifestyle projects, transportive travel and nature writing, and creative nonfiction; fiction: contemporary literary narratives strongly rooted in place); **Alison MacKeen** (idea-driven research books: social scientific, scientific, historical, relationships/parenting, learning and education, sexuality, technology, the life-cycle, health, the environment, politics, economics, psychology, geography, and culture; literary fiction and nonfiction; memoirs; essays; travel writing); **John Maas** (serious nonfiction: business, personal development, science, self-help, health, fitness, lifestyle); **Sarah Passick** (commercial nonfiction: celebrity, food, blogger, lifestyle, health, diet, fitness, fashion).

REPRESENTS Nonfiction, fiction. **Considers these fiction areas:** commercial, juvenile, literary, middle-grade, picture books, science fiction, young adult.

HOW TO CONTACT Query via snail mail. "Please submit a query letter, a synopsis of the work, a brief proposal or the first 3 chapters of the ms, a brief bio or résumé, and an SASE for reply. Original artwork is not accepted. Enclose sufficient postage if you wish to have your materials returned to you. We do not respond to unsolicited e-mail inquiries." Accepts simultaneous submissions.

TERMS Agent receives 15% commission on domestic sales; 20% commission on foreign sales. Offers written contract.

LOWENSTEIN ASSOCIATES INC.

115 E. 23rd St., Floor 4, New York NY 10010. (212)206-1630. **Fax:** (212)727-0280. **E-mail:** assistant@bookhaven.com. **Website:** www.lowensteinassociates.com. **Contact:** Barbara Lowenstein. Member of AAR.

MEMBER AGENTS Barbara Lowenstein, president (nonfiction interests include narrative nonfiction, health, money, finance, travel, multicultural, popular culture, and memoir; fiction interests include literary fiction and women's fiction); **Mary South** (literary fiction and nonfiction on subjects such as neuroscience, bioengineering, women's rights, design, and digital humanities, as well as investigative journalism, essays, and memoir).

REPRESENTS Nonfiction, fiction. **Considers these fiction areas:** commercial, fantasy, literary, middle-grade, science fiction, women's, young adult.

Barbara Lowenstein is currently looking for writers who have a platform and are leading experts in their field, including business, women's issues, psychology, health, science and social issues. She is particularly interested in strong new voices in fiction and narrative nonfiction. Does not want westerns, textbooks, children's picture books, and books in need of translation.

HOW TO CONTACT "For fiction, please send us a one-page query letter, along with the first 10 pages pasted in the body of the e-mail, to assistant@bookhaven.com. If nonfiction, please send a one-page query letter, a table of contents, and, if available, a proposal pasted into the body of the e-mail. Please put the word 'QUERY' and the title of your project in the subject field of your e-mail, and address it to the agent of your choice. Please do not send an attachment as the message will be deleted without being read and no reply will be sent." Accepts simultaneous submissions. Responds in 6 weeks to queries. Obtains most new clients through recommendations from others, solicitations, conferences.

TERMS Agent receives 15% commission on domestic sales; 20% commission on foreign sales. Offers written contract. Charges for large photocopy batches, messenger service, international postage.

TIPS "Know the genre you are working in, and read!"

GINA MACCOBY LITERARY AGENCY

P.O. Box 60, Chappaqua NY 10514. (914)238-5630. **E-mail:** query@maccobylit.com. **Website:** www.publishersmarketplace.com/members/ginamaccoby. **Contact:** Gina Maccoby. Member of AAR, AAR Board of Directors, Royalties and Ethics and Contracts subcommittees, Authors Guild. Represents 25 clients.

MEMBER AGENTS Gina Maccoby.

REPRESENTS Fiction. **Considers these fiction areas:** juvenile, literary, mainstream, mystery, thriller, young adult.

HOW TO CONTACT Query by e-mail only. Accepts simultaneous submissions. Owing to volume of submissions, may not respond to queries unless interested. Obtains most new clients through recommendations from clients and publishers.

TERMS Agent receives 15% commission on domestic sales; 20-25% commission on foreign sales, which includes subagent commissions. May recover certain costs, such as legal fees or the cost of shipping books by air to Europe or Japan.

CAROL MANN AGENCY

55 Fifth Ave., New York NY 10003. (212)206-5635. **Fax:** (212)675-4809. **E-mail:** submissions@carolmannagency.com. **Website:** www.carolmannagency.com. **Contact:** Isabella Ruggiero. Member of AAR. Represents roughly 200 clients.

MEMBER AGENTS **Carol Mann** (health/medical, religion, spirituality, self-help, parenting, narrative nonfiction, current affairs); **Laura Yorke**; **Gareth Esersky**; **Myrsini Stephanides** (nonfiction: pop culture, music, humor, narrative nonfiction, memoir, cookbooks; fiction: offbeat literary fiction, graphic works, edgy young adult fiction); **Joanne Wyckoff** (nonfiction: memoir, narrative nonfiction, personal narrative, psychology, women's issues, education, health and wellness, parenting, serious self-help, natural history; also accepts fiction); **Lydia Shamah** (edgy, modern fiction and timely nonfiction: business, self-improvement, relationship and gift books; particularly interested in female voices and experiences).

REPRESENTS Nonfiction, fiction. **Considers these fiction areas:** commercial, literary, young adult, graphic works.

⊶ Does not want to receive genre fiction (romance, mystery, etc.).

HOW TO CONTACT Please see website for submission guidelines. Accepts simultaneous submissions. Responds in 4 weeks to queries.

TERMS Agent receives 15% commission on domestic sales; 20% commission on foreign sales. Offers written contract.

MARSAL LYON LITERARY AGENCY, LLC

PMB 121, 665 San Rodolfo Dr., 124, Solana Beach CA 92075. **Website:** www.marsallyonliteraryagency.com. **Contact:** Kevan Lyon, Jill Marsal. Member of AAR. Signatory of WGA.

MEMBER AGENTS **Kevan Lyon** (women's fiction with an emphasis on commercial women's fiction, young adult fiction, all genres of romance); **Jill Marsal** (fiction: all types of women's fiction, all types of romance, mysteries, cozies, suspense, thrillers; nonfiction: current events, business, health, self-help, relationships, psychology, parenting, history, science, narrative nonfiction); **Patricia Nelson** (literary and commercial fiction, all types of women's fiction, contemporary and historical romance, young adult, middle-grade, LGBTQ fiction for both young adult and adult); **Deborah Ritchkin** (lifestyle books: food, design, entertaining; pop culture; women's issues; biography; current events; her niche interest is projects about France, including fiction); **Shannon Hassan** (literary and commercial fiction, young adult and middle-grade fiction, select nonfiction).

REPRESENTS Nonfiction, fiction, juvenile books. **Considers these fiction areas:** commercial, juvenile, literary, mainstream, middle-grade, multicultural, mystery, paranormal, romance, suspense, thriller, women's, young adult.

HOW TO CONTACT Query by e-mail. Query only 1 agent at this agency at a time. "Please visit our website to determine who is best suited for your work. Write 'query' in the subject line of your e-mail. Please allow up to several weeks for a reply." Accepts simultaneous submissions.

TIPS "Our agency's mission is to help writers achieve their publishing dreams. We want to work with authors not just for a book but for a career; we are dedicated to building long-term relationships with our authors and publishing partners. Our goal is to help find homes for books that engage, entertain, and make a difference."

THE EVAN MARSHALL AGENCY

Indie Rights Agency, 1 Pacio Court, Roseland NJ 07068-1121 United States. (973)287-6216. **Fax:** (973)488-7910. **E-mail:** evan@evanmarshallagency.com. **E-mail:** evan@evanmarshallagency.com. **Website:** www.evanmarshallagency.com. **Contact:** Evan Marshall. Estab. 1987. Member of AAR; Novelists, Inc. Represents 50+ clients.

Prior to becoming an agent, Evan Marshall held senior editorial positions at Houghton Mifflin, Ariel Books, New American Library, Everest House and Dodd, Mead, where he acquired national and international bestsellers.

MEMBER AGENTS Evan Marshall.

REPRESENTS Fiction. **Considers these fiction areas:** action, adventure, crime, detective, erotica, ethnic, family saga, fantasy, feminist, frontier, gay, glitz, historical, horror, humor, inspirational, lesbian, literary, mainstream, military, multicultural, multimedia, mystery, new adult, New Age, occult, paranormal, police, psychic, regional, religious, satire, science fiction, spiritual, sports, supernatural, suspense, thriller, translation, urban fantasy, war, westerns, women's, young adult, romance (contemporary, gothic, historical, regency).

"We represent all genres of high-quality adult and young-adult full-length fiction."

HOW TO CONTACT Actively seeking new clients. E-mail query letter, synopsis, and first 3 chapters of novel in body of e-mail. Accepts simultaneous submissions. Responds in 1 week to queries; in 1 month to mss. Obtains most clients through queries, recommendations from editors and current clients.

TERMS Agent receives 15% commission on domestic sales; 20% commission on foreign sales. Offers written contract.

RECENT SALES *The Language of Sisters* by Cathy Lamb (Kensington), *A Husband for Mari* by Emma Miller (Love Inspired), *A Taste of Fire* by Hannah Howell (Kensington), *See You at Sunset* by V.K. Sykes (Grand Central Forever), *Murder Has Nine Lives* by Laura Levine (Kensington), *Fortune's Secret Husband* by Karen Rose Smith (Harlequin).

THE MARTELL AGENCY

1350 Avenue of the Americas, Ste. 1205, New York NY 10019. **Fax:** (212)317-2676. **E-mail:** submissions@themartellagency.com. **Website:** www.themartellagency.com. **Contact:** Alice Martell.

REPRESENTS Nonfiction, fiction.

Seeks the following subjects in fiction: literary and commercial, including mystery, suspense and thrillers. Does not want to receive romance, genre mysteries, genre historical fiction, or children's books.

HOW TO CONTACT E-query Alice Martell. This should include a summary of the project and a short biography and any information, if appropriate, as to why you are qualified to write on the subject of your book, including any publishing credits. Send to submissions@themartellagency.com. Accepts simultaneous submissions.

RECENT SALES *New York Times* bestseller *Defending Jacob* by William Landay, Pulitzer Finalist *The Forest Unseen: A Year's Watch in Nature* by David Haskell, *How Paris Became Paris: The Birth of the Modern City* by Joan Dejean, National Book Award Winner *Waiting for Snow in Havana* by Carlos Eire, National Book Award Finalist *The Boy Kings of Texas* by Domingo Martinez.

MARGRET MCBRIDE LITERARY AGENCY

P.O. Box 9128, La Jolla CA 92038. (858)454-1550. **Fax:** (858)454-2156. **E-mail:** staff@mcbridelit.com. **Website:** www.mcbrideliterary.com. **Contact:** Michael Daley, submissions manager. Member of AAR, Authors Guild.

Prior to opening her agency, Ms. McBride worked at Random House, Ballantine Books, and Warner Books.

MEMBER AGENTS Margret McBride, Faye Atchinson.

REPRESENTS Nonfiction, fiction. **Considers these fiction areas:** action, adventure, crime, detective, historical, humor, literary, mainstream, mystery, police, satire, suspense, thriller.

This agency specializes in mainstream fiction and nonfiction. Actively seeking commercial fiction and nonfiction, business, health, self-help. Please do not send screenplays, romance, poetry, or children's.

HOW TO CONTACT Submit a query letter via e-mail (staff@mcbridelit.com). In your letter, provide a brief synopsis of your work as well as any pertinent information about yourself. There are detailed nonfiction proposal guidelines online. Accepts simultaneous submissions. Responds in 8 weeks to queries; in 6-8 weeks to mss.

TERMS Agent receives 15% commission on domestic sales; 25% commission on foreign sales. Charges for overnight delivery and photocopying.

THE MCCARTHY AGENCY, LLC

456 Ninth St., #28, Hoboken NJ 07030. **E-mail:** McCarthylit@aol.com. **Contact:** Shawna McCarthy. Member of AAR.

MEMBER AGENTS Shawna McCarthy.

REPRESENTS Fiction. **Considers these fiction areas:** fantasy, middle-grade, mystery, new adult, science fiction, women's, young adult.

- This agency represents mostly novels. No picture books.

HOW TO CONTACT E-queries only. Accepts simultaneous submissions.

MCCORMICK LITERARY

37 W. 20th St., New York NY 10011. (212)691-9726. **Website:** mccormicklit.com. Member of AAR. Signatory of WGA.

MEMBER AGENTS **David McCormick**; **Pilar Queen** (narrative nonfiction, practical nonfiction, commercial women's fiction); **Bridget McCarthy** (literary and commercial fiction, narrative nonfiction, memoir, cookbooks); **Alia Hanna Habib** (literary fiction, narrative nonfiction, memoir, cookbooks); **Edward Orloff** (literary fiction and narrative nonfiction, especially cultural history, politics, biography, and the arts); **Daniel Menaker**.

HOW TO CONTACT Snail mail queries only. Send an SASE. Accepts simultaneous submissions.

MCINTOSH & OTIS, INC.

353 Lexington Ave., New York NY 10016. (212)687-7400. **Fax:** (212)687-6894. **E-mail:** info@mcintoshandotis.com. **Website:** www.mcintoshandotis.com. **Contact:** Eugene H. Winick, Esq. Estab. 1927. Member of AAR, SCBWI. Signatory of WGA.

MEMBER AGENTS **Elizabeth Winick Rubinstein**, ewrquery@mcintoshandotis.com (literary fiction, women's fiction, historical fiction, mystery/suspense, narrative nonfiction, spiritual/self-help, history, current affairs); **Shira Hoffman**, shquery@mcintoshandotis.com (young adult, middle-grade, mainstream commercial fiction, mystery, literary fiction, women's fiction, romance, urban fantasy, fantasy, science fiction, horror, dystopian); **Christa Heschke**, chquery@mcintoshandotis.com (picture books, middle-grade, young adult, new adult); **Adam Muhlig**, amquery@mcintoshandotis.com (music [from jazz to classical to punk], popular culture, natural history, travel and adventure, sports); **Eugene Winick**; **Shannon Powers**, spquery@mcintoshandotis.com (literary fiction, mystery, horror, popular history, romance, young adult and middle-grade [mysteries and thrillers with high emotional stakes], projects with romantic elements, horror, light science fiction or fantasy, contemporary with a unique premise); **Amelia Appel**, aaquery@mcintoshandotis.com (literary fiction, mystery, thriller, historical fiction, science fiction and fantasy, horror, some young adult).

REPRESENTS **Considers these fiction areas:** fantasy, historical, horror, literary, middle-grade, mystery, new adult, paranormal, picture books, romance, science fiction, suspense, urban fantasy, women's, young adult.

- Actively seeking "books with memorable characters, distinctive voices, and great plots."

HOW TO CONTACT E-mail submissions only. Each agent has a specific e-mail address for submissions. For fiction: Please send a query letter, synopsis, author bio, and the first 3 consecutive chapters (no more than 30 pages) of your novel. For nonfiction: Please send a query letter, proposal, outline, author bio, and 3 sample chapters (no more than 30 pages) of the ms. For children's and young adult: Please send a query letter, synopsis, and the first 3 consecutive chapters (not to exceed 25 pages) of the ms. Accepts simultaneous submissions. Obtains clients through recommendations from others, editors, conferences, queries.

TERMS Agent receives 15% commission on domestic sales; 20% on foreign sales.

WRITERS CONFERENCES Bologna Book Fair, SCBWI New York. Regularly attends other conferences and industry conventions.

SALLY HILL MCMILLAN, LLC

429 E. Kingston Ave., Charlotte NC 28203. (704)334-0897. **E-mail:** mcmagency@aol.com. **Website:** www.publishersmarketplace.com/members/mcmillanagency. **Contact:** Sally Hill McMillan. Member of AAR.

REPRESENTS **Considers these fiction areas:** commercial, literary, mainstream, mystery.

- Do not send science fiction, military, horror, fantasy/adventure, children's, or cookbooks.

HOW TO CONTACT "Please query first with SASE and await further instructions. E-mail queries will be read but not necessarily answered." Accepts simultaneous submissions.

RECENT SALES Clients include Lynne Hinton, Linda Lenhoff, Jennifer Manske Fenske, Joe Martin, Nancy Peacock, Mike Stewart.

BOB MECOY LITERARY AGENCY

460 W. 24th St., Ste. 3E, New York NY 10011. (212)226-1936. **E-mail:** bob.mecoy@gmail.com. **Website:** bobmecoy.com. **Contact:** Bob Mecoy.

MEMBER AGENTS Bob Mecoy.

- Seeking fiction (literary, crime, romance); nonfiction (true crime, finance, memoir, literary, prescriptive self-help, graphic novelists). No westerns.

HOW TO CONTACT Query with sample chapters and synopsis. Accepts simultaneous submissions.

ROBIN MIZELL LITERARY REPRESENTATION

1600 Burnside St., Ste. 205, Beaufort SC 29902. (614)774-7405. **E-mail:** mail@robinmizell.com. **Website:** www.robinmizell.com. **Contact:** Robin Mizell. Member of AAR. Signatory of WGA.

REPRESENTS Nonfiction, fiction. **Considers these fiction areas:** literary, young adult.

- This agency specializes in prescriptive nonfiction, long-form narrative journalism, neuroscience, psychology, sociology, pop culture, literary and upmarket commercial fiction, and young adult.

HOW TO CONTACT E-query with the first 5 pages of your work pasted in the e-mail. More specific submission instructions can be found on the agency website. You should receive a response to your e-mail query within 30 days. Accepts simultaneous submissions.

HOWARD MORHAIM LITERARY AGENCY

30 Pierrepont St., Brooklyn NY 11201. (718)222-8400. **Fax:** (718)222-5056. **Website:** www.morhaimliterary.com. Member of AAR.

MEMBER AGENTS **Howard Morhaim** (no unsolicited submissions), **Kate McKean**, kmckean@morhaimliterary.com (adult fiction: contemporary romance, contemporary women's fiction, literary fiction, historical fiction set in the 20th century, high fantasy, magical realism, science fiction, middle-grade, young adult; nonfiction: books by authors with demonstrable platforms in the areas of sports, food writing, humor, design, creativity, and craft [sewing, knitting, etc.], narrative nonfiction by authors with or without an established platform; some memoir); DongWon Song, dongwon@morhaimliterary.com (science fiction, fantasy, food writing, science, pop culture); Kim-Mei Kirtland, kimmei@morhaimliterary.com (hard science fiction, literary fiction, history, biography, business, economics).

REPRESENTS **Considers these fiction areas:** fantasy, historical, literary, middle-grade, new adult, romance, science fiction, women's, young adult, LGBTQ young adult, magical realism. Fantasy should be high fantasy; historical fiction should be no earlier than the 20th century.

- Kate McKean is open to many subgenres and categories of young adult and middle-grade fiction. Check the website for more details. Actively seeking fiction, nonfiction, and young adult novels.

HOW TO CONTACT Query via e-mail with cover letter and 3 sample chapters. See each agent's listing for specifics. Accepts simultaneous submissions.

MOVEABLE TYPE MANAGEMENT

244 Madison Ave., Ste. 334, New York NY 10016. **E-mail:** achromy@movabletm.com. **Website:** www.movabletm.com. **Contact:** Adam Chromy.

MEMBER AGENTS Adam Chromy.

REPRESENTS Nonfiction, fiction. **Considers these fiction areas:** commercial, crime, detective, erotica, literary, mainstream, mystery, romance, science fiction, sports, suspense, thriller, women's.

- Mr. Chromy is a generalist, meaning that he accepts fiction submissions of virtually any kind (except juvenile books aimed for middle-grade and younger) as well as nonfiction. He has sold books in the following categories: new adult, women's, romance, memoir, pop culture, young adult, lifestyle, horror, how-to, general fiction, and more.

HOW TO CONTACT E-queries only. Responds if interested. For nonfiction: Send a query letter in the body of an e-mail that precisely introduces your topic and approach, and includes a descriptive bio. For journalists and academics, please also feel free to include a CV. Fiction: Send your query letter and the first 10 pages of your novel in the body of an e-mail. Your subject line needs to contain the word "Query" or your message will not reach the agency. No attachments and no snail mail. Accepts simultaneous submissions.

RECENT SALES *The Wedding Sisters* by Jamie Brenner (St. Martin's Press), *Sons of Zeus* by Noble Smith (Thomas Dunne Books), *World Made by Hand* and *Too Much Magic* by James Howard Kunstler (Grove/Atlantic Press), *Dirty Rocker Boys* by Bobbie Brown (Gallery/S&S).

DEE MURA LITERARY

P.O. Box 131, Massapequa NY 11762. (516)795-1616. **E-mail:** info@deemuraliterary.com. **E-mail:** query@deemuraliterary.com. **Website:** www.deemuraliterary.com. **Contact:** Dee Mura. Signatory of WGA. Member of Women's National Book Association, GrubStreet.

Prior to opening her agency, Ms. Mura was a public relations executive with a roster of film and entertainment clients. She is the president and CEO of both Dee Mura Literary and Dee Mura Entertainment.

MEMBER AGENTS Dee Mura, Kimiko Nakamura, Kaylee Davis.

REPRESENTS Nonfiction, fiction, short story collections, juvenile books. **Considers these fiction areas:** action, adventure, comic books, commercial, contemporary issues, crime, detective, erotica, ethnic, family saga, fantasy, feminist, frontier, gay, glitz, historical, horror, humor, inspirational, juvenile, lesbian, literary, mainstream, metaphysical, middle-grade, military, multicultural, multimedia, mystery, new adult, New Age, occult, paranormal, police, psychic, regional, religious, romance, satire, science fiction, short story collections, spiritual, sports, supernatural, suspense, thriller, translation, urban fantasy, war, westerns, women's, young adult, espionage, magical realism, speculative fiction, crossover.

No screenplays, poetry, or children's picture books.

HOW TO CONTACT Query with SASE or e-mail query@deemuraliterary.com (e-mail queries are preferred). Please include the first 25 pages in the body of the e-mail as well as a short author bio and synopsis of the work. Responds to queries in 4-5 weeks; to mss in approximately 8 weeks. Obtains new clients through recommendations, queries, conferences. Accepts simultaneous submissions.

TERMS Agent receives 15% commission on domestic sales; 20% commission on foreign sales. Offers written contract.

RECENT SALES *An Infinite Number of Parallel Universes* by Randy Ribay, *The Number 7* by Jessica Lidh.

WRITERS CONFERENCES BookExpo America, New England Crime Bake, New England SCBWI Agent Day, The Writer's Institute Conference at UW-Madison, Writer's Digest Annual Conference.

TIPS "For more information, please visit us online at deemuraliterary.com."

JEAN V. NAGGAR LITERARY AGENCY, INC.

JVNLA, Inc., 216 E. 75th St., Ste. 1E, New York NY 10021. (212)794-1082. **E-mail:** www.jvnla.com. **Website:** www.jvnla.com. **Contact:** Jennifer Weltz. Estab. 1978. Member of AAR. Other memberships include Women's Media Group, SCBWI, Pace University's Masters in Publishing Board Member. Represents 450 clients.

MEMBER AGENTS Jennifer Weltz (well-researched and original historicals, thrillers with a unique voice, wry dark humor, magical realism, enthralling narrative nonfiction, voice-driven young adult, middle-grade); **Alice Tasman** (literary, commercial, young adult, middle-grade, and nonfiction in the categories of narrative, biography, music, or pop culture); **Laura Biagi** (literary fiction, magical realism, psychological thrillers, young adult novels, middle-grade novels, picture books).

REPRESENTS Nonfiction, fiction, short story collections, novellas, juvenile books, scholarly books, poetry books.

This agency specializes in mainstream fiction and nonfiction and literary fiction with commercial potential as well as young adult, middle-grade, and picture books. Does not want to receive screenplays.

HOW TO CONTACT "Visit our website to send submissions and see what our individual agents are looking for. No snail mail submissions please!" Accepts simultaneous submissions. No responses for queries unless the agent is interested.

TERMS Agent receives 15% commission on domestic sales; 20% commission on foreign sales. Offers written contract. Charges for overseas mailing, messenger services, book purchases, photocopying—all deductible from royalties received.

RECENT SALES *Mort(e)* by Robert Repino, *The Paying Guests* by Sarah Waters, *Violent Crimes* by Phillip Margolin, *An Unseemly Wife* by E.B. Moore, *The Man Who Walked Away* by Maud Casey, *Dietland* by Sarai Walker, *In the Land of Armadillos* by Helen Maryles Shankman, *Not If I See You First* by Eric Lindstrom

TIPS "We recommend courage, fortitude, and patience: the courage to be true to your own vision, the fortitude to finish a novel and polish it again and again before sending it out, and the patience to accept rejection gracefully and wait for the stars to align themselves appropriately for success."

NELSON LITERARY AGENCY

1732 Wazee St., Ste. 207, Denver CO 80202. (303)292-2805. **E-mail:** querykristin@nelsonagency.com. **Website:** www.nelsonagency.com. **Contact:** Kristin Nelson, president. Estab. 2002. Member of AAR, RWA, SCBWI, SFWA. Represents 33 clients.

REPRESENTS Fiction. **Considers these fiction areas:** commercial, fantasy, literary, mainstream, middle-grade, romance, science fiction, women's, young adult.

NLA specializes in representing commercial fiction and high-caliber literary fiction. They represent many pop genre categories, including things like historical romance, steampunk, and all subgenres of young adult. Good stories well told. Please remember that NLA does not look at submissions for nonfiction, memoir, screenplays, short story collections, poetry, children's picture books or early reader chapter books, or material for the Christian/inspirational market.

HOW TO CONTACT "Please visit our website to carefully read our submission guidelines: nelsonagency.com/submission-guidelines." Kristin does not accept any queries by Facebook or Twitter. Query by e-mail only. Put the word "Query" in the e-mail subject line along with the title of your novel. No attachments, but it's okay to include the first 10 pages of your novel in the body of the e-mail. Accepts simultaneous submissions. Tries to respond to all queries within 10 business day. Full ms requests can take 2 months or more.

RECENT SALES Please visit Kristin's Publishers Marketplace page for a list of the latest sales: www.publishersmarketplace.com/members/knelson.

TIPS "If you would like to learn how to write an awesome pitch paragraph for your query letter or would like any info on how publishing contracts work, please visit Kristin's popular industry blog Pub Rants: nelsonagency.com/pub-rants. Insider publishing information is available there for free. Happy reading!"

NEW LEAF LITERARY & MEDIA, INC.

110 W. 40th St., Ste. 2201, New York NY 10018 USA. (646)248-7989. **Fax:** (646)861-4654. **E-mail:** query@newleafliterary.com. **Website:** www.newleafliterary.com. Estab. 2012. Member of AAR.

MEMBER AGENTS **Joanna Volpe** (women's fiction, thriller, horror, speculative fiction, literary fiction and historical fiction, young adult, middle-grade, art-focused picture books); **Kathleen Ortiz**, director of subsidiary rights and literary agent (new voices in young adult and animator/illustrator talent); **Suzie Townsend** (new adult, young adult, middle-grade, romance [all subgenres], fantasy [urban fantasy, science fiction, steampunk, epic fantasy], crime fiction [mysteries, thrillers]); **Pouya Shahbazian**, director of film and television (no unsolicited queries); **Mackenzie Brady** (her taste in nonfiction extends beyond science books to memoirs, lost histories, epic sports narratives, true crime, and gift/lifestyle books; she represents select adult and young adult fiction projects as well); **Peter Knapp** (middle-grade, young adult, general adult fiction, grounded science fiction, genre-agnostic for all); **Jaida Temperly** (fiction: magical realism, historical fiction, literary fiction, stories that are quirky and fantastical, middle-grade; nonfiction: niche, offbeat, a bit strange).

REPRESENTS Nonfiction, fiction, novellas, juvenile books, poetry books. **Considers these fiction areas:** crime, fantasy, historical, horror, literary, mainstream, middle-grade, mystery, new adult, paranormal, picture books, romance, thriller, women's, young adult.

HOW TO CONTACT Send query to query@newleafliterary.com. Please do not query via phone. The word "Query" must be in the subject line, plus the agent's name; for example: "Subject: Query, Suzie Townsend." You may include up to 5 double-spaced sample pages in the body of the e-mail. NO ATTACHMENTS unless specifically requested. Include all necessary contact information. You will receive an auto-response confirming receipt of your query. "We only respond if we are interested in seeing your work." All queries read within 2 weeks.

RECENT SALES Untitled duology by Veronica Roth (HarperCollins), *Red Queen* by Victoria Aveyard (HarperCollins), *Lobster Is the Best Medicine* by Liz Climo (Running Press), *Six of Crows* by Leigh Bardugo (Henry Holt), *A Snicker of Magic* by Natalie Lloyd (Scholastic).

PARK LITERARY GROUP, LLC

270 Lafayette St., Ste. 1504, New York NY 10012. (212)691-3500. **Fax:** (212)691-3540. **E-mail:** queries@parkliterary.com. **Website:** www.parkliterary.com. Estab. 2005.

MEMBER AGENTS **Theresa Park** (plot-driven fiction and serious nonfiction); **Abigail Koons** (popular science, history, politics, current affairs and art, women's fiction).

REPRESENTS Nonfiction, fiction. **Considers these fiction areas:** middle-grade, suspense, thriller, women's, young adult.

⊶ The Park Literary Group represents fiction and nonfiction with a boutique approach: an emphasis on servicing a relatively small number of clients, with the highest professional standards and focused personal attention. Does not want to receive poetry or screenplays.

HOW TO CONTACT Please specify the first and last name of the agent to whom you are submitting in the subject line of the e-mail, and send your query letter and accompanying material to queries@parkliterary.com. All materials must be in the body of the e-mail. Responds if interested. For fiction submissions to Abigail Koons or Theresa Park, please include a query letter with short synopsis and the first 3 chapters of your work. Accepts simultaneous submissions.

RECENT SALES This agency's client list is on their website. It includes bestsellers Nicholas Sparks, Soman Chainani, Emily Giffin, and Debbie Macomber.

AARON M. PRIEST LITERARY AGENCY

200 W. 41st St., 21st Floor, New York NY 10036. (212)818-0344. **Fax:** (212)573-9417. **E-mail:** info@aaronpriest.com. **Website:** www.aaronpriest.com. Estab. 1974. Member of AAR.

MEMBER AGENTS **Aaron Priest**, querypriest@aaronpriest.com (thrillers, commercial fiction, biographies); **Lisa Erbach Vance**, queryvance@aaronpriest.com (contemporary fiction, thrillers/suspense, international fiction, narrative nonfiction); **Lucy Childs Baker**, querychilds@aaronpriest.com (literary and commercial fiction, memoir, edgy women's fiction); **Melissa Edwards**, queryedwards@aaronpriest.com (middle-grade, young adult, women's fiction, thrillers); **Mitch Hoffman** (thrillers, suspense, crime fiction, literary fiction, narrative nonfiction, politics, popular science, history, memoir, current events, pop culture).

REPRESENTS **Considers these fiction areas:** commercial, contemporary issues, crime, literary, middle-grade, suspense, thriller, women's, young adult.

⊶ Does not want to receive poetry, screenplays, horror, or science fiction.

HOW TO CONTACT Query 1 of the agents using the appropriate e-mail listed on the website. "Please do not submit to more than 1 agent at this agency. We urge you to check our website and consider each agent's emphasis before submitting. Your query letter should be about 1 page long and describe your work as well as your background. You may also paste the first chapter of your work in the body of the e-mail. Do not send attachments." Accepts simultaneous submissions. Responds in 4 weeks if interested.

TERMS Agent receives 15% commission on domestic sales.

RECENT SALES *The Hit* by David Baldacci, *Six Years* by Harlan Coben, *Suspect* by Robert Crais, *Permanent Record* by Leslie Stella.

PROSPECT AGENCY

551 Valley Rd., PMB 377, Upper Montclair NJ 07043. (718)788-3217. **Fax:** (718)360-9582. **Website:** www.prospectagency.com. Estab. 2005. Member of AAR. Signatory of WGA.

MEMBER AGENTS **Emily Sylvan Kim**, esk@prospectagency.com (romance, women's, commercial, young adult, new adult); **Rachel Orr**, rko@prospectagency.com (picture books, illustrators, middle-grade, young adult); **Becca Stumpf**, becca@prospectagency.com (young adult and middle-grade: all genres, including fantasy, science fiction, literary, mystery, contemporary, historical, horror/suspense; especially seeking middle-grade and young adult novels featuring diverse protagonists and life circumstances, adult science fiction and fantasy novels with broad appeal, upmarket women's fiction, smart and spicy romance novels); **Carrie Pestritto**, carrie@prospectagency.com (narrative nonfiction, general nonfiction, biography, memoir, commercial fiction with a literary twist, women's fiction, romance, upmarket, historical fiction, high-concept young adult, upper middle-grade); **Teresa Kietlinski**, tk@prospectagency.com (picture book artists and illustrators); **Linda Camacho,** linda@prospectagency.com (middle-grade, young adult, and adult fiction across all genres, especially women's fiction/romance, horror, fantasy/science fiction, graphic novels, contemporary; select literary fiction; fiction featuring diverse/marginalized groups); **Kirsten Carleton**, kcarleton@prospectagency.com (upmarket speculative, thriller, and literary fiction for adult and young adult).

REPRESENTS Nonfiction, fiction, novellas, juvenile books. **Considers these fiction areas:** commercial, contemporary issues, crime, ethnic, family saga, fantasy, feminist, gay, historical, horror, humor, juvenile, lesbian, literary, mainstream, middle-grade, multicultural, mystery, new adult, picture books, romance, science fiction, suspense, thriller, urban fantasy, women's, young adult.

"We're looking for strong, unique voices and unforgettable stories and characters."

HOW TO CONTACT Note that each agent at this agency has a different submission e-mail address and different submission policies. Check the agency website for the latest formal guidelines for each agent. Accepts simultaneous submissions. Obtains new clients through conferences, recommendations, queries, some scouting.

TERMS Agent receives 15% on domestic sales; 20% on foreign sales sold directly; 25% on sales using a subagent. Offers written contract.

RECENT SALES Please see Publishers Marketplace for most recent sales.

RED SOFA LITERARY

P.O. Box 40482, St. Paul MN 55104. (651)224-6670. **E-mail:** dawn@redsofaliterary.com; jennie@redsofaliterary.com; laura@redsofaliterary.com, bree@redsofaliterary.com; amanda@redsofaliterary.com; stacey@redsofaliterary.com; erik@redsofaliterary.com. **Website:** www.redsofaliterary.com. **Contact:** Dawn Frederick, owner/literary agent; Jennie Goloboy, literary agent; Laura Zats, associate literary agent; Amanda Rutter, associate literary agent; Bree Ogden, literary agent; Stacey Graham, associate literary agent; Erik Hane, associate literary agent. Estab. Dec. 2008. Member of Authors Guild, MN Publishers Round Table. Represents 90 clients.

MEMBER AGENTS **Dawn Fredrick** (nonfiction: pop culture, interesting histories, social sciences/advocacy, humor, books that are great conversation starters; fiction: young adult [Gothic, contemporary, historical], middle-grade [fun and lighthearted, more contemporary themes]); **Jennie Goloboy** (adult science fiction and fantasy that's progressive, innovative, and fun); **Laura Zats** (adventurous, fun, STEM-inspired middle-grade fiction; diverse young adult of all kinds, especially the smart, geeky mss; feminist romance and erotica with high-quality writing and fresh takes on tropes; adult science fiction and fantasy that pass the Bechdel Test and/or the Mako Mori Test; "actively searching for diverse and feminist books and authors across all of my representative categories"); **Amanda Rutter** (science fiction/fantasy for adults, young adults, and middle-grade readers); **Bree Ogden** (highly artistic picture books with high-brow art; young adult [no science fiction, fantasy, paranormal, or dystopian]; new adult [any genre as long as it has a strong romantic element]; adult [any genre, but prefers transgressive, horror, noir, crime, mystery, thriller, bizarro, Gothic, romance, erotica, graphic novels]; some select nonfiction [no memoir, academia, humor, pop culture, art books]); **Stacey Graham** (dark middle-grade, horror, humor, humorous memoir, New Age with a strong platform, history [colonial U.S. and British history]; fiction for adults or middle-grade; quirky nonfiction for adults, middle-grade, young adult); **Erik Hane** (literary fiction, nonfiction).

Prior to being an agent, Ms. Frederick was a bookseller in independent, chain, and specialty stores, and was an agent at Sebastian Literary Agency. Ms. Goloboy also writes history and is the author of *Charleston and the Emergence of Middle-Class Culture in the Revolutionary Era* (University of Georgia Press). She writes science fiction and fantasy under her pen name, Nora Fleischer. Ms. Zats previously worked as an editor at a publishing house in London and became an agent in 2013 "quite by accident." Ms. Rutter was previously an acquisitions editor for Strange Chemistry, a freelance editor for Bubblecow and Wise Ink Publishing, and a book blogger. Ms. Ogden has worked in various areas of journalism and started agenting in 2011 after having interned at a literary agency for a year. Ms. Graham is the author of 4 books and multiple short stories, and is a screenwriter, ghostwriter, and editor. Mr. Hane has worked as an editorial assistant, and then assistant editor, at Oxford University Press. He then served as an acquiring editor for The Overlook Press, primarily for upmarket nonfiction (history, biography, pop science) as well as some novels.

REPRESENTS Nonfiction, fiction, juvenile books. **Considers these fiction areas:** erotica, fantasy, feminist, gay, humor, juvenile, lesbian, literary, middle-grade, romance, science fiction, suspense, thriller, young adult.

HOW TO CONTACT Query by e-mail or mail with SASE. No attachments, please. Submit full proposal plus 3 sample chapters (or first 50 pages) and any other pertinent writing samples upon request by the specific agent. Do not send with the query letter. PDF/DOC/DOCX is preferred; no RTF documents, please. Accepts simultaneous submissions. Obtains new clients tThrough queries, recommendations from others, solicitations.

TERMS Agent receives 15% commission on domestic sales; 20% commission on foreign sales. Offers written contract.

RECENT SALES *Branded* (Book 2 of Inked series) by Eric Smith (Bloomsbury Spark), *An Accident of Stars* by Foz Meadows (Angry Robot Books), *The Deeds of Pounce* by Benjamin Wachs (Beating Wind Press), *The Rogue Retrieval* by Dan Koboldt (Voyager Impulse), *Freeze/Thaw* by Chris Bucholz (Apex Books), *The Stumps of Flattop Hill* by Ken Lamug (One Peace Books), *Some Hell* by Patrick Nathan (Graywolf), Book 3 of One Night in Sixes series by Tex Thompson (Solaris Books).

WRITERS CONFERENCES Writer's Digest, SDSU Writers Conference, WorldCon, CONvergence, SCWBI (regional conferences), FWA Conference, DFW Writers Conference, Northern Colorado Writers Conference, Horror World Convention, Loft Literary Conference, Madison Writers Workshop.

TIPS "Always remember the benefits of building an author platform and the accessibility of accomplishing this task in today's industry. Most importantly, research the agents queried. Avoid contacting every literary agent about a book idea. Due to the large volume of queries received, the process of reading queries for unrepresented categories (by the agency) becomes quite the arduous task. Investigate online directories, printed guides (like *Writer's Market*), individual agent websites, and more before beginning the query process. It's good to remember that each agent has a vision of what he or she wants to represent and will communicate this information accordingly. We're simply waiting for those specific book ideas to come in our direction."

REES LITERARY AGENCY

14 Beacon St., Ste. 710, Boston MA 02108. (617)227-9014. **Website:** reesagency.com. Estab. 1983. Member of AAR. Represents more than 100 clients.

MEMBER AGENTS **Ann Collette**, agent10702@aol.com (fiction: literary, upscale commercial women's, crime [including mystery, thriller, and psychological suspense], upscale western, historical, military and war, horror; nonfiction: narrative, military and war, books on race and class, works set in Southeast Asia, biography, pop culture, books on film and opera, humor, memoir); **Lorin Rees**, lorin@reesagency.com (literary fiction, memoirs, business books, self-help, science, history, psychology, and narrative nonfiction); **Rebecca Podos**, rebecca@reesagency.com (young adult and middle-grade fiction, particularly books about complex female relationships, beautifully written contemporary, genre novels with a strong focus on character, romance with more at stake than "will they or won't they," LGBTQ books across all genres).

REPRESENTS Nonfiction, fiction. **Considers these fiction areas:** commercial, crime, historical, horror, literary, middle-grade, mystery, suspense, thriller, westerns, women's, young adult.

HOW TO CONTACT Consult website for each agent's submission guidelines and e-mail addresses, as they differ. Accepts simultaneous submissions. Obtains most new clients through recommendations from others, conferences, submissions.

TERMS Agent receives 15% commission on domestic sales; 20% commission on foreign sales.

RECENT SALES *The Marauders* by Tom Cooper, *Black River* by S.M. Hulse, *The Gentleman's Guide to Vice and Virtue* by Mackenzi Lee, *Regret Nothing* by Sarah Nicolas, *Suffer Love* by Ashley Herring Blake, *Superbosses* by Sydney Finkelstein, *Idyll Threats* by Stephanie Gayle.

REGAL HOFFMANN & ASSOCIATES LLC

242 W. 38th St., Floor 2, New York NY 10018. (212)684-7900. **Fax:** (212)684-7906. **E-mail:** submissions@regal-literary.com. **Website:** www.regal-literary.com. London Office: 36 Gloucester Ave., Primrose Hill, London NW1 7BB, United Kingdom, uk@regal-literary.com. Estab. 2002. Member of AAR. Represents 70 clients.

MEMBER AGENTS **Claire Anderson-Wheeler** (nonfiction: memoirs and biographies, narrative histories, popular science, popular psychology; adult fiction: primarily character-driven literary fiction, but open to genre fiction, high-concept fiction; all genres of young adult/middle-grade fiction); **Markus Hoffmann** (international and literary fiction, crime, pop cultural studies, current affairs, economics, history, music, popular science, travel literature); **Joseph Regal** (literary fiction, international thrillers, history, science, photography, music, culture, whimsy).

REPRESENTS **Considers these fiction areas:** literary, mainstream, middle-grade, thriller, young adult.

"We represent works in a wide range of categories, with an emphasis on literary fiction, outstanding thriller and crime fiction, and serious narrative nonfiction." Actively seeking literary fiction and narrative nonfiction. Does not want romance, science fiction, poetry, or screenplays.

HOW TO CONTACT Query with SASE or via e-mail to submissions@rhaliterary.com. No phone calls. Submissions should consist of a one-page query letter detailing the book in question, as well as the qualifications of the author. For fiction, submissions may also include the first 10 pages of the novel or 1 short story from a collection. Responds if interested. Accepts simultaneous submissions. Responds in 4-8 weeks.

TERMS Agent receives 15% commission on domestic sales; 20% commission on foreign sales. "We charge no reading fees."

RECENT SALES *This Is How It Really Sounds* by Stuart Archer Cohen, *Autofocus* by Lauren Gibaldi, *We've Already Gone This Far* by Patrick Dacey, *A Fierce and Subtle Poison* by Samantha Mabry, *The Life of the World to Come* by Dan Cluchey, *Willful Disregard* by Lena Andersson, *The Sweetheart* by Angelina Mirabella.

TIPS "We are deeply committed to every aspect of our clients' careers, and are engaged in everything from the editorial work of developing a great book proposal or line editing a fiction ms to negotiating state-of-the-art book deals and working to promote and publicize the book when it's published. We are at the forefront of the effort to increase authors' rights in publishing contracts in a rapidly changing commercial environment. We deal directly with co-agents and publishers in every foreign territory and also work directly and with co-agents for feature film and television rights, with extraordinary success in both arenas. Many of our clients' works have sold in dozens of translation markets, and a high proportion of our books have been sold in Hollywood. We have strong relationships with speaking agents, who can assist in arranging author tours and other corporate and college speaking opportunities when appropriate. We also have a staff publicist and marketer to help promote our clients and their work."

THE RIGHTS FACTORY

P.O. Box 499, Station C, Toronto ON M6J 3P6 Canada. (416)966-5367. **E-mail:** sam@therightsfactory.com. **Website:** www.therightsfactory.com. Estab. 2004. Represents ~150 clients.

MEMBER AGENTS **Sam Hiyate**, president (fiction, nonfiction, graphic novels); **Kelvin Kong**, rights manager (clients by referral only); **Ali McDonald**, kidlit agent (young adult and children's literature of all kinds); **Olga Filina**, associate agent (commercial and historical fiction; great genre fiction in the area of romance and mystery; nonfiction in the fields of business, wellness, lifestyle and memoir; young adult and middle-grade novels with memorable characters); **Cassandra Rogers**, associate agent (adult literary and commercial women's fiction; historical fiction; nonfiction on politics, history, science, and finance; humorous, heartbreaking, and inspiring memoir); **Lydia Moed**, associate agent (science fiction and fantasy, historical fiction, diverse voices; narrative nonfiction on a wide variety of topics, including history, popular science, biography, and travel); **Natalie Kimber**, associate agent (literary and commercial fiction and creative nonfiction in categories such as memoir, cooking, pop culture, spirituality, and sustainability); **Harry Endrulat**, associate agent (children's literature, especially author/illustrators and Canadian voices); **Haskell Nussbaum**, associate agent (literature of all kinds).

REPRESENTS Nonfiction, fiction, short story collections, novellas, juvenile books. **Considers these fiction areas:** commercial, crime, family saga, fantasy, gay, hi-lo, historical, horror, juvenile, lesbian, literary, mainstream, middle-grade, multicultural, mystery, new adult, paranormal, picture books, romance, science fiction, short story collections, suspense, thriller, urban fantasy, women's, young adult.

Plays, screenplays, textbooks.

HOW TO CONTACT There is a submission form on this agency's website. You can also query directly via e-mail. Accepts simultaneous submissions. 3-6 weeks

ANGELA RINALDI LITERARY AGENCY

P.O. Box 7875, Beverly Hills CA 90212-7875. (310)842-7665. **Fax:** (310)837-8143. **E-mail:** amr@rinaldiliterary.com. **Website:** www.rinaldiliterary.com. **Contact:** Angela Rinaldi. Member of AAR.

Prior to opening her agency, Ms. Rinaldi was an editor at NAL/Signet, Pocket Books, and

Bantam, and the manager of book development for *The Los Angeles Times*.

REPRESENTS Nonfiction, fiction, TV and motion picture rights (for clients only). **Considers these fiction areas:** commercial, historical, literary, mainstream, mystery, suspense, thriller, women's, contemporary, Gothic, women's book club fiction.

⊶ Actively seeking commercial and literary fiction as well as nonfiction. "For fiction, we do not want to receive humor, CIA espionage, drug thrillers, techno thrillers, category romances, science fiction, fantasy, horror/occult/paranormal, poetry, film scripts, or religion. For nonfiction, please do not send us magazine articles, celebrity bios, or tell alls."

HOW TO CONTACT "E-queries only. E-mail submissions should be sent to info@rinaldiliterary.com. Include the word 'Query' in the subject line. For fiction, please send a brief synopsis and paste the first 10 pages into an e-mail. Nonfiction queries should include a detailed cover letter, your credentials, and platform information as well as any publishing history. Tell us if you have a completed proposal." Accepts simultaneous submissions. Responds in 2-4 weeks.

TERMS Agent receives 15% commission on domestic sales; 25% commission on foreign sales. Offers written contract.

ANN RITTENBERG LITERARY AGENCY, INC.

15 Maiden Lane, Ste. 206, New York NY 10038. **E-mail:** info@rittlit.com. **Website:** www.rittlit.com. **Contact:** Ann Rittenberg, president. Member of AAR.

⊶ This agent specializes in specific fiction genres: upmarket thrillers, literary fiction, and literary nonfiction. Does not want to receive screenplays, straight genre fiction, poetry, self-help.

HOW TO CONTACT Query via postal mail (with SASE) or via e-mail to info@rittlit.com. Submit 3 sample chapters (pasted in e-mail) with your query letter. "If you query by e-mail, we will only respond if interested." Accepts simultaneous submissions. Obtains most new clients through referrals from established writers and editors.

TERMS Agent receives 15% commission on domestic sales; 20% commission on foreign sales. Offers written contract. This agency charges clients for photocopying only.

RECENT SALES *Off the Grid* by C. J. Box, *World Gone By* by Dennis Lehane, *Badlands* by C.J. Box, *The Granite Moth* by Erica Wright, *The Precipice* by Paul Doiron, *The Ravens* by Vidar Sundstol, *The Immune* by David Kazzie, *Ancient Places* by Jack Nisbet.

RLR ASSOCIATES, LTD.

Literary Department, 7 W. 51st St., New York NY 10019. **E-mail:** sgould@rlrassociates.net. **Website:** www.rlrassociates.net. **Contact:** Scott Gould. Member of AAR. Represents 50 clients.

REPRESENTS Nonfiction, fiction. **Considers these fiction areas:** commercial, literary, mainstream, middle-grade, picture books, romance, women's, young adult, genre.

⊶ "We provide a lot of editorial assistance to our clients and have connections." Does not want to receive screenplays.

HOW TO CONTACT Query by either e-mail or snail mail. For fiction, send a query and 1-3 chapters (pasted in body of e-mail). For nonfiction, send query or proposal. Accepts simultaneous submissions. "If you do not hear from us within 3 months, please assume that your work is out of active consideration." Obtains most new clients through recommendations from others.

TERMS Agent receives 15% commission on domestic sales; 20% commission on foreign sales. Offers written contract.

RECENT SALES Clients include Shelby Foote, The Grief Recovery Institute, Don Wade, David Plowden, Nina Planck, Karyn Bosnak, Gerald Carbone, Jason Lethcoe, Andy Crouch.

TIPS "Please check out our website for more details on our agency."

B.J. ROBBINS LITERARY AGENCY

5130 Bellaire Ave., North Hollywood CA 91607-2908. **E-mail:** Robbinsliterary@gmail.com. **Website:** www.publishersmarketplace.com/members/bjrobbins. **Contact:** B.J. Robbins. Estab. 1992. Member of AAR.

Ms. Robbins has spent fifteen years in publishing, starting in publicity at Simon & Schuster and later as marketing director and senior editor at Harcourt.

REPRESENTS Nonfiction, fiction. **Considers these fiction areas:** contemporary issues, crime, detective, ethnic, historical, literary, mainstream, multicultural, mystery, sports, suspense, thriller, women's.

⊶ "We do not represent screenplays, plays, poetry, science fiction, horror, westerns, romance, techno thrillers, religious tracts, dating books or anything with the word 'unicorn' in the title."

HOW TO CONTACT E-query with no attachments. For fiction, it's okay to include first 10 pages in body of e-mail. Accepts simultaneous submissions. Only responds to projects if interested. Obtains most new clients through conferences, referrals.

TERMS Agent receives 15% commission on domestic sales; 20% commission on foreign sales. Offers written contract; three-month notice must be given to terminate contract.

RECENT SALES *Shoot for the Moon: The Perilous Voyage of Apollo 11* by James Donovan (Little, Brown), *Planet Earth 2050* by J. Maarten Troost (Holt), *Mongrels* by Stephen Graham Jones (William Morrow), *Blood Brothers: The Story of the Strange Friendship Between Sitting Bull and Buffalo Bill* by Deanne Stillman (Simon & Schuster), *Reliance, Illinois* by Mary Volmer (Soho Press).

THE ROSENBERG GROUP

23 Lincoln Ave., Marblehead MA 01945. (781)990-1341. **Fax:** (781)990-1344. **Website:** www.rosenberggroup.com. **Contact:** Barbara Collins Rosenberg. Estab. 1998. Member of AAR. Recognized agent of the RWA. Represents 25 clients.

Prior to becoming an agent, Ms. Rosenberg was a senior editor for Harcourt.

REPRESENTS Nonfiction, fiction, textbooks (college only). **Considers these fiction areas:** romance, women's, chick lit.

Ms. Rosenberg is well versed in the romance market (both category and single title). She is a frequent speaker at romance conferences. The Rosenberg Group is accepting new clients working in romance fiction (please see "Areas of Interest" page on website for specific romance subgenres), women's fiction, and chick lit. Does not want to receive inspirational, time travel, futuristic, or paranormal.

HOW TO CONTACT Query via snail mail. Your query letter should not exceed 1 page in length. It should include the title of your work, the genre and/or subgenre, the word count, and a brief description of the work. If you are writing category romance, please be certain to include the line for which your work is intended. Accepts simultaneous submissions. Obtains most new clients through recommendations from others, solicitations, conferences.

TERMS Agent receives 15% commission on domestic sales; 15% commission on foreign sales. Offers written contract; one-month notice must be given to terminate contract. Charges maximum of $350/year for postage and photocopying.

RECENT SALES Sold 27 titles in the last year.

WRITERS CONFERENCES RWA National Conference, BookExpo America.

ANDY ROSS LITERARY AGENCY

767 Santa Ray Ave., Oakland CA 94610 USA. (510)238-8965. **E-mail:** andyrossagency@hotmail.com. **Website:** www.andyrossagency.com. **Contact:** Andy Ross. Estab. 2008. Member of AAR.

Owner of Cody's Books in Berkeley for 30 years.

REPRESENTS Considers these fiction areas: commercial, juvenile, literary, young adult.

"This agency specializes in general nonfiction, politics and current events, history, biography, journalism, and contemporary culture as well as literary, commercial, and young adult fiction." Actively seeking literary, commercial, and young adult fiction. Does not want to receive poetry.

HOW TO CONTACT Queries should be less than a half page. Please put the word "query" in the title header of the e-mail. In the first sentence, state the category of the project. Give a short description of the book and your qualifications for writing. Accepts simultaneous submissions. Responds in 1 week to queries.

TERMS Agent receives 15% commission on domestic sales; 20% commission on foreign sales or other deals made through a subagent. Offers written contract.

JANE ROTROSEN AGENCY LLC

(212)593-4330. **Fax:** (212)935-6985. **Website:** www.janerotrosen.com. Estab. 1974. Member of AAR. Other memberships include Authors Guild. Represents more than 100 clients.

MEMBER AGENTS **Jane Rotrosen Berkey** (not taking on clients); **Andrea Cirillo**, acirillo@janerotrosen.com (general fiction, suspense, women's fiction); **Annelise Robey**, arobey@janerotrosen.com (women's fiction, suspense, mystery, literary fiction, select nonfiction); **Meg Ruley**, mruley@janerotrosen.com (commercial fiction, including suspense, mysteries, romance, and general fiction); **Christina Hogrebe**, chogrebe@janerotrosen.com (young adult, new adult, book club fiction, romantic comedies, mystery, suspense); **Amy Tannenbaum**, atannenbaum@janerotrosen.com (contemporary romance, psychological suspense, thrillers, new adult, women's fiction that falls into that sweet spot between literary and commercial, memoir, narrative and prescriptive nonfiction [health, business, pop culture, humor, and popular psychology]); **Rebecca Scherer** rscherer@janerotrosen.com (women's fiction, mystery, suspense, thriller, romance, upmarket/literary-leaning fiction); **Jessica Errera** (assistant to Christina and Rebecca).

REPRESENTS Nonfiction, fiction. **Considers these fiction areas:** commercial, literary, mainstream, mystery, new adult, romance, suspense, thriller, women's, young adult.

"Jane Rotrosen Agency is best known for representing writers of commercial fiction: thrillers, mystery, suspense, women's fiction, romance, historical novels, mainstream fiction, young adult, etc. We also work with authors of memoirs, narrative, and prescriptive nonfiction."

HOW TO CONTACT "Please e-mail the agent you think would best align with you and your work. Simultaneous e-mail submissions will not be considered. Send a query letter that includes a concise description of your work, relevant biographical information, and any relevant publishing history. Also include a brief synopsis and the first 3 chapters of your novel, or a proposal for nonfiction. Paste all text in the body of your e-mail. We will not open e-mail attachments." Obtains most new clients through recommendations from others.

TERMS Agent receives 15% commission on domestic sales; 20% commission on foreign sales. Offers written contract, binding for 3 years; two-month notice must be given to terminate contract. Charges clients for photocopying, express mail, overseas postage, book purchase.

THE RUDY AGENCY

825 Wildlife Ln., Estes Park CO 80517. (970)577-8500. **E-mail:** mak@rudyagency.com; fred@rudyagency.com; jak@rudyagency.com; claggett@rudyagency.com. **E-mail:** For nonfiction: mak@rudyagency.com; claggett@rudyagency.com; for adult fiction: fred@rudyagency.com; for children's and young adult: jak@rudyagency.com. **Website:** www.rudyagency.com. **Contact:** Maryann Karinch. Estab. 2004. Adheres to AAR canon of ethics. Represents 24 clients.

Prior to becoming an agent, Ms. Karinch was, and continues to be, an author of nonfiction books, covering the subjects of health/medicine and human behavior. Prior to that, she was in public relations and marketing, which are areas of expertise she also applies in her practice as an agent.

MEMBER AGENTS **Maryann Karinch**; **Fred Tribuzzo** (thrillers, historical), **Jak Burke** (children's, young adult), and **Hilary Claggett** (selected nonfiction).

REPRESENTS Nonfiction, fiction, short story collections, juvenile books, scholarly books, textbooks. **Considers these fiction areas:** commercial, crime, historical, juvenile, literary, new adult, thriller.

"We support authors from the proposal stage through promotion of the published work. We work in partnership with publishers to promote the published work and coach authors in their role in the marketing and public relations campaigns for the book." Actively seeking projects with social value, projects that open minds to new ideas and interesting lives, and projects that entertain through good storytelling. Does not want to receive poetry, screenplays/stage plays, art/photo books, novellas, religion books, and joke books.

HOW TO CONTACT "Query us. If we like the query, we will invite a complete proposal (or complete ms if writing fiction). No phone queries, please. We won't hang up on you, but it makes it easier if you send us a note first." Accepts simultaneous submissions. Responds in 8 weeks to mss. Obtains most new clients through recommendations from others, solicitations.

TERMS Agent receives 15% commission on domestic sales. Offers written contract, binding for 1 year.

RECENT SALES *Beethoven's Skull* by Tim Rayborn (Skyhorse), *Advocacy Journalism* by Larry Atkins (Prometheus), *Snipers* by Lena Sisco (Globe Pequot).

TIPS "Present yourself professionally. I tell people all the time to subscribe to *Writer's Digest* (I do), because you will get good advice about how to approach an agent."

VICTORIA SANDERS & ASSOCIATES

440 Buck Rd., Stone Ridge NY 12484. (212)633-8811. **Fax:** (212)633-0525. **E-mail:** queriesvsa@gmail.com. **Website:** www.victoriasanders.com. **Contact:** Victo-

ria Sanders. Estab. 1992. Member of AAR. Signatory of WGA. Represents 135 clients.

MEMBER AGENTS Victoria Sanders, Chris Kepner, Bernadette Baker-Baughman.

REPRESENTS Nonfiction, fiction, juvenile books. **Considers these fiction areas:** action, adventure, comic books, contemporary issues, crime, detective, ethnic, family saga, feminist, lesbian, literary, mainstream, middle-grade, mystery, new adult, picture books, thriller, young adult.

HOW TO CONTACT Query by e-mail only. "We will not respond to e-mails with attachments or attached files." Accepts simultaneous submissions.

TERMS Agent receives 15% commission on domestic sales; 20% commission on foreign/film sales. Offers written contract.

RECENT SALES Sold 20+ titles in the last year.

TIPS "Limit your query to the letter (no calls), and give it your best shot. A good query is going to get a good response."

WENDY SCHMALZ AGENCY

402 Union St., #831, Hudson NY 12534. (518)672-7697. **E-mail:** wendy@schmalzagency.com. **Website:** www.schmalzagency.com. **Contact:** Wendy Schmalz. Estab. 2002. Member of AAR.

REPRESENTS Nonfiction, fiction, juvenile books. **Considers these fiction areas:** literary, mainstream, middle-grade, young adult.

- Not looking for picture books, science fiction, or fantasy.

HOW TO CONTACT Accepts only e-mail queries. Paste synopsis into the e-mail. Do not attach the ms or sample chapters or synopsis. Replies to queries only if they want to read the ms. If you do not hear from this agency within 2 weeks, consider that a no. Accepts simultaneous submissions. Obtains clients through recommendations from others.

TERMS Agent receives 15% commission on domestic sales; 20% on foreign sales; 25% for Asian sales.

⊙ SUSAN SCHULMAN LITERARY AGENCY LLC

454 W. 44th St., New York NY 10036. (212)713-1633. **E-mail:** susan@schulmanagency.com. **Website:** www.publishersmarketplace.com/members/schulman. **Contact:** Susan Schulman. Estab. 1980. Member of AAR. Signatory of WGA. Other memberships include Dramatists Guild, Writers Guild of America East, New York Women in Film, Women's Media Group, Agents' Roundtable, League of New York Theater Women.

REPRESENTS Nonfiction, fiction, juvenile books, feature film, TV scripts, theatrical stage play. **Considers these fiction areas:** commercial, contemporary issues, juvenile, literary, mainstream, new adult, religious, women's, young adult.

- "We specialize in books for, by, and about women and women's issues including nonfiction self-help books, fiction, and theater projects. We also handle the film, television, and allied rights for several agencies as well as foreign rights for several publishing houses." Actively seeking new nonfiction. Considers plays. Does not want to receive poetry, television scripts, or concepts for television.

HOW TO CONTACT "For fiction: query letter with outline and 3 sample chapters, résumé, and SASE. For nonfiction: query letter with complete description of subject, at least 1 chapter, résumé, and SASE. Queries may be sent via regular mail or e-mail. Please do not submit queries via UPS or Federal Express. Please do not send attachments with e-mail queries. Please incorporate the chapters into the body of the e-mail." Accepts simultaneous submissions. Generally responds in less than 1 week to a full query and in 6 weeks to a full ms. Obtains most new clients through recommendations from others, solicitations, conferences.

TERMS Agent receives 15% commission on domestic sales; 20% commission on foreign sales. Offers written contract; 30-day notice must be given to terminate contract.

RECENT SALES Sold 35 titles in the last year, as well as hundreds of subsidiary rights deals.

WRITERS CONFERENCES Geneva Writers Conference (Switzerland), Columbus Writers Conference, Skidmore Conference of the Independent Women's Writers Group. Attends Frankfurt Book Fair, London Book Fair, and BEA annually.

TIPS "Keep writing!"

SCOVIL GALEN GHOSH LITERARY AGENCY, INC.

276 Fifth Ave., Ste. 708, New York NY 10001. (212)679-8686. **Fax:** (212)679-6710. **Website:** www.sgglit.com. **Contact:** Russell Galen. Estab. 1992. Member of AAR. Represents 300 clients.

MEMBER AGENTS **Russell Galen**, russellgalen@sgglit.com (novels that stretch the bounds of reality; strong, serious nonfiction books on almost any subject that teach something new; no books that are merely entertaining, such as diet or pop psych books; serious interests include science, history, journalism, biography, business, memoir, nature, politics, sports, contemporary culture, literary nonfiction, etc.); **Jack Scovil**, jackscovil@sgglit.com; **Anna Ghosh**, annaghosh@sgglit.com (nonfiction proposals on all subjects, including literary nonfiction, history, science, social and cultural issues, memoir, food, art, adventure, and travel; adult commercial and literary fiction); **Ann Behar**, annbehar@sgglit.com (juvenile books for all ages).

HOW TO CONTACT E-mail queries only. Each agent at this agency has his or her own submission e-mail. Accepts simultaneous submissions.

SCRIBE AGENCY, LLC

5508 Joylynne Dr., Madison WI 53716. **E-mail:** whattheshizzle@scribeagency.com. **E-mail:** submissions@scribeagency.com. **Website:** www.scribeagency.com. **Contact:** Kristopher O'Higgins. Represents 11 clients.

"With more than 15 years experience in publishing, with time spent on both the agency and editorial sides, with marketing experience to boot, Scribe Agency is a full-service literary agency, working hands-on with its authors on their projects. Check the website (scribeagency.com) to make sure your work matches the Scribe aesthetic."

MEMBER AGENTS Kristopher O'Higgins.

REPRESENTS Fiction, anthologies. **Considers these fiction areas:** fantasy, literary, science fiction.

"Scribe is currently closed to nonfiction and short fiction collections, and does not represent humor, cozy mysteries, faith-based fiction, screenplays, poetry, or works based on another's ideas."

HOW TO CONTACT E-queries only: submissions@scribeagency.com. See the website for submission info, as it may change. Responds in approximately 6 weeks to queries.

TERMS Agent receives 15% commission on domestic sales; 20% commission on foreign sales. Offers written contract. Charges for postage and photocopying.

WRITERS CONFERENCES BookExpo America, WisCon, Wisconsin Book Festival, World Fantasy Convention, WorldCon.

SECRET AGENT MAN

P.O. Box 1078, Lake Forest CA 92609-1078. (949) 698-6987. **E-mail:** query@secretagentman.net. **Website:** www.secretagentman.net. **Contact:** Scott Mortenson.

REPRESENTS Fiction. **Considers these fiction areas:** action, crime, detective, mystery, suspense, thriller, westerns.

Seeking selective mystery, thriller, suspense, and detective fiction. Does not want to receive scripts or screenplays.

HOW TO CONTACT Query via e-mail only; include sample chapter(s), synopsis, and/or outline. Prefers to read the real thing rather than a description of it. Accepts simultaneous submissions. Responds in 3-6 weeks. Obtains most new clients through recommendations from others.

LYNN SELIGMAN, LITERARY AGENT

400 Highland Ave., Upper Montclair NJ 07043. (973)783-3631. **Contact:** Lynn Seligman.

Prior to opening her agency, Ms. Seligman worked in the subsidiary rights department of Doubleday and Simon & Schuster, and served as an agent with Julian Bach Literary Agency (which became IMG Literary Agency). Foreign rights are represented by Books Crossing Borders, Inc.

REPRESENTS Nonfiction, fiction. **Considers these fiction areas:** commercial, ethnic, fantasy, feminist, historical, horror, humor, literary, mainstream, mystery, new adult, romance, science fiction, women's, young adult.

"This agency specializes in general nonfiction and fiction. I also do illustrated and photography books and have represented several photographers for books."

HOW TO CONTACT Query with SASE. Prefers to read materials exclusively. Accepts simultaneous submissions. Responds in 2 weeks to queries; in 2 months to mss. Obtains most new clients through referrals from other writers and editors.

TERMS Agent receives 15% commission on domestic sales; 25% commission on foreign sales. Charges clients for photocopying, unusual postage, express mail, telephone expenses (checks with author first).

RECENT SALES Sold 10 titles in 2015, including novels by Dee Ernst, Alexandra Hawkins, and Terra Little.

SERENDIPITY LITERARY AGENCY, LLC

305 Gates Ave., Brooklyn NY 11216. **E-mail:** rbrooks@serendipitylit.com; info@serendipitylit.com. **Website:** www.serendipitylit.com; facebook.com/serendipitylit. **Contact:** Regina Brooks. Represents 50 clients.

Prior to becoming an agent, Ms. Brooks was an acquisitions editor for John Wiley & Sons, Inc. and McGraw-Hill Companies.

MEMBER AGENTS **Regina Brooks; Dawn Michelle Hardy** (nonfiction, including sports, pop culture, blog and trend, music, lifestyle, and social science), **Folade Bell** (literary and commercial women's fiction, young adult, literary mysteries and thrillers, historical fiction, African-American issues, gay/lesbian, Christian fiction, humor, and books that deeply explore other cultures; nonfiction that reads like fiction, including blog-to-book or pop culture); **Nadeen Gayle** (romance, memoir, pop culture, inspirational/religious, women's fiction, parenting, young adult, mystery and political thrillers, and all forms of nonfiction); **Chelcee Johns** (narrative nonfiction, investigative journalism, memoir, inspirational self-help, religion/spirituality, international, popular culture, current affairs, literary and commercial fiction).

REPRESENTS **Considers these fiction areas:** commercial, gay, historical, lesbian, literary, middle-grade, mystery, romance, thriller, women's, young adult, Christian.

HOW TO CONTACT "Check the website, as there are online submission forms for fiction, nonfiction, and juvenile. Website will also state if we're temporarily closed to submissions in any areas." Accepts simultaneous submissions. Obtains most new clients through conferences, referrals.

TERMS Agent receives 15% commission on domestic sales; 20% commission on foreign sales. Offers written contract; two-month notice must be given to terminate contract. Charges clients for office fees, which are taken from any advance.

TIPS "See the books *Writing Great Books for Young Adults* and *You Should Really Write a Book: How to Write Sell and Market Your Memoir.* We are looking for high-concept ideas with big hooks. If you get writer's block, try possibiliteas.co. It's a muse in a cup."

THE SEYMOUR AGENCY

475 Miner St., Canton NY 13617. (315)386-1831. **E-mail:** marysue@twcny.rr.com; nicole@theseymouragency.com; julie@theseymouragency.com; lane@theseymouragency.com. **Website:** www.theseymouragency.com. Member of AAR. Signatory of WGA. Other memberships include RWA, Authors Guild, HWA.

Ms. Seymour is a retired New York State certified teacher. Ms. Resciniti was recently named "Agent of the Year" by the ACFW.

MEMBER AGENTS **Mary Sue Seymour** (Christian, inspirational, romance, and nonfiction); **Nicole Resciniti** (all genres of romance, young adult, middle-grade, new adult, suspense, thriller, mystery, science fiction, fantasy); **Julie Gwinn** (Christian and inspirational fiction and nonfiction, women's fiction [contemporary and historical], new adult, Southern fiction, literary fiction, young adult); **Lane Heymont** (science fiction, fantasy, romance, nonfiction).

REPRESENTS Nonfiction, fiction. **Considers these fiction areas:** action, fantasy, inspirational, middle-grade, mystery, new adult, religious, romance, science fiction, suspense, thriller, young adult.

HOW TO CONTACT For Mary Sue: E-query with synopsis, first 50 pages for romance. Accepts e-mail queries. For Nicole, Julie, and Lane: E-mail the query plus first 5 pages of the ms pasted into the e-mail. Accepts simultaneous submissions. Responds in 1 month to queries; in 3 months to mss.

TERMS Agent receives 12-15% commission on domestic sales.

DENISE SHANNON LITERARY AGENCY, INC.

20 W. 22nd St., Ste. 1603, New York NY 10010. **E-mail:** submissions@deniseshannonagency.com. **Website:** www.deniseshannonagency.com. **Contact:** Denise Shannon. Estab. 2002. Member of AAR.

Prior to opening her agency, Ms. Shannon worked for 16 years with Georges Borchardt and International Creative Management.

REPRESENTS Nonfiction, fiction. **Considers these fiction areas:** literary.

"We are a boutique agency with a distinguished list of fiction and nonfiction authors."

HOW TO CONTACT "Queries may be submitted by post, accompanied by an SASE, or by e-mail to submissions@deniseshannonagency.com. Please include a description of the available book project and a brief bio, including details of any prior publications. We will reply and request more material if we are interested. We request that you inform us if you are submitting material simultaneously to other agencies." Accepts simultaneous submissions.

RECENT SALES *Mister Monkey* by Francine Prose (Harper), *Hotel Solitaire* by Gary Shteyngart (Random House), *White Flights* by Jess Row (Graywolf Press), *The Underworld* by Kevin Canty (Norton).

TIPS "Please do not send queries regarding fiction projects until a complete ms is available for review."

WENDY SHERMAN ASSOCIATES, INC.

27 W. 24th St., Ste. 700B, New York NY 10010. (212)279-9027. **E-mail:** submissions@wsherman.com. **Website:** www.wsherman.com. **Contact:** Wendy Sherman. Member of AAR.

Prior to opening the agency, Ms. Sherman served as vice president, executive director, associate publisher, subsidiary rights director, and sales and marketing director for major publishers.

MEMBER AGENTS **Wendy Sherman** (women's fiction that hits that sweet spot between literary and mainstream, Southern voices, historical dramas, suspense with a well-developed protagonist, writing that illuminates the multicultural experience, anything related to food, dogs, mothers, and daughters).

REPRESENTS Nonfiction, fiction. **Considers these fiction areas:** mainstream fiction that hits the sweet spot between literary and commercial.

"We specialize in developing new writers as well as working with more established writers. My experience as a publisher has proven to be a great asset to my clients."

HOW TO CONTACT Query via e-mail only. "We ask that you include your last name, title, and the name of the agent you are submitting to in the subject line. For fiction, please include a query letter and your first 10 pages copied and pasted in the body of the e-mail. We will not open attachments unless they have been requested. For nonfiction, please include your query letter and author bio. Due to the large number of e-mail submissions we receive, we can only reply to e-mail queries in the affirmative. We respectfully ask that you do not send queries to our individual e-mail addresses." Accepts simultaneous submissions. Obtains most new clients through recommendations from other writers.

TERMS Agent receives standard 15% commission. Offers written contract.

RECENT SALES *All Is Not Forgotten* by Wendy Walker; *Z, A Novel of Zelda Fitzgerald* by Therese Anne Fowler; *The Charm Bracelet* by Viol Shipman; *The Silence of Bonaventure Arrow* by Rita Leganski; *Together Tea* by Marjan Kamali; *A Long Long Time Ago* and *Essentially True* by Brigid Pasulka; *Lunch in Paris* by Elizabeth Bard; *The Rules of Inheritance* by Claire Bidwell Smith.

TIPS "The bottom line is: Do your homework. Be as well prepared as possible. Read the books that will help you present yourself and your work with polish. You want your submission to stand out."

SPEILBURG LITERARY AGENCY

E-mail: speilburgliterary@gmail.com. **Website:** speilburgliterary.com. **Contact:** Alice Speilburg. Estab. 2012. Member of SCBWI, MWA, RWA.

Alice Speilburg previously held publishing positions at John Wiley & Sons and Howard Morhaim Literary Agency.

REPRESENTS Nonfiction, fiction. **Considers these fiction areas:** historical, literary, mainstream, middle-grade, mystery, police, science fiction, thriller, women's, young adult.

HOW TO CONTACT If you are interested in submitting your ms or proposal for consideration, please e-mail a query letter along with either 3 sample chapters for fiction, or a TOC and proposal for nonfiction. Accepts simultaneous submissions.

SPENCERHILL ASSOCIATES

8131 Lakewood Main St., Building M, Ste. 205, Lakewood Ranch FL 34202. (941)907-3700. **E-mail:** submission@spencerhillassociates.com. **Website:** www.spencerhillassociates.com. **Contact:** Karen Solem, Nalini Akolekar, Amanda Leuck, Sandy Harding. Member of AAR.

Prior to becoming an agent, Ms. Solem was editor in chief at HarperCollins and an associate publisher.

MEMBER AGENTS Karen Solem, Nalini Akolekar, Amanda Leuck, Sandy Harding.

REPRESENTS Fiction. **Considers these fiction areas:** commercial, erotica, literary, mainstream, mystery, paranormal, romance, thriller.

"We handle mostly commercial women's fiction, historical novels, romance (historical, contemporary, paranormal, urban fantasy), thrillers, and mysteries. We also represent Christian fiction." No nonfiction, poetry, science fiction, children's picture books, or scripts.

HOW TO CONTACT "We accept electronic submissions and are no longer accepting paper queries. Please send us a query letter in the body of an e-mail, pitch us your project, and tell us about yourself: Do you have prior publishing credits? Attach the first 3 chapters and synopsis, preferably in DOC, RTF, or TXT format, to your e-mail. Send all queries to submission@spencerhillassociates.com. We do not have a preference for exclusive submissions but do appreciate knowing if the submission is simultaneous. We receive thousands of submissions a year, and each query receives our attention. Unfortunately, we are unable to respond to each query individually. If we are interested in your work, we will contact you within 12 weeks." Accepts simultaneous submissions.

TERMS Agent receives 15% commission on domestic sales; 20% commission on foreign sales. Offers written contract; three-month notice must be given to terminate contract.

RECENT SALES A full list of sales and clients is available on the agency website.

THE SPIELER AGENCY

27 W. 20 St., Ste. 305, New York NY 10011. **E-mail:** thespieleragency@gmail.com. **Website:** thespieleragency.com. **Contact:** Joe Spieler. Represents 160 clients.

Prior to opening his agency, Mr. Spieler was a magazine editor.

MEMBER AGENTS **Victoria Shoemaker**, victoria@thespieleragency.com (environment and natural history, popular culture, memoir, photography and film, literary fiction and poetry, and books on food and cooking); **John Thornton**, john@thespieleragency.com (nonfiction); **Joe Spieler**, joe@thespieleragency.com (nonfiction and fiction and books for children and young adults); **Helen Sweetland** helen@thespieleragency.com (children's, from board books through young adult fiction; adult general-interest nonfiction, including nature, green living, gardening, architecture, interior design, health, and popular science).

REPRESENTS Nonfiction, fiction, juvenile books. **Considers these fiction areas:** literary, middle-grade, New Age, picture books, thriller, young adult.

HOW TO CONTACT "Before submitting projects to the Spieler Agency, check the listings of our individual agents and see if any particular agent shows a general interest in your subject (e.g., history, memoir, young adult, etc.). Please send all queries either by e-mail or regular mail. If you query us by regular mail, we can only reply to you if you include an SASE." Accepts simultaneous submissions. Cannot guarantee a personal response to all queries. Obtains most new clients through recommendations, listing in *Guide to Literary Agents*.

TERMS Agent receives 15% commission on domestic sales. Charges clients for messenger bills, photocopying, postage.

WRITERS CONFERENCES London Book Fair.

TIPS "Check www.publishersmarketplace.com/members/spielerlit."

NANCY STAUFFER ASSOCIATES

P.O. Box 1203, Darien CT 06820. (203)202-2500. **E-mail:** nancy@staufferliterary.com. **Website:** www.publishersmarketplace.com/members/nstauffer. **Contact:** Nancy Stauffer Cahoon. Other memberships include Authors Guild.

"Over the course of my more than 20-year career, I've held positions in the editorial, marketing, business, and rights departments of *The New York Times*, McGraw-Hill, and Doubleday. Before founding Nancy Stauffer Associates, I was director of foreign and performing rights, then director of subsidiary rights, for Doubleday, where I was honored to have worked with a diverse range of internationally known and best-selling authors of all genres."

REPRESENTS **Considers these fiction areas:** literary.

HOW TO CONTACT Accepts simultaneous submissions. Obtains most new clients through referrals from existing clients.

TERMS Agent receives 15% commission on domestic sales; 20% commission on foreign sales.

RECENT SALES *Thunder Boy Jr.* by Sherman Alexie, *Our Souls At Night* by Kent Haruf, *Bone Fire* by Mark Spragg.

STRACHAN LITERARY AGENCY

P.O. Box 2091, Annapolis MD 21404. **E-mail:** query@strachanlit.com. **Website:** www.strachanlit.com. **Contact:** Laura Strachan. Estab. 1998.

Prior to becoming an agent, Ms. Strachan was (and still is) an attorney.

REPRESENTS Nonfiction, fiction. **Considers these fiction areas:** literary, short story collections, translation, young adult.

"This agency specializes in literary fiction and narrative nonfiction."

HOW TO CONTACT E-mail queries only with brief synopsis and bio; no attachments or samples unless requested. Accepts simultaneous submissions.

ROBIN STRAUS AGENCY, INC.

229 E. 79th St., Ste. 5A, New York NY 10075. (212)472-3282. **Fax:** (212)472-3833. **E-mail:** info@robinstrausagency.com. **Website:** www.robinstrausagency.com. **Contact:** Ms. Robin Straus. Estab. 1983. Member of AAR.

Prior to becoming an agent, Robin Straus served as a subsidiary rights manager at Random House and Doubleday. She began her career in the editorial department of Little, Brown.

REPRESENTS Considers these fiction areas: commercial, literary, mainstream, women's.

Does *not* represent juvenile, young adult, science fiction/fantasy, horror, romance, westerns, poetry, or screenplays.

HOW TO CONTACT E-query, or query via snail mail with SASE. "Send us a query letter with contact information, an autobiographical summary, a brief synopsis or description of your book project, submission history, and information on competition. If you wish, you may also include the opening chapter of your ms (pasted). While we do our best to reply to all queries, you can assume that if you haven't heard from us after 6 weeks, we are not interested." Accepts simultaneous submissions.

TERMS Agent receives 15% commission on domestic sales; 20% commission on foreign sales. Offers written contract.

THE STRINGER LITERARY AGENCY LLC

P.O. Box 770365, Naples FL 34107 USA. **E-mail:** mstringer@stringerlit.com. **E-mail:** Use website form to submit. **Website:** www.stringerlit.com. **Contact:** Marlene Stringer. Estab. 2008. Member of AAR, RWA, MWA, ITW, SBCWI. Signatory of WGA. Represents about 50 clients.

REPRESENTS Fiction. **Considers these fiction areas:** commercial, crime, detective, fantasy, historical, mainstream, multicultural, mystery, new adult, paranormal, police, romance, science fiction, suspense, thriller, urban fantasy, women's, young adult.

This agency specializes in fiction. "We are an editorial agency, and we work with clients to make their mss the best they can be in preparation for submission. We focus on career planning and help our clients reach their publishing goals. We advise clients on marketing and promotional strategies to help them reach their target readership. Because we are so hands-on, we limit the size of our list; however, we are always looking for exceptional voices and stories that demand we read to the end. You never know where the next great story is coming from." This agency is seeking thrillers, crime fiction (not true crime), mystery, women's fiction, single-title and category romance, fantasy (all subgenres), earth-based science fiction (no space opera, aliens, etc.), and young adult/teen. Does not want to receive picture books, middle-grade, plays, short stories, or poetry. This is not the agency for inspirational romance or erotica. The agency is not seeking nonfiction at this time.

HOW TO CONTACT Electronic submissions through website submission form only. "Please make sure your ms is as good as it can be before you submit. Agents are not first readers. For specific information on what we like to see in query letters, refer to the information at www.stringerlit.com under the heading 'Learn.'" Accepts simultaneous submissions. "We strive to respond quickly, but current clients' work always comes first." Obtains new clients through referrals, submissions, conferences.

RECENT SALES *The Conqueror's Wife* by Stephanie Thornton; *When I'm Gone* by Emily Bleeker; *Magic Bitter, Magic Sweet* by Charlie N. Holmberg; *Belle Chasse* by Suzanne Johnson; *Chapel of Ease* by Alex Bledsoe; *Wilds of the Bayou* by Susannah Sandlin; *Summit Lake* by Charlie Donlea; The Jane Doe Series by Liana Brooks; *The Mermaid's Secret* by Katie Schickel; *The Sutherland Scandals* by Anna Bradley; *Fly By Night* by Andrea Thalasinos; The Joe Gale Mystery Series by Brenda Buchanan; The Kate Baer Series by Shannon Baker; Los Nephilim Series by T. Frohock; The Dragonsworn Series by Caitlyn McFarland; *The Devious Dr. Jekyll* by Viola Carr; *The Dragon's Price* by Bethany Wiggins; The Otter Bite Romance Series by Maggie McConnell; *Machinations* by Haley Stone; film rights to *Wreckage* by Emily Bleeker.

WRITERS CONFERENCES RWA National and various other conferences each year.

TIPS "If your ms falls between categories, or you are not sure of the category, query and we'll let you know if we'd like to take a look. We strive to respond as quickly as possible. If you have not received a response in the time period indicated on our website, please re-query."

THE STUART AGENCY

260 W. 52 St., #25C, New York NY 10019. (212)586-2711. **E-mail:** andrew@stuartagency.com. **Website:** stuartagency.com. **Contact:** Andrew Stuart. Estab. 2002.

Prior to his current position, Mr. Stuart was an agent with Literary Group International for 5 years. Prior to becoming an agent, he was an editor at Random House and Simon & Schuster.

MEMBER AGENTS **Andrew Stuart** (history, science, narrative nonfiction, business, current events, memoir, psychology, sports, literary fiction); **Christopher Rhodes**, christopher@stuartagency.com (literary and upmarket fiction [including thriller and horror]; connected stories/essays [humorous and serious]; memoir; creative/narrative nonfiction; history; religion; pop culture; art and design); **Rob Kirkpatrick**, rob@stuartagency.com (memoir, biography, sports, music, pop culture, current events, history, pop science).

REPRESENTS Nonfiction, fiction. **Considers these fiction areas:** horror, literary, thriller.

HOW TO CONTACT Query via online submission form on the agency website. Accepts simultaneous submissions.

RECENT SALES Projects and clients include former Congressman Ron Paul's *New York Times* No. 1 bestseller *The Revolution*; legendary publisher and free speech advocate Larry Flynt; Pulitzer Prize-winning journalists Kathleen Parker, William Dietrich, and Carl Cannon; political scientist Alan Wolfe; Hollywood studio mogul Mike Medavoy; Mark Bauerlein, author of the national bestseller *The Dumbest Generation*; Christopher Ryan, author of the *New York Times* bestseller *Sex at Dawn*; renowned child psychiatrist Bruce Perry; intellectual historian Matthew Stewart, author of *The Courtier and the Heretic*; *New York Times* best-selling novelist Mary Monroe; and the *New York Times* bestseller *The Darwin Awards: Evolution in Action*.

TALCOTT NOTCH LITERARY

31 Cherry St., Ste. 104, Milford CT 06460. (203)876-4959. **Fax:** (203)876-9517. **E-mail:** editorial@talcottnotch.net. **Website:** www.talcottnotch.net. **Contact:** Gina Panettieri, president. Represents 150 clients.

Prior to becoming an agent, Ms. Panettieri was a freelance writer and editor. Ms. Munier was director of acquisitions for Adams Media Corporation and had previously worked for Disney. Ms. Dugas and Ms. Sulaiman had both completed internships with Sourcebooks prior to joining Talcott Notch.

MEMBER AGENTS **Gina Panettieri**, gpanettieri@talcottnotch.net (history, business, self-help, science, gardening, cookbooks, crafts, parenting, memoir, true crime, travel, young adult, middle-grade, women's fiction, paranormal, urban fantasy, horror, science fiction, historical, mystery, thrillers, suspense); **Paula Munier**, pmunier@talcottnotch.net (mystery/thriller, science fiction/fantasy, romance, young adult, memoir, humor, pop culture, health and wellness, cooking, self-help, pop psych, New Age, inspirational, technology, science, writing); **Rachael Dugas**, rdugas@talcottnotch.net (young adult, middle-grade, romance, women's fiction); **Saba Sulaiman**, ssulaiman@talcottnotch.net (upmarket literary and commercial fiction, romance [all subgenres except paranormal], character-driven psychological thrillers, cozy mysteries, memoir, young adult [except paranormal and science fiction], middle-grade, nonfiction humor).

REPRESENTS Nonfiction, fiction, juvenile books. **Considers these fiction areas:** commercial, fantasy, historical, horror, literary, mainstream, middle-grade, mystery, New Age, paranormal, romance, science fiction, suspense, thriller, urban fantasy, women's, young adult.

HOW TO CONTACT Query via e-mail (preferred) with first 10 pages of the ms pasted within the body of the e-mail, not as an attachment. Accepts simultaneous submissions. Responds in 2 weeks to queries; in 6-10 weeks to mss.

TERMS Agent receives 15% commission on domestic sales; 20% commission on foreign sales. Offers written contract, binding for 1 year.

RECENT SALES Agency sold 40 titles in the last year, including *Tier One* by Brian Andrews and Jeffrey Wilson (Thomas & Mercer) and *Beijing Red* (written as Alex Ryan) (Crooked Lane Books), *Firestorm* by Nancy Holzner (Berkley Ace Science Fiction), *The New Jersey Mob* by Scott Deitche (Rowman and Littlefield), *The Homeplace* by Kevin Wolf (St. Martin's Press), *The Goblin Crown* by Robert Hewitt Wolfe (Turner Publishing), *Disintegration* by Richard Thomas (Random House/Alibi), *Red Line* by Brian Thiem (Crooked Lane Books), and more.

TIPS "Know your market and how to reach them. A strong platform is essential in your book proposal. Can you effectively use social media? Are you a strong networker? Are you familiar with the book bloggers in your genre? Are you involved with the interest-specific groups that can help you? What can you do to break through the 'noise' and help present your book to your readers? Check our website for more tips and information on this topic."

TESSLER LITERARY AGENCY, LLC

27 W. 20th St., Ste. 1003, New York NY 10011. (212)242-0466. **Website:** www.tessleragency.com. **Contact:** Michelle Tessler. Estab. 2004. Member of AAR. Women's Media Group.

Prior to forming her own agency, Ms. Tessler worked at the prestigious literary agency Carlisle & Company (now Inkwell Management) and at the William Morris Agency.

REPRESENTS Nonfiction, fiction. **Considers these fiction areas:** commercial, literary, women's.

"Tessler Literary Agency represents a select number of best-selling and emerging authors. Based in the Flatiron District in Manhattan, we are dedicated to writers of high-quality fiction and nonfiction. Our clients include accomplished journalists, scientists, academics, experts in their field, as well as novelists and debut authors with unique voices and stories to tell. We value fresh, original writing that has a compelling point of view. Our list is diverse and far-reaching. In nonfiction, it includes narrative, popular science, memoir, history, psychology, business, biography, food, and travel. In many cases, we sign authors who are especially adept at writing books that cross many of these categories at once. In fiction, we represent literary, women's, and commercial. If your project is in keeping with the kind of books we take on, we want to hear from you." Does not want genre fiction or children's books or anthologies.

HOW TO CONTACT Submit query through online query form only. Accepts simultaneous submissions. New clients by queries/submissions through the website, recommendations from others.

TERMS Receives 15% commission on domestic sales; 20% on foreign sales. Offers written contract.

THOMPSON LITERARY AGENCY

115 W. 29th St., Third Floor, New York NY 10001. (347)281-7685. **E-mail:** info@thompsonliterary.com; meg@thompsonliterary.com. **E-mail:** submissions@thompsonliterary.com. **Website:** thompsonliterary.com. **Contact:** Meg Thompson. Estab. 2014. Member of AAR. Signatory of WGA.

Before her current position, Ms. Thompson was with LJK Literary and the Einstein Thompson Agency.

MEMBER AGENTS **Cindy Uh**, senior agent (picture books, middle-grade, and young adult, including nonfiction queries; loves compelling characters and distinct voices, and more diversity—of all types—is always welcome!); **John Thorn**, affiliate agent; **Sandy Hodgman**, director of foreign rights.

REPRESENTS Nonfiction, fiction, juvenile books. **Considers these fiction areas:** commercial, historical, juvenile, literary, middle-grade, picture books, women's, young adult.

The agency is always on the lookout for both commercial and literary fiction as well as young adult and children's books. "Nonfiction, however, is our specialty, and our interests include biography, memoir, music, popular science, politics, blog-to-book projects, cookbooks, sports, health and wellness, fashion, art, and popular culture. Please note that we do not accept submissions for poetry collections or screenplays, and we only consider picture books by established illustrators."

HOW TO CONTACT "For fiction: Please send a query letter, including any salient biographical information or previous publications, and attach the first 25 pages of your ms. For nonfiction: Please send a query letter and a full proposal, including biographical information, previous publications, credentials that qualify you to write your book, marketing information, and sample material. You should address your query to whichever agent you think is best suited for your project." Accepts simultaneous submissions. Responds in 6 weeks if interested.

THREE SEAS LITERARY AGENCY

P.O. Box 8571, Madison WI 53708. (608)834-9317. **E-mail:** queries@threeseaslit.com. **Website:** threeseasagency.com. **Contact:** Michelle Grajkowski, Cori Deyoe. Estab. 2000. Member of AAR. Other memberships include RWA, SCBWI. Represents 55 clients.

Since its inception, 3 Seas has sold more than 500 titles worldwide. Ms. Grajkowski's authors have appeared on all the major lists, including *The New York Times*, *USA Today*, and *Publishers Weekly*. Prior to joining the agency in 2006, Ms. Deyoe was a multipublished author. She represents a wide range of authors and has sold many projects at auction.

MEMBER AGENTS **Michelle Grajkowski** (romance, women's fiction, young adult, middle-grade, select nonfiction projects); **Cori Deyoe** (all subgenres of romance, women's fiction, young adult, middle-grade, picture books, thrillers, mysteries, select nonfiction); **Linda Scalissi** (women's fiction, thrillers, young adult, mysteries, romance).

REPRESENTS Nonfiction, fiction. **Considers these fiction areas:** middle-grade, mystery, picture books, romance, thriller, women's, young adult.

"We represent more than 50 authors who write romance, women's fiction, science fiction/fantasy, thrillers, young adult and middle-grade fiction, as well as select nonfiction titles. Currently, we are looking for fantastic authors with a voice of their own." 3 Seas does not represent poetry or screenplays.

HOW TO CONTACT E-mail queries only; no attachments, unless requested by agents. For fiction, please e-mail the first chapter and synopsis along with a cover letter. Also, be sure to include the genre and the number of words in your ms, as well as pertinent writing experience in your query letter. For nonfiction, e-mail a complete proposal, including a query letter and your first chapter. For picture books, query with complete text. Accepts simultaneous submissions. Obtains most new clients through recommendations from others, conferences.

TERMS Agent receives 15% commission on domestic sales; 20% commission on foreign sales. Offers written contract.

RECENT SALES Clients include best-selling authors: Jennifer Brown, Katie MacAlister, Kerrelyn Sparks, and C.L. Wilson.

TRANSATLANTIC LITERARY AGENCY

2 Bloor St. E., Ste. 3500, Toronto ON M4W 1A8 Canada. (416)488-9214. **E-mail:** info@transatlanticagency.com. **Website:** transatlanticagency.com.

MEMBER AGENTS **Trena White** (upmarket, accessible nonfiction: current affairs, business, culture, politics, technology, and the environment); **Amy Tompkins** (adult: literary fiction, historical fiction, women's fiction, including smart romance, narrative nonfiction, and quirky or original how-to books; children's: early readers, middle-grade, young adult, new adult); **Stephanie Sinclair** (literary fiction, upmarket women's and commercial fiction, literary thriller and suspense, young adult crossover, narrative nonfiction, memoir, investigative journalism, true crime); **Samantha Haywood** (literary fiction and upmarket commercial fiction, specifically literary thrillers and upmarket mystery, historical fiction, smart contemporary fiction, upmarket women's fiction, and crossover novels; narrative nonfiction, including investigative journalism, politics, women's issues, memoirs, environmental issues, historical narratives, sexuality, true crime; full-length graphic novels [fiction/nonfiction]; story collections; memoirs; biographies; travel narratives); **Jesse Finkelstein** (nonfiction: current affairs, business, culture, politics, technology, religion, the environment); **Marie Campbell** (middle-grade fiction); **Shaun Bradley** (referrals only; adult literary fiction and narrative nonfiction, primarily science and investigative journalism); **Sandra Bishop** (fiction; nonfiction: biography, memoir, and positive or humorous how-to books on advice/relationships, mind/body/spirit, religion, healthy living, finances, life hacks, traveling, living a better life); **Fiona Kenshole** (children's and young adult; only accepting submissions from referrals or conferences she attends as faculty); **Lynn Bennett** (not accepting submissions or new clients); **David Bennett** (children's, young adult, adult).

REPRESENTS Nonfiction, fiction, juvenile books.

"In both children's and adult literature, we market directly into the U.S., the U.K., and Canada." Represents adult and children's authors of all genres, including illustrators. Does not want to receive picture books, musicals, screenplays, or stage plays.

HOW TO CONTACT Always refer to the website, as guidelines will change, and only various agents are open to new clients at any given time. Obtains most new clients through recommendations from others.

TERMS Agent receives 15% commission on domestic sales; 20% commission on foreign sales. Offers written contract; 45-day notice must be given to terminate contract. This agency charges for photocopying and postage when it exceeds $100.

RECENT SALES Sold 250 titles in the last year.

TRIADA U.S. LITERARY AGENCY, INC.

P.O. Box 561, Sewickley PA 15143 USA. (412)401-3376. **E-mail:** uwe@triadaus.com; brent@triadaus.com; laura@triadaus.com; mallory@triadaus.com. **Website:** www.triadaus.com. **Contact:** Dr. Uwe Stender. Estab. 2004. Member of AAR.

MEMBER AGENTS Uwe Stender, Brent Taylor, Laura Crockett, Mallory Brown.

REPRESENTS Nonfiction, fiction, juvenile books. **Considers these fiction areas:** action, adventure, contemporary issues, crime, detective, ethnic, fantasy, gay, historical, horror, juvenile, literary, mainstream, middle-grade, multicultural, mystery, new adult, occult, police, romance, suspense, thriller, urban fantasy, women's, young adult.

"We are looking for great writing and story platforms. Our response time is fairly unique. We recognize that neither we nor the authors have time to waste, so we guarantee a five-day response time. We usually respond within 24 hours." Actively looking for both fiction and nonfiction in all areas.

HOW TO CONTACT E-mail queries preferred. Accepts simultaneous submissions. Obtains most new clients through recommendations from others, conferences.

TERMS Agent receives 15% commission on domestic sales; 20% commission on foreign sales. Offers written contract; 30-day notice must be given to terminate contract.

RECENT SALES *Gettysburg Rebels* by Tom McMillan (Regency), *Who's That Girl* by Blair Thornburgh (Harper Collins Children's), *Perfect Ten* by L.Philips (Viking Children's), *You're Welcome Universe* by Whitney Gardner (Knopf Children's), *Timekeeper* by Tara Sim (Sky Pony), *My Seventh Grade Life in Tights* by Brooks Benjamin (Delacorte), *The Smart Girl's Guide to Polyamory* by Dedeker Winston (Skyhorse), *Raised by Animals* by Jennifer Verdolin (The Experiment), *The Hemingway Thief* by Shaun Harris (Seventh Street), *The Gravedigger's Son* by Patrick Moody (Sky Pony), *Plants You Can't Kill* by Stacy Tornio (Skyhorse), *Thieving Weasels* by Billy Taylor (Dial For Young Readers/Penguin), *Call Me Sunflower* by Miriam Spitzer Franklin (Sky Pony), *Tag You're Dead* by J.C. Lane (Poisoned Pen Press), *Arrivals and Departures* by Dee Romito (Aladdin/Simon & Schuster), *The Land of 10,000 Madonnas* by Kate Hattemer (Knopf Children's).

TIPS "We comment on all requested mss that we reject."

TRIDENT MEDIA GROUP

41 Madison Ave., 36th Floor, New York NY 10010. (212)333-1511. **Website:** www.tridentmediagroup.com. **Contact:** Ellen Levine. Member of AAR.

MEMBER AGENTS **Kimberly Whalen**, ws.assistant@tridentmediagroup (commercial fiction and nonfiction, including women's fiction, romance, suspense, paranormal, and pop culture); **Alyssa Eisner Henkin** (picture books through young adult fiction, including mysteries, period pieces, contemporary school settings, issues of social justice, family sagas, eerie magical realism, and retellings of classics; children's/young adult nonfiction: history, STEM/STEAM themes, memoir) **Scott Miller**, smiller@tridentmediagroup.com (commercial fiction, including thrillers, crime fiction, women's, book club fiction, middle-grade, young adult; nonfiction, including military, celebrity and pop culture, narrative, sports, prescriptive, and current events); **Melissa Flashman**, mflashman@tridentmediagroup.com (nonfiction: pop culture, memoir, wellness, popular science, business and economics, technology; fiction: adult and young adult, literary and commercial); **Don Fehr**, dfehr@tridentmediagroup.com (literary and commercial fiction, young adult fiction, narrative nonfiction, memoirs, travel, science, and health); **John Silbersack**, silbersack.assistant@tridentmediagroup.com (fiction: literary fiction, crime fiction, science fiction and fantasy, children's, thrillers/suspense; nonfiction: narrative nonfiction, science, history, biography, current events, memoirs, finance, pop culture); **Erica Spellman-Silverman; Ellen Levine**, levine.assistant@tridentmediagroup.com (popular commercial fiction and compelling nonfiction, including memoir, popular culture, narrative nonfiction, history, politics, biography, science, and the odd quirky book); **Mark Gottlieb** (fiction: science fiction, fantasy, young adult, graphic novels, historical, middle-grade, mystery, romance, suspense, thrillers; nonfiction: business, finance, history, religious, health, cookbooks, sports, African-American, biography, memoir, travel, mind/body/spirit, narrative nonfiction, science, technology); **Alexander Slater**, aslater@tridentmdiagroup.com (children's, middle-grade, young adult); **Amanda O'Connor**, aoconnor@tridentmediagroup.com; **Tara Carberry**, tcarberry@tridentmediagroup.com (women's commercial fiction, romance, new adult, young adult, select nonfiction); **Alexa Stark**, astark@tridentmediagroup.com (literary fiction, upmarket commercial fiction, young adult, memoir, narrative nonfiction, popular science, cultural criticism, women's issues).

REPRESENTS Considers these fiction areas: commercial, crime, fantasy, historical, juvenile, literary, middle-grade, mystery, new adult, paranormal, picture books, romance, science fiction, suspense, thriller, women's, young adult.

- Actively seeking new or established authors in a variety of fiction and nonfiction genres.

HOW TO CONTACT Submit through the agency's online submission form on the agency website. Query only 1 agent at a time. If you e-query, include no attachments. Accepts simultaneous submissions.

RECENT SALES *Fish Wielder* by J.R.R.R. (Jim) Hardison, *How to Steal the Mona Lisa: And Six Other World-Famous Treasures* by Taylor Bayouth.

TIPS "If you have any questions, please check our FAQ page on the website before e-mailing us."

UNION LITERARY

30 Vandam St., Ste. 5A, New York NY 10013. (212)255-2112. **E-mail:** info@unionliterary.com. **E-mail:** submissions@unionliterary.com. **Website:** unionliterary.com. Member of AAR. Signatory of WGA.

- "Prior to becoming an agent, Trena Keating was editor in chief of Dutton and associate publisher of Plume, both imprints of Penguin, senior editor at HarperCollins, and humanities assistant at Stanford University Press.

MEMBER AGENTS Trena Keating, tk@unionliterary.com (fiction and nonfiction, specifically a literary novel with an exotic setting, a young adult/middle-grade journey or transformation novel, a distinctly modern novel with a female protagonist, a creepy page-turner, a quest memoir that addresses larger issues, nonfiction based on primary research or a unique niche, a great essayist, and a voicy writer who is a great storyteller or makes her laugh); **Sally Wofford-Girand**, swg@unionliterary.com (history, memoir, women's issues, cultural studies, gripping literary fiction); **Jenni Ferrari-Adler**, jenni@unionliterary.com (fiction, cookbook/food, young adult and middle-grade, narrative nonfiction); **Christina Clifford**, christina@unionliterary.com (literary fiction, international fiction, narrative nonfiction, specifically historical biography, memoir, business, and science); **Shaun Dolan,** sd@unionliterary.com (muscular and lyrical literary fiction, narrative nonfiction, memoir, pop culture, and sports narratives).

- "Union Literary is a full-service boutique agency specializing in literary fiction, popular fiction, narrative nonfiction, memoir, social history, business and general big-idea books, popular science, cookbooks, and food writing." The agency does not represent romance, poetry, science fiction, or illustrated books.

HOW TO CONTACT Nonfiction submissions: Include a query letter, a proposal, and a sample chapter. Fiction submissions: Include a query letter, synopsis, and either sample pages or full ms. "Due to the high volume of submissions we receive, we will only be in contact regarding projects that feel like a match for the respective agent." Accepts simultaneous submissions. Responds in 1 month.

RECENT SALES *The Sunlit Night* by Rebecca Dinerstein, *Dept. of Speculation* by Jenny Offill, *Mrs. Houdini* by Victoria Kelly.

UNITED TALENT AGENCY

142 W. 57th St., Sixth Floor, New York NY 10019. (212)581-3100. **Website:** www.theagencygroup.com. **Contact:** Marc Gerald.

- Prior to becoming an agent, Mr. Gerald owned and ran an independent publishing and entertainment agency.

MEMBER AGENTS **Marc Gerald** (no queries); **Juliet Mushens**, U.K. literary division, juliet.mushens@unitedtalent.com (high-concept novels, thrillers, young adult, historical fiction, literary fiction, psychological suspense, reading group fiction, science fiction, fantasy); **Sasha Raskin**, sasah.raskin@unitedtalent.com (popular science, business books, historical narrative nonfiction, narrative and/or literary nonfiction, historical fiction, and genre fiction like science fiction but that fits the crossover space and isn't strictly confined to its genre); **Sarah Manning**, sarah.manning@unitedtalent.com (crime, thrillers, historical fiction, commercial women's fiction, accessible literary fiction, fantasy, young adult); **Diana Beaumont**, U.K. literary division, diana.beaumont@unitedtalent.com (accessible literary fiction with a strong hook, historical fiction, crime, thrillers, women's commercial fiction that isn't too marshmallowy, cookery, lifestyle, celebrity books, memoir with a distinctive voice).

REPRESENTS Nonfiction, fiction. **Considers these fiction areas:** commercial, crime, fantasy, historical, literary, science fiction, suspense, thriller, women's, young adult.

Please do not send Sarah middle-grade, picture books, erotica, or poetry. Please do not send Juliet any books aimed at children (other than young adult), nonfiction, erotica, or romance. Please do not send Diana picture books or middle-grade.

HOW TO CONTACT To query Juliet, please send your cover letter, first 3 chapters, and synopsis by e-mail. Juliet replies to all submissions and aims to respond within 8-12 weeks of receipt of e-mail. To query Sasha, e-query. To query Sarah, please send your cover letter in the body of your e-mail with synopsis and first 3 chapters. She responds to all submissions within 8-12 weeks. Accepts simultaneous submissions.

UPSTART CROW LITERARY

244 Fifth Ave., 11th Floor, New York NY 10001. **E-mail:** danielle.submission@gmail.com. **Website:** www.upstartcrowliterary.com. **Contact:** Danielle Chiotti, Alexandra Penfold. Estab. 2009. Member of AAR. Signatory of WGA.

MEMBER AGENTS **Michael Stearns** (not accepting submissions); **Danielle Chiotti** (all genres of young adult and middle-grade fiction; adult upmarket commercial fiction [not considering romance, mystery/suspense/thriller, science fiction, horror, or erotica]; nonfiction in the areas of narrative/memoir, lifestyle, relationships, humor, current events, food, wine, cooking); **Ted Malawer** (not accepting submissions); **Alexandra Penfold** (not accepting submissions).

REPRESENTS **Considers these fiction areas:** commercial, mainstream, middle-grade, picture books, young adult.

HOW TO CONTACT Submit a query and 20 pages pasted into an e-mail. Accepts simultaneous submissions.

VENTURE LITERARY

2683 Via de la Valle, G-714, Del Mar CA 92014. (619)807-1887. **Fax:** (772)365-8321. **E-mail:** submissions@ventureliterary.com. **Website:** www.ventureliterary.com. **Contact:** Frank R. Scatoni.

Prior to becoming an agent, Mr. Scatoni worked as an editor at Simon & Schuster.

MEMBER AGENTS Frank R. Scatoni, Greg Dinkin.

REPRESENTS Nonfiction, fiction, graphic novels, narratives. **Considers these fiction areas:** action, adventure, crime, detective, historical, literary, mainstream, mystery, police, sports, suspense, thriller, women's.

"We specialize in nonfiction and fiction projects that coincide with our interests—history, sports, business, philanthropy, pop culture, and any narrative that fascinates us. We are accepting queries in all genres except fantasy, science fiction, romance, children's picture books, and westerns."

HOW TO CONTACT Considers e-mail queries only. No unsolicited mss and no snail mail whatsoever. Usually responds within 1 month. See website for complete submission guidelines. Obtains most new clients through recommendations from others.

TERMS Agent receives 15% commission on domestic sales; 20% commission on foreign sales. Offers written contract.

VERITAS LITERARY AGENCY

601 Van Ness Ave., Opera Plaza, Ste. E, San Francisco CA 94102. (415)647-6964. **Fax:** (415)647-6965. **E-mail:** submissions@veritasliterary.com. **Website:** www.veritasliterary.com. **Contact:** Katherine Boyle. Member of AAR. Other memberships include Author's Guild, SCBWI.

MEMBER AGENTS **Katherine Boyle**, katherine@veritasliterary.com (literary fiction, middle-grade, young adult, narrative nonfiction and memoir, historical fiction, crime and suspense, history, pop culture, popular science, business and career); **Michael Carr**, michael@veritasliterary.com (historical fiction, women's fiction, science fiction and fantasy, nonfiction), **Chiara Rosati**, chiara@veritasliterary.com (literary fiction, middle-grade, young adult, new adult, women's studies, narrative nonfiction).

REPRESENTS Nonfiction, fiction. **Considers these fiction areas:** commercial, crime, fantasy, historical, literary, middle-grade, new adult, science fiction, suspense, women's, young adult.

HOW TO CONTACT This agency accepts short queries or proposals via e-mail only. "Fiction: Please include a cover letter listing previously published work, a one-page summary, and the first 5 pages in the body of the e-mail (not as an attachment). Nonfiction: If you are sending a proposal, please include an author biography, an overview, a chapter-by-chapter summary, and an analysis of competitive titles. We do our best to review all queries within 4-6 weeks; however, if you have not heard from us in 12 weeks, consider that a no." Accepts simultaneous submissions.

WALES LITERARY AGENCY, INC.

1508 10th Ave. E., #401, Seattle WA 98102. (206)284-7114. **E-mail:** waleslit@waleslit.com. **E-mail:** waleslit@waleslit.com. **Website:** www.waleslit.com. **Contact:** Elizabeth Wales, Neal Swain. Estab. 1990. Member of AAR, Authors Guild.

Prior to becoming an agent, Ms. Wales worked at Oxford University Press and Viking Penguin.

MEMBER AGENTS Elizabeth Wales, Neal Swain.

REPRESENTS Nonfiction, fiction.

This agency specializes in quality mainstream fiction and narrative nonfiction. Does not handle screenplays, children's picture books, genre fiction, or most category nonfiction (such as self-help or how-to books).

HOW TO CONTACT E-query with no attachments. Accepts simultaneous submissions. Responds in 2 weeks to queries, in 2 months to mss.

TERMS Agent receives 15% commission on domestic sales; 20% commission on foreign sales.

RECENT SALES *Mozart's Starling* by Lyanda Lynn Haupt (Little, Brown, 2017); *The Witness Tree* by Lynda Mapes (Bloomsbury USA, 2017); *Discovering America's Native Bees* by Paige Embry (Timber Press, 2017); *Gaining Lost Ground* by David Montgomery (W.W. Norton, 2017); *The United States of Cheddar* by Gordon Edgar (Chelsea Green, 2016); *Find the Good* by Heather Lende (Algonquin, 2015); *Still Time, a Novel* by Jean Hegland (Arcade, 2015).

TIPS "We are especially interested in work that espouses a progressive cultural or political view, projects a new voice, or simply shares an important, compelling story. We also encourage writers living in the Pacific Northwest, West Coast, Alaska, and Pacific Rim countries, and writers from historically underrepresented groups, such as gay and lesbian writers and writers of color, to submit work. (However, we don't discourage writers outside these areas.) Most importantly, whether in fiction or nonfiction, the agency is looking for talented storytellers."

WAXMAN LEAVELL LITERARY AGENCY, INC.

443 Park Ave. S., Ste. 1004, New York NY 10016. (212)675-5556. **Fax:** (212)675-1381. **Website:** www.waxmanleavell.com.

MEMBER AGENTS **Scott Waxman** (nonfiction: history, biography, health and science, adventure, business, inspirational sports); **Byrd Leavell** (narrative nonfiction, sports, humor, select commercial fiction); **Holly Root** (middle-grade, young adult, women's fiction [commercial and upmarket], urban fantasy, romance, select nonfiction); **Larry Kirschbaum** (fiction and nonfiction, select self-published breakout books); **Rachel Vogel** (nonfiction: subject-driven narratives, memoirs and biography, journalism, popular culture and the occasional humor and gift book; selective fiction); **Julie Stevenson** (literary fiction, atmospheric thrillers, suspense-driven work); **Taylor Haggerty** (young adult, historical, contemporary and historical romance, middle-grade, women's, new adult); **Cassie Hanjian** (fiction: new adult, plot-driven commercial and upmarket women's fiction, historical fiction, psychological suspense, cozy mysteries, contemporary romance; nonfiction: mind/body/spirit, self-help, health and wellness, inspirational memoir, food/wine [narrative and prescriptive], and a limited number of accessible cookbooks); **Fleetwood Robbins** (fantasy and speculative fiction—all subgenres); **Molly O'Neill** (middle-grade and young adult fiction and picture book author/illustrators, and—more selectively—narrative nonfiction [including children's/young adult/middle-grade, pop science/pop culture, and lifestyle/food/travel/cookbook projects by authors with well-established platforms]).

REPRESENTS Nonfiction, fiction. **Considers these fiction areas:** fantasy, historical, literary, mainstream, middle-grade, mystery, paranormal, romance, science fiction, suspense, thriller, urban fantasy, women's, young adult.

HOW TO CONTACT To submit a project, please send a query letter ONLY via e-mail to 1 of the addresses included on the website. Do not send attachments, though for fiction you may include 5-10 pages of your ms in the body of your e-mail. "Due to the high volume of submissions, agents will reach out to you directly if interested. The typical time range for consideration is 6-8 weeks." Accepts simultaneous submissions.

TERMS Agent receives 15% commission on domestic sales; 10% commission on foreign sales. Offers written contract; two-month notice must be given to terminate contract.

O CK WEBBER ASSOCIATES, LITERARY MANAGEMENT

E-mail: carlie@ckwebber.com. **Website:** ckwebber.com. **Contact:** Carlie Webber. Member of AAR. Signatory of WGA.

Ms. Webber's professional publishing experience includes an internship at Writers House and work with the Publish or Perish Agency/New England Publishing Associates and the Jane Rotrosen Agency.

REPRESENTS Nonfiction, fiction. **Considers these fiction areas:** fantasy, literary, mainstream, middle-grade, mystery, new adult, romance, science fiction, suspense, thriller, women's, young adult.

"We are currently not accepting picture books, easy readers, poetry, scripts, and curriculum nonfiction."

HOW TO CONTACT "To submit your work for consideration, please send a query letter, synopsis, and the first 30 pages or 3 chapters of your work, whichever is more, to carlie@ckwebber.com. Put the word 'query' in the subject line of your e-mail. You may include your materials either in the body of your e-mail or as a Word or PDF attachment. Blank emails that include an attachment will be deleted unread. We only accept queries via e-mail." Accepts simultaneous submissions.

◉ WELLS ARMS LITERARY

E-mail: info@wellsarms.com. **Website:** www.wellsarms.com. **Contact:** Victoria Wells Arms. Estab. 2013. Member of SCBWI, Society of Illustrators. Represents 25 clients.

Victoria's career began as an editor at Dial Books for Young Readers, then G.P. Putnam's Sons, and then as the founding editorial director and associate publisher of Bloomsbury USA's Children's Division.

REPRESENTS Fiction, juvenile books, children's book illustrators. **Considers these fiction areas:** juvenile, middle-grade, picture books, young adult.

"We focus on books for young readers of all ages: board books, picture books, readers, chapter books, middle-grade, and young adult fiction. We do not represent to the textbook, magazine, adult romance, or fine art markets."

HOW TO CONTACT E-query. Put "query" and your title in your e-mail subject line. No attachments. Accepts simultaneous submissions. "We try to respond within 1 month."

WOLF LITERARY SERVICES, LLC

Website: wolflit.com. Estab. 2008. Member of AAR. Signatory of WGA.

MEMBER AGENTS **Kirsten Wolf** (no queries); **Kate Johnson** (literary fiction [particularly character-driven stories], psychological investigations, modern-day fables, international tales, magical realism, historical fiction; nonfiction: food, feminism, parenting, art, travel, the environment; loves working with journalists); **Allison Devereux** (literary and upmarket commercial fiction; nonfiction, including examinations of contemporary culture, pop science, and modern feminist perspectives; humor and blog-to-book; illustrated novels or memoir; narrative nonfiction that uses a particular niche topic to explore larger truths about our culture).

REPRESENTS **Considers these fiction areas:** commercial, historical, literary, magical realism.

HOW TO CONTACT To submit a project, please send a query letter along with a 50-page writing sample (for fiction) or a detailed proposal (for nonfiction) to queries@wolflit.com. Samples may be submitted as an attachment or embedded in the body of the e-mail. Accepts simultaneous submissions.

RECENT SALES *A Criminal Magic* by Lee Kelly (Saga Press/Simon & Schuster), *Shallow Graves* by

Kali Wallace (Katherine Tegen Books/HarperCollins), *A Hard and Heavy Thing* by Matthew J. Hefti (Tyrus Books), *What Was Mine* by Helen Klein Ross (S&S/Gallery), *The Extra Woman* by Joanna Scutts (Liveright/Norton), *For the Record* by Charlotte Huang (Delacorte).

● WOLFSON LITERARY AGENCY

P.O. Box 266, New York NY 10276. **E-mail:** query@wolfsonliterary.com. **Website:** www.wolfsonliterary.com. **Contact:** Michelle Wolfson. Estab. 2007. Adheres to AAR canon of ethics.

Prior to forming her own agency in December 2007, Ms. Wolfson spent 2 years with Artists & Artisans, Inc. and 2 years with Ralph Vicinanza, Ltd.

REPRESENTS Nonfiction, fiction. **Considers these fiction areas:** mainstream, mystery, new adult, romance, suspense, thriller, women's, young adult.

Actively seeking commercial fiction: young adult, mainstream, mysteries, thrillers, suspense, women's fiction, romance. For nonfiction, seeking fun, practical advice books in any area, but particularly those that are of interest to women.

HOW TO CONTACT E-queries only. Accepts simultaneous submissions. Responds only if interested. Positive response is generally given within 2-4 weeks. Responds in 3 months to mss. Obtains most new clients through queries or recommendations from others.

TERMS Agent receives 15% commission on domestic sales; 25% commission on foreign sales. Offers written contract; 30-day notice must be given to terminate contract.

TIPS "Be persistent."

⊙ WORDSERVE LITERARY GROUP

7061 S. University Blvd., Ste. 307, Centennial CO 80122. **E-mail:** admin@wordserveliterary.com. **Website:** www.wordserveliterary.com. **Contact:** Greg Johnson. Represents 100 clients.

Prior to becoming an agent in 1994, Mr. Johnson was a magazine editor and freelance writer of more than 20 books and 200 articles.

MEMBER AGENTS Greg Johnson, Nick Harrison, Sarah Freese.

REPRESENTS Nonfiction, fiction. **Considers these fiction areas:** historical, inspirational, literary, mainstream, spiritual, suspense, thriller, women's, young adult.

Materials with a faith-based angle. No gift books, poetry, short stories, screenplays, graphic novels, children's picture books, science fiction, or fantasy. Please do not send mss that are more than 120,000 words.

HOW TO CONTACT E-query admin@wordserveliterary.com. In the subject line, include the word "query." All queries should include the following 3 elements: a pitch for the book, information about you and your platform (for nonfiction) or writing background (for fiction), and the first 5 (or so) pages of the ms pasted into the e-mail. Please view our website for full guidelines: www.wordserveliterary.com/submission-guidlines. Accepts simultaneous submissions. Responds within 60 days. Obtains most new clients through recommendations from others.

TERMS Agent receives 15% commission on domestic sales; 10-15% commission on foreign sales. Offers written contract; up to 60-day notice must be given to terminate contract.

TIPS "We are looking for good proposals, great writing, and authors willing to market their books, as appropriate. Also, we're only looking for projects with a faith element bent. See the website before submitting."

WRITERS HOUSE

21 W. 26th St., New York NY 10010. (212)685-2400. **Fax:** (212)685-1781. **Website:** www.writershouse.com. Estab. 1973. Member of AAR.

MEMBER AGENTS Amy Berkower; Stephen Barr; Susan Cohen; Dan Conaway; Lisa DiMona; Susan Ginsburg; Susan Golomb; Merrilee Heifetz; Brianne Johnson; Daniel Lazar; Simon Lipskar; Steven Malk; Jodi Reamer, Esq.; Robin Rue; Rebecca Sherman; Geri Thoma; Albert Zuckerman; Alec Shane; Stacy Testa; Victoria Doherty-Munro; Beth Miller; Andrea Morrison; Soumeya Roberts.

REPRESENTS Nonfiction, fiction. **Considers these fiction areas:** commercial, fantasy, juvenile, literary, mainstream, middle-grade, picture books, science fiction, women's, young adult.

This agency specializes in all types of popular fiction and nonfiction for both adult and juvenile books as well as illustrators. Does not want to receive scholarly, professional, poetry, plays, or screenplays.

HOW TO CONTACT Individual agent e-mail addresses are available on the website. "Please e-mail us a query letter, which includes your credentials, an explanation of what makes your book unique and special, and a synopsis. Some agents within our agency have different requirements. Please consult their individual Publishers Marketplace profile for details. We respond to all queries, generally within 6-8 weeks." If you prefer to submit by mail, address it to an individual agent, and please include an SASE for our reply. (If submitting to Steven Malk: Writers House, 7660 Fay Ave., #338H, La Jolla CA 92037.) Accepts simultaneous submissions. Obtains most new clients through recommendations from authors and editors.

TERMS Agent receives 15% commission on domestic sales; 20% commission on foreign sales. Offers written contract, binding for 1 year. Agency charges fees for copying mss/proposals and overseas airmail of books.

TIPS "Do not send mss. Write a compelling letter. If you do, we'll ask to see your work. Follow submission guidelines, and please do not simultaneously submit your work to more than 1 Writers House agent."

JASON YOUNG LITERARY AGENCY

3544 Broadway, #68, New York NY 10031. **E-mail:** jason@jasonyarnliteraryagency.com. **Website:** www.jasonyarnliteraryagency.com. Member of AAR. Signatory of WGA.

REPRESENTS Nonfiction, fiction. **Considers these fiction areas:** commercial, fantasy, literary, middle-grade, science fiction, suspense, thriller, young adult, graphic novels, comics.

HOW TO CONTACT Please e-mail your query to jason@jasonyarnliteraryagency.com with the word "Query" in the subject line, and please paste the first 10 pages of your ms or proposal into the text of your e-mail. Do not send any attachments. "Visit the About page on the website for information on what we are interested in, and please note that JYLA does not accept queries for film, TV, or stage scripts." Accepts simultaneous submissions.

RENÉE ZUCKERBROT LITERARY AGENCY

115 W. 29th St., 3rd Floor, New York NY 10001. (212)967-0072. **Fax:** (212)967-0073. **E-mail:** renee@rzagency.com. **E-mail:** submissions@rzagency.com. **Website:** rzagency.com. **Contact:** Renée Zuckerbrot. Member of AAR, PEN, Authors Guild. Represents 30 clients.

Prior to becoming an agent, Ms. Zuckerbrot worked as an editor at Doubleday as well as in the editorial department at Putnam.

REPRESENTS Nonfiction, fiction, short story collections. **Considers these fiction areas:** commercial, ethnic, short story collections, women's.

Narrative nonfiction (focusing on science, history and pop culture). No business books, self-help, spirituality, or romance. No screenplays.

HOW TO CONTACT Query by e-mail to submissions@rzagency.com. Include a synopsis, publication history, and a brief personal bio. You may include up to the first 3 chapters. Accepts simultaneous submissions. Responds in approximately 4-6 weeks.

TERMS Agent receives 15% commission on domestic sales; 25% commission on foreign sales (10% to RZA, 15% to foreign rights co-agent).

MAGAZINES

This section contains magazine listings that fall into one of several categories: literary, consumer, small circulation, and online. Our decision to combine magazines under one section was twofold: All of these magazines represent markets specifically for short fiction, and many magazines now publish both print and online versions, making them more difficult to subcategorize. Below, we outline specifics for literary, online, consumer, and small circulation magazines.

LITERARY MAGAZINES

Although definitions of what constitutes literary writing vary, editors of literary journals agree they want to publish the best fiction they can acquire. Qualities they look for in fiction include fully developed characters, strong and unique narrative voice, flawless mechanics, and careful attention to detail in content and manuscript preparation. Most of the authors writing such fiction are well read and well educated, and many are students or graduates of university creative writing programs.

Stepping Stones to Recognition

Some well-established literary journals pay several hundred or even several thousand dollars for a short story. Most, though, can only pay with contributor's copies or a subscription to their publication. However, being published in literary journals offers the important benefits of experience, exposure, and prestige. Agents and major book publishers regularly read literary magazines in search of new writers. Work from these journals is also selected for inclusion in annual prize anthologies.

You'll find most of the well-known prestigious literary journals listed here. Many, including *The Southern Review* and *Ploughshares*, are associated with universities, while others like *The Paris Review* are independently published.

Selecting the Right Literary Magazine

Once you have browsed through this section and have a list of journals you might like to submit to, read those listings again carefully. Remember, this is information editors provide to help you submit work that fits their needs. Note that you will find some magazines that do not read submissions all year long. Whether limited reading periods are tied to a university schedule or meant to accommodate the capabilities of a very small staff, those periods are noted within listings (when the editors notify us). The staffs of university journals are usually made up of student editors and a managing editor who is also a faculty member. These staffs often change every year. Whenever possible, we indicate this in listings and give the name of the current editor and the length of that editor's term. Also be aware that the schedule of a university journal usually coincides with that university's academic year, meaning that the editors of most university publications are difficult or impossible to reach during the summer.

Furthering Your Search

It cannot be stressed enough that reading the listings for literary journals is only the first part of developing your marketing plan. The second part, equally important, is to obtain fiction guidelines and to read with great care the actual journal you'd like to submit to. Reading copies of these journals helps you determine the fine points of each magazine's publishing style and sensibility. There is no substitute for this type of hands-on research.

Unlike commercial periodicals available at most newsstands and bookstores, it requires a little more effort to obtain some of the literary magazines listed. The super-chain bookstores are doing a better job these days of stocking literaries, and you can find some in independent and college bookstores, especially those published in your area. The Internet is an invaluable resource for submission guidelines, as more and more journals establish an online presence. You may, however, need to send for a sample copy. We include sample copy prices in the listings whenever possible. In addition to reading your sample copies, pay close attention to the **Tips** section of each listing. There you'll often find a very specific description of the style of fiction the editors at that publication prefer.

Another way to find out more about literary magazines is to check out the various prize anthologies and take note of journals whose fiction is being selected for publication in them. Studying prize anthologies not only lets you know which magazines are publishing award-winning work, but it also provides a valuable overview of what is considered to be the best fiction published today. Those anthologies include:

- *Best American Short Stories*, published by Houghton Mifflin
- *New Stories from the South: The Year's Best*, published by Algonquin Books of Chapel Hill
- *The O. Henry Prize Stories*, published by Doubleday/Anchor
- *Pushcart Prize: Best of the Small Presses*, published by Pushcart Press

CONSUMER MAGAZINES

Consumer magazines are publications that reach a broad readership. Many have circulations in the hundreds of thousands or millions. And among the oldest magazines listed in this section are ones not only familiar to us, but also to our parents, grandparents, and even great-grandparents: *The Atlantic Monthly* (1857), *Esquire* (1933), and *Ellery Queen's Mystery Magazine* (1941).

Consumer periodicals make excellent markets for fiction in terms of exposure, prestige, and payment. Because these magazines are well known, however, competition is great. Even the largest consumer publications buy only one or two stories an issue, yet thousands of writers submit to these popular magazines.

Despite the odds, it is possible for talented new writers to break into consumer magazines. Your keys to breaking into these markets include careful research, professional presentation, and, of course, top-quality fiction.

SMALL-CIRCULATION MAGAZINES

Small-circulation magazines include general interest, special interest, regional, and genre magazines with circulations under ten thousand. Although these magazines vary greatly in size, theme, format, and management, the editors are all looking for short stories. Their specific fiction needs present writers of all degrees of expertise and interests with an abundance of publishing opportunities. Among the diverse publications in this section are magazines devoted to almost every topic, every level of writing, and every type of writer. Some of these markets publish fiction about a particular geographic area or by authors who live in that locale.

Although not as high-paying as the large-circulation consumer magazines, you'll find some of the publications listed here do pay writers 10–50¢/word or more. Also, unlike the big consumer magazines, these markets are very open to new writers and relatively easy to break into. Their only criterion is that your story be well written, well presented, and suitable for their particular readership.

ONLINE MARKETS

As production and distribution costs go up and the number of subscribers falls, more and more magazines are giving up print publication and moving online. Relatively inexpensive to maintain and quicker to accept and post submissions, online fiction sites are growing fast in numbers and legitimacy. The benefit for writers is that your stories can get more attention in online journals than in small literary journals. Small journals have small print runs—five hundred to one thousand copies—so there's a limit on how many people will read your work. There is no limit when your work appears online.

There is also no limit to the types of online journals being published, offering outlets for a rich and diverse community of voices. These include genre sites, particularly those for science fiction, fantasy, and horror, and mainstream short fiction markets. Online literary journals range from the traditional to those with a decidedly quirkier bent. Writers will also find online outlets for more highly experimental and multimedia work.

While the medium of online publication is different, the traditional rules of publishing apply to submissions. Writers should research the site and archives carefully, looking for a match in sensibility for their work. Follow submission guidelines exactly and submit courteously. True, these sites aren't bound by traditional print schedules, so your work theoretically may be published more quickly. But that doesn't mean online journals have larger staffs, so exercise patience with editors considering your manuscript.

A final note about online publication: Like literary journals, the majority of these markets are either nonpaying or very low paying. In addition, writers will not receive print copies of the publications because of the medium. So in most cases, do not expect to be paid for your exposure.

SELECTING THE RIGHT MARKET

First, zero in on those markets most likely to be interested in your work. Begin by looking at the Category Index. If your work is more general—or conversely, very specialized—you may wish to browse through the listings, perhaps looking up those magazines published in your state or region.

In addition to browsing through the listings and using the Category Index, check the openness icons at the beginning of listings to find those most likely to be receptive to your work. This is especially true for beginning writers, who should look for magazines that say they are especially open to new writers ○ and for those giving equal weight to both new and established writers ◐. For more explanation about these icons, see the inside back cover of this book.

Once you have a list of magazines you might like to try, read their listings carefully. Much of the material within each listing carries clues that tell you more about the magazine. "How to Use *NSSWM*" describes in detail the listing information common to all the markets in this book.

The physical description appearing near the beginning of the listings can give you clues about the size and financial commitment to the publication. This is not always an indication of quality, but chances are a publication with expensive paper and four-color artwork on the cover has more prestige than a photocopied publication featuring a clip-art cover.

FURTHERING YOUR SEARCH

Most of the magazines listed here are published in the U.S. You will also find some English-speaking markets from around the world. These foreign publications are denoted with a ◕ symbol at the beginning of listings. To make it easier to find Canadian markets, we include a ✪ symbol at the start of those listings.

30 N

(formerly North Central Review), North Central College, CM #235, 30 N. Brainard St., Naperville IL 60540. (630)637-5291. **E-mail:** nccreview@noctrl.edu. **Website:** 30northblog.wordpress.com. *North Central Review,* published semiannually, considers work in all literary genres, including occasional interviews, from undergraduate writers globally. The journal's goal is for college-level, emerging creative writers to share their work publicly and create a conversation with each other. All styles and forms are welcome as submissions. The readers tend to value attention to form (but not necessarily fixed form), voice, and detail. Very long poems or sequences (running more than 4 or 5 pages) may require particular excellence because of the journal's space and budget constraints. Does not want overly sentimental language and hackneyed imagery. These are all-too-common weaknesses that readers see in submissions; recommends revision and polishing before sending work. Considers poetry by teens (undergraduate writers only).

HOW TO CONTACT Submit no more than 2 prose pieces. Accepts e-mail submissions (as Word attachments only); no fax submissions. Cover letter is preferred. Include name, postal address, phone number, and e-mail address (.edu address as proof of student status). If necessary (i.e., .edu address not available), include a photocopy of student ID with number marked out as proof of undergraduate status. Reads submissions September-March, with deadlines in February and October.

TIPS "Don't send anything you just finished moments ago—rethink, revise, and polish. Avoid sentimentalitity and abstraction. That said, *30N* publishes beginners, so don't hesitate to submit and, if rejected, submit again."

34THPARALLEL MAGAZINE

Paris, France. **E-mail:** 34thparallel@gmail.com. **Website:** www.34thparallel.net. **Contact:** Martin Chipperfield. Estab. 2007. *34thParallel Magazine,* published quarterly in digital and print editions, promotes and publishes the exceptional writing of new and emerging writers, writing that experiments with and tests boundaries, that communicates a sense of wonder, reality, tragedy, fantasy, and brilliance.

NEEDS Submit via online submissions manager (Submittable). Length: 1,500-3,500 words.

PAYMENT/TERMS Pays 1 complimentary copy of digital edition.

TIPS "We want it all, but we don't want everything. Take a look at the mag to get a feel for our style."

580 SPLIT, A JOURNAL OF ARTS & LETTERS

Mills College, Graduate English Department, 5000 MacArthur Blvd., Oakland CA 94613-0982. **E-mail:** five80split@gmail.com. **Website:** www.mills.edu/academics/graduate/eng/about/580_split.php. Estab. 1998. "*580 Split* is an annual journal of arts and literature published by graduate students of the English Department at Mills College. This national literary journal includes innovative and risk-taking fiction, creative nonfiction, poetry, and art and is one of the few literary journals carried by the Oakland Public Library. *580 Split* is also distributed in well-known Bay Area bookstores."

HOW TO CONTACT Submit via online submissions manager.

PAYMENT/TERMS Pays 1 contributor's copy.

TIPS "Get a hold of a past issue, read through it, find out what we are about. Check the website for most recent information."

ACM (ANOTHER CHICAGO MAGAZINE)

P.O. Box 408439, Chicago IL 60640. **E-mail:** editors@anotherchicagomagazine.net. **Website:** www.anotherchicagomagazine.net. **Contact:** Caroline Eick Kasner, managing editor; Matt Rowan, fiction editor; David Welch, poetry editor; Colleen O'Connor, nonfiction editor. Estab. 1977. "*Another Chicago Magazine* is a biannual literary magazine that publishes work by both new and established writers. We look for work that goes beyond the artistic and academic to include and address the larger world. The editors read submissions in fiction, poetry, and creative nonfiction year round. The best way to know what we publish is to read what we publish. If you haven't read *ACM* before, order a sample copy to know if your work is appropriate." Sends prepublication galleys.

Work published in *ACM* has been included frequently in *The Best American Poetry* and *The Pushcart Prize.* **Charges $3 submissions fee.**

NEEDS Length: up to 7,500 words.

HOW TO CONTACT Submit complete ms via online submissions manager.

TIPS "Support literary publishing by subscribing to at least 1 literary journal—if not ours, another. Get used to rejection slips, and don't get discouraged. Keep introductory letters short. Make sure ms has name and address on every page, and that it is clean, neat, and proofread. We are looking for stories with freshness and originality in subject angle and style, and work that encounters the world."

THE ADIRONDACK REVIEW

Stanhope St., Brooklyn NY 11237, United States. **E-mail:** editors@theadirondackreview.com. **E-mail:** www.theadirondackreview.submittable.com. **Website:** www.theadirondackreview.com. **Contact:** Angela Leroux-Lindsey, editor in chief; Megan Nolan, fiction editor; Nicholas Samaras, poetry editor; Giovanni Appruzzese, translations editor; Alex Guarco, associate editor. Estab. 2000. *The Adirondack Review* is an online quarterly literary magazine featuring poetry, fiction, art, photography, and translations.

NEEDS Length: up to 6,000 words.

HOW TO CONTACT Submit via online submissions manager.

TIPS "*The Adirondack Review* accepts submissions all year long, so send us your poetry, fiction, nonfiction, translation, reviews, interviews, and art and photography."

AFRICAN VOICES

African Voices Communications, Inc., 270 W. 96th St., New York NY 10025. (212)865-2982. **E-mail:** africanvoicesart@gmail.com. **Website:** www.africanvoices.com. **Contact:** Maitefa Angaza, managing editor; Mariahadessa Ekere Tallie, poetry editor. Estab. 1992. *African Voices*, published quarterly, is an "art and literary magazine that highlights the work of people of color. We publish ethnic literature and poetry on any subject. We also consider all themes and styles: avant-garde, free verse, haiku, light verse, and traditional. We do not wish to limit the reader or author."

NEEDS Length: 500-2,500 words.

HOW TO CONTACT Send complete ms. Include short bio. Accepts submissions by postal mail. Send SASE for return of ms.

PAYMENT/TERMS Pays contributor's copies.

TIPS "A ms stands out if it is neatly typed with a well-written and interesting storyline or plot. Originality is encouraged. We are interested in more horror, erotic, and drama pieces. *AV* wants to highlight the diversity in our culture. Stories must touch the humanity in us all. We strongly encourage new writers/poets to send in their work. Accepted contributors are encouraged to subscribe."

AGNI

Boston University, 236 Bay State Rd., Boston MA 02215. (617)353-7135. **E-mail:** agni@bu.edu. **Website:** www.agnimagazine.org. **Contact:** Sven Birkerts, editor. Estab. 1972. Eclectic literary magazine publishing first-rate poems, essays, translations, and stories.

Reading period is September 1-May 31 only. Online magazine carries original content not found in print edition. All submissions are considered for both. Founding editor Askold Melnyczuk won the 2001 Nora Magid Award for Magazine Editing. Work from *AGNI* has been included and cited regularly in the *Pushcart Prize*, O. Henry, and *Best American* anthologies.

NEEDS Buys short stories. No genre scifi, horror, mystery, or romance.

HOW TO CONTACT Submit online or by regular mail, no more than one story at a time. E-mailed submissions will not be considered. Include a stamped addressed envelope or your e-mail address if sending by mail.

PAYMENT/TERMS Pays $10/page up to $150 (higher some years with grant support), plus a one-year subscription, and, for print publication, 2 contributor's copies and 4 gift copies.

TIPS "We're also looking for extraordinary translations from little-translated languages. It is important to read work published in *AGNI* before submitting, to see if your own might be compatible."

ALASKA QUARTERLY REVIEW

University of Alaska Anchorage, 3211 Providence Dr. (ESH 208), Anchorage AK 99508. **Fax:** (907)786-6916. **E-mail:** uaa_aqr@uaa.alaska.edu. **Website:** www.uaa.alaska.edu/aqr. **Contact:** Ronald Spatz, editor in chief. Estab. 1982. "*Alaska Quarterly Review* is a literary journal devoted to contemporary literary art, publishing fiction, short plays, poetry, photo essays, and literary nonfiction in traditional and experimental styles. The editors encourage new and emerging writers, while continuing to publish award-winning and established writers."

Reads mss August 15-May 15.

NEEDS "Works in *AQR* have certain characteristics: freshness, honesty, and a compelling subject.

MAGAZINES

The voice of the piece must be strong—idiosyncratic enough to create a unique persona. We look for craft, putting it in a form where it becomes emotionally and intellectually complex. Many pieces in *AQR* concern everyday life. We're not asking our writers to go outside themselves and their experiences to the absolute exotic to catch our interest. We look for the experiential and revelatory qualities of the work. We will champion a piece that may be less polished or stylistically sophisticated if it engages me, surprises me, and resonates for me. The joy in reading such a work is in discovering something true. Moreover, in keeping with our mission to publish new writers, we are looking for voices our readers do not know, voices that may not always be reflected in the dominant culture and that, in all instances, have something important to convey." No romance, children's, or inspirational/religious. Length: up to 50 pages.

HOW TO CONTACT Submit complete ms by postal mail. Include cover letter with contact information and SASE for return of ms.

PAYMENT/TERMS Pays contributor's copies and honoraria when funding is available.

TIPS "Although we respond to e-mail queries, we cannot review electronic submissions."

ALBEDO ONE

8 Bachelor's Walk, Dublin 1 , Ireland. **E-mail:** bobn@yellowbrickroad.ie. **Website:** www.albedo1.com. **Contact:** Bob Nielson. Estab. 1993. "We are always looking for thoughtful, well-written fiction. Our definition of what constitutes science fiction, horror, and fantasy is extremely broad, and we love to see material which pushes at the boundaries or crosses between genres."

NEEDS Length: 2,000-8,000 words.

HOW TO CONTACT Submit complete ms by mail or e-mail.

PAYMENT/TERMS Pays €6 per 1,000 words, to a maximum of 8,000 words, and 1 contributor's copy.

TIPS "We look for good writing, good plot, good characters. Read the magazine, and don't give up."

THE ALEMBIC

Providence College, English Dept., Attn: The Alembic Editors, 1 Cunningham Square, Providence RI 02918-0001. **Website:** www.pcc.edu/about/literary-magazines/alembic. **Contact:** Magazine has revolving editor. Editorial term: 1 year. Estab. 1940. "*The Alembic* is an international literary journal featuring the work of both established and student writers and photographers. It is published each April by Providence College in Providence, Rhode Island."

NEEDS "We are open to all styles of fiction." Does not read December 1-July 31. Published Bruce Smith, Robin Behn, Rane Arroyo, Sharon Dolin, Jeff Friedman, and Khalid Mattawa. Length: up to 6,000 words.

HOW TO CONTACT Send complete ms with cover letter. Include brief bio. Send SASE (or IRC) for return of ms. Does not accept online submissions.

PAYMENT/TERMS Pays 2 contributor's copies.

TIPS "We're looking for stories that are wise, memorable, grammatical, economical, poetic in the right places, and end strongly. Take Heraclitus' claim that 'character is fate' to heart and study the strategies, styles, and craft of such masters as Anton Chekov, J. Cheever, Flannery O'Connor, John Updike, Rick Bass, Phillip Roth, Joyce Carol Oates, William Treavor, Lorrie Moore, and Ethan Canin."

ALIMENTUM, THE LITERATURE OF FOOD

P.O. Box 210028, Nashville TN 37221. **E-mail:** editor@alimentumjournal.com. **Website:** www.alimentumjournal.com. **Contact:** Peter Selgin, fiction and nonfiction editor; Esther Cohen, poetry editor. Estab. 2005. "*Alimentum* celebrates the literature and art of food. We welcome work from like-minded writers, musicians, and artists."

Essays appearing in *Alimentium* have appeared in *Best American Essays* and *Best Food Writing.*

NEEDS Has published Mark Kurlansky, Oliver Sacks, Dick Allen, Ann Hood, and Carly Sachs. Publishes short shorts. Also publishes literary essays, poetry, spot illustrations. Rarely comments on/critiques rejected mss. Length: up to 2,000 words.

HOW TO CONTACT Send complete ms by mail. Please include SASE.

PAYMENT/TERMS Pays 1 contributor's copy.

TIPS "No e-mail submissions, only snail mail. Mark outside envelope to the attention of Poetry, Fiction, or Nonfiction Editor."

THE ALLEGHENY REVIEW

Allegheny College Box 32, 520 N. Main St., Meadville PA 16335. **E-mail:** review@allegheny.edu. **Website:** alleghenyreview.wordpress.com. **Contact:** Senior editor. Estab. 1983. "*The Allegheny Review* is one of America's only nationwide literary magazines exclusively for undergraduate works of poetry, fiction, and nonfiction. Our intended audience is persons interested in quality literature."

Has published work by Dianne Page, Monica Stahl, and DJ Kinney.

NEEDS Receives 50 unsolicited mss/month. Accepts 3 mss/issue. Publishes ms 2 months after deadline. Publishes roughly 90% new writers/year. Also publishes short shorts (up to 20 pages), nonfiction, and poetry. Does not want "fiction not written by undergraduates—we accept nothing but fiction by currently enrolled undergraduate students. We consider anything catering to an intellectual audience." Length: up to 20 pages, double-spaced.

HOW TO CONTACT Submit complete ms via online submissions manager.

PAYMENT/TERMS Pays 1 contributor's copy; additional copies $3. Sponsors awards/contests; reading fee $5.

TIPS "We look for quality work that has been thoroughly revised. Unique voice, interesting topic, and playfulness with the English language. Revise, revise, revise! And be careful how you send it—the cover letter says a lot. We definitely look for diversity in the pieces we publish."

ALLEGORY

P.O. Box 2714, Cherry Hill NJ 08034. **E-mail:** submissions@allegoryezine.com. **Website:** www.allegoryezine.com. **Contact:** Ty Drago, editor. Estab. 1998. "We are an e-zine by writers for writers. Our articles focus on the art, craft, and business of writing. Our links and editorial policy all focus on the needs of fiction authors."

Allegory (as Peridot Books) won the Page One Award for Literary Contribution.

NEEDS Receives 150 unsolicited mss/month. Accepts 12 mss/issue; 24 mss/year. Agented fiction 5%. Publishes 10 new writers/year. Also publishes literary essays, literary criticism. Often comments on rejected mss. "No media tie-ins (*Star Trek*, *Star Wars*, etc., or space opera, vampires)." Length: 1,500-7,500 words; average length: 2,500 words.

HOW TO CONTACT "All submissions should be sent by e-mail (no letters or telephone calls) in either TXT or RTF format. Please place 'Submission [Title]-[first and last name]' in the subject line. Include the following in both the body of the e-mail and the attachment: your name, name to use on the story (byline) if different, your preferred e-mail address, your mailing address, the story's title, and the story's word count."

PAYMENT/TERMS Pays $15/story.

TIPS "Give us something original, preferably with a twist. Avoid gratuitous sex or violence. Funny always scores points. Be clever and imaginative, but be able to tell a story with proper mood and characterization. Put your name and e-mail address in the body of the story. Read the site and get a feel for it before submitting."

ALLIGATOR JUNIPER

Prescott College, 220 Grove Ave., Prescott AZ 86301. (928)350-2012. **Website:** alligatorjuniper.wordpress.com. "*Alligator Juniper* features contemporary poetry, fiction, creative nonfiction, and b&w photography. We encourage submissions from writers and photographers at all levels: emerging, early career, and established." Annual magazine comprised of the winners and finalists of national contests. "All entrants pay an $18 submission fee and receive a complementary copy of that year's issue in the spring. First-place winners in each genre receive a $1,000 prize. The first-place winner in photography receives a $500 award. Finalists in writing and images are published and paid in contributor copies. There is currently no avenue for submissions other than the annual contest."

NEEDS "No children's literature or genre work." Length: up to 30 pages.

HOW TO CONTACT Accepts submissions only through annual contest. Submit via online submission form or regular mail. If submitting by regular mail, include $18 entry fee payable to *Alligator Juniper* for each story. Include cover letter with name, address, phone number, and e-mail. Mss should be typed with numbered pages, double-spaced, 12-point font, and 1" margins. Include author's name on first page. "Double-sided submissions are encouraged." No e-mail submissions.

AMERICAN LITERARY REVIEW

University of North Texas, P.O. Box 311307, Denton TX 76203-1307. (940)565-2755. **E-mail:** americanliteraryreview@gmail.com. **Website:** www.americanliteraryreview.com. **Contact:** Bonnie Friedman, editor in chief. Estab. 1990. The *American Literary Review* publishes "excellent poetry, fiction, and nonfiction by writers at all stages of their careers." Beginning in fall 2013, *ALR* became an online publication."

Reading period is from October 1-May 1.

NEEDS "We would like to see more short shorts and stylistically innovative and risk-taking fiction. We like to see stories that illuminate the various layers of characters and their situations with great artistry. Give us distinctive character-driven stories that explore the complexities of human existence." Looks for "the small moments that contain more than at first possible, that surprise us with more truth than we thought we had a right to expect." Has published work by Marylee MacDonald, Michael Isaac Shokrian, Arthur Brown, Roy Bentley, Julie Marie Wade, and Karin Forfota Poklen. No genre works. Length: up to 8,000 words.

HOW TO CONTACT Submit 1 complete ms online through submission manager for a fee of $3. Does not accept submissions via e-mail or postal mail.

TIPS "We encourage writers and artists to examine our journal."

AMERICAN SHORT FICTION

Badgerdog Literary Publishing, P.O. Box 301209, Austin TX 78703. **E-mail:** editors@americanshortfiction.org. **Website:** www.americanshortfiction.org. **Contact:** Rebecca Markovits and Adeena Reitberger, editors. Estab. 1991. "Issued triannually, *American Short Fiction* publishes work by emerging and established voices: stories that dive into the wreck, that stretch the reader between recognition and surprise, that conjure a particular world with delicate expertise—stories that take a different way home."

Stories published by *American Short Fiction* are anthologized in *Best American Short Stories*, *Best American Non-Required Reading*, *The O. Henry Prize Stories*, *The Pushcart Prize: Best of the Small Presses*, and elsewhere.

NEEDS "Open to publishing mystery or speculative fiction if we feel it has literary value." Does not want young adult or genre fiction. Length: open.

HOW TO CONTACT *American Short Fiction* seeks "short fiction by some of the finest writers working in contemporary literature, whether they are established, new, or lesser-known authors." Also publishes stories under 2,000 words online. Submit 1 story at a time via online submissions manager ($3 fee). No paper submissions.

PAYMENT/TERMS Writers receive $250-500, 2 contributor's copies, free subscription to the magazine. Additional copies $5.

TIPS "We publish fiction that speaks to us emotionally, uses evocative and precise language, and takes risks in subject matter and/or form. Try to read a few issues of *American Short Fiction* to get a sense of what we like. Also, to be concise is a great virtue."

ANALOG SCIENCE FICTION & FACT

Dell Magazines, 44 Wall St., Suite 904, New York NY 10005-2401. **E-mail:** analog@dellmagazines.com. **Website:** www.analogsf.com. **Contact:** Trevor Quachri, editor. Estab. 1930. *Analog* seeks "solidly entertaining stories exploring solidly thought-out speculative ideas. But the ideas, and consequently the stories, are always new. Real science and technology have always been important in *ASF*, not only as the foundation of its fiction but as the subject of articles about real research with big implications for the future."

Fiction published in *Analog* has won numerous Nebula and Hugo Awards.

NEEDS "Basically, we publish science fiction stories. That is, stories in which some aspect of future science or technology is so integral to the plot that, if that aspect were removed, the story would collapse. The science can be physical, sociological, psychological. The technology can be anything from electronic engineering to biogenetic engineering. But the stories must be strong and realistic, with believable people (who needn't be human) doing believable things—no matter how fantastic the background might be." No fantasy or stories in which the scientific background is implausible or plays no essential role. Length: 2,000-7,000 words for short stories, 10,000-20,000 words for novelettes and novellas, and 40,000-80,000 for serials.

HOW TO CONTACT Send complete ms via online submissions manager (preferred) or postal mail. Does not accept e-mail submissions.

PAYMENT/TERMS Analog pays 8-10¢/word for short stories up to 7,500 words, 8-8.5¢ for longer material, 6¢/word for serials.

TIPS "I'm looking for irresistibly entertaining stories that make me think about things in ways I've never done before. Read several issues to get a broad feel for our tastes, but don't try to imitate what you read."

ANDERBO.COM

Anderbo Publishing, 270 Lafayette St., Suite 705, New York NY 10012-3364. **E-mail:** rrofihe@yahoo.com. **E-mail:** editors@anderbo.com. **Website:** www.anderbo.com. **Contact:** Rick Rofihe, editor in chief. Online literary magazine/journal. "Quality fiction, poetry, 'fact,' and photography on a website with 'print-feel' design." Member CLMP.

Received the Best New Online Magazine or Journal, *storySouth* Million Writers Award in 2005.

NEEDS Has published Lisa Margonelli, Margot Berwin, Jeffrey Lent, and Susan Breen. Does not want any genre literature. "We're interested only in literary fiction, poetry, and literary 'fact.'" Length: up to 3,500 words.

HOW TO CONTACT Send complete ms in the body of e-mail or as attachment in DOC or RTF format.

TIPS "We are looking for fiction that is unique, urgent, accessible, and involving. Look at our site and read what we've already published."

THE ANTIGONISH REVIEW

St. Francis Xavier University, P.O. Box 5000, Antigonish NS B2G 2W5, Canada. (902)867-3962. **Fax:** (902)867-5563. **E-mail:** tar@stfx.ca. **Website:** www.antigonishreview.com. **Contact:** Bonnie McIsaac, office manager. Estab. 1970. *The Antigonish Review*, published quarterly, tries "to produce the kind of literary and visual mosaic that the modern sensibility requires or would respond to."

NEEDS Send complete ms. Prefers hard copy. No erotica. Length: 500-5,000 words.

HOW TO CONTACT Send complete ms.

PAYMENT/TERMS Pays $50 and 2 contributor's copies for stories.

TIPS "Send for guidelines and/or sample copy. Send ms with cover letter and SASE with submission."

ANTIOCH REVIEW

P.O. Box 148, Yellow Springs OH 45387-0148. (937)769-1365. **E-mail:** ccheck@antiochreview.org. **Website:** www.antiochreview.org. **Contact:** Robert S. Fogarty, editor; Judith Hall, poetry editor. Estab. 1941. Literary and cultural review of contemporary issues and literature for general readership. *The Antioch Review* "is an independent quarterly of critical and creative thought. For well over 70 years, creative authors, poets, and thinkers have found a friendly reception—regardless of formal reputation. We get far more poetry than we can possibly accept, and the competition is keen. Here, where form and content are so inseparable and reaction is so personal, it is difficult to state requirements or limitations. Studying recent issues of *The Antioch Review* should be helpful."

NEEDS Quality fiction only, distinctive in style with fresh insights into the human condition. No science fiction, fantasy, or confessions. Length: generally under 8,000 words.

HOW TO CONTACT Send complete ms with SASE, preferably mailed flat. Fiction submissions are not accepted between June 1-September 1.

PAYMENT/TERMS Pays $20/printed page, plus 2 contributor's copies.

APALACHEE REVIEW

Apalachee Press, P.O. Box 10469, Tallahassee FL 32302. (850) 644-9114. **E-mail:** arsubmissions@gmail.com (for queries outside the U.S.). **Website:** apalacheereview.org. **Contact:** Michael Trammell, editor; Kathleen Laufenberg, nonfiction editor; Mary Jane Ryals, fiction editor; Jay Snodgrass and Chris Hayes, poetry editors. Estab. 1976. "At *Apalachee Review*, we are interested in outstanding literary fiction, but we especially like poetry, fiction, and nonfiction that addresses intercultural issues in a domestic or international setting/context." Annual.

Member CLMP.

NEEDS Receives 60-100 mss/month. Accepts 5-10 mss/issue. Agented fiction: 0.5%. Publishes 1-2 new writers/year. "We prefer fiction that is no longer than 15 pages in length." Has published Lu Vickers, Joe Clark, Joe Taylor, Jane Arrowsmith Edwards, Vivian Lawry, Linda Frysh, Charles Harper Webb, Reno Raymond Gwaltney. Also publishes short shorts. Does not want cliché-filled, genre-oriented fiction. Length: 600-3,300 words; average length: 2,200 words. Average length of short shorts: 250 words.

HOW TO CONTACT Send complete ms with cover letter. Include brief bio, list of publications. Send either SASE (international authors should see website for "international" guidelines: no IRCs, please) for return of ms or disposable copy of ms and #10 SASE for reply only.

PAYMENT/TERMS Pays 2 contributor's copies.

APEX MAGAZINE

Apex Publications, LLC, P.O. Box 24323, Lexington KY 40524. **E-mail:** lesley@apex-magazine.com. **Website:** www.apexbookcompany.com. **Contact:** Lesley Conner, managing editor. Estab. 2004. "An elite repository for new and seasoned authors with an other-worldly interest in the unquestioned and slightly bizarre parts of the universe."

"We want science fiction, fantasy, horror, and mash-ups of all three of the dark, weird stuff down at the bottom of your little literary heart."

NEEDS Length: 100-7,500 words.

HOW TO CONTACT Send complete ms.

PAYMENT/TERMS Pays 6¢/word.

APPALACHIAN HERITAGE

CPO 2166, Berea KY 40404. (859)985-3699. **Fax:** (859)985-3903. **E-mail:** appalachianheritage@berea.edu. **Website:** appalachianheritage.net. **Contact:** Jason Howard, editor. Estab. 1973. "We are seeking poetry, short fiction, literary criticism and biography, book reviews, and creative nonfiction, including memoirs, opinion pieces, and historical sketches. Unless you request not to be considered, all poems, stories, and articles published in *Appalachian Heritage* are eligible for our annual Plattner Award. All honorees are rewarded with a sliding bookrack with an attached commemorative plaque from Berea College Crafts, and First Place winners receive an additional stipend of $200."

Submission period: August 15-March 15.

NEEDS "We do not want to see fiction that has no ties to Southern Appalachia." Length: up to 7,500 words.

HOW TO CONTACT Submit complete ms. Send SASE for reply, return of ms.

PAYMENT/TERMS Pays 3 contributor's copies.

TIPS "Sure, we are *Appalachian Heritage* and we do appreciate the past, but we are a forward-looking contemporary literary quarterly, and, frankly, we receive too many nostalgic submissions. Please spare us the 'Papaw Was Perfect' poetry and the 'Mamaw Moved Mountains' mss and give us some hard-hitting prose, some innovative poetry, some inventive photography, and some original art. Help us be the ground-breaking, stimulating kind of quarterly we aspire to be."

APPLE VALLEY REVIEW: A JOURNAL OF CONTEMPORARY LITERATURE

88 South 3rd St., Suite 336, San Jose CA 95113. **E-mail:** editor@leahbrowning.net. **Website:** www.applevalleyreview.com. **Contact:** Leah Browning, editor. Estab. 2005. *Apple Valley Review: A Journal of Contemporary Literature*, published semiannually online, features "beautifully crafted poetry, short fiction, and essays."

NEEDS Receives 100+ mss/month. Accepts 1-4 mss/issue; 2-8 mss/year. Published Glen Pourciau, Robert Radin, Jessica Rafalko, Thomas Andrew Green, Inderjeet Mani, and Lisa Robertson. Also publishes short shorts. Does not want strict genre fiction, erotica, work containing explicit language, or anything "extremely violent or depressing." Length: 100-4,000+ words. Average length: 2,000 words. Average length of short shorts: 800 words.

HOW TO CONTACT Send complete ms with cover letter.

ARKANSAS REVIEW: A JOURNAL OF DELTA STUDIES

Department of English and Philosophy, P.O. Box 1890, Office: Humanities and Social Sciences, State University AR 72467-1890. (870)972-3043; (870)972-2210. **Fax:** (870)972-3045. **E-mail:** mtribbet@astate.edu. **E-mail:** jcollins@astate.edu; arkansasreview@astate.edu. **Website:** altweb.astate.edu/arkreview. **Contact:** Dr. Marcus Tribbett, general editor. Estab. 1998. "All material, creative and scholarly, published in the *Arkansas Review* must evoke or respond to the natural and/or cultural experience of the Mississippi River Delta region."

NEEDS Receives 30-50 unsolicited mss/month. Accepts 2-3 mss/issue; 5-7 mss/year. Agented fiction 1%. Publishes 3-4 new writers/year. Has published work by Susan Henderson, George Singleton, Scott Ely, and Pia Erhart. "No genre fiction. Must have a Delta focus." Length: up to 10,000 words.

HOW TO CONTACT Send complete ms.

PAYMENT/TERMS Pays 3 contributor's copies.

TIPS "Immerse yourself in the literature of the Delta, but provide us with a fresh and original take on its land, its people, its culture. Surprise us. Amuse us. Recognize what makes this region particular as well as universal, and take risks. Help us shape a new Delta literature."

ARTS & LETTERS JOURNAL OF CONTEMPORARY CULTURE

Georgia College & State University, Milledgeville GA 31061. (478)445-1289. **Website:** al.gcsu.edu. **Contact:** Laura Newbern, editor. Estab. 1999. *Arts & Letters Journal of Contemporary Culture*, published semiannually, is devoted to contemporary arts and literature, featuring ongoing series such as The World Poetry

Translation Series and The Mentors Interview Series. Wants work that is of the highest literary and artistic quality.

Work published in *Arts & Letters Journal* has received the Pushcart Prize.

NEEDS No genre fiction. Length: up to 25 pages typed and double-spaced.

HOW TO CONTACT Submit complete ms via online submissions manager.

PAYMENT/TERMS Pays $10 per printed page (minimum payment: $50) and 1 contributor's copy.

ART TIMES

P.O. Box 730, Mount Marion NY 12456. (845)246-6944. **Fax:** (845)246-6944. **E-mail:** info@arttimesjournal.com. **Website:** www.arttimesjournal.com. **Contact:** Raymond J. Steiner, editor. Estab. 1984. "*Art Times* est. 1984, covers the arts fields with essays about music, dance, theater, film, art, and includes short fiction and poetry as well as editorials is now, after 32 years, exclusively online. Our readers are mostly over 40, affluent, art-conscious and sophisticated. (Italy, France, Germany, Greece, Russia, etc.)."

NEEDS Looks for quality short fiction that aspires to be literary. Publishes 1-2 stories a month "Nothing violent, sexist, erotic, juvenile, racist, romantic, political, off-beat, or related to sports or juvenile fiction." Length: up to 1,500 words.

HOW TO CONTACT Send complete ms.

PAYMENT/TERMS Pays $20.

TIPS "Competition is greater (more submissions received), but keep trying. We publish new as well as published writers. Be familiar with *Art Times* and its special audience."

ASCENT ASPIRATIONS

1560 Arbutus Dr., Nanoose Bay BC C9P 9C8, Canada. **E-mail:** ascentaspirations@shaw.ca. **Website:** www.ascentaspirations.ca. **Contact:** David Fraser, editor. Estab. 1997. "*Ascent Aspirations* magazine publishes monthly online and once in print. The print issues are operated as contests. Please refer to current guidelines before submitting. *Ascent Aspirations* is a quality electronic publication dedicated to the promotion and encouragement of aspiring writers of any genre. The focus, however, is toward interesting experimental writing in dark mainstream, literary, science fiction, fantasy, and horror. Poetry can be on any theme. Essays need to be unique, current, and have social, philosophical commentary."

NEEDS Length: up to 1,000 words. Publishes short shorts.

HOW TO CONTACT Query by e-mail with Word attachment. Include estimated word count, brief bio, and list of publications. "If you have to submit by mail because it is your only avenue, provide a SASE with either International Coupons or Canadian stamps only."

PAYMENT/TERMS "No payment at this time."

TIPS "Short fiction should first of all tell a good story, take the reader to new and interesting imaginary or real places. Short fiction should use language lyrically and effectively, be experimental in either form or content, and take the reader into realms where they can analyze and think about the human condition. Write with passion for your material, be concise and economical, and let the reader work to unravel your story. In terms of editing, always proofread to the point where what you submit is the best it possibly can be. Never be discouraged if your work is not accepted; it may just not be the right fit for a current publication."

ASIMOV'S SCIENCE FICTION

Dell Magazines, 44 Wall St., Suite 904, New York NY 10005. **E-mail:** asimovs@dellmagazines.com. **Website:** www.asimovs.com. **Contact:** Sheila Williams, editor; Victoria Green, senior art director. Estab. 1977. "Magazine consists of science fiction and fantasy stories for adults and young adults. Publishes the best short science fiction available."

Named for a science fiction "legend," *Asimov's* regularly receives Hugo and Nebula Awards.

NEEDS Wants "science fiction primarily. Some fantasy and humor. It is best to read a great deal of material in the genre to avoid the use of some very old ideas." Submit ms via online submissions manager or postal mail; no e-mail submissions. No horror or psychic/supernatural, sword and sorcery, explicit sex or violence that isn't integral to the story. Would like to see more hard science fiction. Length: 750-15,000 words.

PAYMENT/TERMS Pays 8-10¢/word for short stories up to 7,500 words; 8-8.5¢/word for longer material. Works between 7,500-10,000 words by authors who make more than 8¢/word for short stories will receive a flat rate that will be no less than the payment would be for a shorter story.

TIPS "In general, we're looking for 'character-oriented' stories, those in which the characters, rather than the science, provide the main focus for the reader's interest. Serious, thoughtful, yet accessible fiction will constitute the majority of our purchases, but there's always room for the humorous as well."

THE ATLANTIC MONTHLY

The Watergate, 600 New Hampshire Ave., NW, Washington DC 20037. (202)266-6000. **Fax:** (202)266-6001. **E-mail:** submissions@theatlantic.com; pitches@theatlantic.com. **Website:** www.theatlantic.com. **Contact:** Scott Stossel, magazine editor; Ann Hulbert, literary editor. Estab. 1857. General magazine for an educated readership with broad cultural and public-affairs interests. "*The Atlantic* considers unsolicited mss, either fiction or nonfiction. A general familiarity with what we have published in the past is the best guide to our needs and preferences."

NEEDS "Seeks fiction that is clear, tightly written with strong sense of 'story' and well-defined characters." No longer publishes fiction in the regular magazine. Instead, it will appear in a special newsstand-only fiction issue. Receives 1,000 unsolicited mss/month. Accepts 7-8 mss/year. **Publishes 3-4 new writers/year.** Preferred length: 2,000-6,000 words.

HOW TO CONTACT Submit via e-mail with Word document attachment to submissions@theatlantic.com. Mss submitted via postal mail must be typewritten and double-spaced.

PAYMENT/TERMS Payment varies.

TIPS "Writers should be aware that this is not a market for beginner's work (nonfiction and fiction), nor is it truly for intermediate work. Study this magazine before sending only your best, most professional work. When making first contact, cover letters are sometimes helpful, particularly if they cite prior publications or involvement in writing programs. Common mistakes: melodrama, inconclusiveness, lack of development, unpersuasive characters and/or dialogue."

AUTHORSHIP

National Writers Association, 10940 S. Parker Rd., #508, Parker CO 80134. (303)841-0246. **E-mail:** natlwritersassn@hotmail.com. **Website:** www.nationalwriters.com. Estab. 1950s. "Association magazine targeted to beginning and professional writers. Covers how-to, humor, marketing issues. Disk and e-mail submissions preferred."

TIPS "Members of National Writers Association are given preference."

THE AVALON LITERARY REVIEW

CCI Publishing, P.O. Box 780696, Orlando FL 32878. (407)574-7355. **E-mail:** submissions@avalonliteraryreview.com. **Website:** www.avalonliteraryreview.com. **Contact:** Valerie Rubino, managing editor. Estab. 2011. "*The Avalon Literary Review* welcomes work from both published and unpublished writers and poets. We accept submissions of poetry, short fiction, and personal essays. While we appreciate the genres of fantasy, historical romance, science fiction, and horror, our magazine is not the forum for such work." Quarterly magazine.

NEEDS No erotica, science fiction, or horror. Length: 250-2,500.

HOW TO CONTACT Submit complete ms. Only accepts electronic submissions.

PAYMENT/TERMS Pays 5 contributor's copies.

TIPS "The author's voice and point of view should be unique and clear. We seek pieces which spring from the author's life and experiences. Fiction submissions which explore both the sweet and bitter of life, with a touch of humor, and poetry with vivid imagery, are a good fit for our review."

THE AWAKENINGS REVIEW

Awakenings Project, The, P.O. Box 177, Wheaton IL 60187. (630)606-8732. **E-mail:** ar@awakeningsproject.org. **Website:** www.awakeningsproject.org. **Contact:** Robert Lundin, editor. Estab. 1999. *The Awakenings Review* is published by the Awakenings Project. Begun in cooperation with the University of Chicago Center for Psychiatric Rehabilitation in 2000, *The Awakenings Review* has been acclaimed internationally and draws writers from all over the United States and from several other countries including Israel, South Africa, Australia, Finland, Switzerland, the United Kingdom, and Canada.

NEEDS Length: up to 5,000 words.

HOW TO CONTACT No e-mail submissions. Cover letter is preferred. Include SASE and short bio.

PAYMENT/TERMS Pays 1 contributor's copy, plus discount on additional copies.

THE BALTIMORE REVIEW

6514 Maplewood Rd., Baltimore MD 21212. **E-mail:** editor@baltimorereview.org. **Website:** www.baltimorereview.org. **Contact:** Barbara Westwood Diehl, senior editor. Estab. 1996. *The Baltimore Review* publishes poetry, fiction, and creative nonfiction from

Baltimore and beyond. Submission periods are August 1-November 30 and February 1-May 31.

NEEDS Length: 100-6,000 words.

HOW TO CONTACT Send complete ms using online submission form. Publishes 16-20 mss per online issue. Work published online also published in annual anthology.

PAYMENT/TERMS Pays $40.

TIPS "See editor preferences on staff page of website."

BARBARIC YAWP

BoneWorld Publishing, 3700 County Route 24, Russell NY 13684. **Website:** www.boneworldpublishing.com. Estab. 1997. "We publish what we like. Fiction should include some bounce and surprise. Our publication is intended for the intelligent, open-minded reader."

NEEDS "We don't want any pornography, gratuitous violence, or whining."

HOW TO CONTACT Submit complete ms by postal mail. Send SASE for reply and return of ms, or send a disposable copy of ms. Accepts simultaneous, multiple submissions, and reprints.

PAYMENT/TERMS Pays 1 contributor's copy; additional copies $3.

TIPS "Don't give up. Read much, write much, submit much. Observe closely the world around you. Don't borrow ideas from TV or films. Revision is often necessary—grit your teeth and do it. Never fear rejection."

THE BARCELONA REVIEW

Correu Vell 12-2, Barcelona 08002, Spain. (00 34) 93 319 15 96. **E-mail:** editor@barcelonareview.com. **Website:** www.barcelonareview.com. **Contact:** Jill Adams, editor. Estab. 1997. *The Barcelona Review* is "the Web's first multilingual review of international, contemporary, cutting-edge fiction. *TBR* is actually 3 separate reviews—English, Spanish, and Catalan—with occasional translations from 1 language to another. Original texts of other languages are presented along with English and Spanish translations as available."

"We cannot offer money to contributors, but in lieu of pay we can sometimes offer an excellent Spanish translation (worth quite a bit of money in itself). Work is showcased along with 2 or more known authors in a high-quality literary review with an international readership."

NEEDS Length: up to 4,500 words.

HOW TO CONTACT Submit 1 story at a time. To submit via e-mail, send an attached document. Do not send in the body of an e-mail. Include "Submission/Author Name" in the subject box. Accepts hard copies, but they will not be returned. Double-space ms.

TIPS "Send top-drawer material that has been drafted 2, 3, 4 times—whatever it takes. Then sit on it for a while and look at it afresh. Keep the text tight. Grab the reader in the first paragraph and don't let go. Keep in mind that a perfectly crafted story that lacks a punch of some sort won't cut it. Make it new, make it different. Surprise the reader in some way. Read the best of the short fiction available in your area of writing to see how yours measures up. Don't send anything off until you feel it's ready, and then familiarize yourself with the content of the review/magazine to which you are submitting."

BARRELHOUSE

E-mail: yobarrelhouse@gmail.com. **Website:** www.barrelhousemag.com. **Contact:** Dave Housley, Mike Ingram, and Joe Killiany, fiction editors; Tom McAllister, nonfiction editor; Dan Brady, poetry editor. Estab. 2004. "*Barrelhouse* is a biannual print journal featuring fiction, poetry, interviews, and essays about music, art, and the detritus of popular culture."

Stories originally published in *Barrelhouse* have been featured in the *Best American Nonrequired Reading, Best American Science Fiction and Fantasy*, and the Million Writer's Award.

NEEDS Length: open, but prefers pieces under 8,000.

HOW TO CONTACT Submit complete ms via online submissions manager. DOC or RTF files only.

PAYMENT/TERMS Pays $50 and 2 contributor copies.

BATEAU

P.O. Box 1584, Northampton MA 01061. (413)586-2494. **E-mail:** dmahoney@coa.edu. **E-mail:** bateaupress@gmail.com. **Website:** www.bateaupress.org. **Contact:** Daniel Mahoney, editor in chief. Estab. 2007. "*Bateau*, published annually, subscribes to no trend but serves to represent as wide a cross-section of contemporary writing as possible. For this reason, readers will most likely love and hate at least something in each issue. We consider this a good thing. To us, it means *Bateau* is eclectic, open-ended, and not mired in a particular strain."

HOW TO CONTACT Submit via e-mail (bateaupress@gmail.com). Include "SUBMISSION" and the genre in subject heading. Brief bio is encouraged but not required.

PAYMENT/TERMS Pays contributor's copies.

TIPS "Send us your best work. Send us funny work, quirky work, outstanding work, work that is well punctuated or lacks punctuation. Fearless work. Work that wants to crash on our sofa."

BAYOU

Department of English, University of New Orleans, 2000 Lakeshore Dr., New Orleans LA 70148. **E-mail:** bayou@uno.edu. **Website:** bayoumagazine.org. **Contact:** Joanna Leake, editor in chief. Estab. 2002. "A nonprofit journal for the arts, each issue of *Bayou* contains beautiful fiction, nonfiction, and poetry. From quirky shorts to more traditional stories, we are committed to publishing solid work, regardless of style. At *Bayou* we are always interested first in a well-told tale. Our poetry and prose are filled with memorable characters observing their world, acknowledging both the mundane and the sublime, often at once, and always with an eye toward beauty. *Bayou* is packed with a range of material from established, award-winning authors as well as new voices on the rise. Recent contributors include Eric Trethewey, Virgil Suarez, Marilyn Hacker, Sean Beaudoin, Tom Whalen, Mark Doty, Philip Cioffari, Lyn Lifshin, Timothy Liu, and Gaylord Brewer. In 1 issue every year, *Bayou* features the winner of the annual Tennessee Williams/New Orleans Literary Festival One-Act Play Competition."

Does not accept e-mail submissions. Reads submissions August 1-May 1.

NEEDS "Flash fiction and short-shorts are welcome. No novel excerpts, please, unless they can stand alone as short stories." No horror, gothic, or juvenile fiction. Length: up to 7,500 words.

HOW TO CONTACT Send complete ms via online submission system or postal mail.

PAYMENT/TERMS Pays 2 contributor's copies.

TIPS "Do not submit in more than 1 genre at a time. Don't send a second submission until you receive a response to the first."

THE BEAR DELUXE MAGAZINE

Orlo, 240 N. Broadway, #112, Portland OR 97227. **E-mail:** bear@orlo.org. **Website:** www.orlo.org. **Contact:** Tom Webb, editor in chief; Kristin Rogers Brown, art director. Estab. 1993. "*The Bear Deluxe Magazine* is a national independent environmental arts magazine publishing significant works of reporting, creative nonfiction, literature, visual art, and design. Based in the Pacific Northwest, it reaches across cultural and political divides to engage readers on vital issues effecting the environment. Published twice per year, *The Bear Deluxe* includes a wider array and a higher percentage of visual artwork and design than many other publications. Artwork is included both as editorial support and as standalone or independent art. It has included nationally recognized artists as well as emerging artists. As with any publication, artists are encouraged to review a sample copy for a clearer understanding of the magazine's approach. Unsolicited submissions and samples are accepted and encouraged."

NEEDS "We are most excited by high-quality writing that furthers the magazine's goal of engaging new and divergent readers. We appreciate strong aspects of storytelling and are open to new formats, though we wouldn't call ourselves publishers of 'experimental fiction.'" No traditional sci-fi, horror, romance, or crime/action. Length: up to 4,000 words.

HOW TO CONTACT Query or send complete ms. Prefers postal mail submissions.

PAYMENT/TERMS Pays free subscription to the magazine, contributor's copies, and $25-400, depending on piece; additional copies for postage.

TIPS "Offer to be a stringer for future ideas. Get a copy of the magazine and guidelines, and query us with specific nonfiction ideas and clips. We're looking for original, magazine-style stories, not fluff or PR. Fiction, essay, and poetry writers should know we have an open and blind review policy and they should keep sending their best work even if rejected once. Be as specific as possible in queries."

BELLEVUE LITERARY REVIEW

NYU Langone Medical Center, Department of Medicine, 550 First Ave., OBV-A612, New York NY 10016. (212)263-3973. **E-mail:** info@blreview.org. **Website:** www.blreview.org. **Contact:** Stacy Bodziak, managing editor. Estab. 2001. *Bellevue Literary Review*, published semiannually, prints "works of fiction, nonfiction, and poetry that touch upon relationships to the human body, illness, health, and healing."

Work published in *Bellevue Literary Review* has appeared in *The Pushcart Prize* and *Best Amer-*

ican Short Stories. Recently published work by Linda Pastan, Rachel Hadas, and Tom Sleigh. Closed to submissions in July and August.

NEEDS *BLR* "seeks character-driven fiction with original voices and strong settings. While we are always interested in creative explorations in style, we do lean toward classic short stories." No genre fiction. Length: up to 5,000 words. Average length: 2,500 words.

HOW TO CONTACT Submit via online submissions manager.

PAYMENT/TERMS Pays 2 contributor's copies, one-year subscription, and one-year gift subscription.

BELOIT FICTION JOURNAL

Box 11, Beloit College, 700 College St., Beloit WI 53511. (608)363-2079. **E-mail:** bfj@beloit.edu. **Website:** www.beloit.edu/bfj. **Contact:** Chris Fink, editor in chief. Estab. 1985. "*The Beloit Fiction Journal* publishes the best in contemporary short fiction. Traditional and experimental narratives find a home in our pages. We publish new writers alongside established writers. Our fiction-only format allows us to consider very long as well as very short stories. We occasionally publish excerpts."

Reading period: August 1-December 1. Work first appearing in *Beloit Fiction Journal* has been reprinted in award-winning collections, including the Flannery O'Connor and the Milkweed Fiction Prize collections, and has won the Iowa Short Fiction award. Has published work by Dennis Lehane, Silas House, and David Harris Ebenbach.

NEEDS Receives 200 unsolicited mss/month. Accepts 14 mss/year. Publishes ms 9 months after acceptance. **Publishes new writers every year.** Sometimes comments on rejected mss. Wants more experimental and short shorts. Would like to see more "stories with a focus on both language and plot, unusual metaphors and vivid characters." No pornography, religious dogma, science fiction, horror, political propaganda, or genre fiction. Length: 1-60 pages.

HOW TO CONTACT Submit complete ms via online submissions manager ($3 fee) or postal mail.

PAYMENT/TERMS Pays contributor copies.

TIPS "Many of our contributors are writers whose work we had previously rejected. Don't let 1 rejection slip turn you away from our—or any—magazine."

BERKELEY FICTION REVIEW

102 Hearst Gym MC #4500, University of California, Berkeley, Berkeley CA 94720. **E-mail:** berkeleyfictionreview@gmail.com. **Website:** berkeleyfictionreview.com. Estab. 1981. "The *Berkeley Fiction Review* is a UC Berkeley undergraduate, student-run publication. We look for innovative short fiction that plays with form and content, as well as traditionally constructed stories with fresh voices and original ideas."

BFR nominates to O.Henry, *Best American Short Stories* and *Pushcart* prizes. Sponsored by the ASUC.

NEEDS Length: no more than 25 pages.

HOW TO CONTACT Submit via e-mail with "Submission: Name, Title" in subject line. Include cover letter in body of e-mail, with story as an attachment.

PAYMENT/TERMS Pays 1 contributor's copy.

TIPS "Our criteria is fiction that resonates. Voices that are strong and move a reader. Clear, powerful prose (either voice or rendering of subject) with a point. Unique ways of telling stories—these capture the editors. Work hard, don't give up. Ask an honest person to point out your writing weaknesses, and then work on them. We look forward to reading fresh new voices."

BEST NEW WRITING

Hopewell Publications, LLC, P.O. Box 11, Titusville NJ 08560-0011. **E-mail:** info@bestnewwriting.com. **Website:** www.bestnewwriting.com. **Contact:** Brittany Fonte, managing editor. Estab. 2006. "*Best New Writing* is an annual anthology of fiction and creative nonfiction, including the results of The Eric Hoffer Award for short prose and independent books. The Hoffer grand-prize winner and honored stories serve as the centerpiece of *Best New Writing*. Edited by award-winning authors, editors, and masters of the writing craft, *Best New Writing* showcases new works of outstanding literary value that are found outside of the commercial publishing establishment. Entries are previously unpublished (or published with a circulation of less than 500) and nominated by the writing community and the public at large. To submit books or prose or to view previous winners, please visit The Eric Hoffer Award site (www.hofferaward.com).

"Send mss electronically." Pays $250 to Hoffer winner and $250 to Gover Prize winner.

NEEDS Length: up to 10,000 words.

HOW TO CONTACT Send complete ms.

TIPS "Read the guidelines. Read any issue of *Best New Writing*."

BEYOND CENTAURI

White Cat Publications, LLC, 33080 Industrial Rd., Suite 101, Livonia MI 48150. (734)237-8522. **Fax:** (313)557-5162. **E-mail:** beyondcentauri@whitecat-publications.com. **Website:** www.whitecatpublications.com/guidelines/beyond-centauri. Estab. 2003. *Beyond Centauri*, published quarterly, contains fantasy, science fiction, sword and sorcery, very mild horror short stories, poetry, and illustrations for readers ages 10 and up.

NEEDS Looks for themes of science fiction or fantasy. "Science fiction and especially stories that take place in outer space will find great favor with us." Length: up to 2,500 words.

HOW TO CONTACT Submit in the body of an e-mail, or as an RTF attachment.

PAYMENT/TERMS Pays $6/story, $3/reprints, and $2/flash fiction (under 1,000 words), plus 1 contributor's copy.

BIG BRIDGE

Big Bridge Press, P.O. Box 870, Guerniville CA 95446. **E-mail:** walterblue@bigbridge.org. **Website:** www.bigbridge.org. **Contact:** Michael Rothenberg and Terri Carrion, editors. "*Big Bridge* is a webzine of poetry and everything else. If we like it, we'll publish it. We're interested in poetry, fiction, nonfiction essays, journalism, and art (photos, line drawings, performance, installations, siteworks, comics, graphics)."

HOW TO CONTACT Only accepts electronic submissions. Submit via e-mail.

TIPS "We are guided by whimsy and passion and urgency. Each issue will feature an online chapbook."

BIG MUDDY: A JOURNAL OF THE MISSISSIPPI RIVER VALLEY

Southeast Missouri State University Press, 1 University Plaza, MS 2650, Cape Girardeau MO 63701. (573) 651-2044. **E-mail:** upress@semo.edu. **Website:** www.semopress.com/bigmuddy. **Contact:** Susan Swartwout, publisher/editor. Estab. 2000. "*Big Muddy* explores multidisciplinary, multicultural issues, people, and events mainly concerning, but not limited to, the 10-state area that borders the Mississippi River. We publish fiction, poetry, historical essays, creative nonfiction, environmental essays, biography, regional events, photography, art, etc."

NEEDS No romance, fantasy, or children's. Receives 50 unsolicited mss/month. Accepts 20-25 mss/issue. Accepts multiple submissions.

HOW TO CONTACT Submit ms by e-mail.

PAYMENT/TERMS Pays 2 contributor's copies; additional copies $5. Annual short story ($1,000) and flash fiction ($500) contests.

TIPS "We look for clear language, avoidance of clichés except in necessary dialogue, a fresh vision of the theme or issue. Find some excellent and honest readers to comment on your work-in-progress and final draft. Consider their viewpoints carefully. Revise if needed."

BIG PULP

Exter Press, P.O. Box 92, Cumberland MD 21501. **E-mail:** editors@bigpulp.com. **Website:** www.bigpulp.com. **Contact:** Bill Olver, editor. Estab. 2008. *Big Pulp* defines "pulp fiction" very broadly: It's lively, challenging, thought-provoking, thrilling, and fun, regardless of how many or how few genre elements are packed in. Doesn't subscribe to the theory that genre fiction is disposable; a great deal of literary fiction could easily fall under one of their general categories. Places a higher value on character and story than genre elements.

"Submissions are accepted only during certain reading periods. Our website is updated to reflect when we are and are not reading, and what we are looking for."

NEEDS Does not want generic slice-of-life, memoirs, inspirational, political, pastoral odes. Length: up to 10,000 words.

HOW TO CONTACT Submit complete ms.

PAYMENT/TERMS Pays $5-25.

TIPS "We like to be surprised, and we have few boundaries. Fantasy writers may focus on the mundane aspects of a fantastical creature's life or the magic that can happen in everyday life. Romances do not have to be requited or have happy endings, and the object of one's obsession may not be a person. Mysteries need not focus on 'whodunit?' We're always interested in science or speculative fiction focusing on societal issues, but writers should avoid being partisan or shrill. We also like fiction that crosses genre; for example, a science fiction romance or a fantasy crime story. We have an online archive for fiction and poetry and encourage writers to check it out. That said, *Big*

Pulp has a strong editorial bias in favor of stories with monkeys. Especially talking monkeys."

BILINGUAL REVIEW

Arizona State University, Hispanic Research Center, P.O. Box 875303, Tempe AZ 85287-5303. (480)965-3867. **Fax:** (480)965-0315. **E-mail:** brp@asu.edu. **Website:** www.asu.edu/brp/submit. **Contact:** Gary Francisco Keller, publisher. Estab. 1974. *Bilingual Review* is "committed to publishing high-quality writing by both established and emerging writers."

NEEDS Receives 50 unsolicited mss/month. Accepts 3 mss/issue; 9 mss/year. "We do not publish literature about tourists in Latin America and their perceptions of the 'native culture.' We do not publish fiction about Latin America unless there is a clear tie to the U.S."

HOW TO CONTACT Submit via postal mail. Send 2 copies of complete ms with SAE and loose stamps. Does not usually accept e-mail submissions except through special circumstance/prior arrangement.

PAYMENT/TERMS Pays 2 contributor's copies; 30% discount for additional copies.

THE BINNACLE

University of Maine at Machias, 116 O'Brien Ave., Machias ME 04654. **E-mail:** ummbinnacle@maine.edu; ummpublicrelations@maine.edu. **Website:** www.umm.maine.edu/binnacle. Estab. 1957. "We are interested in fresh voices, not Raymond Carver's, and not the Iowa Workshop's. We want the peculiar and the idiosyncratic. We want playful and experimental but understandable. Please see our website for details on our Annual Ultra-Short Competition. (Prize of a minimum of $300.) We accept submissions for the Fall Ultra-Short Edition from December 1-March 15 and report to writers in early June. We accept submissions for the Spring Edition from September 1-November 30 and report to writers between February 1-March 1."

Does not accept paper submissions. Electronic/e-mail submissions only.

NEEDS No extreme erotica, fantasy, horror, or religious, but any genre attuned to a general audience can work. Length: up to 2,500 words.

HOW TO CONTACT Send complete ms via e-mail only.

TIPS "We want fiction, poetry, and images that speak to real people, people who have lives, people who have troubles, people who laugh, too."

THE BITTER OLEANDER

4983 Tall Oaks Dr., Fayetteville NY 13066. **E-mail:** info@bitteroleander.com. **Website:** www.bitteroleander.com. **Contact:** Paul B. Roth, editor and publisher. "We're reading to find a language uncommitted to the commonplace and more integrated with the natural world. A language that helps define the same particulars in nature that exist in us and have not been socialized out of us."

NEEDS Receives 300 unsolicited mss/month. Accepts 4-5 mss/issue; 8-10 mss/year. Does not read in July. Recently published work by Kristiina Ehin (Estonia), Norberto Luis Romero (Spain), Anders Benson, Martín Camps, and Jane Arnold. Publishes short shorts. Also publishes literary essays, poetry. Always comments on rejected mss. Does not want family stories with moralistic plots or fantasy that involves hyper-reality of any sort. Length: 100-2,500 words.

HOW TO CONTACT Query. Send mss by mail with SASE for response. "Whether you live in the U.S. or outside, we accept e-mail submissions or postal mail submissions if SASE is enclosed."

PAYMENT/TERMS Pays 1 contributor's copy.

TIPS "If you are writing poems or short fiction in the tradition of 98% of all journals publishing in this country, then your work will usually not fit for us. If within the first 400 words my mind drifts, the rest rarely makes it. Be yourself, and listen to no one but yourself."

BLACKBIRD

Virginia Commonwealth University Department of English, P.O. Box 843082, Richmond VA 23284. (804)827-4729. **E-mail:** blackbird@vcu.edu. **Website:** www.blackbird.vcu.edu. Estab. 2001. *Blackbird* is published twice a year.

NEEDS "We primarily look for short stories, but novel excerpts are acceptable if self-contained."

HOW TO CONTACT Submit using online submissions manager or by postal mail. Online submission is preferred.

TIPS "We like a story that invites us into its world, that engages our senses, soul, and mind. We are able to publish long works in all genres, but query *Blackbird* before you send a prose piece over 8,000 words or a poem exceeding 10 pages."

BLACK LACE

P.O. Box 83912, Los Angeles CA 90083. (310)410-0808. **Fax:** (310)410-9250. **E-mail:** newsroom@blk.com. **Website:** www.blacklace.org. Estab. 1991. "*Black Lace* seeks stories, articles, photography, models, illustration, and a very limited amount of poetry all related to black women unclothed or in erotic situations."

NEEDS Length: 2,000-4,000 words.

HOW TO CONTACT Submit via postal mail (include SASE if you want your work returned), fax, or e-mail.

PAYMENT/TERMS Pays average of 10¢/word.

TIPS "*Black Lace* seeks erotic material of the highest quality, but it need not be written by professional writers. The most important thing is that the work be erotic and that it feature black women in the life or ITL themes. We are not interested in stories that demean black women or place them in stereotypical situations."

BLACK WARRIOR REVIEW

P.O. Box 862936, Tuscaloosa AL 35486. (205)348-4518. **E-mail:** interns.bwr@gmail.com. **Website:** www.bwr.ua.edu. **Contact:** Bronwyn Valentine, editor. Estab. 1974. "We publish contemporary fiction, poetry, reviews, essays, and art for a literary audience. We publish the freshest work we can find."

Work that appeared in the *Black Warrior Review* has been included in the *Pushcart Prize* anthology, *Harper's Magazine, Best American Short Stories, Best American Poetry,* and *New Stories from the South.*

NEEDS "We are open to good experimental writing and short-short fiction. No genre fiction please." Publishes novel excerpts if under contract to be published. Length: up to 7,000 words.

HOW TO CONTACT One story/chapter per envelope. Wants work that is conscious of form and well-crafted.

PAYMENT/TERMS Pays one-year subscription and nominal lump-sum fee.

TIPS "We look for attention to language, freshness, honesty, a convincing and sharp voice. Send us a clean, well-printed, proofread ms. Become familiar with the magazine prior to submission."

BLUE COLLAR REVIEW

Partisan Press, P.O. Box 11417, Norfolk VA 23517. **E-mail:** red-ink@earthlink.net. **Website:** www.partisanpress.org. **Contact:** A. Markowitz, editor; Mary Franke, co-editor. Estab. 1997. *Blue Collar Review (Journal of Progressive Working Class Literature)*, published quarterly, contains poetry, short stories, and illustrations "reflecting the working-class experience—a broad range from the personal to the societal. Our purpose is to promote and expand working-class literature and an awareness of the connections between workers of all occupations and the social context in which we live. Also to inspire the creativity and latent talent in 'common' working people."

NEEDS Submit ms via postal mail. Your name and address should appear on every page. Cover letter is helpful but not required. Size 10 SASE is required for response. Length: up to 1,000 words.

PAYMENT/TERMS Pays contributor's copies.

BLUELINE

120 Morey Hall, Dept. of English and Communication, Postdam NY 13676. (315)267-2044. **Fax:** (315) 267-3256. **E-mail:** blueline@potsdam.edu. **Website:** bluelinemagadk.com. **Contact:** Donald McNutt, editor; Caroline Downing, art editor; Donald McNutt, nonfiction editor; Stephanie Coyne-Deghett, fiction editor; Rebecca Lehmann, poetry editor. Estab. 1979. "*Blueline* seeks poems, stories, and essays relating to the Adirondacks and regions similar in geography and spirit, or focusing on the shaping influence of nature. Submission period is July-November. *Blueline* welcomes electronic submissions as Word document (DOC or DOCX) attachments. Please identify genre in subject line. Please avoid using compression software."

"Proofread all submissions. It is difficult for our editors to get excited about work containing typographical and syntactic errors."

NEEDS Receives 8-10 unsolicited mss/month. Accepts 2-3 mss/issue. Does not read January-June. Publishes 2 new writers/year. Recently published work by Jim Meirose, Amber Timmerman, Gail Gilliland, Matthew J. Spireng, Roger Sheffer, and Mason Smith. No urban stories or erotica. Length: 500-3,000 words. Average length: 2,500 words.

PAYMENT/TERMS Pays 1 contributor's copy; charges $9 each for 3 or more copies.

TIPS "We look for concise, clear, concrete prose that tells a story and touches upon a universal theme or situation. We prefer realism to romanticism but will consider nostalgia if well done. Pay attention to grammar and syntax. Avoid murky language, sentimentality, cuteness, or folksiness. We would like to see more good, creative nonfiction centered on the literature and/or culture of the Adirondacks, Northern New York, New England, or Eastern Canada. If ms has potential, we work with author to improve and reconsider for publication. Our readers prefer fiction to poetry (in general) or reviews. Write from your own experience, be specific and factual (within the bounds of your story), and if you write about universal features such as love, death, change, etc., write about them in a fresh way. You'll catch our attention if your writing is interesting, vigorous, and polished."

BLUE MESA REVIEW

700 Lomas NE, Suite 108, Albuquerque NM 87102. **E-mail:** bmreditr@unm.edu. **Website:** bluemesareview.org. **Contact:** Has rotating editorial board; see website for current masthead. Estab. 1989. "Originally founded by Rudolfo Anaya, Gene Frumkin, David Johnson, Patricia Clark Smith, and Lee Bartlette in 1989, the *Blue Mesa Review* emerged as a source of innovative writing produced in the Southwest. Over the years the magazine's nuance has changed, sometimes shifting towards more craft-oriented work, other times realigning with its original roots."

Open for submissions from September 30-March 31. Contest: June 1-August 31. Only accepts submissions through online submissions manager.

NEEDS Length: up to 6,000 words.

HOW TO CONTACT Submit via online submissions manager.

TIPS "In general, we are seeking strong voices and lively, compelling narrative with a fine eye for craft. We look forward to reading your best work!"

BLUESTEM

English Deptartment, Eastern Illinois University, **Website:** www.bluestemmagazine.com. **Contact:** Charlotte Pence, editor. Estab. 1966. *Bluestem*, formerly known as *Karamu*, produces a quarterly online issue (December, March, June, September) and an annual print issue. Submissions are accepted September 1-May 1. There is no compensation for online contributors but we will promote your work enthusiastically and widely. Past issues have included themes such as: The Humor Issue, The Music Issue, The Millennium. Produced by the English Department at Eastern Illinois University.

Accepts submissions only through online submissions manager.

NEEDS Length: no more than 5,000 words.

HOW TO CONTACT Submit only 1 short story at a time. Include bio (less than 100 words) with submission. Query if longer than 5,000 words.

PAYMENT/TERMS Pays 1 contributor's copy and discount for additional copies.

BOSTON REVIEW

P.O. Box 425786, Cambridge MA 02142. (617)324-1360. **Fax:** (617)452-3356. **Website:** www.bostonreview.net. Estab. 1975. "The editors are committed to a society and culture that foster human diversity and a democracy in which we seek common grounds of principle amidst our many differences. In the hope of advancing these ideals, the *Review* acts as a forum that seeks to enrich the language of public debate."

Boston Review is a recipient of the Pushcart Prize in Poetry.

NEEDS Looking for "stories that are emotionally and intellectually substantive and also interesting on the level of language. Things that are shocking, dark, lewd, comic, or even insane are fine so long as the fiction is *controlled* and purposeful in a masterly way. Subtlety, delicacy, and lyricism are attractive, too. Simultaneous submissions are fine as long as we are notified of the fact." No romance, erotica, genre fiction. Length: 1,200-5,000 words. Average length: 2,000 words.

HOW TO CONTACT Send complete ms.

PAYMENT/TERMS Pays $25-300 and contributor's copies.

TIPS "The best way to get a sense of the kind of material *Boston Review* is looking for is to read the magazine. "

BOULEVARD

Opojaz, Inc., 6614 Clayton Rd., Box 325, Richmond Heights MO 63117. **E-mail:** richardburgin@netzero.com; jessicarogen@boulevardmagazine.org. **Website:** www.boulevardmagazine.org; boulevard.submittable.com/submit. **Contact:** Jessica Rogen, editor. Estab. 1985. Hosts the Short Fiction Contest for Emerging Writers. **Prize:** $1,500 and publication in *Boulevard*. **Postmarked deadline**: December 31. **Entry fee:** $15 for each individual story, with no limit per author. Entry fee includes a one-year subscription to *Boulevard* (1 per author). Make check payable to *Boulevard*. For contests, make check payable to *Boulevard* or submit online at boulevard.submittable.com/submit. "*Boulevard* is a diverse literary magazine presenting original creative work by well-known authors, as well as by writers of exciting promise." Triannual magazine featuring fiction, poetry, and essays. Sometimes comments on rejected mss. *Boulevard* has been called 'one of the half-dozen best literary journals' by Poet Laureate Daniel Hoffman in *The Philadelphia Inquirer.* We strive to publish the finest in poetry, fiction, and nonfiction. We frequently publish writers with previous credits, and we are very interested in publishing less experienced or unpublished writers with exceptional promise. We've published everything from John Ashbery to Donald Hall to a wide variety of styles from new or lesser known poets. We're eclectic. We are interested in original, moving poetry written from the head as well as the heart. It can be about any topic."

Publishes 10 new writers/year. Recently published work by Joyce Carol Oates, Floyd Skloot, John Barth, Stephen Dixon, David Guterson, Albert Goldbarth, Molly Peacock, Bob Hicok, Alice Friman, Dick Allen, and Tom Disch.

NEEDS Submit by mail or via Submittable. Accepts multiple submissions. Does not accept mss May 1-October 1. SASE for reply. "We do not want erotica, science fiction, romance, western, horror, or children's stories." Length: up to 8,000 words.

PAYMENT/TERMS Pays $50-500 (sometimes higher) for accepted work.

TIPS "Read the magazine first. The work *Boulevard* publishes is generally recognized as among the finest in the country. We continue to seek more good literary or cultural essays. Send only your best work."

BRAIN, CHILD

Erielle Media, LLC, 341 Newtown Turnpike, Wilton CT 06897. **E-mail:** editorial@brainchildmag.com. **Website:** www.brainchildmag.com. **Contact:** Marcelle Soviero, editor in chief. Estab. 2000. "*Brain, Child: The Magazine for Thinking Mothers*, reflects modern motherhood—the way it really is. It is the largest print literary magazine devoted to motherhood. *Brain, Child* is a community for and by mothers who like to think about what raising kids does for (and to) the mind and soul. *Brain, Child* isn't your typical parenting magazine. We couldn't cupcake-decorate our way out of a paper bag. We are more 'literary' than 'how-to,' more *New Yorker* than *Parents.* We shy away from expert advice on childrearing in favor of first-hand reflections by great writers (Jane Smiley, Barbara Ehrenreich, Anne Tyler) on life as a mother. Each quarterly issue is full of essays, features, humor, reviews, fiction, art, cartoons, and our readers' own stories. Our philosophy is pretty simple: Motherhood is worthy of literature. And there are a lot of ways to mother, all of them interesting. We're proud to be publishing articles and essays that are smart, down to earth, sometimes funny, and sometimes poignant."

NEEDS "We publish fiction that has a strong motherhood theme." No genre fiction. Length: 800-4,000 words.

HOW TO CONTACT Send complete ms.

PAYMENT/TERMS Payment varies.

TIPS "We are excited by great writing. It makes our day when we hear from an established writer or publish an author for the first time."

THE BRIAR CLIFF REVIEW

3303 Rebecca St., Sioux City IA 51104. (712)279-5477. **E-mail:** tricia.currans-sheehan@briarcliff.edu; jeanne.emmons@briarcliff.edu. **Website:** bcreview.org. **Contact:** Tricia Currans-Sheehan, Jeanne Emmons, Phil Hey, Paul Weber, editors. Estab. 1989. *The Briar Cliff Review*, published annually in April, is "an attractive, eclectic literary/art magazine." It focuses on, but is not limited to, "Siouxland writers and subjects. We are happy to proclaim ourselves a regional publication. It doesn't diminish us; it enhances us."

Member: CLMP, Humanities International Complete. Reads submissions August 1-November 1 only.

NEEDS Accepts 5 mss/year. **Publishes 10-14 new writers/year.** Publishes ms 3-4 months after acceptance. Recently published work by Leslie Barnard, Daryl Murphy, Patrick Hicks, Siobhan Fallon, Shelley Scaletta, Jenna Blum, Brian Bedard, Rebecca Tuch, Scott H. Andrews, and Josip Novakovich. "No romance, horror, or alien stories." Length: 2,500-5,000 words; average length: 3,000 words.

HOW TO CONTACT Submit by postal mail (send SASE for return of ms) or via Submittable. Does not accept e-mail submissions (unless from overseas). Seldom comments on rejected mss.

PAYMENT/TERMS Pays 2 contributor's copies; additional copies available for $12.

TIPS "So many stories are just telling. We want some action. It has to move. We prefer stories in which there is no gimmick, no mechanical turn of events, no moral except the one we would draw privately."

BRILLIANT CORNERS: A JOURNAL OF JAZZ & LITERATURE

Lycoming College, 700 College Place, Williamsport PA 17701. (570)321-4279. **Fax:** (570)321-4090. **E-mail:** feinstein@lycoming.edu. **Website:** www.lycoming.edu/brilliantcorners. **Contact:** Sascha Feinstein. Estab. 1996. "We publish jazz-related literature—fiction, poetry, and nonfiction. We are open as to length and form." Semiannual.

Does not read mss May 15-September 1.

NEEDS Receives 10-15 unsolicited mss/month. Accepts 1-2 mss/issue; 2-3 mss/year.

HOW TO CONTACT Submit with SASE for return of ms, or send disposable copy of ms. Accepts unpublished work only. No e-mail or fax submissions. Cover letter is preferred.

TIPS "We look for clear, moving prose that demostrates a love of both writing and jazz. We primarily publish established writers, but we read all submissions carefully and welcome work by outstanding young writers."

THE BROADKILL REVIEW

Broadkill Publishing Associates, c/o John Milton & Company, P.O. Box 63, Milton DE 19968. **E-mail:** the_broadkill_review@earthlink.net. **Website:** www.thebroadkillreview.blogspot.com; sites.google.com/site/thebroadkillreview. **Contact:** Jamie Brown, editor; Scott Whitaker, Web editor; Linda Blaskey, poetry editor. Estab. 2005.

"*The Broadkill Review* accepts the best fiction, poetry, and nonfiction by new and established writers. We have published Pushcart-nominated fiction and poetry."

NEEDS No erotica, fantasy, sci-fi "unless these serve some functional, literary purpose; most do not." Length: up to 6,000 words.

HOW TO CONTACT Send complete ms with cover letter online at thebroadkillreview.submittable.com/submit. Include estimated word count, brief bio, list of publications.

PAYMENT/TERMS Pays contributor's copy.

TIPS "Query the editor first. Visit our website to familiarize yourself with the type of material we publish. Request and read a copy of the magazine first!"

BROKEN PENCIL

P.O. Box 203, Station P, Toronto ON M5S 2S7, Canada. **E-mail:** editor@brokenpencil.com. **Website:** www.brokenpencil.com. **Contact:** Alison Lang, editor. Estab. 1995. "*Broken Pencil* is one of the few magazines in the world devoted exclusively to underground culture and the independent arts. We are a great resource and a lively read! *Broken Pencil* reviews the best zines, books, websites, videos, and artworks from the underground and reprints the best articles from the alternative press. From the hilarious to the perverse, *Broken Pencil* challenges conformity and demands attention."

"Please read our magazine (you can order a free trial issue at brokenpencil.com/freeissue) or browse our content at brokenpencil.com before submitting any fiction, nonfiction, or story ideas!"

NEEDS "We're particularly interested in work from emerging writers." Reads fiction submissions February 1-September 15. Length: 50-3,000 words.

HOW TO CONTACT Submit via online submissions manager.

PAYMENT/TERMS Pays $30-300.

TIPS "Remember, we are a guide to alternative and independent culture. We don't want your thoughts on Hollywood movies or your touching tale about coming of age on the prairies! Make sure you have some sense of the kind of work we use before getting in touch. Never send us something if you haven't at least read *Broken Pencil*. Always include your address, phone number, and e-mail, so we know where to find you, and a little something about yourself, so we know who you are."

BUGLE

Rocky Mountain Elk Foundation, 5705 Grant Creek, Missoula MT 59808. (406)523-4500. **Fax:** (800)225-5355. **E-mail:** bugle@rmef.org. **E-mail:** conservationeditor@rmef.org; huntingeditor@rmef.org; assistanteditor@rmef.org; photos@rmef.org. **Website:** www.rmef.org. Estab. 1984. *Bugle* is the membership publication of the Rocky Mountain Elk Foundation, a nonprofit wildlife conservation group. "Our readers are predominantly hunters, many of them conservationists who care deeply about protecting wildlife habitat." Bimonthly.

Magazine: 114-172 pages; 55 lb. Escanaba paper; 80 lb. Steriling cover, b&w, 4-color illustrations; photos.

MAGAZINES

NEEDS "We accept fiction and nonfiction stories pertaining in some way to elk, other wildlife, hunting, habitat conservation, and related issues. We would like to see more humor." Length: 1,500-4,500 words; average length: 2,500 words.

HOW TO CONTACT Query or submit complete ms to appropriate e-mail address; see website for guidelines.

PAYMENT/TERMS Pays 20¢/word and 3 contributor's copies.

TIPS "Hunting stories and essays should celebrate the hunting experience, demonstrating respect for wildlife, the land, and the hunt. Articles on elk behavior or elk habitat should include personal observations and should entertain as well as educate. No freelance product reviews or formulaic how-to articles accepted. Straight action-adventure hunting stories are in short supply, as are 'Situation Ethics' mss."

BURNSIDE REVIEW

P.O. Box 1782, Portland OR 97207. **Website:** www.burnsidereview.org. **Contact:** Sid Miller, founder and editor; Dan Kaplan, managing editor. Estab. 2004. *Burnside Review*, published every 9 months, prints "the best poetry and short fiction we can get our hands on." Each issue includes 1 featured poet with an interview and new poems. "We tend to publish writing that finds beauty in truly unexpected places; that combines urban and natural imagery; that breaks the heart."

Charges a $3 submission fee to cover printing costs.

NEEDS "We like bright, engaging fiction that works to surprise and captivate us." Length: up to 5,000 words.

HOW TO CONTACT Submit complete ms via online submissions manager.

PAYMENT/TERMS Pays $25 and 1 contributor's copy.

BUST MAGAZINE

Bust, Inc., 253 36th St., Suite C307, Brooklyn NY 11232. **E-mail:** debbie@bust.com. **E-mail:** submissions@bust.com. **Website:** www.bust.com. **Contact:** Debbie Stoller, editor in chief/publisher. Estab. 1993. "*Bust* is the groundbreaking, original women's lifestyle magazine and website that is unique in its ability to connect with bright, cutting-edge, influential young women."

"Please include your full name, e-mail address, mailing address, and day and night phone number in your submission. If you're e-mailing your submission, please send it as an attachment. If you're mailing your submission and want us to return it to you, please include a SASE. If we're interested in running your piece, we'll get back to you about it. If we aren't, we will try to let you know, but it may take a very long time and we can't promise you that we'll be able to. *Bust* does not accept poetry. If you are submitting a story idea rather than a story, please also send us clips of your previous writing."

NEEDS "We only publish erotic fiction. All other content is nonfiction." Length: 1,000-1,500 words.

HOW TO CONTACT Query with published clips.

PAYMENT/TERMS Pays up to $50

TIPS "We are always looking for stories that are surprising, and that 'bust' stereotypes about women."

THE CAFE IRREAL

E-mail: editors@cafeirreal.com. **Website:** www.cafeirreal.com. **Contact:** G.S. Evans and Alice Whittenburg, co-editors. Estab. 1998. "Our audience is composed of people who read or write literary fiction with fantastic themes, similar to the work of Franz Kafka, Kobo Abe, or Clarice Lispector. This is a type of fiction (irreal) that has difficulty finding its way into print in the English-speaking world and defies many of the conventions of American literature especially. As a result, ours is a fairly specialized literary publication, and we would strongly recommend that prospective writers look at our current issue and guidelines carefully." Recently published work by Tom Whalen, Venita Blackburn, Agustín Cadena, Michal Ajvaz, Marianne Villanueva, and Eric G. Wilson.

NEEDS Accepts submissions by e-mail. No attachments; include submission in body of e-mail. Include estimated word count. Accepts 6-8 mss/issue; 24-32 mss/year. No horror or 'slice-of-life' stories; no genre or mainstream science fiction or fantasy. Length: up to 2,000 words.

PAYMENT/TERMS Pays 1¢/word, $2 minimum.

TIPS "Forget formulas. Write about what you don't know, take me places I couldn't possibly go, don't try to make me care about the characters. Read short fiction by writers such as Franz Kafka, Jorge Luis Borges,

Donald Barthelme, Magnus Mills, Ana Maria Shua, and Stanislaw Lem. Also read our website and guidelines."

CAHABA RIVER LITERARY JOURNAL

Rivercity Today/X-Press, 2413 Bethel Rd., Logansport LA 71049. (318)564-6031. **E-mail:** cahabariverliteraryjournal@gmail.com. **Website:** cahabariverliteraryjournal.wordpress.com. **Contact:** Marcella Simmons, editor. Estab. 2015. *Cahaba River Literary Journal* publishes quality fiction, poetry, and photography in every genre.

All mss should be submitted with a cover letter, brief bio, and name and address.

NEEDS Length: up to 2,500 words.

HOW TO CONTACT Submit complete ms by e-mail.

TIPS "Present to me your best works: I want to laugh, cry, be sad, or get angry at the story or poem."

CALLALOO: A JOURNAL OF AFRICAN DIASPORA ARTS & LETTERS

Texas A&M University, 249 Blocker Hall, College Station TX 77843-4212, United States. (979)458-3108. **Fax:** (979)458-3275. **E-mail:** callaloo@tamu.edu. **Website:** callaloo.tamu.edu. Estab. 1976. *Callaloo: A Journal of African Diaspora Arts & Letters*, published quarterly, is devoted to poetry dealing with the African Diaspora, including North America, Europe, Africa, Latin and Central America, South America, and the Caribbean. Features about 15-20 poems (all forms and styles) in each issue along with short fiction, interviews, literary criticism, and concise critical book reviews.

NEEDS Would like to see more experimental fiction, science fiction, and well-crafted literary fiction particularly dealing with the black middle class, immigrant communities, and/or the black South. Accepts 3-5 mss/issue; 10-20 mss/year. **Publishes 5-10 new writers/year.** Recently published work by Charles Johnson, Edwidge Danticat, Thomas Glave, Nallo Hopkinson, John Edgar Wideman, Jamaica Kincaid, Percival Everett, and Patricia Powell. Also publishes poetry. Length: up to 10,000 words excluding title page, abstract, bio, and references.

HOW TO CONTACT Submit ms via online submissions manager: callaloo.expressacademic.org/login.php. All fiction submissions are now limited to 1 ms per submission with a maximum of 3 submissions by a single author per calendar year.

TIPS "We look for freshness of both writing and plot, strength of characterization, plausibility of plot. Read what's being written and published, especially in journals such as *Callaloo*."

CALYX

P.O. Box B, Corvallis OR 97339. (541)753-9384. **Fax:** (541)753-0515. **E-mail:** info@calyxpress.org; editor@calyxpress.org. **Website:** www.calyxpress.org. **Contact:** Brenna Crotty, senior editor. Estab. 1976. "*CALYX* exists to publish fine literature and art by women and is dedicated to publishing the work of all women, including women of color, older women, working-class women and other voices that need to be heard. We are committed to discovering and nurturing developing writers."

Annual open submission period is October 1-December 31.

NEEDS Length: up to 5,000 words.

HOW TO CONTACT All submissions should include author's name on each page and be accompanied by a brief (50-word or less) biographical statement, phone number, and e-mail address. Submit using online submissions manager.

PAYMENT/TERMS Pays in contributor's copies and one-volume subscription.

TIPS "A forum for women's creative work—including work by women of color, lesbian and queer women, young women, old women—*CALYX* breaks new ground. Each issue is packed with new poetry, short stories, full-color artwork, photography, essays, and reviews."

CAMAS: THE NATURE OF THE WEST

The University of Montana, Environmental Studies Program, Rankin Hall 1016, Missoula MT 59812. (406)243-6273. **Fax:** (406)243-6090. **E-mail:** camas@mso.umt.edu. **Website:** www.camasmagazine.org. **Contact:** Co-editor. Estab. 1992. Published biannually in Winter and Summer. "*Camas* seeks to create an evocative space that celebrates, explores, and acknowledges the complex relationship of people and land and environment in the American West."

"Please check our website or Facebook page for theme and submission periods."

NEEDS Length: 500-3,000 words

HOW TO CONTACT Submit online via our website.

PAYMENT/TERMS Pays 1 contributor's copy.

TIPS "Submit work that speaks to contemporary social issues associated with environmental concerns of the American West. The link to the region can be tenuous or subtle."

THE CAPILANO REVIEW

281 Industrial Ave., Vancouver BC V6A 2P2, Canada. (604)984-1712. **E-mail:** contact@thecapilanoreview.ca. **Website:** www.thecapilanoreview.ca. **Contact:** Todd Nickel, managing editor. Estab. 1972. Triannual visual and literary arts magazine that "publishes only what the editors consider to be the very best fiction, poetry, drama, or visual art being produced. *TCR* editors are interested in fresh, original work that stimulates and challenges readers. Over the years, the magazine has developed a reputation for pushing beyond the boundaries of traditional art and writing. We are interested in work that is new in concept and in execution."

NEEDS No traditional, conventional fiction. Wants to see more innovative, genre-blurring work. Length: up to 5,000 words

HOW TO CONTACT Send complete ms with SASE and Canadian postage or IRCs. Does not accept submissions through e-mail or on disks.

PAYMENT/TERMS Pays $50-300.

ORSON SCOTT CARD'S INTERGALACTIC MEDICINE SHOW

Hatrack River Publications, P.O. Box 18184, Greensboro NC 27419. **Website:** intergalacticmedicineshow.com; oscigms.com. **Contact:** Edmund R. Schubert, editor. Estab. 2005. "*Orson Scott Card's InterGalactic Medicine Show* is an online fantasy and science fiction magazine. We are a bimonthly publication featuring content from both established and talented new authors. In addition to our bimonthly issues, we offer weekly columns and reviews on books, movies, video games, and writing advice."

NEEDS "We like to see well-developed milieus and believable, engaging characters. We also look for clear, unaffected writing." Length: up to 17,000 words.

HOW TO CONTACT Submit via online submission form. Submit only 1 story at a time. Include estimated word count, e-mail address.

PAYMENT/TERMS Pays 6¢/word.

TIPS "Please note: *IGMS* is a PG-13 magazine and website. That means that while stories can deal with intense and adult themes, we will not accept stories with explicit or detailed sex of the sort that would earn a movie rating more restrictive than PG-13; nor will there be language of the sort that earns an R rating."

THE CARIBBEAN WRITER

University of the Virgin Islands, RR 1, P.O. Box 10,000, Kingshill, St. Croix USVI 00850. (340)692-4152. **Fax:** (340)692-4026. **E-mail:** info@thecaribbeanwriter.org. **E-mail:** submit@thecaribbeanwriter.org. **Website:** www.thecaribbeanwriter.org. **Contact:** Alscess Lewis-Brown, editor. Estab. 1986. "*The Caribbean Writer* features new and exciting voices from the region and beyond that explore the diverse and multi-ethnic culture in poetry, short fiction, personal essays, creative nonfiction, and plays. Social, cultural, economic, and sometimes controversial issues are also explored, employing a wide array of literary devices."

NEEDS Submit complete ms. E-mail as attachment; no fax submissions. Name, address, phone number, e-mail address, and title of ms should appear in cover letter along with brief bio. Title only on ms. Length: up to 3,500 words or 10 pages.

PAYMENT/TERMS Pays 1 contributor's copy.

THE CAROLINA QUARTERLY

CB #3520 Greenlaw Hall, University of North Carolina, Chapel Hill NC 27599-3520. (919)408-7786. **E-mail:** carolina.quarterly@gmail.com. **Website:** www.thecarolinaquarterly.com. Estab. 1948. *The Carolina Quarterly*, published 3 times/year, prints fiction, poetry, reviews, nonfiction, and visual art. No specifications regarding form, length, subject matter, or style. Considers translations of work originally written in languages other than English.

Accepts submissions September through May. Subscription: $24 for individuals, $30 for institutions.

NEEDS Length: up to 7,500 words.

HOW TO CONTACT Submit 1 complete ms via online submissions manager or postal mail (address submissions to Fiction Editor).

CAVEAT LECTOR

400 Hyde St., #606, San Francisco CA 94109. (415)928-7431. **Fax:** (415)928-7431. **E-mail:** editors@caveat-lector.org. **E-mail:** caveatlectormagazine@gmail.com. **Website:** www.caveat-lector.org. **Contact:** Christopher Bernard, co-editor. Estab. 1989. *Caveat Lector*, published 2 times/year, is devoted to the arts and cultural and philosophical commentary. As well as literary work, they publish art, photography, music,

streaming audio of selected literary pieces, and short films. Poetry, fiction, artwork, music, and short films are posted on website. "Don't let those examples limit your submissions. Send what you feel is your strongest work, in any style and on any subject."

All submissions should be sent with a brief bio and SASE, or submitted electronically (poetry submissions only accepted through postal mail). Reads poetry submissions February 1-June 30; reads all other submissions year round.

NEEDS Accepts prose submissions (short stories, excerpts from longer works) throughout the year. Submit complete ms by e-mail or postal mail.

PAYMENT/TERMS Pays contributor's copies.

CEMETERY MOON

Fortress Publishing, Inc., 3704 Hartzdale Dr., Camp Hill PA 17011. **E-mail:** cemeterymoon@yahoo.com. **Website:** www.fortresspublishinginc.com. *Cemetery Moon* is a magazine filled with short stories and poetry devoted to horror, suspense, and Gothic. This magazine brings to light what lurks in the darkness.

NEEDS Length: up to 5,000 words.

HOW TO CONTACT Send complete ms with cover letter by e-mail only.

TIPS "We want compelling stories—if we stop reading your story, so will the reader. We don't care about trick or twist endings; we're more concerned about how you take us there. Don't try to reinvent the wheel. Listen to advice with an open mind. Read your story, reread it, then read it again before you send it anywhere."

CHA

Hong Kong **E-mail:** editors@asiancha.com; j@asiancha.com. **E-mail:** submissions@asiancha.com. **Website:** www.asiancha.com. **Contact:** Tammy Ho Lai-Ming, founding co-editor; Jeff Zroback, founding co-editor; Eddie Tay, reviews editor. Estab. 2007. *Cha* is the first Hong Kong-based English online literary journal; it is dedicated to publishing quality poetry, fiction, creative nonfiction, reviews, photography, and art. *Cha* has a strong focus on Asian-themed creative work and work done by Asian writers and artists. It also publishes established and emerging writers/artists from around the world. *Cha* is an affiliated organisation of the Asia-Pacific Writing Partnership and it is catalogued in the School of Oriental and African Studies (SOAS) Library, among other universities. *Cha* was named Best New Online Magazine of 2008. "At this time, we can only accept work in English or translated into English. If you want to review a book for *Cha*, please also write for further information."

NEEDS Length: 100-5,000 words.

HOW TO CONTACT Submit via e-mail.

TIPS "Please read the guidelines on our website carefully before you submit work to us. Do not send attachments in your e-mail. Include all writing in the body of e-mail. Include a brief biography (100 words)."

THE CHAFFIN JOURNAL

English Department, Eastern Kentucky University, Richmond KY 40475-3102. (859)622-3080. **E-mail:** robert.witt@eku.edu. **Website:** www.english.eku.edu/chaffin_journal. **Contact:** Robert Witt, editor. Estab. 1998. *The Chaffin Journal*, published annually in December, prints quality short fiction and poetry by new and established writers/poets. "We publish fiction on any subject; our only consideration is the quality."

Receives 20 unsolicited mss/month. Accepts 6-8 mss/year. Does not read mss October 1-May 31. Publishes 2-3 new writers/year. Has published work by Meridith Sue Willis, Marie Manilla, Raymond Abbott, Marjorie Bixler, and Chris Helvey.

NEEDS No erotica, fantasy. Length: 10,000 words per submission period; average length: 5,000 words.

HOW TO CONTACT .

PAYMENT/TERMS Pays 1 contributor's copy.

TIPS "All mss submitted are considered."

THE CHATTAHOOCHEE REVIEW

555 N. Indian Creek Dr., Clarkston GA 30021. **E-mail:** gpccr@gpc.edu. **Website:** thechattahoocheereview.gpc.edu. **Contact:** Lydia Ship, managing editor. Estab. 1980. *The Chattahoochee Review*, published quarterly, prints poetry, short fiction, essays, reviews, and interviews. "We publish a number of Southern writers, but *The Chattahoochee Review* is not by design a regional magazine. All themes, forms, and styles are considered as long as they impact the whole person: heart, mind, intuition, and imagination."

Has recently published work by George Garrett, Jim Daniels, Jack Pendarvis, Ignacio Padilla, and Kevin Canty. *The Chattahoochee Review* is 160 pages, digest-sized, professionally printed, flat-spined, with four-color silk-matte card cover. Press run is 1,250; 300 are complimentary copies sent to editors and "miscellaneous VIPs." No e-mail submissions.

NEEDS Length: 500-1,000 words for short shorts; up to 6,000 words for short stories and novellas.

HOW TO CONTACT "*TCR* publishes high-quality literary fiction characterized by interest in language, development of distinctive settings, compelling conflict, and complex, unique characters. Submit 1 story or up to 3 short shorts via online submissions manager.

PAYMENT/TERMS Pays 2 contributor's copies.

CHAUTAUQUA LITERARY JOURNAL

Chautauqua Institution, P.O. Box 28, 1 Ames Ave., Chautauqua NY 14722. **E-mail:** clj@uncw.edu. **Website:** ciweb.org. **Contact:** Jill Gerard and Philip Gerard, editors. Estab. 2003. *Chautauqua*, published annually in June, prints poetry, short fiction, and creative nonfiction. The editors actively solicit writing that expresses the values of Chautauqua Institution broadly construed: a sense of inquiry into questions of personal, social, political, spiritual, and aesthetic importance, regardless of genre. Considers the work of any writer, whether or not affiliated with Chautauqua Institution. Looking for a mastery of craft, attention to vivid and accurate language, a true lyric "ear," an original and compelling vision, and strong narrative instinct. Above all, it values work that is intensely personal, yet somehow implicitly comments on larger public concerns, like work that answers every reader's most urgent question: Why are you telling me this?

Reads submissions February 15-April 15 and August 15-November 15. Work published in *Chautauqua* has been included in *The Pushcart Prize* anthology.

NEEDS "*Chautauqua* short stories, self-contained novel excerpts, or flash fiction demonstrate a sound storytelling instinct, using suspense in the best sense, creating a compulsion in the reader to continue reading. Wants to engage readers' deep interest in the characters and their actions, unsettled issues of action or theme, or in some cases simple delight at the language itself. A superior story will exhibit the writer's attention to language—both in style and content—and should reveal a masterful control of diction and syntax." Length: up to 25 double-spaced pages or 7,000 words.

HOW TO CONTACT Submit through online submissions manager.

PAYMENT/TERMS Pays 2 contributor's copies.

CHICAGO QUARTERLY REVIEW

517 Sherman Ave., Evanston IL 60202. **Website:** www.chicagoquarterlyreview.com. **Contact:** S. Afzal Haider and Elizabeth McKenzie, senior editors. Estab. 1994. "The *Chicago Quarterly Review* is a nonprofit, independent literary journal publishing the finest short stories, poems, translations, and essays by both emerging and established writers. We hope to stimulate, entertain, and inspire."

NEEDS Length: up to 5,000 words; average length: 2,500 words.

HOW TO CONTACT Submit through online submissions manager only.

PAYMENT/TERMS Pays 2 contributor's copies.

TIPS "The writer's voice ought to be clear and unique and should explain something of what it means to be human. We want well-written stories that reflect an appreciation for the rhythm and music of language, work that shows passion and commitment to the art of writing."

CHICAGO REVIEW

Taft House, 935 E. 60th St., Chicago IL 60637. **E-mail:** chicago-review@uchicago.edu. **Website:** chicagoreview.org. **Contact:** Eric Powell, managing editor. Estab. 1946. "Since 1946, *Chicago Review* has published a range of contemporary poetry, fiction, and criticism. Each year typically includes 2 single issues and a double issue with a special feature section."

NEEDS "We will consider work in any literary style but are typically less interested in traditional narrative approaches." Length: up to 5,000 words.

HOW TO CONTACT Submit 1 short story or up to 5 short short stories submitted in 1 file. Submit via online submissions manager. Prefers electronic submissions.

PAYMENT/TERMS Pays contributor's copies.

TIPS "We strongly recommend that authors familiarize themselves with recent issues of *Chicago Review* before submitting. Submissions that demonstrate familiarity with the journal tend to receive more attention than those that appear to be part of a carpet-bombing campaign."

CHIRON REVIEW

Chiron, Inc., 522 E. South Ave., St. John KS 67576-2212. **E-mail:** editor@chironreview.com. **Website:** www.chironreview.com. **Contact:** Michael Hathaway, publisher. Estab. 1982 as *The Kindred Spirit*. *Chiron Review*, published quarterly, presents the widest possible range of contemporary creative writing—fiction and nonfiction, traditional and off-beat—in an attractive, perfect-bound digest, including artwork and photographs. No taboos.

NEEDS Submit complete ms by postal mail with SASE, or by e-mail as DOC attachment. Length: up to 2,500 words.

PAYMENT/TERMS Pays 1 contributor's copy.

TIPS "Please check our website to see if we are open to submissions. When you do send submissions, please have mercy on the editors and follow the guidelines noted here and on our website."

CIMARRON REVIEW

205 Morrill Hall, English Department, Oklahoma State University, Stillwater OK 74078. **E-mail:** cimarronreview@okstate.edu. **Website:** cimarronreview.com. **Contact:** Toni Graham, editor; Lisa Lewis, poetry editor. Estab. 1967. "One of the oldest quarterlies in the nation, *Cimarron Review* publishes work by writers at all stages of their careers, including Pulitzer prize winners, writers appearing in the Best American Series and the Pushcart anthologies, and winners of national book contests. Since 1967, *Cimarron* has showcased poetry, fiction, and nonfiction with a wide-ranging aesthetic. Our editors seek the bold and the ruminative, the sensitive and the shocking, but above all they seek imagination and truth-telling, the finest stories, poems, and essays from working writers across the country and around the world."

Accepts 3-5 mss/issue; 12-15 mss/year. Publishes 2-4 new writers/year. Eager to receive mss from both established and less experienced writers "who intrigue us with their unusual perspective, language, imagery, and character." Has published work by Molly Giles, Gary Fincke, David Galef, Nona Caspers, Robin Beeman, Edward J. Delaney, William Stafford, John Ashbery, Grace Schulman, Barbara Hamby, Patricia Fargnoli, Phillip Dacey, Holly Prado, and Kim Addonizio.

NEEDS No juvenile or genre fiction. Length: up to 25 pages.

HOW TO CONTACT Send complete ms with SASE or submit online through submission manager; include cover letter.

PAYMENT/TERMS Pays 2 contributor's copies.

TIPS "All postal submissions must come with SASE. A cover letter is encouraged. No e-mail submissions from authors living in North America. Query first and follow guidelines. In order to get a feel for the kind of work we publish, please read an issue or two before submitting."

THE CINCINNATI REVIEW

P.O. Box 210069, Cincinnati OH 45221-0069. (513)556-3954. **E-mail:** editors@cincinnatireview.com. **Website:** www.cincinnatireview.com. **Contact:** Michael Griffith, fiction editor; Don Bogen, poetry editor. Estab. 2003. A journal devoted to publishing the best new literary fiction, creative nonfiction, and poetry, as well as book reviews, essays, and interviews.

Reads submissions August 15-March 15.

NEEDS Does not want genre fiction. Length: up to 40 double-spaced pages.

HOW TO CONTACT Submit complete ms via online submissions manager only.

PAYMENT/TERMS Pays $25/page.

TIPS "Each issue includes a translation feature. For more information on translations, please see our website."

THE CLAREMONT REVIEW

Suite 101, 1581-H Hillside Ave., Victoria BC V8T 2C1, Canada. **Website:** www.theclaremontreview.ca. **Contact:** Jody Carrow, editor in chief. The editors of *The Claremont Review* publish first-class poetry, short stories, short plays, visual art, and photography by young adults, aged 13-19, from anywhere in the English speaking world.

"We publish anything from traditional to postmodern but with a preference for works that reveal something of the human condition. By this we mean stories that explore real characters in modern settings. Who are we, what are we doing to the planet, what is our relationship to one another, the earth, or God? Also, reading samples on the website or from past issues will give you a clearer indication of what we are looking for."

NEEDS Submit complete, double-spaced ms by postal mail. Include cover letter with name, age, mailing address, e-mail address, school, and brief bio. Allows up to 6 items in each submission. Does not want science fiction, fantasy, or romance. Only accepts submissions from writers aged 13-19. Length: up to 5,000.

TIPS "Read guidelines before submitting."

CLARK STREET REVIEW

P.O. Box 1377, Berthoud CO 80513. **E-mail:** clarkreview@earthlink.net. **Contact:** Ray Foreman, editor. Estab. 1998. *Clark Street Review*, published 6 times/year, uses narrative poetry and short shorts. Tries "to give writers and poets cause to keep writing by publishing their best work." Press run is 200.

"Editor reads everything with a critical eye of 30 years experience in writing and publishing small-press work."

NEEDS Wants short shorts. Include SASE for reply. No cover letter. No limit on submissions. Length: up to 1,200 words.

CLOUDBANK: JOURNAL OF CONTEMPORARY WRITING

P.O. Box 610, Corvallis OR 97339. (541)752-0075. **E-mail:** michael@cloudbankbooks.com. **Website:** www.cloudbankbooks.com. **Contact:** Michael Malan, editor. Estab. 2009. *Cloudbank* Contest for $200 prize. $15 entry fee. See website for guidelines. *Cloudbank* publishes poetry, short prose, and book reviews.

NEEDS Length: up to 500 words.

HOW TO CONTACT Submit flash fiction by mail with SASE.

PAYMENT/TERMS Pays $200 prize for 1 poem or flash fiction piece per issue.

TIPS "Please consider reading a copy of *Cloudbank* before submitting."

CLOUD RODEO

E-mail: editors@cloudrodeo.org; submit@cloudrodeo.org. **Website:** cloudrodeo.org. "We want your problems deploying a term liek nonelen. We want your isolated photographs of immense locomotives slogged down by the delirium of drunken yet pristine jungles. We want the one eye you caught on fire doing alchemy. The world you collapsed playing architect. We want what you think is too. We want you to anesthetize this aesthetic. Your Enfer, your Ciel, your Qu'importe. We want all your to to sound out."

HOW TO CONTACT Submit 1 prose piece via e-mail as a .doc or .docx attachment.

TIPS "Let's get weird."

O COAL CITY REVIEW

Coal City Press, English Department, University of Kansas, Lawrence KS 66045. **E-mail:** briandal@ku.edu. **Website:** coalcitypress.wordpress.com. **Contact:** Brian Daldorph, editor. "*Coal City Review*, published annually, usually late in the year, publishes poetry, short stories, reviews: "the best material I can find."

NEEDS Accepts mainly mainstream fiction: " Please don't send 'experimental' work our way." Length: up to 4,000 words.

PAYMENT/TERMS Pays contributor's copies.

COLD MOUNTAIN REVIEW

Department of English, Appalachian State University, ASU Box 32052, Boone NC 28608. **E-mail:** coldmountain@appstate.edu. **Website:** www.coldmountain.appstate.edu. *Cold Mountain Review*, published twice/year (Spring and Fall), features poetry, interviews with poets, poetry book reviews, and b&w graphic art. Has published poetry by Sarah Kennedy, Robert Morgan, Susan Ludvigson, Aleida Rodriíguez, R.T. Smith, and Virgil Suaárez.

Reading period is August-May.

NEEDS Considers novel excerpts if the submissions is "an exemplary stand-alone piece." Length: up to 6,000 words.

PAYMENT/TERMS Pays in contributor's copies.

$ COLORADO REVIEW

Center for Literary Publishing, Colorado State University, 9105 Campus Delivery, Fort Collins CO 80523. (970)491-5449. **E-mail:** creview@colostate.edu. **Website:** coloradoreview.colostate.edu. **Contact:** Stephanie G'Schwind, editor in chief and nonfiction editor; Steven Schwartz, fiction editor; Don Revell, Sasha Steensen, and Matthew Cooperman, poetry editors; Dan Beachy-Quick, book review editor. Estab. 1956. Literary magazine published 3 times/year.

Work published in *Colorado Review* has been included in *Best American Poetry, Best New American Voices, Best Travel Writing, Best Food Writing*, and the *Pushcart Prize Anthology*.

NEEDS No genre fiction. Length: up to 10,000 words.

HOW TO CONTACT Send complete ms. Fiction mss are read August 1-April 30. Mss received May 1-July 31 will be returned unread. Send no more than 1 story at a time.

PAYMENT/TERMS Pays $200.

COLUMBIA: A JOURNAL OF LITERATURE AND ART

Columbia University, New York NY 10027. **E-mail:** info@columbiajournal.org. **Website:** columbiajournal.org. **Contact:** Raluca Albu, managing editor. Estab. 1977. *"Columbia: A Journal of Literature and Art* is an annual publication that features the very best in poetry, fiction, nonfiction, and art. We were founded in 1977 and continue to be one of the few national literary journals entirely edited, designed, and produced by students. You'll find that our minds are open, our interests diverse. We solicit mss from writers we love and select the most exciting finds from our virtual submission box. Above all, our commitment is to our readers—to producing a collection that informs, surprises, challenges, and inspires."

Reads submissions March 1-September 15.

HOW TO CONTACT Submit complete ms via online submissions manager.

CONCEIT MAGAZINE

P.O. Box 884223, San Francisco CA 94188-4223. **E-mail:** conceitmagazine2007@yahoo.com. **Website:** sites.google.com/site/conceitmagazine. **Contact:** Perry Terrell, editor. Estab. 2006.

Magazine publishing poetry, short stories, articles, and essays. "Very few guidelines—let me see your creative work."

NEEDS List of upcoming themes available for SASE and on website. Receives 60-70 mss/month. Accepts 20-22 mss/issue; up to 264 mss/year. Ms published 3-10 months after acceptance. Publishes 150 new writers/year. Published D. Neil Simmers, Tamara Fey Turner, Eve J. Blohm, Barbara Hantman, David Body, Milton Kerr, and Juanita Torrence-Thompson. Does not want profanity, porn, gruesomeness. Length: 100-3,000 words. Average length: 1,500-2,000 words. Publishes short shorts. Average length of short shorts: 50-500 words.

HOW TO CONTACT Will read and review your books. "Send review copies to Perry Terrell." Query first or send complete ms with cover letter. Accepts submissions by e-mail and snail mail. Include estimated word count, brief bio, list of publications.

PAYMENT/TERMS Pays 1 contributor's copy. Additional copies $4.50. Pay via PayPal to conceitmagazine@yahoo.com. Pays writers through contests. "Occasionally sponsors contests. Send SASE or check blog on website for details."

TIPS "We are a 'literary sharing' organization. Uniqueness and creativity make a ms stand out. Be brave and confident. Let me see what you created."

CONCHO RIVER REVIEW

Angelo State University, ASU Station #10894, San Angelo TX 76909. (325)486-6137. **E-mail:** crr@angelo.edu. **Website:** conchoriverreview.org. **Contact:** R. Mark Jackson, general editor. Estab. 1987. *"CRR* aims to provide its readers with escape, insight, laughter, and inspiration for many years to come. We urge authors to submit to the journal and readers to subscribe to our publication."

NEEDS "Editors tend to publish traditional stories with a strong sense of conflict, finely drawn characters, and crisp dialogue." Length: 1,500-5,000 words.

HOW TO CONTACT Submit only 1 ms at a time. Electronic submissions preferred. See website for appropriate section editor.

PAYMENT/TERMS Pays 1 contributor's copy.

CONFRONTATION

English Department, LIU Post, Brookville NY 11548. (516)299-2963. **E-mail:** confrontationmag@gmail.com. **Website:** www.confrontationmagazine.org. **Contact:** Jonna Semeiks, editor in chief; Belinda Kremer, poetry editor. Estab. 1968. *"Confrontation* has been in continuous publication since 1968. Our taste and our magazine is eclectic, but we always look for excellence in style, an important theme, a memorable voice. We enjoy discovering and fostering new talent. Each issue contains work by both well-established and new writers. We read August 16-April 15. Do not send mss or e-mail submissions between April 16 and August 15."

Confrontation has garnered a long list of awards and honors, including the Editor's Award for Distinguished Achievement from CLMP (given to Martin Tucker, the founding editor of the magazine) and NEA grants. Work from the magazine has appeared in numerous anthologies, including the *Pushcart Prize*, *Best Short Stories*, and *The O. Henry Prize Stories*.

NEEDS "We judge on quality of writing and thought or imagination, so we will accept genre fiction. However, it must have literary merit or must transcend or challenge genre." No "proselytizing" literature or conventional genre fiction. Length: up to 7,200 words.

HOW TO CONTACT Send complete ms.

PAYMENT/TERMS Pays $175-250; more for commissioned work.

TIPS "We look for literary merit. Keep honing your skills, and keep trying."

CONGRUENT SPACES

820 Taylor St. #5, Medford OR 97504. **E-mail:** congruentspacesmag@gmail.com. **Website:** www.congruentspaces.com. **Contact:** Michael Camarata, editor. Estab. 2011. "*Congruent Spaces* was developed as a common ground for a diverse variety of voices and writing styles within the writing community. In keeping with this sense of community, all submissions are posted directly to the slush pile in our Writer's Lair, where our community of writers and readers come together to read and rate these submissions. For each issue we then select from the top-rated submissions which stories and poems appear within the pages of our magazine. Our magazine covers fantasy, horror, literary/mainstream fiction, poetry, and science fiction."

NEEDS Submit complete ms on website. No erotic/pornographic material. Length: up to 2,500 words.

PAYMENT/TERMS Pays 1 contributor's copy and one-month membership.

TIPS "Don't submit your work unless you truly believe it is ready for publication. Be sure to proof your formatting for readability before posting the ms for our ratings process. The most common error is failing to adequately separate paragraphs after copying and pasting the submission in the submission form. The easier it is to read your ms, the better your chances of receiving a quality rating and being published."

CONTRARY

P.O. Box 806363, Chicago IL 60616-3299. **E-mail:** chicago@contrarymagazine.com. **Website:** www.contrarymagazine.com. **Contact:** Jeff McMahon, editor; Frances Badgett, fiction editor; Shaindel Beers, poetry editor. Estab. 2003. *Contrary* publishes fiction, poetry, and literary commentary, and prefers work that combines the virtues of all those categories. Founded at the University of Chicago, it now operates independently and not-for-profit on the South Side of Chicago. "We like work that is not only contrary in content, but contrary in its evasion of the expectations established by its genre. Our fiction defies traditional story form. For example, a story may bring us to closure without ever delivering an ending. We don't insist on the ending, but we do insist on the closure. And we value fiction as poetic as any poem." Quarterly. Member CLMP.

NEEDS Receives 650 mss/month. Accepts 6 mss/issue; 24 mss/year. Publishes 14 new writers/year. Has published Sherman Alexie, Andrew Coburn, Amy Reed, Clare Kirwan, Stephanie Johnson, Laurence Davies, and Edward McWhinney. Length: up to 2,000 words. Average length: 750 words. Publishes short shorts. Average length of short shorts: 750 words.

HOW TO CONTACT Accepts submissions through website only: www.contrarymagazine.com/Contrary/Submissions.html. Include estimated word count, brief bio, list of publications.

PAYMENT/TERMS Pays $20-60.

TIPS "Beautiful writing catches our eye first. If we realize we're in the presence of unanticipated meaning, that's what clinches the deal. Also, we're not fond of expository fiction. We prefer to be seduced by beauty, profundity, and mystery than to be presented with the obvious. We look for fiction that entrances, that stays the reader's finger above the mouse button. That is, in part, why we favor microfiction, flash fiction, and short shorts. Also, we hope writers will remember that most editors are looking for very particular species of work. We try to describe our particular species in our mission statement and our submission guidelines, but those descriptions don't always convey nuance. That's why many editors urge writers to read the publication itself, in the hope that they will intuit an understanding of its particularities. If you happen to write that particular species of work we favor, your submission may find a happy home with us. If you don't, it does not necessarily reflect on your quality or your ability. It usually just means that your work has a happier home somewhere else."

CONVERGENCE: AN ONLINE JOURNAL OF POETRY AND ART

An Online Journal of Poetry and Art, **E-mail:** clinville@csus.edu. **E-mail:** clinville@csus.edu. **Website:** www.convergence-journal.com. **Contact:** Cynthia Linville, managing editor. Estab. 2003. *Convergence* seeks to unify the literary and visual arts and draw new interpretations of the written word by pairing poems and flash fiction with complementary art. Quarterly. Estab. 2003. Circ. 200. "We look for well-crafted work with fresh images and a strong voice. Work from a series or with a common theme has a greater chance of being accepted. Seasonally-themed work is appreciated (spring and summer for the January deadline, fall and winter for the June deadline). Please include a 75-word bio with your work (bios may be edited for length and clarity). A cover letter is not needed.

Absolutely no simultaneous or previously published submissions."

Deadlines are January 5 and June 5.

NEEDS Accepts 5 mss/issue. Publishes ms 1-6 months after acceptance. Recently published work by Oliver Rice, Simon Perchik, Mary Ocher. Publishes short shorts. Also publishes poetry.

HOW TO CONTACT Send complete ms. E-mail submissions only with "Convergence" in subject line. No simultaneous submissions. Responds in less than a week to queries; in 6 months to mss. Writer's guidelines online. Submit no more than 5 fiction pieces, no longer than 1,000 words each.

PAYMENT/TERMS Acquires first rights.

TIPS "We look for freshness and originality and a mastery of the craft of flash fiction. Working with a common theme has a greater chance of being accepted."

THE COPPERFIELD REVIEW

A Journal for Readers and Writers of Historical Fiction, **E-mail:** copperreview@aol.com. **E-mail:** copperreview@aol.com. **Website:** www.copperfieldreview.com. **Contact:** Meredith Allard, executive editor. Estab. 2000. "We are a quarterly online literary journal that publishes historical fiction, reviews, and interviews related to historical fiction. We believe that by understanding the lessons of the past through historical fiction, we can gain better insight into the nature of our society today, as well as a better understanding of ourselves."

"Remember that we are a journal for readers and writers of historical fiction. We only consider submissions that are historical in nature."

NEEDS "We will consider submissions in most fiction categories, but the setting must be historical in nature. We don't want to see anything not related to historical fiction." Receives 40 unsolicited mss/month. Publishes 30-40% new writers/year. Publishes short shorts. Length: 500-3,000 words.

HOW TO CONTACT Send complete ms. Name and e-mail address should appear on the first page of the submission. Accepts submissions pasted into an e-mail only. "Do not query first. Send the complete ms according to our guidelines."

TIPS "We wish to showcase the very best in historical fiction. Stories that use historical periods to illuminate universal truths will immediately stand out. We are thrilled to receive thoughtful work that is polished, poised, and written from the heart. Be professional, and only submit your very best work. Be certain to adhere to a publication's submission guidelines, and always treat your e-mail submissions with the same care you would use with a traditional publisher."

COTTONWOOD

Room 400 Kansas Union, 1301 Jayhawk Blvd., University of Kansas, Lawrence KS 66045. **E-mail:** tlorenz@ku.edu. **Website:** www2.ku.edu/~englishmfa/cottonwood. **Contact:** Tom Lorenz, fiction editor. Estab. 1965. "Established in the 1960s, *Cottonwood* is the nationally circulated literary review of the University of Kansas. We publish high-quality literary work in poetry, fiction, and creative nonfiction. Over the years authors such as William Stafford, Rita Dove, Connie May Fowler, Virgil Suarez, and Cris Mazza have appeared in the pages of *Cottonwood*, and recent issues have featured the work of Kim Chinquee, Quinn Dalton, Carol Lee Lorenzo, Jesse Kercheval, Joanne Lowery, and Oliver Rice. We welcome submissions from new and established writers. New issues appear once yearly, in the fall."

NEEDS Length: up to 8,500 words.

HOW TO CONTACT Submit with SASE.

PAYMENT/TERMS Pays contributor's copies.

TIPS "We're looking for depth and originality of subject matter, engaging voice and style, emotional honesty, command of the material and the structure. *Cottonwood* publishes high-quality literary fiction, but we are very open to the work of talented new writers. Write something honest and that you care about, and write it as well as you can. Don't hesitate to keep trying us. We sometimes take a piece from a writer we've rejected a number of times. We generally don't like clever, gimmicky writing. The style should be engaging but not claim all the the attention itself."

CRAB CREEK REVIEW

7315 34th Ave. NW, Seattle WA 98117. **E-mail:** crabcreekreview@gmail.com. **Website:** www.crabcreekreview.org. **Contact:** Jenifer Lawrence, editor-in-chief; Martha Silano, poetry editor. *Crab Creek Review* is an 80- to 120-page, perfect-bound paperback. "We are an international journal based in the Pacific Northwest that is looking for poems, stories, and essays that pay attention to craft while still surprising us in positive ways with detail and content. We publish well-known and emerging writers."

Nominates for the Pushcart Prize and offers annual *Crab Creek Review* Editors' Prize of $100 for the best poem, essay, or short story published in the previous year. Annual *Crab Creek Review* poetry prize: $500.

NEEDS Accepts only the strongest fiction. Prefers shorter work. Has published fiction by Shann Ray and Daniel Homan. Length: 3,500 words.

HOW TO CONTACT Send complete ms.

PAYMENT/TERMS Pays 1 contributor's copy.

CRAB ORCHARD REVIEW

Dept. of English, Southern Illinois University Carbondale, Faner Hall 2380, Mail Code 4503, 1000 Faner Dr., Carbondale IL 62901. (618)453-6833. **Fax:** (618)453-8224. **E-mail:** jtribble@siu.edu. **Website:** www.craborchardreview.siu.edu. **Contact:** Jon Tribble, managing editor. Estab. 1995. "We are a general-interest literary journal published twice/year. We strive to be a journal that writers admire and readers enjoy. We publish fiction, poetry, creative nonfiction, fiction translations, interviews, and reviews."

NEEDS No science fiction, romance, western, horror, gothic, or children's. Wants more novel excerpts that also stand alone as pieces. Length: up to 25 pages double-spaced.

HOW TO CONTACT Send SASE for reply, return of ms.

PAYMENT/TERMS Pays $25/published magazine page, $100 minimum, 2 contributor's copies and 1-year subscription.

CRAZYHORSE

College of Charleston, Department of English, 66 George St., Charleston SC 29424. (843)953-4470. **E-mail:** crazyhorse@cofc.edu. **Website:** crazyhorse.cofc.edu. **Contact:** Jonathan Bohr Heinen, managing editor; Emily Rosko, poetry editor; Anthony Varallo, fiction editor; Bret Lott, nonfiction editor. Estab. 1960. "We like to print a mix of writing regardless of its form, genre, school, or politics. We're especially on the lookout for original writing that doesn't fit the categories and that engages in the work of honest communication."

Reads submissions September 1-May 31.

NEEDS Accepts all fiction of fine quality, including short shorts and literary essays. Length: 2,500-8,500 words.

HOW TO CONTACT Submit complete ms via online submissions manager.

PAYMENT/TERMS Pays 2 contributor's copies and $20 per page ($200 maximum).

TIPS "Write to explore subjects you care about. The subject should be one in which something is at stake. Before sending, ask, 'What's reckoned with that's important for other people to read?'"

CREAM CITY REVIEW

c/o UWM Department of English, P.O. Box 413, Milwaukee WI 53201. **E-mail:** info@creamcityreview.org. **Website:** www.creamcityreview.org. **Contact:** Loretta McCormick, editor in chief; Mollie Boutell, managing editor. *Cream City Review* publishes "memorable and energetic fiction, poetry, and creative nonfiction. Features reviews of contemporary literature and criticism as well as author interviews and artwork. We are interested in camera-ready art depicting themes appropriate to each issue."

NEEDS "Would like to see more quality fiction. No horror, formulaic, racist, sexist, pornographic, homophobic, science fiction, romance."

HOW TO CONTACT Submit ms via online submissions manager only.

TIPS "Please include a few lines about your publication history. *CCR* seeks to publish a broad range of writings and a broad range of writers with diverse backgrounds. We accept submissions from August 1-November 1 and December 1-April 1. No e-mail submissions, please."

CREATIVE WITH WORDS PUBLICATIONS

P.O. Box 223226, Carmel CA 93922. **Fax:** (831)655-8627. **E-mail:** geltrich@mbay.net. **Website:** creativewithwords.tripod.com. **Contact:** Brigitta Gisella Geltrich-Ludgate, publisher and editor. Estab. 1975. *Creative with Words* publishes "poetry, prose, illustrations, photos by all ages."

NEEDS No violence or erotica, overly religious fiction, or sensationalism.

HOW TO CONTACT Submit complete ms by mail or e-mail. Always include SASE and legitimate address with postal submissions. Cover letter preferred.

TIPS "We offer a great variety of themes. We look for clean family-type fiction/poetry. Also, we ask the writer to look at the world from a different perspective, research topic thoroughly, be creative, apply brevity, tell the story from a character's viewpoint, tighten dialogue, be less descriptive, proofread before submitting, and be patient. We will not publish every ms we receive. It has to be in standard English, well written, proofread. We do not appreciate receiving mss where we have to do the proofreading and correct the grammar."

CRUCIBLE

Barton College, P.O. Box 5000, Wilson NC 27893. **E-mail:** crucible@barton.edu. **Website:** www.barton.edu/crucible. Estab. 1964. *Crucible*, published annually in the fall, publishes poetry and fiction as part of its Poetry and Fiction Contest run each year. Deadline for submissions: May 1.

NEEDS Length: up to 8,000 words.

HOW TO CONTACT Submit ms by e-mail. Ms accepted only through May 1. Do not include name on ms. Include separate bio.

PAYMENT/TERMS Pays $150 for 1st prize, $100 for 2nd prize, contributor's copies.

CURA: A LITERARY MAGAZINE OF ART AND ACTION

441 E. Fordham Rd., English Department, Dealy 541W, Bronx NY 10548. **E-mail:** curamag@fordham.edu. **Website:** www.curamag.com. **Contact:** Sarah Gambito, editor. Estab. 2011. *CURA: A Literary Magazine of Art and Action* is a multimedia initiative based at Fordham University committed to integrating the arts and social justice. Featuring creative writing, visual art, new media, and video in response to current news, we seek to enable an artistic process that is rigorously engaged with the world at the present moment. *CURA* is taken from the Ignatian educational principle of "cura personalis," care for the whole person. On its own, the word *cura* is defined as guardianship, solicitude, and significantly, written work.

Reading period: October 15 - March 15.

NEEDS Length: up to 6,000 words.

HOW TO CONTACT Submit complete ms.

PAYMENT/TERMS Pays 1 contributor's copy.

CUTTHROAT, A JOURNAL OF THE ARTS

P.O. Box 2414, Durango CO 81302. (970)903-7914. **E-mail:** cutthroatmag@gmail.com. **Website:** www.cutthroatmag.com. **Contact:** Beth Alvarado, fiction editor; William Luvaas, online fiction editor; William Pitt Root, poetry editor. Estab. 2005. "Sponsors the Rick DeMarinis Short Fiction Prize ($1,250 first prize). See separate listing and website for more information." "We publish only high-quality fiction, creative nonfiction, and poetry. We are looking for the cutting edge, the endangered word, fiction with wit, heart, soul, and meaning." *CUTTHROAT* is a literary magazine/journal and "one separate online edition of poetry, translations, short fiction, essays, and book reviews yearly."

Member CLMP.

NEEDS Send review copies to Pamela Uschuk. List of upcoming themes available on website. Receives 100+ mss/month. Accepts 6 mss/issue; 10-12 mss/year. Does not read October 1-March 1 and June 1-July 15. **Publishes 5-8 new writers/year.** Published Michael Schiavone, Rusty Harris, Timothy Rien, Summer Wood, Peter Christopher, Jamey Genna, Doug Frelke, Sally Bellerose, and Marc Levy. Publishes short shorts and book reviews. Does not want romance, horror, historical, fantasy, religious, teen, or juvenile. Length: 500-5,000 words.

HOW TO CONTACT "We prefer online submissions through our submission manager! If submitting by mail, please include cover letter and SASE for response only; mss are recycled."

PAYMENT/TERMS Pays contributor copies. Additional copies: $10.

TIPS "Read our magazine, and see what types of work we've published. The piece must have heart and soul, excellence in craft. "

THE DALHOUSIE REVIEW

Dalhousie University, Halifax NS B3H 4R2, Canada. **E-mail:** dalhousie.review@dal.ca. **Website:** dalhousiereview.dal.ca. **Contact:** Carrie Dawson, editor. Estab. 1921. *Dalhousie Review*, published 3 times/year, is a journal of criticism publishing poetry and fiction. Considers works from both new and established writers.

NEEDS Length: up to 5,000 words.

HOW TO CONTACT Submit via postal mail only. Writers are encouraged "to follow whatever canons of usage might govern the particular work in question and to be inventive with language, ideas, and form."

PAYMENT/TERMS Pays 2 contributor's copies and 10 offprints.

THE DARK

311 Fairbanks Ave., Northfield NJ 08225. **E-mail:** thedarkmagazine@gmail.com. **Website:** www.thedark-

magazine.com. **Contact:** Jack Fisher and Sean Wallace, editors. Estab. 2013.

Stories featured in *The Dark* have appeared in *Best American Science Fiction & Fantasy* and *The Best Horror of the Year.*

NEEDS "Don't be afraid to experiment or to deviate from the ordinary; be different—try us with fiction that may fall out of 'regular' categories. However, it is also important to understand that despite the name, *The Dark* is not a market for graphic, violent horror." Length: 1,000-6,000 words.

HOW TO CONTACT Send complete ms by e-mail attached in Microsoft Word DOC only. No multiple submissions.

PAYMENT/TERMS Pays 3¢/word.

TIPS "All fiction must have a dark, surreal, fantastical bend to it. It should be out of the ordinary and/or experimental. Can also be contemporary."

DARK TALES

Dark Tales, 7 Offley St., Worcester WR3 8BH, United Kingdom. **Website:** www.darktales.co.uk. **Contact:** Sean Jeffery, editor. Estab. 2003. Has occasional contests; see website for details. "We now publish winning stories from our monthly contest. Please see www.darktales.co.uk for full details. We publish horror and speculative short fiction from anybody, anywhere. The publication is professionally illustrated throughout."

NEEDS Length: 500-3,500 words. Average length: 2,500 words. Publishes short shorts. Average length of short shorts: 500 words.

HOW TO CONTACT Currently only publishing from our monthly contest—please see www.darktales.co.uk for details.

PAYMENT/TERMS Pays £100.

TIPS "Have a believable but inspiring plot, sympathetic characters, an original premise, and a human heart no matter how technical or disturbing a story. Read a copy of the magazine! Make sure you get your writing basics spot-on. Don't rehash old ideas—if you must go down the werewolf/vampire route, put a spin on it."

THE DEADLY QUILL

E-mail: lorne@deadlyquill.com. **E-mail:** submissions@deadlyquill.com. **Website:** deadlyquill.com. **Contact:** Lorne McMillan. Estab. 2015. "We are looking to give an outlet for writers of short fiction in the tradition of *The Twilight Zone*, Alfred Hitchcock, and *The Outer Limits*. Make the story grab you and not let go until the very end."

NEEDS The stories should take the reader by the throat and not let go. Does not want anything that doesn't grab you. No violence for the sake of violence. Length: 2,000-5,000 words.

PAYMENT/TERMS Pays 3¢/word.

THE DEAD MULE SCHOOL OF SOUTHERN LITERATURE

NC 27889. **E-mail:** deadmule@gmail.com. **E-mail:** submit.mule@gmail.com. **Website:** www.deadmule.com. **Contact:** Valerie MacEwan, publisher and editor. Estab. 1996. The *Mule* sponsors flash fiction contests with no entry fees. See the site for specifics. Chapbooks published by invitation, also short fiction compilations. "No good southern fiction is complete without a dead mule." *The Dead Mule* is one of the oldest, if not *the* oldest, continuously published online literary journals alive today. Publisher and editor Valerie MacEwan welcomes submissions. *The Dead Mule School of Southern Literature* wants flash fiction, visual poetry, essays, and creative nonfiction. Twenty Years Online. 1996-2016. Celebrate With a Dead Mule.

"*The Dead Mule School of Southern Literature* Institutional Alumni Association recruits year round. We love reading what you wrote."

NEEDS "We welcome the ingenue and the established writer. It's mostly about you entertaining us and capturing our interest. Everyone is South of Somewhere; go ahead, check us out."

HOW TO CONTACT All submissions must be accompanied by a "southern legitimacy statement," details of which can be seen within each page on *The Dead Mule* and within the submishmash entrypage.

PAYMENT/TERMS Pays sporadically "whenever CafePress/*Dead Mule* sales reach an agreeable amount."

TIPS "Read the site to get a feel for what we're looking to publish. Read the guidelines. We look forward to hearing from you. We are nothing if not for our writers. *The Dead Mule* strives to deliver quality writing in every issue. It is in this way that we pay tribute to our authors. Send us something original."

DENVER QUARTERLY

University of Denver, 2000 E. Asbury, Denver CO 80208. (303)871-2892. **E-mail:** denverquarterly@gmail.com. **Website:** www.du.edu/denverquarterly.

Contact: Laird Hunt, editor. Estab. 1965. Publishes fiction, articles, and poetry for a generally well-educated audience, primarily interested in literature and the literary experience. Audience reads *DQ* to find something a little different from a strictly academic quarterly or a creative writing outlet. Quarterly. Reads September 15-May 15.

Denver Quarterly received an Honorable Mention for Content from the American Literary Magazine Awards, and selections have been anthologized in the *Pushcart Prize* anthologies.

NEEDS "We are interested in experimental fiction (minimalism, magic realism, etc.) as well as in realistic fiction and in writing about fiction. No sentimental, science fiction, romance, or spy thrillers." Length: up to 15 pages.

HOW TO CONTACT Submit by postal mail or online submissions manager.

PAYMENT/TERMS Pays $5/page and 2 contributor's copies.

TIPS "We look for serious, realistic, and experimental fiction: stories which appeal to intelligent, demanding readers who are not themselves fiction writers. Nothing so quickly disqualifies a ms as sloppy proofreading and mechanics. Read the magazine before submitting to it. We try to remain eclectic, but the odds for beginners are bound to be small considering the fact that we receive nearly 10,000 mss per year and publish only about 10 short stories."

DESCANT: FORT WORTH'S JOURNAL OF POETRY AND FICTION

TCU Department of English, Box 297270, Ft. Worth TX 76129. (817)257-5907. **Fax:** (817)257-6239. **E-mail:** descant@tcu.edu; m.pitt@tcu.edu. **Website:** www.descant.tcu.edu. **Contact:** Matthew Pitt, editor in chief and fiction editor; Alex Lemon, poetry editor. Estab. 1956. "*descant* seeks high-quality poems and stories in both traditional and innovative form." Member CLMP.

Reading period: September 1-April 1. Offers 4 annual cash awards for work already accepted for publication in the journal: The $500 Frank O'Connor Award for the best story in an issue; the $250 Gary Wilson Award for an outstanding story in an issue; the $500 Betsy Colquitt Award for the best poem in an issue; and the $250 Baskerville Publishers Award for outstanding poem in an issue. Several stories first published by *descant* have appeared in *Best American Short Stories.*

NEEDS Receives 20-30 unsolicited mss/month. Accepts 3-5 mss/year. Publishes ms 1 year after acceptance. Publishes 50% new writers/year. Recently published work by William Harrison, Annette Sanford, Miller Williams, Patricia Chao, Vonesca Stroud, and Walt McDonald. No horror, romance, fantasy, erotica. Length: 1,000-5,000 words; average length: 2,500 words.

HOW TO CONTACT Send complete ms with cover letter. Include estimated word count and brief bio.

PAYMENT/TERMS Pays 2 contributor's copies; additional copies $6.

TIPS "We look for character and quality of prose. Send your best short work."

DIAGRAM

Department of English, University of Arizona, P.O. Box 210067, Tucson AZ 85721-0067. **E-mail:** editor@thediagram.com. **Website:** www.thediagram.com. **Contact:** Ander Monson, editor; T. Fleischmann and Nicole Walker, nonfiction editors; Sarah Blackman and Lauren Slaughter, fiction editors; Heidi Gotz and E.A. Ramey, poetry editors. Estab. 2000. "*DIAGRAM* is an electronic journal of text and art, found and created. We're interested in representations, naming, indicating, schematics, labeling and taxonomy of things; in poems that masquerade as stories; in stories that disguise themselves as indices or obituaries. We specialize in work that pushes the boundaries of traditional genre or work that is in some way schematic. We do publish traditional fiction and poetry, too, but hybrid forms (short stories, prose poems, indexes, tables of contents, etc.) are particularly welcome! We also publish diagrams and schematics (original and found)."

Publishes 6 new writers/year. Bimonthly. Member CLMP. "We sponsor yearly contests for unpublished hybrid essays and innovative fiction. Guidelines on website."

NEEDS Receives 100 unsolicited mss/month. Accepts 2-3 mss/issue; 15 mss/year. "We don't publish genre fiction unless it's exceptional and transcends the genre boundaries." Length: 250-2,000 words.

HOW TO CONTACT Send complete ms. Accepts submissions by online submissions manager; no e-mail. If sending by snail mail, send SASE for return of the ms or send disposable copy of the ms and #10 SASE for reply only.

TIPS "Submit interesting text, images, sound, and new media. We value the insides of things, vivisection, urgency, risk, elegance, flamboyance, work that moves us, language that does something new, or does something old—well. We like iteration and reiteration. Ruins and ghosts. Mechanical, moving parts, balloons, and frenzy. We want art and writing that demonstrates interaction; the processes of things; how functions are accomplished; how things become or expire, move or stand. We'll consider anything."

THE DOS PASSOS REVIEW

Briery Creek Press, Longwood University, Department of English and Modern Languages, 201 High St., Farmville VA 23909. **E-mail:** brierycreek@gmail.com. **E-mail:** dospassosreview@gmail.com. **Website:** brierycreekpress.wordpress.com/the-dos-passos-review. **Contact:** Managing editor. "We are looking for writing that demonstrates characteristics found in the work of John Dos Passos, such as an intense and original exploration of specifically American themes; an innovative quality; and a range of literary forms, especially in the genres of fiction and creative nonfiction. We are not interested in genre fiction, or prose that is experiment for the sake of experiment. We are also not interested in nonfiction that is scholarly or critical in nature. Send us your best unpublished literary prose or poetry."

Reading periods: April 1-July 31 for Fall issue; February 1-May 31 for Spring issue.

NEEDS No genre fiction. Length: up to 3,000 words for short stories; up to 1,000 for flash fiction.

HOW TO CONTACT Submit 1 complete ms by e-mail as attachment. Include cover letter and brief bio.

PAYMENT/TERMS Pays 2 contributor's copies.

O DOWN IN THE DIRT

E-mail: dirt@scars.tv. **Website:** www.scars.tv/dirt. **Contact:** Janet Kuypers, editor. Estab. 2000. *Down in the Dirt*, published every other month online and in print issues sold via Amazon.com throughout the U.S., U.K., and continental Europe, prints "good work that makes you think, that makes you feel like you've lived through a scene instead of merely read it." Also considers poems. *Down in the Dirt* is published "electronically as well as in print, either as printed magazines sold through our printer over the Internet, on the Web, or sold through our printer."

Has published work by Mel Waldman, Ken Dean, Jon Brunette, John Ragusa, and Liam Spencer.

NEEDS No religious, rhyming, or family-oriented material. Average length: 1,000 words. "Contact us if you are interested in submitting very long stories or parts of a novel (if accepted, it would appear in parts in multiple issues)."

HOW TO CONTACT Query editor with e-mail submission. "99.5% of all submissions are via e-mail only, so if you do not have electronic access, there is a strong chance you will not be considered. We recommend you e-mail submissions to us, either as an attachment (TXT, RTF, DOC, or DOCX files, but not PDF) or by placing it directly in the e-mail letter). For samples of what we've printed in the past, visit our website."

DOWNSTATE STORY

1825 Maple Ridge, Peoria IL 61614. (309)688-1409. **E-mail:** ehopkins7@prodigy.net. **Website:** www.wiu.edu/users/mfgeh/dss; www.downstatestory.com. Estab. 1992.

NEEDS Does not want porn. Length: 300-2,000 words.

HOW TO CONTACT Submit complete ms with cover letter and SASE via postal mail.

TIPS "We want more political fiction. We also publish short shorts and literary essays."

DRUNKEN BOAT

119 Main St., Chester CT 06412. **E-mail:** editor@drunkenboat.com. **Website:** www.drunkenboat.com. Estab. 1999. *Drunken Boat*, published 2 times/year online, is a multimedia publication reaching an international audience with an extremely broad aesthetic. "*Drunken Boat* is committed to actively seeking out and promoting the work of marginalized and underrepresented artists, including especially people of color, women, queer, differently abled, and gender nonconforming artists." To cover operational costs, charges a $3 fee for each submission.

NEEDS "Please submit 1 story or piece of longer work. We welcome the well-written in every style, from microfiction to hypertext to pieces of novels, original and in translation (with the writer's permission), American and from around the globe."

TIPS "Submissions should be submitted in Word and RTF format only. (This does not apply to audio, visual, and Web work.) Accepts chapbooks. See our submissions manager system."

DUCTS

P.O. Box 3203, Grand Central Station, New York NY 10163. **E-mail:** vents@ducts.org. **Website:** www.ducts.org. **Contact:** Mary Cool, editor in chief; Tim Tomlinson, fiction editor; Lisa Kirchner, memoir editor; Amy Lemmon, poetry editor; Jacqueline Bishop, art editor. Estab. 1999. *Ducts* is a semiannual webzine of personal stories, fiction, essays, memoirs, poetry, humor, profiles, reviews, and art. "*Ducts* was founded in 1999 with the intent of giving emerging writers a venue to regularly publish their compelling, personal stories. The site has been expanded to include art and creative works of all genres. We believe that these genres must and do overlap. *Ducts* publishes the best, most compelling stories, and we hope to attract readers who are drawn to work that rises above."

NEEDS Accepts all genres. Also accepts graphic narratives (submit to mary@ducts.org).

HOW TO CONTACT Submit to fiction@ducts.org.

PAYMENT/TERMS Pays $20.

TIPS "We prefer writing that tells a compelling story with a strong narrative drive."

ECLECTICA

E-mail: editors@eclectica.org. **Website:** www.eclectica.org. **Contact:** Tom Dooley, managing editor. Estab. 1996. "A sterling-quality literary magazine on the World Wide Web. Not bound by formula or genre, harnessing technology to further the reading experience and dynamic, and interesting in content. *Eclectica* is a quarterly online journal devoted to showcasing the best writing on the Web, regardless of genre. 'Literary' and 'genre' work appear side-by-side in each issue, along with pieces that blur the distinctions between such categories. Pushcart Prize, National Poetry Series, and Pulitzer Prize winners, as well as Nebula Award nominees, have shared issues with previously unpublished authors."

Submission deadlines: December 1 for January/February issue, and March 1 for April/May issue.

NEEDS Needs "high-quality work in any genre." Accepts short stories and novellas. Length: up to 20,000 words for short fiction; longer novella-length pieces accepted.

HOW TO CONTACT Submit via online submissions manager.

TIPS "We pride ourselves on giving everyone (high schoolers, convicts, movie executives, etc.) an equal shot at publication, based solely on the quality of their work. Because we like eclecticism, we tend to favor the varied perspectives that often characterize the work of international authors, people of color, women, alternative lifestylists—but others who don't fit into these categories often surprise us."

ECOTONE

Department of Creative Writing, University of North Carolina Wilmington, 601 S. College Rd., Wilmington NC 28403. (910)962-2547. **Fax:** (910)962-7461. **E-mail:** info@ecotonejournal.com. **Website:** www.ecotonejournal.com. **Contact:** Kate O'Reilly, managing editor; Cathe Shubert, nonfiction editor; Ryan Kaune, fiction editor; Stephanie Trott, poetry editor. "*Ecotone* is a literary journal of place that seeks to publish creative works about the environment and the natural world while avoiding the hushed tones and clichés of much of so-called nature writing."

Reading period is August 15-April 15.

NEEDS Length: up to 30 pages double-spaced.

HOW TO CONTACT Send complete ms via postal mail or online submissions manager.

ECOTONE, REIMAGINING PLACE

University of North Carolina Wilmington, Department of Creative Writing, 601 S. College Rd., Wilmington NC 28403. **E-mail:** info@ecotonejournal.com. **Website:** www.ecotonejournal.com. **Contact:** David Gessner, editor in chief. Estab. 2005. "*Ecotone* is a literary journal of place seeking to publish creative work that illuminates the edges between science and literature, the urban and rural, and the personal and biological." Semiannual.

Reading period: August 15-April 15. "*Ecotone* charges a small fee for electronic submissions. If you are unable to pay this fee, please submit by postal mail."

NEEDS Also publishes literary essays, poetry. Has published Kevin Brockmeier, Michael Branch, Brock Clarke, Daniel Orozco, and Steve Almond, and Pattiann Rogers. Does not want genre (fantasy, horror, sci-fi, etc.) or young adult fiction. Length: up to 30 pages. "We are now considering shorter prose works (under 2,500 words) as well."

HOW TO CONTACT Submit via online submissions manager or postal mail with SASE. Include brief cover letter, listing both the title of the piece and the word count. Do not include identifying information on or within the ms itself.

ELLERY QUEEN'S MYSTERY MAGAZINE

44 Wall St., Suite 904, New York NY 10005-2401. **E-mail:** elleryqueenmm@dellmagazines.com. **Website:** www.themysteryplace.com/eqmm. Estab. 1941. "*Ellery Queen's Mystery Magazine* welcomes submissions from both new and established writers. We publish every kind of mystery short story: the psychological suspense tale, the deductive puzzle, the private eye case—the gamut of crime and detection from the realistic (including the policeman's lot and stories of police procedure) to the more imaginative (including 'locked rooms' and 'impossible crimes'). We look for strong writing, an original and exciting plot, and professional craftsmanship. We encourage writers whose work meets these general criteria to read an issue of *EQMM* before making a submission."

NEEDS "We always need detective stories. Special consideration given to anything timely and original." Publishes ms 6-12 months after acceptance. Agented fiction 50%. **Publishes 10 new writers/year.** Recently published work by Jeffery Deaver, Joyce Carol Oates, and Margaret Maron. Sometimes comments on rejected mss. No explicit sex or violence, no gore or horror. Seldom publishes parodies or pastiches. "We do not want true detective or crime stories." Length: 2,500-8,000 words, but occasionally accepts longer and shorter submissions—including minute mysteries of 250 words, stories up to 12,000 words, and novellas of up to 20,000 words from established authors.

HOW TO CONTACT "*EQMM* uses an online submission system (eqmm.magazinesubmissions.com) that has been designed to streamline our process and improve communication with authors. We ask that all submissions be made electronically, using this system, rather than on paper. All stories should be in standard ms format and submitted in DOC format. We cannot accept DOCX, RTF, or TXT files at this time."

PAYMENT/TERMS Pays 5-8¢/word; occasionally higher for established authors.

TIPS "*EQMM*'s range in the mystery genre is extensive: Almost any story that involves crime or the threat of crime comes within our purview. However, like all magazines, *EQMM* has a distinctive tone and style, and you can only get a sense of whether your work will suit us by reading an issue."

ELLIPSIS

Westminster College, 1840 S. 1300 E., Salt Lake City UT 84105. (801)832-2321. **E-mail:** ellipsis@westminstercollege.edu. **Website:** www.westminstercollege.edu/ellipsis. Estab. 1965. *Ellipsis*, published annually in April, needs good literary poetry, fiction, essays, plays, and visual art.

Reads submissions August 1-January 1. Staff changes from year to year. Check website for an updated list of editors. *Ellipsis* is 120 pages, digest-sized, perfect-bound, with color cover. Accepts about 5% of submissions received. Press run is 2,000; most distributed free through college.

NEEDS Length: up to 6,000 words.

HOW TO CONTACT Submit complete ms via online submissions manager. Include cover letter.

PAYMENT/TERMS Pays $50 and 2 contributor's copies.

EMRYS JOURNAL

P.O. Box 8813, Greenville SC 29604. (864)409-3679. **E-mail:** emrys.info@gmail.com. **Website:** www.emrys.org. **Contact:** Lindsey DeLoach Jones, editor. Estab. 1984. *Emrys Journal* publishes fiction, poetry, and creative nonfiction. "We are pleased to have published works of the highest quality from both emerging and established writers."

Reading period: August 1-November 1.

NEEDS Length: up to 5,000 words.

HOW TO CONTACT Submit complete ms via online submissions manager.

TIPS "Before submitting, please familiarize yourself with our magazine by reading past contributions to the *Emrys Journal*."

EPOCH

251 Goldwin Smith Hall, Cornell University, Ithaca NY 14853-3201. (607)255-3385. **Website:** english.arts.cornell.edu/publications/epoch. **Contact:** Michael Koch, editor; Heidi E. Marschner, managing editor. Estab. 1947. Looking for well-written literary fiction, poetry, personal essays. Newcomers welcome. Open to mainstream and avant-garde writing.

Reads unsolicited submissions September 15-April 15. Publishes 3-4 new writers/year. Has published work by Antonya Nelson, Doris Betts, Heidi Jon Schmidt.

NEEDS No genre fiction. Would like to see more Southern fiction (Southern U.S.).

HOW TO CONTACT Send complete ms. Considers fiction in all forms, short short to novella length.

PAYMENT/TERMS Pay varies; pays up to $150/unsolicited piece.

TIPS "Tell your story, speak your poem, straight from the heart. We are attracted to language and to good writing, but we are most interested in what the good writing leads us to, or where."

EVANSVILLE REVIEW

University of Evansville Creative Writing Department, 1800 Lincoln Ave., Evansville IN 47722. (812)488-1042. **E-mail:** evansvillereview@evansville.edu. **Website:** evansvillereview.evansville.edu. **Contact:** Rachel Wyatt, editor in chief; Kelly Danahy, nonfiction editor; Tia Balmer, fiction editor; Joy Grace Chen, poetry editor. Estab. 1990. "*The Evansville Review* is an annual literary journal published at the University of Evansville. Our award-winning journal includes poetry, fiction, nonfiction, plays, and interviews by a wide range of authors, from emerging writers to Nobel Prize recipients. Past issues have included work by Joyce Carol Oates, Arthur Miller, John Updike, Joseph Brodsky, Elia Kazan, Edward Albee, Willis Barnstone, Shirley Ann Grau, and X.J. Kennedy."

Reading period: September 1-December 1.

NEEDS "We are open to a wide range of styles, though our aim is always the highest literary quality. Hit us with your best language, your most compelling characters. Make us remember your story." Does not want erotica, fantasy, experimental, or children's fiction. Submit up to 3 pieces of flash fiction (1,000 words each) or 1 story (up to 9,000 words).

HOW TO CONTACT Submit online at theevansvillereview.submittable.com/submit.

PAYMENT/TERMS Pays contributor's copies.

EVENING STREET REVIEW

Evening Street Press, Inc., 2701 Corabel LN #27, Sacramento CA 95821. **E-mail:** editor@eveningstreetpress.com. **Website:** www.eveningstreetpress.com. Estab. 2007. "Intended for a general audience, *Evening Street Press* is centered on Elizabeth Cady Stanton's 1848 revision of the Declaration of Independence: 'that all men and women are created equal,' with equal rights to 'life, liberty, and the pursuit of happiness.' It focuses on the realities of experience, personal and historical, from the most gritty to the most dreamlike, including awareness of the personal and social forces that block or develop the possibilities of this new culture."

HOW TO CONTACT Send complete ms. E-mail submissions preferred.

PAYMENT/TERMS Pays 1 contributor's copy.

TIPS "Does not want to see male chauvinism. Mss are read year round. See website for chapbook and book competitions."

FAILBETTER.COM

2022 Grove Ave., Richmond VA 23221. **E-mail:** submissions@failbetter.com. **Website:** www.failbetter.com. **Contact:** Thom Didato, editor. Estab. 2000. "We are a quarterly online magazine published in the spirit of a traditional literary journal—dedicated to publishing quality fiction, poetry, and artwork. While the Web plays host to hundreds, if not thousands, of genre-related sites (many of which have merit), we are not one of them."

Member CLMP.

NEEDS "If you're sending a short story or novel excerpt, send only 1 at a time. Wait to hear from us before sending another."

HOW TO CONTACT Submit work by pasting it into the body of an e-mail. Must put "Submission" in e-mail's subject line. Do not send attachments. Also accepts postal mail submissions.

TIPS "Read an issue. Read our guidelines! We place a high degree of importance on originality, believing that even in this age of trends it is still possible. We are not looking for what is current or momentary. We are not concerned with length: One good sentence may find a home here, as the bulk of mediocrity will not. Most importantly, know that what you are saying could only come from you. When you are sure of this, please feel free to submit."

FAULTLINE

University of California at Irvine, Dept. of English, 435 Humanities Instructional Building, Irvine CA 92697. (949)824-1573. **E-mail:** faultline@uci.edu. **Website:** faultline.sites.uci.edu. Estab. 1992.

Reading period is August 15-January 15. Submissions sent at any other time will not be read. Editors change in September of each year.

NEEDS Length: up to 20 pages.

HOW TO CONTACT Submit complete ms via online submissions manager or postal mail. "While simultaneous submissions are accepted, multiple submissions are not accepted. Please restrict your submissions to one story at a time, regardless of length."

PAYMENT/TERMS Pays contributor copies.

TIPS "Our commitment is to publish the best work possible from well-known and emerging authors with vivid and varied voices."

FICKLE MUSES

Journal of Mythic Poetry, Fiction & Art, 1516 Tijeras Ave. NE, Apt. 35, Albuquerque NM 87106, United States of America. **E-mail:** publisher@ficklemuses.com. **Website:** ficklemuses.com. **Contact:** Sari Krosinsky, publisher and art editor; Jennifer Cunningham and Sherre Vernon, fiction editors; Jennifer Lynn Krohn, poetry editor. Estab. 2007. "*Fickle Muses* is an online journal of poetry, fiction, and art engaged with myth and legend. We feature a poet or fiction writer each week, accompanied by featured artwork. New features are posted on Sundays."

Fiction and poetry submissions should creatively incorporate myth or legend, for example by retelling ancient myths in the context of the contemporary world, reimagining characters and events within earlier contexts, evoking mythologies underlying speculative genres, or otherwise cultivating new growth from our mythic roots. Art submissions are open to any theme or style.

NEEDS Length: up to 5,000 words.

HOW TO CONTACT Submit complete ms through online submissions manager at ficklemuses.com/submission-guidelines. Query at ficklemuses.com/contact. Reading periods are announced on the submission guidelines page.

FICTION

Department of English, The City College of New York, 138th St. & Convent Ave., New York NY 10031. **Website:** www.fictioninc.com. **Contact:** Mark J. Mirsky, editor. Estab. 1972. "As the name implies, we publish only fiction; we are looking for the best new writing available, leaning toward the unconventional. *Fiction* has traditionally attempted to make accessible the inaccessible, to bring the experimental to a broader audience." Reading period for unsolicited mss is September 15-June 15.

Stories first published in *Fiction* have been selected for the *Pushcart Prize: Best of the Small Presses*, *O. Henry Prize Stories*, and *Best American Short Stories*.

NEEDS No romance, science fiction, etc. Length: reads any length, but encourages lengths under 5,000 words.

HOW TO CONTACT Submit complete ms via online submissions manager.

TIPS "The guiding principle of *Fiction* has always been to go to terra incognita in the writing of the imagination and to ask that modern fiction set itself serious questions, if often in absurd and comedic voices, interrogating the nature of the real and the fantastic. It represents no particular school of fiction, except the innovative. Its pages have often been a harbor for writers at odds with each other. As a result of its willingness to publish the difficult, experimental, and unusual, while not excluding the well known, *Fiction* has a unique reputation in the U.S. and abroad as a journal of future directions."

FICTION INTERNATIONAL

San Diego State University, Department of English and Comp. Lit, 5500 Campanile Dr., San Diego CA 92182-6020. **E-mail:** hjaffe@mail.sdsu.edu. **Website:** fictioninternational.sdsu.edu. **Contact:** Harold Jaffe, editor. Estab. 1973. "*Fiction International* is the only literary journal in the United States emphasizing formal innovation and social activism. Each issue revolves around a theme and features a wide variety of fiction, nonfiction, indeterminate prose, and visuals by leading writers and artists from around the world."

Has published works by William Burroughs, Clarice Lispector (Brazil), Robert Coover, Edmund White, Joyce Carol Oates, Walter Abish, and Kathy Acker.

NEEDS Each issue is themed; see website for details. No genre fiction. Length: up to 5,500 words.

HOW TO CONTACT Submit complete ms via online submissions manager.

FICTION TERRIFICA

17 Ninth Ave. NW, Suite C, Glen Burnie MD 21061. 4436941695. **E-mail:** dschaff@fictionterrifica.com; dwest@fictionterrifica.com. **E-mail:** submissions@fictionterrifica.com. **Website:** www.fictionterrifica.com. **Contact:** Destiny West, managing editor. Estab. 2014. "*Fiction Terrifica* is a website/bimonthly e-zine

dedicated to helping small press writers and previously unpublished writers publish their mss. We are a royalty-based publishing site. We promote writers on Facebook and Twitter, along with any works they may have currently for sale. Our only requirement for acceptance is that the work be horror, dark fiction, science fiction, or fantasy related. We host links to our authors works available at other sites. We also offer Kindle publishing on a royalty basis."

NEEDS Length: 1,500-10,000 words.

HOW TO CONTACT Query before submitting.

TIPS "The best advice I can give is to write a good story, article, or personal experience publishing piece and submit it. We are always looking to promote new and upcoming writers. Have your piece polished and ready for publication."

THE FIDDLEHEAD

University of New Brunswick, Campus House, 11 Garland Court, Box 4400, Fredericton NB E3B 5A3, Canada. (506)453-3501. **Fax:** (506)453-5069. **E-mail:** fiddlehd@unb.ca. **Website:** www.thefiddlehead.ca. **Contact:** Kathryn Taglia, managing editor; Ross Leckie, editor; Mark Anthony Jarman and Gerard Beirne, fiction editors; Phillip Crymble, Ian LeTourneau, and Rebecca Salazar, poetry editors; Sabine Campbell and Ross Leckie, reviews editors. Estab. 1945. "Canada's longest living literary journal, *The Fiddlehead* is published 4 times/year at the University of New Brunswick, with the generous assistance of the University of New Brunswick, the Canada Council for the Arts, and the Province of New Brunswick. It is experienced, wise enough to recognize excellence, and always looking for freshness and surprise. *The Fiddlehead* publishes short stories, poems, book reviews, and a small number of personal essays. Our full-color covers have become collectors' items and feature work by New Brunswick artists and from New Brunswick museums and art galleries. The journal is open to good writing in English from all over the world, looking always for freshness and surprise. Our editors are always happy to see new unsolicited works in fiction and poetry. Work is read on an ongoing basis; the acceptance rate is around 1-2%. Apart from our annual contest, we have no deadlines for submissions."

"No criteria for publication except quality. For a general audience, including many poets and writers." Has published work by George Elliott Clarke, Kayla Czaga, Daniel Woodrell, and Clea Young. *The Fiddlehead* also sponsors an annual writing contest.

NEEDS Receives 100-150 unsolicited mss/month. Accepts 4-5 mss/issue; 20-40 mss/year. Agented fiction: small percentage. Publishes high percentage of new writers/year. Length: up to 6,000 words. Also publishes short shorts.

HOW TO CONTACT Send SASE and *Canadian* stamps or IRCs for return of mss. No e-mail, fax, or disc submissions. Simultaneous submissions only if stated on cover letter; must contact immediately if accepted elsewhere.

PAYMENT/TERMS Pays up to $40 (Canadian)/published page and 2 contributor's copies.

TIPS "If you are serious about submitting to *The Fiddlehead*, you should subscribe or read several issues to get a sense of the journal. Contact us if you would like to order sample back issues ($10-15 plus postage)."

F.U.

FILLING STATION

P.O. Box 22135, Bankers Hall, Calgary AB T2P 4J5, Canada. **E-mail:** mgmt@fillingstation.ca; poetry@fillingstation.ca; fiction@fillingstation.ca; nonfiction@fillingstation.ca; art@fillingstation.ca. **Website:** www.fillingstation.ca. **Contact:** Paul Zits, managing editor. Estab. 1993. *filling Station*, published 3 times/year, prints contemporary poetry, fiction, visual art, interviews, reviews, and articles. "We are looking for all forms of contemporary writing, but especially that which is innovative and/or experimental."

HOW TO CONTACT E-mail up to 10 pages to fiction@fillingstation.ca. "We receive any of the following fiction, or a combination thereof: flash fiction, postcard fiction, short fiction, experimental fiction, or a novel excerpt that can stand alone. A submission lacking mailing address and/or bio will be considered incomplete."

TIPS "*filling Station* accepts singular or simultaneous submissions of previously unpublished poetry, fiction, creative nonfiction, nonfiction, or art. We are always on the hunt for great writing!"

THE FIRST LINE

Blue Cubicle Press, LLC, P.O. Box 250382, Plano TX 75025. (972)824-0646. **E-mail:** submission@thefirstline.com. **Website:** www.thefirstline.com. **Contact:** Robin LaBounty, ms coordinator. Estab. 1999. "*The First Line* is an exercise in creativity for writers and a chance for readers to see how many different directions we can take when we start from the same place. The purpose of *The First Line* is to jumpstart the imagination—to help writers break through the block that is the blank page. Each issue contains short stories that stem from a common first line; it also provides a forum for discussing favorite first lines in literature."

NEEDS "We only publish stories that start with the first line provided. We are a collection of tales—of different directions writers can take when they start from the same place. " Length: 300-5,000 words.

HOW TO CONTACT Submit complete ms.

PAYMENT/TERMS Pays $25-50.

TIPS "Don't just write the first story that comes to mind after you read the sentence. If it is obvious, chances are other people are writing about the same thing. Don't try so hard. Be willing to accept criticism."

FLINT HILLS REVIEW

Department of English, Modern Languages, and Journalist (Box 4019), Emporia State University, 1 Kellogg Circle, Emporia KS 66801. **E-mail:** bluestem@emporia.edu. **E-mail:** bluestem@emporia.edu. **Website:** www.emporia.edu/fhr. **Contact:** Kevin Rabas. Estab. 1996. *Flint Hills Review*, published annually, is "a regionally focused journal presenting writers of national distinction alongside new authors. *FHR* seeks work informed by a strong sense of place or region, especially Kansas and the Great Plains region. We seek to provide a publishing venue for writers of the Great Plains and Kansas while also publishing authors whose work evidences a strong sense of place, writing of literary quality, and accomplished use of language and depth of character development."

Has published work by Julene Bair, Elizabeth Dodd, Dennis Etzel Jr., Patricia Lawson, and Amanda Frost. Reads mss November to mid-March.

NEEDS "No religious, inspirational, children's." Wants to see more "writing of literary quality with a strong sense of place." Publishes short shorts and short stories. Include short bio. Reads submissions November-March. Length: 1-4 pages for short shorts; 5-25 pages for short stories.

HOW TO CONTACT Submit complete ms.

PAYMENT/TERMS Pays 2 contributor's copies; additional copies at discounted price.

TIPS "Submit writing that has strong imagery and voice, writing that is informed by place or region, writing of literary quality with depth of character development. Hone the language down to the most literary depiction possible in the shortest space that still provides depth of development without excess length."

THE FLORIDA REVIEW

Department of English, University of Central Florida, P.O. Box 161346, Orlando FL 32816-1346. **E-mail:** flreview@ucf.edu. **Website:** floridareview.cah.ucf.edu. **Contact:** Lisa Roney, editor. Estab. 1972. "We publish fiction and essays of high literary quality—stories that delight, instruct, and take risks. Our audience consists of avid readers of fiction, poetry, graphic narrative, and creative nonfiction."

Recently published work by Gerald Vizenor, Billy Collins, Sherwin Bitsui, Kelly Clancy, Denise Duhamel, Tony Hoagland, Baron Wormser, Marcia Aldrich, and Patricia Foster. As of November 2015, *The Florida Review* no longer accepts mailed submissions.

NEEDS No genre fiction. Length: 3-25 pages.

HOW TO CONTACT Submit complete ms via online submissions manager.

TIPS "We're looking for writers with fresh voices and original stories. We like risk."

FLOYD COUNTY MOONSHINE

720 Christiansburg Pike, Floyd VA 24091. (540)745-5150. **E-mail:** floydshine@gmail.com. **Website:** www.floydcountymoonshine.org. **Contact:** Aaron Lee Moore, editor in chief. Estab. 2008. *Floyd County Moonshine*, published biannually, is a "literary and arts magazine in Floyd, Virginia, and the New River Valley. We accept poetry, short stories, and essays addressing all manner of themes; however, preference is given to those works of a rural or Appalachian nature. *Floyd County Moonshine* publishes a variety of home-grown Appalachian writers in addition to writers from across the country. The mission of *Floyd County Moonshine* is to publish thought-provoking, well-crafted, free-thinking, uncensored prose and poetry. Our literature explores the dark and Gothic as well as the bright and pleasant in order to give an honest portrayal of the human condition. We aspire to publish quality literature in the local color genre, specifically writing that relates to Floyd, Virginia, and the New River Valley. Floyd and local Appalachian authors are given priority consideration; however, to stay versatile we also aspire to publish some writers

from all around the country in every issue. We publish both well-established and beginning writers."

Wants "literature addressing rural or Appalachian themes." Has published poetry by Steve Kistulentz, Louis Gallo, Ernie Wormwood, R.T. Smith, Chelsea Adams, and Justin Askins.

NEEDS "Any and all subject matter is welcome, although we gravitate toward Local Color (especially stories set in Floyd, the New River Valley, or a specific rural setting) and the Southern Gothic." Length: up to 8,000 words.

HOW TO CONTACT Accepts e-mail (preferred). Submit a Word document as attachment. Accepts previously published works and simultaneous submissions on occasion. Cover letter is unnecessary. Include brief bio. Reads submissions year round.

PAYMENT/TERMS Pays 1 contributor's copy.

TIPS "If we favor your work, it may appear in several issues, so prior contributors are also encouraged to resubmit. Every year we choose at least 1 featured author for an issue. We also nominate for Pushcart prizes, and we will do book reviews if you mail us the book."

FLYWAY

Department of English, 206 Ross Hall, Iowa State University, Ames IA 50011-1201. **E-mail:** flywayjournal@gmail.com; flyway@iastate.edu. **Website:** www.flyway.org. **Contact:** Elizabeth A. Giorgi, managing editor. Estab. 1995. Based out of Iowa State University, *Flyway: Journal of Writing and Environment* publishes poetry, fiction, nonfiction, and visual art exploring the many complicated facets of the word environment—at once rural, urban, and suburban—and its social and political implications. Also open to all different interpretations of'environment.

Reading period is September 15-May 15. Has published work by Rick Bass, Jacob M. Appel, Madison Smartt Bell, Jane Smiley. Also sponsors the annual fall "Notes from the Field" nonfiction contest, and the spring "Sweet Corn Prize in Fiction" short story contest. Details on website.

NEEDS Length: up to 5,000 words. Average length: 3,000 words. Also publishes short shorts of up to 1,000 words. Average length: 500 words.

HOW TO CONTACT Submit mss only via online submission manager. Receives 50-100 mss monthly. Accepts 3-5 stories per issue; up to 10 per year. Also reviews novels and short-story collections. Submit 1 short story or up to 3 short shorts.

PAYMENT/TERMS Pays one-year subscription to *Flyway*.

TIPS "For *Flyway*, there should be tension between the environment or setting of the story and the characters in it. A well-known place should appear new, even alien and strange through the eyes and actions of the characters. We want to see an active environment, too—a setting that influences actions, triggers it's one events."

FOGGED CLARITY

Fogged Clarity and Nicotine Heart Press, P.O. Box 1016, Muskegon MI 49443-1016. (231)670-7033. **E-mail:** editor@foggedclarity.com; submissions@foggedclarity.com. **Website:** www.foggedclarity.com. **Contact:** Editors. Estab. 2008. "*Fogged Clarity* is an arts review that accepts submissions of poetry, fiction, nonfiction, music, visual art, and reviews of work in all mediums. We seek art that is stabbingly eloquent. Our print edition is released once every year, while new issues of our online journal come out at the beginning of every month. Artists maintain the copyrights to their work until they are monetarily compensated for said work. If your work is selected for our print edition and you consent to its publication, you will be compensated."

"By incorporating music and the visual arts and releasing a new issue monthly, *Fogged Clarity* aims to transcend the conventions of a typical literary journal. Our network is extensive, and our scope is as broad as thought itself; we are, you are, unconstrained. With that spirit in mind, *Fogged Clarity* examines the work of authors, artists, scholars, and musicians, providing a home for exceptional art and thought that warrants exposure."

NEEDS Length: up to 8,000 words.

HOW TO CONTACT Submit 1-2 complete ms by e-mail (submissions@foggedclarity.com) as attached .DOC or .DOCX file. Subject line should be formatted as: "Last Name: Medium of Submission." For example, "Evans: Fiction." Include brief cover letter, complete contact information, and a third-person bio.

TIPS "The editors appreciate artists communicating the intention of their submitted work and the influences behind it in a brief cover letter. Any artists with proposals for features or special projects should feel free to contact Ben Evans directly at editor@foggedclarity.com."

FOLIATE OAK LITERARY MAGAZINE

University of Arkansas-Monticello, Arts & Humanities, 562 University Dr., Monticello AR 71656. **E-mail:** foliateoak@gmail.com. **Website:** www.foliateoak.com. **Contact:** Diane Payne, faculty advisor. Estab. 1973. "The *Foliate Oak Literary Magazine* is a student-run magazine accepting hybrid prose, poetry, fiction, flash, creative nonfiction and artwork."

"After you receive a rejection/acceptance notice, please wait 1 month before submitting new work. **Submission Period: August 1-April 24.** We do not read submissions during summer break. If you need to contact us for anything other than submitting your work, please write to foliateoak@gmail.com." No e-mail submissions.

NEEDS Does not want horror or confession, pornographic, racist, or homophobic content. Length: 200-2,500 words.

HOW TO CONTACT Send complete ms through online submission manager. "Remember to include your brief third-person bio."

TIPS "Please submit all material via our online submission manager. Read our guidelines before submitting. We are eager to include multimedia submissions of videos, music, and collages. Submit your best work."

FOLIO, A LITERARY JOURNAL AT AMERICAN UNIVERSITY

Department of Literature, American University, Washington DC 20016. (202)885-2971. **Fax:** (202)885-2938. **E-mail:** folio.editors@gmail.com. **Website:** www.american.edu/cas/literature/folio. **Contact:** Editor in chief and managing editor. Estab. 1984. "*Folio* is a nationally recognized literary journal sponsored by the College of Arts and Sciences at American University in Washington, DC. Since 1984, we have published original creative work by both new and established authors. Past issues have included work by Michael Reid Busk, Billy Collins, William Stafford, and Bruce Weigl, and interviews with Michael Cunningham, Charles Baxter, Amy Bloom, Ann Beattie, and Walter Kirn. We look for well-crafted poetry and prose that is bold and memorable."

Reads submissions September 1-January 1.

NEEDS Length: up to 5,000 words.

HOW TO CONTACT Submit via online submission form at foliolitjournal.submittable.com/submit. "Cover letters must contain all of the following: brief bio, e-mail address, snail mail address, phone number, and title(s) of work enclosed."

FOURTEEN HILLS

Department of Creative Writing, San Francisco State University, 1600 Holloway Ave., San Francisco CA 94132. **Website:** www.14hills.net. Estab. 1994. "*Fourteen Hills* publishes the highest-quality innovative fiction and poetry for a literary audience." Editors change each year. Always sends prepublication galleys.

Reading periods: September 1-December 1 for summer issue; March 1-June 1 for winter issue.

NEEDS Has published work by Susan Straight, Yiyun Li, Alice LaPlante, Terese Svoboda, Peter Rock, Stephen Dixon, and Adam Johnson. Length: up to 25 pages for short stories; up to 10 pages for experimental or cross-genre literature (including graphic stories).

HOW TO CONTACT Submit complete ms via online submissions manager.

PAYMENT/TERMS Pays 2 contributor's copies and offers discount on additional copies.

TIPS "Please read an issue of *Fourteen Hills* before submitting."

THE FOURTH RIVER

Chatham University, Woodland Rd., Pittsburgh PA 15232. **E-mail:** 4thriver@gmail.com. **Website:** thefourthriver.com. Estab. 2005. *The Fourth River*, an annual publication of Chatham University's MFA in Creative Writing Programs, features literature that engages and explores the relationship between humans and their environments. Wants writings that are richly situated at the confluence of place, space, and identity, or that reflect upon or make use of landscape and place in new ways.

The Fourth River's contributors have been published in *Glimmer Train, Alaska Quarterly Review, The Missouri Review, The Best American Short Stories, The O. Henry Prize Stories*, and *The Best American Travel Writing.*

NEEDS Length: up to 7,000 words.

HOW TO CONTACT Submit complete ms via online submissions manager.

FREEFALL MAGAZINE

Freefall Literary Society of Calgary, 922 Ninth Ave. SE, Calgary AB T2G 0S4, Canada. **E-mail:** editors@

freefallmagazine.ca. **Website:** www.freefallmagazine.ca. **Contact:** Ryan Stromquist, managing editor. Estab. 1990. "Magazine published triannually containing fiction, poetry, creative nonfiction, essays on writing, interviews, and reviews. We are looking for exquisite writing with a strong narrative."

NEEDS Length: up to 4,000 words.

HOW TO CONTACT Submit via website form. Attach submission file (file name format is 'lastname_firstname_storytitle' in DOC, DOCX, or PDF format).

PAYMENT/TERMS Pays $10/printed page in the magazine, to a maximum of $100, and 1 contributor's copy.

TIPS "Our mission is to encourage the voices of new, emerging, and experienced Canadian writers and provide a platform for their quality work."

FREEXPRESSION

P.O. Box 4, West Hoxton NSW 2171, Australia. (02)96075559. **E-mail:** editor@freexpression.com.au. **Website:** www.freexpression.com.au. **Contact:** Peter F. Pike, managing editor. Estab. 1993. *FreeXpresSion*, published monthly, contains "creative writing, how-to articles, short stories, and poetry, including cinquain, haiku, etc., and bush verse." Open to all forms. "Christian themes OK. Humorous material welcome. No gratuitous sex; bad language OK. We don't want to see anything degrading."

HOW TO CONTACT Submit prose via e-mail.

THE FROGMORE PAPERS

21 Mildmay Rd., Lewes, East Sussex BN7 1PJ, England. **Website:** www.frogmorepress.co.uk. **Contact:** Jeremy Page, editor. Estab. 1983. *The Frogmore Papers*, published semiannually, is a literary magazine with emphasis on new poetry and short stories.

Reading periods: October 1-31 for March issue and April 1-30 for September issue.

NEEDS Length: up to 2,000 words.

HOW TO CONTACT Submit by e-mail or mail (postal submissions only accepted from within the UK).

PAYMENT/TERMS Pays 1 contributor's copy.

FUGUE LITERARY MAGAZINE

200 Brink Hall, University of Idaho, P.O. Box 44110, Moscow ID 83844. **E-mail:** fugue@uidaho.edu. **Website:** www.fuguejournal.com. **Contact:** Alexandra Teague, faculty advisor. Estab. 1990. Biannual literary magazine. "Submissions are accepted online only. Poetry, fiction, and nonfiction submissions are accepted September 1-April 1. All material received outside of this period will not be read." $3 submission fee per entry. See website for submission instructions.

Work published in *Fugue* has won the Pushcart Prize and has been cited in *Best American Essays*.

HOW TO CONTACT Submit complete ms via online submissions manager. "Please send no more than 2 short shorts or 1 story at a time. Submissions in more than 1 genre should be submitted separately. All multiple submissions will be returned unread. Once you have submitted a piece to us, wait for a response on this piece before submitting again."

PAYMENT/TERMS Pays 2 contributor's copies and additional payment.

TIPS "The best way, of course, to determine what we're looking for is to read the journal. As the name *Fugue* indicates, our goal is to present a wide range of literary perspectives. We like stories that satisfy us both intellectually and emotionally, with fresh language and characters so captivating that they stick with us and invite a second reading. We are also seeking creative literary criticism which illuminates a piece of literature or a specific writer by examining that writer's personal experience."

GARBLED TRANSMISSIONS MAGAZINE

5813 NW 20th St., Margate FL 33063. **E-mail:** jamesrobertpayne@yahoo.com. **E-mail:** editor@garbledtransmission.com. **Website:** www.garbledtransmission.com. **Contact:** James Payne, editor in chief. Estab. 2011. Daily online literary magazine featuring fiction and book, movie, and comic book reviews.

"Stories should have a dark/strange/twisted slant to them and should be original ideas, or have such a twist to them that they redefine the genre. We like authors with an original voice. That being said, we like Stephen King, Richard Matheson, Neil Gaiman, A. Lee Martinez, Chuck Palahniuk, and Clive Barker. Movies and TV shows that inspire us include "Lost," *The Matrix*, *Fight Club*, *3:10 to Yuma*, *Dark City*, *The Sixth Sense*, "X-Files," and *Super 8*."

NEEDS "No romance or corny sci-fi or fantasy. Nothing contrived or a blatant rip-off." Length: 500-15,000 words.

HOW TO CONTACT Send complete ms by e-mail with subject line "Garbled Transmissions Submission."

TIPS "The best way to see what we like is to visit our website and read some of the stories we've published to get a taste of what style we seek."

GARGOYLE

Paycock Press, 3819 13th St. N, Arlington VA 22201. (703)525-9296. **E-mail:** rchrdpeabody9@gmail.com. **Website:** www.gargoylemagazine.com. **Contact:** Richard Peabody, editor; Lucinda Ebersole, co-editor. Estab. 1976. "*Gargoyle* has always been a scallywag magazine, a maverick magazine, a bit too academic for the underground and way too underground for the academics. We are a writer's magazine in that we are read by other writers and have never worried about reaching the masses." Annual.

The submission window for 2016 is from August 1 until full; in 2015 that took 17 days to fill a 500+ pages. Recently published work by Abdul Ali, Nin Andrews, Claudia Apablaza, Sara Backer, Tina Barr, Stacy Barton, Alessandra Bava, Bill Beverly, Mary Biddinger, Matthew Blasi, Gerri Brightwell, Dana Cann, Michael Casey, Karen Chase, Kelly Cherry, Joan Colby, Katherine Coles, Nicelle Davis, Jennifer K. Dick, Gabriel Don, Lauren Fairbanks, Angela Featherstone, April L. Ford, Thaisa Frank, Myronn Hardy, Lola Haskins, Allison Hedge-Coke, Nancy Hightower, Paul House, Laird Hunt, Gerry LaFemina, Louise Wareham Leonard, Gilles Leroy, Susan Lewis, Peter Tieryas Liu, Duane Locke, Jonathan Lyons, James Magruder, Margaret McCarthy, Dora E. McQuaid, Ana Merino, Joe Mills, Gloria Mindock, Sheryl L. Nelms, Rodney Nelson, Amanda Newell, Rebecca Nison, Kevin O'Cuinn, W.P. Osborn, Abbey Mei Otis, Jose Padua, Theresa Pappas, Kit Reed, Doug Rice, Lou Robinson, Gregg Shapiro, Rose Solari, Marilyn Stablein, Janet Steen, D.E. Steward, Dariel Suarez, Art Taylor, Virgie Townsend, Dan Vera, Elisha Wagman, Vallie Lynn Watson, Tim Wendel, Theodore Wheeler, and Kirby Wright.

NEEDS Wants "edgy realism or experimental works. We run both." Wants to see more Canadian, British, Australian, and Third World fiction. Receives 300 unsolicited mss/week during submission period. Accepts 20-50 mss/issue. Agented fiction 5%. **Publishes 2-3 new writers/year.** Publishes 1-2 titles/year. Format: trade paperback originals. No romance, horror, science fiction. Length: up to 5,000 words. "We have run 2 novellas in the past 40 years."

PAYMENT/TERMS Pays 1 contributor's copy and offers 50% discount on additional copies.

TIPS "We have to fall in love with a particular fiction."

A GATHERING OF THE TRIBES

P.O. Box 20693, Tompkins Square Station, New York NY 10009. (212)777-2038. **E-mail:** gatheringofthetribes@gmail.com. **E-mail:** tribes.editor@gmail.com. **Website:** www.tribes.org. **Contact:** Steve Cannon. Estab. 1992. *A Gathering of the Tribes* is a multicultural and multigenerational publication featuring poetry, fiction, interviews, essays, visual art, and musical scores. Audience is anyone interested in the arts from a diverse perspective."

Has published work by Carl Watson, Ishle Park, Wang Pang, and Hanif Kureishi. Sponsors awards/contests.

NEEDS "Would like to see more satire/humor. We are open to all work; just no poor writing/grammar/syntax." Length: 2,500-5,000 words.

HOW TO CONTACT Send complete ms by postal mail or e-mail.

PAYMENT/TERMS Pays 1 contributor's copy.

TIPS "Make sure your work has substance."

THE GEORGIA REVIEW

The University of Georgia, Main Library, Room 706A, 320 S. Jackson St., Athens GA 30602. (706)542-3481. **Fax:** (706)542-0047. **E-mail:** garev@uga.edu. **Website:** thegeorgiareview.com. **Contact:** Stephen Corey, editor. Estab. 1947. "Our readers are inquisitive people and avid consumers of art and literature. All work submitted should be marked by singularity of vision, exceptional skillfulness of craft, and thoughtful engagement with the contemporary world." Electronic submissions available for $3 fee. Reading period: August 15-May 15.

NEEDS "We seek original, excellent short fiction not bound by type. Ordinarily we do not publish novel excerpts or works translated into English, and we discourage authors from submitting these."

HOW TO CONTACT Send complete ms via online submissions manager or postal mail.

PAYMENT/TERMS Pays $50/published page.

GERTRUDE

P.O. Box 28281, Portland OR 97228. **E-mail:** editor@gertrudepress.org. Estab. 1999. *Gertrude*, the annual literary arts journal of Gertrude Press, is a "publication featuring the voices and visions of the gay, lesbian, bisexual, transgender, and supportive community."

NEEDS Has published work by Carol Guess, Demrie Alonzo, Henry Alley, and Scott Pomfret. Length: up to 3,000 words.

HOW TO CONTACT Submit 1-2 pieces via online submissions manager, double-spaced. Include word count for each piece in cover letter.

TIPS "We look for strong characterization and imagery, and new, unique ways of writing about universal experiences. Follow the construction of your work until the ending. Many stories start out with zest, then flipper and die. Show us, don't tell us."

THE GETTYSBURG REVIEW

Gettysburg College, Gettysburg College, 300 N. Washington St., Gettysburg PA 17325. (717)337-6770. **Fax:** (717)337-6775. **E-mail:** mdrew@gettysburg.edu. **Website:** www.gettysburgreview.com. **Contact:** Mark Drew, editor; Ellen Hathaway, managing editor. Estab. 1988. Published quarterly, *The Gettysburg Review* considers unsolicited submissions of poetry, fiction, and essays. "Our concern is quality. Mss submitted here should be extremely well written." Reading period September 1-May 31.

NEEDS Wants high-quality literary fiction. "We require that fiction be intelligent and esthetically written." No genre fiction. Length: 2,000-7,000 words.

HOW TO CONTACT Send complete ms with SASE.

PAYMENT/TERMS Pays $15/printed page, a one-year subscription, and 1 contributor's copy.

GINOSKO LITERARY JOURNAL

73 Sais Ave., San Anselmo CA 94960. (415)785-3160. **E-mail:** editorginosko@aol.com. **Website:** www.ginoskoliteraryjournal.com. **Contact:** Robert Paul Cesaretti, editor. Estab. 2002. *Ginosko* Flash Fiction Contest: Deadline is March 1; $5 entry fee; $250 prize. "*Ginosko* (ghin-océ-koe): To perceive, understand, realize, come to know; knowledge that has an inception, a progress, an attainment. The recognition of truth by experience." Accepting short fiction and poetry, creative nonfiction, interviews, social justice concerns, and literary insights for www.ginoskoliteraryjournal.com.

Reads year round. Length of articles flexible; accepts excerpts. Publishing as semiannual e-zine. Print anthology every 2 years. Check downloadable issues on website for tone and style. Downloads free; accepts donations. Member CLMP.

HOW TO CONTACT Submit via postal mail, e-mail (prefers attachments: WPS, DOC, or RTF), or online submissions manager (ginosko.submittable.com/submit).

GLIMMER TRAIN STORIES

Glimmer Train Press, Inc., P.O. Box 80430, Portland OR 97280. **Fax:** (503)221-0837. **E-mail:** eds@glimmertrain.org. **Website:** www.glimmertrain.org. Estab. 1991. "We are interested in literary short stories, particularly by new and emerging writers."

Recently published work by Benjamin Percy, Laura van den Berg, Manuel Muñoz, Claire Vaye Watkins, Abby Geni, Peter Ho Davies, William Trevor, Thisbe Nissen, and Yiyun Li.

NEEDS Length: 1,200-12,000 words.

HOW TO CONTACT Submit via the website at www.glimmertrain.org. "In a pinch, send a hard copy and include SASE for response." Receives 36,000 unsolicited mss/year. Accepts 15 mss/issue; 45 mss/year. Agented fiction 2%. Publishes 20 new writers/year.

PAYMENT/TERMS Pays $700 for standard submissions, up to $2,500 for contest-winning stories.

TIPS "In the last 2 years, over half of the first-place stories have been their authors' very first publications. See our contest listings in Contests & Awards section."

GRAIN

P.O. Box 3986, Regina SK S4P 3R9, Canada. (306)791-7749. **Fax:** (306)565-8554. **E-mail:** grainmag@skwriter.com. **Website:** www.grainmagazine.ca. Estab. 1973. "*Grain, The Journal of Eclectic Writing* is a literary quarterly that publishes engaging, diverse, and challenging writing and art by some of the best Canadian and international writers and artists. Every issue features superb new writing from both developing and established writers. Each issue also highlights the unique artwork of a different visual artist. *Grain* has garnered national and international recognition for its distinctive, cutting-edge content and design."

Submissions are read September 1-May 31 only. Mss postmarked June 1-August 31 will not be read.

NEEDS No romance, confession, science fiction, vignettes, mystery. Length: up to 3,500 words.

HOW TO CONTACT Postal submissions only. Send typed, unpublished material only (considers work published online to be previously published). Please only submit work in 1 genre at a time.

PAYMENT/TERMS Pays $50/page ($250 maximum) and 3 contributor's copies.

TIPS "Only work of the highest literary quality is accepted. Read several back issues."

GRASSLIMB

P.O. Box 420816, San Diego CA 92142. **E-mail:** editor@grasslimb.com. **Website:** www.grasslimb.com. **Contact:** Valerie Polichar, editor. Estab. 2002. "*Grasslimb* publishes literary prose, poetry, and art. Fiction is best when it is short and avant-garde or otherwise experimental."

NEEDS "Fiction in an experimental, avant-garde, or surreal mode is often more interesting to us than a traditional story." "Although general topics are welcome, we're less likely to select work regarding romance, sex, aging, and children." Length: up to 2,500 words; average length: 1,500 words.

HOW TO CONTACT Send complete ms via e-mail or postal mail with SASE.

PAYMENT/TERMS Pays $10-70 and 2 contributor's copies.

TIPS "We publish brief fiction work that can be read in a single sitting over a cup of coffee. Work is generally 'literary' in nature rather than mainstream. Experimental work welcome. Remember to have your work proofread and to send short work. We cannot read over 3,000 words and prefer under 2,000 words. Include word count."

GREEN HILLS LITERARY LANTERN

Truman State University, Department of English, Truman State University, Kirksville MO 63501. **E-mail:** adavis@truman.edu. **Website:** ghll.truman.edu. **Contact:** Adam Brooke Davis, managing editor; Joe Benevento, poetry editor. Estab. 1990. *Green Hills Literary Lantern* is published annually, in June, by Truman State University. Historically, the print publication ran between 200-300 pages, consisting of poetry, fiction, reviews, and interviews. The digital magazine is of similar proportions and artistic standards. Open to the work of new writers, as well as more established writers.

NEEDS "We are interested in stories that demonstrate a strong working knowledge of the craft. Avoid genre fiction or mainstream religious fiction. Otherwise, we are open to short stories of various settings, character conflict, and styles, including experimental. Above all, we demand that work be 'striking.' Language should be complex, with depth, through analogy, metaphor, simile, understatement, irony, etc.—but all this must not be overwrought or self-consciously literary. If style is to be at center stage, it must be interesting and provocative enough for the reader to focus on style alone. 'Overdone' writing surely is not either." No word limit.

HOW TO CONTACT Submit complete ms.

GREEN MOUNTAINS REVIEW

Johnson State College, 337 College Hill, Johnson VT 05656. (802)635-1350. **E-mail:** gmr@jsc.edu. **Website:** greenmountainsreview.com. **Contact:** Elizabeth Powell, editor; Jessica Hendry Nelson, nonfiction editor; Jacob White, fiction editor; Ben Aleshire, assistant poetry editor. Semiannual magazine covering poems, stories, and creative nonfiction by both well-known authors and promising newcomers.

The editors are open to a wide range of styles and subject matter. Open reading period: September 1-March 1.

NEEDS Recently published work by Tracy Daugherty, Terese Svoboda, Walter Wetherell, T.M. McNally, J. Robert Lennon, Louis B. Jones, and Tom Whalen. Publishes short shorts. Also publishes literary criticism, poetry. Sometimes comments on rejected mss. Length: up to 25 pages, double-spaced.

HOW TO CONTACT Submit ms via online submissions manager.

PAYMENT/TERMS Pays contributor's copies, one-year subscription, and small honorarium, depending on grants.

TIPS "We encourage you to order some of our back issues to acquaint yourself with what has been accepted in the past."

THE GREENSBORO REVIEW

MFA Writing Program, 3302 HHRA Building, UNC-Greensboro, Greensboro NC 27402. (336)334-5459. **E-mail:** jlclark@uncg.edu. **Website:** greensbororeview.submittable.com/submit. **Contact:** Jim Clark, editor. Estab. 1965. "A local lit mag with an international reputation. We've been 'old school' since 1965."

Stories for *The Greensboro Review* have been included in *Best American Short Stories, The O. Henry Awards Prize Stories, New Stories from The South*and *Pushcart Prize*. Does not accept e-mail submissions.

NEEDS Length: up to 7,500 words.

HOW TO CONTACT Submit complete ms via online submission form. Include cover letter and estimated word count.

PAYMENT/TERMS Pays contributor's copies.

TIPS "We want to see the best being written regardless of theme, subject, or style."

THE GRIFFIN

Gwynedd Mercy College, 1325 Sumneytown Pike, P.O. Box 901, Gwynedd Valley PA 19437-0901. (215)641-5518. **Fax:** (215)641-5552. **E-mail:** allego.d@gmercyu.edu. **Website:** www.gmercyu.edu/about-gwynedd-mercy/publications/griffin. **Contact:** Dr. Donna M. Allego, editor. Estab. 1999. Published by Gwynedd Mercy University, *The Griffin* is a literary journal for the creative writer—subscribing to the belief that improving the human condition requires dedication to and respect for the individual and the community. Seeks works which explore universal qualities—truth, justice, integrity, compassion, mercy. Publishes poetry, short stories, short plays, and reflections.

NEEDS All genres considered. No slashers, graphic violence, or sex, however. Length: up to 2,500 words.

HOW TO CONTACT Submit complete ms via e-mail or on disk with a hard copy. Include short author bio.

TIPS "Pay attention to the word length requirements, the mission of the magazine, and how to submit ms as set forth. These constitute the writer's guidelines listed online."

GUERNICA MAGAZINE

112 W. 27th St., Suite 600, New York NY 10001. **E-mail:** editors@guernicamag.com; art@guernicamag.com; publisher@guernicamag.com. **Website:** www.guernicamag.com. **Contact:** See masthead online for specific editors. Estab. 2005. "*Guernica* is called a 'great online literary magazine' by *Esquire*. *Guernica* contributors come from dozens of countries and write in nearly as many languages."

Received Caine Prize for African Writing, Best of the Net.

NEEDS "*Guernica* strongly prefers fiction with a diverse international outlook—or if American, from an underrepresented or alternative perspective. (No stories about American tourists in other countries, please.)" Has published Jesse Ball, Elizabeth Crane, Josh Weil, Justo Arroyo, Sergio Ramírez Mercado, Matthew Derby, E.C. Osondu (Winner of the 2009 Caine Prize for African Writing). No genre fiction or satire. Length: 1,200-4,500 words.

HOW TO CONTACT Submit complete ms via online submissions manager.

TIPS "Please read the magazine first before submitting. Most stories that are rejected simply do not fit our approach. Submission guidelines available online."

GULF COAST: A JOURNAL OF LITERATURE AND FINE ARTS

4800 Calhoun Rd., Houston TX 77204-3013. (713)743-3223. **E-mail:** editors@gulfcoastmag.org. **Website:** www.gulfcoastmag.org. **Contact:** Adrienne Perry, editor; Martin Rock, managing editor; Carlos Hernandez, digital editor; Henk Rossouw, Luisa Muradyan, and Erika Jo Brown, poetry editors; Jennifer McFarland, Dino Piacentini, and Joshua Foster, fiction editors; Georgia Pearle and Nathan Stabenfeldt, nonfiction editors; Matthew Salesses, online fiction editor; Christopher Murray, online poetry editor; Melanie Brkich, online nonfiction editor. Estab. 1986.

NEEDS "Please do not send multiple submissions; we will read only 1 submission per author at a given time, except in the case of our annual contests." No children's, genre, religious/inspirational.

HOW TO CONTACT *Gulf Coast* reads general submissions, submitted by post or through the online submissions manager, September 1-March 1. Submissions e-mailed directly to the editors or postmarked March 1-September 1 will not be read or responded to. "Please visit our contest page for contest submission guidelines." Receives 500 unsolicited mss/month. Accepts 6-8 mss/issue; 12-16 mss/year. Agented fiction: 5%. Publishes 2-8 new writers/year. Recently published work by Alan Heathcock, Anne Carson, Bret Anthony Johnston, John D'Agata, Lucie Brock-Broido, Clancy Martin, Steve Almond, Sam Lipsyte, Carl Phillips, Dean Young, and Eula Biss. Publishes short shorts.

PAYMENT/TERMS Pays $50/page.

TIPS "Submit only previously unpublished works. Include a cover letter. Online submissions are strongly preferred. Stories or essays should be typed, double-spaced, and paginated with your name, address, and phone number on the first page and the title on subsequent pages. Poems should have your name, address, and phone number on the first page of each." The Annual Gulf Coast Prizes award publication and $1,500 each in poetry, fiction, and nonfiction; opens in December of each year. Honorable mentions in each category will receive a $250 second prize. Postmark/online entry deadline: March 22 of each year. Winners and honorable mentions will be announced in May. **Entry fee:** $23 (includes one-year subscription). Make checks payable to *Gulf Coast*. Guidelines available on website.

GULF STREAM MAGAZINE

English Department, FIU, Biscayne Bay Campus, 3000 NE 151 St., AC1-335, North Miami FL 33181. **E-mail:** gulfstreamlitmag@gmail.com. **Website:** www.gulfstreamlitmag.com. **Contact:** Miguel Pichardo, editor-in-chief. Estab. 1989. "*Gulf Stream Magazine* has been publishing emerging and established writers of exceptional fiction, nonfiction, and poetry since 1989. We also publish interviews and book reviews. Past contributors include Sherman Alexie, Steve Almond, Jan Beatty, Lee Martin, Robert Wrigley, Dennis Lehane, Liz Robbins, Stuart Dybek, David Kirby, Ann Hood, Ha Jin, B.H. Fairchild, Naomi Shihab Nye, F. Daniel Rzicznek, and Connie May Fowler. *Gulf Stream Magazine* is supported by the Creative Writing Program at Florida International University in Miami, Florida. Each year we publish 2 online issues."

NEEDS Does not want romance, historical, juvenile, or religious work.

HOW TO CONTACT "Submit online only. Please read guidelines on website in full. Submissions that do not conform to our guidelines will be discarded. We do not accept e-mailed or mailed submissions. We read from September 1-November 1 and January 1-March 1."

PAYMENT/TERMS Pays contributor's copies.

TIPS "Looks for fresh, original writing—well-plotted stories with unforgettable characters, fresh poetry, and experimental writing. Usually longer stories do not get accepted. There are exceptions, however."

HAIGHT ASHBURY LITERARY JOURNAL

558 Joost Ave., San Francisco CA 94127. (415)584-8264. **E-mail:** haljeditor@gmail.com. **Website:** haightashburyliteraryjournal.wordpress.com; www.facebook.com/pages/haight-ashbury-literary-journal/365542018331. **Contact:** Alice Rogoff and Cesar Love, editors. Estab. 1979. *Haight Ashbury Literary Journal*, publishes "well-written poetry and fiction. *HALJ*'s voices are often of people who have been marginalized, oppressed, or abused. *HALJ* strives to bring literary arts to the general public, to the San Francisco community of writers, to the Haight Ashbury neighborhood, and to people of varying ages, genders, ethnic groups, and sexual preferences. The *Journal* is produced as a tabloid to maintain an accessible price for low-income people."

NEEDS Submit 1-3 short stories or 1 long story. Submit only once every 6 months. No e-mail submissions (unless overseas); postal submissions only. "Put name and address on every page, and include SASE. No bio." Sometimes publishes theme issues (each issue changes its theme and emphasis).

$ HANGING LOOSE

Hanging Loose Press, 231 Wyckoff St., Brooklyn NY 11217. **E-mail:** print225@aol.com. **Website:** www.hangingloosepress.com. **Contact:** Robert Hershon and Mark Pawlak, editors. Estab. 1966. *Hanging Loose*, published in April and October, concentrates on the work of new writers. Wants excellent, energetic poems and short stories.

HOW TO CONTACT Submit 1 complete ms by postal mail with SASE.

PAYMENT/TERMS Pays small fee and 2 contributor's copies.

HARPER'S MAGAZINE

666 Broadway, 11th Floor, New York NY 10012. (212)420-5720. **E-mail:** readings@harpers.org; scg@harpers.org. **Website:** www.harpers.org. **Contact:** Ellen Rosenbush, editor. Estab. 1850. *Harper's Magazine* encourages national discussion on current and significant issues in a format that offers arresting facts and intelligent opinions. By means of its several shorter journalistic forms—Harper's Index, Readings, Forum, and Annotation—as well as with its acclaimed essays, fiction, and reporting, *Harper's* continues the tradition begun with its first issue in 1850: to inform readers across the whole spectrum of political, literary, cultural, and scientific affairs.

Harper's Magazine will neither consider nor return unsolicited nonfiction mss that have not been preceded by a written query. *Harper's* will consider unsolicited fiction. Unsolicited poetry will not be considered or returned. No queries or mss will be considered unless they are accompanied by a SASE. All submissions and written queries (with the exception of Readings submissions) must be sent by mail to above address.

NEEDS Will consider unsolicited fiction. Has published work by Rebecca Curtis, George Saunders, Haruki Murakami, Margaret Atwood, Allan Gurganus, Evan Connell, and Dave Bezmosgis. Length: 3,000-5,000 words.

HOW TO CONTACT Submit complete ms by postal mail.

PAYMENT/TERMS Generally pays 50¢-$1/word.

TIPS "Some readers expect their magazines to clothe them with opinions in the way that Bloomingdale's dresses them for the opera. The readers of *Harper's Magazine* belong to a different crowd. They strike me as the kind of people who would rather think in their own voices and come to their own conclusions."

HARPUR PALATE

English Department, Binghamton University, P.O. Box 6000, Binghamton NY 13902-6000. **E-mail:** harpur.palate@gmail.com. **Website:** harpurpalate.blogspot.com. **Contact:** Sri Siddhi N. Upadhyay, editor in chief; Liam Meilleur, editor in chief and fiction editor; Carolyn Keller, managing editor and nonfiction editor; Brian Kelly, poetry editor; Roberta Borger, fiction editor. Estab. 2000. *Harpur Palate*, published biannually, is "dedicated to publishing the best poetry and prose, regardless of style, form, or genre. We have no restrictions on subject matter or form. Quite simply, send us your highest-quality fiction and poetry."

Submission periods are September 1-November 15 for the Winter issue and February 1-April 15 for the Summer issue.

NEEDS Receives 400 unsolicited mss/month. Accepts 5-10 mss/issue; 12-20 mss/year. Publishes 5 new writers/year. Has published work by Darryl Crawford and Tim Hedges, Jesse Goolsby, Ivan Faute, and Keith Meatto. Does not accept novel excerpts. Length: up to 6,000 words.

HOW TO CONTACT Prefers submissions through online submissions manager, or send complete ms by postal mail with SASE. No more than 1 submission per envelope.

PAYMENT/TERMS Pays 2 contributor copies.

TIPS "We are interested in high-quality writing of all genres but especially literary poetry and fiction. We also sponsor a fiction contest for the Summer issue and a poetry and nonfiction contest for the Winter issue with $500 prizes."

HARVARD REVIEW

Lamont Library, Harvard University, Cambridge MA 02138. (617)495-9775. **E-mail:** info@harvardreview.org. **Website:** harvardreview.fas.harvard.edu. **Contact:** Christina Thompson, editor; Suzanne Berne, fiction editor; Major Jackson, poetry editor. Estab. 1992. Semiannual magazine covering poetry, fiction, essays, drama, graphics, and reviews in the spring and fall by an eclectic range of international writers. "Previous contributors include John Updike, Alice Hoffman, Joyce Carol Oates, Miranda July, and Jim Crace. We also publish the work of emerging and previously unpublished writers."

Does not accept e-mail submissions. Reading period: November 1-May 31.

NEEDS No genre fiction (romance, horror, detective, etc.). Length: up to 7,000 words.

HOW TO CONTACT Submit using online submissions manager or by mail (with SASE).

TIPS "Writers at all stages of their careers are invited to apply; however, we can only publish a very small fraction of the material we receive. We recommend that you familiarize yourself with *Harvard Review* before you submit your work."

HAWAI'I PACIFIC REVIEW

1060 Bishop St., Honolulu HI 96813. **Website:** hawaiipacificreview.org. **Contact:** Tyler McMahon, editor; Christa Cushon and Jordana Dintruff, managing editors. Estab. 1987. "*Hawai'i Pacific Review* is the online literary magazine of Hawai'i Pacific University. It features poetry and prose by authors from Hawai'i, the mainland, and around the world. *HPR* was started as a print annual in 1987. In 2013, it began to publish exclusively online. *HPR* publishes work on a rolling basis. Poems, stories, and essays are posted 1 piece at a time, several times a month. All contents are archived on the site."

NEEDS Prefers literary work to genre work. Length: up to 4,000 words.

HOW TO CONTACT Submit 1 ms via online submissions manager.

TIPS "We look for the unusual or original plot, and prose with the texture and nuance of poetry. Character development or portrayal must be unusual/original; humanity shown in an original insightful way (or characters); sense of humor where applicable. Be sure it's a draft that has gone through substantial changes, with supervision from a more experienced writer, if you're a beginner. Write about intense emotion and feeling, not just about someone's divorce or shaky relationship. No soap-opera-like fiction."

HAWAI'I REVIEW

University of Hawaii Board of Publications, 2445 Campus Rd., Hemenway Hall 107, Honolulu HI 96822. (808)956-3030. **Fax:** (808)956-3083. **E-mail:** hawaiireview@gmail.com. **Website:** www.kaleo.org/hawaii_review. Estab. 1973. *Hawai'i Review* is a student-run biannual literary and visual arts print journal featuring national and international writing and visual art, as well as regional literature and visual art of Hawai'i and the Pacific.

Accepts submissions online through Submittable only. Offers yearly award with $500 prizes in poetry and fiction.

NEEDS Length: up to 7,000 words for short stories, up to 2,500 words for flash fiction.

HOW TO CONTACT Send 1 short story or 2 pieces of flash fiction via online submission manager.

TIPS "Make it new."

HAYDEN'S FERRY REVIEW

c/o Dept. of English,, Arizona State University, P.O. Box 870302, Tempe AZ 85287. **Website:** haydensferryreview.com. **Contact:** Editorial staff changes every year; see website for current masthead. Estab. 1986. "*Hayden's Ferry Review* publishes the best-quality fiction, poetry, and creative nonfiction from new, emerging, and established writers."

Work from *Hayden's Ferry Review* has been selected for inclusion in *Pushcart Prize* anthologies and *Best Creative Nonfiction*. No longer accepts postal mail or e-mail submissions.

NEEDS Word length open, but typically does not accept submissions over 25 pages.

HOW TO CONTACT Send complete ms via online submissions manager.

PAYMENT/TERMS Pays 2 contributor's copies and one-year subscription.

HELIOTROPE

E-mail: heliotropeditor@gmail.com. **Website:** www.heliotropemag.com. Estab. 2006. *Heliotrope* is a quarterly e-zine that publishes fiction, articles, and poetry.

NEEDS "If your story is something we can't label, we're interested in that, too." Length: up to 5,000 words.

HOW TO CONTACT Submit complete ms via e-mail.

PAYMENT/TERMS Pays 10¢/word.

THE HELIX

Central Connecticut State University English Dept., **E-mail:** helixmagazine@gmail.com. **Website:** helixmagazine.org. **Contact:** See masthead online for current editorial staff. "*The Helix* is a Central Connecticut State University publication, and it puts out an issue every semester. It accepts submissions from all over the globe. The magazine features writing from CCSU students, writing from the Hartford County community, and an array of submissions from all over the world. The magazine publishes multiple genres of literature and art, including poetry, fiction, drama, nonfiction, paintings, photography, watercolor, collage, stencil, and computer-generated artwork. It is a student-run publication and is funded by the university."

NEEDS Length: up to 3,000 words.

HOW TO CONTACT Submit complete ms by online submissions manager.

TIPS "Please see our website for specific deadlines, as it changes every semester based on a variety of factors, but we typically leave the submission manager open sometime starting in the summer to around the end of October for the Fall issue, and during the winter to late February or mid-March for the Spring issue. Contributions are invited from all members of the campus community, as well as the literary community at large."

HELLOHORROR

Houston TX **E-mail:** info@hellohorror.com. **E-mail:** submissions@hellohorror.com. **Website:** www.hellohorror.com. **Contact:** Brent Armour, editor in chief. Estab. 2012. "*HelloHorror* is an online literary magazine. We are currently in search of literary pieces, photography, and visual art, including film from writers and artists that have a special knack for inducing goose bumps and raised hairs. This genre has become, especially in film, noticeably saturated in gore and high shock-value aspects as a crutch to avoid the true challenge of bringing about real, psychological fear to an audience that's persistently more and more numb to its tactics. While we are not opposed to the extreme, blood and guts need bones and cartilage. Otherwise it's just a sloppy mess."

"Specifically, we are looking for pieces grounded in psychological fear rather than gore. We will not automatically pass on a gore drenched story, but it needs to have its foundations in psychological horror."

NEEDS "We don't want fiction that can in no way be classified as horror. Some types of dark science fiction are acceptable, depending on the story." Length: 6-20 pages for short stories; up to 1,000 words for flash fiction.

HOW TO CONTACT Submit complete ms via e-mail.

TIPS "We like authors that show consideration for their readers. A great horror story leaves an impression on the reader long after it is finished. Consider your reader and consider yourself. What really scares you as opposed to what's stereotypically supposed to scare you? Bring us and our readers into that place of fear with you."

ALFRED HITCHCOCK'S MYSTERY MAGAZINE

Dell Magazines, 44 Wall St., Suite 904, New York NY 10005. **E-mail:** alfredhitchcockmm@dellmagazines.com. **Website:** www.themysteryplace.com/ahmm. Estab. 1956.

NEEDS Wants "original and well-written mystery and crime fiction. Because this is a mystery magazine, the stories we buy must fall into that genre in some sense or another. We are interested in nearly every kind of mystery: stories of detection of the classic kind, police procedurals, private eye tales, suspense, courtroom dramas, stories of espionage, and so on. We ask only that the story be about crime (or the threat or fear of one). We sometimes accept ghost stories or supernatural tales, but those also should involve a crime." No sensationalism. Length: up to 12,000 words.

HOW TO CONTACT Send complete ms.

PAYMENT/TERMS Payment varies.

TIPS "No simultaneous submissions, please. Submissions sent to *Alfred Hitchcock's Mystery Magazine* are not considered for or read by *Ellery Queen's Mystery Magazine*, and vice versa."

HOTEL AMERIKA

Columbia College, English Department, 600 S. Michigan Ave., Chicago IL 60605. (312)369-8175. **Website:** www.hotelamerika.net. **Contact:** David Lazar, editor; Lisa Wagner, managing editor. Estab. 2002. *Hotel Amerika* is a venue for both well-known and emerging writers. Publishes exceptional writing in all forms. Strives to house the most unique and provocative poetry, fiction, and nonfiction available.

Mss will be considered between September 1 and May 1. Materials received after May 1 and before September 1 will be returned unread. Send submissions only via mail, with SASE. Work published in *Hotel Amerika* has been included in *The Pushcart Prize* and *The Best American Poetry* and featured on *Poetry Daily*.

NEEDS Welcomes submissions in all genres of creative writing, generously defined. Does not publish book reviews as such, although considers review-like essays that transcend the specific objects of consideration.

THE HUDSON REVIEW

The Hudson Review, Inc., 33 W. 67th St., New York NY 10023. (212)650-0020. **Website:** hudsonreview.com. **Contact:** Paula Deitz, editor. Estab. 1948.

Send with SASE. Mss sent outside accepted reading period will be returned unread if SASE contains sufficient postage.

NEEDS Length: up to 10,000 words.

HOW TO CONTACT Send complete ms by postal mail between **September 1-November 30** only.

TIPS "We do not specialize in publishing any particular 'type' of writing; our sole criterion for accepting unsolicited work is literary quality. The best way for you to get an idea of the range of work we publish is to read a current issue. Unsolicited mss submitted outside of specified reading times will be returned unread. Do not send submissions via e-mail."

HUNGER MOUNTAIN

Vermont College of Fine Arts, 36 College St., Montpelier VT 05602. (802)828-8517. **E-mail:** hungermtn@vcfa.edu. **Website:** www.hungermtn.org. **Contact:** Samantha Kolber, managing editor. Estab. 2002. Accepts high-quality work from unknown, emerging, or successful writers. Publishing fiction, creative nonfiction, poetry, and young adult & children's writing. Four writing contests annually.

Member: CLMP.

NEEDS "We look for work that is beautifully crafted and tells a good story, with characters that are alive and kicking, storylines that stay with us long after we've finished reading, and sentences that slay us with their precision." No genre fiction, meaning science fiction, fantasy, horror, detective, erotic, etc. Length: up to 10,000 words.

HOW TO CONTACT Submit ms using online submissions manager: hungermtn.submittable.com/submit.

PAYMENT/TERMS Pays $50 for general fiction.

TIPS "Mss must be typed, prose double-spaced. No multiple genre submissions. Fresh viewpoints and human interest are very important, as is originality and diversity. We are committed to publishing an outstanding journal of the arts. Do not send entire novels, mss, or short story collections. Do not send previously published work."

I-70 REVIEW

Writing from the Middle and Beyond, 913 Joseph Dr., Lawrence KS 66049. **E-mail:** i70review@gmail.com. **Website:** www.fieldinfoserv.com. **Contact:** Gary Lechliter, Maryfrances Wagner, Greg Field, and Jan Duncan-O'Neal, editors. Estab. 1998. *I-70 Review* is an annual literary magazine. "Our interests lie in writing grounded in fresh language, imagery, and metaphor. We prefer free verse in which the writer pays attention to the sound and rhythm of the language. We appreciate poetry with individual voice and a good lyric or a strong narrative. In fiction, we like short pieces that are surprising and uncommon. We want writing that captures the human spirit with unusual topics or familiar topics with different perspective or approaches. We reject stereotypical and clichéd writing, as well as sentimental work or writing that summarizes and tells instead of shows. We look for writing that pays attention to words, sentences, and style. We publish literary writing. We do not publish anything erotic, religious, or political."

Open submission period is July 1-December 31.

NEEDS Rejects anything over 1,000 words, unless solicited. Not interested in anything political, religious, spiritual, didactic, or erotic. Accepts mainly flash fiction and very short literary fiction. Pays in contributor copies. Length: up to 1,000 words.

HOW TO CONTACT Submit complete ms by e-mail.

PAYMENT/TERMS Pays contributor copies.

ICONOCLAST

1675 Amazon Rd., Mohegan Lake NY 10547-1804. **Website:** www.iconoclastliterarymagazine.com. **Contact:** Phil Wagner, editor and publisher. Estab. 1992. *Iconoclast* seeks and chooses the best new writing and poetry available—of all genres and styles and entertainment levels. Its mission is to provide a serious publishing opportunity for unheralded, unknown, but deserving creators, whose work is often overlooked or trampled in the commercial, university, or Internet marketplace.

NEEDS "Subjects and styles are completely open (within the standards of generally accepted taste—though exceptions, as always, can be made for unique and visionary works)." No slice-of-life stories, stories containing alcoholism, incest, and domestic or public violence. Accepts most genres, "with the exception of mysteries."

HOW TO CONTACT Submit by postal mail; include SASE. Cover letter not necessary.

PAYMENT/TERMS Pays 1¢/word and 2 contributor's copies. Contributors get 40% discount on extra copies.

TIPS "Please don't send preliminary drafts—rewriting is half the job. If you're not sure about the story, don't truly believe in it, or are unenthusiastic about the subject (we will not recycle your term papers or thesis), then don't send it. This is not a lottery (luck has nothing to do with it)."

THE IDAHO REVIEW

Boise State University, 1910 University Dr., Boise ID 83725. **E-mail:** mwieland@boisestate.edu. **Website:** idahoreview.org. **Contact:** Mitch Wieland, editor. Estab. 1998. *The Idaho Review* is the literary journal of Boise State University.

Recent stories appearing in *The Idaho Review* have been reprinted in *The Best American Short Stories*, *The O. Henry Prize Stories*, *The Pushcart Prize*, and *New Stories from the South*.

NEEDS No genre fiction of any type. Length: up to 25 double-spaced pages.

HOW TO CONTACT Prefers submissions using online submissions manager, but will accept submissions by postal mail.

PAYMENT/TERMS Pays $100/story and contributor's copies.

TIPS "We look for strongly crafted work that tells a story that needs to be told. We demand vision and intelligence and mystery in the fiction we publish."

IDIOM 23

Central Queensland University, Rockhampton QLD 4702, Australia. **E-mail:** idiom@cqu.edu.au. **Website:** www.cqu.edu.au/idiom23. Estab. 1988. *Idiom 23*, published annually, is "named for the Tropic of Capricorn and is dedicated to developing the literary arts throughout the Central Queensland region. Submissions of original short stories, poems, articles, and b&w drawings and photographs are welcomed by the editorial collective. *Idiom 23* is not limited to a particular viewpoint but, on the contrary, hopes to encourage and publish a broad spectrum of writing. The collective seeks out creative work from community groups with as varied backgrounds as possible."

NEEDS Length: up to 3,000 words.

HOW TO CONTACT Submit complete ms via online submissions manager.

IMAGE

3307 Third Ave. W., Seattle WA 98119. (206)281-2988. **Fax:** (206)281-2979. **E-mail:** image@imagejournal.org. **Website:** www.imagejournal.org. **Contact:** Gregory Wolfe, publisher and editor. Estab. 1989. "*Image* is a unique forum for the best writing and artwork that is informed by—or grapples with—religious faith. We have never been interested in art that merely regurgitates dogma or falls back on easy answers or didacticism. Instead, our focus has been on writing and visual artwork that embody a spiritual struggle, that seek to strike a balance between tradition and a profound openness to the world. Each issue explores this relationship through outstanding fiction, poetry, painting, sculpture, architecture, film, music, interviews, and dance. *Image* also features 4-color reproductions of visual art."

NEEDS "No sentimental, preachy, moralistic, obvious stories, or genre stories (unless they manage to transcend their genre)." Length: 3,000-6,000 words.

HOW TO CONTACT Send complete ms by postal mail (with SASE for reply or return of ms) or online submissions manager. Does not accept e-mail submissions.

PAYMENT/TERMS Pays $10/page ($150 maximum) and 4 contributor's copies.

TIPS "Fiction must grapple with religious faith, though subjects need not be overtly religious."

INDIANA REVIEW

Ballantine Hall 529, 1020 E. Kirkwood Ave., Indiana University, Bloomington IN 47405. **E-mail:** inreview@indiana.edu. **Website:** indianareview.org. **Contact:** See masthead for current editorial staff. Estab. 1976. "*Indiana Review*, a nonprofit organization run by IU graduate students, is a journal of innovative fiction, nonfiction, and poetry. We're interested in energy, originality, and careful attention to craft. While we publish many well-known writers, we also welcome new and emerging poets and fiction writers."

See website for open reading periods.

NEEDS "We look for daring stories which integrate theme, language, character, and form. We like polished writing, humor, and fiction which has consequence beyond the world of its narrator." No genre fiction. Length: up to 8,000 words.

HOW TO CONTACT Submit via online submissions manager.

PAYMENT/TERMS Pays $5/page ($10 minimum), plus 2 contributor's copies

TIPS "Read us before you submit. Only submit work to journals you would proudly subscribe to, then subscribe to a few. Take care to read the latest 2 issues and specifically mention work you identify with and why. Submit work that 'stacks up' with the work we've published." Offers annual poetry, fiction, and short short/prose poem prizes. See website for full guidelines.

INTERPRETER'S HOUSE

36 College Bounds, Old Aberdeen Aberdeen AB24 3DS, England. **E-mail:** theinterpretershouse@aol.com. **Website:** www.theinterpretershouse.com. **Contact:** Martin Malone, editor. Estab. 1996. *The Interpreter's House*, published 3 times/year in February, June, and October, prints short stories and poetry.

Submission windows: October for the Spring issue, February for the Summer issue, June for the Autumn issue.

NEEDS Length: up to 2,000 words.

HOW TO CONTACT Submit up to 2 short stories by mail (with SASE) or e-mail.

PAYMENT/TERMS Pays contributor's copies.

THE IOWA REVIEW

308 EPB, The University of Iowa, Iowa City IA 52242. (319)335-0462. **E-mail:** iowa-review@uiowa.edu. **Website:** www.iowareview.org. **Contact:** Harilaos Stecopoulos. Estab. 1970. *The Iowa Review*, published 3 times/year, prints fiction, poetry, essays, reviews, and, occasionally, interviews. Receives about 5,000 submissions/year, accepts up to 100. Press run is 2,900; 1,500 distributed to stores.

This magazine uses the help of colleagues and graduate assistants. Its reading period for unsolicited work is September 1-December 1. From January through April, the editors read entries to the annual Iowa Review Awards competition. Check the website for further information.

NEEDS "We are open to a range of styles and voices and always hope to be surprised by work we then feel we need." Receives 600 unsolicited mss/month. Accepts 4-6 mss/issue; 12-18 mss/year. Does not read mss January-August. Publishes ms an average of 12-18 months after acceptance. Agented fiction less than 2%. **Publishes some new writers/year.** Recently published work by Johanna Hunting, Bennett Sims, and Pedro Mairal.

HOW TO CONTACT Send complete ms with cover letter. Don't bother with queries. SASE for return of ms. Accepts mss by snail mail (SASE required for response) and online submission form at iowareview.submittable.com/submit; no e-mail submissions.

PAYMENT/TERMS Pays 8¢/word ($100 minimum), plus 2 contributor's copies.

TIPS "We publish essays, reviews, novel excerpts, stories, poems, and photography. We have no set guidelines regarding content but strongly recommend that writers read a sample issue before submitting."

IRIS

E-mail: submissions@creatingiris.org. **E-mail:** editorial@creatingiris.org. **Website:** www.creatingiris.org. Estab. 2014. "*Iris* seeks works of fiction and poetry that speak to LGBT young adults and their allies. We are interested in creative, thoughtful, original work that engages our young readers. We seek writing that challenges them and makes them think. We're looking for stories that capture their imaginations and characters that are relatable. We think there's a need in the young adult literary market for writing that speaks to the everyday experiences of LGBT adolescents: Themes of identity, friendship, coming out, families, etc., are especially welcome. The protagonist need not identify as LGBT, but we do ask that there be some kind of LGBT angle to your story. We welcome all genres of fiction and poetry!"

"Because we publish for a young demographic, work submitted to *Iris* may not include depictions of sex, drug use, and violence. They can certainly be discussed and referenced, but not directly portrayed."

NEEDS Length: up to 3,000 words.

HOW TO CONTACT Submit complete ms via e-mail as attachment. Include cover letter in text of e-mail.

ISLAND

P.O. Box 4703, Hobart Tasmania 7000, Australia. **E-mail:** admin@islandmag.com. **Website:** www.islandmag.com. **Contact:** Geordie Williamson, editor at large. Estab. 1979. *Island* seeks quality fiction, poetry, and essays. It is "one of Australia's leading literary magazines, tracing the contours of our national, and international, culture while still retaining a uniquely Tasmanian perspective."

Only publishes the work of subscribers; you can submit if you are not currently a subscriber, but if your piece is chosen, the subscription will be taken from the fee paid for the piece.

HOW TO CONTACT Submit 1 piece via online submissions manager.

PAYMENT/TERMS Pay varies.

JABBERWOCK REVIEW

Department of English, Mississippi State University, Drawer E, Mississippi State MS 39762. **E-mail:** jabberwockreview@english.msstate.edu. **Website:** www.jabberwockreview.org.msstate.edu. **Contact:** Becky Hagenston, editor. Estab. 1979. "*Jabberwock Review* is a literary journal published semi-annually by students and faculty of Mississippi State University. The journal consists of poetry, fiction, and nonfiction from around the world. Funding is provided by the Office of the Provost, the College of Arts & Sciences, the Shackouls Honors College, the Department of English, fundraisers, and subscriptions."

Submissions accepted August 15-October 20 and January 15-March 15.

NEEDS No science fiction or romance.

HOW TO CONTACT Submit no more than 1 story at a time.

PAYMENT/TERMS Pays contributor's copies.

TIPS "It might take a few months to get a response from us, but your ms will be read with care. Our editors enjoy reading submissions (really!) and will remember writers who are persistent and committed to getting a story 'right' through revision."

J JOURNAL: NEW WRITING ON JUSTICE

524 W. 59th St., Seventh Floor, New York NY 10019. (212)237-8697. **E-mail:** jjournal@jjay.cuny.edu. **Website:** www.jjournal.org. **Contact:** Adam Berlin and Jeffrey Heiman, editors. Estab. 2008. "*J Journal* publishes literary fiction, creative nonfiction, and poetry on the justice theme—social, political, criminal, gender, racial, religious, economic. While the justice theme is specific, it need not dominate the work. We're interested in innovative writing that examines justice from all creative perspectives. Tangential connections to justice are often better than direct."

Several stories in *J Journal* have been recognized in the Pushcart anthology.

NEEDS Receives 100 mss/month. Accepts 20 mss/issue; 40 mss/year. Length: 750-6,000 words. Average length: 4,000 words.

HOW TO CONTACT Send complete ms with cover letter. Include estimated word count, brief bio, list of publications.

PAYMENT/TERMS Pays 2 contributor's copies. Additional copies $10.

TIPS "We're looking for literary fiction, memoir, personal narrative, or poetry with a connection, direct or tangential, to the theme of justice."

THE JOURNAL

The Ohio State University, 164 Annie and John Glenn Ave., Columbus OH 43210. (614)292-6065. **Fax:** (614)292-7816. **E-mail:** managingeditor@thejournalmag.org. **Website:** thejournalmag.org. Estab. 1973. "We are interested in quality fiction, poetry, nonfiction, art, and reviews of new books of poetry, fiction, and nonfiction. We impose no restrictions on category, type, or length of submission for fiction, poetry, and nonfiction. We are happy to consider long stories and self-contained excerpts of novels. Please double-space all prose submissions. Please send 3-5 poems in 1 submission. We only accept online submissions and will not respond to mailed submissions."

"We're open to all forms; we tend to favor work that gives evidence of a mature and sophisticated sense of the language."

NEEDS No romance, science fiction, or religious/devotional.

HOW TO CONTACT Does not accept queries. Send full ms via online submission system at thejournal.submittable.com. "Mss are rejected because of lack of understanding of the short story form, shallow plots, undeveloped characters. Cure: Read as much well-written fiction as possible. Our readers prefer 'psychological' fiction rather than stories with intricate plots. Take care to present a clean, well-typed submission."

PAYMENT/TERMS Pays 2 contributor's copies and a one-year subscription.

KAIMANA: LITERARY ARTS HAWAI'I

Hawai'i Literary Arts Council, P.O. Box 11213, Honolulu HI 96828. **E-mail:** reimersa001@hawaii.rr.com. **Website:** www.hawaii.edu/hlac. Estab. 1974. *Kaimana: Literary Arts Hawai'i*, published annually, is the magazine of the Hawai'i Literary Arts Council. Wants submissions with "some Pacific reference—Asia, Polynesia, Hawai'i—but not exclusively."

HOW TO CONTACT Submit ms with SASE. No e-mail submissions. Cover letter is preferred.

PAYMENT/TERMS Pays 2 contributor's copies.

TIPS "Hawai'i gets a lot of 'travelling regionalists,' visiting writers with inevitably superficial observations. We also get superb visiting observers who are careful craftsmen anywhere. *Kaimana* is interested in the latter, to complement our own best Hawai'i writers."

KALEIDOSCOPE

701 S. Main St., Akron OH 44311-1019. (330)762-9755. **Fax:** (330)762-0912. **E-mail:** kaleidoscope@udsakron.org. **Website:** www.kaleidoscopeonline.org. **Contact:** Gail Willmott, editor in chief. Estab. 1979. "*Kaleidoscope* magazine creatively focuses on the experiences of disability through literature and the fine arts. Unique to the field of disability studies, this award-winning publication expresses the diversity of the disability experience from a variety of perspectives including: individuals, families, friends, caregivers, educators, and healthcare professionals, among others."

Kaleidoscope has received awards from the Great Lakes Awards Competition and Ohio

Public Images; received the Ohioana Award of Editorial Excellence.

NEEDS Wants short stories with a well-crafted plot and engaging characters. No fiction that is stereotypical, patronizing, sentimental, erotic, or maudlin. No romance, religious or dogmatic fiction; no children's literature. Length: up to 5,000 words.

HOW TO CONTACT Submit complete ms by website or e-mail. Include cover letter.

PAYMENT/TERMS Pays $10-100.

TIPS "The material chosen for *Kaleidoscope* challenges and overcomes stereotypical, patronizing, and sentimental attitudes about disability. We accept the work of writers with and without disabilities; however the work of a writer without a disability must focus on some aspect of disability. The criteria for good writing apply: effective technique, thought-provoking subject matter, and, in general, a mature grasp of the art of storytelling. Writers should avoid using offensive language and always put the person before the disability."

KANSAS CITY VOICES

Whispering Prairie Press, P.O. Box 410661, Kansas City MO 64141. **E-mail:** info@wppress.org. **Website:** www.wppress.org/kansas-city-voices. **Contact:** Jessica Conoley, managing editor. Estab. 2003. *Kansas City Voices*, published annually, features an eclectic mix of fiction, poetry, and art. "We seek exceptional written and visual creations from established and emerging voices."

Submission period: December 15-March 15.

NEEDS Length: up to 2,500 words.

HOW TO CONTACT Submit up to 2 complete mss via online submissions manager.

PAYMENT/TERMS Pays small honorarium and 1 contributor's copy.

TIPS "There is no 'type' of work we are looking for, and while we would love for you to read through our previous issues, it is not an indicator of what kind of work we actively seek. Our editors rotate, our tastes evolve, and good work is just *good work*. We want to feel something when we encounter a piece. We want to be excited, surprised, thoughtful, and interested. We want to have a reaction. We want to share the best voices we find. Send us that one."

KASMA MAGAZINE

Kasma Publications, **E-mail:** editors@kasmamagazine.com. **Website:** www.kasmamagazine.com. **Contact:** Alex Korovessis, editor. Estab. 2009. Online magazine. "We publish the best science fiction, from promising new and established writers. Our aim is to provide stories that are well written, original and thought provoking."

NEEDS No erotica, excessive violence/language. Length: 1,000-5,000 words.

HOW TO CONTACT Submit complete ms via e-mail.

PAYMENT/TERMS Pays 2¢/word (Canadian).

TIPS "The type of stories I enjoy the most usually come as a surprise: I think I know what is happening, but the underlying reality is revealed to me as I read on. That said, I've accepted many stories that don't fit this model. Sometimes I'm introduced to a new story structure. Sometimes the story I like reminds me of another story, but it introduces a slightly different spin on it. Other times, the story introduces such interesting and original ideas that structure and style don't seem to matter as much."

THE KELSEY REVIEW

Liberal Arts Division, Mercer County Community College, P.O. Box 17202, Trenton NJ 08690. **E-mail:** kelsey.review@mccc.edu. **Website:** www.mccc.edu/community_kelsey-review.shtml. **Contact:** Ed Carmien, co-editor. Estab. 1988. *The Kelsey Review*, published annually online in September by Mercer County Community College, serves as "an outlet for literary talent of people living and working in Mercer County, New Jersey."

Submission deadline: May 31.

NEEDS Has no specifications as to form, subject matter, or style. Length: up to 4,000 words.

HOW TO CONTACT Submit via online submissions manager. Submissions are limited to people who live, work, or give literary readings in Mercer County, New Jersey.

TIPS "See *The Kelsey Review* website for current guidelines. Note: We only accept submissions from the Mercer County, New Jersey area."

THE KENYON REVIEW

Finn House, 102 W. Wiggin, Gambier OH 43022. (740)427-5208. **Fax:** (740)427-5417. **E-mail:** kenyonreview@kenyon.edu. **Website:** www.kenyonreview.org. **Contact:** Alicia Misarti. Estab. 1939. "An international journal of literature, culture, and the arts, dedicated to an inclusive representation of the best in new writing (fiction, poetry, essays, interviews, criticism) from established and emerging writers."

The *Kenyon Review* receives about 8,000 submissions/year. Also publishes *KR Online*, a separate and complementary online literary magazine.

NEEDS Receives 800 unsolicited mss/month. Unsolicited mss accepted September 15-December 15 only. Recently published work by Alice Hoffman, Beth Ann Fennelly, Romulus Linney, John Koethe, Albert Goldbarth, Erin McGraw. Length: 3-15 typeset pages preferred.

HOW TO CONTACT Only accepts mss via online submissions program; visit website for instructions. Do not submit via e-mail or snail mail.

PAYMENT/TERMS Pays 8¢/published word of prose (minimum payment $80; maximum payment $450); word count does not include title, notes, or citations.

TIPS "We no longer accept mailed or e-mailed submissions. Work will only be read if it is submitted through our online program on our website. Reading period is September 15 through December 15. We look for strong voice, unusual perspective, and power in the writing."

LADY CHURCHILL'S ROSEBUD WRISTLET

150 Pleasant St., #306, Easthampton MA 01027. **E-mail:** smallbeerpress@gmail.com. **Website:** www.smallbeerpress.com/lcrw. **Contact:** Gavin Grant, editor. Estab. 1996. *Lady Churchill's Rosebud Wristlet* accepts fiction, nonfiction, poetry, and b&w art. "The fiction we publish tends toward, but is not limited to, the speculative. This does not mean only quietly desperate stories. We will consider items that fall out with regular categories. We do not accept multiple submissions."

Semiannual.

NEEDS Receives 100 unsolicited mss/month. Accepts 4-6 mss/issue; 8-12 mss/year. Publishes 2-4 new writers/year. Also publishes literary essays, poetry. Has published work by Ted Chiang, Gwenda Bond, Alissa Nutting, and Charlie Anders. "We do not publish gore, sword and sorcery, or pornography. We can discuss these terms if you like. There are places for them all; this is not one of them." Length: 200-7,000 words.

HOW TO CONTACT Send complete ms with a cover letter. Include estimated word count. Send SASE (or IRC) for return of ms, or send a disposable copy of ms and #10 SASE for reply only.

PAYMENT/TERMS Pays $25.

TIPS "We recommend you read *Lady Churchill's Rosebud Wristlet* before submitting. You can pick up a copy from our website or from assorted book shops."

LAKE EFFECT: A JOURNAL OF THE LITERARY ARTS

School of Humanities & Social Sciences, Penn State Erie, The Behrend College, 4951 College Dr., Erie PA 16563-1501. (814)898-6281. **Fax:** (814)898-6032. **E-mail:** gol1@psu.edu. **Website:** www.pserie.psu.edu/lakeeffect. **Contact:** George Looney, editor in chief. Estab. 1978. *Lake Effect* is a publication of the School of Humanities and Social Sciences at Penn State Erie, The Behrend College.

NEEDS "*Lake Effect* is looking for stories that emerge from character and language as much as from plot. *Lake Effect* does not, in general, publish genre fiction, but literary fiction. *Lake Effect* seeks work from both established and new and emerging writers." Length: up to 15 pages, if longer, query first.

HOW TO CONTACT Submit complete ms with SASE.

LANDFALL: NEW ZEALAND ARTS AND LETTERS

Otago University Press, P.O. Box 56, Dunedin 9054, New Zealand. (64)(3)479-4155. **E-mail:** landfall.press@otago.ac.nz. **Website:** www.otago.ac.nz/press/landfall. **Contact:** Editor. Estab. 1947. *Landfall: New Zealand Arts and Letters* contains literary fiction and essays, poetry, extracts from work in progress, commentary on New Zealand arts and culture, work by visual artists including photographers and reviews of local books. (*Landfall* does not accept unsolicited reviews.)

Deadlines for submissions: January 10 for the May issue, June 10 for the November issue. "*Landfall* is open to work by New Zealand and Pacific writers or by writers whose work has a connection to the region in subject matter or location. Work from Australian writers is occasionally included as a special feature."

NEEDS Length: up to 3,000 words.

HOW TO CONTACT Submit up to 3 pieces at a time. Prefers e-mail submissions. Include cover letter with contact info and bio of about 30 words.

LEADING EDGE MAGAZINE

4087 JKB, Provo UT 84602. **E-mail:** editor@leadingedgemagazine.com; fiction@leadingedgemagazine.com; art@leadingedgemagazine.com; poetry@leadingedgemagazine.com; nonfiction@leadingedgemagazine.com. **Website:** www.leadingedgemagazine.com. **Contact:** Leah Welker, editor in chief. Estab. 1981. "*Leading Edge* is a magazine dedicated to new and upcoming talent in the fields of science fiction and fantasy. We strive to encourage developing and established talent and provide high-quality speculative fiction to our readers." Does not accept mss with sex, excessive violence, or profanity.

Accepts unsolicited submissions.

NEEDS Length: up to 15,000 words.

HOW TO CONTACT Send complete ms with cover letter and SASE. Include estimated word count.

PAYMENT/TERMS Pays 1¢/word; $50 maximum.

TIPS "Buy a sample issue to know what is currently selling in our magazine. Also, make sure to follow the writer's guidelines when submitting."

LILITH MAGAZINE: INDEPENDENT, JEWISH & FRANKLY FEMINIST

250 W. 57th St., Suite 2432, New York NY 10107. (212)757-0818. **Fax:** (212)757-5705. **E-mail:** info@lilith.org. **Website:** www.lilith.org. **Contact:** Susan Weidman Schneider, editor in chief; Naomi Danis, managing editor. Estab. 1976. *Lilith Magazine: Independent, Jewish & Frankly Feminist*, published quarterly, welcomes submissions of high-quality, lively writing: reportage, opinion pieces, memoirs, fiction, and poetry on subjects of interest to Jewish women.

For all submissions: Make sure name and contact information appear on each page of mss. Include a short bio (1-2 sentences), written in third person. Accepts submissions year round.

NEEDS Length: up to 3,000 words.

HOW TO CONTACT Send complete ms via online submissions form or mail.

TIPS "Read a copy of the publication before you submit your work. Please be patient."

THE LISTENING EYE

Kent State University Geauga Campus, 14111 Claridon-Troy Rd., Burton OH 44021. (440)286-3840. **E-mail:** grace_butcher@msn.com. **E-mail:** Only from other countries. **Contact:** Grace Butcher, editor. Estab. 1970. "We look for powerful, unusual imagery, content, and plot in our short stories."

Magazine: 5.5×8.5; 60 pages; photographs. "We publish the occasional very short stories (750 words/3 pages double-spaced) in any subject and any style, but the language must be strong, unusual, free from cliché and vagueness. We are a shoestring operation from a small campus, but we publish high-quality work." Reads submissions January 1-April 15 only.

NEEDS "Pretty much anything will be considered except porn." Recently published work by Simon Perchik, Lyn Lifshin, and John Hart. Publishes short shorts. Also publishes poetry. Sometimes comments on rejected mss.

HOW TO CONTACT Send SASE for return of ms or disposable copy of ms with SASE for reply only.

LITERAL LATTÉ

200 E. Tenth St., Suite 240, New York NY 10003. (212)260-5532. **E-mail:** litlatte@aol.com. **Website:** www.literal-latte.com. **Contact:** Jenine Gordon Bockman and Jeffrey Michael Bockman, editors and publishers. Estab. 1994. Bimonthly online publication. Print anthologies featuring the best of the website. "We want great writing in all styles and subjects. A feast is made of a variety of flavors."

NEEDS Accepts all styles and genres. General Submissions, Fiction Award ($1,000 prize), Short Short Contest ($500 prize). Length: up to 6,000 words.

HOW TO CONTACT Submit via online submissions manager or postal mail.

PAYMENT/TERMS Pays minimum of anthology copies and maximum of $1,000.

TIPS "Keeping free thought free and challenging entertainment are not mutually exclusive. Words make a ms stand out, words beautifully woven together in striking and memorable patterns."

LITERARY JUICE

Issaquah WA 98027. **E-mail:** info@literaryjuice.com. **Website:** www.literaryjuice.com. **Contact:** Sara Rajan, editor in chief; Andrea O'Connor and Dinesh Rajan, managing editors. Estab. 2011. Bimonthly online literary magazine that publishes original, unpublished works of fiction, poetry, art, and photography. Does not publish works of nonfiction, essays, or interviews.

NEEDS "We do not publish works with intense sexual content." Length: 100-2,500 words.

HOW TO CONTACT Submit complete ms via online submissions manager.

TIPS Looking for works that are not only thought-provoking, but venture into unconventional territory as well. Avoid submitting mainstream stories and poems (stories about zombies or politics fall into this category). Instead, take the reader to a new realm that has yet to be explored.

LITERARY MAMA

E-mail: lminfo@literarymama.com. **Website:** www.literarymama.com. **Contact:** Maria Scala, editor in chief. Estab. 2003. "Online monthly magazine that features writing about the complexities and many faces of motherhood. Departments include columns, creative nonfiction, fiction, literary reflections, poetry, profiles, and book reviews. We prefer previously unpublished work and are interested in work that offers a fresh perspective."

"*Literary Mama* is not currently a paying market. We are all volunteers here: editors, writers, and editorial assistants. With the publication of each issue, we make a concerted effort to promote the work of our contributors via Facebook, Twitter, and our ezine."

NEEDS Length: up to 5,000 words.

TIPS "We seek top-notch creative writing. We also look for quality literary criticism about mother-centric literature and profiles of mother writers. We publish writing with fresh voices, superior craft, and vivid imagery. Please send submission (copied into e-mail) to appropriate departmental editors. Include a brief cover letter. We tend to like stark revelation (pathos, humor, and joy); clarity; concrete details; strong narrative development; ambiguity; thoughtfulness; delicacy; irreverence; lyricism; sincerity; the elegant."

THE LITERARY REVIEW

285 Madison Ave., Madison NJ 07940. (973)443-8564. **Fax:** (973)443-8364. **E-mail:** info@theliteraryreview.org. **Website:** www.theliteraryreview.org. **Contact:** Minna Proctor, editor. Estab. 1957.

Work published in *The Literary Review* has been included in *Editor's Choice*, *Best American Short Stories*, and *Pushcart Prize* anthologies. Uses online submissions manager.

NEEDS Wants works of high literary quality only. Does not want to see "overused subject matter or pat resolutions to conflicts." Length: up to 7,000 words.

HOW TO CONTACT Submit electronically only. Does not accept paper submissions.

PAYMENT/TERMS Pays 2 contributor's copies and a one-year subscription.

TIPS "We want original dramatic situations with complex moral and intellectual resonance and vivid prose. We don't want versions of familiar plots and relationships. Too much of what we are seeing today is openly derivative in subject, plot, and prose style. We pride ourselves on spotting new writers with fresh insight and approach."

LITTLE PATUXENT REVIEW

P.O. Box 6084, Columbia MD 21045. **E-mail:** editor@littlepatuxentreview.org. **Website:** www.littlepatuxentreview.org. **Contact:** Steven Leyva, editor. Estab. 2006. "*Little Patuxent Review* (*LPR*) is a community-based, biannual print journal devoted to literature and the arts, primarily in the Mid-Atlantic region. We profile the work of a major poet or fiction writer and a visual artist in each issue. We celebrate the launch of each issue with a series of readings and broadcast highlights on *LPR*'s YouTube channel. All forms and styles considered. Please see our website for the current theme."

NEEDS Length: up to 5,000 words.

HOW TO CONTACT Submit complete ms by online submissions manager; no mail or e-mail submissions. Include word count and 75-word bio.

PAYMENT/TERMS Pays 1 contributor's copy.

TIPS "Please see our website for the current theme. Poetry and prose must exhibit the highest quality to be considered. Please read a sample issue before submitting."

THE LONDON MAGAZINE

11 Queen's Gate, London SW7 5EL, United Kingdom. (44)(0)20 7584 5977. **E-mail:** admin@thelondonmagazine.org. **Website:** www.thelondonmagazine.org. **Contact:** Steven O'Brien, editor. Estab. 1732. "We publish literary writing of the highest quality. We look for poetry and short fiction that startles and entertains us. Reviews, essays, memoir pieces, and features should be erudite, lucid, and incisive. We are obviously interested in writing that has a London fo-

cus, but not exclusively so, since London is a world city with international concerns."

NEEDS "Short fiction should address mature and sophisticated themes. Moreover, it should have an elegance of style, structure and characterization. We do not normally publish science fiction or fantasy writing, or erotica." Length: up to 4,000 words.

HOW TO CONTACT Send complete ms. Submit via online submissions manager, e-mail (as an attachment), or postal mail (enclose SASE).

TIPS "Please look at *The London Magazine* before you submit work so that you can see the type of material we publish."

O THE LONG STORY

18 Eaton St., Lawrence MA 01843. (978)686-7638. **E-mail:** rpburnham@mac.com. **Website:** www.longstorylitmag.com. **Contact:** R.P. Burnham. Estab. 1983. For serious, educated, literary people. "We publish high literary quality of any kind but especially look for stories that have difficulty getting published elsewhere: committed fiction, working class settings, left-wing themes, etc."

NEEDS Receives 25-35 unsolicited mss/month. Accepts 6-7 mss/issue. Publishes 90% new writers/year. No science fiction, adventure, romance, etc. Length: 8,000-20,000 words; average length: 8,000-12,000 words.

HOW TO CONTACT Submit complete ms by postal mail. Include SASE.

PAYMENT/TERMS Pays 2 contributor's copies; $6 charge for extras.

TIPS "Read us first and make sure submitted material is the kind we're interested in. Send clear, legible mss. We're not interested in commercial success; rather we want to provide a place for long stories, the most difficult literary form to publish in our country."

THE LOS ANGELES REVIEW

P.O. Box 2458, Redmond WA 98073. (626)356-4760. **Fax:** (626)356-9974. **E-mail:** lareviewеditor@gmail.com. **Website:** losangelesreview.org. **Contact:** Alisa Trager, managing editor. Estab. 2003.

NEEDS "We're looking for hard-to-put-down shorties under 500 words and lengthier shorts up to 4,000 words—lively, vivid, excellent literary fiction." Does not accept multiple submissions. Does not want pornography. Length: 500-4,000 words.

HOW TO CONTACT "Submishmash, our online submission form, is now our preferred method of submission, though you may still submit through postal mail. Please see our guidelines online."

TIPS "Read a few recent issues to see what we're about. Pay close attention to the submission guidelines. We like cover letters, but please keep them brief."

LOST LAKE FOLK OPERA

Shipwreckt Books Publishing Company, 309 W. Stevens Ave., Rushford MN 55971. **E-mail:** contact@shipwrecktbooks.com. **Website:** www.shipwrecktbooks.com. **Contact:** Tom Driscoll, managing editor. Estab. 2013. *Lost Lake Folk Opera* magazine accepts submissions of critical journalism, short fiction, poetry, and graphic art. Published twice annually.

NEEDS Length: 250-3,500 words.

HOW TO CONTACT Query with sample.

PAYMENT/TERMS Does not offer payment.

TIPS " When in doubt, edit and cut. Please remember to read your submission. Don't expect *LLFO* to wash your car and detail it. Send clean copies of your work."

LOUISIANA LITERATURE

SLU Box 10792, Hammond LA 70402. **E-mail:** lalit@selu.edu. **Website:** www.louisianaliterature.org. **Contact:** Jack B. Bedell, editor. Estab. 1984. "Since 1984, *Louisiana Literature* has featured some of the finest writing published in America. The journal has always striven to spotlight local talent alongside nationally recognized authors. Whether it's work from established writers or from first-time publishers, *Louisiana Literature* is always looking to print the finest poetry and fiction available."

May not read mss June-July. Publishes 4 new writers/year. Publishes theme issues. Has published work by Anthony Bukowski, Aaron Gwyn, Robert Phillips, and R.T. Smith. Work first published in *Louisiana Literature* is regularly reprinted in collections and is nominated for prizes from the National Book Awards for both genres and the Pulitzer. Recently, stories by Aaron Gwyn and Robert Olen Butler were selected for inclusion in *New Stories from the South*.

NEEDS Reviews fiction. "No sloppy, ungrammatical mss." Length: 1,000-6,000 words; average length: 3,500 words.

HOW TO CONTACT Submit ms via online submissions manager. Ms should be double-spaced.

PAYMENT/TERMS Pays 2 contributor's copies.

TIPS "Cut out everything that is not a functioning part of the story. Make sure your ms is professionally presented. Use relevant, specific detail in every scene. We love detail, local color, voice, and craft. Any professional ms stands out."

THE LOUISIANA REVIEW

Division of Liberal Arts, Louisiana State University Eunice, P.O. Box 1129, Eunice LA 70535. (337)550-1315. **E-mail:** bfonteno@lsue.edu. **Website:** web.lsue.edu/la-review. **Contact:** Dr. Billy Fontenot, fiction editor; Dr. Jude Meche, poetry editor; Dr. Diane Langlois, art editor. Estab. 1999. *The Louisiana Review*, published annually during the fall or spring semester, offers "Louisiana poets, writers, and artists a place to showcase their most beautiful pieces. Others may submit Louisiana- or Southern-related poetry, stories, and art. Publishes photographs. Sometimes publishes nonfiction." Wants "strong imagery, metaphor, and evidence of craft."

NEEDS Receives 25 unsolicited mss/month. Accepts 5-7 mss/issue. Reads year round. Has published work by Ronald Frame, Tom Bonner, Laura Cario, and Sheryl St. Germaine. Also publishes short shorts. Length: up to 9,000 words; average length: 2,000 words.

HOW TO CONTACT Send SASE for return of ms. Accepts multiple submissions.

PAYMENT/TERMS Pays 1 contributor's copy.

TIPS "We do like to have fiction play out visually as a film would, rather than be static and undramatized. Louisiana or Gulf Coast settings and themes preferred."

LULLWATER REVIEW

P.O. Box 122036, Atlanta GA 30322. **E-mail:** emorylullwaterreview@gmail.com. **Website:** www.lullwaterreview.wordpress.com. **Contact:** Aneyn M. O'Grady, editor-in-chief; Gabriel Unger, managing editor. Estab. 1990. "We're a small, student-run literary magazine published out of Emory University in Atlanta, Georgia with 2 issues yearly—once in the fall and once in the spring. You can find us in the *Index of American Periodical Verse*, the *American Humanities Index* and as a member of the Council of Literary Magazines and Presses. We welcome work that brings a fresh perspective, whether through language or the visual arts."

NEEDS Recently published work by Greg Jenkins, Thomas Juvik, Jimmy Gleacher, Carla Vissers, and Judith Sudnolt. No romance or science fiction, please. 5,000 words maximum.

HOW TO CONTACT Send complete ms via e-mail. *Does not accept postal mail submissions.*

PAYMENT/TERMS Pays 3 contributor's copies.

TIPS "We at the *Lullwater Review* look for clear cogent writing, strong character development and an engaging approach to the story in our fiction submissions. Stories with particularly strong voices and well-developed central themes are especially encouraged. Be sure that your ms is ready before mailing it off to us. Revise, revise, revise! Be original, honest, and of course, keep trying."

LUMINA

Sarah Lawrence College, **E-mail:** lumina@gm.slc.edu. **Website:** luminajournal.com. **Contact:** Sarah Dean, editor in chief; Steven Wolf, fiction editor; Melanie Anagnos, nonfiction editor; Marie Marandola, poetry editor. Estab. 2000. "*LUMINA*'s mission is to provide a journal where emerging and established writers and visual artists come together in exploration of the new and appreciation of the traditional. We want to see sonnets sharing space with experimental prose; we want art that pushes boundaries and bends rules with eloquence."

NEEDS Length: up to 5,000 words.

HOW TO CONTACT Submit via online submissions manager. All submissions are read blind; do not include personal information on submission documents.

LUNGFULL!MAGAZINE

316 23rd St., Brooklyn NY 11215. **E-mail:** customerservice@lungfull.org. **Website:** lungfull.org. **Contact:** Brendan Lorber, editor/publisher. Estab. 1994. "*LUNGFULL!* Magazine World Headquarters in Brooklyn is home to a team of daredevils who make it their job to bring you only the finest in typos, misspellings, and awkward phrases. That's because *LUNGFULL!magazine* is the only literary and art journal in America that prints the rough drafts of people's work so you can see the creative process as it happens."

LUNGFULL! was the recipient of a grant from the New York State Council for the Arts.

NEEDS Publishes rough drafts.

HOW TO CONTACT Submit up to 15 pages of prose. Include cover letter.

MĀNOA: A PACIFIC JOURNAL OF INTERNATIONAL WRITING

English Department, University of Hawaii, Honolulu HI 96822. (808)956-3070. **Fax:** (808)956-3083. **E-mail:** mjournal-l@lists.hawaii.edu. **Website:** manoajournal.hawaii.edu. **Contact:** Frank Stewart, editor. Estab. 1989. *Mānoa* is seeking "high-quality literary fiction, poetry, essays, and translations. In general, each issue is devoted to new work from Pacific and Asian areas. Our audience is international. US writing need not be confined to Pacific settings or subjects. Please note that we seldom publish unsolicited work; you may query us at our website."

Mānoa has received numerous awards, and work published in the magazine has been selected for prize anthologies. See website for recently published issues.

NEEDS Query first. No Pacific exotica. Length: 1,000-7,500 words.

HOW TO CONTACT Send complete ms.

PAYMENT/TERMS Pays $100-500 ($25/printed page).

TIPS "Not accepting unsolicited mss at this time because of commitments to special projects. Please query before sending mss as e-mail attachments."

THE MACGUFFIN

Schoolcraft College, 18600 Haggerty Rd., Livonia MI 48152, United States. (734)462-4400, ext 5327. **E-mail:** macguffin@schoolcraft.edu. **E-mail:** macguffin@schoolcraft.edu. **Website:** www.schoolcraft.edu/macguffin. **Contact:** Steven A. Dolgin, editor; Gordon Krupsky, managing editor;. Estab. 1984. "Our purpose is to encourage, support and enhance the literary arts in the Schoolcraft College community, the region, the state, and the nation. We also sponsor annual literary events and give voice to deserving new writers as well as established writers."

NEEDS Length: 5,000 words.

HOW TO CONTACT Submit 2 stories, maximum. Prose should be typed and double-spaced. Include word count. Send SASE or e-mail.

PAYMENT/TERMS Pays 2 contributor's copies.

MAD HATTERS' REVIEW

Wales. **E-mail:** askalice@madhatarts.com; marc@madhatarts.com. **Website:** www.madhattersreview.com. **Contact:** Marc Vincenz, publisher and editor in chief. *Mad Hatters' Review* "seeks to foster the work of writers and poets: explosive, lyrical, passionate, deeply wrought voices and aesthetic experiments that stretch the boundaries of language, narrative, and image, vital and enduring literary voices that sing on the page as well as in the mind. The name of our annual reflects our view of the world as essentially demented and nonsensical, too frequently a nightmare or 'non-dream' that needs to be exposed to the light for what it is, as well as what it is not. We're particularly interested in risky, thematically broad (i.e., saying something about the world and its creatures), psychologically and philosophically sophisticated works. Humor, satire, irony, magical realism, and surrealism are welcome. We look for originality, surprise, intellectual and emotional strength, lyricism, and rhythm. We love writers who stretch their imaginations to the limits and challenge conventional notions of reality and style; we care little for categories. We also adore collaborative ventures, between/among writers, visual artists, and composers."

Mad Hatters' Review has received an Artistry Award from Sixty Plus Design, 2006-2007 Web Design Award from Invision Graphics, and a Gold Medal Award of Excellence for 2006-7 from ArtSpace2000.com. Member: CLMP.

NEEDS Submissions are open briefly for each issue: check guidelines periodically for dates. **Publishes 1 new writer/year.** Has published Alastair Gray, Kass Fleisher, Vanessa Place, Harold Jaffe, Andrei Codrescu, Sheila Murphy, Simon Perchik, Terese Svoboda, Niels Hav, Martin, Nakell, and Juan Jose Millas (translated from the Spanish). Does not want mainstream prose/story that doesn't exhibit a love of language and a sophisticated mentality. No religious or inspirational writings, confessionals, boys sowing oats, sentimental and coming-of-age stories. Length: up to 3,000 words. Average length: 1,500-2,500 words. Publishes short shorts. Average length of short shorts: 500-800 words.

HOW TO CONTACT Submit via online submissions manager.

TIPS "Imagination, skill with and appreciation of language, inventiveness, rhythm, sense of humor/

irony/satire, and compelling style make a ms stand out. Read the magazine. Don't necessarily follow the rules you've been taught in the usual MFA program or workshop."

THE MADISON REVIEW

University of Wisconsin, 600 N. Park St., 6193 Helen C. White Hall, Madison WI 53706. **E-mail:** madisonrevw@gmail.com. **Website:** www.english.wisc.edu/madisonreview. **Contact:** Will Conley and Sam Zisser, fiction editors; Mckenna Kohlenberg and Cody Dunn, poetry editors. Estab. 1972. *The Madison Review* is a student-run literary magazine that looks to publish the best available fiction and poetry.

Does not publish unsolicited interviews or genre fiction. Send all submissions through online submissions manager.

NEEDS Wants well-crafted, compelling fiction featuring a wide range of styles and subjects. Does not read May-September. No genre: horror, fantasy, erotica, etc. Length: 500-30,000 words, up to 30 pages.

HOW TO CONTACT Send complete ms.

PAYMENT/TERMS Pays 2 contributor's copies, $5 for additional copies.

TIPS "Our editors have very eclectic tastes, so don't specifically try to cater to us. Above all, we look for original, high-quality work."

THE MAGAZINE OF FANTASY & SCIENCE FICTION

P.O. Box 3447, Hoboken NJ 07030. (201) 876-2551. **E-mail:** fandsf@aol.com. **Website:** www.fandsf.com; submissions.ccfinlay.com/fsf. **Contact:** C.C. Finlay, editor. Estab. 1949. "*The Magazine of Fantasy and Science Fiction* publishes various types of science fiction and fantasy short stories and novellas, making up about 80% of each issue. The balance of each issue is devoted to articles about science fiction, a science column, book and film reviews, cartoons, and competitions." Bimonthly.

The Magazine of Fantasy and Science Fiction won a Nebula Award for Best Novelet for *A Guide to the Fruits of Hawai'i* by Alaya Dawn Johnson in 2015. Many other works published by *F&SF* received award nominations and reprints in various "Best of the Year" anthologies.

NEEDS "Prefers character-oriented stories. We receive a lot of fantasy fiction but never enough science fiction." Length: up to 25,000 words.

HOW TO CONTACT Send complete ms.

PAYMENT/TERMS Pays 7-12¢/word.

TIPS "Good storytelling makes a submission stand out. Regarding mss, a well-prepared ms (i.e., one that follows the traditional format, like that described here: www.sfwa.org/writing/vonda/vonda.htm) stands out more than any gimmicks. Read an issue of the magazine before submitting. New writers should keep their submissions under 15,000 words—we rarely publish novellas by new writers."

THE MAGNOLIA QUARTERLY

P.O. Box 10294, Gulfport MS 39505. **E-mail:** writerpllevin@gmail.com. **Website:** www.gcwriters.org. **Contact:** Phil Levin, editor. Estab. 1985. *The Magnolia Quarterly* publishes poetry, fiction, nonfiction, and reviews. **For members of GCWA only.**

The Magnolia Quarterly is 40 pages, pocket-sized, stapled, with glossy cover, includes ads. Editing service offered on all prose.

NEEDS Length: about 700 words.

HOW TO CONTACT E-mail submissions in .doc format as attachments.

PAYMENT/TERMS No payment.

THE MAIN STREET RAG

P.O. Box 690100, Charlotte NC 28227-7001. (704)573-2516. **E-mail:** editor@mainstreetrag.com. **Website:** www.mainstreetrag.com. **Contact:** M. Scott Douglass, editor/publisher. Estab. 1996. *The Main Street Rag*, published quarterly, prints "poetry, short fiction, essays, interviews, reviews, photos, and art. We like publishing good material from people who are interested in more than notching another publishing credit, people who support small independent publishers like ourselves." Will consider "almost anything," but prefers "writing with an edge—either gritty or bitingly humorous. Contributors are advised to visit our website prior to submission to confirm current needs."

NEEDS Length: up to 6,000 words.

HOW TO CONTACT E-mail submissions only. Cover letter preferred. "No bios or credits—let the work speak for itself."

PAYMENT/TERMS Pays 1 contributor's copy.

THE MALAHAT REVIEW

The University of Victoria, P.O. Box 1700, STN CSC, Victoria BC V8W 2Y2, Canada. (250)721-8524. **E-mail:** malahat@uvic.ca (for queries only). **Website:** www.malahatreview.ca. **Contact:** John Barton, editor. Estab. 1967. Quarterly magazine covering poetry, fiction, creative nonfiction, and reviews. "We try to achieve a balance of views and styles in each issue. We strive for a mix of the best writing by both established and new writers."

NEEDS Length: up to 8,000 words.

HOW TO CONTACT Submit via online submissions manager: malahatreview.ca/submission_guidelines.html#submittable.

PAYMENT/TERMS Pays $50/magazine page.

TIPS "Please do not send more than 1 submission at a time: 3-5 poems, 1 piece of creative nonfiction, or 1 short story (do not mix poetry and prose in the same submission). See *The Malahat Review*'s Open Season Awards for poetry and short fiction, creative nonfiction, long poem, and novella contests in the Awards section of our website."

THE MASSACHUSETTS REVIEW

University of Massachusetts, Photo Lab 309, Amherst MA 01003. (413)545-2689. **E-mail:** massrev@external.umass.edu. **Website:** www.massreview.org. **Contact:** Emily Wojcik, managing editor. Estab. 1959. Seeks a balance between established writers and promising new ones. Interested in material of variety and vitality relevant to the intellectual and aesthetic questions of our time. Aspire to have a broad appeal.

Does not respond to mss without SASE.

NEEDS Wants short stories. Accepts 1 short story per submission. Include name and contact information on the first page. Encourages page numbers. Has published work by Ahdaf Soueif, Elizabeth Denton, and Nicholas Montemarano. Length: up to 30 pages or 8,000 words.

HOW TO CONTACT Send complete ms.

PAYMENT/TERMS Pays $50 and 2 contributor's copies.

TIPS "No mss are considered May-September. Electronic submission process can be found on website. No fax or e-mail submissions. Shorter rather than longer stories preferred (up to 28-30 pages)." Looks for works that "stop us in our tracks." Mss that stand out use "unexpected language, idiosyncrasy of outlook, and are the opposite of ordinary."

MERIDIAN

University of Virginia, P.O. Box 400145, Charlottesville VA 22904-4145. **E-mail:** meridianuva@gmail.com; meridianpoetry@gmail.com; meridianfiction@gmail.com. **Website:** www.readmeridian.org. Estab. 1998. *Meridian* Editors' Prize Contest offers annual $1,000 award. Submit online only; see website for formatting details. **Entry fee:** $8.50, includes one-year electronic subscription to *Meridian* for all U.S. entries or 1 copy of the prize issue for all international entries. **Deadline:** December or January; see website for current deadline. *Meridian*, published semiannually, prints poetry, fiction, nonfiction, interviews, and reviews. "*Meridian* is interested in writing that is vibrant, moving, and alive, and welcomes contributions from a variety of aesthetic approaches. Has published such poets as Alexandra Teague, Gregory Pardlo, Sandra Meek, and Bob Hicok, and such fiction writers as Matt Bell, Kate Milliken, and Ron Carlson. Has recently interviewed C. Michael Curtis, Ann Beatty, and Claire Messud, among other luminaries. Also publishes a recurring feature called 'Lost Classic,' which resurrects previously unpublished work by celebrated writers and which has included illustrations from the mss of Jorge Luis Borges, letters written by Elizabeth Bishop, Stephen Crane's deleted chapter from *The Red Badge of Courage*, and a letter written by Flannery O'Connor about her novel *Wise Blood*."

Work published in *Meridian* has appeared in *The Best American Poetry* and *The Pushcart Prize Anthology*.

NEEDS Submit complete ms via online submissions manager. Length: up to 6,500 words.

PAYMENT/TERMS Pays 2 contributor's copies (additional copies available at discount).

MICHIGAN QUARTERLY REVIEW

0576 Rackham Bldg., 915 E. Washington, Ann Arbor MI 48109-1070. (734)764-9265. **E-mail:** mqr@umich.edu. **Website:** www.michiganquarterlyreview.com. **Contact:** Jonathan Freedman, editor; Vicki Lawrence, managing editor. Estab. 1962. *Michigan Quarterly Review* is an eclectic interdisciplinary journal of arts and culture that seeks to combine the best of poetry, fiction, and creative nonfiction with outstanding critical essays on literary, cultural, social, and political matters. The flagship journal of the University of Michigan, *MQR* draws on lively minds here and elsewhere, seeking to present accessible work of all varieties for sophisticated readers from within and without the academy.

NEEDS "No restrictions on subject matter or language. We are very selective. We like stories that are unusual in tone and structure, and innovative in language. No genre fiction written for a market. Would like to see more fiction about social, political, and cultural matters, not just centered on a love relationship or dysfunctional family." Receives 300 unsolicited mss/month. Accepts 3-4 mss/issue; 12-16 mss/year. Publishes 1-2 new writers/year. Has published work by Rebecca Makkai, Peter Ho Davies, Laura Kasischke, Gerald Shapiro, and Alan Cheuse. Length: 1,500-7,000 words; average length: 5,000 words.

HOW TO CONTACT Send complete ms.

PAYMENT/TERMS Payment varies but is usually in the range of $50-$150.

TIPS "Read the journal and assess the range of contents and the level of writing. We have no guidelines to offer or set expectations; every ms is judged on its unique qualities. On essays, query with a very thorough description of the argument and a copy of the first page. Watch for announcements of special issues, which are usually expanded issues and draw upon a lot of freelance writing. Be aware that this is a university quarterly that publishes a limited amount of fiction and poetry and that it is directed at an educated audience, one that has done a great deal of reading in all types of literature."

MID-AMERICAN REVIEW

Bowling Green State University, Dept. of English, Bowling Green OH 43403. (419)372-2725. **E-mail:** mar@bgsu.edu; marsubmissions.bgsu.edu. **Website:** www.bgsu.edu/midamericanreview. **Contact:** Abigail Cloud, editor in chief; Lydia Munnell, fiction editor. Estab. 1981. "We aim to put the best possible work in front of the biggest possible audience. We publish contemporary fiction, poetry, creative nonfiction, translations, and book reviews."

NEEDS Publishes traditional, character-oriented, literary, experimental, prose poem, and short-short stories. No genre fiction. Length: 6,000 words maximum.

HOW TO CONTACT Submit ms by post with SASE or with online submission manager. Agented fiction 5%. Recently published work by Mollie Ficek and J. David Stevens.

TIPS "We are seeking translations of contemporary authors from all languages into English; submissions must include the original and proof of permission to translate. We would also like to see more creative nonfiction."

MIDWAY JOURNAL

77 Liberty Avenue #10, Somerville MA 02144. (763)516-7463. **E-mail:** editors@midwayjournal.com. **Website:** www.midwayjournal.com. **Contact:** Christopher Lowe, nonfiction editor; Ralph Pennel, fiction editor; Paige Riehl, poetry editor. Estab. 2006. "Just off of I-94 and on the border between St. Paul and Minneapolis, the Midway, like any other state fairgrounds, is alive with a mix of energies and people. Its position as mid-way, as a place of boundary crossing, also reflects our vision for this journal. The work here complicates and questions the boundaries of genre, binary, and aesthetic. It offers surprises and ways of re-seeing, re-thinking, and re-feeling: a veritable banquet of literary fare. Which is why, in each new issue, we are honored to present work by both new and established writers alike."

Member CLMP.

NEEDS No length limit.

HOW TO CONTACT Submit 1 piece of fiction or 2 pieces of flash/sudden fiction via online submissions manager.

TIPS "An interesting story with engaging writing, both in terms of style and voice, make a ms stand out. Round characters are a must. Writers who take chances either with content or with form grab an editor's immediate attention. Spend time with the words on the page. Spend time with the language. The language and voice are not vehicles; they, too, are tools."

MINAS TIRITH EVENING-STAR: JOURNAL OF THE AMERICAN TOLKIEN SOCIETY

American Tolkien Society, P.O. Box 97, Highland MI 48357-0097. **E-mail:** editor@americantolkiensociety.org; americantolkiensociety@yahoo.com. **Website:** www.americantolkiensociety.org. **Contact:** Amalie A. Helms, editor. Estab. 1967. *Minas Tirith Evening-Star: Journal of the American Tolkien Society*, published quarterly, publishes poetry, book reviews, essays, and fan fiction. *Minas Tirith Evening-Star* is digest-sized, offset-printed from typescript, with cartoon-like b&w graphics. Press run is 400. Single copy: $3.50; subscription: $12.50. Sample: $3. Make checks payable to American Tolkien Society.

HOW TO CONTACT Submit complete ms by mail or e-mail.

PAYMENT/TERMS Pays 1 contributor's copy.

THE MINNESOTA REVIEW

Virginia Tech, ASPECT, 202 Major Williams Hall (0192), Blacksburg VA 24061. **E-mail:** editors@theminnesotareview.org. **Website:** minnesotareview.wordpress.com. **Contact:** Janell Watson, editor. Estab. 1960. *The Minnesota Review*, published biannually, is a journal featuring creative and critical work from writers on the rise or who are already established. Each issue is about 200 pages, digest-sized, flat-spined, with glossy card cover. Press run is 1,000 (400 subscribers). Also available online. Subscription: $30/2 years for individuals, $60/year for institutions. Sample: $15.

Open to submissions August 1-November 1 and January 1-April 1. Accepts submissions via online submissions manager.

NEEDS Length: 10,000 words for short stories, 1,000 words for flash fiction.

HOW TO CONTACT Limit submissions to 1 short story or 4 flash fiction pieces.

MISSISSIPPI REVIEW

University of Southern Mississippi, 118 College Dr., #5144, Hattiesburg MS 39406-0001. (601)266-4321. **Fax:** (601)266-5757. **E-mail:** msreview@usm.edu. **Website:** www.usm.edu/mississippi-review. **Contact:** Andrew Malan Milward, editor in chief; Caleb Tankersley and Allison Campbell, associate editors. Estab. 1972. *Mississippi Review* "is one of the most respected literary journals in the country. Raymond Carver, an early contributor to the magazine, once said that *Mississippi Review* 'is one of the most remarkable and indispensable literary journals of our time.' Well-known and established writers have appeared in the pages of the magazine, including Pulitzer and Nobel Prize winners, as well as new and emerging writers who have gone on to publish books and to receive awards."

NEEDS No juvenile or genre fiction. Length: 30 pages maximum.

THE MISSOURI REVIEW

357 McReynolds Hall, University of Missouri, Columbia MO 65211. (573)882-4474. **Fax:** (573)884-4671. **E-mail:** mutmrquestion@moreview.com. **Website:** www.missourireview.com. **Contact:** Speer Morgan, editor; Kate McIntyre, managing editor, Evelyn Somers, associate editor; Chun Ye, poetry editor. Estab. 1978. The William Peden Prize of $1,000 is awarded annually to the best piece of fiction to have appeared in the previous volume year. The winner is chosen by an outside judge from stories published in *TMR*. There is no separate application process. Publishes contemporary fiction, poetry, interviews, personal essays, cartoons, special features—such as History as Literature series, Found Text series, and Curio Cabinet art features—for the literary and the general reader interested in a wide range of subjects.

NEEDS No genre or flash fiction. Length: 15-25 pp. average

HOW TO CONTACT Send complete ms.

PAYMENT/TERMS Pays $40/printed page.

TIPS "Send your best work."

MOBIUS

505 Christianson St., Madison WI 53714. **E-mail:** fmschep@charter.net. **Website:** www.mobiusmagazine.com. **Contact:** Fred Schepartz, publisher and executive editor. Estab. 1989. *Mobius: The Journal of Social Change* is online-only journal, published quarterly in March, June, September, and December. "At *Mobius* we believe that writing is power and good writing empowers both the reader and the writer. We feel strongly that alternatives are needed to an increasingly corporate literary scene. *Mobius* strives to provide an outlet for writers disenfranchised by a bottom-line marketplace, and challenging writing for those who feel that today's literary standards are killing us in a slow, mind-numbing fashion."

NEEDS Wants fiction dealing with themes of social change. "We like social commentary, but mainly we like good writing. No porn, no racist, sexist or any other kind of *-ist*. No Christian or spirituality proselytizing fiction." Length: up to 5,000 words.

HOW TO CONTACT Submit no more than 1 story at a time via e-mail (preferred) or mail.

TIPS "We like high impact. We like plot- and character-driven stories that function like theater of the mind. We look first and foremost for good writing. Prose must be crisp and polished; the story must pique my interest and make me care due to a certain intellectual, emotional aspect. *Mobius* is about social change. We want stories that make some statement about the society we live in, either on a macro or micro level. Not that your story needs to preach from a soapbox (actually, we prefer that it doesn't), but your story needs to have something to say."

THE MOCHILA REVIEW

Missouri Western State University, 525 Downs Dr., St. Joseph MO 64507. **E-mail:** mochila@missouriwestern.edu. **Website:** www.missouriwestern.edu/orgs/mochila/homepage.htm. **Contact:** Marianne Kunkel, editor. Estab. 2000. "We are looking for writing that has a respect for the sound of language. We value poems that have to be read aloud so your mouth can feel the shape of the words. Send us writing that conveys a sense of urgency, writing that the writer can't *not* write. We crave fresh and daring work."

NEEDS Length: 1 piece of no more than 5,000 words.

HOW TO CONTACT Submit complete ms by postal mail. Include cover letter, contact information, SASE.

PAYMENT/TERMS Pays in contributor's copies.

TIPS "Mss with fresh language, energy, passion, and intelligence stand out. Study the craft and be entertaining and engaging."

MYTHIC DELIRIUM

3514 Signal Hill Ave. NW, Roanoke VA 24017-5148. **E-mail:** mythicdelirium@gmail.com. **Website:** www.mythicdelirium.com. **Contact:** Mike Allen, editor. Estab. 1998. "*Mythic Delirium* is an online and e-book venue for fiction and poetry that ranges through science fiction, fantasy, horror, interstitial, and cross-genre territory—we love blurred boundaries and tropes turned on their heads. We are interested in work that demonstrates ambition, that defies traditional approaches to genre, that introduces readers to the legends of other cultures, that re-evaluates the myths of old from a modern perspective, that twists reality in unexpected ways. We are committed to diversity and are open to and encourage submissions from people of every race, gender, nationality, sexual orientation, political affiliation and religious belief. We publish 12 short stories and 24 poems a year. Our quarterly ebooks in PDF, EPUB, and MOBI formats, published in July, October, January, and April, will each contain 3 stories and 6 poems. We will also publish 1 story and 2 poems on our website each month." Reading period: August 1-October 1 annually.

NEEDS "No unsolicited reprints or multiple submissions. Please use the words 'fiction submission' in the e-mail subject line. Stories should be sent in standard ms format as .rtf or .doc attachments." Length: up to 4,000 words (firm).

PAYMENT/TERMS Pays 2¢/word.

TIPS "*Mythic Delirium* isn't easy to get into, but we publish newcomers in every issue. Show us how ambitious you can be, and don't give up."

NA'AMAT WOMAN

505 Eighth Ave., Suite 12A04, New York NY 10018. (212)563-5222. **E-mail:** naamat@naamat.org; judith@naamat.org. **Website:** www.naamat.org. **Contact:** Judith Sokoloff, editor. Estab. 1926. "Magazine covering a wide variety of subjects of interest to the Jewish community—including political and social issues, arts, profiles; many articles about Israel and women's issues. Fiction must have a Jewish theme. Readers are the American Jewish community." Circ. 15,000. "Magazine covering a wide variety of subjects of interest to the Jewish community—including political and social issues, arts, profiles; many articles about Israel and women's issues. Fiction must have a Jewish theme. Readers are the American Jewish community."

NEEDS Ethnic/multicultural, historical, humor/satire, literary, novel excerpts, women-oriented. Receives 10 unsolicited mss/month. Accepts 1-3 mss/year. "We want serious fiction, with insight, reflection and consciousness." "We do not want fiction that is mostly dialogue. No corny Jewish humor. No Holocaust fiction." Length: 2,000-3,000 words.

HOW TO CONTACT Query with published clips or send complete mss. Responds in 6 months to queries; 6 months to mss. Sample copy for 9×11½ SAE and $2 postage or look online. Sample copy for $2. Writer's guidelines for #10 SASE, or by e-mail. Query with published clips or send complete ms.

PAYMENT/TERMS Pays 10¢/word and 2 contributor's copies. Pays on publication for first North American serial, first, one time, second serial (reprint) rights, makes work-for-hire assignments. Pays 10-20¢/word for assigned articles and for unsolicited articles.

TIPS "No maudlin nostalgia or romance; no hackneyed Jewish humor."

NARRATIVE MAGAZINE

2443 Fillmore St. #214, San Francisco CA 94115. **E-mail:** contact@narrativemagazine.com. **Website:** www.narrativemagazine.com. **Contact:** Michael Croft, senior editor; Mimi Kusch, managing editor; Michael Wiegers, poetry editor. Estab. 2003. "*Narrative* publishes high-quality contemporary literature in a full range of styles, forms, and lengths. Submit poetry, fiction, and nonfiction, including stories, short shorts, novels, novel excerpts, novellas, personal es-

says, humor, sketches, memoirs, literary biographies, commentary, reportage, interviews, and short audio recordings of short-short stories and poems. We welcome submissions of previously unpublished mss of all lengths, ranging from short-short stories to complete book-length works for serialization. In addition to submissions for issues of *Narrative* itself, we also encourage submissions for our Story of the Week, literary contests, and Readers' Narratives. Please read our Submission Guidelines for all information on mss formatting, word lengths, author payment, and other policies. We accept submissions only through our electronic submission system. We do not accept submissions through postal services or e-mail. You may send us mss for the following submission categories: General Submissions, Narrative Prize, Story of the Week, Readers' Narrative, iPoem, iStory, Six-Word Story, or a specific Contest. Your ms must be in one of the following file forms: DOC, RTF, PDF, DOCX, TXT, WPD, ODF, MP3, MP4, MOV. or FLV."

Narrative has received recognitions in *New Stories from the South, Best American Mystery Stories, O. Henry Prize Stories, Best American Short Stories, Best American Essays*, and the *Pushcart Prize Collection.* In an article on the business of books, the National Endowment for the Arts featured *Narrative* as the model for the evolution of both print and digital publishing.

NEEDS Has published work by Alice Munro, Tobias Wolff, Marvin Bell, Jane Smiley, Joyce Carol Oates, E.L. Doctorow, Min Jin Lee, and Alice Munro. Publishes new and emerging writers.

HOW TO CONTACT Send complete ms.

PAYMENT/TERMS Pays on publication between $150-1,000, $1,000-5,000 for book length, plus annual prizes of more than $32,000 awarded.

TIPS "Log on and study our magazine online. Narrative fiction, graphic art, and multimedia are selected, first and foremost, for quality."

◐ THE NASSAU REVIEW

Nassau Community College, Nassau Community College, English Dept., 1 Education Dr., Garden City NY 11530. **E-mail:** nassaureview@ncc.edu. **Website:** www.ncc.edu/nassaureview. **Contact:** Christina M. Rau, editor in chief. Estab. 1964. *The Nassau Review* welcomes submissions of many genres, preferring work that is "innovative, captivating, well-crafted, and unique, work that crosses boundaries of genre and tradition. You may be serious. You may be humorous. You may be somewhere in between. We are looking simply for quality. New and seasoned writers are welcome."

All open submissions are under consideration for the Writer Awards.

NEEDS Accepts simultaneous submissions: "Please let us know they are simultaneous when you submit them." Does not want "children's literature; cliché, unoriginal work; fan fiction." Length: 100-3,000 words.

HOW TO CONTACT Submit via online submissions manager. Include title, word count, and bio of up to 100 words.

PAYMENT/TERMS Pays 1 contributor's copy.

NATURAL BRIDGE

Dept. of English, University of Missouri-St. Louis, One University Blvd., St. Louis MO 63121. (314)516-7327. **E-mail:** natural@umsl.edu. **Website:** www.umsl.edu/~natural. Estab. 1999. *Natural Bridge*, published biannually in May and December, invites submissions of poetry, fiction, personal essays, and translations.

No longer accepts submissions via e-mail. Accepts submissions through online submission form and postal mail only.

NEEDS Literary. Submit year round; however, "we do not read May 1-August 1." Recently published work by Tayari Jones, Steve Stern, Jamie Wriston Colbert, Lex Williford, and Mark Jay Mirsky. Also publishes literary essays, poetry. Sometimes comments on rejected mss.

HOW TO CONTACT Submit 1 ms through online submissions manager ($3 fee for nonsubscribers) or by postal mail (free).

PAYMENT/TERMS Pays 2 contributor's copies and one-year subscription.

NEBO

Arkansas Tech University, Department of English, Russellville AR 72801. **E-mail:** nebo@atu.edu. **Website:** www.atu.edu/worldlanguages/nebo.php. **Contact:** Editor. Estab. 1983. *Nebo*, published in the spring and fall, publishes fiction, poetry, creative nonfiction, drama, comics, and art from Arkansas Tech students and unpublished writers as well as nationally known writers.

Reads submissions August 15-January 31.

NEEDS Accepts all genres. Length: up to 5,000 words.

HOW TO CONTACT Submit complete ms by e-mail or postal mail.

TIPS "Avoid pretentiousness. Write something you genuinely care about. Please edit your work for spelling, grammar, cohesiveness, and overall purpose. Many of the mss we receive should be publishable with a little polishing. Mss should never be submitted handwritten or on 'onion skin' or colored paper."

NEON MAGAZINE

UK. **E-mail:** info@neonmagazine.co.uk. **Website:** www.neonmagazine.co.uk. **Contact:** Krishan Coupland. Quarterly website and print magazine covering alternative work of any form of poetry and prose, short stories, flash fiction, artwork and reviews. "Genre work is welcome. Experimentation is encouraged. We like stark poetry and weird prose. We seek work that is beautiful, shocking, intense, and memorable. Darker pieces are generally favored over humorous ones."

Neon was previously published as *FourVolts Magazine.*

NEEDS "No nonsensical prose; we are not appreciative of sentimentality." No word limit.

PAYMENT/TERMS Pays royalties.

TIPS "Send several poems, 1 or 2 pieces of prose or several images via form e-mail. Include the word 'submission' in your subject line. Include a short biographical note (up to 100 words). Read submission guidelines before submitting your work."

THE NEW CRITERION

900 Broadway, Suite 602, New York NY 10003. **Website:** www.newcriterion.com. **Contact:** Roger Kimball, editor and publisher. Estab. 1982. "A monthly review of the arts and intellectual life, *The New Criterion* began as an experiment in critical audacity—a publication devoted to engaging, in Matthew Arnold's famous phrase, with 'the best that has been thought and said.' This also meant engaging with those forces dedicated to traducing genuine cultural and intellectual achievement, whether through obfuscation, politicization, or a commitment to nihilistic absurdity. We are proud that *The New Criterion* has been in the forefront both of championing what is best and most humanely vital in our cultural inheritance and in exposing what is mendacious, corrosive, and spurious. Published monthly from September through June, *The New Criterion* brings together a wide range of young and established critics whose common aim is to bring you the most incisive criticism being written today."

NEW ENGLAND REVIEW

Middlebury College, Middlebury VT 05753. (802)443-5075. **E-mail:** nereview@middlebury.edu. **Website:** www.nereview.com. **Contact:** Marcia Parlow, managing editor. Estab. 1978. *New England Review* is a prestigious, nationally distributed literary journal. Reads September 1 through May 31 (postmarked dates).

Does not accept mss June-August.

NEEDS Send 1 story at a time, unless it is very short. Serious literary only, novel excerpts. Publishes approximately 10 new writers/year. Has published work by Steve Almond, Christine Sneed, Roy Kesey, Thomas Gough, Norman Lock, Brock Clarke, Carl Phillips, Lucia Perillo, Linda Gregerson, and Natasha Trethewey. Length: not strict on word count.

HOW TO CONTACT Send complete ms via online submission manager. No e-mail submissions. "Will consider simultaneous submissions, but must be stated as such and you must notify us immediately if the ms accepted for publication elsewhere."

PAYMENT/TERMS Pays $20/page ($20 minimum), and 2 contributor's copies.

TIPS "We consider short fiction, including short shorts, novellas, and self-contained extracts from novels in both traditional and experimental forms. In nonfiction, we consider a variety of general and literary but not narrowly scholarly essays; we also publish long and short poems, screenplays, graphics, translations, critical reassessments, statements by artists working in various media, testimonies, and letters from abroad. We are committed to exploration of all forms of contemporary cultural expression in the U.S. and abroad. With few exceptions, we print only work not published previously elsewhere."

NEW LETTERS

University of Missouri-Kansas City, 5101 Rockhill Rd., Kansas City MO 64110. (816)235-1168. **Fax:** (816)235-2611. **E-mail:** newletters@umkc.edu. **Website:** www.newletters.org. **Contact:** Robert Stewart, editor in chief. Estab. 1934. "*New Letters* continues to seek the best new writing, whether from established writers or those ready and waiting to be discovered. In addition, it supports those writers, readers, and listeners who want to experience the joy of writing that can both surprise and inspire us all."

Submissions are not read May 1 through October 1.

NEEDS No genre fiction. Length: up to 5,000 words.

HOW TO CONTACT Send complete ms.

PAYMENT/TERMS Pays $30-75.

TIPS "We aren't interested in essays that are footnoted or essays usually described as scholarly or critical. Our preference is for creative nonfiction or personal essays. We prefer shorter stories and essays to longer ones (an average length is 3,500-4,000 words). We have no rigid preferences as to subject, style, or genre, although commercial efforts tend to put us off. Even so, our only fixed requirement is good writing."

NEW MADRID

Journal of Contemporary Literature, Murray State University, Department of English and Philosophy, 7C Faculty Hall, Murray KY 42071-3341. (270)809-4730. **E-mail:** msu.newmadrid@murraystate.edu. **Website:** newmadridjournal.org. **Contact:** Ann Neelon, editor. "*New Madrid* is the national journal of the low-residency MFA program at Murray State University. It takes its name from the New Madrid seismic zone, which falls within the central Mississippi Valley and extends through western Kentucky."

See website for guidelines and upcoming themes. "We have 2 reading periods, one from August 15-October 15, and one from January 15-March 15." Also publishes poetry and creative nonfiction. Rarely comments on/critiques rejected mss.

NEEDS Length: up to 20 pages double-spaced.

HOW TO CONTACT Accepts submissions by online submissions manager only. Include brief bio, list of publications. Considers multiple submissions.

PAYMENT/TERMS Pays 2 contributor's copies.

TIPS "Quality is the determining factor for breaking into *New Madrid*. We are looking for well-crafted, compelling writing in a range of genres, forms, and styles."

NEW OHIO REVIEW

English Department, 360 Ellis Hall, Ohio University, Athens OH 45701. (740)597-1360. **E-mail:** noreditors@ohio.edu. **Website:** www.ohiou.edu/nor. **Contact:** David Wanczyk, editor. Estab. 2007. *New Ohio Review*, published biannually in spring and fall, publishes fiction, nonfiction, and poetry. Member CLMP. Reading period is September 15-December 15 and January 15-April 15.

NEEDS Considers literary short fiction; no novel excerpts.

HOW TO CONTACT Send complete ms.

PAYMENT/TERMS Pays $30 minimum in addition to 2 contributor's copies and one-year subscription.

NEW ORLEANS REVIEW

Box 195, Loyola University, New Orleans LA 70118. (504)865-2295. **E-mail:** noreview@loyno.edu. **Website:** neworleansreview.org. **Contact:** Heidi Braden, managing editor. Estab. 1968. *New Orleans Review* is an annual journal of contemporary literature and culture, publishing new poetry, fiction, nonfiction, art, photography, film and book reviews.

NEEDS Length: up to 6,500 words.

HOW TO CONTACT "We are now using an online submission system and require a $3 fee." See website for details.

PAYMENT/TERMS Pays $25-50 and 2 contributor's copies.

TIPS "We're looking for dynamic writing that demonstrates attention to the language and a sense of the medium, writing that engages, surprises, moves us. We're not looking for genre fiction or academic articles. We subscribe to the belief that in order to truly write well, one must first master the rudiments: grammar and syntax, punctuation, the sentence, the paragraph, the line, the stanza. We receive about 3,000 mss a year and publish about 3% of them. Check out a recent issue, send us your best, proofread your work, be patient, be persistent."

THE NEW QUARTERLY

St. Jerome's University, 290 Westmount Rd. N., Waterloo ON N2L 3G3, Canada. (519)884-8111, ext. 28290. **E-mail:** editor@tnq.ca; info@tnq.ca. **Website:** www.tnq.ca. Estab. 1981. "Emphasis on emerging writers and genres, but we publish more traditional work as well if the language and narrative structure are fresh."

Open to Canadian writers only. Reading periods: March 1-August 31; September 1-February 28.

NEEDS "*Canadian work only.* We are not interested in genre fiction. We are looking for innovative, beautifully crafted, deeply felt literary fiction."

HOW TO CONTACT Send complete ms with submission cover sheet and bio. Does not accept submissions by e-mail. Accepts simultaneoues submissions if indicated in cover letter.

PAYMENT/TERMS Pays $250/story.

TIPS "Reading us is the best way to get our measure. We don't have preconceived ideas about what we're looking for other than that it must be Canadian work (Canadian writers, not necessarily Canadian content). We want something that's fresh, something that will repay a second reading, something in which the language soars and the feeling is complexly rendered."

NEW SOUTH

English Dept., Georgia State University, P.O Box 3970, Atlanta GA 30302-3970. (404)413-5874. **E-mail:** newsoutheditors@gmail.com. **Website:** www.newsouthjournal.com. Estab. 1980. Semiannual magazine dedicated to finding and publishing the best work from artists around the world. Wants original voices searching to rise above the ordinary. Seeks to publish high-quality work, regardless of genre, form, or regional ties.

New South is 160+ pages. Press run is 2,000; 500 distributed free to students. The *New South* Annual Writing Contest offers $1,000 for the best poem and $1,000 for the best story or essay; one-year subscription to all who submit. Submissions must be unpublished. Submit up to 3 poems, 1 story, or 1 essay on any subject or in any form. Guidelines available online. Competition receives 300 entries. Past judges include Sharon Olds, Jane Hirschfield, Anthony Hecht, Phillip Levine, and Jake Adam York. Winner will be announced in the Fall issue.

NEEDS Receives 200 unsolicited mss/month. Publishes and welcomes short shorts. Length: up to 9,000 words (short stories); up to 1,000 words (short shorts).

HOW TO CONTACT Submit 1 short story or up to 5 short shorts through Submittable.

PAYMENT/TERMS Pays 2 contributor's copies.

TIPS "We want what's new, what's fresh, and what's different—whether it comes from the Southern United States, the South of India, or the North, East or West of Anywhere."

NEW WELSH REVIEW

P.O. Box 170, Aberystwyth, Ceredigion SY23 1 WZ, United Kingdom. 01970-626230. **E-mail:** editor@newwelshreview.com. **E-mail:** submissions@newwelshreview.com. **Website:** www.newwelshreview.com. **Contact:** Gwen Davies, editor. "*NWR*, a literary quarterly ranked in the top 5 of British literary magazines, publishes stories, poems, and critical essays. The best of Welsh writing in English, past and present, is celebrated, discussed, and debated. We seek poems, short stories, reviews, special features/articles, and commentary." Quarterly.

HOW TO CONTACT Send hard copy only with SASE or international money order for return. Outside the UK, submission by e-mail only.

PAYMENT/TERMS Pays "cheque on publication and 1 free copy."

THE NEW YORKER

1 World Trade Center, New York NY 10007. **E-mail:** themail@newyorker.com. **Website:** www.newyorker.com. **Contact:** David Remnick, editor in chief. Estab. 1925. A quality weekly magazine of distinct news stories, articles, essays, and poems for a literate audience.

The New Yorker receives approximately 4,000 submissions per month.

NEEDS Publishes 1 ms/issue.

HOW TO CONTACT Send complete ms by e-mail (as PDF attachment) or mail (address to Fiction Editor).

PAYMENT/TERMS Payment varies.

TIPS "Be lively, original, not overly literary. Write what you want to write, not what you think the editor would like."

NIMROD: INTERNATIONAL JOURNAL OF POETRY AND PROSE

University of Tulsa, 800 S. Tucker Dr., Tulsa OK 74104-3189. (918)631-3080. **Fax:** (918)631-3033. **E-mail:** nimrod@utulsa.edu. **Website:** www.utulsa.edu/nimrod. **Contact:** Eilis O'Neal, editor-in-chief. Estab. 1956. "*Nimrod*'s mission is the discovery and support of new writing of vigor and quality from this country and abroad. The journal seeks new, unheralded writers; writers from other lands who become accessible to the English-speaking world through translation; and established authors who have vigorous new work to present that has not found a home within the establishment. We believe in a living literature; that it is possible to search for, recognize, and reward contemporary writing of content and vigor, without reliance on a canon."

Publishes 10-15 new writers/year. Reading period: January 1 through November 30. Online submissions accepted at nimrodjournal.submittable.com/submit. Does not accept submissions by e-mail unless the writer is living outside the U.S. and cannot submit using the submissions manager. Poetry published in *Nimrod* has been included in *The Best American Poetry.*

NEEDS Wants "vigorous writing, characters that are well developed, dialogue that is realistic without being banal." Length: up to 7,500 words.

HOW TO CONTACT Submit complete ms by mail or through the online submissions manager. Include SASE for work submitted by mail.

PAYMENT/TERMS Pays 2 contributor's copies.

NINTH LETTER

Department of English, University of Illinois, 608 S. Wright St., Urbana IL 61801. (217)300-4315. **E-mail:** info@ninthletter.com; editor@ninthletter.com. **Website:** www.ninthletter.com. **Contact:** Jodee Stanley, editor. "*Ninth Letter* accepts submissions of fiction, poetry, and essays from September 1-February 28 (postmark dates). *Ninth Letter* is published semiannually at the University of Illinois, Urbana-Champaign. We are interested in prose and poetry that experiment with form, narrative, and nontraditional subject matter, as well as more traditional literary work."

Ninth Letter won Best New Literary Journal 2005 from the Council of Editors of Learned Journals (CELJ) and has had poetry selected for *Best American Poetry, The Pushcart Prize, Best New Poets,* and *The Year's Best Fantasy and Horror.*

NEEDS Length: up to 8,000 words.

HOW TO CONTACT "Please send only 1 story at a time. All mailed submissions must include an SASE for reply."

PAYMENT/TERMS Pays $25 per printed page and 2 contributor's copies.

NITE-WRITER'S INTERNATIONAL LITERARY ARTS JOURNAL

158 Spencer Ave., Suite 100, Pittsburgh PA 15227. (412)882-5171. **E-mail:** nitewritersliteraryarts@gmail.com. **Website:** sites.google.com/site/nitewriterinternational/home. **Contact:** John Thompson. Estab. 1994. *Nite-Writer's International Literary Arts Journal* is an online literary arts journal. "We are 'dedicated to the emotional intellectual' with a creative perception of life."

Journal is open to beginners as well as professionals.

NEEDS Length: up to 1,200 words.

HOW TO CONTACT All literary works should be in MS Word at 12-point font.

TIPS "Read a lot of what you write—study the market. Don't fear rejection, but use it as a learning tool to strengthen your work before resubmitting."

THE NORMAL SCHOOL

The Press at the California State University—Fresno, 5245 N. Backer Ave., M/S PB 98, Fresno CA 93740-8001. **E-mail:** editors@thenormalschool.com. **Website:** thenormalschool.com. **Contact:** Steven Church, editor. Estab. 2008. Semiannual magazine that accepts outstanding work by beginning and established writers.

Mss are read from September 1-December 1 and from January 15-April 15. Address submissions to the appropriate editor. Charges $3 fee for each online submission, due to operational costs.

NEEDS Also publishes short shorts (fewer than 1,500 words). Sponsors The Normal Prizes in Fiction Contest and Creative Nonfiction Contest. Does not want any genre writing. Length: up to 12,000 words.

HOW TO CONTACT Submit complete ms.

NORTH AMERICAN REVIEW

University of Northern Iowa, 1222 W. 27th St., Cedar Falls IA 50614. (319)273-6455. **Fax:** (319)273-4326. **E-mail:** nar@uni.edu. **Website:** northamericanreview.org. Estab. 1815. "The *NAR* is the oldest literary magazine in America and one of the most respected; though we have no prejudices about the subject matter of material sent to us, our first concern is quality."

This is the oldest literary magazine in the country and one of the most prestigious. Also one of the most entertaining—and a tough market for the young writer.

NEEDS "No flat narrative stories where the inferiority of the character is the paramount concern." Wants to see more "well-crafted literary stories that emphasize family concerns. We'd also like to see more stories engaged with environmental concerns." Reads fiction mss all year. **Publishes 2 new writers/year.** Recently published work by Lee Ann Roripaugh, Dick Allen, Rita Welty Bourke.

HOW TO CONTACT Accepts submissions by USPS mail only. Send complete ms with SASE.

TIPS "We like stories that start quickly and have a strong narrative arc. Poems that are passionate about subject, language, and image are welcome, whether they are traditional or experimental, whether in formal or free verse (closed or open form). Nonfiction should combine art and fact with the finest writing."

NORTH CAROLINA LITERARY REVIEW

East Carolina University, Mailstop 555 English, Greenville NC 27858-4353. (252)328-1537. **Fax:** (252)328-4889. **E-mail:** nclrsubmissions@ecu.edu; bauerm@ecu.edu. **Website:** www.nclr.ecu.edu. **Contact:** Margaret Bauer. Estab. 1992. "Articles should have a North Carolina slant. Fiction, creative nonfiction, and poetry accepted through yearly contests. First consideration is always for quality of work. Although we treat academic and scholarly subjects, we do not wish to see jargon-laden prose; our readers, we hope, are found as often in bookstores and libraries as in academia. We seek to combine the best elements of a magazine for serious readers with the best of a scholarly journal."

Accepts submissions through Submittable.

NEEDS Length: up to 6,000 words.

HOW TO CONTACT Submit fiction for the Doris Betts Fiction Prize competition via Submittable.

PAYMENT/TERMS First-place winners of contests receive a prize of $250. Other writers whose stories are selected for publication receive comp copies.

TIPS "By far the easiest way to break in is with special issue sections. We are especially interested in reports on conferences, readings, meetings that involve North Carolina writers, and personal essays or short narratives with a strong sense of place. See back issues for other departments. Interviews are probably the other easiest place to break in; no discussions of poetics/theory, etc., except in reader-friendly (accessible) language. Interviews should be personal, more like conversations, that explore connections between a writer's life and his/her work."

NORTH DAKOTA QUARTERLY

University of North Dakota, 276 Centennial Dr. Stop 7209, Merrifield Hall Room 15, Grand Forks ND 58202. (701)777-3322. **Fax:** (701)777-2373. **E-mail:** ndq@und.edu. **Website:** www.ndquarterly.org. **Contact:** Kate Sweney, managing editor. Estab. 1911. "*North Dakota Quarterly* strives to publish the best fiction, poetry, and essays that in our estimation we can. Our tastes and interests are best reflected in what we have been recently publishing, and we suggest that you look at some current issues for guidance."

Only reads fiction and poetry between September 1-May 1. Work published in *North Dakota Quarterly* was selected for inclusion in *The O. Henry Prize Stories*, *The Pushcart Prize Series*, and *Best American Essays*.

NEEDS No length restrictions.

HOW TO CONTACT Submit hard copies only.

NOTRE DAME REVIEW

University of Notre Dame, B009C McKenna Hall, Notre Dame IN 46556. **Website:** ndreview.nd.edu. Estab. 1995. "The *Notre Dame Review* is an indepenent, noncommercial magazine of contemporary American and international fiction, poetry, criticism, and art. Especially interested in work that takes on big issues by making the invisible seen, that gives voice to the voiceless. In addition to showcasing celebrated authors like Seamus Heaney and Czelaw Milosz, the *Notre Dame Review* introduces readers to authors they may have never encountered before but who are doing innovative and important work. In conjunction with the *Notre Dame Review*, the online companion to the printed magazine, the *nd[re]view* engages readers as a community centered in literary rather than commercial concerns, a community we reach out to through critique and commentary as well as aesthetic experience."

Does not accept e-mail submissions. Only reads hardcopy submissions September-November and January-March.

NEEDS "We're eclectic. Upcoming theme issues planned. List of upcoming themes or editorial calendar available for SASE." No genre fiction. Length: up to 3,000 words.

HOW TO CONTACT Send complete ms with cover letter. Include 4-sentence bio. Send SASE for response, return of ms, or send a disposable copy of ms.

PAYMENT/TERMS Pays $5-25.

TIPS "We're looking for high-quality work that takes on big issues in a literary way. Please read our back issues before submitting."

NOW & THEN: THE APPALACHIAN MAGAZINE

East Tennessee State University, Box 70556, Johnson City TN 37614-1707. (423)439-5348. **Fax:** (423)439-6340. **E-mail:** nowandthen@etsu.edu. **E-mail:** sandersr@etsu.edu. **Website:** www.etsu.edu/cass/nowandthen. **Contact:** Randy Sanders, managing editor; Wayne Winkler, music editor; Charlie Warden, photo editor. Estab. 1984. Literary magazine published twice/year. "*Now & Then* accepts a variety of writing genres: fiction, poetry, nonfiction, essays, interviews, memoirs, and book reviews. All submissions must relate to Appalachia and to the issue's specific theme. Our readership is educated and interested in the region."

Now & Then tells the stories of Appalachia and presents a fresh, revealing picture of life in Appalachia, past and present, with engaging articles, personal essays, fiction, poetry, and photography.

NEEDS "Absolutely has to relate to Appalachian theme. Can be about adjustment to new environment, themes of leaving and returning, for instance. Nothing unrelated to region." Accepts 1-2 mss/issue. Publishes ms 4 months after acceptance. Publishes some new writers/year. Length: 1,000-1,500 words.

HOW TO CONTACT Send complete ms. Accepts submissions by mail, e-mail, with a strong preference for e-mail. Include "information we can use for contributor's note." SASE (or IRC). Rarely accepts simultaneous submissions. Reviews fiction.

PAYMENT/TERMS Pays $50 for each accepted article. Pays on publication.

TIPS "Keep in mind that *Now & Then* only publishes material related to the Appalachian region. Plus we only publish fiction that has some plausible connection to a specific issue's themes. We like to offer first-time publication to promising writers."

NTH DEGREE

1219-M Gaskins Rd., Henrico VA 23238. **E-mail:** submissions@nthzine.com. **Website:** www.nthzine.com. **Contact:** Michael D. Pederson. Estab. 2002. Free online fanzine to promote up-and-coming new science fiction and fantasy authors and artists. Also supports the world of fandom and conventions.

No longer accepts hard copy submissions.

NEEDS Length: up to 7,500 words.

HOW TO CONTACT Submit complete ms via e-mail.

PAYMENT/TERMS Pays in contributor's copies.

TIPS "Don't submit anything that you may be ashamed of 10 years later."

NUTHOUSE

P.O. Box 119, Ellenton FL 34222. **Website:** www.nuthousemagazine.com. *Nuthouse*, published every 3 months, uses humor of all kinds, including homespun and political.

NEEDS "We publish all genres, from the homespun to the horrific. We don't automatically dismiss crudity or profanity. We're not prudes. Yet we consider such elements cheap and insulting unless essential to the gag. *Nuthouse* seeks submissions that are original, tightly written, and laugh-out-loud funny." Length: up to 1,000 words. "The shorter, the better."

HOW TO CONTACT Send complete ms with SASE and cover letter. Include estimated word count, bio (paragraph), and list of publications. No e-mail submissions.

PAYMENT/TERMS Pays 1 contributor's copy.

OBSIDIAN

Brown University, **E-mail:** obsidianatbrown@gmail.com. **Website:** obsidian-magazine.tumblr.com. **Contact:** Maya Finoh, managing editor. Estab. 1975. *Obsidian* is a "literary and visual space to showcase the creativity and experiences of black people, specifically at Brown University, formed out of the need for a platform made for us, by us." It is "actively intersectional, safe, and open: a space especially for the stories and voices of black women, black queer and trans people, and black people with disabilities."

NEEDS Length: up to 4,000 words.

HOW TO CONTACT Submit by e-mail. Include brief bio up to 3 sentences.

TIPS "Following proper format is essential. Your title must be intriguing and text clean. Never give up. Some of the writers we publish were rejected many times before we published them."

OHIO TEACHERS WRITE

1209 Heather Run, Wilmington OH 45177. **E-mail:** ohioteacherswrite@octela.org. **Website:** www.octela.org/OTW.html. **Contact:** Eimile Máiréad Green, editor. Estab. 1995. "*Ohio Teachers Write* is a literary magazine published annually by the Ohio Council of Teachers of English Language Arts. This publication seeks to promote both poetry and prose of Ohio teachers and to provide an engaging collection of writing for our readership of educators and other like-minded adults. Invites electronic submissions from both active and retired Ohio educators for our annual literary print magazine."

NEEDS Submissions are limited to Ohio Educators. Length: up to 1,500 words.

HOW TO CONTACT Submit by e-mail.

PAYMENT/TERMS Pays 2 contributor's copies.

TIPS Check website for yearly theme.

ON SPEC

P.O. Box 4727, Station South, Edmonton AB T6E 5G6, Canada. (780)628-7121. **E-mail:** onspec@onspec.ca. **Website:** www.onspec.ca. Estab. 1989. "We publish speculative fiction and poetry by new and established writers, with a strong preference for Canadian-authored works."

See website guidelines for submission announcements. "Please refer to website for information regarding submissions, as we are not open year round."

NEEDS No media tie-in or shaggy-alien stories. No condensed or excerpted novels, religious/inspirational stories, fairy tales. Length: 1,000-6,000 words.

HOW TO CONTACT Send complete ms. Electronic submissions preferred.

TIPS "We want to see stories with plausible characters, a well-constructed, consistent, and vividly described setting, a strong plot, and believable emotions; characters must show us (not tell us) their emotional responses to each other and to the situation and/or challenge they face. Also: Don't send us stories written for television. We don't like media tie-ins, so don't watch TV for inspiration! Read instead! Strong preference given to submissions by Canadians."

ON THE PREMISES: A GOOD PLACE TO START

On the Premises, LLC, 4323 Gingham Court, Alexandria VA 22310. **E-mail:** questions@onthepremises.com. **Website:** www.onthepremises.com. **Contact:** Tarl Roger Kudrick or Bethany Granger, co-publishers. Estab. 2006. Stories published in *On the Premises* are winning entries in contests that are held every 6 months. Each contest challenges writers to produce a great story based on a broad premise that our editors supply as part of the contest. *On the Premises* aims to promote newer and/or relatively unknown writers who can write what we feel are creative, compelling stories told in effective, uncluttered, and evocative prose. Entrants pay no fees, and winners receive cash prizes in addition to publication. Also holds four "mini-contests" a year in which authors are asked to write extremely short fiction (50 words or so) in accordance with special challenges.

Does not read March or September. Receives 50-150 mss/month. Accepts 4-7 mss/issue; 8-14 mss/year. Has published a few well-known authors such as multiple award winner Ken Liu, as well as dozens of lesser known authors and quite a few first-time fiction sellers. Member Small Press Promotions.

NEEDS Themes are announced the day each contest is launched. List of past and current premises available on website. "All genres considered. All stories must be based on the broad premise supplied as part of the contest. Sample premise, taken from the first issue: 'One or more characters are traveling in a vehicle, and never reach their intended destination. Why not? What happens instead?'" No young adult, children's, or "preachy" fiction. "In general, we don't like stories that were written solely to make a social or political point, especially if the story seems to assume that no intelligent person could possibly disagree with the author. Save the ideology for editorial and opinion pieces, please. But above all, we *never ever* want to see stories that do not use the contest premise! Use the premise, and make it 'clear' and 'obvious' that you are using the premise." Length: 1,000-5,000 words. Average length: 3,500 words.

HOW TO CONTACT Submit stories only via submission form at onthepremises.submittable.com/submit. "We no longer accept e-mailed submissions."

PAYMENT/TERMS Pays $60-220.

TIPS "Make sure you use the premise, not just interpret it. If the premise is 'must contain a real live dog,' then think of a creative, compelling way to use a real dog. Revise your draft, then revise again and again. Remember, we judge stories blindly, so craftmanship and creativity matter, not how well known you are."

OPEN MINDS QUARTERLY

NISA/Northern Initiative for Social Action, Northern Initiative for Social Action, 36 Elgin St., 2nd Floor, Sudbury ON P3C 5B4, Canada. (705)222-6472 ext. 303. **E-mail:** openminds@nisa.on.ca. **Website:** www.

openmindsquarterly.com. **Contact:** Dinah Laprairie, editor. Estab. 1997. *Open Minds Quarterly* provides a venue for individuals who have experienced mental illness to express themselves via poetry, short fiction, essays, first-person accounts of living with mental illness, and book/movie reviews. Wants unique, well-written, provocative poetry. Does not want overly graphic or sexual violence.

NEEDS Length: 1,000-3,000 words.

HOW TO CONTACT Submit through website. Cover letter is required. Information in cover letter: indicate your lived experience with mental illness. Reads submissions year round.

PAYMENT/TERMS Pays contributor's copies.

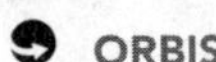 ORBIS

17 Greenhow Ave., West Kirby Wirral CH48 5EL, United Kingdom. **E-mail:** carolebaldock@hotmail.com. **Website:** www.orbisjournal.com. **Contact:** Carole Baldock, editor; Noel Williams, reviews editor. Estab. 1969. "*Orbis* has long been considered one of the top 20 small-press magazines in the UK. We are interested in social inclusion projects and encouraging access to the Arts, young people, Under 20s, and 20-somethings. Subjects for discussion: 'day in the life,' technical, topical."

Please see guidelines on website before submitting.

NEEDS Length: 1,000 words max.

TIPS "Any publication should be read cover to cover because it's the best way to improve your chances of getting published. Enclose SAE with all correspondence. Overseas: 2 IRCs, 3 if work is to be returned."

OXFORD MAGAZINE

OxMag, Miami University, Oxford OH 45056. **Website:** www.oxfordmagazine.org. Estab. 1984. *Oxford Magazine*, published annually online in May, is open in terms of form, content, and subject matter. "Since our premiere in 1984, our magazine has received Pushcart Prizes for both fiction and poetry and has published authors such as Charles Baxter, William Stafford, Robert Pinsky, Stephen Dixon, Helena Maria Viramontes, Andre Dubus, and Stuart Dybek."

Work published in *Oxford Magazine* has been included in the *Pushcart Prize* anthology. Does not read submissions June through August.

NEEDS Length: up to 3,000 words.

HOW TO CONTACT Submit complete ms via online submissions manager.

OYEZ REVIEW

Roosevelt University, Dept. of Literature & Languages, 430 S. Michigan Ave., Chicago IL 60605. **E-mail:** oyezreview@roosevelt.edu. **Website:** oyezreview.wordpress.com. Estab. 1965. Annual magazine of the Creative Writing Program at Roosevelt University, publishing fiction, creative nonfiction, poetry, and art. There are no restrictions on style, theme, or subject matter.

Reading period is August 1-October 1. The journal has featured work from such writers as Charles Bukowski, James McManus, Carla Panciera, Michael Onofrey, Tim Foley, John N. Miller, Gary Fincke, and Barry Silesky, and visual artists Vivian Nunley, C. Taylor, Jennifer Troyer, and Frank Spidale.

NEEDS "We publish short stories and flash fiction on their merit as contemporary literature rather than the category within the genre." Length: up to 5,000 words.

HOW TO CONTACT Send complete ms via online submissions manager or postal mail.

PAYMENT/TERMS Pays 2 contributor's copies.

OYSTER BOY REVIEW

P.O. Box 1483, Pacifica CA 94044. **E-mail:** email_2015@oysterboyreview.com. **Website:** www.oysterboyreview.com. **Contact:** Damon Sauve, editor/publisher. Estab. 1993. Electronic and print magazine. *Oyster Boy Review*, published annually, is interested in "the underrated, the ignored, the misunderstood, and the varietal. We'll make some mistakes."

NEEDS Wants "fiction that revolves around characters in conflict with themselves or each other; a plot that has a beginning, a middle, and an end; a narrative with a strong moral center (not necessarily 'moralistic'); a story with a satisfying resolution to the conflict; and an ethereal something that contributes to the mystery of a question but does not necessarily seek or contrive to answer it." Submit complete ms by postal mail or e-mail. No genre fiction.

PAYMENT/TERMS Pays 2 contributor's copies.

TIPS "Keep writing, keep submitting, keep revising."

PACIFICA LITERARY REVIEW

E-mail: pacificalitreview@gmail.com. **Website:** www.pacificareview.com. **Contact:** Matt Muth, editor-in-chief; Courtney Johnson, managing editor. "*Pacifica*

Literary Review is a small literary arts magazine based in Seattle. Our print editions are published biannually in winter and summer and we publish year-round on the web. *PLR* is now accepting submissions of poetry, fiction, creative nonfiction, author interviews, and b&w photography. Submission period: September 15-December 15 and Jan 15-May 15."

NEEDS Wants literary fiction and flash fiction. Length: up to 6,000 words for literary fiction; 300-1,000 words for flash fiction.

HOW TO CONTACT Submit complete ms.

PACIFIC REVIEW

Dept. of English and Comparative Literature, San Diego State University, 5500 Campanile Dr., MC6020, San Diego CA 92182-6020. **E-mail:** pacrevjournal@gmail.com. **Website:** pacificreview.sdsu.edu. **Contact:** Ryan Kelly, editor in chief. "We welcome submissions of previously published poems, short stories, translations, and creative nonfiction, including essays and reviews." For information on theme issues see website. **Publishes 15 new writers/year.** Recently published work by Ai, Alurista, Susan Daitch, Lawrence Ferlinghetti, and William T. Vollmann.

Does not accept e-mail submissions. See website for theme.

NEEDS Length: up to 5,000 words.

HOW TO CONTACT Submit ms via online submissions manager. Include cover letter with name, postal address, e-mail addresss, phone number, and short bio.

PAYMENT/TERMS Pays 2 contributor's copies.

TIPS "We welcome all submissions, especially those created in or in the context of the West Coast/California and the space of our borders."

PACKINGTOWN REVIEW

111 S. Lincoln St., Batavia IL 60510. **E-mail:** editors@packingtownreview.com. **E-mail:** packingtownreview@gmail.com. **Website:** www.packingtownreview.com. Estab. 2008. *Packingtown Review* publishes imaginative and critical prose and poetry by emerging and established writers. Welcomes submissions of poetry, scholarly articles, drama, creative nonfiction, fiction, and literary translation, as well as genre-bending pieces.

NEEDS Does not want to see uninspired or unrevised work. Wants to avoid fantasy, science fiction, overtly religious, or romantic pieces. Length: up to 4,000 words.

HOW TO CONTACT Send complete ms with cover letter. Include estimated word count, brief bio, SASE.

PAYMENT/TERMS Pays 2 contributor's copies.

TIPS "We are looking for well-crafted prose. We are open to most styles and forms. We are also looking for prose that takes risks and does so successfully. We will consider articles about prose."

PAINTED BRIDE QUARTERLY

Drexel University, Department of English and Philosophy, 3141 Chestnut St., Philadelphia PA 19104. **E-mail:** pbq@drexel.edu. **Website:** pbq.drexel.edu. Estab. 1973. *Painted Bride Quarterly* seeks literary fiction (experimental and traditional), poetry, and artwork and photographs.

NEEDS Publishes theme-related work; check website. Holds annual fiction contests. Length: up to 5,000 words.

HOW TO CONTACT Send complete ms.

PAYMENT/TERMS Pays contributor's copy.

TIPS "We look for freshness of idea incorporated with high-quality writing. We receive an awful lot of nicely written work with worn-out plots. We want quality in whatever—we hold experimental work to as strict standards as anything else. Many of our readers write fiction; most of them enjoy a good reading. We hope to be an outlet for quality. A good story gives, first, enjoyment to the reader. We've seen a good many of them lately, and we've published the best of them."

PANK

PANK, Department of Humanities, 1400 Townsend Dr., Houghton MI 49931-1200. **E-mail:** mbartley@pankmagazine.com. **Website:** www.pankmagazine.com. **Contact:** M. Bartley Seigel, editor. Estab. 2006. "*PANK* Magazine fosters access to emerging and experimental poetry and prose, publishing the brightest and most promising writers for the most adventurous readers. To the end of the road, up country, a far shore, the edge of things, to a place of amalgamation and unplumbed depths, where the known is made and unmade, and where unimagined futures are born, a place inhabited by contradictions, a place of quirk and startling anomaly. *PANK*, no soft pink hands allowed."

NEEDS "Bright, new, energetic, passionate writing, writing that pushes our tender little buttons and gets us excited. Push our tender buttons, excite us, and we'll publish you."

HOW TO CONTACT Send complete ms through online submissions manager.

PAYMENT/TERMS Pays $20, a one-year subscription, and a *PANK* t-shirt.

TIPS "To read *PANK* is to know *PANK*. Or, read a lot within the literary magazine and small press universe—there's plenty to choose from. Unfortunately, we see a lot of submissions from writers who have clearly read neither *PANK* nor much else. Serious writers are serious readers. Read. Seriously."

PAPERPLATES

19 Kenwood Ave., Toronto ON M6C 2R8, Canada. (416)651-2551. **E-mail:** magazine@paperplates.org. **Website:** www.paperplates.org. **Contact:** Bernard Kelly, publisher. Estab. 1990. *paperplates* is a literary quarterly published in Toronto. "We make no distinction between veterans and beginners. Some of our contributors have published several books; some have never before published a single line."

No longer accepts IRCs.

NEEDS Length: up to 7,500 words.

HOW TO CONTACT Submit by mail or e-mail. "Do not send fiction as an e-mail attachment. Copy the first 300 words or so into the body of your message. If you prefer not to send a fragment, you have the option of using surface mail." Include short bio with submission.

THE PARIS REVIEW

544 W. 27th St., New York NY 10001. (212)343-1333. **E-mail:** queries@theparisreview.org. **Website:** www.theparisreview.org. **Contact:** Lorin Stein, editor; Robyn Creswell, poetry editor. *The Paris Review* publishes "fiction and poetry of superlative quality, whatever the genre, style, or mode. Our contributors include prominent, as well as less well-known and previously unpublished writers. The Writers at Work interview series includes important contemporary writers discussing their own work and the craft of writing."

Address submissions to proper department. Do not make submissions via e-mail.

NEEDS Study the publication. Annual Plimpton Prize award of $10,000 given to a new voice published in the magazine. Recently published work by Ottessa Moshfegh, John Jeremiah Sullivan, and Lydia Davis. Length: no limit.

HOW TO CONTACT Send complete ms.

PAYMENT/TERMS Pays $1,000-3,000.

PASSAGER

Passager Press, 1420 N. Charles St., Baltimore MD 21201. **E-mail:** editors@passagerbooks.com. **Website:** www.passagerbooks.com. Estab. 1990. "*Passager* has a special focus on older writers. Its mission is to encourage, engage, and strengthen the imagination well into old age and to give mature readers oppertunities that are sometimes closed off to them in our youth-oriented culture. We are dedicated to honoring the creativity that takes hold in later years and to making public the talents of those over the age of 50." Passager publishes 2 issues/year, an Open issue (fall/winter) and a Poetry Contest issue (spring/summer).

NEEDS Accepts submissions from writers over 50. Has published Miriam Karme, Lucille Schulberg Warner, Sally Bellerose, and Craig Hartglass. Length: up to 4,000 words.

HOW TO CONTACT Send complete ms with cover letter. Check website for guidelines. Include estimated word count, brief bio, list of publications. Send either SASE (or IRC) for return of ms or disposable copy of ms and #10 SASE for reply only.

PAYMENT/TERMS Pays 1 contributor's copy.

TIPS "Stereotyped images of old age will be rejected immediately. Write humorous, tongue-in-cheek essays. Read the publication, or at least visit the website."

PASSAGES NORTH

English Department, Northern Michigan University, 1401 Presque Isle Ave., Marquette MI 49855. (906)227-1203. **E-mail:** passages@nmu.edu. **Website:** www.passagesnorth.com. **Contact:** Jennifer A. Howard, editor in chief; Matt Weinkam and Robin McCarthy, managing editors; Matthew Gavin Frank, hybrids editor; Rachel May, nonfiction editor; Patricia Killelea, poetry editor; Monica McFawn, fiction editor. Estab. 1979. *Passages North*, published annually in spring, prints poetry, short fiction, creative nonfiction, essays, and interviews.

NEEDS "Don't be afraid to surprise us." No genre fiction, science fiction, "typical commercial-press work." Length: up to 7,000 words.

HOW TO CONTACT Send 1 short story or as many as 3 short-short stories (paste them all into 1 document).

TIPS "We look for voice, energetic prose, writers who take risks. We look for an engaging story in which the author evokes an emotional response from the reader through carefully rendered scenes, complex characters, and a smart, narrative design. Revise, revise. Read what we publish."

PENNSYLVANIA ENGLISH

Indiana University of Pennsylvania, Department of English, Indiana University of Pennsylvania, HSS 506A, 981 Grant St., Indiana PA 15705. (724)357-2262. **E-mail:** mtwill@iup.edu. **Website:** https://paenglish.submittable.com/submit. **Contact:** Dr. Michael T. Williamson, editor (mtwill@iup.edu); Dr. Michael Cox, nonfiction and fiction editor (mwcox@pitt.edu); Dr. Anthony Vallone, poetry editor (avallone@psu.edu); Dr. John Marsden, literary criticism editor (marsden@iup.edu). Estab. 1985. *Pennsylvania English*, published annually, is "sponsored by the Pennsylvania College English Association. Our philosophy is quality. We publish literary fiction (and poetry and nonfiction). Our intended audience is literate, college-educated people."

Reads mss during the summer. Publishes 4-6 new writers/year. Has published work by Dave Kress, Dan Leone, Paul West, Liz Rosenberg, Walt MacDonald, Amy Pence, Jennifer Richter, and Jeff Schiff.

NEEDS No genre fiction or romance.

HOW TO CONTACT Submit via the online submission manager at https://paenglish.submittable.com/submit. "For all submissions, please include a brief bio for the contributors' page. Be sure to include your name, address, phone number, e-mail address, institutional affiliation (if you have one), the title of your short story, and any other relevant information. We will edit if necessary for space."

PAYMENT/TERMS Pays 1 contributor's copy.

TIPS "Quality of the writing is our only measure. We're not impressed by long-winded cover letters detailing awards and publications we've never heard of. Beginners and professionals have the same chance with us. We receive stacks of competently written but boring fiction. For a story to rise from the rejection pile, it takes more than the basic competence."

PENNSYLVANIA LITERARY JOURNAL

Anaphora Literary Press, 2419 Southdale Drive, Hephzibah GA 30815, USA. (470)289-6395. **E-mail:** director@anaphoraliterary.com. **Website:** anaphoraliterary.com. **Contact:** Anna Faktorovich, editor/director. Estab. 2009. "*Pennsylvania Literary Journal* is a printed, peer-reviewed journal that publishes critical essays, book reviews, short stories, interviews, photographs, art, and poetry. Published tri-annually, it features special issues on a wide variety of different fields from film studies to literary criticism to interviews with bestsellers. Submissions in all genres from emerging and established writers are warmly welcomed."

NEEDS Detailed, descriptive, and original short stories are preferred. No word limit.

HOW TO CONTACT Send complete ms via e-mail.

PAYMENT/TERMS Does not provide payment.

TIPS "We are just looking for great writing. Send your materials; if they are good and you don't mind working for free, we'll take it."

PENNY DREADFUL: TALES & POEMS OF FANTASTIC TERROR

P.O. Box 719, Radio City Station, Hell's Kitchen NY 10101-0719. **E-mail:** mmpendragon@aol.com. **Website:** www.mpendragon.com/pennydreadful.html. Estab. 1996. *Penny Dreadful: Tales & Poems of Fanastic Terror*, published irregularly (about once a year), features goth-romantic poetry and prose. Publishes poetry, short stories, essays, letters, listings, reviews, and b&w artwork "which celebrate the darker aspects of Man, the World, and their Creator." Wants "literary horror in the tradition of Poe, M.R. James, Shelley, M.P. Shiel, and LeFanu—dark, disquieting tales and verses designed to challenge the reader's perception of human nature, morality, and man's place within the Darkness. Stories and poems should be set prior to 1910 and/or possess a timeless quality." Does not want "references to 20th- and 21st-century personages/events, graphic sex, strong language, excessive gore and shock elements."

"Works appearing in *Penny Dreadful* have been reprinted in *The Year's Best Fantasy and Horror.*" *Penny Dreadful* nominates best tales and poems for Pushcart Prizes.

NEEDS Length: up to 5,000 words.

HOW TO CONTACT Submit complete ms by mail or e-mail. "Mss should be submitted in the standard, professional format: typed, double-spaced, name and address on the first page, name and title of work on all subsequent pages, etc. Include SASE for reply. Also include brief cover letter with a brief bio and publication history."

PAYMENT/TERMS Pays 1 contributor's copy.

PERMAFROST: A LITERARY JOURNAL

c/o English Dept., Univ. of Alaska Fairbanks, P.O. Box 755720, Fairbanks AK 99775. **E-mail:** editor@permafrostmag.com. **Website:** permafrostmag.com. Estab. 1977. *Permafrost Magazine*, a literary journal, contains poems, short stories, creative nonfiction, b&w drawings, photographs, and prints. We print both new and established writers, hoping and expecting to see the best work out there. We have published work by E. Ethelbert Miller, W. Loran Smith, Peter Orlovsky, Jim Wayne Miller, Allen Ginsberg, and Andy Warhol.

NEEDS Length: up to 8,000 words.

HOW TO CONTACT Submit complete ms via online submissions manager at permafrostmag.submittable.com; "e-mail submissions will not be read."

PAYMENT/TERMS Pays 1 contributor's copy. Reduced contributor rate of $5 on additional copies.

PERSIMMON TREE: MAGAZINE OF THE ARTS BY WOMEN OVER SIXTY

1534 Campus Dr., Berkeley CA 94708. (510)486-2332. **E-mail:** editor@persimmontree.org. **E-mail:** submissions@persimmontree.org. **Website:** www.persimmontree.org. **Contact:** Sue Leonard, editor. "*Persimmon Tree*, an online magazine, is a showcase for the creativity and talent of women over sixty. Too often older women's artistic work is ignored or disregarded, and only those few who are already established receive the attention they deserve. Yet many women are at the height of their creative abilities in their later decades and have a great deal to contribute. *Persimmon Tree* is committed to bringing this wealth of fiction, nonfiction, poetry, and art to a broader audience, for the benefit of all."

NEEDS Length: under 3,500 words.

HOW TO CONTACT Submit complete ms via e-mail. "Note: You must be signed onto the e-mail newsletter to be considered for publication."

TIPS "High quality of writing and an interesting or unique point of view make a ms stand out. Make it clear that you're familiar with the magazine. Tell us why the piece would work for our audience."

PERSPECTIVES

c/o Jason Lief, Dordt College, 498 Fourth Ave. NE, Sioux Center, Sioux Center IA 51250. **E-mail:** submissions@perspectivesjournal.org. **Website:** perspectivesjournal.org. **Contact:** Jason Lief. "*Perspectives* is a journal of theology in the broad Reformed tradition. We seek to express the Reformed faith theologically; to engage issues that Reformed Christians meet in personal, ecclesiastical, and societal life; and thus to contribute to the mission of the church of Jesus Christ.The editors are interested in submissions that contribute to a contemporary Reformed theological discussion. Our readers tend to be affiliated with the Presbyterian Church (USA), the Reformed Church in America, and the Christian Reformed Church. Some of our subscribers are academics or pastors, but we also gear our articles to thoughtful, literate laypeople who want to engage in Reformed theological reflection on faith and culture."

NEEDS Length: up to 3,000 words.

HOW TO CONTACT Submit complete ms by e-mail.

PHILADELPHIA STORIES

Fiction/Art/Poetry of the Delaware Valley, 93 Old York Rd., Suite 1/#1-753, Jenkintown PA 19046. **E-mail:** christine@philadelphiastories.org; info@philadelphiastories.org. **Website:** www.philadelphiastories.org. **Contact:** Christine Weiser, executive director/co-publisher. Estab. 2004. *Philadelphia Stories*, published quarterly, publishes "fiction, poetry, essays, and art written by authors living in, or originally from, Pennsylvania, Delaware, or New Jersey. *Philadelphia Stories* also hosts 2 national writing contests: The Marguerite McGlinn Short Story Contest ($2,000 first-place prize; $500 second-place prize; $250 third-place prize) and the Sandy Crimmins National Poetry Contest ($1,000 first-place prize, 3 $100 runner-up prizes). Visit our website for details." *Philadelphia Stories* also launched a "junior" version in 2012 for Philadelphia-area writers ages 12 and younger and a "teen" version for writers aged 13-18. Visit www.philadelphiastories.org/junior for details.

Member: CLMP.

NEEDS Receives 45-80 mss/month. Accepts 3-4 mss/issue for print, additional 1-2 online; 12-16 mss/year for print, 4-8 online. Publishes 50% new writers/year. Also publishes book reviews. Send review queries to: info@philadelphiastories.org. "We will consider anything that is well written but are most inclined to publish literary or mainstream fiction. We are *not* particularly interested in most genres (sci fi/fantasy, romance, etc.)." Length: up to 5,000 words. Average length: 4,000 words. Also publishes short shorts; average length: 800 words.

PAYMENT/TERMS Pays $25 honorarium from the Conrad Weiser Author Fund and 2+ contributor's copies.

TIPS "We look for exceptional, polished prose, a controlled voice, strong characters and place, and interesting subjects. Follow guidelines. We cannot stress this enough. Read every guideline carefully and thoroughly before sending anything out. Send out only polished material. We reject many quality pieces for various reasons; try not to take rejection personally. Just because your piece isn't right for one publication doesn't mean it's bad. Selection is an extremely subjective process."

PHOEBE: A JOURNAL OF LITERATURE AND ART

MSN 2C5, George Mason University, 400 University Dr., Fairfax VA 22030. **Website:** www.phoebejournal.com. Estab. 1971. Publishes poetry, fiction, nonfiction, and visual art. "*Phoebe* prides itself on supporting up-and-coming writers, whose style, form, voice, and subject matter demonstrate a vigorous appeal to the senses, intellect, and emotions of our readers."

NEEDS No romance or erotica. Length: up to 4,000 words.

HOW TO CONTACT Submit 1 fiction submission via online submission manager.

PAYMENT/TERMS Pays 2 contributor's copies and $500 for contest winner.

THE PINCH

English Department, University of Memphis, Memphis TN 38152. (901)678-4591. **E-mail:** editor@pinchjournal.com. **Website:** www.pinchjournal.com. **Contact:** Tim Johnston, editor in chief; Derek Moseley, managing editor. Estab. 1980. Semiannual literary magazine. "We publish fiction, creative nonfiction, poetry, and art of literary quality by both established and emerging artists."

"The Pinch Literary Awards in Fiction, Poetry, and Nonfiction offer a $1,000 prize and publication. Check our website for details."

NEEDS Wants "character-based" fiction with a "fresh use of language." No genre fiction. Length: up to 5,000 words.

HOW TO CONTACT "We do not accept submissions via e-mail. Submissions sent via e-mail will not receive a response. To submit, see guidelines." Submit through mail or via online submissions manager.

TIPS "We have a new look and a new edge. We're soliciting work from writers with a national or international reputation as well as strong, interesting work from emerging writers."

THE PINK CHAMELEON

E-mail: dpfreda@juno.com. **Website:** www.thepinkchameleon.com. **Contact:** Dorothy Paula Freda, editor/publisher. Estab. 2000. *The Pink Chameleon*, published annually online, contains "family-oriented, upbeat poetry, stories, essays, and articles, any genre in good taste that gives hope for the future."

Reading period is January 1-April 30 and September 1-October 31.

NEEDS "No violence for the sake of violence." No novels or novel excerpts. Length: 500-2,500 words; average length: 2,000 words.

HOW TO CONTACT Send complete ms in the body of the e-mail. No attachments. Accepts reprints. Has published work by Deanne F. Purcell, Martin Green, Albert J. Manachino, James W. Collins, Ron Arnold, Sally Kosmalski, Susan Marie Davniero, and Glenn D. Hayes.

PAYMENT/TERMS No payment.

TIPS Wants "simple, honest, evocative emotion; upbeat fiction and nonfiction submissions that give hope for the future; well-paced plots; stories, poetry, articles, essays that speak from the heart. Read guidelines carefully. Use a good, but not ostentatious, opening hook. Stories should have a beginning, middle, and end that make the reader feel the story was worth his or her time. This also applies to articles and essays. In the latter 2, wrap your comments and conclusions in a neatly packaged final paragraph. Turnoffs include violence and bad language. Simple, genuine, and sensitive work does not need to shock with vulgarity to be interesting and enjoyable."

PMS POEMMEMOIRSTORY

University of Alabama at Birmingham, HB 217, 1530 Third Ave. S., Birmingham AL 35294. (205)934-2641. **Fax:** (205)975-8125. **E-mail:** poemmemoirstory@gmail.com. **Website:** pms-journal.org. **Contact:** Kerry Madden, editor in chief. "*PMS poemmemoirstory* appears once a year. We accept unpublished, original submissions of poetry, memoir, and short fiction during our January 1-March 31 reading period. We accept simultaneous submissions; however, we ask that you please contact us immediately if your piece is published elsewhere so we may free up space for other authors. While *PMS* is a journal of exclusively women's writing, the subject field is wide open."

"*PMS* has gone all-digital on Submittable. There is now a $3 fee, which covers costs associated with our online submissions system. Please send all submissions to poemmemoirstory.submittable.com/submit."

NEEDS Length: up to 15 pages or 4,300 words.

HOW TO CONTACT Submit through online submissions manager.

PAYMENT/TERMS Pays 2 contributor's copies.

TIPS "We strongly encourage you to familiarize yourself with *PMS* before submitting. You can find links to some examples of what we publish in the pages of *PMS 8* and *PMS 9*. We look forward to reading your work."

POCKETS

The Upper Room, P.O. Box 340004, Nashville TN 37203. (615)340-7333. **E-mail:** pockets@upperroom.org. **Website:** pockets.upperroom.org. **Contact:** Lynn W. Gilliam, editor. Estab. 1981. In addition to receiving regular submissions, *Pockets* sponsors a fiction contest each year. Magazine published 11 times/year. "*Pockets* is a Christian devotional magazine for children ages 6-12. All submissions should address the broad theme of the magazine. Each issue is built around a theme with material which can be used by children in a variety of ways. Scripture stories, fiction, poetry, prayers, art, graphics, puzzles and activities are included. Submissions do not need to be overtly religious. They should help children experience a Christian lifestyle that is not always a neatly wrapped moral package but is open to the continuing revelation of God's will. Seasonal material, both secular and liturgical, is desired."

Does not accept e-mail or fax submissions.

NEEDS "Stories should contain lots of action, use believable dialogue, be simply written, and be relevant to the problems faced by this age group in everyday life." Length: 600-1,000 words.

HOW TO CONTACT Submit complete ms by mail. No e-mail submissions.

TIPS "Theme stories, role models, and retold scripture stories are most open to freelancers. Poetry is also open. It is very helpful if writers read our writers' guidelines and themes on our website."

POETICA MAGAZINE, CONTEMPORARY JEWISH WRITING

P.O. Box 11014, Norfolk VA 23517. **E-mail:** poeticapublishing@aol.com. **Website:** www.poeticamagazine.com. Estab. 2002. *Poetica Magazine, Contemporary Jewish Writing*, published in print 3 times/year, offers "an outlet for the many writers who draw from their Jewish background and experiences to create poetry/prose/short stories, giving both emerging and recognized writers the opportunity to share their work with the larger community."

NEEDS Length: up to 4 pages.

HOW TO CONTACT Submit ms through online submissions manager. Include e-mail, bio, and mailing address.

PAYMENT/TERMS Pays 1 contributor's copy.

TIPS "We publish original, unpublished works by Jewish and non-Jewish writers alike. We are interested in works that have the courage to acknowledge, challenge, and celebrate modern Jewish life beyond distinctions of secular and sacred. We like accessible works that find fresh meaning in old traditions that recognize the challenges of our generation. We evaluate works on several levels, including its skillful use of craft, its ability to hold interest, and layers of meaning."

PORTLAND REVIEW

Portland State University, P.O. Box 751, Portland OR 97207. **Website:** portlandreview.org. **Contact:** Alex Dannemiller, editor-in-chief. Estab. 1956. Portland Review has been publishing exceptional writing and artwork by local and international artists since 1956.

NEEDS Publishes 40 mss per year.

HOW TO CONTACT Guidelines available online: portlandreview.submittable.com/submit.

PAYMENT/TERMS Pays contributor's copies.

TIPS Please visit portlandreview.org for access to our submission manager and for more information.

POTOMAC REVIEW: A JOURNAL OF ARTS & HUMANITIES

Montgomery College, 51 Mannakee St., MT/212, Rockville MD 20850. (240)567-4100. **E-mail:** PotomacReviewEditor@montgomerycollege.edu. **E-mail:** potomacreview.submittable.com. **Website:** blogs.montgomerycollege.edu/potomacreview/. **Contact:**

Julie Wakeman-Linn, editor-in-chief; Kathleen Smith, poetry editor; John W. Wang, fiction editor; J. Howard, technology editor. Estab. 1994. *Potomac Review: A Journal of Arts & Humanities*, published semiannually in August and February, welcomes poetry and fiction from across the spectrum, both traditional and nontraditional poetry, free verse and in-form (translations accepted). We like traditional fiction and experimental or meta fiction and flash fiction. Essays and creative nonfiction are also welcome.

Reading period: Year round, although slower in the summer. Has published work by David Wagoner, Jacob Appel, Sandra Beasley, Marilyn Kallet, Katie Cortese, and Amy Holman.

NEEDS Length: up to 5,000 words.

HOW TO CONTACT Submit electronically through website.

THE PRAIRIE JOURNAL

P.O. Box 68073, 28 Crowfoot Terrace NW, Calgary AB Y3G 3N8, Canada. **E-mail:** editor@prairiejournal.org (queries only); prairiejournal@yahoo.com. **Website:** www.prairiejournal.org. **Contact:** A.E. Burke, literary editor. Estab. 1983. "The audience is literary, university, library, scholarly, and creative readers/writers."

"Use our mailing address for submissions and queries with samples or for clippings."

NEEDS No genre (romance, horror, western—sagebrush or cowboys), erotic, science fiction, or mystery. Length: 100-3,000 words.

HOW TO CONTACT Send complete ms. No e-mail submissions.

PAYMENT/TERMS Pays $10-75.

TIPS "We publish many, many new writers and are always open to unsolicited submissions because we are 100% freelance. Do not send U.S. stamps; always use IRCs. We have poems, interviews, stories, and reviews online (query first)."

PRAIRIE SCHOONER

The University of Nebraska Press, Prairie Schooner, 110 Andrews Hall, University of Nebraska, Lincoln NE 68588. (402)472-0911. **E-mail:** prairieschooner@unl.edu. **Website:** prairieschooner.unl.edu. **Contact:** Ashley Strosnider, managing editor. Estab. 1926. "We look for the best fiction, poetry, and nonfiction available to publish, and our readers expect to read stories, poems, and essays of extremely high quality. We try to publish a variety of styles, topics, themes, points of view, and writers with a variety of backgrounds in all stages of their careers. We like work that is compelling—intellectually or emotionally—either in form, language, or content."

Submissions must be received between September 1 and May 1. Poetry published in *Prairie Schooner* has been selected for inclusion in *The Best American Poetry* and *The Pushcart Prize*.

NEEDS "We try to remain open to a variety of styles, themes, and subject matter. We look for high-quality writing, 3-D characters, well-wrought plots, setting, etc. We are open to realistic and/or experimental fiction."

HOW TO CONTACT Send complete ms with SASE and cover letter listing previous publications (where, when).

PAYMENT/TERMS Pays 3 copies of the issue in which the writer's work is published.

TIPS "Send us your best, most carefully crafted work, and be persistent. Submit again and again. Constantly work on improving your writing. Read widely in literary fiction, nonfiction, and poetry. Read *Prairie Schooner* to know what we publish."

PREMONITIONS

13 Hazely Combe, Arrenton Isle of Wight PO30 3AJ, United Kingdom. **E-mail:** mail@pigasuspress.co.uk. **Website:** www.pigasuspress.co.uk. **Contact:** Tony Lee, editor. "Science fiction and horror stories, plus genre poetry and fantastic artwork."

NEEDS Wants "original, high-quality SF/fantasy. Horror must have a science fiction element and be psychological or scary, rather than simply gory. Cutting-edge SF and experimental writing styles (cross-genre scenarios, slipstream, etc.) are always welcome." "No supernatural fantasy-horror." Length: 500-6,000 words. Send 1 story at a time.

HOW TO CONTACT Submit via mail and include SAE or IRC if you want material returned. "Use a standard ms format: double-spaced text, no right-justify, no staples." Do not send submissions via e-mail, unless by special request from editor. Include personalized cover letter with brief bio and publication credits.

PAYMENT/TERMS Pays minimum $5 or £5 per 1,000 words, plus copy of magazine.

TIPS "Potential contributors are advised to study recent issues of the magazine."

PRISM INTERNATIONAL

Dept. of Creative Writing, Buch E462, 1866 Main Mall, University of British Columbia, Vancouver British Columbia V6T 1Z1, Canada. (604)822-2514. **Fax:** (604)822-3616. **E-mail:** prismcirculation@gmail.com. **Website:** www.prismmagazine.ca. Estab. 1959. A quarterly international journal of contemporary writing—fiction, poetry, drama, creative nonfiction and translation. *PRISM international* is 80 pages, digest-sized, elegantly printed, flat-spined, with original color artwork on a glossy card cover. Readership: public and university libraries, individual subscriptions, bookstores—a world-wide audience concerned with the contemporary in literature. "We have no thematic or stylistic allegiances: Excellence is our main criterion for acceptance of mss." Receives 1,000 submissions/year, accepts about 80. Circulation is for 1,200 subscribers. Subscription: $35/year for Canadian subscriptions, $40/year for US subscriptions, $45/year for international. Sample: $13.

NEEDS Experimental, traditional. New writing that is contemporary and literary. Short stories and self-contained novel excerpts (up to 25 double-spaced pages). Works of translation are eagerly sought and should be accompanied by a copy of the original. Would like to see more translations.

HOW TO CONTACT Send complete ms by mail: Department of Creative Writing, Buch E462, 1866 Main Mall, University of British Columbia, Vancouver BC V6T 1Z1 Canada; or submit online through prismmagazine.ca. "Keep it simple. U.S. contributors take note: Do not send SASEs with U.S. stamps, they are not valid in Canada. Send International Reply Coupons instead." Responds in 4 months to queries; 3-6 months to mss.

PAYMENT/TERMS Pays $20/printed page of prose, $40/printed page of poetry, and 2 copies of issue.

TIPS "We are looking for new and exciting fiction. Excellence is still our No. 1 criterion. As well as poetry, imaginative nonfiction and fiction, we are especially open to translations of all kinds, very short fiction pieces and drama which work well on the page. Translations must come with a copy of the original language work."

PSEUDOPOD

Escape Artists, Inc., P.O. Box 965609, Marietta GA 30066. **E-mail:** editor@pseudopod.org. **Website:** pseudopod.org. **Contact:** Shawn M. Garrett and Alex Hofelich, co-editors. Estab. 2006. "*Pseudopod* is the premier horror podcast magazine. Every week we bring you chilling short stories from some of today's best horror authors, in convenient audio format for your computer or MP3 player."

NEEDS Guidelines available at pseudopod.org/guidelines/. Submit via pseudopod.submittable.com/submit. Length: 2,000-6,000 words (short fiction); 500-1,500 words (flash fiction).

PAYMENT/TERMS Pays 6¢/word for original fiction, $100 for short fiction reprints, $20 for flash fiction.

TIPS "Let the writing be guided by a strong sense of who the (hopefully somewhat interesting) protagonist is, even if zero time is spent developing any other characters. Preferably, tell the story using standard past tense, third person, active voice."

A PUBLIC SPACE

323 Dean St., Brooklyn NY 11217. (718)858-8067. **E-mail:** general@apublicspace.org. **Website:** www.apublicspace.org. **Contact:** Brigid Hughes, founding editor; Anne McPeak, managing editor. *A Public Space*, published quarterly, is an independent magazine of literature and culture. "In an era that has relegated literature to the margins, we plan to make fiction and poetry the stars of a new conversation. We believe that stories are how we make sense of our lives and how we learn about other lives. We believe that stories matter."

Accepts unsolicited submissions from September 15-April 15. Submissions accepted through Submittable or by mail (with SASE).

NEEDS No word limit.

HOW TO CONTACT Submit 1 complete ms via online submissions manager.

PUERTO DEL SOL

New Mexico State University, English Dept., P.O. Box 30001, MSC 3E, Las Cruces NM 88003. (575)646-3931. **E-mail:** puertodelsoljournal@gmail.com. **Website:** www.puertodelsol.org. **Contact:** Evan Lavender-Smith, editor in chief; Carmen Gimenez Smith, poetry editor; Lily Hoang, prose editor. Estab. 1964. Publishes innovative work from emerging and established writers and artists. Wants poetry, fiction, nonfiction, drama, theory, artwork, interviews, reviews, and interesting combinations thereof.

Reading period is September 15-December 1 and January 1-March 1.

NEEDS Accepts 8-12 mss/issue; 16-24 mss/year. Publishes several new writers/year. Has published work by David Trinidad, Molly Gaudry, Ray Gonzalez, Cynthia Cruz, Steve Tomasula, Denise Leto, Rae Bryant, Joshua Cohen, Blake Butler, Trinie Dalton, and Rick Moody.

HOW TO CONTACT Send 1 short story or 2-4 short short stories at a time through online submission manager.

PAYMENT/TERMS Pays 2 contributor's copies.

TIPS "We are especially pleased to publish emerging writers who work to push their art form or field of study in new directions."

QUANTUM FAIRY TALES

E-mail: editor@quantumfairytales.com. **Website:** quantumfairytales.com. **Contact:** The Gnomies. Estab. October 2012. *Quantum Fairy Tales* is a nonprofit, all-volunteer, all-donation, quarterly e-zine showcasing art and literature with elements of science fiction, fantasy, and the supernatural, with weekly website articles and author/artist highlights. "The best part about *QFT* is that real, live gnomies reply with feedback to every submission."

NEEDS Length: up to 7,000 words. Seeking all varieties of speculative fiction.

HOW TO CONTACT E-mail fiction submissions with title, type of submission, and word count in submission line.

TIPS "Your writing and art work must fall in the category of speculative fiction for us to consider it. Every submission gets a free critique whether published or not. If you do not hear from us within 3 months, please give us a nudge. Thank you!"

QUARTER AFTER EIGHT

Ohio University, 360 Ellis Hall, Athens OH 45701. **Website:** www.quarteraftereight.org. **Contact:** Patrick Swaney and Claire Eder, editors. "*Quarter After Eight* is an annual literary journal devoted to the exploration of innovative writing. We celebrate work that directly challenges the conventions of language, style, voice, or idea in literary forms. In its aesthetic commitment to diverse forms, *QAE* remains a unique publication among contemporary literary magazines." Reading period: October 15-April 15.

Holds annual short prose (any genre) contest with grand prize of $1,000. Deadline is November 30.

NEEDS Length: no more than 10,000 words.

HOW TO CONTACT Submit through online submissions manager.

PAYMENT/TERMS Pays 2 contributor's copies.

TIPS "We look for prose and poetry that is innovative, exploratory, and—most importantly—well written. Please subscribe to our journal and read what is published to get acquainted with the *QAE* aesthetic."

QUARTERLY WEST

University of Utah, 255 S. Central Campus Dr., Room 3500, Salt Lake City UT 84112. **E-mail:** quarterlywest@gmail.com. **Website:** www.quarterlywest.com. **Contact:** Claire Wahmanholm and Sara Eliza Johnson, editors. Estab. 1976. "We publish fiction, poetry, nonfiction, and new media in long and short formats, and will consider experimental as well as traditional works."

Quarterly West was awarded first place for Editorial Content from the American Literary Magazine Awards. Work published in the magazine has been selected for inclusion in the *Pushcart Prize* anthology, the *Best of the Net* anthology, and *The Best American Short Stories* anthology.

NEEDS No preferred lengths; interested in longer, fuller short stories and short shorts. Accepts 6-10 mss/year. No detective, science fiction, or romance.

HOW TO CONTACT Send complete ms using online submissions manager only.

TIPS "We publish a special section of short shorts every issue, and we also sponsor an annual novella contest. We are open to experimental work—potential contributors should read the magazine! Don't send more than 1 story per submission. Novella competition guidelines available online. We prefer work with interesting language and detail—plot or narrative are less important. We don't do religious work."

QUEEN'S QUARTERLY

144 Barrie St., Queen's University, Kingston ON K7L 3N6, Canada. (613)533-2667. **E-mail:** queens.quarterly@queensu.ca. **Website:** www.queensu.ca/quarterly. **Contact:** Joan Harcourt, literary editor (fiction and poetry); Boris Castel, nonfiction editor (articles, essays and reviews). Estab. 1893. *Queen's Quarterly* is "a general interest intellectual review featuring articles on science, politics, humanities, arts and letters, extensive book reviews, and some poetry and fiction."

Has published work by Gail Anderson-Dargatz, Tim Bowling, Emma Donohue, Viktor Carr, Mark Jarman, Rick Bowers, and Dennis Bock.

NEEDS Length: 2,500-3,000 words. "Submissions over 3,000 words shall not be accepted."

HOW TO CONTACT Send complete ms with SASE and/or IRC. No reply with insufficient postage. Accepts 2 mss/issue; 8 mss/year. Publishes 5 new writers/year.

PAYMENT/TERMS "Payment to new writers will be determined at time of acceptance."

QUIDDITY INTERNATIONAL LITERARY JOURNAL AND PUBLIC-RADIO PROGRAM

Benedictine University at Springfield, 1500 N. 5th St., Springfield IL 62702. **E-mail:** quidditylit@gmail.com. **Website:** www.quidditylit.com. **Contact:** Joanna Beth Tweedy, founding editor; John McCarthy, managing editor. *Quiddity*, published semi-annually, is a print journal and public-radio program featuring poetry, prose, and artwork by new, emerging, and established contributors from around the world. Has published work by J.O.J. Nwachukwu-Agbada, Kevin Stein, Karen An-Hwei Lee, and Haider Al-Kabi.

NEEDS Length: up to 5,000 words.

HOW TO CONTACT Send complete ms. Submit online through submissions manager.

THE RAG

P.O. Box 17463, Portland OR 97217. **E-mail:** submissions@raglitmag.com. **Website:** raglitmag.com. **Contact:** Seth Porter, editor; Dan Reilly, editor. Estab. 2011. *The Rag* focuses on the grittier genres that tend to fall by the wayside at more traditional literary magazines. *The Rag*'s ultimate goal is to put the literary magazine back into the entertainment market while rekindling the social and cultural value short fiction once held in North American literature.

Fee to submit online ($3) is waived if you subscribe or purchase a single issue.

NEEDS Accepts all styles and themes. Length: up to 10,000 words.

HOW TO CONTACT Send complete ms.

PAYMENT/TERMS Pays 5¢/word, the average being $250/story.

TIPS "We like gritty material: material that is psychologically believable and that has some humor in it, dark or otherwise. We like subtle themes, original characters, and sharp wit."

RALEIGH REVIEW LITERARY & ARTS MAGAZINE

Box 6725, Raleigh NC 27628-6725. **E-mail:** info@raleighreview.org. **Website:** www.raleighreview.org. **Contact:** Rob Greene, editor; Landon Houle, fiction editor; Bryce Emley, poetry editor. Estab. 2010. "*Raleigh Review* is a national nonprofit magazine of poetry, short fiction (including flash), and art. We believe that great literature inspires empathy by allowing us to see the world through the eyes of our neighbors, whether across the street or across the globe. Our mission is to foster the creation and availability of accessible yet provocative contemporary literature. We look for work that is emotionally and intellectually complex.

NEEDS "We prefer work that is physically grounded and accessible, though complex and rich in emotional or intellectual power. We delight in stories from unique voices and perspectives. Any fiction that is born from a relatively unknown place grabs our attention. We are not opposed to genre fiction, so long as it has real, human characters and is executed artfully." Length: 250-7,500 words. "While we accept fiction up to 7,500 words, we are more likely to publish work in the 4,500- to 5,000-word range."

HOW TO CONTACT Submit complete ms.

PAYMENT/TERMS Pays $10 maximum.

TIPS "Please be sure to read the guidelines and look at sample work on our website. Every piece is read for its intrinsic value, so new/emerging voices are often published alongside nationally recognized, award-winning authors."

RATTAPALLAX

Rattapallax Press, 217 Thompson St., Suite 353, New York NY 10012. **E-mail:** devineni@rattapallax.com. **Website:** www.rattapallax.com. **Contact:** Ram Devineni, founder & president; Flávia Rocha, editor in chief. Estab. 1999. Receives 15 unsolicited mss/month. Accepts 3 mss/issue; 6 mss/year. Agented fiction 15%. Receives about 5,000 poems/year; accepts 2%. Publishes 3 new writers/year. Has published work by Stuart Dybek, Howard Norman, Molly Giles, Rick Moody, Anthony Hecht, Sharon Olds, Lou Reed, Marilyn Hacker, Billy Collins, and Glyn Maxwell. *Rattapallax*, published semiannually, is named for "Wallace Stevens's word for the sound of thunder. The magazine includes a DVD featuring poetry films and audio files. *Rattapallax* is looking for the extraordinary in modern poetry and prose that reflect the diversity of world cultures. Our goals are to create international dialogue using literature and focus on what is relevant to our society."

Rattapallax is 112 pages, magazine-sized, offset-printed, perfect-bound, with 12-pt. CS1 cover; some illustrations; photos. Press run is 2,000 (100 subscribers, 50 libraries, 1,200 shelf sales); 200 distributed free to contributors, reviews, and promos.

NEEDS Length: up to 2,000 words.

HOW TO CONTACT Submit via online submissions manager at rattapallax.submittable.com/submit.

PAYMENT/TERMS Pays 2 contributor's copies.

THE RAVEN CHRONICLES

A Journal of Art, Literature, & the Spoken Word, 15528 12th Ave. NE, Shoreline WA 98155. (206)941-2955. **E-mail:** editors@ravenchronicles.org. **Website:** www.ravenchronicles.org. Estab. 1991. "*The Raven Chronicles* publishes work which reflects the cultural diversity of the Pacific Northwest, Canada, and other areas of America. We promote art, literature and the spoken word for an audience that is hip, literate, funny, informed, and lives in a society that has a multicultural sensibility. We publish fiction, talk art/spoken word, poetry, essays, reflective articles, reviews, interviews, and contemporary art. We look for work that reflects the author's experiences, perceptions, and insights."

NEEDS "Experimental work is always of interest." Length: up to 4,000 words or 3 flash fiction/lyric prose fiction. "Check with us for maximum length. We sometimes print longer pieces."

HOW TO CONTACT Submit complete ms via online submissions manager.

THE READER

The Reader Organisation, Calderstones Mansion, Calderstones Park, Liverpool L18 3JB, United Kingdom. **E-mail:** magazine@thereader.org.uk; info@thereader.org.uk. **Website:** www.thereader.org.uk. **Contact:** Philip Davis, editor. Estab. 1997. "*The Reader* is a quarterly literary magazine aimed at the intelligent 'common reader'—from those just beginning to explore serious literary reading to professional teachers, academics, and writers. As well as publishing short fiction and poetry by new writers and established names, the magazine features articles on all aspects of literature, language, and reading; regular features, including a literary quiz and a section on the Reading Revolution, reporting on The Reader Organisation's outreach work; reviews; and readers' recommendations of books that have made a difference to them. *The Reader* is unique among literary magazines in its focus on reading as a creative, important, and pleasurable activity, and in its combination of high-quality material and presentation with a genuine commitment to ordinary but dedicated readers." Also publishes literary essays, literary criticism, poetry.

NEEDS Wants short fiction and (more rarely) novel excerpts. Has published work by Karen King Arbisala, Ray Tallis, Sasha Dugdale, Vicki Seal, David Constantine, Jonathan Meades, and Ramesh Avadhani. Length: 1,000-2,500 words. Average length: 2,300 words. Publishes short shorts. Average length of short shorts: 1,500 words.

HOW TO CONTACT No e-mail submissions. Send complete ms with cover letter. Include estimated word count, brief bio, list of publications.

TIPS "The style or polish of the writing is less important than the deep structure of the story (though, of course, it matters that it's well written). The main persuasive element is whether the story moves us—and that's quite hard to quantify. It's something to do with the force of the idea and the genuine nature of enquiry within the story. When fiction is the writer's natural means of thinking things through, that'll get us. "

REAL: REGARDING ARTS & LETTERS

Stephen F. Austin State University, P.O. Box 13007, SFA Station, Nacogdoches TX 75962-3007. **E-mail:** brininsta@sfasu.edu. **Website:** regardingartsandletters.wordpress.com. **Contact:** Andrew Brininstool, editor. Estab. 1968. "*REAL: Regarding Arts & Letters* was founded in 1968 as an academic journal which occasionally published poetry. Now, it is an international creative magazine dedicated to publishing the best contemporary fiction, poetry, and nonfiction." Features both established and emerging writers.

NEEDS "We're not interested in genre fiction—science fiction or romance or the like—unless you're doing some cheeky genre-bending. Otherwise, send us your best literary work." Publishes short shorts. Length: up to 8,000 words.

HOW TO CONTACT Submit via online submissions manager. Include cover letter addressed to Andrew Brininstool or John McDermott.

PAYMENT/TERMS Pays contributor's copies

TIPS "We are looking for the best work, whether you are established or not."

REDACTIONS: POETRY & POETICS

604 N. 31st Ave., Apt. D-2, Hattiesburg MS 39401. **E-mail:** redactionspoetry@yahoo.com. **E-mail:** redactionspoetry@yahoo.com. **Website:** www.redactions.com. **Contact:** Tom Holmes. Estab. 2002. *Redactions*, released every 9 months, covers poems, reviews of new books of poems, translations, manifestos, interviews, essays concerning poetry, poetics, poetry movements, or concerning a specific poet or a group of poets; and anything dealing with poetry.

TIPS "We only accept submissions by e-mail. We read submissions throughout the year. E-mail submission as an attach in one Word, Wordpad, Notepad, RTF, or TXT document, or place in the body of an e-mail. Include brief bio and your snail-mail address. E-mails that have no subject line or have nothing written in the body of the e-mail will be deleted. We do not accept blank e-mails with only an attachment. Query after 90 days if you haven't heard from us. See website (redactions.com/submission-and-ordering.asp) for full guidelines, including for cover artwork."

REDIVIDER

Department of Writing, Literature, and Publishing, Emerson College, 120 Boylston St., Boston MA 02116. **E-mail:** editor@redividerjournal.org. **Website:** www.redividerjournal.org. Estab. 1986. *Redivider*, a journal of literature and art, is published twice a year by graduate students in the Writing, Literature, and Publishing Department of Emerson College. Prints new art, fiction, nonfiction, and poetry from new, emerging, and established artists and writers.

Every spring, *Redivider* hosts the Beacon Street Prize Writing Contest, awarding a cash prize and publication to the winning submission in fiction, poetry, and nonfiction categories. Hosts the Blurred Genre Contest each fall, awarding cash prizes and publication for flash fiction, flash nonfiction, and prose poetry. See www.redividerjournal.org for details.

NEEDS Length: no more than 8,000 words.

HOW TO CONTACT Submit electronically.

PAYMENT/TERMS Pays 2 contributor's copies.

TIPS To get a sense of what we publish, pick up an issue!

RED ROCK REVIEW

College of Southern Nevada, CSN Department of English, J2A, 3200 E. Cheyenne Ave., North Las Vegas NV 89030. (702)651-4094. **Fax:** (702)651-4455. **E-mail:** redrockreview@csn.edu. **Website:** sites.csn.edu/english/redrockreview. **Contact:** Erica Vital-Lazare, senior editor; Jacob Elison, associate editor. Estab. 1994. Dedicated to the publication of fine contemporary literature and poetry.

NEEDS "We're looking for the very best literature. Stories need to be tightly crafted, strong in character development, built around conflict." Length: up to 5,000 words.

HOW TO CONTACT Send ms by e-mail as Word, RTF, or PDF file attachment.

PAYMENT/TERMS Pays 2 contributor's copies.

TIPS "Open to short fiction and poetry submissions from year-round. See guidelines online."

RED WHEELBARROW

De Anza College, 21250 Stevens Creek Blvd., Cupertino CA 95014. **Website:** www.deanza.edu/redwheelbarrow. Estab. 1976 as *Bottomfish*; 2000 as *Red Wheelbarrow.*

"We seek to publish a diverse range of styles and voices from around the country and the world." Publishes a student edition and a national edition.

NEEDS Length: up to 4,000 words.

HOW TO CONTACT Send complete ms by mail (include SASE) or e-mail with brief bio.

TIPS "Write freely, rewrite carefully. Resist clichés and stereotypes. We are not affiliated with Red Wheelbarrow Press or any similarly named publication."

REED MAGAZINE

San Jose State University, Dept. of English, One Washington Square, San Jose CA 95192. **E-mail:** mail@reedmag.org; cathleen.miller@sjsu.edu. **Website:** www.reedmag.org. **Contact:** Cathleen Miller, editor in chief. Estab. 1867. *Reed Magazine* is the oldest literary journal west of the Mississippi. We publish works of short fiction, nonfiction, poetry, and art, and offer cash prizes in each category.

Accepts electronic submissions only.

NEEDS Does not want children's, young adult, fantasy, or erotic. Length: up to 5,000 words.

HOW TO CONTACT Submit complete ms via online submissions manager.

PAYMENT/TERMS Contest contributors receive 1 free copy; additional copies: $10.

TIPS Well-writen, original, clean grammatical prose is essential. We are interested in established authors as well as fresh new voices. Keep submitting!

RHINO

The Poetry Forum, Inc., P.O. Box 591, Evanston IL 60204. **E-mail:** editors@rhinopoetry.org. **Website:** rhinopoetry.org. "This independent, eclectic annual journal of 40 years accepts poetry, flash fiction (500 words max), and poetry-in-translation that experiments, provokes, compels. Emerging and established poets are showcased." Accepts general submissions April 1-August 31 and Founders' Prize submissions September 1-October 31.

NEEDS Length: up to 500 words.

PAYMENT/TERMS Pays 1 contributor's copy and offers contributor discounts for additional copies.

TIPS "Our diverse group of editors looks for the very best in contemporary writing, and we have created a dynamic process of soliciting and reading new work by local, national, and international writers. We are open to all styles and look for idiosyncratic, rigorous, well-crafted, lively, and passionate work."

THE ROCKFORD REVIEW

The Rockford Writers Guild, P.O. Box 858, Rockford IL 61105. **E-mail:** rwg@rockfordwritersguild.com; editor@rockfordwritersguild.com. **Website:** www.rockfordwritersguild.com. **Contact:** Connie Kluntz. Estab. 1947. "Published twice/year. Members only edition in summer-fall and winter-spring edition which is open to all writers. Open season to submit for the winter-spring edition of the Rock Review is August. If pubished in the winter-spring edition of the Rockford Review, payment is one copy of magazine and $5 per published piece. Credit line given. Check website for frequent updates. We are also on Facebook under Rockford Writers' Guild."

Poetry 50 lines or less, prose 1,300 words or less.

NEEDS "Prose should express fresh insights into the human condition." No sexist, pornographic, or supremacist content. Length: no more than 1,300 words.

TIPS "We're wide open to new and established writers alike—particularly short satire."

ROOM

West Coast Feminist Literary Magazine Society, P.O. Box 46160, Station D, Vancouver BC V6J 5G5, Canada. **E-mail:** contactus@roommagazine.com. **Website:** www.roommagazine.com. Estab. 1975. "*Room* is Canada's oldest feminist literary journal. Published quarterly by a collective based in Vancouver, *Room* showcases fiction, poetry, reviews, art work, interviews, and profiles by writers and artists who identify as women or genderqueer. Many of our contributors are at the beginning of their writing careers, looking for an opportunity to get published for the first time. Some later go on to great acclaim. *Room* is a space where women can speak, connect, and showcase their creativity. Each quarter we publish original, thought-provoking works that reflect women's strength, sensuality, vulnerability, and wit."

Room is digest-sized; illustrations, photos. Press run is 1,600 (900 subscribers, 50-100 libraries, 100-350 shelf sales).

NEEDS Accepts literature that illustrates the female experience—short stories, creative nonfiction, poetry—by, for and about women.

HOW TO CONTACT Submit complete ms via online submissions manager.

PAYMENT/TERMS Pays $50-120 (Canadian), 2 contributor's copies, and a one-year subscription.

SACRED CITY PRODUCTIONS

Sacred City Productions, Ltd., 5781 Springwood Ct., Mentor on the Lake OH 44060. (440)290-9325. **E-mail:** info@sacredcityproductions.com. **E-mail:** info@sacredcityproductions.com. **Website:** sacredcityproductions.com. **Contact:** Erin Garlock, editor/owner. Estab. 2011. Sacred City Productions is dedicated to creative endeavors that promote the ideals of a positive faith life. "We ask people to think about what they believe and to take action on those beliefs. Our own actions reflect our Christian beliefs as we reach out in ministry to extend an uplifting hand to those around us."

NEEDS Sacred City Production's fiction focus is on speculative Christian fiction for publication in short story anthologies. "Historical romance stories in the style of Beverly Lewis isn't what we are looking for." Length: 500-8,000 words.

HOW TO CONTACT Submit completed story via online submission form.

PAYMENT/TERMS Pays $10 for stories over 500 words, $20 for stories over 2,000 words. Once royalties earned by the publication equal the total amount paid out to all contributors, a 50/50 pro-rate share of the anthology's earnings, if any, will be paid as royalties at a ratio, to the aforementioned rates, relevant to the number of contributors. A royalty breakdown sheet will be supplied at the end of a project.

TIPS "We are very interested in submissions from first-time authors and authors with a very limited record."

SALMAGUNDI

Skidmore College, 815 North Broadway, Saratoga Springs NY 12866. **Fax:** (518)580-5188. **E-mail:** salmagun@skidmore.edu. **E-mail:** Only accepting hard copy submissions with SASE from now on. **Website:** cms.skidmore.edu/salmagundi. Estab. 1965. "*Salmagundi* publishes an eclectic variety of materials, ranging from short-short fiction to novellas from the surreal to the realistic. Our audience is a generally literate population of people who read for pleasure."

Salmagundi authors are regularly represented in *Pushcart* collections and *Best American Short Story* collections. Reading period: November 1 through December 1.

NEEDS Length: up to 12,000 words.

HOW TO CONTACT Submit hard copy only by snail mail with SASE.

PAYMENT/TERMS Pays 6-10 contributor's copies and one-year subscription.

TIPS "I look for excellence and a very unpredictable ability to appeal to the interests and tastes of the editors. Be brave. Don't be discouraged by rejection. Keep stories in circulation. Of course, it goes without saying: Work hard on the writing. Revise tirelessly. Study other magazines as well as this one and send only to those whose sensibility matches yours."

SALT HILL JOURNAL

Creative Writing Program, Syracuse University, English Deptartment, 401 Hall of Languages, Syracuse University, Syracuse NY 13244. **Website:** salthilljournal.net. **Contact:** Emma DeMilta and Jessica Poli, editors. "*Salt Hill* is published through Syracuse University's Creative Writing MFA program. We strive to publish a mix of the best contemporary and emerging talent in poetry, fiction, and nonfiction. Your work, if accepted, would appear in a long tradition of exceptional contributors, including Steve Almond, Mary Caponegro, Kim Chinquee, Edwidge Danticat, Denise Duhamel, Brian Evenson, B.H. Fairchild, Mary Gaitskill, Terrance Hayes, Bob Hicok, Laura Kasischke, Etgar Keret, Phil Lamarche, Dorianne Laux, Maurice Manning, Karyna McGlynn, Ander Monson, David Ohle, Lucia Perillo, Tomaž Šalamun, Zachary Schomburg, Christine Schutt, David Shields, Charles Simic, Patricia Smith, Dara Wier, and Raúl Zurita among many others."

Only accepts submissions by online submission form; does not accept unsolicited e-mail submissions.

NEEDS Length: up to 30 pages.

HOW TO CONTACT Submit via online submissions manager; contact fiction editor via e-mail for retractions and queries only.

THE SAME

P.O. Box 494, Mount Union PA 17066. **E-mail:** editors@thesamepress.com. **E-mail:** submissions@thesamepress.com. **Website:** www.thesamepress.com. **Contact:** Nancy Eldredge, managing editor. Estab. 2000. *The Same*, published biannually, prints nonfiction (essays, reviews, literary criticism), poetry, and short fiction.

HOW TO CONTACT Query before submitting.

THE SANDY RIVER REVIEW

University of Maine at Farmington, 114 Prescott St., Farmington ME 04938. **E-mail:** srreview@gmail.com. **E-mail:** submissions@sandyriverreview.com. **Website:** sandyriverreview.com. **Contact:** Nicole Byrne, editor. "*The Sandy River Review* seeks prose, poetry, and art submissions twice a year for our Spring and Fall issues. Prose submissions may be either fiction or creative nonfiction and should be a maximum of 3,500 words in length, 12-point, Times New Roman font, and double-spaced. Most of our art is published in b&w and must be submitted as 300-dpi quality, CMYK color mode, and saved as a TIFF file. We publish a wide variety of work from students as well as professional, established writers. Your submission should be polished and imaginative with strongly drawn characters and an interesting, original narrative. The review is the face of the University of Maine at Farmington's venerable BFA Creative Writing program, and we strive for the highest quality prose and poetry standard."

NEEDS Submit via e-mail. "The review is a literary journal—please, no horror, science fiction, romance." Length: up to 3,5000 words.

HOW TO CONTACT Send complete ms.

PAYMENT/TERMS Pays 3 contributor's copies.

TIPS "We recommend that you take time with your piece. As with all submissions to a literary journal, submissions should be fully completed, polished final drafts that require minimal to no revision once accepted. Double-check your prose pieces for basic grammatical errors before submitting."

SANTA CLARA REVIEW

Santa Clara Review, Santa Clara University, 500 El Camino Real, Box 3212, Santa Clara CA 95053-3212. (408)554-4484. **E-mail:** santaclarareview@gmail.com. **Website:** www.santaclarareview.com. Estab. 1869. "*SCR* is one of the oldest literary publications in the West. Entirely student-run by undergraduates at Santa Clara University, the magazine draws upon submissions from SCU affiliates as well as contributors from around the globe. The magazine is published in February and May each year. In addition to publishing the magazine, the Review staff organizes a writing practicum, open mic nights, and retreats for writers and artists, and hosts guest readers. Our printed magazine is also available to view free online. For contacts, queries, and general info, visit our website. *SCR* accepts submissions year round.

NEEDS Length: up to 5,000 words.

HOW TO CONTACT Submit via online submissions manager or mail (include SASE for return of ms).

SANTA MONICA REVIEW

Santa Monica College, 1900 Pico Blvd., Santa Monica CA 90405. **Website:** www.smc.edu/sm_review. **Contact:** Andrew Tonkovich, editor. Estab. 1988. The *Santa Monica Review*, published twice yearly in fall and spring, is a nationally distributed literary arts journal sponsored by Santa Monica College. It currently features fiction and nonfiction.

NEEDS "No crime and detective, mysogyny, footnotes, TV, dog stories. We want more self-conscious, smart, political, humorous, digressive, meta-fiction."

HOW TO CONTACT Submit complete ms with SASE. No e-mail submissions.

PAYMENT/TERMS Pays in contributor's copies and subscription.

THE SARANAC REVIEW

Dept. of English, Champlain Valley Hall, 101 Broad St., Plattsburgh NY 12901. (518)564-2241. **Fax:** (518)564-2140. **E-mail:** saranacreview@plattsburgh.edu. **Website:** www.saranacreview.com. **Contact:** J.L. Torres, executive editor. Estab. 2004. "*The Saranac Review* is committed to dissolving boundaries of all kinds, seeking to publish a diverse array of emerging and established writers from Canada and the U.S. *The Saranac Review* aims to be a textual clearing in which a space is opened for cross-pollination between American and Canadian writers. In this way the magazine reflects the expansive, bright spirit of the etymology of its name, Saranac, meaning 'cluster of stars.'" Published annually.

Publishes both digital and print-on-demand versions. Has published Lawrence Raab, Jacob M. Appel, Marilyn Nelson, Tom Wayman, Colette Inez, Louise Warren, Brian Campbell, Gregory Pardlo, Myfanwy Collins, William Giraldi, Xu Xi, Julia Alvarez, and other fine emerging and established writers.

NEEDS "We're looking for well-crafted fiction that demonstrates respect for and love of language. Fiction that makes us feel and think, that edifies without being didactic or self-indulgent and ultimately connects us to our sense of humanity." No genre material (fantasy, sci-fi, etc.) or light verse. Length: up to 7,000 words.

HOW TO CONTACT Submit complete ms via online submissions manager (Submittable).

PAYMENT/TERMS Pays 1 contributor's copies and offers discount on additional copies.

THE SAVAGE KICK LITERARY MAGAZINE

Murder Slim Press, 29 Alpha Rd., Gorleston Norfolk NR31 0EQ, United Kingdom. **E-mail:** moonshine@murderslim.com. **Website:** www.murderslim.com. Estab. 2005. "*Savage Kick* primarily deals with viewpoints outside the mainstream: honest emotions told in a raw, simplistic way. It is recommended that you are very familiar with the *SK* style before submitting. Ensure you have a distinctive voice and story to tell."

NEEDS "Real-life stories are preferred, unless the work is distinctively extreme within the crime genre. No poetry of any kind, no mainstream fiction, Oprah-style fiction, Internet/chat language, teen issues, excessive Shakespearean language, surrealism, overworked irony, or genre fiction (horror, fantasy, science fiction, western, erotica, etc.)." Length: 500-6,000 words.

HOW TO CONTACT Send complete ms.

PAYMENT/TERMS Pays $35.

SCREAMINMAMAS

Harmoni Productions, LLC, 1911 Cleveland St., Hollywood FL 33020. **E-mail:** screaminmamas@gmail.com. **Website:** www.screaminmamas.com. **Contact:** Darlene Pistocchi, editor; Lena, submissions coordinator. Estab. 2012. "We are the voice of everyday moms. We share their stories, revelations, humorous rants, photos, talent, children, ventures, etc."

NEEDS Does not want vulgar, obscene, derogatory, or negative fiction. Length: 800-1,200 words.

HOW TO CONTACT Send complete ms.

TIPS "Visit our submissions page and themes page on our website."

THE SEATTLE REVIEW

Box 354330, University of Washington, Seattle WA 98195. (206)543-2302. **E-mail:** seaview@uw.edu. **Website:** www.seattlereview.org. **Contact:** Andrew Feld, editor in chief. Estab. 1978. *The Seattle Review* includes poetry, fiction, and creative nonfiction.

NEEDS Only publishes novellas. "Currently, we do not consider, use, or have a place for genre fiction (sci-fi, detective, etc.) or visual art." Length: at least 40 double-spaced pages.

HOW TO CONTACT Send complete ms. Accepts electronic submissions only.

PAYMENT/TERMS Pays 2 contributor's copies and 1-year subscription.

TIPS "Know what we publish; no genre fiction. Look at our magazine and decide if your work might be appreciated. Beginners do well in our magazine if they send clean, well-written mss. We've published a lot of 'first stories' from all over the country and take pleasure in discovery."

$ SEEK

Standard Publishing, 4050 Lee Vance View Dr., Colorado Springs CO 80918. (800)323-7543. **E-mail:** seek@standardpublishing.com. **Website:** www.standardpub.com. Estab. 1970. "Inspirational stories of faith-in-action for Christian adults; a Sunday School take-home paper." Quarterly.

NEEDS List of upcoming themes available online. Accepts 150 mss/year. Send complete ms. Prefers submissions by e-mail. "*SEEK* corresponds to the topics of Standard Publishing's adult curriculum line and is designed to further apply these topics to everyday life." Unsolicited mss must be written to a theme list. Does not want poetry. Length: 850-1,000 words.

HOW TO CONTACT Send complete ms. Prefers submissions by e-mail.

PAYMENT/TERMS Pays 7¢/word.

TIPS "Write a credible story with a Christian slant—no preachments; avoid overworked themes such as joy in suffering, generation gaps, etc. Most mss are rejected by us because of irrelevant topic or message, unrealistic story, or poor character and/or plot development. We use fiction stories that are believable."

SEQUESTRUM

Sequestrum Publishing, 1023 Garfield Ave., Ames IA 50014. **E-mail:** sequr.info@gmail.com. **Website:** www.sequestrum.org. **Contact:** R.M. Cooper, managing editor. Estab. 2014. All publications are paired with a unique visual component. Regularly holds contests and features well-known authors, as well as promising new and emerging voices.

NEEDS Length: 5,000 words max.

HOW TO CONTACT Submit complete ms via online submissions manager.

PAYMENT/TERMS Pays $10-15/story.

TIPS "Reading a past issue goes a long way; there's little excuse not to: Our entire archive is available online to preview and subscription rates are variable. Send your best, most interesting work. General submissions are open, and we regularly hold contests and offer awards which are themed."

THE SEWANEE REVIEW

University of the South, 735 University Ave., Sewanee TN 37383-1000. (931)598-1000. **E-mail:** sreview@sewanee.edu. **Website:** review.sewanee.edu. **Contact:** George Core, editor. Estab. 1892. *The Sewanee Review* is America's oldest continuously published literary quarterly. Publishes original fiction, poetry, essays on literary and related subjects, and book reviews for well-educated readers who appreciate good American and English literature. Only erudite work representing depth of knowledge and skill of expression is published.

Does not read mss June 1-August 31.

NEEDS No erotica, science fiction, fantasy, or excessively violent or profane material. Length: 3,500-7,500 words. No short-short stories.

HOW TO CONTACT Submit complete ms by mail; no electronic submissions.

PAYMENT/TERMS Pays $10-12/printed page, plus 2 contributor's copies.

SIERRA NEVADA REVIEW

999 Tahoe Blvd., Incline Village NV 89451. **E-mail:** sncreview@sierranevada.edu. **Website:** blog.sierranevada.edu/sierranevadareview/. Estab. 1990. "*Sierra Nevada Review*, published annually in May, features poetry, short fiction, and literary nonfiction by new and established writers. Wants "writing that leans toward the unconventional, surprising, and risky."

Reads submissions September 1-February 15 only.

NEEDS Length: up to 4,000 words.

PAYMENT/TERMS Pays 2 contributor's copies.

SLOW TRAINS LITERARY JOURNAL

P.O. 4741, Denver CO 80155. **E-mail:** editor@slowtrains.com. **Website:** www.slowtrains.com. **Contact:** Susannah Grace Indigo, editor. Estab. 2000. Looking for fiction, essays, and poetry that reflect the spirit of adventure, the exploration of the soul, the energies of imagination, and the experience of Big Fun. Music, travel, sex, humor, love, loss, art, spirituality, childhood/coming of age, baseball, and dreams, but most of all, *Slow Trains* wants to read about the things you are passionate about.

NEEDS Genre writing is not encouraged. No sci-fi, erotica, horror, romance, though elements of those may naturally be included. Length: up to 5,000 words.

HOW TO CONTACT Submit via e-mail only.

SONORA REVIEW

University of Arizona's Creative Writing MFA Program, University of Arizona, Dept. of English, Tucson AZ 85721. **E-mail:** sonorareview2@gmail.com. **Website:** sonorareview.com. Estab. 1980. University of Arizona's Creative Writing MFA Program, University of Arizona, Dept. of English, Tucson AZ 85721. **E-mail:** sonora@email.arizona.edu. **Website:** www.coh.arizona.edu/sonora. **Contact:** Jake Levine, Jon Walter, editors. "We look for the highest-quality poetry, fiction, and nonfiction, with an emphasis on emerging writers. Our magazine has a long-standing tradition of publishing the best new literature and writers. Check out our website for a sample of what we publish and our submission guidelines, or write us for a sample back issue."

NEEDS Ethnic/multicultural, experimental, literary, mainstream, novel excerpts. Receives 200 unsolicited mss/month. Accepts 2-3 mss/issue; 6-8 mss/year. Does not read in the summer (June-August). Publishes ms 3-4 months after acceptance. **Publishes 1-3 new writers/year.** Recently published work by Michael Martone, Sawako Nakayasu. Also publishes literary essays, literary criticism, poetry. Sometimes comments on rejected mss. Length: 1,000-6,000 words.

HOW TO CONTACT Send complete ms. Send disposable copy of the ms and #10 SASE for reply only. Responds in 2-5 weeks to queries; in 3 months to mss. Accepts simultaneous, multiple submissions.

PAYMENT/TERMS Pays 2 contributor's copies; additional copies for $4.

TIPS "We have no length requirements, but we usually do not consider poems, stories, or essays that are over 20 pages in length, because of space."

SOUL FOUNTAIN

Website: www.antarcticajournal.com. **Contact:** Tone Bellizzi, editor. Estab. 1997. *Soul Fountain* is produced by The Antarctica Journal, a not-for-profit arts project of the Hope for the Children Foundation, committed to empowering young and emerging artists of all disciplines at all levels to develop and share their talents through performance, collaboration, and networking. Digitally publishes poetry, art, photography, short fiction, and essays on the website. Open to all. Publishes quality submitted work, and specializes in emerging voices. Favors visionary, challenging, and consciousness-expanding material.

HOW TO CONTACT Submit by e-mail only. No cover letters, please.

SOUTH DAKOTA REVIEW

The University of South Dakota, Dept. of English, 414 E. Clark St., Vermillion SD 57069. (605)677-5184. **E-mail:** sdreview@usd.edu. **Website:** www.usd.edu/sdreview. **Contact:** Lee Ann Roripaugh, editor in chief. Estab. 1963. "*South Dakota Review*, published quarterly, is committed to cultural and aesthetic diversity. First and foremost, we seek to publish exciting and compelling work that reflects the full spectrum of the contemporary literary arts. Since its inception in 1963, *South Dakota Review* has maintained a tradition of supporting work by contemporary writers writing from or about the American West. We hope to retain this unique flavor through particularly welcoming works by American Indian writers, writers addressing the complexities and contradictions of the 'New West,' and writers exploring themes of landscape, place, and/or eco-criticism in surprising and innovative ways. At the same time, we'd like to set these ideas and themes in dialogue with and within the context of larger global literary communities. Single copy: $12; subscription: $40/year, $65/2 years. Sample: $8.

Writing from *South Dakota Review* has appeared in *Pushcart* and *Best American Essays* anthologies. Press run is 500-600 (more than 500 subscribers, many of them libraries).

NEEDS "Our aesthetic is eclectic, but we tend to favor deft use of language in both our poetry and prose selections, nuanced characterization in our fiction, and either elegantly or surprisingly executed formal strategies. As part of our unique flavor, a small handful works in each issue will typically engage with aspects of landscape, ecocritical issues, or place (oftentimes with respect to the American West)." Length: up to 6,000 words.

HOW TO CONTACT Submit via online submissions manager. Include cover letter.

PAYMENT/TERMS Pays 2 contributor's copies.

THE SOUTHEAST REVIEW

Department of English, Florida State University, Tallahassee FL 32306. **Website:** southeastreview.org. **Contact:** Erin Hoover, editor. Estab. 1979. "The mission of *The Southeast Review* is to present emerging writers on the same stage as well-established ones. In each semiannual issue, we publish literary fiction, creative nonfiction, poetry, interviews, book reviews, and art. With nearly 60 members on our editorial staff who come from throughout the country and the world, we strive to publish work that is representative of our diverse interests and aesthetics, and we celebrate the eclectic mix this produces. We receive approximately 400 submissions per month, and we accept less than 1-2% of them."

Publishes 4-6 new (not previously published) writers/year. Has published work by A. A. Balaskovits, Hannah Gamble, Michael Homolka, Brandon Lingle, and Colleen Morrissey.

NEEDS "We try to respond to submissions within 2-4 months. If after 4 months you have not heard back regarding your submission, you may query the appropriate section editor. *SER* accepts simultaneous submissions, but we request that you withdraw the submission by way of our online submission manager if your piece is accepted elsewhere." Length: up to 7,500 words.

PAYMENT/TERMS Pays 2 contributor's copies.

TIPS "*The Southeast Review* accepts regular submissions for publication consideration year-round exclusively through the online submission manager. **Except in the case of contests, paper submissions sent through regular postal mail will not be read or returned**. Avoid trendy experimentation for its own sake (present-tense narration, observation that isn't also revelation). Fresh stories; moving, interesting characters; and a sensitivity to language are still fiction mainstays. We also publish the winner and runners-up of the World's Best Short Story Contest, Poetry Contest, and Creative Nonfiction Contest."

THE SOUTHERN REVIEW

338 Johnston Hall, Louisiana State University, Baton Rouge LA 70803. (225)578-5104. **Fax:** (225)578-6461. **E-mail:** southernreview@lsu.edu. **Website:** thesouthernreview.org. **Contact:** Jessica Faust, co-editor and poetry editor; Emily Nemens, co-editor and prose editor. Estab. 1935. "*The Southern Review* is one of the nation's premiere literary journals. Hailed by *Time* as 'superior to any other journal in the English language,' we have made literary history since our founding in 1935. We publish a diverse array of fiction, nonfiction, and poetry by the country's—and the world's—most respected contemporary writers." Reading period: September 1 through December 1 (prose); September 1 through February 1 (poetry). All mss submitted during outside the reading period will be recycled.

NEEDS Wants short stories of lasting literary merit, with emphasis on style and technique; novel excerpts. "We emphasize style and substantial content. No mystery, fantasy, or religious mss." Length: up to 8,000 words.

HOW TO CONTACT Submit 1 ms at a time by mail or through online submission form. "We rarely publish work that is longer than 8,000 words. We consider novel excerpts if they stand alone."

PAYMENT/TERMS Pays $25/printed page (max $200), 2 contributor's copies, and 1-year subscription.

TIPS "Careful attention to craftsmanship and technique combined with a developed sense of the creation of story will always make us pay attention."

SOUTHWESTERN AMERICAN LITERATURE

Center for the Study of the Southwest, Texas State University, Brazos Hall, 601 University Dr., San Marcos TX 78666-4616. (512)245-2224. **Fax:** (512)245-7462. **E-mail:** wj13@txstate.edu. **E-mail:** swpublications@txstate.edu. **Website:** www.txstate.edu/cssw/publications/sal.html. **Contact:** William Jensen, editor. Estab. 1971. *Southwestern American Literature* is a biannual scholarly journal that includes literary criticism, fiction, poetry, and book & film reviews concerning the Greater Southwest.

NEEDS Fiction must deal with the Southwest. Stories set outside our region will be rejected. We are always looking for stories that examine the relationship between the tradition of Southwestern American literature and the writer's own imagination. We like stories that move beyond stereotype. Length: up to 6,000 words/25 pages.

HOW TO CONTACT Submit using online submissions manager.

PAYMENT/TERMS Pays 2 contributor's copies.

TIPS Fiction and poetry must deal with the greater Southwest. We look for crisp language, an interesting approach to material. Read widely, write often, revise carefully. We seek stories that, as William Faulkner noted in his Nobel Prize acceptance speech, treat subjects central to good literature—the old verities of the human heart, such as honor and courage and pity and suffering, fear and humor, love and sorrow.

SOUTHWEST REVIEW

P.O. Box 750374, Dallas TX 75275-0374. (214)768-1037. **Fax:** (214)768-1408. **E-mail:** swr@smu.edu. **Website:** www.smu.edu/southwestreview. **Contact:** Willard Spiegelman, editor-in-chief. Estab. 1915. The majority of readers are well-read adults who wish to stay abreast of the latest and best in contemporary fiction, poetry, and essays in all but the most specialized disciplines. Published quarterly.

Has published work by Alice Hoffman, Sabina Murray, Alix Ohlin. The Elizabeth Matchett Stover Memorial Award presents $250 to the author of the best poem or groups of poems (chosen by editors) published in the preceding year. Also offers The Morton Marr Poetry Prize and the David Nathan Meyerson Prize for Fiction.

NEEDS Publishes fiction in widely varying styles. Prefers stories of character development, of psychological penetration, to those depending chiefly on plot. No specific requirements as to subject matter. Length: 3,500-8,000 words preferred.

HOW TO CONTACT Submissions accepted online for a $2 fee. No fee for submissions sent by mail. Submit one story at a time. Reading period: September 1-May 31.

PAYMENT/TERMS Accepted pieces receive nominal payment upon publication and copies of the issue.

TIPS "Despite the title, we are not a regional magazine. Before you submit your work, it's a good idea to take a look at recent issues to familiarize yourself with the magazine. We strongly advise all writers to include a cover letter. Keep your cover letter professional and concise, and don't include extraneous personal information, a story synopsis, or a résumé. When authors ask what we look for in a strong story submission, the answer is simple regardless of graduate degrees in creative writing, workshops, or whom you know: We look for good writing, period."

SPACE AND TIME

458 Elizabeth Ave., Somerset NJ 08873. **Website:** www.spaceandtimemagazine.com. **Contact:** Hildy Silverman, publisher. Estab. 1966. *Space and Time* is the longest continually published small-press genre fiction magazine still in print. We pride ourselves in having published the first stories of some of the great writers in science fiction, fantasy, and horror.

We love stories that blend elements—horror and science fiction, fantasy with science fiction elements, etc. We challenge writers to try something new and send us their hard to classify works-—what other publications reject because the work doesn't fit in their "pigeonholes."

NEEDS "We are looking for creative blends of science fiction, fantasy, and/or horror." "Do not send children's stories." Length: 1,000-10,000 words. Average length: 6,500 words. Average length of short shorts: 1,000 words.

HOW TO CONTACT Submit electronically as a Word document or RTF attachment ONLY during open reading periods. Anything sent outside those period will be rejected out of hand.

PAYMENT/TERMS Pays 1¢/word.

SPITBALL: THE LITERARY BASEBALL MAGAZINE

5560 Fox Rd., Cincinnati OH 45239. **E-mail:** spitball5@hotmail.com. **Website:** www.spitballmag.com.

Contact: Mike Shannon, editor in chief. Estab. 1981. *Spitball: The Literary Baseball Magazine*, published semiannually, is a unique magazine devoted to poetry, fiction, and book reviews exclusively about baseball. Newcomers are very welcome, but they must know the subject. "Perhaps a good place to start for beginners is one's personal reactions to the game, a game, a player, etc., and take it from there." Writers submitting to *Spitball* for the first time must buy a sample copy (waived for subscribers). "This is a one-time-only fee, which we regret, but economic reality dictates that we insist those who wish to be published in *Spitball* help support it, at least at this minimum level."

Spitball is 96 pages, digest-sized, computer-typeset, perfect-bound. Receives about 1,000 submissions/year, accepts about 40. Press run is 1,000. Subscription: $12. Sample: $6.

NEEDS Length: 5-15 pages, double-spaced. Short stories longer than 20 pages must be exceptionally good.

HOW TO CONTACT Submit with a biography and SASE.

PAYMENT/TERMS Pays 2 contributor's copies.

TIPS "Take the subject seriously. We do. In other words, get a clue (if you don't already have one) about the subject and about the poetry that has already been done and published about baseball. Learn from it—think about what you can add to the canon that is original and fresh—and don't assume that just anybody with the feeblest of efforts can write a baseball poem worthy of publication. And most importantly, stick with it. Genius seldom happens on the first try."

STAND MAGAZINE

School of English, Leeds LS2 9JT, United Kingdom. (44)(113)233-4794. **E-mail:** stand@leeds.ac.uk. **Website:** www.standmagazine.org. **Contact:** Jon Glover, managing editor. Estab. 1952. *Stand Magazine* is concerned with what happens when cultures and literatures meet, with translation in its many guises, with the mechanics of language, with the processes by which the policy receives or disables its cultural makers. *Stand* promotes debate of issues that are of radical concern to the intellectual community worldwide. U.S. submissions can be made through the Virginia office (see separate listing).

Does not accept e-mail submissions.

NEEDS Does not want genre fiction. Length: up to 3,000 words.

ST. ANTHONY MESSENGER

Franciscan Media, 28 W. Liberty St., Cincinnati OH 45202-6498. (513)241-5615. **Fax:** (513)241-0399. **E-mail:** magazineeditors@franciscanmedia.org. **Website:** www.stanthonymessenger.org. **Contact:** John Feister, editor-in-chief. Estab. 1893. *St. Anthony Messenger* is a Catholic family magazine which aims to help its readers lead more fully human and Christian lives. "We publish articles that report on a changing church and world, opinion pieces written from the perspective of Christian faith and values, personality profiles, and fiction which entertains and informs."

NEEDS "We do not want mawkishly sentimental or preachy fiction. Stories are most often rejected for poor plotting and characterization, bad dialogue (listen to how people talk), and inadequate motivation. Many stories say nothing, are 'happenings' rather than stories. No fetal journals, no rewritten Bible stories." Length: 2,000-2,500 words.

HOW TO CONTACT Send complete ms.

PAYMENT/TERMS Pays 20¢/word maximum and 2 contributor's copies; $1 charge for extras.

TIPS "The freelancer should consider why his or her proposed article would be appropriate for us, rather than for *Redbook* or *Saturday Review.* We treat human problems of all kinds, but from a religious perspective. Articles should reflect Catholic theology, spirituality, and employ a Catholic terminology and vocabulary. We need more articles on prayer, scripture, Catholic worship. Get authoritative information (not merely library research); we want interviews with experts. Write in popular style; use lots of examples, stories, and personal quotes. Word length is an important consideration."

STEPPING STONES MAGAZINE

P.O. Box 902, Norristown PA 19404-0902. **E-mail:** info@ssmalmia.com. **Website:** ssmalmia.com. **Contact:** Trinae Ross, publisher. Estab. 1996. "*Stepping Stones Magazine* is a not-for-profit organization dedicated to presenting awesome writing and art created by people from all lifestyles." Publishes fiction, nonfiction, and poetry."

Has published poetry by Richard Fenwick, Karlanna Lewis, and Stephanie Kaylor. Receives about 600 poems/year, accepts about 10-15%.

NEEDS Fiction should be able to hold the reader's interest in the first paragraph and sustain that interest throughout the rest of the story. Length: up to 4,000 words.

HOW TO CONTACT Send up to 3 mss via postal mail, e-mail (fiction@ssmalmia.com), or online submissions manager. Include brief bio.

STILL CRAZY

(614)746-0859. **E-mail:** editor@crazylitmag.com. **Website:** www.crazylitmag.com. **Contact:** Barbara Kussow, editor. Estab. 2008. *Still Crazy*, published biannually in January and July, features poetry, short stories, and essays written by or about people over age 50. The editor is particularly interested in material that challenges the stereotypes of older people and that portrays older people's inner lives as rich and rewarding. Wants writing by people over age 50 and writing by people of any age if the topic is about people over 50.

Accepts 3-4 short stories per issue; 5-7 essays; 12-14 poems. Reads submissions year round.

NEEDS Publishes short shorts. Ms published 6-12 months after acceptance. Sometimes features a "First Story," a story by an author who has not been published before. Does not want material that is "too sentimental or inspirational, 'Geezer' humor, or anything too grim." Length: up to 3,500 words, but stories fewer than 3,000 words are more likely to be published.

HOW TO CONTACT Upload submissions via submissions manager on website. Include estimated word count, brief bio, age of writer or "Over 50."

PAYMENT/TERMS Pays 1 contributor's copy.

TIPS Looking for interesting characters and interesting situations that might interest readers of all ages. Humor and lightness welcomed.

STIRRING: A LITERARY COLLECTION

Sundress Publications, **E-mail:** stirring@sundresspublications.com. **E-mail:** stirring.fiction@gmail.com; stirring.poetry@gmail.com; stirring.nonfiction@gmail.com. **Website:** www.sundresspublications.com/stirring. **Contact:** Luci Brown, Managing Editor

Andrew Koch, Managing Editor

Sarah Einstein, Managing Editor. Estab. 1999. "*Stirring* is one of the oldest continually-published literary journals on the web. *Stirring* is a monthly literary magazine that publishes poetry, short fiction, creative nonfiction, and photography by established and emerging writers."

NEEDS Length: up to 5,000 words.

HOW TO CONTACT Submit complete ms by e-mail to stirring.fiction@gmail.com

STORIE

Via Suor Celestina Donati 13/E, Rome 00167, Italy. (+39)06-454-33670. **Fax:** (+39)06-454-33670. **E-mail:** info@storie.it. **Website:** www.storie.it/english. Estab. 1986. "*Storie* is one of Italy's leading cultural and literary magazines. Committed to a truly crossover vision of writing, the bilingual (Italian/English) review publishes high-quality fiction and poetry, interspersed with the work of alternative wordsmiths such as filmmakers and musicians. Through writings bordering on narratives and interviews with important contemporary writers, it explores the culture and craft of writing."

HOW TO CONTACT "Mss may be submitted directly by regular post without querying first; however, we do not accept unsolicited mss via e-mail. Please query via e-mail first. We only contact writers if their work has been accepted. We also arrange for and oversee a high-quality, professional translation of the piece."

PAYMENT/TERMS Pays $30-600 and 2 contributor's copies.

TIPS "More than erudite references or a virtuoso performance, we're interested in a style merging news writing with literary techniques in the manner of new journalism. *Storie* reserves the right to include a brief review of interesting submissions not selected for publication in a special column of the magazine."

STORYSOUTH

3302 MHRA Building, UNCG, Greensboro NC 27412, USA. **E-mail:** terry@storysouth.com. **Website:** www.storysouth.com. **Contact:** Terry Kennedy, editor; Cynthia Nearman, creative nonfiction editor; Drew Perry, fiction editor; Luke Johnson, poetry editor. Estab. 2001. "*storySouth* accepts unsolicited submissions of fiction, poetry, and creative nonfiction during 2 submission periods annually: May 15-July 1 and November 15-January 1. Long pieces are encouraged. Please make only 1 submission in a single genre per reading period."

NEEDS No word limit.

HOW TO CONTACT Submit 1 story via online submissions manager.

TIPS "What really makes a story stand out is a strong voice and a sense of urgency—a need for the reader to keep reading the story and not put it down until it is finished."

THE STORYTELLER

65 Highway 328 West, Maynard AR 72444. (870)647-2137. **E-mail:** storytellermag1@yahoo.com. **Website:** www.thestorytellermagazine.com. **Contact:** Regina Riney (Williams), editor. Estab. 1996. "We are here to help writers however we can and to help start them on their publishing career. Proofread! Make sure you know what we take and what we don't and also make sure you know the word count."

NEEDS Does not want pornography, erotica, horror, graphic language or violence, children's stories, or anything deemed racial or biased toward any religion, race, or moral preference.

HOW TO CONTACT Send complete ms with cover letter and SASE.

TIPS "*The Storyteller* is one of the best places you will find to submit your work, especially new writers. Our best advice, be professional. You have one chance to make a good impression. Don't blow it by being unprofessional."

O STRAYLIGHT

UW-Parkside, English Department, University of Wisconsin-Parkside, 900 Wood Rd., Kenosha WI 53141. **E-mail:** submissions@straylightmag.com. **Website:** www.straylightmag.com. Estab. 2005. *Straylight*, published biannually, seeks fiction and "poetry of almost any style as long as it's inventive."

Literary magazine/journal: 6x9, 115 pages, quality paper, uncoated index stock cover. Contains illustrations, photographs.

NEEDS "*Straylight* is interested in publishing high-quality, character-based fiction of any style. We tend not to publish strict genre pieces, though we may query them for future special issues. We do not publish erotica." Publishes short shorts and novellas. Does not read May through August. Agented fiction 10%. Length: 1,000-5,000 words for short stories; under 1,000 words for flash fiction; 17,500-45,000 for novellas. Average length: 1,500-3,000 words.

HOW TO CONTACT Submissions can be submitted here: straylight.submittable.com/submit.

PAYMENT/TERMS Pays 2 contributor's copies.

TIPS "We tend to publish character-based and inventive fiction with cutting-edge prose. We are unimpressed with works based on strict plot twists or novelties. Read a sample copy to get a feel for what we publish."

O STRUGGLE: A MAGAZINE OF PROLETARIAN REVOLUTIONARY LITERATURE

P.O. Box 28536, Detroit MI 48228. (313)273-9039. **E-mail:** timhall11@yahoo.com. **Website:** www.strugglemagazine.net. **Contact:** Tim Hall, editor. Estab. 1985. "A quarterly magazine featuring African American, Latino, and other writers of color; prisoners; disgruntled workers; activists in the anti-war, anti-racist, and other mass movements; and many writers discontented with Obama and with the Republicans, their joint austerity campaign against the workers and the poor, and their continuing aggressive wars and drone murders abroad. While we urge literature in the direction of revolutionary working-class politics and a vision of socialism as embodying a genuine workers' power, in distinction to the state-capitalist regimes of the former Soviet Union, present-day China, North Korea, Cuba, etc., we accept a broader range of rebellious viewpoints in order to encourage creativity and dialogue."

NEEDS "Readers would like fiction about anti-globalization, the fight against racism, global militarism including the Afghanistan war, the struggle of immigrants, and the disillusionment with the Obama Administration as it reveals its craven service to the rich billionaires. Would also like to see more fiction that depicts life, work, and struggle of the working class of every background, especially young workers in the struggle for a $15/hour wage and unionization in fast food and Walmart; also the struggles of the 1930s and 1960s illustrated and brought to life." No romance, psychic, mystery, western, erotica, or religious. Length: 4,000 words; average length: 1,000-3,000 words.

HOW TO CONTACT Submit ms via e-mail or postal mail.

PAYMENT/TERMS Pays 1 contributor's copy.

STUDIO, A JOURNAL OF CHRISTIANS WRITING

727 Peel St., Albury NSW 2640, Australia. (61)(2)6021-1135. **E-mail:** studio00@bigpond.net.au. **Contact:** Paul Grover, publisher. Estab. 1980. *Studio, A Journal of Christians Writing*, published three times a year, prints poetry and prose of literary merit, offering a venue for previously published, new, and aspiring

writers and seeking to create a sense of community among Christians writing. Also publishes occasional articles as well as news and reviews of writing, writers, and events of interest to members. People who send material should be comfortable being published under this banner: *Studio, A Journal of Christians Writing*.

NEEDS Cover letter is required. Include brief details of previous publishing history, if any. SAE with IRC required. "Submissions must be typed and double-spaced on 1 side of A4 white paper. Name and address must appear on the reverse side of each page submitted."

PAYMENT/TERMS Pays 1 contributor's copy.

SUBTERRAIN

Strong Words for a Polite Nation, P.O. Box 3008, MPO, Vancouver BC V6B 3X5, Canada. (604)876-8710. **Fax:** (604)879-2667. **E-mail:** subter@portal.ca. **Website:** www.subterrain.ca. **Contact:** Brian Kaufman, editor in chief. Estab. 1988. "*subTerrain* magazine is published 3 times/year from modest offices just off of Main Street in Vancouver, BC. We strive to produce a stimulating fusion of fiction, poetry, photography, and graphic illustration from uprising Canadian, U.S., and international writers and artists."

NEEDS Receives 100 unsolicited mss/month. Accepts 4 mss/issue; 10-15 mss/year. Recently published work by J.O. Bruday, Lisa Pike, and Peter Babiak. Does not want genre fiction or children's fiction. **3,000 words max.**

HOW TO CONTACT Send complete ms. Include disposable copy of the ms and SASE for reply only. Accepts multiple submissions.

PAYMENT/TERMS Pays $50/page for prose.

TIPS "Read the magazine first. Get to know what kind of work we publish."

THE SUMMERSET REVIEW

25 Summerset Dr., Smithtown NY 11787. **E-mail:** editor@summersetreview.org. **Website:** www.summersetreview.org. **Contact:** Joseph Levens, editor. Estab. 2002. "Our goal is simply to publish the highest-quality literary fiction, nonfiction, and poetry intended for a general audience. This is a simple online literary journal of high-quality material, so simple you can call it unique."

NEEDS No sci-fi, horror, or graphic erotica. Length: up to 8,000 words; average length: 3,000 words. Publishes short shorts.

HOW TO CONTACT Send complete ms by e-mail as attachment or by postal mail with SASE.

TIPS "Style counts. We prefer innovative or at least very smooth, convincing voices. Even the dullest premises or the complete lack of conflict make for an interesting story if it is told in the right voice and style. We like to find little, interesting facts and/or connections subtly sprinkled throughout the piece. Harsh language should be used only if/when necessary. If we are choosing between light and dark subjects, the light will usually win."

THE SUN

107 N. Roberson St., Chapel Hill NC 27516. (919)942-5282. **Fax:** (919)932-3101. **Website:** www.thesunmagazine.org. **Contact:** Sy Safransky, editor. Estab. 1974. *The Sun* publishes essays, interviews, fiction, and poetry. "We are open to all kinds of writing, though we favor work of a personal nature."

NEEDS Open to all fiction. Receives 800 unsolicited mss/month. Accepts 20 short stories/year. Recently published work by Sigrid Nunez, Susan Straight, Lydia Peelle, Stephen Elliott, David James Duncan, Linda McCullough Moore, and Brenda Miller. No science fiction, horror, fantasy, or other genre fiction. "Read an issue before submitting." Length: up to 7,000 words.

HOW TO CONTACT Send complete ms. Accepts reprint submissions.

PAYMENT/TERMS Pays $300-1,500 and 1-year subscription.

TIPS "Do not send queries except for interviews. We're open to unusual work. Read the magazine to get a sense of what we're about. Our submission rate is extremely high. Please be patient after sending us your work and include return postage."

SUSPENSE MAGAZINE

Suspense Publishing, 26500 W. Agoura Rd., Suite 102-474, Calabasas CA 91302. **Fax:** (310)626-9670. **E-mail:** editor@suspensemagazine.com; john@suspensemagazine.com. **E-mail:** stories@suspensemagazine.com. **Website:** www.suspensemagazine.com. **Contact:** John Raab, publisher/CEO/editor in chief. Estab. 2007.

NEEDS No explicit scenes. Length: 1,500-5,000 words.

HOW TO CONTACT Submit story in body of e-mail. "Attachments will not be opened."

TIPS "Unpublished writers are welcome and encouraged to query. Our emphasis is on horror, suspense, thriller, and mystery."

SYCAMORE REVIEW

Purdue University Department of English, 500 Oval Dr., West Lafayette IN 47907. (765) 494-3783. **Fax:** (765) 494-3780. **E-mail:** sycamore@purdue.edu. **Website:** www.sycamorereview.com. **Contact:** Anthony Sutton, editor in chief; Bess Cooley, managing editor. *Sycamore Review* is Purdue University's internationally acclaimed literary journal, affiliated with Purdue's College of Liberal Arts and the Dept. of English. Strives to publish the best writing by new and established writers. Looks for well-crafted and engaging work, works that illuminate our lives in the collective human search for meaning. Would like to publish more work that takes a reflective look at national identity and how we are perceived by the world. Looks for diversity of voice, pluralistic worldviews, and political and social context.

Reading period: September 1-March 31.

NEEDS No genre fiction.

HOW TO CONTACT Submit complete ms via online submissions manager.

PAYMENT/TERMS Pays in contributor's copies and $50/short story.

TIPS "We look for originality, brevity, significance, strong dialogue, and vivid detail. We sponsor the Wabash Prize for Poetry (deadline: December 1) and Fiction (deadline: April 17), $1,000 award for each. All contest submissions will be considered for regular inclusion in the *Sycamore Review*."

TAKAHĒ

P.O. Box 13-335, Christchurch 8141, New Zealand. **E-mail:** admin@takahe.org.nz. **Website:** www.takahe.org.nz. The Takahē Collective Trust is a nonprofit organization that aims to support emerging and published writers, poets, artists, and cultural commentators.

Takahē magazine is a New Zealand-based literary and arts magazine that appears 3 times/year with a mix of print and online issues. It publishes short stories, poetry, and art by established and emerging writers and artists as well as essays, interviews, and book reviews (by invitation) in these related areas.

NEEDS "We look for stories that have something special about them: an original idea, a new perspective, an interesting narrative style or use of language, an ability to evoke character and/or atmosphere. Above all, we like some depth, an extra layer of meaning, an insight—something more than just an anecdote or a straightforward narration of events." Length: 1,500-3,000 words, "although we do occasionally accept flash fiction, or longer work, up to 5,000 words, for online issues only."

HOW TO CONTACT E-mail submissions are preferred (fiction@takahe.org.nz). Overseas submissions are only accepted by e-mail.

PAYMENT/TERMS Pays small honorarium to New Zealand authors, or one-year subscription to overseas writers.

TIPS "Editorials, book reviews, artwork, and literary commentaries are by invitation only."

TALKING RIVER

Division of Literature and Languages, 500 8th Ave., Lewiston ID 83501. (208)792-2189. **Fax:** (208)792-2324. **E-mail:** talkingriver@lcmail.lcsc.edu. **Website:** www.lcsc.edu/talking-river. **Contact:** Kevin Goodan, editorial advisor. Estab. 1994. "We look for new voices with something to say to a discerning general audience." Wants more well-written, character-driven stories that surprise and delight the reader with fresh, arresting yet unself-conscious language, imagery, metaphor, revelation. Reads mss September 1-May 1 only. Recently published work by Chris Dombrowski, Sherwin Bitsui, and Lia Purpura, Jim Harrison, David James Duncan, Dan Gerber, Alison Hawthorne Deming.

Submission period runs August 1-April 1.

NEEDS No stories that are sexist, racist, homophobic, erotic for shock value; no genre fiction. Length: 4,000 words; average length: 3,000 words.

HOW TO CONTACT Send complete ms with cover letter by postal mail. Include estimated word count, two-sentence bio, and list of publications. Send SASE for reply and return of ms, or send disposable copy of ms.

PAYMENT/TERMS Pays contributor's copies; additional copies $6.

TIPS "We look for the strong, the unique; we reject clichéd images and predictable climaxes."

TAMPA REVIEW

University of Tampa Press, 401 W. Kennedy Blvd., Tampa FL 33606. (813)253-6266. **Fax:** (813)258-7593. **E-mail:** utpress@ut.edu. **Website:** www.ut.edu/tampareview. **Contact:** Richard Mathews, editor; Elizabeth Winston and Daniel Dooghan, nonfiction editors; Yuly Restrepo and Andrew Plattner, fiction editors; Erica Dawson, poetry editor. Estab. 1988. An international literary journal publishing art and literature from Florida and Tampa Bay as well as new work and translations from throughout the world.

NEEDS "We are far more interested in quality than in genre. Nothing sentimental as opposed to genuinely moving, nor self-conscious style at the expense of human truth." Length: up to 5,000 words.

HOW TO CONTACT Send complete ms via mail or online submissions manager.

PAYMENT/TERMS Pays $10/printed page, 1 contributor's copy, and offers 40% discount on additional copies.

TIPS "Send a clear cover letter stating previous experience or background. Our editorial staff considers submissions between September and December for publication in the following year."

TEARS IN THE FENCE

Portman Lodge, Durweston, Blandford Forum, Dorset DT11 0QA, England. **E-mail:** tearsinthefence@gmail.com. **Website:** tearsinthefence.com. Estab. 1984. *Tears in the Fence*, published 2 times/year, is a "small-press magazine of poetry, fiction, interviews, essays, and reviews. We are open to a wide variety of poetic styles and work that shows social and poetic awareness whilst prompting close and divergent readings. However, we like to publish a variety of work."

NEEDS Length: up to 5,000 words.

HOW TO CONTACT Submit complete ms via e-mail as attachment.

PAYMENT/TERMS Pays 1 contributor's copy.

TEKKA

134 Main St., Watertown MA 02472. (617)924-9044. **E-mail:** editor@tekka.net. **E-mail:** bernstein@eastgate.com. **Website:** www.tekka.net. **Contact:** Mark Bernstein, publisher. Estab. 2003. "*Tekka* takes a close look at serious ideas that intertwingle computing and expression: hypertext, new media, software aesthetics, and the changing world that lies beyond the new economy. *Tekka* is always seeking new writers who can enhance our understanding, tempt our palate, and help explore new worlds and advance the state of the art. We welcome proposals for incisive, original features, reviews, and profiles from freelance writers. Our rates vary by length, department, and editorial requirements but are generally in line with the best Web magazines. We welcome proposals from scholars as well. We also publish short hypertext fiction, as well as fiction that explores the future of reading, writing, media, and computing. We are probably the best market for Web fiction, but we are extremely selective.

HOW TO CONTACT Query.

PAYMENT/TERMS Pay rates vary.

TELLURIDE MAGAZINE

Big Earth Publishing, Inc., P.O. Box 888, Telluride CO 81435. (970)728-4245. **Fax:** (866)936-8406. **E-mail:** deb@telluridemagazine.com. **Website:** www.telluridemagazine.com. **Contact:** Deb Dion Kees, editor in chief. Estab. 1982. "*Telluride Magazine* speaks specifically to Telluride and the surrounding mountain environment. Telluride is a resort town supported by the ski industry in winter, festivals in summer, outdoor recreation year round, and the unique lifestyle all of that affords. As a National Historic Landmark District with a colorful mining history, it weaves a tale that readers seek out. The local/visitor interaction is key to Telluride's success in making profiles an important part of the content. Telluriders are an environmentally minded and progressive bunch who appreciate efforts toward sustainability and protecting the natural landscape and wilderness that are the region's number one draw."

NEEDS "Please contact us; we are very specific about what we will accept." Length: 800-1,200 words.

HOW TO CONTACT Query with published clips.

TERRAIN.ORG: A JOURNAL OF THE BUILT + NATURAL ENVIROMENTS

Terrain.org, P.O. Box 19161, Tucson AZ 85731-9161. **E-mail:** contact2@terrain.org. **Website:** www.terrain.org. **Contact:** Simmons B. Buntin, editor in chief. Receives 25 mss/month. Accepts 12-15 mss/year. Agented fiction 5%. **Publishes 1-3 new writers/year.** Published Al Sim, Jacob MacAurthur Mooney, T.R. Healy, Deborah Fries, Andrew Wingfield, Braden Hepner, Chavawn Kelly, Tamara Kaye Sellman. *Terrain.org* is based on, and thus welcomes quality submissions from, new and experienced authors and artists alike. Our online journal accepts only the finest poetry, essays, fiction, articles, artwork, and other contributions' material that reaches deep into the earth's fiery core, or humanity's incalculable core, and brings forth new insights and wisdom. *Terrain.org* is searching for that interface—the integration among the built and natural environments, that might be called the soul of place. The works contained within *Terrain.org* ultimately examine the physical realm around us and how those environments influence us and each other physically, mentally, emotionally, and spiritually."

NEEDS Does not want erotica. Length: up to 6,000 words. Average length: 5,000 words. Publishes short shorts. Average length of short shorts: 750 words.

HOW TO CONTACT Accepts submissions online at sub.terrain.org. Include brief bio. Send complete ms with cover letter. Reads September 1-May 30 for regular submissions; contest submissions open year round.

TIPS "We have 3 primary criteria in reviewing fiction: (1) The story is compelling and well crafted. (2) The story provides some element of surprise; whether in content, form, or delivery we are unexpectedly delighted in what we've read. (3) The story meets an upcoming theme, even if only peripherally. Read fiction in the current issue and perhaps some archived work, and if you like what you read—and our overall enviromental slant—then send us your best work. Make sure you follow our submission guidelines (including cover note with bio), and that your mss is as error-free as possible."

◐ TEXAS REVIEW

Texas Review Press, Department of English, Sam Houston State University, Box 2146, Huntsville TX 77341-2146. (936)294-1992. **Fax:** (936)294-3070. **E-mail:** eng_pdr@shsu.edu; cww006@shsu.edu. **Website:** www.shsu.edu/~www_trp. **Contact:** Dr. Paul Ruffin, editor/director; Greg Bottoms, essay editor; Eric Miles Williamson, fiction editor; Nick Lantz, poetry editor. Estab. 1976. "We publish top-quality poetry, fiction, articles, interviews, and reviews for a general audience." Semiannual.

Publishes some new writers/year. Does not read mss May-September. A member of the Texas A&M University Press consortium.

NEEDS "We are eager enough to consider fiction of quality, no matter what its theme or subject matter. No juvenile fiction."

HOW TO CONTACT Send complete ms. No mss accepted via fax. Send disposable copy of ms and #10 SASE for reply only. Accepts multiple submissions.

PAYMENT/TERMS Pays contributor's copies and one-year subscription.

◐$ THEMA

Thema Literary Society, P.O. Box 8747, Metairie LA 70011-8747. **E-mail:** thema@cox.net. **Website:** themaliterarysociety.com. **Contact:** Gail Howard, poetry editor. Estab. 1988. "*THEMA* is designed to stimulate creative thinking by challenging writers with unusual themes, such as 'Golden Isn't Silent' and 'Lost in the Zoo.' Appeals to writers, teachers of creative writing, and general reading audience."

NEEDS All stories must relate to one of *THEMA*'s upcoming themes (**indicate the target theme on submission of ms**). See website for themes. No erotica. from 300 to 6,000 words (one to twenty double-spaced pages)

HOW TO CONTACT Send complete ms with SASE, cover letter; include "name and address, brief introduction, **specifying the intended target issue for the mss.**" SASE. Accepts simultaneous, multiple submissions, and reprints. Does not accept e-mailed submissions except from non-USA addresses.

PAYMENT/TERMS $10 for under 1,000 words; $25 for stories over 1,000 words, plus one contributor copy

THIRD COAST

Western Michigan University, English Dept., 1903 W. Michigan Ave., Kalamazoo MI 49008-5331. **Website:** www.thirdcoastmagazine.com. **Contact:** S.Marie LaFata-Clay, editor in chief. Estab. 1995. Sponsors an annual fiction contest. First Prize: $1,000 and publication. Guidelines available on website. **Entry fee:** $16, includes 1-year subscription to *Third Coast*. "*Third Coast* publishes poetry, fiction (including traditional and experimental fiction, shorts, and novel excerpts, but not genre fiction), creative nonfiction (including reportage, essay, memoir, and fragments), drama, and translations."

Reads mss from September through December of each year.

NEEDS Has published work by Bonnie Jo Campbell, Peter Ho Davies, Robin Romm, Lee Martin, Caitlin Horrocks, and Peter Orner. No genre fiction. Length: up to 8,000 words or 25 pages. Query for longer works.

HOW TO CONTACT Send complete ms via online submissions manager.

PAYMENT/TERMS Pays 2 contributor's copies and 1-year subscription.

TIPS "We will consider many different types of fiction and favor those exhibiting a freshness of vision and approach."

THE THREEPENNY REVIEW

P.O. Box 9131, Berkeley CA 94709. (510)849-4545. **E-mail:** wlesser@threepennyreview.com. **Website:** www.threepennyreview.com. **Contact:** Wendy Lesser, editor. Estab. 1980. "We are a general-interest, national literary magazine with coverage of politics, the visual arts, and the performing arts." Reading period: January 1-June 30.

NEEDS No fragmentary, sentimental fiction. Length: 800-4,000 words.

HOW TO CONTACT Send complete ms.

PAYMENT/TERMS Pays $400.

TIPS Nonfiction (political articles, memoirs, reviews) is most open to freelancers.

TIMBER JOURNAL

E-mail: timberjournal@gmail.com. **Website:** www.timberjournal.com. *Timber* is a literary journal, run by students in the MFA program at the University of Colorado Boulder, dedicated to the promotion of innovative literature. Publishes work that explores the boundaries of poetry, fiction, creative nonfiction, and digital literatures. Produces both an online journal that explores the potentials of the digital medium and an annual print anthology.

Reading period: August-March (submit just once during this time). Staff changes regularly; see website for current staff members.

NEEDS Length: up to 4,000 words.

HOW TO CONTACT Submit via online submissions manager. Include 30-50 word bio.

PAYMENT/TERMS Pays 1 contributor's copy.

TIPS "We are looking for innovative poetry, fiction, creative nonfiction, and digital lit (screenwriting, digital poetry, multimedia lit, etc.)."

TOASTED CHEESE

E-mail: editors@toasted-cheese.com. **E-mail:** submit@toasted-cheese.com. **Website:** www.toasted-cheese.com. Estab. 2001. *Toasted Cheese* accepts submissions of previously unpublished fiction, flash fiction, creative nonfiction, poetry, and book reviews. "Our focus is on quality of work, not quantity. Some issues will therefore contain fewer or more pieces than previous issues. We don't restrict publication based on subject matter. We encourage submissions from innovative writers in all genres and actively seek diverse voices."

NEEDS *Toasted Cheese* actively seeks submissions from those with diverse voices. See site for submission guidelines and samples of what *Toasted Cheese* publishes. No simultaneous submissions. Be mindful that final notification of acceptance or rejection may take 4 months. No chapters or excerpts unless they read as a standalone story. No first drafts.

PAYMENT/TERMS *Toasted Cheese* is a nonpaying market.

TIPS "We are looking for clean, professional work from writers and poets of any experience level. Accepted stories and poems will be concise and compelling with a strong voice. We're looking for writers who are serious about the craft: tomorrow's literary stars before they're famous. Take your submission seriously, yet remember that levity is appreciated."

TORCH LITERARY ARTS

TORCH: Creative Writing by Black Women, 3720 Gattis School Rd., Suite 800, Round Rock TX 78664. **E-mail:** torchliteraryarts@gmail.com. **E-mail:** torchliteraryarts@gmail.com. **Website:** www.torchliteraryarts.org. **Contact:** Amanda Johnston, founder/editor. Estab. 2006. *TORCH: Creative Writing by Black Women* , published semiannually online, provides "a place to publish contemporary poetry, prose, and short stories by experienced and emerging writers alike. We prefer our contributors to take risks, and offer a diverse body of work that examines and challenges preconceived notions regarding race, ethnicity, gender roles, and identity." Has published poetry by Sharon Bridgforth, Patricia Smith, Crystal Wilkinson, Tayari Jones, and Natasha Trethewey. Reads submissions April 15-August 31 only. Sometimes comments on rejected poems. Always sends prepublication galleys. No payment. "Within *TORCH*, we offer a special section called Flame that features an interview, biography, and work sample by an established writer as well as an introduction to their Spark—an emerging writer who inspires them and adds to the boundless voice of creative writing by Black women." A free online newsletter is available; see website.

TRIQUARTERLY

School of Professional Studies, Northwestern University, 339 E. Chicago Ave., Chicago IL 60611. **E-mail:** triquarterly@northwestern.edu. **Website:** www.triquarterly.org. **Contact:** Adrienne Gunn, managing editor. Estab. 1964. *TriQuarterly*, the literary magazine of Northwestern University, welcomes submissions of fiction, creative nonfiction, poetry, short drama, and hybrid work. "We also welcome short-short prose pieces." Reading period: October 15-May 1.

NEEDS Length: up to 5,000 words.

HOW TO CONTACT Submit complete ms via online submissions manager.

PAYMENT/TERMS Pays honoraria.

TIPS "We are especially interested in work that embraces the world and continues, however subtly, the ongoing global conversation about culture and society that *TriQuarterly* pursued from its beginning in 1964."

TULANE REVIEW

Tulane University, Suite G08A Lavin-Bernick Center, Tulane University, New Orleans LA 70118. **E-mail:** litsoc@tulane.edu. **Website:** www.tulane.edu/~litsoc/index.html. Estab. 1988. *Tulane Review*, published biannually, is a national literary journal seeking quality submissions of prose, poetry, and art.

NEEDS Length: up to 4,000 words.

HOW TO CONTACT Submit via online submissions manager only. Include a brief biography, an e-mail address, and a return address in cover letter.

PAYMENT/TERMS Pays 2 contributor's copies.

VAMPIRES 2 MAGAZINE

Man's Story 2 Publishing Co., 1321 Snapfinger Rd., Decatur GA 30032. **E-mail:** vampires2com2@aol.com. **Website:** www.vampires2.us. **Contact:** Carlos Dunn, founder and editor. Estab. 1999. "Online e-zine that strives to re-create vampire romance in the pulp fiction style of the 1920s through the 1970s with strong emphasis on 3D graphic art." Also features illustrated stories, online magazine, online photo galleries, and more.

"We publish books, publish online, and operate websites. In 2000 we became one of *Writer's Digest*'s top 100 markets for fiction writers and have since become listed with 20 other outstanding writers organizations."

NEEDS Length: up to 3,500 words or up to 10,000 words (two options offered; see website for details).

HOW TO CONTACT Send complete ms via e-mail as a .doc attachment. Include short summary of story.

TIPS "Your story must come to us edited, error free, and ready to publish. We prefer stories that have a strong romantic angle and a tastefully written love-making scene. Your story must have a compelling plot, nonstop action, and a satisfying ending, and you must tell a story well."

VAN GOGH'S EAR: BEST WORLD POETRY & PROSE

French Connection Press, 12 Rue Lamartine, Paris 75009, France. (33)(1)4016-1147. **E-mail:** tinafayeayres@gmail.com. **Website:** www.frenchcx.com/press; theoriginalvangoghsearanthology.com. Estab. 2002. *Van Gogh's Ear*, published annually in April, is an anthology series "devoted to publishing powerful poetry and prose in English and English translations by major voices and innovative new talents from around the globe."

NEEDS Length: up to 1,500 words.

HOW TO CONTACT Submit up to 2 prose pieces by e-mail. Cover letter is preferred, along with a brief bio of up to 120 words.

PAYMENT/TERMS Pays 1 contributor's copy.

TIPS "As a 501(c)(3) nonprofit enterprise, *Van Gogh's Ear* needs the support of individual poets, writers, and readers to survive. Any donation, large or small, will help *Van Gogh's Ear* continue to publish the best cross-section of contemporary poetry and prose. Because of being an anglophone publication based in France, *Van Gogh's Ear* is unable to get any grants or funding. Your contribution will be tax-deductible. Make donation checks payable to Committee on Poetry-*VGE*, and mail them (donations **only**) to the Allen Ginsberg Trust, P.O. Box 582, Stuyvesant Station, New York NY 10009."

VANILLEROTICA LITERARY EZINE

Cleveland OH 44102. (216)799-9775. **E-mail:** talentdripseroticpublishing@yahoo.com. **Website:** eroticatalentdrips.wordpress.com. **Contact:** Kimberly Steele, founder. Estab. 2007. *Vanillerotica*, published monthly online, focuses solely on showcasing new erotic fiction.

NEEDS Length: 5,000-10,000 words.

HOW TO CONTACT Submit short stories by e-mail to talentdripseroticpublishing@yahoo.com. Stories should be pasted into body of message. Reads submissions during publication months only.

PAYMENT/TERMS Pays $15 for each accepted short story.

TIPS "Please read our take on the difference between *erotica* and *pornography*; it's on the website. *Vanillerotica* does not accept pornography. And please keep poetry 30 lines or less."

VERANDAH LITERARY & ART JOURNAL

Faculty of Arts, Deakin University, 221 Burwood Hwy., Burwood, Victoria 3125, Australia. (61)(3)9251-7134. **E-mail:** verandah@deakin.edu.au. **Website:** verandahjournal.wordpress.com/. Estab. 1985. *Verandah*, published annually in August, is a high-quality literary journal edited by professional writing students. It aims to give voice to new and innovative writers and artists.

Submission period: February 1 through June 5. Has published work by Christos Tsiolka, Dorothy Porter, Seamus Heaney, Les Murray, Ed Burger, and John Muk Muk Burke. *Verandah* is 120 pages, professionally printed on glossy stock, flat-spined, with full-color glossy card cover.

NEEDS Length: 350-2,500 words.

HOW TO CONTACT Submit by mail or e-mail. However, electronic version of work must be available if accepted by *Verandah*. Do not submit work without the required submission form (available for download on website). Reads submissions by June 5 deadline (postmark).

PAYMENT/TERMS Pays 1 contributor's copy, "with prizes awarded accordingly."

VESTAL REVIEW

127 Kilsyth Road, Apt. 3, Brighton MA 02135. **E-mail:** submissions@vestalreview.net. **Website:** www.vestalreview.org. Semi-annual print magazine specializing in flash fiction.

Vestal Review's stories have been reprinted in the *Mammoth Book of Miniscule Fiction*, *Flash Writing*, *E2Ink Anthologies*, and in the *WW Norton Anthology Flash Fiction Forward*. Reading periods: February-May and August-November.

NEEDS No porn, racial slurs, excessive gore, or obscenity. No children's or preachy stories. Length: 50-500 words.

HOW TO CONTACT Publishes flash fiction. "We accept submissions only through our submission manager."

PAYMENT/TERMS Pays 3-10¢/word and 1 contributor's copy; additional copies for $10 (plus postage).

TIPS "We like literary fiction with a plot that doesn't waste words. Don't send jokes masked as stories."

THE VIRGINIA QUARTERLY REVIEW

VQR, P.O. Box 400223, Charlottesville VA 22904. **E-mail:** editors@vqronline.org. **Website:** www.vqronline.org. **Contact:** Allison Wright, managing editor. Estab. 1925. "*VQR*'s primary mission has been to sustain and strengthen Jefferson's bulwark, long describing itself as 'A National Journal of Literature and Discussion.' And for good reason. From its inception in prohibition, through depression and war, in prosperity and peace, *The Virginia Quarterly Review* has been a haven—and home—for the best essayists, fiction writers, and poets, seeking contributors from every section of the United States and abroad. It has not limited itself to any special field. No topic has been alien: literary, public affairs, the arts, history, the economy. If it could be approached through essay or discussion, poetry or prose, *VQR* has covered it." Press run is 4,000.

NEEDS "We are generally not interested in genre fiction (such as romance, science fiction, or fantasy)." Length: 2,000-10,000 words.

HOW TO CONTACT Accepts online submissions only at virginiaquarterlyreview.submittable.com/submit.

PAYMENT/TERMS Pays $1,000-2,500 for short stories; $1,000-4,000 for novellas and novel excerpts.

WEB DEL SOL

Wed del Sol Association, 2020 Pennsylvania Ave. NW, Suite 443, Washington D.C. 20006. **E-mail:** editor@webdelsol.com. **Website:** www.webdelsol.com. **Contact:** Michael Neff, editor in chief. Estab. 1994. Electronic magazine. "The goal of *Web Del Sol* is to use the medium of the Internet to bring the finest in contemporary literary arts to a larger audience. To that end, *WDS* not only web-publishes collections of work by accomplished writers and poets, but hosts over 25 literary arts publications on the WWW such as *Del Sol Review, North American Review, Global City Review, The Literary Review*, and *The Prose Poem*." Estab. 1994.

NEEDS Literary. "*WDS* publishes work considered to be literary in nature, i.e. non-genre fiction. *WDS* also publishes poetry, prose poetry, essays and experimental types of writing." **Publishes 100-200 new writers/year.**

HOW TO CONTACT "Submissions by e-mail from September through November and from January through March only. Submissions must contain some brief bio, list of prior publications (if any), and a short work or portion of that work, neither to exceed 1,000 words. Editors will contact if the balance of work is required." Sample copy online.

TIPS "*WDS* wants fiction that is absolutely cutting edge, unique and/or at a minimum, accomplished with a crisp style and concerning subjects not usually considered the objects of literary scrutiny. Read works in such publications as *Conjunctions* (www.conjunctions.com) and *North American Review* (webdelsol.com/NorthAmReview/NAR) to get an idea of what we are looking for."

WEST BRANCH

Stadler Center for Poetry, Bucknell University, Lewisburg PA 17837-2029. (570)577-1853. **Fax:** (570)577-1885. **E-mail:** westbranch@bucknell.edu. **Website:** www.bucknell.edu/westbranch. **Contact:** G.C. Waldrep, editor. *West Branch* publishes poetry, fiction, and nonfiction in both traditional and innovative styles.

Reading period: August 15-April 1. No more than 3 submissions from a single contributor in a given reading period.

NEEDS No genre fiction. Length: no more than 30 pages.

HOW TO CONTACT Send complete ms.

PAYMENT/TERMS Pays 5¢/word, up to $100.

TIPS "All submissions must be sent via our online submission manager. Please see website for guidelines. We recommend that you acquaint yourself with the magazine before submitting."

WESTERLY

University of Western Australia, The Westerly Centre (M202), Crawley WA 6009, Australia. (61)(8)6488-3403. **Fax:** (61)(8)6488-1030. **E-mail:** westerly@uwa.edu.au. **Website:** westerlymag.com.au. **Contact:** Catherine Noske, editor. Estab. 1956. *Westerly*, published in July and November, prints quality short fiction, poetry, literary criticism, socio-historical articles, and book reviews with special attention given to Australia, Asia, and the Indian Ocean region. "We assume a reasonably well-read, intelligent audience. Past issues of *Westerly* provide the best guides. Not consciously an academic magazine."

Deadline for July edition: March 31; deadline for November edition: August 31.

NEEDS Length: up to 3,500 words.

HOW TO CONTACT Submit complete ms by mail, e-mail, or online submissions form.

PAYMENT/TERMS Pays $150 and contributor's copies.

WESTERN HUMANITIES REVIEW

University of Utah, English Department, 255 S. Central Campus Dr., Salt Lake City UT 84112-0494. (801)581-6070. **Fax:** (801)585-5167. **E-mail:** whr@mail.hum.utah.edu. **Website:** ourworld.info/whrweb/. **Contact:** Barry Weller, editor; Nate Liederbach, managing editor. Estab. 1947. *Western Humanities Review* is a journal of contemporary literature and culture housed in the University of Utah English Department. Publishes poetry, fiction, nonfiction essays, artwork, and work that resists categorization.

Reading period: September 1 through April 15. All submissions must be sent through online submissions manager.

NEEDS Does not want genre (romance, science fiction, etc.). Length: 5,000 words.

HOW TO CONTACT Send complete ms.

PAYMENT/TERMS Pays $5/published page (when funds available).

TIPS "Because of changes in our editorial staff, we urge familiarity with recent issues of the magazine. We do not publish writer's guidelines because we think that the magazine itself conveys an accurate picture of our requirements. Please, no e-mail submissions."

WHISKEY ISLAND MAGAZINE

English Dept., Cleveland State University, 2121 Euclid Ave., Cleveland OH 44115. (216)687-3951. **E-mail:** whiskeyisland@csuohio.edu. **Website:** whiskeyislandmagazine.com. "*Whiskey Island* is a nonprofit literary magazine that has been published in one form or another by students of Cleveland State University for over 30 years."

Reading periods: August 15 through November 15 and January 15 through April 15. Paper and e-mail submissions are not accepted. No multiple submissions.

NEEDS "No translations, please." Length: 1,500-8,000 words for short stories; up to 1,500 words for flash fiction.

HOW TO CONTACT Submit via online submissions manager.

PAYMENT/TERMS Pays 2 contributor's copies.

WICKED ALICE

Dancing Girl Press & Studio, 410 S. Michigan #921, Chicago IL 60605. **E-mail:** wickedalicepoetry@yahoo.com. **Website:** www.sundresspublications.com/wickedalice. **Contact:** Kristy Bowen, editor. Estab. 2001. "*Wicked Alice* is a women-centered online journal dedicated to publishing quality work by both sexes, depicting and exploring the female experience." Wants "work that has a strong sense of image and music. Work that is interesting and surprising, with innovative, sometimes unusual, use of language. We love humor when done well, strangeness, wackiness. Hybridity, collage, intertexuality."

HOW TO CONTACT Submit complete ms by e-mail.

WILD VIOLET

P.O. Box 39706, Philadelphia PA 19106. **E-mail:** wildvioletmagazine@yahoo.com. **Website:** www.wildviolet.net. **Contact:** Alyce Wilson, editor. Estab. 2001. *Wild Violet*, published weekly online, aims "to make the arts more accessible, to make a place for the arts in modern life, and to serve as a creative forum for writers and artists. Our audience includes English-speaking readers from all over the world who are interested in both 'high art' and pop culture."

NEEDS Receives 30 unsolicited mss/month. Accepts 3-5 mss/issue; 135 mss/year. **Publishes 70 new writers/year.** Recently published work by Bill Gaythwaite, Jonathan Lowe, and Nancy Christie. Also publishes literary essays, literary criticism, poetry. Sometimes comments on rejected mss. "No stories where sexual or violent content is just used to shock the reader. No racist writings." Length: 500-6,000 words; average length: 3,000 words.

HOW TO CONTACT Send complete ms. Accepts submissions by e-mail and postal mail. Include estimated word count and brief bio. Send SASE for return of ms or send a disposable copy of ms and #10 SASE for reply only. Accepts simultaneous, multiple submissions.

PAYMENT/TERMS Writers receive bio and links on contributor's page. Sponsors awards/contests.

TIPS "We look for stories that are well-paced and show character and plot development. Even short shorts should do more than simply paint a picture. Mss stand out when the author's voice is fresh and engaging. Avoid muddying your story with too many characters, and don't attempt to shock the reader with an ending you have not earned. Experiment with styles and structures, but don't resort to experimentation for its own sake."

WILLARD & MAPLE

163 S. Willard St., Box #3636, Burlington VT 05401. (802)860-2700 ext.2462. **E-mail:** willardandmaple@champlain.edu. **Website:** willardandmaple.com. Estab. 1994. *Willard & Maple*, published annually in spring, is a student-run literary magazine from Champlain College's Professional Writing Program that considers short fiction, essays, reviews, fine art, and poetry by adults, children, and teens. Wants creative work of the highest quality.

Willard & Maple is 200 pages, digest-sized, digitally printed, perfect-bound. Receives about 500 poems/year, accepts about 20%. Press run is 600 (80 subscribers, 4 libraries); 200 are distributed free to the Champlain College writing community.

HOW TO CONTACT Send complete ms via e-mail or postal mail. Send SASE for return of ms or send disposable copy of mss and #10 SASE for reply only.

PAYMENT/TERMS Pays 2 contributor's copies.

TIPS "The power of imagination makes us infinite."

WILLOW REVIEW

College of Lake County Publications, College of Lake County, 19351 W. Washington St., Grayslake IL 60030-1198. (847)543-2956. **E-mail:** com426@clcillinois.edu. **Website:** www.clcillinois.edu/community/willowreview.asp. **Contact:** Michael Latza, editor. Estab. 1969. Prizes totaling $400 are awarded to the best poetry and short fiction/creative nonfiction in each issue. *Willow Review*, published annually, is interested in poetry, creative nonfiction, and fiction of high quality. "We have no preferences as to form, style, or subject, as long as each piece stands on its own as art and communicates ideas."

The editors award prizes for best poetry and prose in the issue. Prize awards vary contingent on the current year's budget but normally range from $100-400. There is no reading fee or separate application for these prizes. All accepted mss are eligible." *Willow Review* can be found on EBSCOhost databases, assuring a broader targeted audience for our authors' work. *Willow Review* is a nonprofit journal partially supported by a grant from the Illinois Arts Council (a state agency), College of Lake County Publications, private contributions, and sales."

NEEDS Accepts short fiction. Considers simultaneous submissions "if indicated in the cover letter" and multiple submissions.

HOW TO CONTACT Send complete ms with cover letter. Include estimated word count, brief bio, list of publications. Send either SASE (or IRC) for return of ms or disposable copy of ms and #10 SASE for reply only.

PAYMENT/TERMS Pays 2 contributor's copies.

WILLOW SPRINGS

668 N. Riverpoint Blvd. 2 RPT, #259, Spokane WA 99202. (509)359-7435. **E-mail:** willowspringsewu@gmail.com. **Website:** willowsprings.ewu.edu. **Contact:** Samuel Ligon, editor. Estab. 1977. *Willow Springs* is a semiannual magazine covering poetry, fiction, literary nonfiction and interviews of notable writers. Published twice a year, in spring and fall.

Reading period: September 1-May 31 for fiction and poetry; year-round for nonfiction. Reading fee: $3/submission.

NEEDS "We accept any good piece of literary fiction. Buy a sample copy." Does not want to see genre fiction that does not transcend its subject matter. Length: open for short stories; up to 750 words for short shorts.

HOW TO CONTACT Submit via online submissions manager.

PAYMENT/TERMS Pays $100 and 2 contributor's copies for short stories; $40 and 2 contributor's copies for short shorts.

TIPS "While we have no specific length restrictions, we generally publish fiction and nonfiction no longer than 10,000 words and poetry no longer than 120 lines, though those are not strict rules. *Willow Springs* values poems and essays that transcend the merely autobiographical and fiction that conveys a concern for language as well as story."

WINDHOVER

A Journal of Christian Literature, P.O. Box 8008, 900 College St., Belton TX 76513. (254)295-4563. **E-mail:** windhover@umhb.edu. **Website:** undergrad.umhb.edu/english/windhover-journal. **Contact:** Dr. Nathaniel Hansen, editor. Estab. 1997. "*Windhover* is devoted to promoting writers and literature with Christian perspectives and with a broad definition of those perspectives. We accept poetry, short fiction, nonfiction, and creative nonfiction."

Reading period is February 1-August 1.

NEEDS Receives 30 unsolicited mss/month. Recently published work by Walt McDonald, Cleatus Rattan, Greg Garrett, and Barbara Crooker. No erotica. Length: 1,500-4,000 words. Average length: 3,000 words.

PAYMENT/TERMS Pays 1 contributor's copy.

TIPS "We are looking for writing that avoids the didactic, the melodramatic, the trite, the obvious. Eschew tricks and gimmicks. We want writing that invites rereading."

WISCONSIN REVIEW

University of Wisconsin Oshkosh, 800 Algoma Blvd., Oshkosh WI 54901. (920)424-2267. **E-mail:** wisconsinreview@uwosh.edu. **Website:** www.uwosh.edu/wisconsinreview. Estab. 1966. *Wisconsin Review*, published biannually, is a "contemporary poetry, prose, and art magazine run by students at the University of Wisconsin Oshkosh."

Reading period: May through October for Spring issue; November through April for Fall issue.

NEEDS "Standard or experimental styles will be considered, although we look for outstanding characterization and unique themes." Submit via postal mail (include SASE) or online submission manager. There is a $2 reading fee for online submissions. Length: up to 15 pages, double-spaced with 12-point font.

PAYMENT/TERMS Pays 2 contributor's copies.

TIPS "We are open to any poetic form and style, and look for outstanding imagery, new themes, and fresh voices—poetry that induces emotions."

WITCHES AND PAGANS

BBI Media, Inc., P.O. Box 687, Forest Grove OR 97116. (888)724-3966. **E-mail:** editor2@bbimedia.com. **Website:** www.witchesandpagans.com. Estab. 2002. "*Witches and Pagans* is dedicated to witches, wiccans, neo-pagans, and various other earth-based, pre-Christian, shamanic, and magical practitioners. We hope to reach not only those already involved in what we cover but the curious and completely new as well."

"Devoted exclusively to promoting and covering contemporary Pagan culture, *W&P* features exclusive interviews with the teachers, writers, and activists who create and lead our traditions, visits to the sacred places and people who inspire us, and in-depth discussions of our ever-evolving practices. You'll also find practical daily magic, ideas for solitary ritual and devotion, God/dess-friendly craft-projects, Pagan poetry and short fiction, reviews, and much more in every 88-page issue. *W&P* is available in either traditional paper copy sent by postal mail or as a digital PDF e-zine download that is compatible with most computers and readers."

NEEDS Does not want faction (fictionalized retellings of real events). Avoid gratuitous sex, violence, sentimentality, and pagan moralizing. Don't beat our readers with the Rede or the Threefold Law. Length: 1,000-5,000 words.

HOW TO CONTACT Send complete ms.

TIPS "Read the magazine, do your research, write the piece, send it in. That's really the only way to get started as a writer; everything else is window dressing."

THE WORCESTER REVIEW

1 Ekman St., Worcester MA 01607. (508)797-4770. **E-mail:** twr.diane@gmail.com. **Website:** www.theworcesterreview.org. **Contact:** Diane Vanaskie Mulligan, managing editor. Estab. 1972. *The Worcester Review*, published annually by the Worcester County Poetry Association, encourages "critical work with a New England connection; no geographic limitation on poetry and fiction." Wants "work that is crafted, intuitively honest and empathetic. We like high-quality, creative poetry, artwork, and fiction. Critical articles should be connected to New England."

NEEDS Accepts about 10% unsolicited mss. Agented fiction less than 10%. Recently published work by Robert Pinsky, Marge Piercy, Wes McNair, and Ed Hirsch. Length: 1,000-4,000 words. Average length: 2,000 words.

HOW TO CONTACT Send complete ms via online submissions manager. "Send only 1 short story—reading editors do not like to read 2 by the same author at the same time. We will use only 1."

PAYMENT/TERMS Pays 2 contributor's copies and honorarium if possible.

TIPS "We generally look for creative work with a blend of craftsmanship, insight, and empathy. This does not exclude humor. We won't print work that is shoddy in any of these areas."

WORD RIOT

P.O. Box 414, Middletown NJ 07748-3143. (732)706-1272. **Fax:** (732)706-5856. **E-mail:** wr.submissions@gmail.com. **Website:** www.wordriot.org. **Contact:** Jackie Corley, publisher; Kevin O'Cuinn, fiction editor; Doug Paul Case, poetry editor; Antonia Crane, creative nonfiction editor. Estab. 2002. "*Word Riot* publishes the forceful voices of up-and-coming writers and poets. We like edgy. We like challenging. We like unique voices. Each month we provide readers with book reviews, author interviews, and, most importantly, writing from some of the best and brightest making waves on the literary scene."

Online magazine. Member CLMP.

NEEDS Accepts 20-25 mss/issue; 240-300 mss/year. Agented fiction 5%. Publishes 8-10 new writers/year. "No fantasy, science fiction, romance." Length: 1,000-6,500 words.

HOW TO CONTACT Submit via online submissions manager at wordriot.submittable.com/submit. Do not send submissions by mail.

TIPS "We're always looking for something edgy or quirky. We like writers who take risks."

WORKERS WRITE!

Blue Cubicle Press, LLC, P.O. Box 250382, Plano TX 75025. **E-mail:** info@workerswritejournal.com. **Website:** www.workerswritejournal.com. **Contact:** David LaBounty, managing editor. Estab. 2005. "*Workers Write!* is an annual print journal published by Blue Cubicle Press, an independent publisher dedicated to giving voice to writers trapped in the daily grind. Each issue focuses on a particular workplace; check website for details. Submit your stories via e-mail or send a hard copy."

NEEDS "We need your stories (5,000-12,000 words) about the workplace from our Overtime series. Every 3 months, we'll release a chapbook containing 1 story that centers on work." Length: 500-5,000 words.

HOW TO CONTACT Send complete ms.

PAYMENT/TERMS Payment: $5-50 (depending on length and rights requested).

THE WRITE PLACE AT THE WRITE TIME

E-mail: submissions@thewriteplaceatthewritetime.org. **Website:** www.thewriteplaceatthewritetime.org. **Contact:** Nicole M. Bouchard, editor in chief. Estab. 2008. Online literary magazine, published 3 times/year. Publishes fiction, personal nonfiction, craft essays by professionals, and poetry that "speaks to the heart and mind."

"Our writers range from previously unpublished to having written for *The New York Times*, *Time* magazine, *The New Yorker*, *The Wall Street Journal*, *Glimmer Train*, *Newsweek*, and *Business Week*, and they come from all over the world. Interview subjects include *NYT* best-selling authors such as Dennis Lehane, Janet Fitch, Alice Hoffman, Joanne Harris, Arthur Golden, Jodi Picoult, and Frances Mayes."

NEEDS Considers literary and most genre fiction if thought-provoking and emotionally evocative. No erotica, explicit horror/gore/violence, political. Length: up to 3,500 words. Average length of stories: 3,000 words. Average length of short-shorts: 1,000 words. "If we feel the strength of the submission merits added length, we are happy to consider exceptions."

HOW TO CONTACT Send complete ms with cover letter by e-mail—no attachments. Include estimated word count and brief bio. Accepts multiple submissions, up to 3 stories at a time. Accepts simultaneous submissions if indicated; other publications must be notified immediately upon acceptance. "If accepted elsewhere, we must be notified." Accepts 90-100 mss/year; receives 500-700 mss/year.

TIPS "Through our highly personalized approach to content, feedback, and community, we aim to give a very human visage to the publishing process. We wish to speak deeply of the human condition through pieces that validate the entire spectrum of emotions and the real circumstances of life. Every piece has a unique power and presence that stands on its own; we've had writers write about surviving an illness, losing a child, embracing a foreign land, learning of their parent's suicide, discovering love, finding humor in dark hours, and healing from abuse. Our collective voice, from our aesthetic to our artwork to the words, looks at and highlights aspects of life through a storytelling lens that allows for or promotes a universal understanding."

THE WRITING DISORDER

P.O. Box 93613, Los Angeles CA 90093. (323)336-5822. **E-mail:** submit@thewritingdisorder.com. **Website:** www.writingdisorder.com. **Contact:** C.E. Lukather, editor; Paul Garson, managing editor; Julianna Woodhead, poetry editor; Pamela Ramos Langley, fiction editor; C.E. Lukather, nonfiction editor. Estab. 2009. "*The Writing Disorder* is an online literary magazine devoted to literature, art, and culture. The mission of the magazine is to showcase new and emerging writers—particularly those in writing programs—as well as established ones. The magazine also features original artwork, photography, and comic art. Although we strive to publish original and experimental work, *The Writing Disorder* remains rooted in the classic art of storytelling."

NEEDS Does not want to see romance, religious, or fluff. Length: 7,500 words maximum.

HOW TO CONTACT Query.

PAYMENT/TERMS Pays contributor's copies.

TIPS "We are looking for work from new writers, writers in writing programs, and students and faculty of all ages."

XAVIER REVIEW

Xavier University of Louisiana, 1 Drexel Dr., Box 89, New Orleans LA 70125-1098. **Website:** www.xula.edu/review. **Contact:** Ralph Adamo, editor. Estab. 1980. "*Xavier Review* accepts poetry, fiction, translations, creative nonfiction, and critical essays. Content focuses on African American, Caribbean, and Southern literature, as well as works that touch on issues of religion and spirituality. We do, however, accept quality work on all themes. (Please note: This is not a religious publication.)"

NEEDS Has published work by Andrei Codrescu, Terrance Hayes, Naton Leslie, and Patricia Smith. Also publishes literary essays and literary criticism.

HOW TO CONTACT Send complete ms. Include 2-3 sentence bio and SASE. "We rarely accepts mss over 20 pages."

PAYMENT/TERMS Pays 2 contributor's copies; offers 40% discount on additional copies.

THE YALE REVIEW

Yale University, P.O. Box 208243, New Haven CT 06520-8243. (203)432-0499. **Fax:** (203)432-0510.

Website: www.yale.edu/yalereview. **Contact:** J.D. McClatchy, editor. Estab. 1911. "Like Yale's schools of music, drama, and architecture, like its libraries and art galleries, *The Yale Review* has helped give the University its leading place in American education. In a land of quick fixes and short view and in a time of increasingly commercial publishing, the journal has an authority that derives from its commitment to bold established writers and promising newcomers, to both challenging literary work and a range of essays and reviews that can explore the connections between academic disciplines and the broader movements in American society, thought, and culture. With independence and boldness, with a concern for issues and ideas, with a respect for the mind's capacity to be surprised by speculation and delighted by elegance, *The Yale Review* proudly continues into its third century."

HOW TO CONTACT Submit complete ms with SASE. All submissions should be sent to the editorial office.

PAYMENT/TERMS Pays $400-500.

THE YALOBUSHA REVIEW

University of Mississippi, **E-mail:** yreditors@gmail.com. **Website:** yr.olemiss.edu. **Contact:** Maggie Woodward and Marty Cain, senior editors. Estab. 1995.

NEEDS Length: up to 5,000 words for short stories; up to 1,000 words for flash fiction.

HOW TO CONTACT Submit 1 short story or up to 3 pieces of flash fiction via online submissions manager.

YEMASSEE

University of South Carolina, Department of English, Columbia SC 29208. **E-mail:** editor@yemasseejournal.com. **Website:** yemasseejournal.com. Estab. 1993. "*Yemassee* is the University of South Carolina's literary journal. Our readers are interested in high-quality fiction, poetry, and creative nonfiction. We have no editorial slant; quality of work is our only concern. We publish in the fall and spring, printing 5-7 stories, 2-3 essays, and 12-15 poems per issue. We tend to solicit reviews, essays, and interviews but welcome unsolicited queries. We do not favor any particular aesthetic or school of writing."

Stories from *Yemassee* have been published in *New Stories From the South*. Only accepts submissions through online submissions manager.

NEEDS "We are open to a variety of subjects and writing styles. Our essential consideration for acceptance is the quality of the work. No romance, religious/inspirational, young adult/teen, children's/juvenile, erotica. Wants more experimental work." Length: up to 5,000 words.

HOW TO CONTACT Send complete ms. "Submissions for all genres should include a cover letter that lists the titles of the pieces included, along with your contact information (including author's name, address, e-mail address, and phone number)." Yemassee Short Fiction Contest: $1,000 award. Check website for deadline.

PAYMENT/TERMS Pays 2 contributor's copies.

ZEEK: A JEWISH JOURNAL OF THOUGHT AND CULTURE

125 Maiden Ln., 8th Floor, New York NY 10038. (212)453-9435. **E-mail:** zeek@zeek.net. **Website:** www.zeek.net. **Contact:** Erica Brody, editor in chief. Estab. 2001. *ZEEK* "relaunched in late February 2013 as a hub for the domestic Jewish social justice movement, one that showcases the people, ideas, and conversations driving an inclusive and diverse progressive Jewish community. At the same time, we've reaffirmed our commitment to building on *ZEEK*'s reputation for original, ahead-of-the-curve Jewish writing and arts, culture and spirituality content, incubating emerging voices and artists, as well as established ones." *ZEEK* seeks "great writing in a variety of styles and voices, original thinking, and accessible content. That means we're interested in hearing your ideas for first-person essays, reflections and commentary, reporting, profiles, Q&As, analysis, infographics, and more. For the near future, *ZEEK* will focus on domestic issues. Our discourse will be civil."

NEEDS "Calls for fiction submissions are issued periodically. Follow *ZEEK* on Twitter @ZEEKMag for announcements and details."

ZOETROPE: ALL-STORY

Zoetrope: All-Story, The Sentinel Bldg., 916 Kearny St., San Francisco CA 94133. (415)788-7500. **Website:** www.all-story.com. **Contact:** fiction editor. Estab. 1997. *Zoetrope: All Story* presents a new generation of classic stories.

NEEDS Length: up to 7,000 words. "Excerpts from larger works, screenplays, treatments, and poetry will be returned unread."

HOW TO CONTACT "Writers should submit only 1 story at a time and no more than 2 stories a year. We do not accept artwork or design submissions. We do not accept unsolicited revisions nor respond to writers who don't include an SASE." Send complete ms by mail.

PAYMENT/TERMS Pays up to $1,000.

TIPS "Before submitting, nonsubscribers should read several issues of the magazine to determine if their works fit with *All-Story*. Electronic versions of the magazine are available to read, in part, at the website, and print versions are available for purchase by single-issue order and subscription."

ZYZZYVA

57 Post St., Suite 604, San Francisco CA 94104. (415)757-0465. **E-mail:** editor@zyzzyva.org. **Website:** www.zyzzyva.org. **Contact:** Laura Cogan, editor; Oscar Villalon, managing editor. Estab. 1985. "Every issue is a vibrant mix of established talents and new voices, providing an elegantly curated overview of contemporary arts and letters with a distinctly San Francisco perspective."

Accepts submissions January 1-May 31 and August 1-November 30. Does not accept online submissions.

NEEDS Length: no limit.

HOW TO CONTACT Send complete ms by mail. Include SASE and contact information.

PAYMENT/TERMS Pays $50.

TIPS "We are not currently seeking work about any particular theme or topic; that said, reading recent issues is perhaps the best way to develop a sense for the length and quality we are looking for in submissions."

BOOK PUBLISHERS

In this section, you will find many of the "big name" book publishers. Many of these publishers remain tough markets for new writers or for those whose work might be considered literary or experimental. Indeed, some only accept work from established authors, and then often only through an author's agent. Although having your novel published by one of the big commercial publishers listed in this section is difficult, it is not impossible. The trade magazine *Publishers Weekly* regularly features interviews with writers whose first novels are being released by top publishers. Many editors at large publishing houses find great satisfaction in publishing a writer's first novel.

In the References section, you'll find the publishing industry's "family tree," which maps out each of the large book publishing conglomerates' divisions, subsidiaries, and imprints. Remember, most manuscripts are acquired by imprints, not their parent company, so avoid submitting to the conglomerates themselves.

Also listed here are "small presses," which publish four or more titles annually. Included among them are independent presses, university presses, and other nonprofit publishers. Introducing new writers to the reading public has become an increasingly important role of these smaller presses at a time when the large conglomerates are taking fewer chances on unknown writers. Many of the successful small presses listed in this section have built their reputations and their businesses in this way and have become known for publishing prize-winning fiction.

These smaller presses also tend to keep books in print longer than larger houses. And, since small presses publish a smaller number of books, each title is equally important to the publisher and each is promoted in much the same way and with the same commitment. Editors also stay at small presses longer because they have more of a stake in the business—often they own the business. Many smaller book publishers are writers themselves and know firsthand the importance of a close editor-author or publisher-author relationship.

TYPES OF BOOK PUBLISHERS

Large or small, the publishers in this section publish books "for the trade." That is, unlike textbook, technical, or scholarly publishers, trade publishers publish books to be sold to the general consumer through bookstores, chain stores, or other retail outlets. Within the trade book field, however, there are a number of different types of books.

The easiest way to categorize books is by their physical appearance and the way they are marketed. Hardcover books are the more expensive editions of a book, sold through bookstores and carrying a price tag of around $20 and up. Trade paperbacks are softbound books, also sold mostly in bookstores, but they carry a more modest price tag of usually around $10 to $20. Today a lot of fiction is published in this form because it means a lower financial risk than hardcover.

Mass-market paperbacks are another animal altogether. These are the smaller "pocket-size" books available at bookstores, grocery stores, drugstores, chain retail outlets, etc. Much genre or category fiction is published in this format. This area of the publishing industry is very open to the work of talented new writers who write in specific genres such as science fiction, romance, and mystery.

At one time, publishers could be easily identified and grouped by the type of books they produce. Today, however, the lines between hardcover and paperback books are blurred. Many publishers known for publishing hardcover books also publish trade paperbacks and have paperback imprints. This enables them to offer established authors (and a very few lucky newcomers) hard-soft deals in which their book comes out in both versions. Thanks to the mergers of the past decade, too, the same company may own several hardcover and paperback subsidiaries and imprints, even though their editorial focuses may remain separate.

CHOOSING A BOOK PUBLISHER

In addition to checking the bookstores and libraries for books by publishers that interest you, you may want to refer to the Category Index at the back of this book to find publishers divided by specific subject categories. The subjects listed in the index are general. Read individual listings to find which subcategories interest a publisher. For example, you will find several romance publishers listed, but you should read the listings to find which type of romance is considered: gothic, contemporary, regency, futuristic, and so on.

The icons appearing before the names of the publishers will also help you in selecting a publisher. These codes are especially important in this section, because many of the publishing houses listed here require writers to submit through an agent. The ● symbol indicates that a publisher accepts agented submissions only. A ● icon identifies those that mostly publish established and agented authors, while a ○ points to publishers most open to new writers. See the inside back cover of this book for a complete list and explanations of symbols used in this book.

IN THE LISTINGS

We include several symbols to help you narrow your search. English-speaking foreign markets are denoted by a ●. The maple leaf symbol ● identifies Canadian presses. If you are not a Canadian writer but are interested in a Canadian press, check the listing carefully. Many small presses in Canada receive grants and other funds from their provincial or national government and are, therefore, restricted to publishing Canadian authors.

We also include editorial comments set off by a bullet (●) within listings. This is where we include information about any special requirements or circumstances that will help you know even more about the publisher's needs and policies. The ● symbol identifies publishers who have recently received honors or awards for their books. The ● denotes publishers who produce comics and graphic novels.

Each listing includes a summary of the houses's editorial mission, an overarching principle that ties together what they publish. Under the heading **Contact** we list one or more editors, often with their specific area of expertise.

Book editors asked us again this year to emphasize the importance of paying close attention to the **Needs** and **How to Contact** subheads of listings for book publishers. Unlike magazine editors, who want to see complete manuscripts of short stories, most of the book publishers listed here ask that writers send a query letter with an outline and/or synopsis and several chapters of their novel. "The Business of Fiction Writing," found earlier in this book, outlines how to prepare work to submit directly to a publisher.

There are no subsidy book publishers listed in *Novel & Short Story Writer's Market.* By subsidy, we mean any arrangement in which the writer is expected to pay all or part of the cost of producing, distributing, and marketing his book. We feel a writer should not be asked to share in any cost of turning his manuscript into a book. All the book publishers listed here told us that they do not charge writers for publishing their work. If any of the publishers listed here ask you to pay any part of publishing or marketing your manuscript, please let us know.

A NOTE ABOUT AGENTS

Some publishers are willing to look at unsolicited submissions, but most feel having an agent is in the writer's best interest. In this section more than any other, you'll find a number of publishers who prefer submissions from agents. That's why we've included a section of agents open to submissions from fiction writers (see the Literary Agents section of the listings). For even more agents, along with a great deal of helpful articles about approaching and working with them, refer to *Guide to Literary Agents*.

If you use the Internet or another resource to find an agent not listed in this book, be wary of any agents who charge large sums of money for reading a manuscript. Reading fees do not guarantee representation. Think of an agent as a potential business partner and feel free to ask tough questions about his or her credentials, experience, and business practices.

⊘ ABBEVILLE FAMILY

Abbeville Press, 116 W. 23rd St., New York NY 10011. (212)366-5585. **Fax:** (212)366-6966. **E-mail:** abbeville@abbeville.com. **Website:** www.abbeville.com. Estab. 1977. "Our list is full for the next several seasons." Not accepting unsolicited book proposals at this time.

NEEDS Picture books: animal, anthology, concept, contemporary, fantasy, folktales, health, hi-lo, history, humor, multicultural, nature/environment, poetry, science fiction, special needs, sports, suspense. Average word length 300-1,000 words.

HOW TO CONTACT Please refer to website for submission policy.

ABDO PUBLISHING CO.

8000 W. 78th St., Ste. 310, Edina MN 55439. (800)800-1312. **Fax:** (952)831-1632. **E-mail:** nonfiction@abdopublishing.com. **E-mail:** fiction@abdopublishing.com; illustration@abdopublishing.com. **Website:** www.abdopublishing.com. **Contact:** Paul Abdo, editor in chief. Estab. 1985. ABDO publishes nonfiction children's books (pre-kindergarten to eighth grade) for school and public libraries—mainly history, sports, biography, geography, science, and social studies. "Please specify each submission as either nonfiction, fiction, or illustration." Publishes hardcover originals. Guidelines online.

ABINGDON PRESS

Imprint of The United Methodist Publishing House, 201 Eighth Ave. S., P.O. Box 801, Nashville TN 37202. (615)749-6000. **Fax:** (615)749-6512. **E-mail:** submissions@umpublishing.org. **Website:** www.abingdonpress.com. Estab. 1789. "Abingdon Press, America's oldest theological publisher, provides an ecumenical publishing program dedicated to serving the Christian community—clergy, scholars, church leaders, musicians, and general readers—with quality resources in the areas of Bible study, the practice of ministry, theology, devotion, spirituality, inspiration, prayer, music and worship, reference, Christian education, and church supplies." Publishes hardcover and paperback originals. Book catalog available free. Guidelines online.

NEEDS Publishes stories of faith, hope, and love that encourage readers to explore life.

HOW TO CONTACT Agented submissions only for fiction.

TERMS Pays 7.5% royalty on retail price. Responds in 2 months to queries.

ACADEMY CHICAGO PUBLISHERS

814 N. Franklin St., Chicago IL 60610. (312)337-0747. **Fax:** (312)337-5985. **Website:** www.academychicago.com. **Contact:** Yuval Taylor, senior editor. Estab. 1975. "We publish quality fiction and nonfiction. Our audience is literate and discriminating. No novelized biography, history, or science fiction." No electronic submissions. Publishes hardcover and some paperback originals and trade paperback reprints. Book catalog online. Guidelines online.

NEEDS "We look for quality work, but we do not publish experimental, avant garde, horror, science fiction, or thrillers."

HOW TO CONTACT Submit proposal package, synopsis, 3 sample chapters, and short bio.

TERMS Pays 7-10% royalty on wholesale price. Responds in 3 months.

TIPS "At the moment, we are looking for good nonfiction; we certainly want excellent original fiction, but we are swamped. No fax queries, no disks. No electronic submissions. We are always interested in reprinting good out-of-print books."

Ⓐ⊘ ACE SCIENCE FICTION AND FANTASY

Imprint of the Berkley Publishing Group, Penguin Group (USA), Inc., 375 Hudson St., New York NY 10014. (212)366-2000. **Website:** www.us.penguingroup.com. Estab. 1953. Ace publishes science fiction and fantasy exclusively. Publishes hardcover, paperback, and trade paperback originals and reprints.

As imprint of Penguin, Ace is not open to unsolicited submissions.

NEEDS No other genre accepted. No short stories.

HOW TO CONTACT Due to the high volume of mss received, most Penguin Group (USA) Inc. imprints do not normally accept unsolicited mss.

TERMS Pays royalty. Pays advance.

⊘ ALADDIN

Simon & Schuster, 1230 Avenue of the Americas, Fourth Floor, New York NY 10020. (212)698-7000. **Website:** www.simonandschuster.com. **Contact:** Acquisitions Editor. Aladdin publishes picture books, beginning readers, chapter books, middle-grade and tween fiction and nonfiction, and graphic novels and nonfiction in hardcover and paperback, with an emphasis on commercial, kid-friendly titles. Publishes hardcover/paperback originals and imprints of Simon & Schuster Children's Publishing Children's Division.

HOW TO CONTACT Simon & Schuster does not review, retain, or return unsolicited materials or artwork. "We suggest prospective authors and illustrators submit their mss through a professional literary agent."

⊘ ALGONQUIN BOOKS OF CHAPEL HILL

Workman Publishing, P.O. Box 2225, Chapel Hill NC 27515-2225. (919)967-0108. **Website:** www.algonquin.com. **Contact:** Editorial Department. "Algonquin Books publishes quality literary fiction and literary nonfiction." Publishes hardcover originals. Guidelines online.

IMPRINTS Algonquin Young Readers.

HOW TO CONTACT Does not accept unsolicited submissions at this time.

ALGONQUIN YOUNG READERS

P.O. Box 2225, Chapel Hill NC 27515. **Website:** algonquinyoungreaders.com. Algonquin Young Readers is a new imprint that features books for readers 7-17. "From short illustrated novels for the youngest independent readers to timely and topical crossover young adult fiction, what ties our books together are unforgettable characters, absorbing stories, and superior writing." Guidelines online.

NEEDS Algonquin Young Readers publishes fiction and a limited number of narrative nonfiction titles for middle-grade and young adult readers. "We don't publish poetry, picture books, or genre fiction."

HOW TO CONTACT Query with 15-20 sample pages and SASE.

ALLEN & UNWIN

406 Albert St., East Melbourne VIC 3002, Australia. (61)(3)9665-5000. **E-mail:** fridaypitch@allenandunwin.com. **Website:** www.allenandunwin.com. Allen & Unwin publishes over 80 new books for children and young adults each year, many of these from established authors and illustrators. "However, we know how difficult it can be for new writers to get their work in front of publishers, which is why we've decided to extend our innovative and pioneering Friday Pitch service to emerging writers for children and young adults." Guidelines online.

AMBERJACK PUBLISHING

P.O. Box 4668 #89611, New York NY 10163. (888)959-3352. **Website:** www.amberjackpublishing.com. Amberjack Publishing offers authors the freedom to write without burdening them with having to promote the work themselves. They retain all rights. "You will have no rights left to exploit, so you cannot resell, republish, or use your story again."

NEEDS Amberjack Publishing is always on the lookout for the next great story. "We are interested in fiction, children's books, graphic novels, science fiction, fantasy, humor, and everything in between."

HOW TO CONTACT Submit via online query form with book proposal and first 10 pages of ms.

AMG PUBLISHERS

AMG International, Inc., 6815 Shallowford Rd., Chattanooga TN 37421-1755. (423)894-6060. **Fax:** (423)894-9511. **E-mail:** ricks@amgpublishers.com. **Website:** www.amgpublishers.com. **Contact:** Rick Steele, product development/acquisitions. Estab. 1985. "Publishing division of AMG International began in 1985 with release of the *Hebrew-Greek Key Word Study Bible* in the King James Version. This groundbreaking study Bible is now published in 4 other Bible translations. In-depth study and examination of original biblical languages provide some of our core Bible study and reference tools. In 1998, AMG launched the successful Following God Bible study series (primarily for women) that examines key characters of the Bible along with life application principles. AMG has also been publishing young adult inspirational fantasy fiction since 2005 but is not currently accepting fiction mss. Profits from sales of our books and Bibles are funneled back into world missions and childcare efforts of parent organization, AMG Publishers." Publishes hardcover and trade paperback originals, electronic originals, and audio Bible and book originals. Book catalog and guidelines online.

IMPRINTS Living Ink Books; God and Country Press; AMG Bible Studies.

NEEDS "We are not presently acquiring fiction of any genre, though we continue to publish a number of titles in the young adult inspirational fantasy category."

TERMS Pays 10-16% royalty on net sales. Advance negotiable. Responds in 1 month to queries; 4 months to proposals/mss.

TIPS "AMG is open to well-written, niche Bible study, reference, and devotional books that meet immediate needs."

AMULET BOOKS

Imprint of Abrams, 115 W. 18th St., Sixth Floor, New York NY 10001. **Website:** www.amuletbooks.com. Estab. 2004.

Does not accept unsolicited mss or queries.

NEEDS Middle readers: adventure, contemporary, fantasy, history, science fiction, sports. Young adults/teens: adventure, contemporary, fantasy, history, science fiction, sports, suspense.

ANDERSEN PRESS

20 Vauxhall Bridge Rd., London SW1V 2SA, United Kingdom. **E-mail:** anderseneditorial@randomhouse.co.uk. **Website:** www.andersenpress.co.uk. Andersen Press is a specialist children's publisher. "We publish picture books, for which the required text would be approximately 500 words (maximum 1,000); juvenile fiction, for which the text would be approximately 3,000-5,000 words; and older fiction up to 75,000 words. We do not publish adult fiction, nonfiction, poetry, or short story anthologies." Guidelines online.

HOW TO CONTACT Send all submissions by post: Query and full ms for picture books; query with synopsis and 3 chapters for longer fiction.

ANKERWYCKE

American Bar Association, 321 N. Clark St., Chicago IL 60654. **Website:** www.ababooks.org. **Contact:** Tim Brandhorst, director of new product development. Estab. 1878. "In 1215, the Magna Carta was signed underneath the ancient Ankerwycke Yew tree, starting the process which led to rule by constitutional law—in effect, giving rights and the law to the people. And today, the ABA's Ankerwycke line of books continues to bring the law to the people. With legal fiction, true crime books, popular legal histories, public policy handbooks, and prescriptive guides to current legal and business issues, Ankerwycke is a contemporary and innovative line of books for everyone from a trusted and vested authority." Publishes hardcover and trade paperback originals. Book catalog and ms guidelines online.

NEEDS "We're actively acquiring legal fiction with extreme verisimilitude."

HOW TO CONTACT Query with cover letter, outline or TOC, and CV/bio including other credits. Include e-mail address for response.

TERMS Responds in 1 month to queries and proposals; 3 months to mss.

ANNICK PRESS, LTD.

15 Patricia Ave., Toronto ON M2M 1H9, Canada. (416)221-4802. **Fax:** (416)221-8400. **Website:** www.annickpress.com. **Contact:** The Editors. "Annick Press maintains a commitment to high-quality books that entertain and challenge. Our publications share fantasy and stimulate imagination, while encouraging children to trust their judgment and abilities." Does not accept unsolicited mss. Publishes picture books, juvenile and young adult fiction and nonfiction; specializes in trade books. Book catalog and guidelines online.

NEEDS Publisher of children's books. Not accepting picture books at this time.

TERMS Pays authors royalty of 5-12% based on retail price. Offers advances (average amount: $3,000). Pays illustrators royalty of 5% minimum.

ANTARCTIC PRESS

7272 Wurzbach, Ste. 204, San Antonio TX 78240. (210)614-0396. **E-mail:** submissions@antarctic-press.com. **Website:** www.antarctic-press.com. **Contact:** David Hutchison. Estab. 1985. "Antarctic Press is a Texas-based company that was started in 1984. Since then, we have grown to become one of the largest publishers of comics in the U.S. Over the years we have produced more than 850 titles with a total circulation of more than 5 million. Among our titles are some of the most respected and longest-running independent series in comics today. Since our inception, our main goal has been to establish a series of titles that are unique, entertaining, and high in both quality and profitability. The titles we currently publish exhibit all these traits and appeal to a wide audience. Antarctic Press is among the top 10 publishers of comics in the United States. However, the difference in market shares between the top five publishers and the next five publishers is dramatic. Most of the publishers ranked above us have a far greater share of the market place. That being the case, we are an independent publisher with a small staff, and many of our employees have multiple responsibilities. Bigger companies would spread these responsibilities out among a larger staff. Additionally, we don't have the same financial power as a larger company. We cannot afford to pay high page rates; instead, we work on an advance and royalty system, which is determined by sales or potential sales of a particular book. We pride ourselves on being a company that gives new talent a chance to get published and take a shot at comic stardom."

NEEDS Comic books, graphic novels.

TERMS Pays royalty on net receipts; ms guidelines online.

ANVIL PRESS

P.O. Box 3008 MPO, Vancouver BC V6B 3X5, Canada. (604)876-8710. **Fax:** (604)879-2667. **E-mail:** info@anvilpress.com. **Website:** www.anvilpress.com. Estab. 1988. "Anvil Press publishes contemporary adult fiction, poetry, and drama, giving voice to up-and-coming Canadian writers, exploring all literary genres, and discovering, nurturing, and promoting new Canadian literary talent. Currently emphasizing urban-/suburban-themed fiction and poetry; de-emphasizing historical novels." Canadian authors only. No e-mail submissions. Publishes trade paperback originals. Book catalog for 9x12 SAE with 2 first-class stamps. Guidelines online.

NEEDS Contemporary, modern literature; no formulaic or genre.

HOW TO CONTACT Query with 20-30 pages and SASE.

TERMS Pays advance. Average advance is $500-2,000, depending on the genre. Responds in 2 months to queries; 6 months to mss.

TIPS "Audience is informed, educated, aware, with an opinion, culturally active (films, books, the performing arts). No U.S. authors. Research the appropriate publisher for your work."

ARBORDALE PUBLISHING

612 Johnnie Dodds, Ste. A2, Mt. Pleasant SC 29464. (843)971-6722. **Fax:** (843)216-3804. **E-mail:** katie@arbordalepublishing.com. **E-mail:** katie@arbordalelpublishing.com. **Website:** www.arbordalepublishing.com. **Contact:** Katie Hall. Estab. 2004. "The picture books we publish are usually, but not always, fictional stories with nonfiction woven into the story that relate to science or math. All books should subtly convey an educational theme through a warm story that is fun to read and that will grab a child's attention. Each book has a four-page 'For Creative Minds' section to reinforce the educational component. This section will have a craft and/or game as well as 'fun facts' to be shared by the parent, teacher, or other adult. Authors do not need to supply this information with their submission, but if their ms is accepted, they may be asked to provide additional information for this section. Mss should be less than 1,000 words and meet all of the following 4 criteria: (1) must be fun to read—mostly fiction with nonfiction facts woven into the story; (2) must have national or regional in scope; (3) must tie in to early elementary school curriculum; (4) must be marketable through a niche market such as a zoo, aquarium, or museum gift shop." Publishes hardcover, trade paperback, and electronic originals. Book catalog and guidelines online. "All mss should be submitted via e-mail to Katie Hall. Mss should be less than 1,000 words."

NEEDS Picture books: animal, folktales, nature/environment, math-related. Word length—picture books: no more than 1,500.

TERMS Pays 6-8% royalty on wholesale price. Pays small advance. Accepts electronic submissions only. Snail mail submissions are discarded without being opened.

Acknowledges receipt of ms submission within 1 month.

TIPS "Please make sure that you have looked at our website to read our complete submission guidelines and to see if we are looking for a particular subject. Mss must meet all four of our stated criteria. We look for fairly realistic, bright and colorful art-no cartoons. We want the children excited about the books. We envision the books being used at home and in the classroom."

ARCADE PUBLISHING

Skyhorse Publishing, 307 W. 36th St., 11th Floor, New York NY 10018. (212)643-6816. **Fax:** (212)643-6819. **E-mail:** arcadesubmissions@skyhorsepublishing.com. **Website:** www.arcadepub.com. **Contact:** Acquisitions Editor. Estab. 1988. "Arcade prides itself on publishing top-notch literary nonfiction and fiction, with a significant proportion of foreign writers." Publishes hardcover originals, trade paperback reprints. Book catalog and ms guidelines for #10 SASE.

NEEDS No romance, historical, science fiction.

HOW TO CONTACT Submit proposal with brief query, one- to two-page synopsis, chapter outline, market analysis, sample chapter, bio.

TERMS Pays royalty on retail price and 10 author's copies. Pays advance. Responds in 2 months if interested.

ARCHAIA

Imprint of Boom! Studios, 5670 Wilshire Blvd., Ste. 450, Los Angeles CA 90036. **Website:** www.archaia.com. **Contact:** Mark Smylie, chief creative officer. Use online submission form.

NEEDS Looking for graphic novel submissions that include finished art. "Archaia is a multi-award-winning graphic novel publisher with more than 75 renowned publishing brands, including such domestic and international hits as *Artesia, Mouse Guard*, and a line of Jim Henson graphic novels including *Fraggle Rock* and *The Dark Crystal*. Publishes creator-shared comic books and graphic novels in the adventure, fantasy, horror, pulp noir, and science fiction genres that contain idiosyncratic and atypical writing and art. *Archaia does not generally hire freelancers or arrange for freelance work, so submissions should only be for completed book and series proposals.*"

ARCH STREET PRESS

1122 County Line Rd., Bryn Mawr PA 19010. (877)732-ARCH. **E-mail:** contact@archstreetpress.org. **Website:** www.archstreetpress.org. **Contact:** Robert Rimm, managing editor. Estab. 2010. Arch Street Press is an independent nonprofit publisher dedicated to the collaborative work of creative visionaries, social entrepreneurs, and leading scholars worldwide. Arch Street Press is part of the Institute for Leadership Education, Advancement, and Development, a Pennsylvania-based 501(c)(3) nonprofit with offices in Philadelphia and Bryn Mawr. It has served as a key force for community leadership development since 1995, fostering a degreed citizenry to tangibly improve and sustain the economic, civic, and social well-being of communities throughout the U.S. Please visit our website for further information, including our Innovate podcast series with international CEOs and leaders, current and upcoming books, and a wide-ranging blog. Publishes hardcover, trade paperback, mass market paperback, and electronic originals. Book catalog and guidelines online.

HOW TO CONTACT Query with SASE. Submit proposal package, including outline and 3 sample chapters.

TERMS Pays 6-20% royalty on retail price. Responds in 1-2 months.

ARROW PUBLICATIONS, LLC

20411 Sawgrass Dr., Montgomery Village MD 20886. (301)299-9422. **Fax:** (240)632-8477. **E-mail:** arrow_info@arrowpub.com. **Website:** www.arrowpub.com. **Contact:** Tom King, managing editor; Maryan Gibson, acquisition editor. Estab. 1987. Guidelines online.

No graphic novels until further notice.

NEEDS "We are looking for outlines of stories heavy on romance with elements of adventure/intrigue/mystery. We will consider other romance genres, such as fantasy, western, inspirational, and historical, as long as the romance element is strong."

HOW TO CONTACT Query with outline first with SASE. Consult submission guidelines online before submitting.

TERMS Makes outright purchase of accepted completed scripts. Responds in 2 month to queries; 1 month to mss sent upon request.

TIPS "Our audience is primarily women 18 and older. Send query with outline only."

ARSENAL PULP PRESS

#202-211 E. Georgia St., Vancouver BC V6A 1Z6, Canada. (604)687-4233. **Fax:** (604)687-4283. **E-mail:** info@arsenalpulp.com. **Website:** www.arsenalpulp.com. **Contact:** Editorial Board. Estab. 1980. "We are interested in literature that traverses uncharted territories, publishing books that challenge and stimulate and ask probing questions about the world around us." Publishes trade paperback originals and trade paperback reprints. Book catalog for 9x12 SAE with IRCs or online. Guidelines online.

NEEDS No children's books or genre fiction, i.e., westerns, romance, horror, mystery, etc.

HOW TO CONTACT Submit proposal package, outline, clips, 2-3 sample chapters.

TERMS Responds in 2-4 months.

ARTE PUBLICO PRESS

University of Houston, 4902 Gulf Fwy., Bldg. 19, Room 100, Houston TX 77204-2004. **Fax:** (713)743-2847. **E-mail:** submapp@uh.edu. **Website:** artepublicopress.com. **Contact:** Nicolas Kanellos, editor. Estab. 1979. Arte Publico Press is the oldest and largest publisher of Hispanic literature for children and adults in the U.S. "We are a showcase for Hispanic literary creativity, arts and culture. Our endeavor is to provide a national forum for U.S.-Hispanic literature." Publishes hardcover originals, trade paperback originals ,and reprints. Book catalog available free. Guidelines online.

NEEDS "Written by U.S.-Hispanics."

HOW TO CONTACT Submissions made through online submission form.

TERMS Pays 10% royalty on wholesale price. Provides 20 author's copies; 40% discount on subsequent copies. Pays $1,000-3,000 advance. Responds in 1 month to queries and proposals; 4 months to mss.

TIPS "Include cover letter in which you 'sell' your book—why we should publish the book, who will want to read it, why does it matter, etc. Use our ms submission online form. Format files accepted: DOC, TXT, RTF files. Other formats will not be accepted. Ms files cannot be larger than 5MB. Once editors review your ms, you will receive an e-mail with the decision. Revision process could take up to 4 months."

ⒶⓈ ATHENEUM BOOKS FOR YOUNG READERS

Simon & Schuster, 1230 Avenue of the Americas, New York NY 10020. **Website:** kids.simonandschuster.com. Estab. 1961. Publishes hardcover originals. Guidelines for #10 SASE.

NEEDS Juvenile books. "We have few specific needs except for books that are fresh, interesting, and well written. Fad topics are dangerous, as are works you haven't polished to the best of your ability. We also don't need safety pamphlets, ABC books, coloring books, or board books. In writing picture book texts, avoid the coy and 'cutesy,' such as stories about characters with alliterative names." Agented submissions only. No paperback romance-type fiction.

TIPS "Study our titles."

AUTUMN HOUSE PRESS

87½ Westwood St., Pittsburgh PA 15211. (412)381-4261. **E-mail:** info@autumnhouse.org. **Website:** www.autumnhouse.org. **Contact:** Christine Stroud, senior editor. Estab. 1998. "We are a nonprofit literary press specializing in high-quality poetry, fiction, and nonfiction. Our editions are beautifully designed and printed, and they are distributed nationally. Approximately one-third of our sales are to college literature and creative writing classes." Member CLMP and Academy of American Poets. "We distribute our own titles. We do extensive national promotion through ads, web-marketing, reading tours, book fairs, and conferences. We are open to all genres. The quality of writing concerns us, not the genre. You can also learn about our annual Fiction Prize, Poetry Prize, Nonfiction Prize, and Chapbook Award competitions, as well as our online journal, *Coal Hill Review*." (Please note that Autumn House accepts unsolicited mss *only* through these competitions.) Publishes hardcover, trade paperback, and electronic originals. Format: acid-free paper; offset printing; perfect and casebound (cloth) bound; sometimes contains illustrations. Average print order: 1,000. Debut novel print order: 1,000. Catalog online. Guidelines online.

NEEDS Holds competition/award for short stories, novels, story collections, memoirs, nonfiction. "We ask that all submissions from authors new to Autumn House come through 1 of our annual contests." See website for official guidelines. Responds to queries in 2 days. Accepts mss only through contest. Never critiques/comments on rejected mss.

HOW TO CONTACT "Submit only through our annual contest. The competition is tough, so submit only your best work!"

TERMS Pays 7% royalty on wholesale price. Pays $0-2,500 advance. Responds in 1-3 days on queries and proposals; 3 months on mss.

AVON ROMANCE

Harper Collins Publishers, 10 E. 53 St., New York NY 10022. **E-mail:** info@avonromance.com. **Website:** www.avonromance.com. Estab. 1941. "Avon has been publishing award-winning books since 1941. It is recognized for having pioneered the historical romance category and continues to bring the best of commercial literature to the broadest possible audience." Publishes paperback and digital originals and reprints.

HOW TO CONTACT Submit a query and ms via the online submission form at www.avonromance.com/impulse.

BAEN BOOKS

P.O. Box 1188, Wake Forest NC 27588. (919)570-1640. **E-mail:** info@baen.com. **Website:** www.baen.com. Estab. 1983. "We publish only science fiction and fantasy. Writers familiar with what we have published in the past will know what sort of material we are most likely to publish in the future: powerful plots with solid scientific and philosophical underpinnings are the sine qua non for consideration for science fiction submissions. As for fantasy, any magical system must be both rigorously coherent and integral to the plot, and overall the work must at least strive for originality."

NEEDS "Style: Simple is generally better; in our opinion, good style, like good breeding, never calls attention to itself." Length: 100,000-130,000 words. "Generally we are uncomfortable with mss under 100,000 words, but if your novel is really wonderful, send it along regardless of length."

HOW TO CONTACT "Query letters are not necessary. We prefer to see complete mss accompanied by a synopsis. We prefer not to see simultaneous submissions. Electronic submissions are strongly preferred. *We no longer accept submissions by e-mail.* Send ms by using the submission form at: ftp.baen.com/slush/submit.aspx. No disks unless requested. Attach ms as a Rich Text Format (RTF) file. Any other format will not be considered."

TERMS Responds to mss within 12-18 months.

BAILIWICK PRESS

309 E. Mulberry St., Fort Collins CO 80524. (970)672-4878. **Fax:** (970)672-4731. **E-mail:** info@bailiwickpress.com. **E-mail:** aldozelnick@gmail.com. **Website:** www.bailiwickpress.com. "We're a micropress that produces books and other products that inspire and tell great stories. Our motto is 'books with something to say.' We are now considering submissions, agented and unagented, for children's and young adult fiction. We're looking for smart, funny, and layered writing that kids will clamor for. Authors who already have a following have a leg up. We are only looking for humorous children's fiction. Please do not submit work for adults. Illustrated fiction is desired but not required. (Illustrators are also invited to send samples.) Make us laugh out loud, ooh and aah, and cry, 'Eureka!'"

HOW TO CONTACT "Please read the Aldo Zelnick series to determine if we might be on the same page, then fill out our submission form. Please do not send submissions via snail mail or phone calls. You must complete the online submission form to be considered. If, after completing and submitting the form, you also need to send us an e-mail attachment (such as sample illustrations or excerpts of graphics), you may e-mail them to aldozelnick@gmail.com."

TERMS Responds in 6 months.

Ⓐ BALLANTINE BANTAM DELL

Imprint of Penguin Random House, Inc., 1745 Broadway, 18th Floor, New York NY 10019. (212)782-9000. **Website:** www.penguinrandomhouse.com. Estab. 1952. Ballantine Bantam Dell publishes a wide variety of nonfiction and fiction. Publishes hardcover, trade paperback, mass market paperback originals. Guidelines online.

HOW TO CONTACT Agented submissions only.

Ⓐ BALZER & BRAY

HarperCollins Children's Books, 10 E. 53rd St., New York NY 10022. **Website:** www.harpercollinschildrens.com. Estab. 2008. "We publish bold, creative, groundbreaking picture books and novels that appeal directly to kids in a fresh way."

NEEDS Picture books, young readers: adventure, animal, anthology, concept, contemporary, fantasy, history, humor, multicultural, nature/environment, poetry, science fiction, special needs, sports, suspense. Middle readers, young adults/teens: adventure, animal, anthology, contemporary, fantasy, history, humor, multicultural, nature/environment, poetry, science fiction, special needs, sports, suspense.

HOW TO CONTACT Agented submissions only.

TERMS Offers advances. Pays illustrators by the project.

Ⓐ BANCROFT PRESS

P.O. Box 65360, Baltimore MD 21209-9945. (410)358-0658. **Fax:** (410)764-1967. **E-mail:** bruceb@bancroftpress.com. **Website:** www.bancroftpress.com. **Contact:** Bruce Bortz, editor/publisher (health, investments, politics, history, humor, literary novels, mystery/thrillers, chick lit, young adult). "Bancroft Press is a general trade publisher. We publish young adult fiction and adult fiction, as well as occasional nonfiction. Our only mandate is 'books that enlighten.'" Publishes hardcover and trade paperback originals. Guidelines online.

NEEDS "Our current focuses are young adult fiction, women's fiction, and literary fiction."

HOW TO CONTACT Submit complete ms.

TERMS Pays 6-8% royalty. Pays various royalties on retail price. Pays $750 advance. Responds in 6-12 months.

TIPS "We advise writers to visit our website and to be familiar with our previous work. Patience is the no. 1 attribute contributors must have. It takes us a very long time to get through submitted material, because we are such a small company. Also, we only publish 4-6 books per year, so it may take a long time for your optioned book to be published. We like to be able to market our books to be used in schools and in libraries. We prefer fiction that bucks trends and moves in a new direction. We are especially interested in mysteries and humor (especially humorous mysteries)."

Ⓐ⊘ BANTAM BOOKS

Imprint of Penguin Random House, Inc., 1745 Broadway, New York NY 10019. (212)782-9000. **Website:** www.randomhousebooks.com. Not seeking mss at this time.

Ⓐ BARBOUR PUBLISHING, INC.

P.O. Box 719, Urichsville OH 44683. **E-mail:** submissions@barbourbooks.com. **Website:** www.barbourbooks.com. Estab. 1981. "Barbour Books publishes inspirational/devotional material that is nondenominational and evangelical in nature. We're a Christian evangelical publisher." Specializes in short, easy-to-read Christian bargain books. "Faithfulness to the Bible and Jesus Christ are the bedrock values behind every book Barbour's staff produces."

"We no longer accept unsolicited submissions unless they are submitted through professional literary agencies. For more information, we encourage new fiction authors to join a professional writers organization like American Christian Fiction Writers."

FREDERIC C. BEIL, PUBLISHER, INC.

609 Whitaker St., Savannah GA 31401. (912)233-2446. **E-mail:** fcb@beil.com. **Website:** www.beil.com. **Contact:** Frederic Beil. Estab. 1982. Frederic C. Beil publishes books in the subject areas of history, literature, and biography. Publishes original titles in hardcover, softcover, and e-book. Catalog online.

IMPRINTS The Sandstone Press.

HOW TO CONTACT Query with SASE.

TERMS Pays 7.5% royalty on retail price. Responds in 1 week to queries.

TIPS "Our objectives are to offer to the reading public carefully selected texts, to adhere to high standards in the choice of materials and in bookmaking craftsmanship, to produce books that exemplify good taste in format and design, and to maintain the lowest cost consistent with quality."

BELLEBOOKS

P.O. Box 300921, Memphis TN 38130. (901)344-9024. **E-mail:** bellebooks@bellebooks.com. **Website:** www.bellebooks.com. Estab. 1999. BelleBooks began by publishing Southern fiction. It has become a "second home" for many established authors, who also continue to publish with major publishing houses. Guidelines online.

NEEDS "Yes, we'd love to find the next Harry Potter, but our primary focus for the moment is publishing for the teen market."

HOW TO CONTACT Query e-mail with brief synopsis and credentials/credits with full ms attached (RTF format preferred).

TIPS "Our list aims for the teen reader and the crossover market. If you're a 'Southern Louise Rennison,' that would catch our attention. Humor is always a plus. We'd love to see books featuring teen boys as protagonists. We're happy to see dark, edgy books on serious subjects."

BELLEVUE LITERARY PRESS

New York University School of Medicine, Dept. of Medicine, NYU School of Medicine, 550 First Avenue, OBV 612, New York NY 10016. (212)263-7802. **E-mail:** blpsubmissions@gmail.com. **Website:** blpress.org. **Contact:** Erika Goldman, publisher/editorial director. Estab. 2005. "Publishes literary and authoritative fiction and nonfiction at the nexus of the arts and the sciences, with a special focus on medicine. As our authors explore cultural and historical representations of the human body, illness, and health, they address the impact of scientific and medical practice on the individual and society."

HOW TO CONTACT Submit complete ms.

TIPS "We are a project of New York University's School of Medicine, and while our standards reflect NYU's excellence in scholarship, humanistic medicine, and science, our authors need not be affiliated with NYU. We are not a university press and do not receive any funding from NYU. Our publishing operations are financed exclusively by foundation grants, private donors, and book sales revenue."

Ⓐ⊘ BERKLEY/NAL

Penguin Group (USA) Inc., 375 Hudson St., New York NY 10014. **Website:** penguin.com. **Contact:** Leslie Gelbman, president and publisher. Estab. 1955. The Berkley Publishing Group publishes a variety of general nonfiction and fiction, including the traditional categories of romance, mystery, and science fiction. Publishes paperback and mass market originals and reprints.

"Due to the high volume of mss received, most Penguin Group (USA) Inc. imprints do not normally accept unsolicited mss. The preferred and standard method for having mss considered for publication by a major publisher is to submit them through an established literary agent."

IMPRINTS Ace, Jove, Heat, Sensation, Berkley Prime Crime, Berkley Caliber.

NEEDS No occult fiction.

HOW TO CONTACT Prefers agented submissions.

BETHANY HOUSE PUBLISHERS

Division of Baker Publishing Group, 6030 E. Fulton Rd., Ada MI 49301. (616)676-9185. **Fax:** (616)676-9573. **Website:** bakerpublishinggroup.com/bethanyhouse. Estab. 1956. Bethany House Publishers specializes in books that communicate Biblical truth and assist people in both spiritual and practical areas of life. Considers unsolicited work only through a professional literary agent or through ms submission services, Authonomy or Christian Manuscript Submissions. Guidelines online. All unsolicited mss returned unopened. Publishes hardcover and trade paperback originals, mass market paperback reprints. Book catalog for 9x12 envelope and 5 first-class stamps.

TERMS Pays royalty on net price. Pays advance. Responds in 3 months to queries.

TIPS "Bethany House Publishers' publishing program relates Biblical truth to all areas of life—whether in the framework of a well-told story, of a challenging book for spiritual growth, or of a Bible reference work. We are seeking high-quality fiction and nonfiction that will inspire and challenge our audience."

BIRCH BOOK PRESS

Birch Brook Impressions, P.O. Box 81, Delhi NY 13753. **Fax:** (607)746-7453. **E-mail:** birchbrook@copper.net. **Website:** www.birchbrookpress.info. **Contact:** Tom Tolnay, editor/publisher; Leigh Eckmair, art and research editor; Joyce Tolnay, account services. Estab. 1982. Birch Brook Press "is a book printer/typesetter/designer that uses monies from these activities to publish several titles of its own each year with cultural and literary interest." Specializes in literary work, flyfishing, baseball, outdoors, themed short fiction anthologies, and books about books. Occasionally publishes trade paperback originals. Book catalog online.

NEEDS "Mostly we do anthologies around a particular theme generated in-house. We make specific calls for fiction when we are doing an anthology."

HOW TO CONTACT Query with SASE and submit sample chapter(s), synopsis.

TERMS Pays modest royalty on acceptance. Responds in 3-6 months.

TIPS "Write well on subjects of interest to BBP, such as outdoors, flyfishing, baseball, music, literary stories, fine poetry, books about books."

BKMK PRESS

University of Missouri—Kansas City, 5101 Rockhill Rd., Kansas City MO 64110-2499. (816)235-2558. **Fax:** (816)235-2611. **E-mail:** bkmk@umkc.edu. **Website:** newletters.org. Estab. 1971. "BkMk Press publishes fine literature. Reading period February-June." Publishes trade paperback originals. Guidelines online.

HOW TO CONTACT Query with SASE.

TERMS Responds in 4-6 months to queries.

TIPS "We skew toward readers of literature, particularly contemporary writing. Because of our limited number of titles published per year, we discourage apprentice writers or 'scattershot' submissions."

BLACK HERON PRESS

P.O. Box 13396, Mill Creek WA 98082. **Website:** www.blackheronpress.com. Estab. 1984. "Black Heron Press publishes primarily literary fiction." Publishes hardcover and trade paperback originals, trade paperback reprints. Catalog available online.

NEEDS "All of our fiction is character driven. We don't want to see fiction written for the mass market. If it sells to the mass market, fine, but we don't see ourselves as a commercial press."

HOW TO CONTACT Submit proposal package, including cover letter and first 40-50 pages of your completed novel.

TERMS Pays 8% royalty on retail price. Responds in 6 months.

TIPS "Our readers love good fiction—they are scattered among all social classes, ethnic groups, and zip code areas. If you can't read our books, at least check out our titles on our website."

BLACK LAWRENCE PRESS

326 Bigham St., Pittsburgh PA 15211. **E-mail:** editors@blacklawrencepress.com. **Website:** www.black-

lawrencepress.com. **Contact:** Diane Goettel, executive editor. Estab. 2003. Black Lawrence press seeks to publish intriguing books of literature—novels, short story collections, poetry collections, chapbooks, anthologies, and creative nonfiction. Will also publish the occasional translation from German. Publishes 15-20 books/year, mostly poetry and fiction. Mss are selected through open submission and competition. Books are 20-400 pages, offset-printed or high-quality POD, perfect-bound, with 4-color cover.

HOW TO CONTACT Submit complete ms.

TERMS Pays royalties. Responds in 6 months to mss.

O BLACK LYON PUBLISHING, LLC

P.O. Box 567, Baker City OR 97814. **E-mail:** info@blacklyonpublishing.com. **E-mail:** queries@blacklyonpublishing.com. **Website:** www.blacklyonpublishing.com. **Contact:** The Editors. Estab. 2007. "Black Lyon Publishing is a small, independent publisher. We are very focused on giving new novelists a launching pad into the industry." Publishes paperback and e-book originals. Guidelines online.

HOW TO CONTACT Prefers e-mail queries.

TERMS Responds in 2-3 months to queries.

TIPS "Write a good, solid romance with a setting, premise, character, or voice just a little 'different' than what you might usually find on the market. We like unique books—but they still need to be romances."

BLACK VELVET SEDUCTIONS PUBLISHING

E-mail: ric@blackvelvetseductions.com. **Website:** www.blackvelvetseductions.com. **Contact:** Richard Savage, acquisitions editor. Estab. 2005. "We publish 2 types of material: (1) romance novels and short stories and (2) romantic stories involving spanking between consenting adults. We look for well-crafted stories with a high degree of emotional impact. No first-person point of view. All material must be in third-person point of view." Publishes trade paperback and electronic originals. "We have a high interest in republishing backlist titles in electronic and trade paperback formats once rights have reverted to the author." Accepts only complete mss. Query with SASE. Submit complete ms. Catalog free or online. Guidelines online.

NEEDS All stories must have a strong romance element. "There are very few sexual taboos in our erotic line. We tend to give our authors the widest latitude. If it is safe, sane, and consensual we will allow our authors latitude to show us the eroticism. However, we will not consider mss with any of the following: bestiality (sex with animals), necrophilia (sex with dead people), pedophilia (sex with children)."

HOW TO CONTACT Only accepts electronic submissions.

TERMS Pays 10% royalty for paperbacks; 50% royalty for electronic books. Responds in 6 months to queries; 8 months to proposals; 8-12 months to mss.

TIPS "We publish romance and erotic romance. We look for books written in very deep point of view. Shallow point of view remains the no. 1 reason we reject mss in which the storyline generally works."

JOHN F. BLAIR, PUBLISHER

1406 Plaza Dr., Winston-Salem NC 27103. (336)768-1374. **Fax:** (336)768-9194. **E-mail:** editorial@blairpub.com. **Website:** www.blairpub.com. **Contact:** Carolyn Sakowski, president. Estab. 1954. No poetry, young adult, children's, science fiction. Fiction must be set in southern U.S., or author must have strong Southern connection. Catalog online. Guidelines online.

NEEDS "We specialize in regional books, with an emphasis on nonfiction categories such as history, travel, folklore, and biography. We publish only 1 or 2 works of fiction each year. Fiction submitted to us should have some connection with the Southeast. We do not publish children's books, poetry, or category fiction such as romances, science fiction, or spy thrillers. We do not publish collections of short stories, essays, or newspaper columns." Does not want fiction set outside southern U.S.

HOW TO CONTACT Accepts unsolicited mss. Any fiction submitted should have some connection with the Southeast, either through setting or author's background. Send a cover letter, giving a synopsis of the book. Include the first 2 chapters (at least 50 pages) of the ms. "You may send the entire ms if you wish. If you choose to send only samples, please include the projected word length of your book and estimated completion date in your cover letter. Send a biography of the author, including publishing credits and credentials."

TERMS Pays royalties. Pays negotiable advance. Responds in 3-6 months.

TIPS "We are primarily interested in nonfiction titles. Most of our titles have a tie-in with North Carolina or the southeastern U.S. We do not accept short story collections. Please enclose a cover letter and outline with the ms. We prefer to review queries before we are sent complete mss. Queries should include an approximate word count."

BLAZEVOX [BOOKS]

131 Euclid Ave., Kenmore NY 14217. **E-mail:** editor@blazevox.org. **Website:** www.blazevox.org. **Contact:** Geoffrey Gatza, editor/publisher. Estab. 2005. "We are a major publishing presence specializing in innovative fictions and wide-ranging fields of innovative forms of poetry and prose. Our goal is to publish works that are challenging, creative, attractive, and yet affordable to individual readers. Articles of submission depend on many criteria, but, overall, items submitted must conform to 1 ethereal trait: Your work must not suck. Put plainly, bad art should be punished; we will not promote it. However, all submissions will be reviewed and the author will receive feedback. We are human, too." Guidelines online.

NEEDS Submit complete ms via e-mail.

TERMS Pays 10% royalties on fiction and poetry books, based on net receipts. This amount may be split across multiple contributors. "We do not pay advances."

TIPS "We actively contract and support authors who tour, read, and perform their work; play an active part of the contemporary literary scene; and seek a readership."

BOA EDITIONS, LTD.

P.O. Box 30971, Rochester NY 14603. (585)546-3410. **Fax:** (585)546-3913. **E-mail:** contact@boaeditions.org. **Website:** www.boaeditions.org. **Contact:** Jenna Fisher, director of marketing and production; Peter Conners, publisher. Estab. 1976. BOA Editions, Ltd., a not-for-profit publisher of poetry, short fiction, and poetry-in-translation, fosters readership and appreciation of contemporary literature. By identifying, cultivating, and publishing both new and established poets and selecting authors of unique literary talent, BOA brings high-quality literature to the public. Publishes hardcover, trade paperback, and digital e-book originals. Book catalog online. Guidelines online.

NEEDS "BOA publishes literary fiction through its American Reader Series. While aesthetic quality is subjective, our fiction will be by authors more concerned with the artfulness of their writing than the twists and turns of plot. Our strongest current interest is in short story collections (and short short story collections). We strongly advise you to read our published fiction collections." Temporarily closed to novel/collection submissions.

TERMS Negotiates royalties. Pays variable advance. Responds in 1 week to queries; 5 months to mss.

BOLD STROKES BOOKS, INC.

P.O. Box 249, Valley Falls NY 12185. (518)677-5127. **Fax:** (518)677-5291. **E-mail:** sandy.boldstrokes@gmail.com. **E-mail:** bsbsubmissions@gmail.com. **Website:** www.boldstrokesbooks.com. **Contact:** Sandy Lowe, senior editor. Publishes trade paperback originals and reprints, electronic originals and reprints. Guidelines online.

IMPRINTS BSB Fiction, Victory Editions Lesbian Fiction, Liberty Editions Gay Fiction, Soliloquy Young Adult, Heat Stroke Erotica.

NEEDS "Submissions should have a gay, lesbian, transgendered, or bisexual focus and should be positive and life affirming."

HOW TO CONTACT Submit completed ms with bio, cover letter, and synopsis—electronically only.

TERMS Sliding scale based on sales volume and format. Responds in 1 month to queries; 2 months to proposals; 4 months to mss.

TIPS "We are particularly interested in authors who are interested in craft enhancement, technical development, and exploring and expanding traditional genre definitions and boundaries and are looking for a long-term publishing relationship."

BOOKFISH BOOKS

E-mail: bookfishbooks@gmail.com. **Website:** bookfishbooks.com. **Contact:** Tammy Mckee, acquisitions editor. BookFish Books is looking for novel-length young adult, new adult, and middle-grade works in all subgenres. Both published and unpublished, agented or unagented authors are welcome to submit. "Sorry, but we do not publish novellas, picture books, early reader/chapter books, or adult novels." Responds to every query. Guidelines online.

HOW TO CONTACT Query via e-mail with a brief synopsis and first 3 chapters of ms.

TIPS "We only accept complete mss. Please do not query us with partial mss or proposals."

BOOKOUTURE

StoryFire Ltd., 23 Sussex Rd., Ickenham UB10 8P, United Kingdom. **E-mail:** questions@bookouture.com. **E-mail:** pitch@bookouture.com. **Website:** www.bookouture.com. **Contact:** Oliver Rhodes, founder and publisher. Estab. 2012. Publishes mass market paperback and electronic originals and reprints. Book catalog online.

IMPRINTS Imprint of StoryFire Ltd.

NEEDS "We are looking for entertaining fiction targeted at modern women. That can be anything from steampunk to erotica, historicals to thrillers. A distinctive author voice is more important than a particular genre or ms length."

HOW TO CONTACT Submit complete ms.

TERMS Pays 45% royalty on wholesale price. Responds in 1 month.

TIPS "The most important questions we ask of submissions are: 'Why would a reader buy the next book? What's distinctive or different about your storytelling that will make readers want to come back for more?' We look to acquire global English-language rights for e-book and print-on-demand."

BOREALIS PRESS, LTD.

8 Mohawk Crescent, Napean ON K2H 7G6, Canada. (613)829-0150. **Fax:** (613)829-7783. **E-mail:** drt@borealispress.com. **Website:** www.borealispress.com. Estab. 1972. "Our mission is to publish work that will be of lasting interest in the Canadian book market." Currently emphasizing Canadian fiction, nonfiction, drama, poetry. De-emphasizing children's books. Publishes hardcover and paperback originals and reprints. Book catalog online. Guidelines online.

IMPRINTS Tecumseh Press.

NEEDS Only material Canadian in content and dealing with significant aspects of the human situation.

HOW TO CONTACT Query with SASE. Submit clips, 1-2 sample chapters. No unsolicited mss.

TERMS Pays 10% royalty on net receipts; plus 3 free author's copies. Responds in 2 months to queries; 4 months to mss.

BROADWAY BOOKS

Penguin Random House, 1745 Broadway, New York NY 10019. (212)782-9000. **Fax:** (212)782-9411. **Website:** crownpublishing.com/imprint/broadway-books. Estab. 1995. "Broadway publishes high-quality general interest nonfiction and fiction for adults." Publishes hardcover and trade paperback books.

IMPRINTS Broadway Books, Broadway Business, Doubleday, Doubleday Image, Doubleday Religious Publishing, Main Street Books, Nan A. Talese.

HOW TO CONTACT Agented submissions only.

TERMS Pays royalty on retail price. Pays advance.

BRONZE MAN BOOKS

Millikin University, 1184 W. Main, Decatur IL 62522. (217)424-6264. **E-mail:** rbrooks@millikin.edu. **Website:** www.bronzemanbooks.com. **Contact:** Dr. Randy Brooks, editorial board; Edwin Walker, editorial board. Estab. 2006. A student-owned and operated press located on Millikin University's campus in Decatur, Ill., Bronze Man Books is dedicated to integrating quality design and meaningful content. The company exposes undergraduate students to the process of publishing by combining the theory of writing, publishing, editing, and designing with the practice of running a book publishing company. This emphasis on performance learning is a hallmark of Millikin's brand of education. Publishes hardcover, trade paperback, literary chapbooks, and mass market paperback originals.

NEEDS Subjects include art, graphic design, exhibits, general.

HOW TO CONTACT Submit completed ms.

TERMS Outright purchase based on wholesale value of 10% of a press run. Responds in 1-3 months.

TIPS "The art books are intended for serious collectors and scholars of contemporary art, especially of artists from the Midwestern U.S. These books are published in conjunction with art exhibitions at Millikin University or the Decatur Area Arts Council. The children's books have our broadest audience, and the literary chapbooks are intended for readers of contemporary fiction, drama, and poetry."

THE BRUCEDALE PRESS

P.O. Box 2259, Port Elgin ON N0H 2C0, Canada. (519)832-6025. **E-mail:** info@brucedalepress.ca. **Website:** brucedalepress.ca. The Brucedale Press publishes books and other materials of regional interest and merit, as well as literary, historical, and/or pictorial works. Publishes hardcover and trade paperback originals. Book catalog online. "Unless responding to an invitation to submit, query first by Canada Post with outline and sample chapter to book-length mss. Send full mss for work intended for children." Guidelines online.

Accepts works by Canadian authors only. Book submissions reviewed November to January. Submissions to *The Leaf Journal* accepted in September and March only. Mss must be in

English and thoroughly proofread before being sent. Use Canadian spellings and style.

TERMS Pays royalty.

TIPS "Our focus is very regional. In reading submissions, I look for quality writing with a strong connection to the Queen's Bush area of Ontario. All authors should visit our website, get a catalog, and read our books before submitting."

BULLITT PUBLISHING

P.O. Box, Austin TX 78729. **E-mail:** bullittpublishing@yahoo.com. **E-mail:** submissions@bullittpublishing.com. **Website:** bullittpublishing.com. **Contact:** Pat Williams, editor. Estab. 2012. "Bullitt Publishing is a royalty-offering publishing house specializing in smart, contemporary romance. We are proud to provide print-on-demand distribution through the world's most comprehensive distribution channel, including amazon.com and barnesandnoble.com. Digital distribution is available through the world's largest distibutor of e-books and can be downloaded to reading devices such as the iPhone, Ipod Touch, Amazon Kindle, Sony Reader, or Barnes & Noble nook. E-books are distributed to the Apple iBookstore, Barnes & Noble, Sony, Kobo, and the Diesel eBook Store. Whether this is your first novel or your 101st novel, Bullitt Publishing will treat you with the same amount of professionalism and respect. While we expect well-written, entertaining mss from all of our authors, we promise to provide a high-quality, professional product in return." Publishes trade paperback and electronic originals.

IMPRINTS Tempo Romance.

BUSTER BOOKS

16 Lion Yard, Tremadoc Rd., London WA SW4 7NQ, United Kingdom. (020)7720-8643. **Fax:** (022)7720-8953. **E-mail:** enquiries@mombooks.com. **Website:** www.busterbooks.co.uk. "We are dedicated to providing irresistible and fun books for children of all ages. We typically publish b&w nonfiction for children aged 8-12 and novelty titles—including doodle books."

TIPS "We do not accept picture book or poetry submissions. Please do not send original artwork as we cannot guarantee its safety." Visit website before submitting.

BY LIGHT UNSEEN MEDIA

20 Heald St, Pepperell MA 01463. (978)433-8866. **Fax:** (978)433-8866. **E-mail:** vyrdolak@bylightunseenmedia.com. **Website:** bylightunseenmedia.com. **Contact:** Inanna Arthen, owner/editor in chief. Estab. 2006. The only small press owned and operated by a recognized expert in vampire folklore, media, and culture, By Light Unseen Media was founded in 2006. "Our mission is to explore and celebrate the variety, imagination, and ambiguities of the vampire theme in fiction, history, and the human psyche. No other mythic trope remotely approaches the vampire as an ever-changing and evolving mirror of the zeitgeist, deepest fears, and most fervent fantasies of each successive generation—and none ever will. Particular trends and treatments rise and fall in popularity, but the vampire will never go out of style. By Light Unseen Media offers fiction and nonfiction that transcends the popular clichés of the day and demonstrates the creative variety and infinite potential of the vampire motif." Publishes hardcover, paperback, and electronic originals. Catalog online. Ms guidelines online.

NEEDS "We are a niche small press that *only* publishes fiction relating in some way to vampires. Within that guideline, we're interested in almost any genre that includes a vampire trope; the more creative and innovative, the better. Restrictions are noted in the submission guidelines (no derivative fiction based on other works, such as *Dracula*, no gore-for-gore's-sake 'splatter' horror, etc.) We do not publish anthologies." Does not want anything that does not focus on vampires as the major theme.

HOW TO CONTACT Submit proposal package, including synopsis, 3 sample chapters, brief author bio. "We encourage electronic submissions." Unsolicited mss will not be considered.

TERMS Pays royalty of 50-70% on net as explicitly defined in contract. Payment quarterly. No advance. Responds in 3 months.

TIPS "We strongly urge authors to familiarize themselves with the vampire genre and not imagine that they're doing something new and amazingly different just because they're not imitating the current fad."

CALAMARI PRESS

Via Titta Scarpetta #28, Rome 00153, Italy. **E-mail:** derek@calamaripress.net. **Website:** www.calamaripress.com. Calamari Press publishes books of literary text and art. Mss are selected by invitation. Occasionally has open submission period—check website. Helps to be published in *SleepingFish* first. Publishes paperback originals. Guidelines online.

HOW TO CONTACT Query with outline/synopsis and 3 sample chapters. Accepts queries by e-mail only. Include brief bio. Send SASE or IRC for return of ms.

TERMS Pays in author's copies. Responds to mss in 2 weeks.

CALKINS CREEK

Boyds Mills Press, 815 Church St., Honesdale PA 18431. **Website:** www.calkinscreekbooks.com. Estab. 2004. "We aim to publish books that are a well-written blend of creative writing and extensive research, which emphasize important events, people, and places in U.S. history." Guidelines online.

HOW TO CONTACT Submit outline/synopsis and 3 sample chapters.

TERMS Pays authors royalty or work purchased outright.

TIPS "Read through our recently published titles and review our catalog. When selecting titles to publish, our emphasis will be on important events, people, and places in U.S. history. Writers are encouraged to submit a detailed bibliography, including secondary and primary sources, and expert reviews with their submissions."

CANDLEWICK PRESS

99 Dover St., Somerville MA 02144. (617)661-3330. **Fax:** (617)661-0565. **E-mail:** bigbear@candlewick.com. **Website:** www.candlewick.com. Estab. 1991. "Candlewick Press publishes high-quality, illustrated children's books for ages infant through young adult. We are a truly child-centered publisher." Publishes hardcover and trade paperback originals, and reprints.

Candlewick Press is not accepting queries or unsolicited mss at this time.

NEEDS Picture books: animal, concept, contemporary, fantasy, history, humor, multicultural, nature/environment, poetry. Middle readers, young adults: contemporary, fantasy, history, humor, multicultural, poetry, science fiction, sports, suspense/mystery.

HOW TO CONTACT "We currently do not accept unsolicited editorial queries or submissions. If you are an author or illustrator and would like us to consider your work, please read our submissions policy (online) to learn more."

TERMS Pays authors royalty of 2.5-10% based on retail price. Offers advance.

TIPS "We no longer accept unsolicited mss. See our website for further information about us."

CANTERBURY HOUSE PUBLISHING, LTD.

4535 Ottawa Trail, Sarasota FL 34233. (941)312-6912. **Website:** www.canterburyhousepublishing.com. **Contact:** Sandra Horton, editor. Estab. 2009. "Our audience is made up of readers looking for wholesome fiction with good Southern stories with elements of mystery, romance, and inspiration and/or are looking for true stories of achievement and triumph over challenging circumstances. We are very strict on our submission guidelines due to our small staff and our target market of Southern regional settings." Publishes hardcover, trade paperback, and electronic originals. Book catalog online. Guidelines online.

HOW TO CONTACT Query with SASE and through website.

TERMS Pays 10-15% royalty on wholesale price. Responds in 1 month to queries; 3 months to mss.

TIPS "Because of our limited staff, we prefer authors who have good writing credentials and submit edited mss. We also look at authors who are business and marketing savvy and willing to help promote their books."

CARNEGIE MELLON UNIVERSITY PRESS

5032 Forbes Ave., Pittsburgh PA 15289-1021. (412)268-2861. **Fax:** (412)268-8706. **E-mail:** carnegiemellonuniversitypress@gmail.com. **Website:** www.cmu.edu/universitypress. Estab. 1972. Publishes hardcover and trade paperback originals. Book catalog and guidelines online.

CAROLINA WREN PRESS

120 Morris St., Durham NC 27701. (919)560-2738. **E-mail:** carolinawrenpress@earthlink.net. **Website:** www.carolinawrenpress.org. **Contact:** Andrea Selch, president. Estab. 1976. "We publish poetry, fiction, and memoirs by and/or about people of color, women, gay/lesbian issues, and work by writers from, living in, or writing about the U.S. South." Guidelines online.

Accepts simultaneous submissions, but "let us know if work has been accepted elsewhere."

NEEDS "We are no longer publishing children's literature on any topic." Books: 6×9 paper; typeset; various bindings; illustrations. Distributes titles through amazon.com, Barnes & Noble, Baker & Taylor, and on their website. "We very rarely accept any unsolicited mss, but we accept submissions for the Doris Bakwin Award for Writing by a Woman in Jan-March of even-numbered years."

HOW TO CONTACT Query by mail. "We will accept e-mailed queries—a letter in the body of the e-mail describing your project—but please do not send large attachments."

TERMS Responds in 3 months to queries; 6 months to mss.

TIPS "Best way to get read is to submit to a contest."

CARTWHEEL BOOKS

Imprint of Scholastic Trade Division, 557 Broadway, New York NY 10012. (212)343-6100. **Website:** www.scholastic.com. Estab. 1991. Cartwheel Books publishes innovative books for children up to age 8. "We are looking for 'novelties' that are books first, play objects second. Even without its gimmick, a Cartwheel Book should stand alone as a valid piece of children's literature." Publishes novelty books, easy readers, board books, hardcover and trade paperback originals. Guidelines available free.

NEEDS "Again, the subject should have mass market appeal for very young children. Humor can be helpful, but not necessary. Mistakes writers make are a reading level that is too difficult, a topic of no interest or too narrow, or mss that are too long."

HOW TO CONTACT Accepts mss from agents only.

CAVE BOOKS

Cave Research Foundation, Hamilton Valley Rd., Cave City KY 42127. (609)530-9743. **E-mail:** editor@cavebooks.com. **Website:** www.cavebooks.com. **Contact:** Elizabeth Winkler, managing editor. Estab. 1980. Cave Books publishes books only on caves, karst, and speleology. Publishes hardcover and trade paperback originals and reprints.

NEEDS "Must be realistic and centrally concerned with cave exploration. The cave and action in the cave must be central, authentic, and realistic. No Gothic, no science fiction, no fantasy, no romance, no mystery, or no poetry. No novels that are not entirely about caves. We will not respond to mss that do not fit this very limited category."

HOW TO CONTACT Query with SASE. Submit complete ms.

TERMS Pays 10% royalty on retail price. Responds in 2 weeks to queries; 3 months to mss.

TIPS "Our readers are interested only in caves, karst, and speleology. Please do not send mss on other subjects."

CAVE HOLLOW PRESS

P.O. Drawer J, Warrensburg MO 64093. **E-mail:** gbcrump@cavehollowpress.com. **Website:** www.cavehollowpress.com. **Contact:** G.B. Crump, editor. Estab. 2001. Publishes trade paperback originals. Available online. Guidelines available free.

NEEDS "We publish fiction by Midwestern authors and/or with Midwestern themes and/or settings. Our website is updated frequently to reflect the current type of fiction Cave Hollow Press is seeking."

HOW TO CONTACT Query with SASE.

TERMS Pays 7-12% royalty on wholesale price. Pays negotiable amount in advance. Responds in 1-2 months to queries and proposals; 3-6 months to mss.

TIPS "Our audience varies based on the type of book we are publishing. We specialize in Missouri and Midwest regional fiction. We are interested in talented writers from Missouri and the surrounding Midwest. Check our submission guidelines on the website for what type of fiction we are interested in currently."

CEDAR FORT, INC.

2373 W. 700 S, Springville UT 84663. (801)489-4084. **Fax:** (801)489-1097. **Website:** www.cedarfort.com. Estab. 1986. "Each year we publish well over 100 books, and many of those are by first-time authors. At the same time, we love to see books from established authors. As one of the largest book publishers in Utah, we have the capability and enthusiasm to make your book a success, whether you are a new author or a returning one. We want to publish uplifting and edifying books that help people think about what is important in life, books people enjoy reading to relax and feel better about themselves, and books to help improve lives. Although we do put out several children's books each year, we are extremely selective. Our children's books must have strong religious or moral values and must contain outstanding writing and an excellent storyline." Publishes hardcover, trade paperback originals and reprints, mass market paperback and electronic reprints. Catalog and guidelines online.

IMPRINTS Council Press, Sweetwater Books, Bonneville Books, Front Table Books, Hobble Creek Press, CFI, Plain Sight Publishing, Horizon Publishers, Pioneer Plus.

HOW TO CONTACT Submit completed ms.

TERMS Pays 10-12% royalty on wholesale price. Pays $2,000-50,000 advance. Responds in 1 month on queries; 2 months on proposals; 4 months on mss.

TIPS "Our audience is rural, conservative, mainstream. The first page of your ms is very important because we start reading every submission, but good-writing and plot keep us reading."

CHANGELING PRESS LLC

315 N. Centre St., Martinsburg WV 25404. **E-mail:** submissions@changelingpress.com. **Website:** www.changelingpress.com. **Contact:** Margaret Riley, publisher. Estab. 2004. Erotic romance, novellas only (8,000-25,000 words). "We're currently looking for contemporary and futuristic short fiction, single title, series, and serials in the following genres and themes: science fiction/futuristic, dark and urban fantasy, paranormal, BDSM, action adventure, guilty pleasures (adult contemporary kink), new adult, menage, bisexual and more, gay, interracial, BBW, cougar (M/F), silver fox (M/M), men and women in uniform, vampires, werewolves, elves, dragons and magical creatures, other shape shifters, magic, dark desires (demons and horror), and hentai (tentacle monsters)." Publishes e-books. Catalog online. Guidelines available.

IMPRINTS Razor's Edge Press.

NEEDS Accepts unsolicited submissions. No lesbian fiction submissions without prior approval, please. Absolutely no lesbian fiction written by men.

HOW TO CONTACT E-mail submissions only.

TERMS Pays 35% gross royalties on site, 50% gross off site monthly. Does not pay advance. Responds in 1 week to queries.

CHARLESBRIDGE PUBLISHING

85 Main St., Watertown MA 02472. (617)926-0329. **Fax:** (617)926-5720. **E-mail:** tradeeditorial@charlesbridge.com. **E-mail:** yasubs@charlesbridge.com. **Website:** www.charlesbridge.com. Estab. 1980. "Charlesbridge publishes high-quality books for children with a goal of creating lifelong readers and lifelong learners. Our books encourage reading and discovery in the classroom, library, and home. We believe that books for children should offer accurate information, promote a positive worldview, and embrace a child's innate sense of wonder and fun. To this end, we continually strive to seek new voices, new visions, and new directions in children's literature. As of September 2015, we are now accepting young adult novels for consideration." Publishes hardcover and trade paperback nonfiction and fiction, children's books for the trade and library markets. Guidelines online.

NEEDS Strong stories with enduring themes. Charlesbridge publishes both picture books and transitional bridge books (books ranging from early readers to middle-grade chapter books). "Our fiction titles include lively, plot-driven stories with strong, engaging characters." No alphabet books, board books, coloring books, activity books, or books with audiotapes or CD-ROMs.

HOW TO CONTACT Please submit only 1 ms at a time. For picture books and shorter bridge books, please send a complete ms. For fiction books longer than 30 ms pages, please send a detailed plot synopsis, a chapter outline, and 3 chapters of text. If sending a young adult novel, mark the front of the envelope with "YA NOVEL ENCLOSED." Please note, for young adult, e-mail submissions are preferred to the following address; yasubs@charlesbridge.com. Only responds if interested. Full guidelines on site.

TERMS Pays royalty. Pays advance. Responds in 3 months.

TIPS "To become acquainted with our publishing program, we encourage you to review our books and visit our website where you will find our catalog."

CHRISTIAN FOCUS PUBLICATIONS

Geanies House, Fearn, Tain Ross-shire Scotland IV20 1TW, United Kingdom. (44)1862-871-011. **Fax:** (44)1862-871-699. **E-mail:** submissions@christianfocus.com. **Website:** www.christianfocus.com. **Contact:** Director of Publishing. Estab. 1975. Specializes in Christian material, nonfiction, fiction, educational material.

NEEDS Picture books, young readers, adventure, history, religion. Middle readers: adventure, problem novels, religion. Young adult/teens: adventure, history, problem novels, religion. Average word length: young readers—5,000; middle readers—max 10,000; young adult/teen—max 20,000.

TERMS Responds to queries in 2 weeks; mss in 3 to 6 months.

TIPS "Be aware of the international market in regard to writing style/topics as well as illustration styles. Our company sells rights to European as well as Asian countries. Fiction sales are not as good as they were. Christian fiction for youngsters is not a product that is performing well in comparison to nonfiction such as Christian biography/Bible stories/church history, etc."

CHRONICLE BOOKS

680 Second St., San Francisco CA 94107. **E-mail:** submissions@chroniclebooks.com. **Website:** www.chroniclebooks.com. "We publish an exciting range of books, stationery, kits, calendars, and novelty formats. Our list includes children's books and interactive formats; young adult books; cookbooks; fine art, design, and photography; pop culture; craft, fashion, beauty, and home decor; relationships, mind/body/spirit; innovative formats such as interactive journals, kits, decks, and stationery; and much, much more." Book catalog for 9x12 SAE and 8 first-class stamps. Ms guidelines for #10 SASE.

NEEDS Only interested in fiction for children and young adults. No adult fiction.

HOW TO CONTACT Submit complete ms (picture books); submit outline/synopsis and 3 sample chapters (for older readers). Will not respond to submissions unless interested. Will not consider submissions by fax, e-mail, or disk. Do not include SASE; do not send original materials. No submissions will be returned.

TERMS Generally pays authors in royalties based on retail price, "though we do occasionally work on a flat-fee basis." Advance varies. Illustrators paid royalty based on retail price or flat fee. Responds to queries in 1 month.

CHRONICLE BOOKS FOR CHILDREN

680 Second St., San Francisco CA 94107. (415)537-4200. **Fax:** (415)537-4460. **E-mail:** submissions@chroniclebooks.com. **Website:** www.chroniclekids.com. "Chronicle Books for Children publishes an eclectic mixture of traditional and innovative children's books. Our aim is to publish books that inspire young readers to learn and grow creatively while helping them discover the joy of reading. We're looking for quirky, bold artwork and subject matter." Publishes hardcover and trade paperback originals. Book catalog for 9x12 envelope and 3 first-class stamps. Guidelines online.

NEEDS Does not accept proposals by fax, via e-mail, or on disk. When submitting artwork, either as a part of a project or as samples for review, do not send original art.

TERMS Pays variable advance. Responds in 2-4 weeks to queries; 6 months to mss.

TIPS "We are interested in projects that have a unique bent to them—be it in subject matter, writing style, or illustrative technique. As a small list, we are looking for books that will lend our list a distinctive flavor. Primarily we are interested in fiction and nonfiction picture books for children up to 8 years old, and nonfiction books for children up to 12 years old. We publish board, pop-up, and other novelty formats as well as picture books. We are also interested in early chapter books, middle-grade fiction, and young adult projects."

CINCO PUNTOS PRESS

701 Texas Ave., El Paso TX 79901. (915)838-1625. **Fax:** (915)838-1635. **E-mail:** info@cincopuntos.com. **Website:** www.cincopuntos.com. **Contact:** Lee Byrd, acquisitions editor. "We don't always know what we're looking for until we actually see it, but what matters to us is that the writing is good, that it is work that comes from the heart and soul of the author, and that it fits well with the concerns of our press." Call first for submission details.

NEEDS "We do not look at unsolicited mss or at work that comes via e-mail."

CLARION BOOKS

Houghton Mifflin Co., 215 Park Ave. S., New York NY 10003. **Website:** www.hmhco.com. Estab. 1965. "Clarion Books publishes picture books, nonfiction, and fiction for infants through grade 12. Avoid telling your stories in verse unless you are a professional poet. We are no longer responding to your unsolicited submission unless we are interested in publishing it. Please do not include a SASE. Submissions will be recycled, and you will not hear from us regarding the status of your submission unless we are interested. We regret that we cannot respond personally to each submission, but we do consider each and every submission we receive." Publishes hardcover originals for children. Guidelines online.

NEEDS "Clarion is highly selective in the areas of historical fiction, fantasy, and science fiction. A novel must be superlatively written in order to find a place on the list. Mss that arrive without an SASE of adequate size will *not* be responded to or returned. Accepts fiction translations."

HOW TO CONTACT Submit complete ms. No queries, please. Send to only *1* Clarion editor.

TERMS Pays 5-10% royalty on retail price. Pays minimum of $4,000 advance. Responds in 2 months to queries.

TIPS "Looks for freshness, enthusiasm—in short, life."

CLEIS PRESS

Cleis Press & Viva Editions, 101 Hudson St., 37th Floor, Ste. 3705, Jersey City NJ 07302. **Fax:** (510)845-8001. **E-mail:** kthomas@cleispress.com. **Website:** www.cleispress.com. **Contact:** Karen Thomas, publisher. Estab. 1980. Cleis Press publishes provocative, intelligent books in the areas of sexuality, gay and lesbian studies, erotica, fiction, gender studies, and human rights. Publishes books that inform, enlighten, and entertain. Areas of interest include gift, inspiration, health, family and childcare, self-help, women's issues, reference, cooking. "We do our best to bring readers quality books that celebrate life, inspire the mind, revive the spirit, and enhance lives all around. Our authors are practical visionaries; people who offer deep wisdom in a hopeful and helpful manner."

NEEDS "We are looking for high-quality fiction and nonfiction."

HOW TO CONTACT Submit complete ms. Include brief bio, list of publishing credits. Send SASE for return of ms, or send a disposable ms and SASE for reply only.

TERMS Responds in 2 month to queries.

TIPS "Be familiar with publishers' catalogs; be absolutely aware of your audience; research potential markets; present fresh new ways of looking at your topic; avoid 'PR' language and include publishing history in query letter."

COACH HOUSE BOOKS

80 bpNichol Ln., Toronto ON M5S 3J4, Canada. (416)979-2217. **Fax:** (416)977-1158. **E-mail:** editor@chbooks.com. **Website:** www.chbooks.com. **Contact:** Alana Wilcox, editorial director. Publishes trade paperback originals by Canadian authors. Guidelines online.

HOW TO CONTACT "Electronic submissions are welcome. Please send your complete ms, along with an introductory letter that describes your work and compares it to at least 2 current Coach House titles, explaining how your book would fit our list, and a literary CV listing your previous publications and relevant experience. If you would like your ms back, please enclose a large-enough SAE with adequate postage. If you don't want your ms back, a small stamped envelope or e-mail address is fine. We prefer electronic submissions. Please e-mail PDF files to editor@chbooks.com and include the cover letter and CV as a part of the ms. Please send your ms only once. Revised and updated versions will not be read, so make sure you're happy with your text before sending. You can also mail your ms. Please do not send it by ExpressPost or Canada Post courier—regular Canada Post mail is much more likely to arrive here. Be patient. We try to respond promptly, but we do receive hundreds of submissions, so it may take us several months to get back to you. Please do not call or e-mail to check on the status of your submission. We will answer you as promptly as possible."

TERMS Pays 10% royalty on retail price. Responds in 6-8 months to queries.

TIPS "We are not a general publisher and publish only Canadian poetry, fiction, select nonfiction, and drama. We are interested primarily in innovative or experimental writing."

COFFEE HOUSE PRESS

79 13th NE, Ste. 110, Minneapolis MN 55413. (612)338-0125. **Fax:** (612)338-4004. **E-mail:** info@coffeehousepress.org. **Website:** www.coffeehousepress.org. **Contact:** Molly Fuller, production editor. Estab. 1984. This successful nonprofit small press has received numerous grants from various organizations including the NEA, the McKnight Foundation and Target. Books published by Coffee House Press have won numerous honors and awards. For example, *The Book of Medicines* by Linda Hogan won the Colorado Book Award for Poetry and the Lannan Foundation Literary Fellowship. Publishes hardcover and trade paperback originals. Book catalog and ms guidelines online.

NEEDS Seeks literary novels, short story collections and poetry.

HOW TO CONTACT Query first with outline and samples (20-30 pages) during annual reading periods (March 1-31 and September 1-30).

TERMS Responds in 4-6 weeks to queries; up to 6 months to mss.

TIPS "Look for our books at stores and libraries to get a feel for what we like to publish. No phone calls, e-mails, or faxes."

CONSTABLE & ROBINSON, LTD.

50 Victoria Embankment, London EC4Y 0DZ, United Kingdom. **E-mail:** info@littlebrown.co.uk. **Website:** www.littlebrown.co.uk/constablerobinson/about-constable-publisher.page. Publishes hardcover and trade paperback originals. Book catalog available free.

NEEDS Publishes "crime fiction (mysteries) and historical crime fiction." Length: 80,000 words minimum; 130,000 words maximum.

HOW TO CONTACT Agented submissions only.

TERMS Pays royalty. Pays advance. Responds in 1-3 months.

COTEAU BOOKS

Thunder Creek Publishing Co-operative Ltd., 2517 Victoria Ave., Regina SK S4P 0T2, Canada. (306)777-0170. **Fax:** (306)522-5152. **E-mail:** coteau@coteaubooks.com. **Website:** www.coteaubooks.com. **Contact:** Geoffrey Ursell, publisher. Estab. 1975. "Our mission is to publish the finest in Canadian fiction, nonfiction, poetry, drama, and children's literature, with an emphasis on Saskatchewan and prairie writers. De-emphasizing science fiction, picture books." Publishes chapter books for young readers aged 9-12 and novels for older kids ages 13-15 and ages 15 and up. Publishes trade paperback originals and reprints. Book catalog available free. Guidelines online.

NEEDS No science fiction. No children's picture books.

HOW TO CONTACT Query.

TERMS Pays 10% royalty on retail price. Responds in 3 months.

TIPS "Look at past publications to get an idea of our editorial program. We do not publish romance, horror, or picture books but are interested in juvenile and teen fiction from Canadian authors. Submissions, even queries, must be made in hard copy only. We do not accept simultaneous/multiple submissions. Check our website for new submission timing guidelines."

COVENANT COMMUNICATIONS, INC.

920 E. State Rd., Ste. F, P.O. Box 416, American Fork UT 84003. (801)756-1041. **Fax:** (801)756-1049. **E-mail:** submissionsdesk@covenant-lds.com. **Website:** www.covenant-lds.com. **Contact:** Kathryn Gordon, managing editor. Estab. 1958. "Currently emphasizing inspirational, doctrinal, historical, biography, and fiction." Guidelines online.

NEEDS "Mss do not necessarily have to include LDS/Mormon characters or themes, but cannot contain profanity, sexual content, gratuitous violence, witchcraft, vampires, and other such material."

HOW TO CONTACT Submit complete ms.

TERMS Pays 6-15% royalty on retail price. Responds in 1 month on queries; 4-6 months on mss.

TIPS "We are actively looking for new, fresh regency romance authors."

CRAIGMORE CREATIONS

PMB 114, 4110 SE Hawthorne Blvd., Portland OR 97124. (503)477-9562. **E-mail:** info@craigmorecreations.com. **Website:** www.craigmorecreations.com. Estab. 2009.

HOW TO CONTACT Submit proposal package. See website for detailed submission guidelines.

CRESCENT MOON PUBLISHING

P.O. Box 1312, Maidstone Kent ME14 5XU, United Kingdom. (44)(162)272-9593. **E-mail:** cresmopub@yahoo.co.uk. **Website:** www.crmoon.com. **Contact:** Jeremy Robinson, director (arts, media, cinema, literature); Cassidy Hughes (visual arts). Estab. 1988. "Our mission is to publish the best in contemporary work, in poetry, fiction, and critical studies, and selections from the great writers. Currently emphasizing nonfiction (media, film, music, painting). De-emphasizing children's books." Publishes hardcover and trade paperback originals. Book catalog and ms guidelines free.

IMPRINTS Joe's Press, Pagan America Magazine, Passion Magazine.

NEEDS "We do not publish much fiction at present but will consider high-quality new work."

HOW TO CONTACT Query with SASE. Submit outline, clips, 2 sample chapters, bio.

TERMS Pays royalty. Pays negotiable advance. Responds in 2 months to queries; 4 months to proposals and mss.

TIPS "Our audience is interested in new contemporary writing."

CRESTON BOOKS

P.O. Box 9369, Berkeley CA 94709. **E-mail:** submissions@crestonbooks.co. **Website:** crestonbooks.co. Creston Books is author-illustrator driven, with talented, award-winning creators given more editorial freedom and control than in a typical New York house. Catalog online. Guidelines available.

HOW TO CONTACT Please paste text of picture books or first chapters of novels in the body of e-mail. Words of Advice for submitting authors listed on the site.

TERMS Pays advance.

CRIMSON ROMANCE

Adams Media, a division of F+W Media, Inc., 57 Littlefield St., Avon MA 02322. (508)427-7100. **E-mail:** editorcrimson@gmail.com. **Website:** crimsonromance.com. **Contact:** Tara Gelsomino, executive editor. "Direct-to-e-book romance imprint of Adams Media." Publishes electronic originals.

NEEDS "We're open to romance submissions in 5 popular subgenres: romantic suspense, contemporary, paranormal, historical, and erotic romance. Within those subgenres, we are flexible about what happens. It's romance, so there must be a happily-ever-after, but we're open to how your characters get there. You won't come up against preconceived ideas about what can or can't happen in romance or what kind of characters you can or can't have. Our only rule is everyone has to be a consenting adult. Other than that, we're looking for smart, savvy heroines; fresh voices; and new takes on old favorite themes." Length: 55,000-90,000 words.

HOW TO CONTACT Please see current submission guidelines online.

Ⓐ⊘ CROWN PUBLISHING GROUP

Penguin Random House, 1745 Broadway, New York NY 10019. (212)782-9000. **E-mail:** crownosm@randomhouse.com. **Website:** crownpublishing.com. Estab. 1933. Publishes popular fiction and nonfiction hardcover originals. Agented submissions only. See website for more details.

IMPRINTS Amphoto Books, Back Stage Books, Billboard Books, Broadway Books, Clarkson Potter, Crown, Crown Archetype, Crown Business, Crown Forum, Harmony Books, Image Books, Potter Craft, Potter Style, Ten Speed Press, Three Rivers Press, Waterbrook Multnomah, Watson-Guptill.

CRYSTAL SPIRIT PUBLISHING, INC.

P.O. Box 12506, Durham NC 27709. **E-mail:** crystalspiritinc@gmail.com. **E-mail:** submissions@crystalspiritinc.com. **Website:** www.crystalspiritinc.com. **Contact:** Vanessa S. O'Neal, senior managing editor. Estab. 2004. "Our readers are lovers of high-quality books that are sold as direct sales in bookstores and gift shops, and placed in libraries and schools. They support independent authors, and they expect works that will provide them with entertainment, inspiration, romance, and education. Our audience loves to read and will embrace niche authors who love to write." Publishes hardcover, trade paperback, mass market paperback, and electronic originals. Book catalog and ms guidelines online. Guidelines for submissions are stated on the website.

HOW TO CONTACT Submit cover letter, synopsis, and 30 pages by USPS mail, e-mail, or website submission.

TERMS Pays 20-45% royalty on retail price. Responds in 1-3 months to mss.

TIPS "Submissions are accepted for publication throughout the year. Works should be positive and nonthreatening. Typed pages only. Nontyped entries will not be reviewed or returned. Ensure that all contact information is correct, abide by the submission guidelines, and do not send follow-up e-mails or calls."

CURIOSITY QUILLS

Whampa, LLC, P.O. Box 2160, Reston VA 20195. (800)998-2509. **Fax:** (800)998-2509. **E-mail:** editor@curiosityquills.com. **Website:** curiosityquills.com. **Contact:** Alisa Gus. Estab. 2011. Curiosity Quills is a publisher of hard-hitting dark science fiction, speculative fiction, and paranormal works aimed at adults, young adults, and new adults. Firm publishes science fiction, speculative fiction, steampunk, paranormal, and urban fantasy, and corresponding romance titles under its new Rebel Romance imprint. Catalog available. Guidelines online.

IMPRINTS Curiosity Quills Press, Rebel Romance.

NEEDS Looking for "thought-provoking, mind-twisting rollercoasters—challenge our mind, turn our world upside-down, and make us question. Those are the makings of a true literary marauder."

HOW TO CONTACT Submit ms using online submission form or e-mail to acquisitions@curiosityquills.com.

TERMS Pays variable royalty. Does not pay advance. Responds in 1-6 weeks.

CURIOUS FOX

Brunel Rd., Houndmills, Basingstoke Hants RG21 6XS, United Kingdom. **E-mail:** submissions@curious-fox.com. **Website:** www.curious-fox.com. "Do you love telling good stories? If so, we'd like to hear from you. Curious Fox is on the lookout for U.K.-based authors, whether new talent or established authors with exciting ideas. We take submissions for books aimed at ages 3 to young adult. If you have story ideas that are bold, fun, and imaginative, then please do get in touch!" Guidelines online.

HOW TO CONTACT "Send your submission via e-mail to submissions@curious-fox.com. Include the following in the body of the e-mail, not as attachments: sample chapters, résumé, list of previous publishing credits, if applicable. We will respond only if your writing samples fit our needs."

DAW BOOKS, INC.

Penguin Random House, 375 Hudson St., New York NY 10014-3658. (212)366-2096. **Fax:** (212)366-2090. **E-mail:** daw@us.penguingroup.com. **Website:** www.dawbooks.com. **Contact:** Peter Stampfel, submissions editor. Estab. 1971. DAW Books publishes science fiction and fantasy. Publishes hardcover and paperback originals and reprints. Guidelines online.

NEEDS "Currently seeking modern urban fantasy and paranormals. We like character-driven books with appealing protagonists, engaging plots, and well-constructed worlds. We accept both agented and unagented mss."

HOW TO CONTACT Submit entire ms, cover letter, SASE. "Do not submit your only copy of anything. The average length of the novels we publish varies but is almost never less than 80,000 words."

TERMS Pays in royalties with an advance negotiable on a book-by-book basis. Responds in 3 months.

KATHY DAWSON BOOKS

Penguin Random House, 375 Hudson St., New York NY 10014. (212)366-2000. **Website:** kathydawsonbooks.tumblr.com. **Contact:** Kathy Dawson, vice-president and publisher. Estab. 2014. Mission statement: "Publish stellar novels with unforgettable characters for children and teens that expand their vision of the world, sneakily explore the meaning of life, celebrate the written word, and last for generations. The imprint strives to publish tomorrow's award contenders: quality books with strong hooks in a variety of genres with universal themes and compelling voices—books that break the mold and the heart." Guidelines online.

HOW TO CONTACT Accepts fiction queries via snail mail only. Include cover sheet with one-sentence elevator pitch, main themes, author version of catalog copy for book, first 10 pages of ms (double-spaced, Times New Roman, 12 point type), and publishing history. No SASE needed. Responds only if interested.

TERMS Responds only if interested.

DEL REY BOOKS

Penguin Random House, 1745 Broadway, 18th Floor, New York NY 10019. (212)782-9000. **Website:** www.penguinrandomhouse.com. Estab. 1977. Del Rey publishes top-level fantasy, alternate history, and science fiction. Publishes hardcover, trade paperback, and mass market originals and mass market paperback reprints.

IMPRINTS Del Rey/Manga, Del Rey/Lucas Books.

HOW TO CONTACT Agented submissions only.

TERMS Pays royalty on retail price. Pays competitive advance.

TIPS "Del Rey is a reader's house. Pay particular attention to plotting, strong characters, and dramatic, satisfactory conclusions. It must be/feel believable. That's what the readers like. In terms of mass market, we basically created the field of fantasy bestsellers. Not that it didn't exist before, but we put the mass into mass market."

DIAL BOOKS FOR YOUNG READERS

Penguin Random House, 345 Hudson St., New York NY 10014. (212)366-2000. **Website:** www.penguin.com/children. Estab. 1961. "Dial Books for Young Readers publishes quality picture books for ages 18 months-6 years; lively, believable novels for middle readers and young adults; and occasional nonfiction for middle readers and young adults." Publishes hardcover originals. Book catalog and guidelines online.

NEEDS "Especially looking for lively and well-written novels for middle-grade and young adult children involving a convincing plot and believable characters. The subject matter or theme should not already be overworked in previously published books. The approach must not be demeaning to any minority group, nor should the roles of female characters (or others) be stereotyped, though we don't think books should be didactic or in any way message-y. No topics inappropriate for the juvenile, young adult, and middle-grade audiences. No plays."

HOW TO CONTACT Accepts unsolicited queries and up to 10 pages for longer works and unsolicited mss for picture books. Will only respond if interested.

TERMS Pays royalty. Pays varies advance. Responds in 4-6 months to queries.

TIPS "Our readers are anywhere from preschool age to teenage. Picture books must have strong plots, lots of action, unusual premises, or universal themes treated with freshness and originality. Humor works well in these books. A very well-thought-out and intelligently presented book has the best chance of being taken on. Genre isn't as much of a factor as presentation."

DIVERTIR

P.O. Box 232, North Salem NH 03073. **E-mail:** info@divertirpublishing.com. **E-mail:** query@divertirpublishing.com. **Website:** www.divertirpublishing.com. **Contact:** Kenneth Tupper, publisher. Estab. 2009. Divertir Publishing is an independent publisher located in Salem, NH. "Our goal is to provide interesting and entertaining books to our readers, as well as to offer new and exciting voices in the writing community the opportunity to publish their work. We seek to combine an understanding of traditional publishing with a unique understanding of the modern market to best serve both our authors and readers." Publishes trade paperback and electronic originals. Catalog online. Guidelines online.

NEEDS "We are particularly interested in the following: science fiction, fantasy, historical, alternate history, contemporary mythology, mystery and suspense, paranormal, and urban fantasy." Does not consider erotica or mss with excessive violence.

HOW TO CONTACT Electronically submit proposal package, including synopsis and query letter with author's bio.

TERMS Pays 10-15% royalty on wholesale price (for novels and nonfiction). Does not pay advance. Responds in 1-3 months on queries; 3-4 months on proposals and mss.

TIPS "Please see our Author Info page (online) for more information."

DOWN THE SHORE PUBLISHING

P.O. Box 100, West Creek NJ 08092. **Fax:** (609)597-0422. **E-mail:** info@down-the-shore.com. **Website:** www.down-the-shore.com. **Contact:** Acquisitions Editor. "Bear in mind that our market is regional-New Jersey, the Jersey Shore, the mid-Atlantic, and seashore and coastal subjects." Publishes hardcover and trade paperback originals and reprints. Book catalog online. Guidelines online.

HOW TO CONTACT Query with SASE. Submit proposal package, clips, 1-2 sample chapters.

TERMS Pays royalty on wholesale or retail price, or makes outright purchase. Responds in 3 months to queries.

TIPS "Carefully consider whether your proposal is a good fit for our established market."

DUFOUR EDITIONS

P.O. Box 7, 124 Byers Rd., Chester Springs PA 19425. (610)458-5005. **Fax:** (610)458-7103. **Website:** www.dufoureditions.com. Estab. 1948. "We publish literary fiction by good writers which is well received and achieves modest sales. De-emphsazing poetry and nonfiction." Publishes hardcover originals, trade paperback originals and reprints. Book catalog available free.

NEEDS "We like books that are slightly off-beat, different, and well-written."

HOW TO CONTACT Query with SASE.

TERMS Pays $100-500 advance. Responds in 3-6 months.

Ⓐ⊘ THOMAS DUNNE BOOKS

Imprint of St. Martin's Press, 175 Fifth Ave., New York NY 10010. (212)674-5151. **E-mail:** thomasdunnebooks@stmartins.com. **Website:** www.thomasdunnebooks.com. Estab. 1986. "Thomas Dunne Books publishes popular trade fiction and nonfiction. With an output of approximately 175 titles each year, his group covers a range of genres, including commercial and literary fiction, thrillers, biography, politics, sports, popular science, and more. The list is intentionally eclectic and includes a wide range of fiction and nonfiction, from first books to international bestsellers." Publishes hardcover and trade paperback originals, and reprints. Book catalog and ms guidelines free.

HOW TO CONTACT Accepts agented submissions only.

DUTTON ADULT TRADE

Penguin Random House, 375 Hudson St., New York NY 10014. (212)366-2000. **Website:** penguin.com. Estab. 1852. "Dutton currently publishes 45 hardcovers a year, roughly half fiction and half nonfiction." Publishes hardcover originals. Book catalog online.

HOW TO CONTACT Agented submissions only. No unsolicited mss.

TERMS Pays royalty. Pays negotiable advance.

TIPS "Write the complete ms and submit it to an agent or agents. They will know exactly which editor will be interested in a project."

DUTTON CHILDREN'S BOOKS

Penguin Random House, 375 Hudson St., New York NY 10014. **Website:** www.penguin.com. **Contact:** Julie Strauss-Gabel, vice president and publisher. Estab. 1852. Dutton Children's Books publishes high-quality fiction and nonfiction for readers, ranging from preschoolers to young adults, on a variety of subjects. Currently emphasizing middle-grade and young adult novels that offer a fresh perspective. De-emphasizing photographic nonfiction and picture books that teach a lesson. Publishes hardcover originals as well as novelty formats.

"Cultivating the creative talents of authors and illustrators and publishing books with purpose and heart continue to be the mission and joy at Dutton."

NEEDS Dutton Children's Books has a diverse, general interest list that includes picture books; easy-to-read books; and fiction for all ages, from first chapter books to young adult readers.

HOW TO CONTACT Query. Responds only if interested.

TERMS Pays royalty on retail price. Pays advance.

THE ECCO PRESS

195 Broadway, New York NY 10007. (212)207-7000. **Fax:** (212)702-2460. **Website:** www.harpercollins.com. Estab. 1970. Publishes hardcover and trade paperback originals and reprints.

NEEDS Literary, short story collections. "We can publish possibly 1 or 2 original novels a year."

HOW TO CONTACT Does not accept unsolicited mss.

TERMS Pays royalty. Pays negotiable advance.

TIPS "We are always interested in first novels and feel it's important that they be brought to the attention of the reading public."

EDGE SCIENCE FICTION AND FANTASY PUBLISHING

Hades Publications, Box 1714, Calgary AB T2P 2L7, Canada. (403)254-0160. **Website:** www.edgewebsite.com. **Contact:** Editorial Manager. Estab. 1996. EDGE publishes thought-provoking full-length novels and anthologies of science fiction, fantasy, and horror. Featuring works by established authors and emerging new voices, EDGE is pleased to provide quality literary entertainment in both print and pixels. Publishes hardcover, trade paperback, and e-book originals. Catalog online. Guidelines online.

IMPRINTS EDGE, EDGE-Lite, Absolute XPress.

NEEDS "We are looking for all types of fantasy, science fiction, and horror— except juvenile, erotica, and religious fiction. Short stories and poetry are only required for announced anthologies." Length: 75,000-100,000 words. Does not want juvenile, erotica, and religious fiction.

HOW TO CONTACT Submit first 3 chapters and synopsis. Check website for guidelines. Include estimated word count.

TERMS Pays 10% royalty on net price. Negotiable advance. Responds in 4-5 months to mss.

WILLIAM B. EERDMANS PUBLISHING CO.

2140 Oak Industrial Dr. NE, Grand Rapids MI 49505. (616)459-4591. **Fax:** (616)459-6540. **E-mail:** info@eerdmans.com. **E-mail:** submissions@eerdmans.com. **Website:** www.eerdmans.com. Estab. 1911. "The majority of our adult publications are religious and most of these are academic or semi-academic in character (as opposed to inspirational or celebrity books), though we also publish general trade books on the Christian life. Our nonreligious titles, most of them in regional history or on social issues, aim, similarly, at an educated audience." Publishes hardcover and paperback originals and reprints. Book catalog and ms guidelines free.

HOW TO CONTACT Query with SASE.

TERMS Responds in 4 weeks.

ELLORA'S CAVE PUBLISHING, INC.

1056 Home Ave., Akron OH 44310. **E-mail:** submissions@ellorascave.com. **Website:** www.ellorascave.com. Estab. 2000. Publishes electronic originals and reprints, print books. Guidelines online. "Read and follow detailed submission instructions."

NEEDS Erotic romance and erotica fiction of every subgenre, including gay/lesbian, menage and more, and BDSM. All must have abundant, explicit, and graphic erotic content.

HOW TO CONTACT Submit electronically only; cover e-mail as defined in our submission guidelines plus 1 attached DOCX file containing full synopsis, first 3 chapters, and last chapter.

TERMS Pays 45% royalty on amount received. Responds in 2-4 months to mss. No queries.

TIPS "Our audience is romance readers who want explicit sexual detail. They come to us because we offer sex with romance, plot, emotion. In addition to erotic romance with happy-ever-after endings, we also publish pure erotica, detailing sexual adventure and experimentation."

ELLYSIAN PRESS

E-mail: publisher@ellysianpress.com. **E-mail:** submissions@ellysianpress.com. **Website:** www.ellysianpress.com. **Contact:** Maer Wilson. Estab. 2014. "At Ellysian Press, we seek to create a sense of home for our authors, a place where they can find fulfillment as artists. Just as exceptional mortals once sought a place in the Elysian Fields, now exceptional authors can find a place here at Ellysian Press. We are accepting submissions in the following genres: fantasy, science fiction, paranormal, paranormal romance, horror, along with young/new adult in these genres. Please submit polished mss. It's best to have work read by critique groups or beta readers prior to submission." Publishes fantasy, science fiction, paranormal, paranormal romance, horror, young/new adult in these genres. Catalog online. Guidelines online.

HOW TO CONTACT "We accept online submissions only. Please submit a query letter, a synopsis, and the first 10 pages of your ms in the body of your e-mail. The subject line should be as follows: 'QUERY—Your Last Name, TITLE, Genre.' If we choose to request more, we will request the full ms in standard format. This means your ms should be formatted as follows: 1" margins on all sides and a nonjustified right margin, 12 pt. Times New Roman font, double-spaced, DOC or DOCX file format. Ensure that your paragraph indentations are done via the ruler; please DO NOT use the TAB key. There are many online guides that explain how to use the ruler. We accept simultaneous submissions. We accept submissions directly from the author or from an agent. We answer every query and submission. If you do not hear back from us within 1 week, we most likely did not receive your query. Please feel free to check with us. We are currently accepting the following genres only: fantasy, science fiction, paranormal, paranormal romance, horror, young adult/new adult in these genres. Please do not submit queries for any genres not listed above. You may e-mail queries to submissions@ellysianpress.com.

TERMS Pays quarterly. Does not pay advance. Responds in 1 week for queries; 4-6 weeks for partials and fulls.

ELM BOOKS

1175 Hwy. 130, Laramie WY 82070. (610)529-0460. **E-mail:** leila.elmbooks@gmail.com. **Website:** www.elm-books.com. **Contact:** Leila Monaghan, publisher. "We are eager to publish stories by new writers who have real stories to tell. We are looking for short stories (5,000-10,000 words) with real characters, and true-to-life stories. Whether your story is fictionalized autobiography, or other stories of real-life mayhem and debauchery, we are interested in reading them!"

NEEDS "We are looking for short stories (1,000-5,000 words) about kids of color that will grab readers' attentions—mysteries, adventures, humor, suspense, set in the present, near past, or near future, that reflect the realities and hopes of life in diverse communities." Also looking for middle-grade novels (20,000-50,000 words).

HOW TO CONTACT Send complete ms for short stories; synopsis and 3 sample chapters for novels.

TERMS Pays royalties.

ENTANGLED TEEN

Website: www.entangledteen.com. "Entangled Teen and Entangled digiTeen, our young adult imprints, publish the swoonworthy young adult romances readers crave. Whether they're dark and angsty or fun and sassy, contemporary, fantastical, or futuristic, we are seeking fresh voices with interesting twists on popular genres."

IMPRINTS Teen Crush, Teen Crave.

NEEDS "We are seeking novels in the subgenres of romantic fiction for contemporary, upper young adult with crossover appeal."

HOW TO CONTACT E-mail using site. "All submissions must have strong romantic elements. Young adult novels should be 50,000-100,000 words in length. Revised backlist titles will be considered on a case-by-case basis." Agented and unagented considered.

TERMS Pays royalty.

FAMILIUS

1254 Commerce Way, Sanger CA 93657. (559)876-2170. **Fax:** (559)876-2180. **E-mail:** bookideas@familius.com. **Website:** familius.com. **Contact:** Michele Robbins, acquisitions editor. Estab. 2011. Familius is all about strengthening families. Collective, the authors and staff have experienced a wide slice of the family-life spectrum. Some come from broken homes. Some are married and in the throes of managing a bursting household. Some are preparing to start families of their own. Together, they publish books and articles that help families be happy. Publishes hardcover, trade paperback, and electronic originals and reprints. Catalog online. Guidelines online.

NEEDS All fiction must align with Familius values statement listed on the website footer.

HOW TO CONTACT Submit a proposal package, including a synopsis, 3 sample chapters, and your author platform.

TERMS Authors are paid 10-30% royalty on wholesale price. Responds in 1 month to queries and proposals; 2 months to mss.

FANTAGRAPHICS BOOKS, INC.

7563 Lake City Way NE, Seattle WA 98115. (206)524-1967. **Fax:** (206)524-2104. **Website:** www.fantagraphics.com. **Contact:** Submissions Editor. Estab. 1976. Publishes comics for thinking readers. Does not want mainstream genres of superhero, vigilante, horror, fantasy, or science fiction. Publishes original trade paperbacks. Book catalog online. Guidelines online.

NEEDS "Fantagraphics is an independent company with a modus operandi different from larger, factory-like corporate comics publishers. If your talents are limited to a specific area of expertise (i.e., inking, writing, etc.), then you will need to develop your own team before submitting a project to us. We want to see an idea that is fully fleshed-out in your mind, at least, if not on paper. Submit a minimum of 5 fully inked pages of art, a synopsis, SASE, and a brief note stating approximately how many issues you have in mind."

TERMS Responds in 2-3 months to queries.

TIPS "Take note of the originality and diversity of the themes and approaches to drawing in such Fantagraphics titles as *Love & Rockets* (stories of life in Latin America and Chicano L.A.), *Palestine* (journalistic autobiography in the Middle East), *Eightball* (surrealism mixed with kitsch culture in stories alternately humorous and painfully personal), and *Naughty Bits* (feminist humor and short stories which both attack and commiserate). Try to develop your own, equally individual voice; originality, aesthetic maturity, and graphic storytelling skill are the signs by which Fantagraphics judges whether or not your submission is ripe for publication."

FARRAR, STRAUS & GIROUX

18 W. 18th St., New York NY 10011. (646)307-5151. **Website:** us.macmillan.com/fsg. **Contact:** Editorial Department. Estab. 1946. "We publish original and well-written material for all ages." Publishes hardcover originals and trade paperback reprints. Catalog available by request. Guidelines online.

NEEDS Do not query picture books; just send ms. Do not fax or e-mail queries or mss.

HOW TO CONTACT Send cover letter describing submission with first 50 pages.

TERMS Pays 2-6% royalty on retail price for paperbacks, 3-10% for hardcovers. Pays $3,000-25,000 advance. Responds in 2-3 months.

FARRAR, STRAUS & GIROUX FOR YOUNG READERS

Macmillan Children's Publishing Group, 175 Fifth Ave., New York NY 10010. (212)741-6900. **Fax:** (212)633-2427. **E-mail:** childrens.editorial@fsgbooks.com. **Website:** www.fsgkidsbooks.com. Estab. 1946. Book catalog available by request. Ms guidelines online.

NEEDS All levels: all categories. "Original and well-written material for all ages."

HOW TO CONTACT Submit cover letter, first 50 pages by mail only.

TIPS "Study our catalog before submitting. We will see illustrators' portfolios by appointment. Don't ask for criticism and/or advice—due to the volume of submissions we receive, it's just not possible. Never send originals. Always enclose SASE."

FAT FOX BOOKS

The Den, P.O. Box 579, Tonbridge TN9 9NG, United Kingdom. (44)(0)1580-857249. **E-mail:** hello@fatfoxbooks.com. **Website:** fatfoxbooks.com. "Can you write engaging, funny, original, and brilliant stories? We are looking for fresh new talent as well as exciting new ideas from established writers and illustrators. We publish books for children ages 3-14, and if we think the story is brilliant and fits our list, then as one of the few publishers who accepts unsolicited material, we will take it seriously. We will consider books of all genres." Guidelines online. Currently closed to submissions.

HOW TO CONTACT For picture books, send complete ms; for longer works, send first 3 chapters and estimate of final word count.

FAWCETT

The Ballantine Publishing Group, A Division of Penguin Random House, 1745 Broadway, New York NY 10019. **Website:** www.penguinrandomhouse.com. Estab. 1955. Major publisher of mystery mass market and trade paperbacks. Publishes paperback originals and reprints.

HOW TO CONTACT Agented submissions only. All unsolicited mss returned.

FEIWEL AND FRIENDS

Macmillan Children's Publishing Group, 175 Fifth Ave., New York NY 10010. (646)307-5151. **Website:** us.macmillan.com. Feiwel and Friends is a publisher of innovative children's fiction and nonfiction literature, including hardcover, paperback series, and individual titles. The list is eclectic and combines quality and commercial appeal for readers ages 0-16. The imprint is dedicated to "book by book" publishing, bringing the work of distinctive and oustanding authors, illustrators, and ideas to the marketplace. This market does not accept unsolicited mss due to the volume of submissions; they also do not accept unsolicited queries for interior art. The best way to submit a ms is through an agent. Catalog online.

FENCE BOOKS

Science Library 320, Univ. of Albany, 1400 Washington Ave., Albany NY 12222. (518)591-8162. **E-mail:** fencesubmissions@gmail.com. **Website:** www.fenceportal.org. **Contact:** Submissions Manager. "Fence Books publishes poetry, fiction, and critical texts and anthologies, and prioritizes sustained support for its authors, many of whom come to us through our book contests and then go on to publish second, third, or fourth books." Publishes hardcover originals. Guidelines online.

HOW TO CONTACT Submit via contests and occasional open reading periods.

DAVID FICKLING BOOKS

31 Beamont St., Oxford OX1 2NP, United Kingdom. (018)65-339000. **Fax:** (018)65-339009. **Website:** www.davidficklingbooks.co.uk. **Contact:** Simon Mason, managing editor. David Fickling Books is a story house." For nearly 12 years DFB has been run as an imprint—first as part of Scholastic, then of Random House. Now we've set up as an independent business." Guidelines online. Closed to submissions. Check website for when they open to submissions and for details on the Inkpot competition.

NEEDS Considers all categories.

HOW TO CONTACT Submit cover letter and 3 sample chapters as PDF attachment saved in format "Author Name_Full Title."

TERMS Responds to mss in 3 months if interested.

TIPS "We adore stories for all ages, in both text and pictures. Quality is our watch word."

FLUX

Llewellyn Worldwide, Ltd., Llewellyn Worldwide, Ltd., 2143 Wooddale Dr., Woodbury MN 55125. (651)312-8613. **Fax:** (651)291-1908. **Website:** www.fluxnow.com. Estab. 2005. "Flux seeks to publish authors who see young adult as a point of view, not a reading level. We look for books that try to capture a slice of teenage experience, whether in real or imagined worlds." Book catalog and guidelines online.

NEEDS Young adults: adventure, contemporary, fantasy, history, humor, problem novels, religion, science fiction, sports, suspense. Average word length: 50,000.

HOW TO CONTACT Accepts agented submissions only.

TERMS Pays royalties of 10-15% based on wholesale price.

TIPS "Read contemporary teen books. Be aware of what else is out there. If you don't read teen books, you probably shouldn't write them. Know your audience. Write incredibly well. Do not condescend."

FLYING EYE BOOKS

62 Great Eastern St., London EC2A 3QR, United Kingdom. (44)(0)207-033-4430. **E-mail:** picturbksubs@nobrow.net. **Website:** www.flyingeyebooks.com. Estab.

2013. Flying Eye Books is the children's imprint of award-winning visual publishing house Nobrow. FEB seeks to retain the same attention to detail and excellence in illustrated content as its parent publisher, but with a focus on the craft of children's storytelling and nonfiction. Guidelines online.

FOLDED WORD

79 Tracy Way, Meredith NH 03253. **Website:** www.foldedword.com. **Contact:** Barbara Flaherty, submissions editor. Estab. 2008. Folded Word is a literary micropress that explores the world, one voice at a time. "Our list includes globally distributed work by authors from 4 continents. We give individualized attention to the editing and design of each title." Catalog online. Guidelines online.

NEEDS "We are seeking nonformulaic narratives that have a strong sense of place and/or time, especially the exploration of unfamiliar place/time. We are looking for mss that are an escape from the everyday, be it a cleansing laugh, a cathartic cry, a virtual holiday, or even a respite from predictable plots. We are also looking for mss that are ecologically aware. We enjoy quirky characters, voices that take a chance, humor, and word play. Please, surprise us."

HOW TO CONTACT "We are especially seeking 5,000-word short stories that can be published as standalone chapbooks and chapbook-length collections of flash fiction."

TERMS Pays royalty. Advance only in rare cases with solicited books. Responds in 60 days for queries. If a full ms is requested, it may take 6 months for a final decision.

TIPS "Please be sure you have read some of our titles prior to submitting; our e-books are reasonably priced to make exploring our list easier."

FORWARD MOVEMENT

412 Sycamore St., Cincinnati OH 45202. (513)721-6659; (800)543-1813. **Fax:** (513)721-0729. **E-mail:** editorial@forwardmovement.org. **Website:** www.forwardmovement.org. **Contact:** Richelle Thompson, managing editor. Estab. 1934. "Forward Movement was established to help reinvigorate the life of the church. Many titles focus on the life of prayer, where our relationship with God is centered, death, marriage, baptism, recovery, joy, the Episcopal Church, and more. Currently emphasizing prayer/spirituality." Book catalog free. Guidelines online.

TERMS Responds in 1 month.

TIPS "Audience is primarily Episcopalians and other Christians."

FOUR WAY BOOKS

Box 535, Village Station, New York NY 10014. **E-mail:** editors@fourwaybooks.com. **Website:** www.fourwaybooks.com. **Contact:** Martha Rhodes, director. Estab. 1993. "Four Way Books is a not-for-profit literary press dedicated to publishing poetry and short fiction by emerging and established writers. Each year, Four Way Books publishes the winners of its national poetry competitions, as well as collections accepted through general submission, panel selection, and solicitation by the editors."

NEEDS Open reading period: June 1-30. Accepts book-length story collections and novellas. Submission guidelines will be posted online at end of May. Does not want novels or translations.

FRANCES LINCOLN CHILDREN'S BOOKS

Frances Lincoln, 74-77 White Lion St., Islington, London N1 9PF, United Kingdom. (44)(20)7284-4009. **Website:** www.franceslincoln.com. Estab. 1977. "Our company was founded by Frances Lincoln in 1977. We published our first books 2 years later, and we have been creating illustrated books of the highest quality ever since, with special emphasis on gardening, walking and the outdoors, art, architecture, design, and landscape. In 1983, we started to publish illustrated books for children. Since then we have won many awards and prizes with both fiction and nonfiction children's books."

NEEDS Average word length: picture books—1,000; young readers—9,788; middle readers—20,653; young adults—35,407.

HOW TO CONTACT Query by e-mail.

TERMS Responds in 6 weeks to mss.

FREE SPIRIT PUBLISHING, INC.

6325 Sandburg Rd., Ste. 100, Golden Valley MN 55427-3674. (612)338-2068. **Fax:** (612)337-5050. **E-mail:** acquisitions@freespirit.com. **Website:** www.freespirit.com. Estab. 1983. "We believe passionately in empowering kids to learn to think for themselves and make their own good choices." Free Spirit does not accept general fiction, poetry or storybook submissions. Publishes trade paperback originals and reprints. Book catalog and ms guidelines online.

NEEDS "Please review catalog and author guidelines (both available online) for details before submitting proposal. If you'd like material returned, enclose a SASE with sufficient postage."

HOW TO CONTACT Accepts queries only—not submissions—by e-mail.

TERMS Pays advance. Responds to proposals in 2-6 months.

TIPS "Our books are issue oriented, jargon free, and solution focused. Our audience is children, teens, teachers, parents, and youth counselors. We are especially concerned with kids' social and emotional wellbeing and look for books with ready-to-use strategies for coping with today's issues at home or in school, written in everyday language. We are not looking for academic or religious materials, or books that analyze problems with the nation's school systems. Instead, we want books that offer practical, positive advice so kids can help themselves, and parents and teachers can help kids succeed."

GERTRUDE PRESS

P.O. Box 28281, Portland OR 97228. (503)515-8252. **E-mail:** editor@gertrudepress.org. **Website:** www.gertrudepress.org. Estab. 2005. "Gertrude Press is a nonprofit organization developing and showcasing the creative talents of lesbian, gay, bisexual, trans, queer-identified, and allied individuals. We publish limited-edition fiction and poetry chapbooks plus the biannual literary journal, *Gertrude*." Reads chapbook mss only through contests.

TIPS Sponsors poetry and fiction chapbook contest. Prize is $175 and 50 contributor's copies. Submission guidelines and fee information on website. "Read the journal and sample published work. We are not impressed by pages of publications; your work should speak for itself."

⊘ GIANT SQUID BOOKS

E-mail: editors@giantsquidbooks.com. **Website:** giantsquidbooks.com. "Our mission is to publish, support, and promote debut authors—and help them navigate the world of online publishing." Guidelines online.

NEEDS Giant Squid Books is currently closed to submissions. "See website or follow us on Twitter @giantsquidbooks to be notified when we reopen submissions." Accepts young adult novels in any genre.

HOW TO CONTACT Query with the first 3 chapters or 50 pages of book.

TIPS "We read every submission and try to respond within 2 weeks, but due to a high volume of submissions we sometimes get behind! If it's been more than 2 weeks since you queried us, please feel free to send a follow-up e-mail."

GIVAL PRESS

Gival Press, LLC, P.O. Box 3812, Arlington VA 22203. (703)351-0079. **E-mail:** givalpress@yahoo.com. **Website:** www.givalpress.com. **Contact:** Robert L. Giron, editor in chief (area of interest: literary). Estab. 1998. "We publish literary works: fiction, nonfiction (essays, academic), and poetry in English, Spanish, and French." Publishes trade paperback, electronic originals, and reprints. Book catalog online. Guidelines online.

HOW TO CONTACT Always query first via e-mail; provide description, author's bio, and supportive material.

TERMS Pays royalty. Responds in 3-5 months.

TIPS "Our audience is those who read literary works with depth to the work. Visit our website—there is much to be read/learned from the numerous pages."

O THE GLENCANNON PRESS

P.O. Box 1428, El Cerrito CA 94530. (510)528-4216. **E-mail:** merships@yahoo.com. **Website:** www.glencannon.com. **Contact:** Bill Harris (maritime, maritime children's). Estab. 1993. "We publish quality books about ships and the sea." Average print order: 1,000. Member PMA, BAIPA. Distributes titles through Baker & Taylor. Promotes titles through direct mail, magazine advertising, and word of mouth. Accepts unsolicited mss. Often comments on rejected mss. Publishes hardcover and paperback originals and hardcover reprints.

IMPRINTS Smyth.

HOW TO CONTACT Submit complete ms. Include brief bio, list of publishing credits. Send SASE for return of ms, or send a disposable ms and SASE for reply only.

TERMS Pays 10-20% royalty. Responds in 1 month to queries; 2 months to mss.

TIPS "Write a good story in a compelling style."

Ⓐ⊘ DAVID R. GODINE, PUBLISHER

15 Court Square, Ste. 320, Boston MA 02108. (617)451-9600. **Fax:** (617)350-0250. **E-mail:** info@godine.com.

Website: www.godine.com. Estab. 1970. "We publish books that matter for people who care." This publisher is no longer considering unsolicited mss of any type. Only interested in agented material.

IMPRINTS Black Sparrow Books, Verba Mundi, Nonpareil.

GOOSE LANE EDITIONS

500 Beaverbrook Ct., Ste. 330, Fredericton NB E3B 5X4, Canada. (506)450-4251. **Fax:** (506)459-4991. **E-mail:** submissions@gooselane.com. **Website:** www.gooselane.com. **Contact:** Angela Williams, publishing assistant. Estab. 1954. "Goose Lane publishes literary fiction and nonfiction from well-read and highly skilled Canadian authors." Publishes hardcover and paperback originals and occasional reprints.

NEEDS "Our needs in fiction never change: substantial, character-centered literary fiction." No children's, young adult, mainstream, mass market, genre, mystery, thriller, confessional, or science fiction.

HOW TO CONTACT Query with SAE, Canadian stamps or IRCs. No U.S. stamps.

TERMS Pays 8-10% royalty on retail price. Pays $500-3,000, negotiable advance. Responds in 6 months to queries.

TIPS "Writers should send us outlines and samples of books that show a very well-read author with highly developed literary skills. Our books are almost all by Canadians living in Canada; we seldom consider submissions from outside Canada. We consider submissions from outside Canada only when the author is Canadian and the book is of extraordinary interest to Canadian readers. We do not publish books for children or for the young adult market."

GRAYWOLF PRESS

250 Third Ave. N., Ste. 600, Minneapolis MN 55401. (651)641-0077. **Fax:** (651)641-0036. **Website:** www.graywolfpress.org. Estab. 1974. "Graywolf Press is an independent, nonprofit publisher dedicated to the creation and promotion of thoughtful and imaginative contemporary literature essential to a vital and diverse culture." Publishes trade cloth and paperback originals. Book catalog free. Guidelines online.

NEEDS "Familiarize yourself with our list first." No genre books (romance, western, science fiction, suspense).

HOW TO CONTACT Agented submissions only.

TERMS Pays royalty on retail price. Pays $1,000-25,000 advance. Responds in 3 months to queries.

GREENWILLOW BOOKS

HarperCollins Publishers, 10 E. 53rd St., New York NY 10022. (212)207-7000. **Website:** www.greenwillowblog.com. Estab. 1974. Does not accept unsolicited mss. "Unsolicited mail will not be opened and will not be returned." Publishes hardcover originals, paperbacks, e-books, and reprints.

HOW TO CONTACT Agented submissions only.

TERMS Pays 10% royalty on wholesale price for first-time authors. Offers variable advance.

GREY GECKO PRESS

565 S. Mason Rd., Ste. 154, Katy TX 77450. **Phone/Fax:** (866)535-6078. **E-mail:** info@greygeckopress.com. **E-mail:** submissions@greygeckopress.com. **Website:** www.greygeckopress.com. **Contact:** Submissions Coordinator. Estab. 2011. Grey Gecko focuses on new and emerging authors and great books that might not otherwise get a chance to see the light of day. "We publish all our titles in hardcover, trade paperback, and e-book formats (both Kindle and ePub), as well as audiobook and foreign-language editions. Our books are available worldwide, for readers of all types, kinds, and interests." Publishes hardcover, trade paperback, audiobook, and electronic originals. Catalog online. Guidelines online.

NEEDS "We do not publish extreme horror, erotica, or religious fiction. New and interesting stories by unpublished authors will always get our attention. Innovation is a core value of our company." Does not want extreme horror (e.g., *Saw* or *Hostel*), religious, or erotica.

HOW TO CONTACT Use online submission page.

TERMS Pays 50-75% royalties on net revenue. Does not pay advance. Responds in 6-12 months.

TIPS "Be willing to be a part of the Grey Gecko family. Publishing with us is a partnership, not indentured servitude. Authors are expected and encouraged to be proactive and contribute to their book's success."

GROUNDWOOD BOOKS

128 Sterling Road, Lower Level, Attention: Submissions, Toronto Ontario M6R 2B7, Canada. (416)363-4343. **Fax:** (416)363-1017. **E-mail:** submissions@groundwoodbooks.com. **Website:** groundwoodbooks.com. "We are always looking for new authors of novel-length fiction for children of all ages. Our mandate

is to publish high-quality, character-driven literary fiction. We do not generally publish stories with an obvious moral or message, or genre fiction such as thrillers or fantasy." Publishes 19 picture books/year; 2 young readers/year; 3 middle readers/year; 3 young adult titles/year, approximately 2 nonfiction titles/year. Visit website for guidelines: www.houseofanansi.com/groundwoodsubmissions.aspx.

NEEDS Recently published *Lost Girl Found* by Leah Bassoff and Laura Deluca, *A Simple Case of Angels* by Carolnie Adderson, *This One Summer* by Mariko Tamaki and Jillian Tamaki.

HOW TO CONTACT Submit a cover letter, synopsis and sample chapters via e-mail. "Due to the large number of submissions we receive, Groundwood regrets that we cannot accept unsolicited mss for picture books."

TERMS Offers advances. Responds to mss in 6-8 months.

GROVE/ATLANTIC, INC.

154 W. 14th St., 12th Floor, New York NY 10011. **E-mail:** info@groveatlantic.com. **Website:** www.groveatlantic.com. Estab. 1917. "Due to limited resources of time and staffing, Grove/Atlantic cannot accept mss that do not come through a literary agent. In today's publishing world, agents are more important than ever, helping writers shape their work and navigate the main publishing houses to find the most appropriate outlet for a project." Publishes hardcover and trade paperback originals, and reprints. Book catalog available online.

IMPRINTS Black Cat, Atlantic Monthly Press, Grove Press.

HOW TO CONTACT Agented submissions only.

TERMS Pays 7.5-12.5% royalty. Makes outright purchase of $5-500,000. Responds in 1 month to queries; 2 months to proposals; 4 months to mss.

GUERNICA EDITIONS

1569 Heritage Way, Oakville Ontario L6M 2Z7, Canada. (905)599-5304. **Fax:** (416)981-7606. **E-mail:** michaelmirolla@guernicaeditions.com. **Website:** www.guernicaeditions.com. **Contact:** Michael Mirolla, editor/publisher (poetry, nonfiction, short stories, novels). Estab. 1978. Guernica Editions is a literary press that produces works of poetry, fiction, and nonfiction, often by writers who are ignored by the mainstream. Publishes trade paperback originals and reprints. Book catalog available online. Queries and submissions accepted via e-mail.

IMPRINTS MiroLand.

NEEDS "We wish to open up into the fiction world and focus less on poetry. We specialize in European, especially Italian, translations."

HOW TO CONTACT E-mail queries only.

TERMS Pays 8-10% royalty on retail price, or makes outright purchase of $200-5,000. Pays $450-750 advance. Responds in 1 month to queries. Responds in 6 months to proposals; 1 year to mss.

HACHAI PUBLISHING

527 Empire Blvd., Brooklyn NY 11225. (718)633-0100. **Fax:** (718)633-0103. **Website:** www.hachai.com. **Contact:** Devorah Leah Rosenfeld, editor. Estab. 1988. Hachai is dedicated to producing high-quality Jewish children's literature, for ages 2-10. Story should promote universal values such as sharing, kindness, etc. Publishes hardcover originals. Guidelines online.

"All books have spiritual/religious themes, specifically traditional Jewish content. We're seeking books about morals and values; the Jewish experience in current and Biblical times; and Jewish observance, Sabbath, and holidays."

NEEDS Picture books and young readers: contemporary, historical fiction, religion. Middle readers: adventure, contemporary, problem novels, religion. Does not want to see fantasy, animal stories, romance, problem novels depicting drug use or violence.

HOW TO CONTACT Submit complete ms.

TERMS Work purchased outright from authors for $800-1,000. Responds in 2 months to mss.

TIPS "We are looking for books that convey the traditional Jewish experience in modern times or long ago; traditional Jewish observance such as Sabbath and holidays and mitzvos such as mezuzah, blessings etc.; positive character traits (middos) such as honesty, charity, respect, sharing, etc. We are also interested in historical fiction for young readers (ages 7-10) written with a traditional Jewish perspective and highlighting the relevance of Torah in making important choices. Please, no animal stories, romance, violence, preachy sermonizing. Write a story that incorporates a moral, not a preachy morality tale. Originality is the key. We feel Hachai publications will appeal to a wider readership as parents become more interested in positive values for their children."

HADLEY RILLE BOOKS

P.O. Box 25466, Overland Park KS 66225. **E-mail:** contact@hadleyrillebooks.com. **E-mail:** subs@hadleyrillebooks.com. **Website:** hadleyrillebks.wordpress.com. **Contact:** Eric T. Reynolds, editor/publisher. Estab. 2005. Currently closed to submissions. Check website for future reading periods.

TIPS "We aim to produce books that are aligned with current interest in the genres. Anthology markets are somewhat rare in science fiction these days. We feel there aren't enough good anthologies being published each year, and part of our goal is to present the best that we can. We like stories that fit well within the guidelines of the particular anthology for which we are soliciting mss. Aside from that, we want stories with strong characters (not necessarily characters with strong personalities; flawed characters are welcome). We want a sense of wonder and awe. We want to feel the world around the character, and so scene description is important (however, this doesn't always require a lot of text—just set the scene well so we don't wonder where the character is). We strongly recommend workshopping the story or having it critiqued in some way by readers familiar with the genre. We prefer clichés be kept to a bare minimum in the prose. Avoid reworking old storylines."

HAMPTON ROADS PUBLISHING CO., INC.

665 Third St., Ste. 400, San Francisco CA 94107. **E-mail:** submissions@rwwbooks.com. **Website:** www.redwheelweiser.com. Estab. 1989. "Our reason for being is to impact, uplift, and contribute to positive change in the world. We publish books that will enrich and empower the evolving consciousness of mankind. Though we are not necessarily limited in scope, we are most interested in mss on the following subjects: body/mind/spirit, health and healing, self-help. Please be advised that at the moment we are not accepting: fiction or novelized material that does not pertain to body/mind/spirit, channeled writing." Publishes and distributes hardcover and trade paperback originals on subjects including metaphysics, health, complementary medicine, visionary fiction, and other related topics. Guidelines online.

"Please know that we only publish a handful of books every year, and that we pass on many well-written, important works simply because we cannot publish them all. We review each and every proposal very carefully. However, due to the volume of inquiries, we cannot respond to them all individually. Please give us 30 days to review your proposal. If you do not hear back from us within that time, this means we have decided to pursue other book ideas that we feel fit better within our plan."

NEEDS Fiction should have 1 or more of the following themes: spiritual, inspirational, metaphysical (i.e., past-life recall, out-of-body experiences, near-death experience, paranormal).

HOW TO CONTACT Query with SASE. Submit outline, 2 sample chapters, clips. Submit complete ms.

TERMS Pays royalty. Pays $1,000-50,000 advance. Responds in 2-4 months to queries; 1 month to proposals; 6-12 months to mss.

HARCOURT, INC., TRADE DIVISION

Imprint of Houghton Mifflin Harcourt Book Group, 215 Park Ave. S., New York NY 10003. **Website:** www.harcourtbooks.com. Publishes hardcover and trade paperback originals and trade paperback reprints. Book catalog for 9x12 envelope and first-class stamps. Guidelines available online.

HOW TO CONTACT Agented submissions only.

TERMS Pays 6-15% royalty on retail price. Pays $2,000 minimum advance.

HARLEQUIN AMERICAN ROMANCE

225 Duncan Mill Rd., Don Mills ON M3B 3K9, Canada. **E-mail:** submisssions@harlequin.com. **Website:** www.harlequin.com. **Contact:** Kathleen Scheibling, senior editor. "Upbeat and lively, fast paced, and well plotted, American Romance celebrates the pursuit of love in the backyards, big cities, and wide-open spaces of America." Publishes paperback originals and reprints. Books: newspaper print paper, web printing, perfect bound. Length: 55,000 words. "American Romance features heartwarming romances with strong family elements. These are stories about the pursuit of love, marriage, and family in America today." Guidelines online.

NEEDS Needs "all-American stories with a range of emotional and sensual content that are supported by a sense of community within the plot's framework. In the confident and caring heroine, the tough but tender hero, and their dynamic relationship that is at the center of this series, real-life love is showcased as the best fantasy of all!"

HOW TO CONTACT Submit online.

TERMS Pays royalty. Offers advance.

HARLEQUIN BLAZE

225 Duncan Mill Rd., Don Mills ON M3B 3K9, Canada. (416)445-5860. **Website:** www.harlequin.com. **Contact:** Kathleen Scheibling, senior editor. "Harlequin Blaze is a red-hot series. It is a vehicle to build and promote new authors who have a strong sexual edge to their stories. It is also the place to be for seasoned authors who want to create a sexy, sizzling, longer contemporary story." Publishes paperback originals. Guidelines online.

NEEDS "Sensuous, highly romantic, innovative plots that are sexy in premise and execution. The tone of the books can run from fun and flirtatious to dark and sensual. Submissions should have a very contemporary feel—what it's like to be young and single today. We are looking for heroes and heroines in their early 20s and up. There should be a strong emphasis on the physical relationship between the couples. Fully described love scenes, along with a high level of fantasy and playfulness." Length: 55,000-60,000 words.

TIPS "Are you a *Cosmo* girl at heart? A fan of *Sex and the City*? Or maybe you have a sexually adventurous spirit. If so, then Blaze is the series for you!"

HARLEQUIN DESIRE

233 Broadway, Ste. 1001, New York NY 10279. (212)553-4200. **Website:** www.harlequin.com. **Contact:** Stacy Boyd, senior editor. Always powerful, passionate, and provocative. "Desire novels are sensual reads, and a love scene or scenes are still needed. But there is no set number of pages that needs to be fulfilled. Rather, the level of sensuality must be appropriate to the storyline. Above all, every Silhouette Desire novel must fulfill the promise of a powerful, passionate, and provocative read." Publishes paperback originals and reprints. Guidelines online.

NEEDS Looking for novels in which "the conflict is an emotional one, springing naturally from the unique characters you've chosen. The focus is on the developing relationship, set in a believable plot. Sensuality is key, but lovemaking is never taken lightly. Secondary characters and subplots need to blend with the core story. Innovative new directions in storytelling and fresh approaches to classic romantic plots are welcome." Manuscripts must be 50,000-55,000 words.

TERMS Pays royalty. Offers advance.

HARLEQUIN HQN

Imprint of Harlequin, 225 Duncan Mill Rd., Don Mills ON M3B 3K9, Canada. **Website:** harlequin.com. **Contact:** Margo Lipschultz, senior editor. "HQN publishes romance in all subgenres—historical, contemporary, romantic suspense, paranormal—as long as the story's central focus is romance. Prospective authors can familiarize themselves with the wide range of books we publish by reading work by some of our current authors. The imprint is looking for a wide range of authors, from known romance stars to first-time authors. At the moment, we are accepting only agented submissions—unagented authors may send a query letter to determine if their project suits our needs. Please send your projects to our New York editorial office." Publishes hardcover, trade paperback, and mass market paperback originals.

HOW TO CONTACT Accepts unagented material. Length: 90,000 words.

TERMS Pays royalty. Pays advance.

HARLEQUIN INTRIGUE

225 Duncan Mill Rd., Don Mills ON M3B 3K9, Canada. **Website:** www.harlequin.com. **Contact:** Denise Zaza, senior editor. Wants crime stories tailored to the series romance market packed with a variety of thrilling suspense and whodunit mystery. Word count: 55,000-60,000. Guidelines online.

HOW TO CONTACT Submit online.

HARLEQUIN SUPERROMANCE

225 Duncan Mill Rd., Don Mills ON M3B 3K9, Canada. **Website:** www.harlequin.com. **Contact:** Victoria Curran, senior editor. "The Harlequin Superromance line focuses on believable characters triumphing over true-to-life drama and conflict. At the heart of these contemporary stories should be a compelling romance that brings the reader along with the hero and heroine on their journey of overcoming the obstacles in their way and falling in love. Because of the longer length, relevant subplots and secondary characters are welcome but not required. This series publishes a variety of story types—family sagas, romantic suspense, Westerns, to name a few—and tones from light to dramatic, emotional to suspenseful. Settings also vary from vibrant urban neighborhoods to charming small towns. The unifying element of Harlequin Superromance stories is the realistic treatment of character and plot. The characters should seem familiar

to readers—similar to people they know in their own lives—and the circumstances within the realm of possibility. The stories should be layered and complex in that the conflicts should not be easily resolved. The best way to get an idea of what we're looking for is to read what we're currently publishing. The aim of Superromance novels is to produce a contemporary, involving read with a mainstream tone in its situations and characters, using romance as the major theme. To achieve this, emphasis should be placed on individual writing styles and unique and topical ideas." Publishes paperback originals. Guidelines online.

NEEDS "The criteria for Superromance books are flexible. Aside from length (80,000 words), the determining factor for publication will always be quality. Authors should strive to break free of stereotypes, clichés, and worn-out plot devices to create strong, believable stories with depth and emotional intensity. Superromance novels are intended to appeal to a wide range of romance readers."

HOW TO CONTACT Submit online.

TERMS Pays royalties. Pays advance.

TIPS "A general familiarity with current Superromance books is advisable to keep abreast of ever-changing trends and overall scope, but we don't want imitations. We look for sincere, heartfelt writing based on true-to-life experiences the reader can identify with. We are interested in innovation."

Ⓐ⊘ HARLEQUIN TEEN

Harlequin, 195 Broadway, 24th Floor, New York NY 10007. **Website:** www.harlequin.com. **Contact:** Natashya Wilson, executive editor. Harlequin Teen is a single-title program dedicated to building authors and publishing unique, memorable young adult fiction.

NEEDS Harlequin Teen looks for fresh, authentic fiction featuring extraordinary characters and extraordinary stories set in contemporary, paranormal, fantasy, science fiction, and historical worlds. Wants commercial, high-concept stories that capture the teen experience and will speak to readers with power and authenticity. All subgenres are welcome, so long as the book delivers a relevant reading experience that will resonate long after the book's covers are closed. Expects that most stories will include a compelling romantic element.

HOW TO CONTACT Agented submissions only.

HARMONY INK PRESS

5032 Capital Circle SW, Ste. 2 PMB 279, Tallahassee FL 32305. (850)632-4648. **Fax:** (888)308-3739. **E-mail:** submissions@harmonyinkpress.com. **Website:** harmonyinkpress.com. Harmony Ink is accepting mss for teen and new adult fiction featuring at least 1 strong LGBTQ+ main character who shows significant personal growth through the course of the story.

NEEDS "We are looking for stories in all subgenres, featuring primary characters across the whole LGBTQ+ spectrum between the ages of 14 and 21 that explore all the facets of young adult, teen, and new adult life. Sexual content should be appropriate for the characters and the story."

HOW TO CONTACT Submit complete ms.

TERMS Pays royalty. Pays $500-1,000 advance.

Ⓐ⊘ HARPERCOLLINS

195 Broadway, New York NY 10007. (212)207-7000. **Website:** www.harpercollins.com. HarperCollins, one of the largest English language publishers in the world, is a broad-based publisher with strengths in academic, business and professional, children's, educational, general interest, and religious and spiritual books, as well as multimedia titles. Publishes hardcover and paperback originals and paperback reprints.

NEEDS "We look for a strong story line and exceptional literary talent."

HOW TO CONTACT Agented submissions only. All unsolicited mss returned.

TERMS Pays royalty. Pays negotiable advance.

TIPS "We do not accept any unsolicited material."

⊘ HARPERCOLLINS CANADA, LTD.

2 Bloor St. E., 20th Floor, Toronto ON M4W 1A8, Canada. (416)975-9334. **Fax:** (416)975-5223. **Website:** www.harpercollins.ca. Estab. 1989. *HarperCollins Canada is not accepting unsolicited material at this time.*

Ⓐ HARPERCOLLINS CHILDREN'S BOOKS/ HARPERCOLLINS PUBLISHERS

195 Broadway, New York NY 10007. (212)207-7000. **Website:** www.harpercollins.com. HarperCollins, one of the largest English-language publishers in the world, is a broad-based publisher with strengths in academic, business and professional, children's, educational, general interest, and religious and spiritual books, as well as multimedia titles. Publishes hard-

cover and paperback originals and paperback reprints. Catalog online.

IMPRINTS **HarperCollins Australia/New Zealand:** Angus & Robertson, Fourth Estate, HarperBusiness, HarperCollins, HarperPerenniel, HarperReligious, HarperSports, Voyager; **HarperCollins Canada**: HarperFlamingoCanada, PerennialCanada; **HarperCollins Children's Books Group:** Amistad, Julie Andrews Collection, Avon, Joanna Cotler Books, Eos, Laura Geringer Books, Greenwillow Books, HarperAudio, HarperCollins Children's Books, HarperFestival, HarperTempest, HarperTrophy, Rayo, Katherine Tegen Books; **HarperCollins General Books Group:** Access, Amistad, Avon, Caedmon, Ecco, Eos, Fourth Estate, HarperAudio, HarperBusiness, HarperCollins, HarperEntertainment, HarperLargePrint, HarperResource, HarperSanFrancisco, HarperTorch, Harper Design International, Perennial, PerfectBound, Quill, Rayo, ReganBooks, William Morrow, William Morrow Cookbooks; **HarperCollins UK:** Collins Bartholomew, Collins, HarperCollins Crime & Thrillers, Collins Freedom to Teach, HarperCollins Children's Books, Thorsons/Element, Voyager Books; **Zondervan:** Inspirio, Vida, Zonderkidz, Zondervan.

NEEDS "We look for a strong storyline and exceptional literary talent."

HOW TO CONTACT Agented submissions only. All unsolicited mss returned.

TERMS Negotiates payment upon acceptance. Responds in 1 month, only if interested. Does not accept any unsolicted texts.

TIPS "We do not accept any unsolicited material."

Ⓐ HARPERTEEN

195 Broadway, New York NY 10007. (212)207-7000. **Website:** www.harpercollins.com. HarperTeen is a teen imprint that publishes hardcovers, paperback reprints, and paperback originals.

HarperCollins Children's Books is not accepting unsolicited and/or unagented mss or queries. Unfortunately the volume of these submissions is so large that they cannot receive the attention they deserve. Such submissions will not be reviewed or returned.

Ⓐ⊘ HARPER VOYAGER

Imprint of HarperCollins General Books Group, 195 Broadway, New York NY 10007. (212)207-7000. **Website:** www.harpercollins.com. Estab. 1998. Eos publishes quality science fiction/fantasy with broad appeal. Publishes hardcover originals, trade and mass market paperback originals, and reprints. Guidelines online.

NEEDS No horror or juvenile.

HOW TO CONTACT Agented submissions only. All unsolicited mss returned.

TERMS Pays royalty on retail price. Pays variable advance.

Ⓐ⊘ HARVEST HOUSE PUBLISHERS

990 Owen Loop N., Eugene OR 97402. (541)343-0123. **Fax:** (541)302-0731. **Website:** www.harvesthousepublishers.com. Estab. 1974. Publishes hardcover, trade paperback, and mass market paperback originals and reprints.

NEEDS No unsolicited mss, proposals, or artwork.

HOW TO CONTACT Agented submissions only.

TERMS Pays royalty.

TIPS "For first-time/nonpublished authors, we suggest building their literary résumé by submitting to magazines, or perhaps accruing book contributions."

HENDRICK-LONG PUBLISHING CO., INC.

10635 Tower Oaks, Ste. D, Houston TX 77070. (832)912-READ. **Fax:** (832)912-7353. **E-mail:** hendrick-long@worldnet.att.net. **Website:** hendricklongpublishing.com. **Contact:** Vilma Long. Estab. 1969. "Hendrick-Long publishes historical fiction and nonfiction about Texas and the Southwest for children and young adults." Publishes hardcover and trade paperback originals and hardcover reprints. Book catalog available. Guidelines online.

HOW TO CONTACT Query with SASE. Submit outline, clips, 2 sample chapters.

TERMS Pays royalty on selling price. Pays advance. Responds in 3 months to queries.

HEYDAY BOOKS

c/o Acquisitions Editor, Box 9145, Berkeley CA 94709. **Fax:** (510)549-1889. **E-mail:** heyday@heydaybooks.com. **Website:** www.heydaybooks.com. **Contact:** Gayle Wattawa, acquisitions and editorial director. Estab. 1974. "Heyday Books publishes nonfiction books and literary anthologies with a strong California focus. We publish books about Native Americans, natural history, history, literature, and recreation, with a strong California focus." Publishes hardcover originals, trade paperback originals and reprints. Book catalog online. Guidelines online.

NEEDS Publishes picture books, beginning readers, and young adult literature.

HOW TO CONTACT Submit complete ms for picture books; proposal with sample chapters for longer works. Include a chapter-by-chapter summary. Mark submission with 'Attention: Children's Submission.' Reviews ms/illustration packages, but may consider art and text separately. Tries to respond to query within 3 months.

TERMS Pays 8% royalty on net price. Responds in 3 months.

HIGHLAND PRESS PUBLISHING

P.O. Box 2292, High Springs FL 32655. **E-mail:** the.highland.press@gmail.com; submissions.hp@gmail.com. **Website:** www.highlandpress.org. **Contact:** Leanne Burroughs, CEO (fiction); she will forward all mss to appropriate editor. Estab. 2005. "With our focus on historical romances, Highland Press Publishing is known as your 'Passport to Romance.' We focus on historical romances and our award-winning anthologies. Our short stories/novellas are heart warming. As for our historicals, we publish historical novels like many of us grew up with and loved. History is a big part of the story and is tactfully woven throughout the romance. We have opened our submissions up to all genres, with the exception of erotica. Our newest lines are inspirational, regency, and young adult." Publishes paperback originals, both historical and contemporary. Also publishes some nonfiction books. Catalog and guidelines online.

HOW TO CONTACT Query with proposal and sample chapters. Accepts queries by snail mail, e-mail. Include estimated word count, target market, promotional strategy.

TERMS Pays royalties. Responds in 3 months to queries; 3-12 months to mss.

TIPS "I don't publish based on industry trends. We buy what we like and what we believe readers are looking for. However, often this proves to be the genres and time periods larger publishers are not currently interested in. Be professional at all times. Present your ms in the best possible light. Be sure you have run a spell-check and that the ms has been vetted by at least 1 critique partner, preferably more. Many times we receive mss that have wonderful stories involved but would take far too much time to edit to make it marketable."

HIPSO MEDIA

8151 E. 29th Ave., Denver CO 80238. **Website:** www.hipsomedia.com. Estab. 2012. Publishes trade and mass market paperback and electronic originals. Catalog online. Guidelines online.

HOW TO CONTACT Query via online form.

TERMS Authors receive between 15-30% on royalty. Responds in 1 month.

TIPS Describes ideal audience as "hip readers of e-books. We are going digital first, so tell us why someone would want to read your book."

HOLIDAY HOUSE, INC.

425 Madison Ave., New York NY 10017. (212)688-0085. **Fax:** (212)421-6134. **E-mail:** info@holidayhouse.com. **Website:** holidayhouse.com. Estab. 1935. "Holiday House publishes children's and young adult books for the school and library markets. We have a commitment to publishing first-time authors and illustrators. We specialize in quality hardcovers from picture books to young adult, both fiction and nonfiction, primarily for the school and library market." Publishes hardcover originals and paperback reprints. Guidelines for #10 SASE.

NEEDS Children's books only.

HOW TO CONTACT Query with SASE. No phone calls, please.

TERMS Pays royalty on list price, range varies. Responds in 4 months.

TIPS "We need mss with strong stories and writing."

HOPEWELL PUBLICATIONS

P.O. Box 11, Titusville NJ 08560. **Website:** www.hopepubs.com. **Contact:** E. Martin, publisher. Estab. 2002. "Hopewell Publications specializes in classic reprints—books with proven sales records that have gone out of print—and the occasional new title of interest. Our catalog spans from 1-60 years of publication history. We print fiction and nonfiction, and we accept agented and unagented materials. Submissions are accepted online only." Publishes hardcover, trade paperback, and electronic originals; trade paperback and electronic reprints. Catalog online. Guidelines online.

IMPRINTS Egress Books, Legacy Classics.

HOW TO CONTACT Query online using online guidelines.

TERMS Pays royalty on retail price. Responds in 3 months to queries; 6 months to proposals; 9 months to mss.

HOUGHTON MIFFLIN HARCOURT BOOKS FOR CHILDREN

Imprint of Houghton Mifflin Trade & Reference Division, 222 Berkeley St., Boston MA 02116. (617)351-5000. **Fax:** (617)351-1111. **Website:** www.houghtonmifflinbooks.com. Houghton Mifflin Harcourt gives shape to ideas that educate, inform, and, above all, delight. Does not respond to or return mss unless interested. Publishes hardcover originals and trade paperback originals and reprints. Guidelines online.

HOW TO CONTACT Submit complete ms.

TERMS Pays 5-10% royalty on retail price. Pays variable advance. Responds in 4-6 months to queries.

HOUSE OF ANANSI PRESS

128 Sterling Rd., Lower Level, Toronto ON M6R 2B7, Canada. (416)363-4343. **Fax:** (416)363-1017. **Website:** www.anansi.ca. Estab. 1967. House of Anansi publishes literary fiction and poetry by Canadian and international writers.

NEEDS Publishes literary fiction that has a unique flair, memorable characters, and a strong narrative voice.

HOW TO CONTACT Query with SASE.

TERMS Pays 8-10% royalties. Pays $750 advance and 10 author's copies.

IDW PUBLISHING

2765 Truxtun Rd., San Diego CA 92106. **E-mail:** letters@idwpublishing.com. **Website:** www.idwpublishing.com. Estab. 1999. IDW Publishing currently publishes a wide range of comic books and graphic novels, including titles based on *GI Joe, Star Trek, Terminator: Salvation*, and *Transformers*. Creator-driven titles include *Fallen Angel* by Peter David and JK Woodward, *Locke & Key* by Joe Hill and Gabriel Rodriguez, and a variety of titles by writer Steve Niles, including *Wake the Dead, Epilogue*, and *Dead, She Said*. Publishes hardcover, mass market, and trade paperback originals.

ILIUM PRESS

2407 S. Sonora Dr., Spokane WA 99037. (509)701-8866. **E-mail:** iliumpress@outlook.com. **E-mail:** iliumpress@outlook.com. **Contact:** John Lemon, owner/editor. Estab. 2010. "Ilium is a small, one-man press that I run in my spare time. It was created to cultivate and promote the relevance of epic poetry in today's world. I am very selective about my projects, but I provide extensive editorial care to those I take on." Publishes trade paperback originals and reprints, electronic originals and reprints.

TERMS Pays 20-50% royalties on receipts. Does not pay advance. Responds in 6 months.

ILLUSIO & BAQER

1827 W. Shannon Ave., Spokane WA **E-mail:** submissions@zharmae.com. **Website:** illusiobaqer.com. Illusio & Baqer publishes high-quality middle-grade, young adult, and new adult fiction of all genres. "We are a young adult, new adult, and middle-grade imprint of The Zharmae Publishing Press."

HOW TO CONTACT Query with synopsis and 3-5 sample chapters.

IMAGE COMICS

2001 Center St., Sixth Floor, Berkeley CA 94704. **E-mail:** submissions@imagecomics.com. **Website:** www.imagecomics.com. **Contact:** Eric Stephenson, publisher. Estab. 1992. Publishes creator-owned comic books, graphic novels. See this company's website for detailed guidelines. Does not accept writing samples without art.

HOW TO CONTACT Query with one-page synopsis and 5 pages or more of samples. "We do not accept writing samples (that is, plots, scripts, etc.)! If you're an established pro, we might be able to find somebody willing to work with you, but it would be nearly impossible for us to read through every script that might find its way our direction. Do not send your script or your plot unaccompanied by art—it will be discarded unread."

TIPS "We are not looking for any specific genre or type of comic book. We are looking for comics that are well written and well drawn, by people who are dedicated and can meet deadlines."

IMMEDIUM

P.O. Box 31846, San Francisco CA 94131. (415)452-8546. **Fax:** (360)937-6272. **Website:** www.immedium.com. Estab. 2005. "Immedium focuses on publishing eye-catching children's picture books, Asian American topics, and contemporary arts, popular culture, and multicultural issues." Publishes hardcover and trade paperback originals. Catalog online. Guidelines online.

HOW TO CONTACT Submit complete ms.

TERMS Pays 5% royalty on wholesale price. Pays on publication. Responds in 1-3 months.

TIPS "Our audience is children and parents. Please visit our site."

IMMORTAL INK PUBLISHING

E-mail: immortalinkpublishing@gmail.com. **Website:** www.immortalinkpublishing.com. Immortal Ink Publishing is open to most genres but specifically wants literary fiction, women's fiction, crime/mystery/thriller, young adult, and dark and paranormal fiction that is original, character-based, and literary in flavor. Immortal Ink Publishing is currently closed to submissions.

HOW TO CONTACT Submit query with first 10 pages via e-mail.

TIPS "Due to time constraints, we will not be giving reasons for our rejections (as you really shouldn't be making changes just because of something we personally didn't like anyway), but we will get back to you with either a 'no thanks' or a request for your full ms."

INSOMNIAC PRESS

520 Princess Ave., London ON N6B 2B8, Canada. (416)504-6270. **E-mail:** mike@insomniacpress.com. **Website:** www.insomniacpress.com. **Contact:** Mike O'Connor, publisher. Estab. 1992. Publishes trade paperback originals and reprints, mass market paperback originals, and electronic originals and reprints. Guidelines online.

NEEDS "We publish a mix of commercial (mysteries) and literary fiction."

HOW TO CONTACT Query via e-mail, submit proposal.

TERMS Pays 10-15% royalty on retail price. Pays $500-1,000 advance.

TIPS "We envision a mixed readership that appreciates up-and-coming literary fiction and poetry as well as solidly researched and provocative nonfiction. Peruse our website and familiarize yourself with what we've published in the past."

INTERLINK PUBLISHING GROUP, INC.

46 Crosby St., Northampton MA 01060. (413)582-7054. **Fax:** (413)582-7057. **E-mail:** info@interlinkbooks.com. **Website:** www.interlinkbooks.com. Estab. 1987. Interlink is an independent publisher of general trade adult fiction and nonfiction with an emphasis on books that have a wide appeal while also meeting high intellectual and literary standards. Publishes hardcover and trade paperback originals. Book catalog and guidelines online.

NEEDS "We are looking for translated works relating to the Middle East, Africa, or Latin America." No science fiction, romance, plays, erotica, fantasy, horror.

HOW TO CONTACT Query with SASE. Submit outline, sample chapters.

TERMS Pays 6-8% royalty on retail price. Pays small advance. Responds in 3-6 months to queries.

TIPS "Any submissions that fit well in our publishing program will receive careful attention. We recommend a visit to our website, your local bookstore, or a library to look at some of our books before you send in your submission."

INVERTED-A

P.O. Box 267, Licking MO 65542. **E-mail:** amnfn@well.com. **Contact:** Aya Katz, chief editor (poetry, novels, political); Nets Katz, science editor (scientific, academic). Estab. 1985. Books: POD. Distributes through Amazon, Bowker, Barnes Noble. Publishes paperback originals. Guidelines for SASE.

HOW TO CONTACT Does not accept unsolicited mss. Query with SASE. Reading period open from January 2-March 15. Accepts queries by e-mail. Include estimated word count.

TERMS Pays 10 author's copies. Responds in 1 month to queries; 3 months to mss.

TIPS "Read our books. Read the *Inverted-A Horn*. We are different. We do not follow industry trends."

ITALICA PRESS

595 Main St., Ste. 605, New York NY 10044-0047. (917)371-0563. **E-mail:** inquiries@italicapress.com. **Website:** www.italicapress.com. **Contact:** Ronald G. Musto and Eileen Gardiner, publishers. Estab. 1985. "Italica Press publishes English translations of modern Italian fiction and medieval and Renaissance nonfiction." Publishes hardcover and trade paperback originals. Book catalog and guidelines online.

NEEDS "First-time translators published. We would like to see translations of Italian writers who are well known in Italy and are not yet translated for an American audience."

HOW TO CONTACT Query via e-mail.

TERMS Pays 7-15% royalty on wholesale price; author's copies. Responds in 1 month to queries; 4 months to mss.

TIPS "We are interested in considering a wide variety of medieval and Renaissance topics (not historical fiction), and for modern works we are only interested in translations from Italian fiction by well-known Italian authors. *Only* fiction that has been previously published in Italian. A *brief* e-mail saves a lot of time; 90% of proposals we receive are completely off base—but we are very interested in things that are right on target."

JEWISH LIGHTS PUBLISHING

LongHill Partners, Inc., Sunset Farm Offices, Rt. 4, P.O. Box 237, Woodstock VT 05091. (802)457-4000. **Fax:** (802)457-4004. **E-mail:** editorial@jewishlights.com; sales@jewishlights.com. **Website:** www.jewishlights.com. **Contact:** Acquisitions Editor. Estab. 1990. "Jewish Lights publishes books for people of all faiths and all backgrounds who yearn for books that attract, engage, educate, and spiritually inspire. Our authors are at the forefront of spiritual thought and deal with the quest for the self and for meaning in life by drawing on the Jewish wisdom tradition. Our books cover topics including history, spirituality, life cycle, children, self-help, recovery, theology, and philosophy. We do not publish autobiography, biography, fiction, haggadot, poetry, or cookbooks. At this point we plan to do only 2 books for children annually, and 1 will be for younger children (ages 4-10)." Publishes hardcover and trade paperback originals, trade paperback reprints. Book catalog and guidelines online.

NEEDS Picture books, young readers, middle readers: spirituality. "We are not interested in anything other than spirituality."

HOW TO CONTACT Query with outline/synopsis and 2 sample chapters; submit complete ms for picture books.

TERMS Pays authors royalty of 10% of revenue received; 15% royalty for subsequent printings. Responds in 6 months to queries.

TIPS "We publish books for all faiths and backgrounds that also reflect the Jewish wisdom tradition. Explain in your cover letter why you're submitting your project to us in particular. Make sure you know what we publish."

JOLLY FISH PRESS

P.O. Box 1773, Provo UT 84603. **E-mail:** submit@jollyfishpress.com. **Website:** jollyfishpress.com. Guidelines online.

NEEDS "We accept literary fiction, fantasy, science fiction, mystery, suspense, horror, thriller, children's literature, young adult, trade."

HOW TO CONTACT Submit query with synopsis and first 3 chapters.

TERMS Does not pay advance.

JOURNEYFORTH

Imprint of BJU Press, 1700 Wade Hampton Blvd., Greenville SC 29614. (864)770-1317 or (800)845-5731. **Fax:** (864)271-8151 or (800)525-8398. **E-mail:** journeyforth@bjupress.com. **Website:** www.journeyforth.com. Estab. 1974. "Small independent publisher of trustworthy novels and biographies for readers in primary school through high school from a conservative Christian perspective as well as Christian living books and Bible studies for teens and adults." Publishes paperback originals. Book catalog available free or online. Guidelines online.

NEEDS "Our fiction is all based on a Christian worldview." Does not want short stories.

HOW TO CONTACT Submit 5 sample chapters, synopsis, market analysis of competing works.

TERMS Pays royalty. Responds in 1 month to queries; 3 months to mss.

TIPS "Study the publisher's guidelines. No picture books. Fiction for the youth market only."

⊘ JUPITER GARDENS PRESS

Jupiter Gardens, LLC, P.O. Box 191, Grimes IA 50111. **Website:** www.jupitergardens.com. **Contact:** Mary Wilson, publisher. Estab. 2007. Format publishes in trade paperback originals and reprints; electronic originals and reprints. Catalog online. Guidelines online.

NEEDS "We only publish romance (all subgenres), science fiction and fantasy, and metaphysical fiction. Our science fiction and fantasy covers a wide variety of topics, such as feminist fantasy, or more hard science fiction and fantasy which looks at the human condition. Our young adult imprint, Jupiter Storm, with thought-provoking reads that explore the full range of speculative fiction, includes science fiction or fantasy and metaphysical fiction. These readers would enjoy edgy contemporary works. Our romance readers love seeing a couple, no matter the gender, overcome obstacles and grow in order to find true love. Like our readers, we believe that love can come in many forms."

HOW TO CONTACT Use online submission form. Currently closed to submissions.

TERMS Pays 40% royalty on retail price. Responds in 1 month on proposals; 2 months on mss.

TIPS "No matter which line you're submitting to, know your genre and your readership. We publish a diverse catalog, and we're passionate about our main focus. We want romance that takes your breath away and leaves you with that warm feeling that love does conquer all. Our science fiction takes place in wild and alien worlds, and our fantasy transports readers to mythical realms and finds strange worlds within our own. And our metaphysical nonfiction will help readers gain new skills and awareness for the coming age. We want authors who engage with their readers and who aren't afraid to use social media to connect. Read and follow our submission guidelines."

JUST US BOOKS, INC.

P.O. Box 5306, East Orange NJ 07019. (973)672-7701. **Fax:** (973)677-7570. **Website:** justusbooks.com. Estab. 1988. "Just Us Books is the nation's premier independent publisher of Black-interest books for young people. Our books focus primarily on the culture, history, and contemporary experiences of African Americans." Guidelines online.

IMPRINTS Marimba Books.

NEEDS Just Us Books is currently accepting queries for chapter books and middle reader titles only. "We are not considering any other works at this time."

TIPS "We are looking for realistic, contemporary characters, and stories and interesting plots that introduce both conflict and resolution. We will consider various themes and storylines, but before an author submits a query we urge them to become familiar with our books."

KAEDEN BOOKS

P.O. Box 16190, Rocky River OH 44116. **Website:** www.kaeden.com. Estab. 1986. "Children's book publisher for education K-3 market: reading stories, fiction/nonfiction, chapter books, science, and social studies materials." Publishes paperback originals. Book catalog and guidelines online.

NEEDS "We are looking for stories with humor, surprise endings, and interesting characters that will appeal to children in kindergarten through third grade." No sentence fragments. Please do not submit queries, ms summaries, or résumés; mss that stereotype or demean individuals or groups; or mss that present violence as acceptable behavior.

HOW TO CONTACT Submit complete ms. "Can be as minimal as 25 words for the earliest reader or as much as 2,000 words for the fluent reader. Beginning chapter books are welcome. Our readers are in kindergarten to third grade, so vocabulary and sentence structure must be appropriate for young readers. Make sure that all language used in the story is of an appropriate level for the students to read independently. Sentences should be complete and grammatically correct."

TERMS Work purchased outright from authors. Pays royalties to previous authors. Responds only if interested.

TIPS "Our audience ranges from kindergarten to third-grade school children. We are an educational publisher. We are particularly interested in humorous stories with surprise endings and beginning chapter books."

Ⓐ KANE/MILLER BOOK PUBLISHERS

4901 Morena Blvd., Ste. 213, San Diego CA 92117. (858)456-0540. **Fax:** (858)456-9641. **E-mail:** submissions@kanemiller.com. **Website:** www.kanemiller.com. **Contact:** Editorial Department. Estab. 1985. "Kane/Miller Book Publishers is a division of EDC Publishing, specializing in award-winning children's books from around the world. Our books bring the children of the world closer to each other, sharing stories and ideas, while exploring cultural differences and similarities. Although we continue to look for books from other countries, we are now actively seeking works that convey cultures and communities within the U.S. We are committed to expanding our picture book list and are interested in great stories with engaging characters, especially those with particularly American subjects. When writing about the experiences of a particular community, we will express a preference for stories written from a firsthand experience." Submission guidelines on site.

NEEDS Picture books: concept, contemporary, health, humor, multicultural. Young readers: contemporary, multicultural, suspense. Middle readers: contemporary, humor, multicultural, suspense. "At this time, we are not considering holiday stories (in any age range) or self-published works."

TERMS If interested, responds in 90 days to queries.

TIPS "We like to think that a child reading a Kane/Miller book will see parallels between his own life and what might be the unfamiliar setting and characters of the story. And that by seeing how a character who is somehow or in some way dissimilar—an outsider—finds a way to fit comfortably into a culture or community or situation while maintaining a healthy sense of self and self-dignity, she might be empowered to do the same."

KAR-BEN PUBLISHING

Lerner Publishing Group, 241 First Ave. N., Minneapolis MN 55401. (612)215-6229. **E-mail:** editorial@karben.com. **Website:** www.karben.com. Estab. 1974. Kar-Ben publishes exclusively children's books on Jewish themes. Publishes hardcover, trade paperback, and electronic originals. Book catalog online; free upon request. Guidelines online.

NEEDS "We seek picture book mss, 800-1,000 words, on Jewish-themed topics for children." Picture books: Adventure, concept, folktales, history, humor, multicultural, religion, special needs; must be on a Jewish theme. Average word length: picture books—1,000. Recently published titles: *The Count's Hanukkah Countdown, Sammy Spider's First Book of Jewish Holidays, The Cats of Ben Yehuda Street.*

HOW TO CONTACT Submit full ms. Picture books only.

TERMS Pays 5% royalty on net sale. Pays $500-2,500 advance. Responds in 6 weeks.

TIPS "Authors: Do a literature search to make sure a similar title doesn't already exist. Illustrators: Look at our online catalog for a sense of what we like—bright colors and lively composition."

KAYA PRESS

c/o USC ASE, 3620 S. Vermont Ave. KAP 462, Los Angeles CA 90089. (213) 740-2285. **E-mail:** info@kaya.com. **Website:** www.kaya.com. **Contact:** Sunyoung Lee, editor. Estab. 1994. Kaya is an independent literary press dedicated to the publication of innovative literature from the Asian Pacific diaspora. Publishes hardcover originals and trade paperback originals and reprints. Book catalog available free. Guidelines online.

HOW TO CONTACT Submit 2-4 sample chapters, clips, SASE.

TERMS Responds in 6 months to mss.

TIPS "Audience is people interested in a high standard of literature and who are interested in breaking down easy approaches to multicultural literature."

KELSEY STREET PRESS

Poetry by Women, 2824 Kelsey St., Berkeley CA 94705. **E-mail:** info@kelseyst.com. **Website:** www.kelseyst.com. Estab. 1974. "A Berkeley, California, press publishing collaborations between women poets and artists. Many of the press's collaborations focus on a central theme or conceit, like the sprawl and spectacle of New York in *Arcade* by Erica Hunt and Alison Saar." Hardcover and trade paperback originals and electronic originals.

KENSINGTON PUBLISHING CORP.

119 W. 40th St., New York NY 10018. (212)407-1500. **Fax:** (212)935-0699. **E-mail:** jscognamiglio@kensingtonbooks.com. **Website:** www.kensingtonbooks.com. **Contact:** John Scognamiglio, editorial director, fiction (historical romance, Regency romance, women's contemporary fiction, gay and lesbian fiction and nonfiction, mysteries, suspense, mainstream fiction); Michaela Hamilton, editor in chief, Citadel Press (thrillers, mysteries, mainstream fiction, true crime, current events); Selena James, executive editor, Dafina Books (African American fiction and nonfiction, inspirational, young adult, romance); Peter Senftleben, assistant editor (mainstream fiction, women's contemporary fiction, gay and lesbian fiction, mysteries, suspense, thrillers, romantic suspense, paranormal romance). Estab. 1975. "Kensington focuses on profitable niches and uses aggressive marketing techniques to support its books." Publishes hardcover and trade paperback originals, mass market paperback originals and reprints. Book catalog and guidelines online.

NEEDS No science fiction/fantasy, experimental fiction, business texts, or children's titles.

HOW TO CONTACT Query.

TERMS Pays 6-15% royalty on retail price. Makes outright purchase. Pays a minimum $2,000 advance. Responds in 1 month to queries and proposals; 4 months to mss.

TIPS "Agented submissions only, except for submissions to romance lines. For those lines, query with

SASE or submit proposal package, including 3 sample chapters, synopsis."

KIDS CAN PRESS

25 Dockside Dr., Toronto ON M5A 0B5, Canada. (416)479-7000. **Fax:** (416)960-5437. **Website:** www.kidscanpress.com. **Contact:** Corus Quay, acquisitions. Estab. 1973.

Kids Can Press is currently accepting unsolicited mss from Canadian adult authors only.

NEEDS Picture books, young readers: concepts. "We do not accept young adult fiction or fantasy novels for any age." Adventure, animal, contemporary, folktales, history, humor, multicultural, nature/environment, special needs, sports, suspense/mystery. Average word length: picture books—1,000-2,000; young readers—750-1,500; middle readers—10,000-15,000; young adults—over 15,000.

HOW TO CONTACT Submit outline/synopsis and 2-3 sample chapters. For picture books submit complete ms.

TERMS Responds in 6 months only if interesed.

DENIS KITCHEN PUBLISHING CO., LLC

P.O. Box 2250, Amherst MA 01004. (413)259-1627. **Fax:** (413)259-1812. **E-mail:** help@deniskitchen.com. **Website:** www.deniskitchen.com. **Contact:** Denis Kitchen, publisher. Publishes hardcover and trade paperback originals and reprints.

This publisher strongly discourages e-mail submissions.

NEEDS "We do not want pure fiction. We seek cartoonists or writer/illustrator teams who can tell compelling stories with a combination of words and pictures." No pure fiction (meaning text only).

HOW TO CONTACT Query with SASE. Submit sample illustrations/comic pages. Submit complete ms.

TERMS Pays 6-10% royalty on retail price. Occasionally makes deals based on percentage of wholesale if idea and/or bulk of work is done in-house. Pays $1-5,000 advance. Responds in 4-6 weeks.

TIPS "Our audience is readers who embrace the graphic novel revolution, who appreciate historical comic strips and books, and who follow popular and alternative culture. We like to discover new talent. The artist who has a day job but a great idea is encouraged to contact us. The pop culture historian who has a new take on an important figure is likewise encouraged. We have few preconceived notions about mss or ideas, though we are decidedly selective. Historically, we have published many first-time authors and artists, some of whom developed into award-winning creators with substantial followings. Artists or illustrators who do not have confidence in their writing should send us self-promotional postcards (our favorite way of spotting new talent)."

KNOPF

Imprint of Penguin Random House, 1745 Broadway, New York NY 10019. **Fax:** (212)940-7390. **Website:** knopfdoubleday.com/imprint/knopf. Estab. 1915. Publishes hardcover and paperback originals.

NEEDS Publishes book-length fiction of literary merit by known or unknown writers. Length: 40,000-150,000 words.

HOW TO CONTACT Usually only accepts mss submitted by agents. However, writers may submit sample 25-50 pages with SASE.

TERMS Royalties vary. Offers advance. Responds in 2-6 months to queries.

KNOX ROBINSON PUBLISHING

Knox Robinson Holdings, LLC, 3104 Briarcliff Rd. NE #98414, Atlanta GA 30345. (404)478-8696. **E-mail:** info@knoxrobinsonpublishing.com. **E-mail:** subs@knoxrobinsonpublishing.com. **Website:** www.knoxrobinsonpublishing.com. **Contact:** Dr. Dana Celeste Robinson, publisher. Estab. 2010. Knox Robinson Publishing began as an international, independent, specialist publisher of historical fiction, historical romance, and fantasy. Now open to well-written literature in all genres. Publishes fiction and nonfiction. Catalog available. Guidelines online.

IMPRINTS Under the Maple Tree Books (children's literature), Mithras Books (young adult literature).

NEEDS "We are seeking historical fiction featuring obscure historical figures."

HOW TO CONTACT Submit first 3 chapters and author questionnaire found on website.

TERMS Pays royalty. Responds within 6 months to submissions of first 3 chapters. "We do not accept proposals."

KREGEL PUBLICATIONS

2450 Oak Industrial Dr. NE, Grand Rapids MI 49505. (616)451-4775. **Fax:** (616)451-9330. **E-mail:** kregelbooks@kregel.com. **Website:** www.kregelpublications.com. **Contact:** Dennis R. Hillman, publisher.

Estab. 1949. "Our mission as an evangelical Christian publisher is to provide—with integrity and excellence—trusted, Biblically based resources that challenge and encourage individuals in their Christian lives. Works in theology and Biblical studies should reflect the historic, orthodox Protestant tradition." Publishes hardcover and trade paperback originals and reprints. Guidelines online.

IMPRINTS Kregel Publications, Kregel Academic, Kregel Childrens, Kregel Classics.

NEEDS Fiction should be geared toward the evangelical Christian market. Wants books with fast-paced, contemporary storylines presenting a strong Christian message in an engaging, entertaining style.

HOW TO CONTACT Finds works through The Writer's Edge and Christian Manuscript Submissions ms screening services.

TERMS Pays royalty on wholesale price. Pays negotiable advance. Responds in 2-3 months.

TIPS "Our audience consists of conservative, evangelical Christians, including pastors and ministry students."

KWELA BOOKS

Imprint of NB Publishers, P.O. Box 6525, Roggebaai 8012, South Africa. (27)(21)406-3605. **Fax:** (27)(21)406-3712. **E-mail:** kwela@kwela.com. **Website:** www.kwela.com. Estab. 1994.

LANTANA PUBLISHING

London, United Kingdom. **E-mail:** info@lantanapublishing.com. **E-mail:** submissions@lantanapublishing.com. **Website:** www.lantanapublishing.com. Estab. 2014. "Lantana Publishing is an independent publishing company committed to addressing the widespread lack of cultural diversity in children's publishing in the U.K. As a publishing house with a strong social mission to increase the availability and visibility of diverse children's writing, we provide opportunities for authors and illustrators of minority backgrounds to create children's books that are resonant of their own experiences, places and cultures." Guidelines online.

"We are currently focusing on picture books for 4- to 8-year-olds."

NEEDS "We love writing that is new, unusual or quirky, and that interweaves mythic, historical or spiritual elements into fun, contemporary stories full of color and excitement. We particularly like stories with modern-day settings and strong role models, positive relationships between communities and their environment, and evocative storylines that can provide a glimpse into the belief systems, traditions, or worldviews of other cultures." No nonfiction.

HOW TO CONTACT "If you are a picture book author, please send us the complete text of your ms. Illustrations are not necessary. If we like your story, we will commission an illustrator to work with you. A picture book ms should not normally exceed 1,000 words. If your story does exceed this word limit, please include a justification for its length in your cover letter."

TERMS Pays royalty. Pays advance. Responds in 6 weeks.

LEAPFROG PRESS

Box 505, Fredonia NY 14063. (508)274-2710. **E-mail:** leapfrog@leapfrogpress.com. **E-mail:** acquisitions@leapfrogpress.com. **Website:** www.leapfrogpress.com. **Contact:** Rebecca Schwab, acquisitions editor; Layla Al-Bedawi, publicity. Estab. 1996. Guidelines online.

NEEDS "We search for beautifully written literary titles and market them aggressively to national trade and library accounts. We also sell film, translation, foreign, and book club rights." Publishes paperback originals. Books: acid-free paper; sewn binding. Average print order: 3,000. First novel print order: 2,000 (average). Member: Publishers Marketing Association, PEN. Distributes titles through Consortium Book Sales and Distribution, St. Paul, MN. Promotes titles through all national review media, bookstore readings, author tours, website, radio shows, chain store promotions, advertisements, book fairs. "Genres often blur; we look for good writing. We are most interested in works that are quirky, that fall outside of any known genre, and, of course, that are well written and finely crafted. We are most interested in literary fiction."

HOW TO CONTACT Query by e-mail only. Send letter and first 5-10 ms pages within e-mail message. No attachments. Responds in 2-3 weeks to queries by e-mail; 6 months to mss. May consider simultaneous submissions.

TERMS Pays 10% royalty on net receipts. Average advance: negotiable. Response time varies.

TIPS "We like anything that is superbly written and genuinely original. We like the idiosyncratic and the peculiar. We rarely publish nonfiction. Send only your best work, and send only completed work that is ready. That means the completed ms has already been through extensive editing and is ready to be judged. We consider submissions from both previously published and unpublished writers. We are uninterested in an impressive author bio if the work is poor; if the work is excellent, the author bio is equally unimportant."

LEE & LOW BOOKS

95 Madison Ave., #1205, New York NY 10016. (212)779-4400. **E-mail:** general@leeandlow.com. **Website:** www.leeandlow.com. Estab. 1991. "Our goals are to meet a growing need for books that address children of color, and to present literature that all children can identify with. We only consider multicultural children's books. Sponsors a yearly New Voices Award for first-time picture book authors of color. Contest rules online at website or for SASE." Publishes hardcover originals and trade paperback reprints. Book catalog available online. Guidelines available online or by written request with SASE.

NEEDS Picture books, young readers: anthology, contemporary, history, multicultural, poetry. Picture book, middle reader: contemporary, history, multicultural, nature/environment, poetry, sports. Average word length: picture books—1,000-1,500 words. "We do not publish folklore or animal stories."

HOW TO CONTACT Submit complete ms.

TERMS Pays net royalty. Pays authors advance against royalty. Pays illustrators advance against royalty. Pays photographers advance against royalty. Responds in 6 months to mss if interested.

TIPS "Check our website to see the kinds of books we publish. Do not send mss that don't fit our mission."

⊘ LERNER PUBLISHING GROUP

1251 Washington Ave. N., Minneapolis MN 55401. (800)452-7236; (612)332-3344. **Fax:** (612)337-7615. **E-mail:** editorial@karben.com. **Website:** www.karben.com; www.lernerbooks.com. Estab. 1957. Lerner Publishing primarily publishes books for children ages 7-18. List includes titles in geography, natural and physical science, current events, ancient and modern history, high interest, sports, world cultures, and numerous biography series. Kar-Ben Publishing, the Jewish-themed imprint of Lerner Publishing Group, primarily publishes books for children ages Pre-K-9. Lerner's list includes titles in geography, natural and physical science, current events, ancient and modern history, high interest, sports, world cultures, and numerous biography series. Kar-Ben's list includes only books on Jewish themes for children and families. Lerner Publishing does not accept unsolicited mss. Kar-Ben does accept unsolicited mss. **Illustrators:** Please submit samples that show skill in children's book illustration. Digital portfolios preferred. Please DO NOT send original art. **Writers:** Kar-Ben considers fiction and nonfiction for preschool through middle school, including holiday books, life-cycle stories, Bible tales, folktales, and board books. In particular, Kar-Ben is looking for stories that reflect the cultural diversity of today's Jewish community. Kar-Ben DOES NOT publish games, textbooks, or books in Hebrew. "Your story should be concise, have interesting, believable characters, and action that holds the readers' attention. Good prose is far better than tortured verse." Contact editorial@karben.com.

Lerner Publishing Group no longer accepts submission in any of their imprints except for Kar-Ben Publishing.

HOW TO CONTACT "We will continue to seek targeted solicitations at specific reading levels and in specific subject areas. The company will list these targeted solicitations on our website and in national newsletters, such as the SCBWI *Bulletin*."

LES ÉDITIONS DU VERMILLON

305 Saint Patrick St., Ottawa ON K1N 5K4, Canada. (613)241-4032. **Fax:** (613)241-3109. **E-mail:** lesditionsduvermillon@rogers.com. **Website:** www.leseditionsduvermillon.ca. Publishes trade paperback originals. Book catalog available free.

TERMS Pays 10% royalty. Responds in 6 months to mss.

LES FIGUES PRESS

P.O. Box 7736, Los Angeles CA 90007. **E-mail:** info@lesfigues.com. **Website:** www.lesfigues.com. **Contact:** Teresa Carmody, director. Les Figues Press is an independent, nonprofit publisher of poetry, prose, visual art, conceptual writing, and translation. With a mission to create aesthetic conversations between readers, writers, and artists, Les Figues Press favors projects which push the boundaries of genre, form, and general acceptability. Submissions are only reviewed through its annual NOS Book Contest.

LETHE PRESS

118 Heritage Ave., Maple Shade NJ 08052. (609)410-7391. **E-mail:** lethepress@aol.com. **Website:** www.lethepressbooks.com. Estab. 2001. "Welcomes submis-

sions from authors of any sexual or gender identity." Guidelines online.

NEEDS "Named after the Greek river of memory and forgetfulness (and pronounced *Lee-Thee*), Lethe Press is a small press devoted to ideas that are often neglected or forgotten by mainstream, profit-oriented publishers." Distributes/promotes titles. Lethe Books are distributed by Ingram Publications and Bookazine, and are available at all major bookstores as well as the major online retailers.

HOW TO CONTACT Query via e-mail.

ARTHUR A. LEVINE BOOKS

Scholastic, Inc., 557 Broadway, New York NY 10012. (212)343-4436. **Fax:** (212)343-6143. **Website:** www.arthuralevinebooks.com. Estab. 1996. Publishes hardcover, paperback, and e-book editions. Picture books: Send query letter and full text of pb. Novels: Send query letter, first 2 chapters, and synopsis. Other: Send query letter, 10-page sample, and synopsis/proposal.

NEEDS "Arthur A. Levine is looking for distinctive literature, for children and young adults, for whatever's extraordinary." Averages 18-20 total titles/year.

HOW TO CONTACT Query.

TERMS Responds in 1 month to queries; 5 months to mss.

LILLENAS PUBLISHING CO.

Imprint of Lillenas Drama Resources, P.O. Box 419527, Kansas City MO 64141. (800)877-0700. **Fax:** (816)412-8390. **E-mail:** drama@lillenas.com. **Website:** www.lillenasdrama.com. "We purchase only original, previously unpublished materials. Also, we require that all scripts be performed at least once before they are submitted for consideration. We do not accept scripts that are sent via fax or e-mail. Direct all mss to the Drama Resources Editor." Publishes mass market paperback and electronic originals. Guidelines online.

NEEDS "Looking for sketch and monologue collections for all ages—adults, children and youth. For these collections, we request 12-15 scripts to be submitted at 1 time. Unique treatments of spiritual themes, relevant issues, and biblical messages are of interest. Contemporary full-length and one-act plays that have conflict, characterization, and a spiritual context that is neither a sermon nor an apologetic for youth and adults. We also need wholesome, so-called secular, full-length scripts for dinner theaters and schools." No musicals.

TERMS Pays royalty on net price. Makes outright purchase. Responds in 4-6 months to material.

TIPS "We never receive too many mss."

R.C. LINNELL PUBLISHING

2100 Tyler Ln., Louisville KY 40205. **E-mail:** info@linnellpublishing.com. **Website:** www.linnellpublishing.com. **Contact:** Cheri Powell, owner. Estab. 2010. "We are currently very small and have published a limited number of books. We review books on other subjects on a case-by-case basis. If a book is well written and has an audience, we consider it. We offer publishing services. Please review our Web page to understand our business model and what we can do for you." Publishes print-on-demand paperbacks. Book catalog and guidelines online.

HOW TO CONTACT Submit complete ms.

TERMS Pays 10-40% royalty on retail price. Responds in 1 month to mss.

TIPS "Visit our website to understand the business model and the relationship with authors. All sales are through the Internet. Author should have a marketing plan in mind. We can help expand the plan, but we do not market books. Authors should be comfortable with using the Internet and should know their intended readers. We are especially interested in books that inspire, motivate, amuse, and challenge readers."

LIQUID SILVER BOOKS

10509 Sedgegrass Dr., Indianapolis IN 46235. **E-mail:** submissions@liquidsilverbooks.com. **Website:** www.lsbooks.com. **Contact:** Chrissie Henderson, editorial director. Estab. 1999. Liquid Silver Books is an imprint of Atlantic Bridge Publishing, a royalty-paying, full-service e-publisher. Atlantic Bridge has been in business since June 1999. Liquid Silver Books is dedicated to bringing high-quality erotic romance to our readers.

"We are foremost an e-publisher. We believe the market will continue to grow for e-books. It is our prime focus. At this time our print publishing is on hiatus. We will update the submission guidelines if we reinstate this aspect of our publishing."

NEEDS Needs contemporary, gay and lesbian, paranormal, supernatural, science fiction, fantasy, historical, suspense, and western romances. "We do not accept literary erotica submissions."

HOW TO CONTACT E-mail entire ms as an attachment in RTF format in Arial 12 pt. font. "Include in the body of the e-mail: author bio, your thoughts on e-publishing, a blurb of your book, including title and series title if applicable. Ms must include pen name, real name, and snail mail and e-mail contact information on the first page, top left corner."

TERMS Responds to mss in 10-15 days.

Ⓐ⊘ LITTLE, BROWN AND CO. ADULT TRADE BOOKS

1290 Avenue of the Americas, New York NY 10104. **Website:** www.littlebrown.com. Estab. 1837. "The general editorial philosophy for all divisions continues to be broad and flexible, with high quality and the promise of commercial success as always the first considerations." Publishes hardcover originals and paperback originals and reprints. Guidelines online.

HOW TO CONTACT Agented submissions only.

TERMS Pays royalty. Offer advance.

LITTLE PICKLE PRESS

3701 Sacramento St., #494, San Francisco CA 94118. (415)340-3344. **Fax:** (415)366-1520. **E-mail:** info@littlepicklepress.com. **Website:** www.littlepicklepress.com. Little Pickle Press is a 21st-century publisher dedicated to helping parents and educators cultivate conscious, responsible little people by stimulating explorations of the meaningful topics of their generation through a variety of media, technologies, and techniques. Submit through submission link on site. Includes young adult imprint Relish Media. Uses author.me for submissions for Little Pickle and young adult imprint Relish Media. Guidelines available on site.

TIPS "We have lots of mss to consider, so it will take up to 8 weeks before we get back to you."

⊘ LIVINGSTON PRESS

University of West Alabama, 100 N. Washington St., Station 22, University of West Alabama, Livingston AL 35470. **Fax:** (205)653-3717. **E-mail:** jwt@uwa.edu. **Website:** www.livingstonpress.uwa.edu. **Contact:** Joe Taylor, director. Estab. 1974. "Livingston Press, as do all literary presses, looks for authorial excellence in style. Currently emphasizing novels." Reading in June only. Check back for details. Publishes hardcover and trade paperback originals, plus Kindle. Book catalog online. Guidelines online.

IMPRINTS Swallow's Tale Press.

NEEDS "We are interested in form and, of course, style." No genre fiction, please.

TERMS Pays 100 contributor's copies, after sales of 1,500, standard royalty. Responds in 4 months to queries; 6-12 months to mss.

TIPS "Our readers are interested in literature, often quirky literature that emphasizes form and style. Please visit our website for current needs."

LOOSE ID

P.O. Box 806, San Francisco CA 94104. **E-mail:** submissions@loose-id.com. **Website:** www.loose-id.com. **Contact:** Treva Harte, editor in chief. Estab. 2004. "Loose Id is love unleashed. We're taking romance to the edge." Publishes e-books and some print books. Distributes/promotes titles. "The company promotes itself through Web and print advertising wherever readers of erotic romance may be found, creating a recognizable brand identity as the place to let your id run free and the people who unleash your fantasies. It is currently pursuing licensing agreements for foreign translations, and has a print program of 2-5 titles per month." Guidelines online.

"Loose Id is actively acquiring stories from both aspiring and established authors."

NEEDS Wants nontraditional erotic romance stories, including gay, lesbian, heroes and heroines, multi-culturalism, cross-genre, fantasy, science fiction, straight contemporary or historical romances.

HOW TO CONTACT Query with outline/synopsis and 3 sample chapters. Accepts queries by e-mail. Include estimated word count, list of publishing credits, and why your submission is love unleashed. "Before submitting a query or proposal, please read the guidelines on our website. Please don't hesitate to contact us by e-mail for any information you don't see there."

TERMS Pays e-book royalties of 40%. Responds to queries in 1 month.

MAGE PUBLISHERS, INC.

1780 Crossroads Dr., Odenton MD 21113. (202)342-1642. **Fax:** (202)342-9269. **E-mail:** as@mage.com. **Website:** www.mage.com. Estab. 1985. Mage publishes books relating to Persian/Iranian culture. Publishes hardcover originals and reprints, trade paperback originals. Book catalog available free. Guidelines online.

NEEDS Must relate to Persian/Iranian culture.

HOW TO CONTACT Submit outline, SASE. Query via mail or e-mail.

TERMS Pays royalty. Responds in 1 month to queries.

TIPS "Audience is the Iranian-American community in America and Americans interested in Persian culture."

MAGINATION PRESS

750 First St. NE, Washington DC 20002. (202)336-5618. **Fax:** (202)336-5624. **E-mail:** magination@apa.org. **Website:** www.apa.org. Estab. 1988. Magination Press is an imprint of the American Psychological Association. "We publish books dealing with the psycho/therapeutic resolution of children's problems and psychological issues with a strong self-help component." Submit complete ms. Full guidelines available on site. Materials returned only with SASE.

NEEDS All levels: psychological and social issues, self-help, health, parenting concerns, and special needs. Picture books, middle school readers.

TERMS Responds to queries in 1-2 months; mss in 2-6 months.

MANDALA PUBLISHING

Mandala Publishing and Earth Aware Editions, 800 A St., San Rafael CA 94901. **E-mail:** info@mandalapublishing.com. **Website:** www.mandalaeartheditions.com. Estab. 1989. "In the traditions of the East, wisdom, truth, and beauty go hand-in-hand. This is reflected in the great arts, music, yoga, and philosophy of India. Mandala Publishing strives to bring to its readers authentic and accessible renderings of thousands of years of wisdom and philosophy from this unique culture—timeless treasures that are our inspirations and guides. At Mandala, we believe that the arts, health, ecology, and spirituality of the great Vedic traditions are as relevant today as they were in sacred India thousands of years ago. As a distinguished publisher in the world of Vedic literature, lifestyle, and interests today, Mandala strives to provide accessible and meaningful works for the modern reader." Publishes hardcover, trade paperback, and electronic originals. Book catalog online.

HOW TO CONTACT Query with SASE.

TERMS Pays 3-15% royalty on retail price. Responds in 6 months.

MANOR HOUSE PUBLISHING, INC.

452 Cottingham Crescent, Ancaster ON L9G 3V6, Canada. **E-mail:** mbdavie@manor-house.biz. **E-mail:** mbdavie@manor-house.biz. **Website:** www.manor-house.biz. **Contact:** Mike Davie, president (novels and nonfiction). Estab. 1998. Publishes hardcover, trade paperback, and mass market paperback originals and reprints. Book catalog online. Guidelines available via e-mail.

NEEDS Stories should have Canadian settings and characters should be Canadian, but content should have universal appeal to wide audience.

HOW TO CONTACT Query via e-mail. Submit proposal package, clips, bio, 3 sample chapters. Submit complete ms.

TERMS Pays 10% royalty on retail price. Queries and mss to be sent by e-mail only. "We will respond in 30 days if interested—if not, there is no response. Do not follow up unless asked to do so."

TIPS "Our audience includes everyone—the general public/mass audience. Self-edit your work first, make sure it is well written, with strong Canadian content."

MARTIN SISTERS PUBLISHING COMPANY, INC

P.O. Box 1154, Barbourville KY 40906-1499. **E-mail:** submissions@martinsisterspublishing.com. **Website:** www.martinsisterspublishing.com. **Contact:** Publisher/Editor (fiction/nonfiction). Estab. 2011. Firm/imprint publishes trade and mass market paperback originals; electronic originals. Catalog and guidelines online.

HOW TO CONTACT "Please place query letter, marketing plan, and the first 5-10 pages of your ms (if you are submitting fiction) directly into your e-mail." Guidelines available on site.

TERMS Pays 7.5% maximum net royalty on print. Pays 35% maximum net royalty on e-books. No advance offered. Responds in 1 month on queries; 2 months on proposals; 3-6 months on mss.

MARVEL COMICS

135 W. 50th St., Seventh Floor, New York NY 10020. **Website:** www.marvel.com. Publishes hardcover originals and reprints, trade paperback reprints, mass market comic book originals, electronic reprints. Guidelines online.

NEEDS "Our shared universe needs new heroes and villains; books for younger readers and teens needed."

HOW TO CONTACT Submit inquiry letter, idea submission form (download from website), SASE.

TERMS Pays on a per-page, work-for-hire basis, or creator-owned, which is then contracted. Pays negotiable advance. Responds in 3-5 weeks to queries.

MCBOOKS PRESS

ID Booth Building, 520 N. Meadow St., Ithaca NY 14850. (607)272-2114. **E-mail:** mcbooks@mcbooks.com. **Website:** www.mcbooks.com. **Contact:** Alexander G. Skutt, publisher. Estab. 1979. Publishes trade paperback and hardcover originals and reprints. Guidelines online.

"Currently not accepting submissions or queries for fiction or nonfiction." The only exception that we would look at is excellent nautical historical fiction that could be expanded into a series.

NEEDS Publishes Julian Stockwin, John Biggins, Colin Sargent, and Douglas W. Jacobson. Distributes titles through Independent Publishers Group.

TIPS "We are currently only publishing authors with whom we have a pre-existing relationship. If this policy changes, we will announce the change on our website."

MCCLELLAND & STEWART, LTD.

The Canadian Publishers, 320 Front St. W., Ste. 1400, Toronto ON M5V 3B6, Canada. (416)364-4449. **Fax:** (416)598-7764. **Website:** www.mcclelland.com. Publishes hardcover, trade paperback, and mass market paperback originals and reprints.

NEEDS "We publish work by established authors as well as the work of new and developing authors."

HOW TO CONTACT Query. All unsolicited mss returned unopened.

TERMS Pays 10-15% royalty on retail price (hardcover rates). Pays advance. Responds in 3 months to proposals.

THE MCDONALD & WOODWARD PUBLISHING CO.

695 Tall Oaks Dr., Newark OH 43055. (740)641-2691. **Fax:** (740)641-2692. **E-mail:** mwpubco@mwpubco.com. **Website:** www.mwpubco.com. **Contact:** Jerry N. McDonald, publisher. Estab. 1986. McDonald & Woodward publishes books in natural history, cultural history, and natural resources. Currently emphasizing travel, natural and cultural history, and natural resource conservation. Publishes hardcover and trade paperback originals. Book catalog online. Guidelines free on request, by e-mail.

HOW TO CONTACT Query with SASE.

TERMS Pays 10% royalty. Responds in less than 1 month.

TIPS "Our books are meant for the curious and educated elements of the general population."

MARGARET K. MCELDERRY BOOKS

Imprint of Simon & Schuster Children's Publishing Division, 1230 Sixth Ave., New York NY 10020. (212)698-7200. **Website:** imprints.simonandschuster.biz/margaret-k-mcelderry-books. Estab. 1971. "Margaret K. McElderry Books publishes hardcover and paperback trade books for children from preschool age through young adult. This list includes picture books, middle-grade and teen fiction, poetry, and fantasy. The style and subject matter of the books we publish is almost unlimited. We do not publish textbooks, coloring and activity books, greeting cards, magazines, pamphlets, or religious publications." Guidelines for #10 SASE.

NEEDS No unsolicited mss.

HOW TO CONTACT Agented submissions only.

TERMS Pays authors royalty based on retail price. Pays illustrators by the project. Pays photographers by the project. Original artwork returned at job's completion. Offers $5,000-8,000 advance for new authors.

TIPS "Read! The children's book field is competitive. See what's been done and what's out there before submitting. We look for high quality: an originality of ideas, clarity and felicity of expression, a well-organized plot, and strong character-driven stories. We're looking for strong, original fiction, especially mysteries and middle-grade humor. We are always interested in picture books for the youngest-age reader. Study our titles."

MEDALLION PRESS

4222 Meridian Pkwy., Aurora IL 60504. (630)513-8316. **E-mail:** emily@medallionpress.com. **Website:** medallionpress.com. **Contact:** Emily Steele, editorial director. Estab. 2003. "We are an independent, innovative publisher looking for compelling, memorable stories told in distinctive voices." Publishes trade paperback, hardcover, e-book originals, book apps, and TREEbook. Guidelines online. Currently closed to submissions.

NEEDS Word count: 40,000-90,000 for young adult; 60,000-120,000 for all others. No short stories, anthologies, erotica.

HOW TO CONTACT Submit first 3 consecutive chapters and a synopsis through our online submission form. Please check if submissions are currently open before submitting.

TERMS Offers advance. Responds in 2-3 months to mss.

TIPS "We are not affected by trends. We are simply looking for well-crafted, original, compelling works of fiction and nonfiction. Please visit our website for the most current guidelines prior to submitting anything to us. Please check if submissions are currently open before submitting."

MELANGE BOOKS, LLC

White Bear Lake MN 55110-5538. **E-mail:** melangebooks@melange-books.com. **E-mail:** submissions@melange-books.com. **Website:** www.melange-books.com. **Contact:** Nancy Schumacher, publisher and acquiring editor for Melange and Satin Romance; Caroline Andrus, acquiring editor for Fire and Ice for Young Adult. Estab. 2011. Melange is a royalty-paying company publishing e-books and print books. Publishes trade paperback originals and electronic originals. Send SASE for book catalog. Guidelines online.

IMPRINTS Fire and Ice (young and new adult), Satin Romance.

NEEDS Submit a clean mss by following guidelines on website.

HOW TO CONTACT Query electronically by clicking on "submissions" on website. Include a synopsis and 4 chapters.

TERMS Authors receive a minimum of 20% royalty on print sales, 40% on electronic book sales. Does not offer an advance. Responds in 1 month on queries; 2 months on proposals; 4-6 months on mss.

MERRIAM PRESS

133 Elm St., Ste. 3R, Bennington VT 05201. (802)447-0313. **E-mail:** ray@merriam-press.com. **Website:** www.merriam-press.com. Estab. 1988. "Merriam Press specializes in military history, particularly World War II history. We are also branching out into other genres, including fiction, historical fiction, poetry, children's." Publishes hardcover and softcover trade paperback originals and reprints. Many titles are also made available in PDF and e-book editions. Book catalog and guidelines online.

NEEDS Especially, but not limited to, military history.

HOW TO CONTACT Query with SASE or by e-mail first.

TERMS Pays 10% royalty on actual selling price. Does not pay advance. Responds quickly (e-mail preferred) to queries.

TIPS "Our military history books are geared for military historians, collectors, model kit builders, wargamers, veterans, general enthusiasts. We now publish some historical fiction and poetry and will consider well-written books on a variety of nonmilitary topics."

MESSIANIC JEWISH PUBLISHERS

6120 Day Long Ln., Clarksville MD 21029. (410)531-6644. **E-mail:** editor@messianicjewish.net. **Website:** www.messianicjewish.net. Publishes hardcover and trade paperback originals and reprints. Guidelines via e-mail.

NEEDS "We publish very little fiction. Jewish or Biblical themes are a must. Text must demonstrate keen awareness of Jewish culture and thought."

HOW TO CONTACT Query with SASE. Unsolicited mss are not return.

TERMS Pays 7-15% royalty on wholesale price.

MICHIGAN STATE UNIVERSITY PRESS

1405 S. Harrison Rd., Ste. 25, East Lansing MI 48823. (517)355-9543. **Fax:** (517)432-2611. **E-mail:** msupress@msu.edu. **Website:** msupress.org. **Contact:** Alex Schwartz and Julie Loehr, acquisitions. Estab. 1947. Michigan State University Press has notably represented both scholarly publishing and the mission of Michigan State University with the publication of numerous award-winning books and scholarly journals. In addition, they publish nonfiction that addresses, in a more contemporary way, social concerns, such as diversity and civil rights. They also publish literary fiction and poetry. Publishes hardcover and softcover originals. Book catalog and ms guidelines online.

NEEDS Publishes literary fiction.

HOW TO CONTACT Submit proposal.

TERMS Pays variable royalty.

MILKWEED EDITIONS

1011 Washington Ave. S., Ste. 300, Minneapolis MN 55415. (612)332-3192. **Fax:** (612)215-2550. **Website:** www.milkweed.org. **Contact:** Patrick Thomas, managing editor. Estab. 1979. "Milkweed Editions publishes with the intention of making a humane impact on society, in the belief that literature is a transformative art uniquely able to convey the essential experiences of the human heart and spirit. To that end, Milkweed Editions publishes distinctive voices of literary merit in handsomely designed, visually dynamic books, exploring the ethical, cultural, and esthetic issues that free societies need continually to address." Publishes hardcover, trade paperback, and electronic originals; trade paperback and electronic reprints. Book catalog online. Only accepts submissions during open submission periods. See website for guidelines.

NEEDS Novels for adults and for readers 8-13. High literary quality. For adult readers: literary fiction, nonfiction, poetry, essays. Middle readers: adventure, contemporary, fantasy, multicultural, nature/environment, suspense/mystery. Average length: middle readers—90-200 pages. No romance, mysteries, science fiction.

HOW TO CONTACT "Please submit a query letter with 3 opening chapters (of a novel) or 3 representative stories (of a collection)."

TERMS Pays authors variable royalty based on retail price. Offers advance against royalties. Pays varied advance from $500-10,000. Responds in 6 months.

TIPS "We are looking for excellent writing with the intent of making a humane impact on society. Please read submission guidelines before submitting and acquaint yourself with our books in terms of style and quality before submitting. Many factors influence our selection process, so don't get discouraged. Nonfiction is focused on literary writing about the natural world, including living well in urban environments."

MILKWEED FOR YOUNG READERS

Milkweed Editions, Open Book Building, 1011 Washington Ave. S., Ste. 300, Minneapolis MN 55415. (612)332-3192. **Fax:** (612)215-2550. **Website:** www.milkweed.org. **Contact:** Patrick Thomas, managing editor. Estab. 1984. "We are looking first of all for high-quality literary writing. We publish books with the intention of making a humane impact on society." Publishes hardcover and trade paperback originals. Book catalog for $1.50. Guidelines online.

HOW TO CONTACT "Milkweed Editions now accepts mss online through our Submission Manager. If you're a first-time submitter, you'll need to fill in a simple form and then follow the instructions for selecting and uploading your ms. Please make sure that your ms follows the submission guidelines."

TERMS Pays 7% royalty on retail price. Pays variable advance. Responds in 6 months to queries.

MONDIAL

203 W. 107th St., Ste. 6C, New York NY 10025. 212-864-7095. **Fax:** (208)361-2863. **E-mail:** contact@mondialbooks.com. **Website:** www.mondialbooks.com; www.librejo.com. **Contact:** Andrew Moore, editor. Estab. 1996. Publishes hardcover, trade paperback originals and reprints. Guidelines available online.

HOW TO CONTACT Query through online submission form.

TERMS Pays 10% royalty on wholesale price. Responds to queries in 3 months. Responds only if interested.

MOODY PUBLISHERS

Moody Bible Institute, 820 N. LaSalle Blvd., Chicago IL 60610. (800)678-8812. **Fax:** (312)329-4157. **E-mail:** authors@moody.edu. **Website:** www.moodypublishers.org. **Contact:** Acquisitions Coordinator. Estab. 1894. "The mission of Moody Publishers is to educate and edify the Christian and to evangelize the non-Christian by ethically publishing conservative, evangelical Christian literature and other media for all ages around the world, and to help provide resources for Moody Bible Institute in its training of future Christian leaders." Publishes hardcover, trade, and mass market paperback originals. Book catalog for 9x12 envelope and 4 first-class stamps. Guidelines online.

HOW TO CONTACT Agented submissions only.

TERMS Royalty varies. Responds in 2-3 months to queries.

TIPS "In our fiction list, we're looking for Christian storytellers rather than teachers trying to present a message. Your motivation should be to delight the reader. Using your skills to create beautiful works is glorifying to God."

THE NAUTICAL & AVIATION PUBLISHING CO. OF AMERICA

845 A Lowcountry Blvd., Mt. Pleasant SC 29464. (843)856-0561. **Fax:** (843)856-3164. **E-mail:** nauticalaviationpublishing@comcast.net. **Website:** www.nauticandaviation.com. Estab. 1979. Publishes hard-

cover and trade paperback originals and reprints. Book catalog and guidelines available free.

HOW TO CONTACT Submit complete ms with cover letter and brief synopsis.

TERMS Pays royalty.

TIPS "We are primarily a nonfiction publisher, but we will review historical fiction of military interest with strong literary merit."

NBM PUBLISHING

160 Broadway, Ste. 700, East Bldg., New York NY 10038. **E-mail:** nbmgn@nbmpub.com. **Website:** nbmpub.com. **Contact:** Terry Nantier, editor/art director. Estab. 1976. "One of the best-regarded quality graphic novel publishers. Our catalog is determined by what will appeal to a wide audience of readers." Publishes hardcover originals, paperback originals. Format: offset printing; perfect binding, e-books. Average print order: 3,000-4,000; average debut writer's print order: 2,000. Publishes 1 debut writer/year. Publishes 20 titles/year. Member: IBPA, CBC. Distributed/promoted by IPG. Imprints: ComicsLit (literary comics), Eurotica (erotic comics). Publishes graphic novels for an audience of young adult/adults. Types of books include fiction, mystery, and social parodies. Catalog online.

NEEDS literary fiction mostly, children's/juvenile (especially fairy tales, classics), creative nonfiction (especially true crime), erotica, ethnic/multicultural, humor (satire), manga, mystery/suspense, translations, young adult/teen. Does not want superhero or overly violent comics.

HOW TO CONTACT Prefers submissions from writer-artists, creative teams. Send a one-page synopsis of story along with a few pages of comics (copies, NOT originals) and SASE, or submit by e-mail. Attends San Diego Comicon. Agented submissions: 2%. Responds to queries in 1 week; to ms/art packages in 3-4 weeks. Sometimes comments on rejected mss.

TERMS Royalties and advance negotiable. Publishes ms 1 year after acceptance. Writer's guidelines on website. Artist's guidelines on website. Book catalog free upon request. Advance negotiable. Responds to e-mail in 1-2 days; to mail in 1 week.

THOMAS NELSON, INC.

HarperCollins Christian Publishing, Box 141000, Nashville TN 37214. (615)889-9000. **Website:** www.thomasnelson.com. Thomas Nelson publishes Christian lifestyle nonfiction and fiction, and general nonfiction. Publishes hardcover and paperback orginals.

NEEDS Publishes authors of commercial fiction who write for adults from a Christian perspective.

HOW TO CONTACT Does not accept unsolicited mss. No phone queries.

TERMS Rates negotiated for each project. Pays advance.

TOMMY NELSON

Imprint of Thomas Nelson, Inc., P.O. Box 141000, Nashville TN 37214-1000. (615)889-9000. **Fax:** (615)902-2219. **Website:** www.tommynelson.com. "Tommy Nelson publishes children's Christian nonfiction and fiction for boys and girls up to age 14. We honor God and serve people through books, videos, software, and Bibles for children that improve the lives of our customers." Publishes hardcover and trade paperback originals. Guidelines online.

NEEDS No stereotypical characters.

HOW TO CONTACT Does not accept unsolicited mss.

TIPS "Know the Christian Booksellers Association market. Check out the Christian bookstores to see what sells and what is needed."

NEW DIRECTIONS

80 Eighth Ave., New York NY 10011. **Fax:** (212)255-0231. **E-mail:** editorial@ndbooks.com. **Website:** www.ndbooks.com. **Contact:** Editorial Assistant. Estab. 1936. "Currently, New Directions focuses primarily on fiction in translation, avant-garde American fiction, and experimental poetry by American and foreign authors. If your work does not fall into one of those categories, you would probably do best to submit your work elsewhere." Hardcover and trade paperback originals. Book catalog and guidelines online.

NEEDS No juvenile or young adult; occult or paranormal; genre fiction (formula romances, science fiction or westerns); arts and crafts; and inspirational poetry.

HOW TO CONTACT Brief query only.

TERMS Responds in 3-4 months to queries.

TIPS "Our books serve the academic community."

NEWEST PUBLISHERS LTD.

201, 8540-109 St., Edmonton AB T6G 1E6, Canada. (780)432-9427. **Fax:** (780)433-3179. **E-mail:** info@newestpress.com. **E-mail:** submissions@newestpress.com. **Website:** www.newestpress.com. Estab. 1977. NeWest publishes Western Canadian fiction, nonfiction, poetry, and drama. Publishes trade paperback originals. Book catalog for 9x12 SASE. Guidelines online.

HOW TO CONTACT Submit complete ms.

TERMS Pays 10% royalty. Responds in 6-8 months to queries.

NEW LIBRI PRESS

4907 Meridian Ave. N., Seattle WA 98103. **E-mail:** query@newlibri.com. **Website:** www.newlibri.com. **Contact:** Michael Muller, editor; Stanislav Fritz, editor. Estab. 2011. "We only accept e-mail submissions, not USPS." Publishes trade paperback, electronic originals, electronic reprints. Catalog online. Guidelines online. Electronic submissions only.

NEEDS "Open to most ideas right now; this will change as we mature as a press. As a new press, we are more open than most, and time will probably shape the direction. That said, trite as it is, we want good writing that is fun to read. While we currently are not looking for some subgenres, if it is well written and a bit off the beaten path, submit to us. We are e-book focused. We may not create a paper version if the e-book does not sell, which means some fiction may be less likely to currently sell (e.g., picture books are problematic).

HOW TO CONTACT Submit query, synopsis, and full ms (so we don't have to ask for it later if we like it. We will read about 50 pages to start).

TERMS Pays 20-35% royalty on wholesale price. No advance. Responds in 3 months to mss.

TIPS "Our audience is someone who is comfortable reading an e-book, or someone who is tired of the recycled authors of mainstream publishing but still wants a good, relatively fast reading experience. The industry is changing, and while we accept for the traditional model, we are searching for writers who are interested in sharing the risk and controlling their own destiny. We embrace writers with no agent."

NEW RIVERS PRESS

1104 Seventh Ave. S., Moorhead MN 56563. **Website:** www.newriverspress.com. **Contact:** Nayt Rundquist, managing editor. Estab. 1968. New Rivers Press publishes collections of poetry, novels, nonfiction, translations of contemporary literature, and collections of short fiction and nonfiction. "We continue to publish books regularly by new and emerging writers, but we also welcome the opportunity to read work of every character and to publish the best literature available nationwide. Each fall, through the Many Voices Project competition, we choose 2 books: 1 poetry and 1 prose."

NEEDS Sponsors American Fiction Prize to find best unpublished short stories by American writers.

NIGHTSCAPE PRESS

P.O. Box 1948, Smyrna TN 37167. **E-mail:** info@nightscapepress.com. **E-mail:** submissions@nightscapepress.com. **Website:** www.nightscapepress.com. Estab. 2012. Nightscape Press is seeking quality, book-length words of at least 50,000 words (40,000 for young adult). Guidelines online. Currently closed to submissions. Will announce on site when they reopen to submissions.

NEEDS "We are not interested in erotica or graphic novels."

HOW TO CONTACT Query.

TERMS Pays monthly royalties. Offers advance.

NORTIA PRESS

Santa Ana CA **E-mail:** acquisitions@nortiapress.com. **Website:** www.nortiapress.com. Estab. 2009. Publishes trade paperback and electronic originals.

NEEDS "We focus mainly on nonfiction as well as literary and historical fiction, but are open to other genres. No vampire stories, science fiction, or erotica, please."

HOW TO CONTACT Submit a brief e-mail query. Please include a short bio, approximate word count of book, and expected date of completion (fiction titles should be completed before sending a query and should contain a sample chapter in the body of the e-mail). All unsolicited snail mail or attachments will be discarded without review.

TERMS Pays negotiable royalties on wholesale price. Responds in 1 month.

TIPS "We specialize in working with experienced authors who seek a more collaborative and fulfilling relationship with their publisher. As such, we are less likely to accept pitches from first-time authors, no matter how good the idea. As with any pitch, please make your e-mail very brief and to the point, so the reader is not forced to skim it. Always include some biographic information. Your life is interesting."

W.W. NORTON & COMPANY, INC.

500 Fifth Ave., New York NY 10110. (212)354-5500. **Fax:** (212)869-0856. **Website:** www.wwnorton.com.

Estab. 1923. "W.W. Norton & Company, the oldest and largest publishing house owned wholly by its employees, strives to carry out the imperative of its founder to 'publish books not for a single season, but for the years' in fiction, nonfiction, poetry, college textbooks, cookbooks, art books, and professional books. Due to the workload of our editorial staff and the large volume of materials we receive, Norton is no longer able to accept unsolicited submissions. If you are seeking publication, we suggest working with a literary agent who will represent you to the house."

NOSY CROW PUBLISHING

The Crow's Nest, 10a Lant St., London SE1 1QR, United Kingdom. (44)(0)207-089-7575. **Fax:** (44)(0)207-089-7576. **E-mail:** hello@nosycrow.com. **E-mail:** submissions@nosycrow.com. **Website:** nosycrow.com. "We publish books for children 0-14. We're looking for 'parent-friendly' books, and we don't publish books with explicit sex, drug use, or serious violence, so no edgy young adult or edgy cross-over. And whatever new adult is, we don't do it. We also publish apps for children from 2-7 and may publish apps for older children if the idea feels right." Guidelines online.

NEEDS "As a rule, we don't like books with 'issues' that are in any way overly didactic."

HOW TO CONTACT Prefers submissions by e-mail, but post works if absolutely necessary.

TIPS "Please don't be too disappointed if we reject your work! We're a small company and can only publish a few new books and apps each year, so do try other publishers and agents: Publishing is necessarily a hugely subjective business. We wish you luck!"

OAK TREE PRESS

1700 Dairy Ave., #49, Corcoran CA 93212. **E-mail:** query@oaktreebooks.com. **Website:** www.oaktreebooks.com. **Contact:** Billie Johnson, publisher. Estab. 1998. Oak Tree Press is an independent publisher that is looking for mainstream, genre fiction especially mysteries, narrative nonfiction, how-to. Sponsors 3 contests annually: Dark Oak Mystery, Timeless Love Romance, and CopTales for true crime and other stories of law enforcement professionals." Publishes trade paperback and hardcover books. Catalog and guidelines online. "We require a marketing plan and author participation in the book promotion process."

IMPRINTS Dark Oak Mysteries, Timeless Love, Wild Oaks (stories of the old West).

NEEDS Emphasis on mystery and romance novels. "No science fiction or fantasy novels, or stories set far into the future. Next, novels substantially longer than our stated word count are not considered, regardless of genre. We look for mss of 70,000-90,000 words. If the story really charms us, we will bend some on either end of the range. No right-wing political or racist agendas; gratuitous sex or violence; especially against women; or work that depicts harm of animals."

HOW TO CONTACT Does not accept or return unsolicited mss. Query with SASE. Accepts queries by e-mail. Include estimated word count, brief bio, list of publishing credits, brief description of ms.

TERMS Royalties based on sales. Does not pay advance. Responds in 4-6 weeks.

TIPS "Perhaps my most extreme pet peeve is receiving queries on projects which we've clearly advertised we don't want: science fiction, fantasy, epic tomes, bigoted diatribes, and so on. Second to that is a practice I call 'over-taping,' or the use of yards and yards of tape, or worse yet, the filament tape, so that it takes forever to open the package. Finding story pitches on my voice mail is also annoying."

OCEANVIEW PUBLISHING

595 Bay Isles Rd., Ste. 120-G, Longboat Key FL 34228. **E-mail:** mail@oceanviewpub.com. **E-mail:** submissions@oceanviewpub.com. **Website:** www.oceanviewpub.com. **Contact:** Robert Gussin, CEO. Estab. 2006. "Independent publisher of nonfiction and fiction, with primary interest in original mystery, thriller, and suspense titles. Accepts new and established writers." Publishes hardcover and electronic originals. Catalog and guidelines online.

NEEDS Accepting adult mss with a primary interest in the mystery, thriller, and suspense genres—from new and established writers. No children's or young adult literature, poetry, cookbooks, technical manuals, or short stories.

HOW TO CONTACT Within body of e-mail only, include author's name and brief bio (indicate if this is an agent submission), ms title and word count, author's mailing address, phone number, and e-mail address. Attached to the e-mail should be the following: a synopsis of 750 words or fewer, the first 30 pages of the ms. "Please note that we accept only Word documents as attachments to the submission e-mail." Do not send query letters or proposals.

TERMS Responds in 3 months on mss.

ONSTAGE PUBLISHING

190 Lime Quarry Rd., Ste. 106-J, Madison AL 35758-8962. (256)461-0661. **E-mail:** onstage123@knology.net. **Website:** www.onstagepublishing.com. **Contact:** Dianne Hamilton, senior editor. Estab. 1999. "At this time, we only produce fiction books for ages 8-18. We have added an e-book-only side of the house for mysteries for grades 6-12. See our website for more information. We will not do anthologies of any kind. Query first for nonfiction projects, as nonfiction projects must spark our interest. Now accepting e-mail queries and submissions. For submissions: Put the first 3 chapters in the body of the e-mail. Do not use attachments! We will no longer return any mss. Only an SASE envelope is needed. Send complete ms if under 20,000 words; otherwise send synopsis and first 3 chapters."

Suggested ms lengths: Chapter books: 3,000-9,000 words; middle-grade novels: 10,000-40,000 words; young adult novels: 40,000-60,000 words.

NEEDS Middle readers: adventure, contemporary, fantasy, history, nature/environment, science fiction, suspense/mystery. Young adults: adventure, contemporary, fantasy, history, humor, science fiction, suspense/mystery. Average word length: chapter books—3,000-9,000 words; middle readers—10,000 words and up; young adults—40,000 and up. Recently published *Mission: Shanghai* by Jamie Dodson (an adventure for boys ages 12+); *Birmingham, 1933: Alice* (a chapter book for grades 3-5). "We do not produce picture books."

TERMS Pays authors/illustrators/photographers advance plus royalties.

TIPS "Study our titles and get a sense of the kind of books we publish, so that you know whether your project is likely to be right for us."

OOLICHAN BOOKS

P.O. Box 2278, Lantzville BC V0R 1M0, Canada. (250)390-4839. **Fax:** (866)299-0026. **E-mail:** info@oolichan.com. **Website:** www.oolichan.com. Estab. 1974. Publishes hardcover and trade paperback originals and reprints. Book catalog online. Guidelines online.

Only publishes Canadian authors.

NEEDS "We try to publish at least 2 literary fiction titles each year. We receive many more deserving submissions than we are able to publish, so we publish only outstanding work. We try to balance our list between emerging and established writers, and have published many first-time writers who have gone on to win or be shortlisted for major literary awards, both nationally and internationally."

HOW TO CONTACT Submit proposal package, publishing history, clips, bio, cover letter, 3 sample chapters, SASE.

TERMS Pays royalty on retail price. Responds in 1-3 months.

TIPS "Our audience is adult readers who love good books and good literature. Our audience is regional and national, as well as international. Follow our submission guidelines. Check out some of our titles at your local library or bookstore to get an idea of what we publish. Don't send us the only copy of your ms. Let us know if your submission is simultaneous, and inform us if it is accepted elsewhere. Above all, keep writing!"

OOLIGAN PRESS

369 Neuberger Hall, 724 SW Harrison St., Portland OR 97201. (503)725-9410. **E-mail:** acquisitions@ooliganpress.pdx.edu. **Website:** ooligan.pdx.edu. **Contact:** Acquisitions Co-Managers. Estab. 2001. "We seek to publish regionally significant works of literary, historical, and social value. We define the Pacific Northwest as Northern California, Oregon, Idaho, Washington, British Columbia, and Alaska. We recognize the importance of diversity, particularly within the publishing industry, and are committed to building a literary community that includes traditionally underrepresented voices; therefore, we are interested in works originating from, or focusing on, marginalized communities of the Pacific Northwest." Publishes trade paperbacks, electronic originals, and reprints. Catalog online. Guidelines online.

NEEDS "We seek to publish regionally significant works of literary, historical, and social value. We define the Pacific Northwest as Northern California, Oregon, Idaho, Washington, British Columbia, and Alaska. We recognize the importance of diversity, particularly within the publishing industry, and are committed to building a literary community that includes traditionally underrepresented voices; therefore, we are interested in works originating from, or focusing on, marginalized communities of the Pacific

Northwest." Does not want romance, horror, westerns, incomplete mss.

HOW TO CONTACT Query with SASE. *"At this time we cannot accept science fiction or fantasy submissions."*

TERMS Pays negotiable royalty on retail price. Responds in 2 weeks for queries; 3 months for proposals.

TIPS "Search the blog for tips."

ORCA BOOK PUBLISHERS

P.O. Box 5626, Stn. B, Victoria BC V8R 6S4, Canada. (250)380-1229. **Fax:** (877)408-1551. **E-mail:** orca@orcabook.com. **Website:** www.orcabook.com. **Contact:** Amy Collins, editor (picture books); Sarah Harvey, editor (young readers); Andrew Wooldridge, editor (juvenile and teen fiction); Bob Tyrrell, publisher (young adult, teen); Ruth Linka, associate editor (rapid reads). Estab. 1984. Only publishes Canadian authors. Publishes hardcover and trade paperback originals, and mass market paperback originals and reprints. Book catalog for 8.5x11 SASE. Guidelines online.

NEEDS Picture books: animals, contemporary, history, nature/environment. Middle readers: contemporary, history, fantasy, nature/environment, problem novels, graphic novels. Young adults: adventure, contemporary, hi-lo (Orca Soundings), history, multicultural, nature/environment, problem novels, suspense/mystery, graphic novels. Average word length: picture books—500-1,500; middle readers—20,000-35,000; young adult—25,000-45,000; Orca Soundings—13,000-15,000; Orca Currents—13,000-15,000. No romance, science fiction.

HOW TO CONTACT Query with SASE. Submit proposal package, outline, clips, 2-5 sample chapters, SASE.

TERMS Pays 10% royalty. Responds in 1 month to queries; 2 months to proposals and mss.

TIPS "Our audience is students in grades K-12. Know our books, and know the market."

ORCHARD BOOKS (US)

557 Broadway, New York NY 10012. **Website:** www.scholastic.com. Orchard is not accepting unsolicited mss.

NEEDS Picture books, early readers, and novelty: animal, contemporary, history, humor, multicultural, poetry.

TERMS Most commonly offers an advance against list royalties.

RICHARD C. OWEN PUBLISHERS, INC.

P.O. Box 585, Katonah NY 10536. (914)232-3903; (800)262-0787. **E-mail:** richardowen@rcowen.com. **Website:** www.rcowen.com. **Contact:** Richard Owen, publisher. Estab. 1982. "We publish child-focused books, with inherent instructional value, about characters and situations with which 5-, 6-, and 7-year-old children can identify—books that can be read for meaning, entertainment, enjoyment, and information. We include multicultural stories that present minorities in a positive and natural way. Our stories show the diversity in America." Not interested in lesson plans, or books of activities for literature studies or other content areas. Submit complete ms and cover letter. Book catalog available with SASE. Ms guidelines with SASE or online.

"Due to high volume and long production time, we are currently limiting to nonfiction submissions only."

TERMS Pays authors royalty of 5% based on net price or outright purchase (range: $25-500). Offers no advances. Pays illustrators by the project (range: $100-2,000) or per photo (range: $50-150). Responds to mss in 1 year.

PETER OWEN PUBLISHERS

81 Bridge Rd., London N8 9NP, United Kingdom. (44)(208)350-1775. **Fax:** (44)(208)340-9488. **E-mail:** info@peterowen.com. **Website:** www.peterowen.com. "We are far more interested in proposals for nonfiction than fiction at the moment. No poetry or short stories." Publishes hardcover originals and trade paperback originals and reprints. Book catalog for SASE, SAE with IRC, or on website.

NEEDS "No first novels. Authors should be aware that we publish very little new fiction these days."

HOW TO CONTACT Query with synopsis, sample chapters.

TERMS Pays 7.5-10% royalty. Pays negotiable advance. Responds in 2 months to queries; 3 months to proposals and mss.

OXFORD UNIVERSITY PRESS: SOUTHERN AFRICA

P.O. Box 12119, NI City Cape Town 7463, South Africa. (27)(21)596-2300. **Fax:** (27)(21)596-1234. **E-mail:** oxford.za@oup.com. **Website:** www.oxford.co.za. Academic publisher known for its educational books for southern African schools. Also publishes general and reference titles. Book catalog online. Guidelines online.

HOW TO CONTACT Submit cover letter, synopsis.

PACIFIC PRESS PUBLISHING ASSOCIATION

Trade Book Division, 1350 N. Kings Rd., Nampa ID 83687. (208)465-2500. **Fax:** (208)465-2531. **Website:** www.pacificpress.com. Estab. 1874. "We publish books that fit Seventh-day Adventist beliefs only. All titles are Christian and religious. For guidance, see www.adventist.org/beliefs/index.html. Our books fit into the categories of this retail site: www.adventistbookcenter.com." Publishes hardcover and trade paperback originals and reprints. Guidelines online.

NEEDS "Pacific Press rarely publishes fiction, but we're interested in developing a line of Seventh-day Adventist fiction in the future. Only proposals accepted; no full mss."

TERMS Pays 8-16% royalty on wholesale price. Responds in 3 months to queries.

TIPS "Our primary audience is members of the Seventh-day Adventist denomination. Almost all are written by Seventh-day Adventists. Books that do well for us relate the Biblical message to practical human concerns and focus more on the experiential rather than theoretical aspects of Christianity. We are assigning more titles, using less unsolicited material—although we still publish mss from freelance submissions and proposals."

PAGESPRING PUBLISHING

PageSpring Publishing, P.O. Box 21133, Columbus OH 43221. **E-mail:** submissions@pagespringpublishing.com. **Website:** www.pagespringpublishing.com. Estab. 2012. PageSpring Publishing is a small independent publisher with 2 imprints: Cup of Tea Books and Lucky Marble Books. Cup of Tea Books publishes women's fiction, with particular emphasis on mystery and humor. Lucky Marble Books publishes young adult and middle-grade fiction. Publishes trade paperback and electronic originals. Guidelines online.

"We are looking for engaging characters and well-crafted plots that keep our readers turning the page. We accept e-mail queries only; see our website for details."

IMPRINTS Cup of Tea Books and Lucky Marble Books.

NEEDS Cup of Tea Books publishes women's fiction. Lucky Marble Books publishes middle-grade and young adult novels. No children's picture books.

HOW TO CONTACT Submit proposal package via e-mail only. Include synopsis and 30 sample pages.

TERMS Pays royalty. Responds in 3 months.

TIPS "Cup of Tea Books is particularly interested in cozy mystery novels. Lucky Marble Books is looking for funny, age-appropriate tales for middle-grade and young adult readers."

PAJAMA PRESS

181 Carlaw Ave., Ste. 207, Toronto ON M4M 2S1, Canada. **E-mail:** info@pajamapress.ca. **E-mail:** annfeatherstone@pajamapress.ca. **Website:** pajamapress.ca. "We publish picture books—both for the very young and for school-aged readers—as well as novels for middle-grade readers and for young adults aged 12+. Our nonfiction titles typically contain a strong narrative element."

HOW TO CONTACT Query with an excerpt. Guidelines on site.

PANKHEARST

Website: pankhearst.wordpress.com. Estab. 2012. Pankhearst is a collective of independent writers. "We exist to develop and promote new writers, and to learn while doing. We have published 4 spiffing full-length collections of fiction, 2 novels, and more than a dozen Kindle 'singles' to date. We've also published 2 collections of poetry and flash fiction." Guidelines online.

TIPS "Pankhearst welcomes everybody, regardless of age, color, disability, familial or parental status, gender identity, marital status, national origin, race, religion, sex, sexual orientation, and anything else you or we can think of."

PANTHEON BOOKS

Penguin Random House, 1745 Broadway, New York NY 10019. **Website:** www.pantheonbooks.com. Estab. 1942. Publishes hardcover and trade paperback originals and trade paperback reprints.

Pantheon Books publishes both Western and non-Western authors of literary fiction and important nonfiction. "We only accept mss submitted by an agent."

HOW TO CONTACT *Does not accept unsolicited mss.* Agented submissions only.

PANTS ON FIRE PRESS

2062 Harbor Cove Way, Winter Garden FL 34787. (863)546-0760. **E-mail:** submission@pantsonfirepress.com. **Website:** www.pantsonfirepress.com. **Contact:** Becca Goldman, senior editor; Emily Gerety, editor. Estab. 2012. Pants On Fire Press is an award-winning book publisher of picture, middle-grade, young adult, and adult books. They are a digital-first book publisher, striving to follow a high degree of excellence while maintaining quality standards. Publishes hardcover originals and reprints, trade paperback originals and reprints, and electronic originals and reprints. Catalog online. Guidelines online.

NEEDS Publishes big story ideas with high concepts, new worlds, and meaty characters for children, teens, and discerning adults. Always on the lookout for action, adventure, animals, comedic, dramatic, dystopian, fantasy, historical, paranormal, romance, science fiction, supernatural, and suspense stories.

HOW TO CONTACT Submit a proposal package including a synopsis, 3 sample chapters, and a query letter via e-mail.

TERMS Pays 10-50% royalties on wholesale price. Responds in 3 months.

PAPERCUTZ

160 Broadway, Ste. 700E, New York NY 10038. (646)559-4681. **Fax:** (212)643-1545. **Website:** www.papercutz.com. Estab. 2004. Publisher of graphic novels.

NEEDS "Independent publisher of graphic novels based on popular existing properties aimed at the teen and tween market."

TIPS "Be familiar with our titles—that's the best way to know what we're interested in publishing. If you are somehow attached to a successful tween or teen property and would like to adapt it into a graphic novel, we may be interested."

PARADISE CAY PUBLICATIONS

P.O. Box 29, Arcata CA 95518-0029. (800)736-4509. **Fax:** (707)822-9163. **E-mail:** info@paracay.com. **Website:** www.paracay.com. "Paradise Cay Publications, Inc. is a small independent publisher specializing in nautical books, videos, and art prints. Our primary interest is in mss that deal with the instructional and technical aspects of ocean sailing. We also publish and will consider fiction if it has a strong nautical theme." Publishes hardcover and trade paperback originals and reprints. Book catalog and ms guidelines free on request or online.

IMPRINTS Pardey Books.

NEEDS All fiction must have a nautical theme.

HOW TO CONTACT Query with SASE. Submit proposal package, clips, 2-3 sample chapters.

TERMS Pays 10-15% royalty on wholesale price. Makes outright purchase of $1,000-10,000. Does not normally pay advances to first-time or little-known authors. Responds in 1 month to queries/proposals; 2 months to mss.

TIPS "Audience is recreational sailors. Call Matt Morehouse (publisher)."

PAUL DRY BOOKS

1700 Sansom St., Ste. 700, Philadelphia PA 19103. (215)231-9939. **Fax:** (215)231-9942. **E-mail:** editor@pauldrybooks.com. **E-mail:** pdry@pauldrybooks.com. **Website:** pauldrybooks.com. "We publish fiction (both novels and short stories) and nonfiction, (biography, memoirs, history, and essays), covering subjects from Homer to Chekhov, bird watching to jazz music, New York City to shogunate Japan." Hardcover and trade paperback originals, trade paperback reprints. Book catalog available online. Guidelines available online.

"Take a few minutes to familiarize yourself with the books we publish. Then if you think your book would be a good fit in our line, we invite you to submit the following: a one- or two-page summary of the work (be sure to tell us how many pages or words the full book will be), a sample of 20-30 pages, your bio, and a brief description of how you think the book (and you, the author) could be marketed."

HOW TO CONTACT Submit sample chapters, clips, bio.

TIPS "Our aim is to publish lively books 'to awaken, delight, and educate'—to spark conversation. We publish fiction and nonfiction, and essays covering subjects from Homer to Chekhov, bird watching to jazz music, New York City to shogunate Japan."

PAYCOCK PRESS

3819 N. 13th St., Arlington VA 22201. (703)525-9296. **E-mail:** rchrdpeabody9@gmail.com. **Website:** www.gargoylemagazine.com. **Contact:** Richard Peabody. Estab. 1976. "Too academic for the underground, too outlaw for the academic world. We tend to be edgy and look for ultra-literary work." Publishes paperback originals. Books: POD printing. Average print order: 500. Averages 1 total title/year. Member CLMP. Distributes through Amazon and website.

HOW TO CONTACT Accepts unsolicited mss. Accepts queries by e-mail. Include brief bio. Send SASE for return of ms or send a disposable ms and SASE for reply only.

TERMS Responds to queries in 1 month; mss in 4 months.

TIPS "Check out our website. Two of our favorite writers are Paul Bowles and Jeanette Winterson."

PEACHTREE PUBLISHERS, LTD.

Peachtree Publishers, Ltd., 1700 Chattahoochee Ave., Atlanta GA 30318-2112. (404)876-8761. **Fax:** (404)875-2578. **E-mail:** hello@peachtree-online.com. **Website:** www.peachtree-online.com. **Contact:** Helen Harriss, submissions editor. "We publish a broad range of subjects and perspectives, with emphasis on innovative plots and strong writing." Publishes hardcover and trade paperback originals. Book catalog for 6 first-class stamps. Guidelines online.

NEEDS Looking for very well-written middle-grade and young adult novels. No adult fiction. No collections of poetry or short stories; no romance or science fiction.

HOW TO CONTACT Submit complete ms with SASE.

TERMS Pays royalty on retail price. Responds in 6 months and mss.

PEDLAR PRESS

113 Bond St., St. John's NL A16 1T6, Canada. (709)738-6702. **E-mail:** feralgrl@interlog.com. **Website:** www.pedlarpress.com. **Contact:** Beth Follett, owner/editor.

NEEDS Experimental, feminist, gay/lesbian, literary, short story collections. Canadian writers only.

HOW TO CONTACT Query with SASE, sample chapter(s), synopsis.

TERMS Pays 10% royalty on retail price. Average advance: $200-400.

TIPS "I select mss according to my taste, which fluctuates. Be familiar with some if not most of Pedlar's recent titles."

PELICAN PUBLISHING COMPANY

1000 Burmaster St., Gretna LA 70053. (504)368-1175. **Fax:** (504)368-1195. **E-mail:** editorial@pelicanpub.com. **Website:** www.pelicanpub.com. Estab. 1926. "We believe ideas have consequences. One of the consequences is that they lead to a best-selling book. We publish books to improve and uplift the reader. Currently emphasizing business and history titles." Publishes 20 young readers/year; 1 middle reader/year. "Our children's books (illustrated and otherwise) include history, biography, holiday, and regional. Pelican's mission is to publish books of quality and permanence that enrich the lives of those who read them." Publishes hardcover, trade paperback and mass market paperback originals and reprints. Book catalog and ms guidelines online.

NEEDS We publish no adult fiction. Young readers: history, holiday, science, multicultural and regional. Middle readers: Louisiana History. Multicultural needs include stories about African-Americans, Irish-Americans, Jews, Asian-Americans, and Hispanics. Does not want animal stories, general Christmas stories, "day at school" or "accept yourself" stories. Maximum word length: young readers—1,100; middle readers—40,000. No young adult, romance, science fiction, fantasy, gothic, mystery, erotica, confession, horror, sex, or violence. Also no psychological novels.

HOW TO CONTACT Submit outline, clips, 2 sample chapters, SASE. Full guidelines on website.

TERMS Pays authors in royalties; buys ms outright "rarely." Illustrators paid by "various arrangements." Advance considered. Responds in 1 month to queries; 3 months to mss. Requires exclusive submission.

TIPS "We do extremely well with cookbooks, popular histories, and business. We will continue to build in these areas. The writer must have a clear sense of the market and knowledge of the competition. A query letter should describe the project briefly, give the author's writing and professional credentials, and promotional ideas."

PENGUIN GROUP: SOUTH AFRICA

P.O. Box 9, Parklands 2121, South Africa. (27)(11)327-3550. **Fax:** (27)(11)327-3660. **E-mail:** fiction@penguinrandomhouse.co.za. **E-mail:** nonfiction@penguinrandomhouse.co.za. **Website:** www.penguinbooks.co.za. Seeks adult fiction (literary and mass market titles) and adult nonfiction (travel, sports, politics, current affairs, business). No children's, young adult, poetry, or short stories.

HOW TO CONTACT Submit intro letter, 3 sample chapters.

TERMS Pays royalty.

PENGUIN GROUP USA

375 Hudson St., New York NY 10014. (212)366-2000. **Website:** www.penguin.com. General interest publisher of both fiction and nonfiction. *No unsolicited mss.* Submit work through a literary agent. DAW Books is the lone exception. Guidelines online.

PENGUIN RANDOM HOUSE, LLC

Division of Bertelsmann Book Group, 1745 Broadway, New York NY 10019. (212)782-9000. **Website:** www.penguinrandomhouse.com. Estab. 1925. Penguin Random House LLC is the world's largest English-language general trade book publisher. *Agented submissions only. No unsolicited mss.*

IMPRINTS Crown Publishing Group; Knopf Doubleday Publishing Group; Random House Publishing Group; Random House Children's Books; RH Digital Publishing Group; RH International.

THE PERMANENT PRESS

Attn: Judith Shepard, 4170 Noyac Rd., Sag Harbor NY 11963. (631)725-1101. **Fax:** (631)725-8215. **E-mail:** judith@thepermanentpress.com; shepard@thepermanentpress.com. **Website:** www.thepermanentpress.com. **Contact:** Judith and Martin Shepard, acquisitions/co-publishers. Estab. 1978. Mid-size, independent publisher of literary fiction. "We keep titles in print and are active in selling subsidiary rights." Average print order: 1,000-2,500. Averages 16 total titles. Accepts unsolicited mss. Pays 10-15% royalty on wholesale price. Offers $1,000 advance. *Will not accept simultaneous submissions.* Publishes hardcover originals.

NEEDS Promotes titles through reviews. Literary, mainstream/contemporary, mystery. Especially looking for high-line literary fiction, "artful, original and arresting." Accepts any fiction category as long as it is a "well-written, original full-length novel."

TERMS Pays 10-15% royalty on wholesale price. Offers $1,000 advance. Responds in weeks or months.

TIPS "We are looking for good books—be they 10th novels or first ones, it makes little difference. The fiction is more important than the track record. Send us the first 25 pages; it's impossible to judge something that begins on page 302. Also, no outlines—let the writing present itself."

PERSEA BOOKS

277 Broadway, Ste. 708, New York NY 10007. (212)260-9256. **Fax:** (212)267-3165. **E-mail:** info@perseabooks.com. **Website:** www.perseabooks.com. Estab. 1975. The aim of Persea is to publish works that endure by meeting high standards of literary merit and relevance. "We have often taken on important books other publishers have overlooked, or have made significant discoveries and rediscoveries, whether of a single work or writer's entire oeuvre. Our books cover a wide range of themes, styles, and genres. We have published poetry, fiction, essays, memoir, biography, titles of Jewish and Middle Eastern interest, women's studies, American Indian folklore, and revived classics, as well as a notable selection of works in translation." Guidelines online.

HOW TO CONTACT Queries should include a cover letter, author background and publication history, a detailed synopsis of the proposed work, and a sample chapter. Please indicate if the work is simultaneously submitted.

TERMS Responds in 8 weeks to proposals; 10 weeks to mss.

PHILOMEL BOOKS

Imprint of Penguin Group (USA), Inc., 375 Hudson St., New York NY 10014. (212)414-3610. **Website:** www.penguin.com. **Contact:** Michael Green, president/publisher. Estab. 1980. "We look for beautifully written, engaging mss for children and young adults." Publishes hardcover originals.

HOW TO CONTACT *No unsolicited mss.*

TERMS Pays authors in royalties. Average advance payment "varies." Illustrators paid by advance and in royalties. Pays negotiable advance.

PIANO PRESS

P.O. Box 85, Del Mar CA 92014. (619)884-1401. **Fax:** (858)755-1104. **E-mail:** pianopress@pianopress.com. **Website:** www.pianopress.com. **Contact:** Elizabeth C. Axford, editor. Estab. 1984. "We publish music-related books, either fiction or nonfiction, music-related coloring books, songbooks, sheet music, CDs, and music-related poetry." Book catalog available online.

NEEDS Picture books, young readers, middle readers, young adults: folktales, multicultural, poetry, music. Average word length: picture books—1,500-2,000.

TERMS Pays authors, illustrators, and photographers royalties based on the retail price. Electronic queries ONLY may be sent to: pianopress@pianopress.com. Please include a brief bio and/or web link(s) with your inquiry. Please DO NOT send MP3s, ms .docs, or picture .jpgs unless requested to do so by the acquisitions editor. Responds if interested.

TIPS "We are looking for music-related material only for the juvenile market. Please do not send non-music-related materials. Query by e-mail first before submitting anything."

PIÑATA BOOKS

Imprint of Arte Publico Press, University of Houston, 4902 Gulf Fwy., Bldg. 19, Room 100, Houston TX 77204-2004. (713)743-2845. **Fax:** (713)743-3080. **E-mail:** submapp@uh.edu. **Website:** www.artepublicopress.com. Estab. 1994. "Piñata Books is dedicated to the publication of children's and young adult literature focusing on U.S. Hispanic culture by U.S. Hispanic authors. Arte Publico's mission is the publication, promotion and dissemination of Latino literature for a variety of national and regional audiences, from early childhood to adult, through the complete gamut of delivery systems, including personal performance as well as print and electronic media." Publishes hardcover and trade paperback originals. Book catalog and guidelines online.

HOW TO CONTACT Submissions made through online submission form.

TERMS Pays 10% royalty on wholesale price. Pays $1,000-3,000 advance. Responds in 2-3 months to queries; 4-6 months to mss.

TIPS "Include cover letter with submission explaining why your ms is unique and important, why we should publish it, who will buy it, etc."

PIATKUS BOOKS

Little, Brown Book Group, Carmelite House, 50 Victoria Embankment, London EC4Y 0DZ, United Kingdom. (020)3122-7000. **Fax:** (020)3122-7000. **E-mail:** info@littlebrown.co.uk. **Website:** piatkus.co.uk. Estab. 1979. Publishes hardcover originals, paperback originals, and paperback reprints. Guidelines online.

NEEDS Romance fiction, women's fiction, bookclub fiction.

HOW TO CONTACT *Agented submissions only.*

PICADOR USA

MacMillan, 175 Fifth Ave., New York NY 10010. (212)674-5151. **Website:** us.macmillan.com/picador. Estab. 1994. Picador publishes high-quality literary fiction and nonfiction. "We are open to a broad range of subjects, well written by authoritative authors." Publishes hardcover and trade paperback originals and reprints. Does not accept unsolicited mss. *Agented submissions only.*

TERMS Pays 7-15% on royalty. Advance varies.

PINEAPPLE PRESS, INC.

P.O. Box 3889, Sarasota FL 34230. (941)706-2507. **Fax:** (800)746-3275. **E-mail:** info@pineapplepress.com. **Website:** www.pineapplepress.com. **Contact:** June Cussen, executive editor. Estab. 1982. "We are seeking quality nonfiction on diverse topics for the library and book trade markets. Our mission is to publish good books about Florida." Publishes hardcover and trade paperback originals. Book catalog for 9×12 SAE with $1.32 postage. Guidelines online.

NEEDS Picture books, young readers, middle readers, young adults: animal, folktales, history, nature/environment.

HOW TO CONTACT Query or submit outline/synopsis and 3 sample chapters.

TERMS Pays authors royalty of 10-15%. Responds in 2 months.

TIPS "Quality first novels will be published, though we usually only do one or two novels per year and they must be set in Florida. We regard the author/editor relationship as a trusting relationship with communication open both ways. Learn all you can about the publishing process and about how to promote your book once it is published. A query on a novel without a brief sample seems useless."

PLAYLAB PRESS

P.O. Box 3701, South Brisbane BC 4101, Australia. **E-mail:** info@playlab.org.au. **Website:** www.playlab.org.au. Estab. 1978. Guidelines online.

HOW TO CONTACT Submit 2 copies of ms, cover letter.

TERMS Responds in 3 months to mss.

TIPS "Playlab Press is committed to the publication of quality writing for and about theatre and performance, which is of significance to Australia's cultural life. It values socially just and diverse publication outcomes and aims to promote these outcomes in local, national, and international contexts."

PLEXUS PUBLISHING, INC.

143 Old Marlton Pike, Medford NJ 08055. (609)654-6500. **Fax:** (609)654-4309. **E-mail:** rcolding@plexuspublishing.com. **Website:** www.plexuspublishing.com. **Contact:** Rob Colding, Book Marketing Manager. Estab. 1977. Plexus publishes regional-interest

(southern New Jersey and the greater Philadelphia area) fiction and nonfiction including mysteries, field guides, nature, travel and history. Publishes hardcover and paperback originals. Book catalog and book proposal guidelines for 10x13 SASE.

NEEDS Mysteries and literary novels with a strong regional (southern New Jersey) angle.

HOW TO CONTACT Query with SASE.

TERMS Pays $500-1,000 advance. Responds in 3 months to proposals.

POCKET BOOKS

Simon & Schuster, 1230 Avenue of the Americas, New York NY 10020. (212)698-7000. **Website:** www.simonandschuster.com. Estab. 1939. Pocket Books publishes commercial fiction and genre fiction (WWE, Downtown Press, Star Trek). Publishes paperback originals and reprints, mass market and trade paperbacks. Book catalog available free. Guidelines online.

HOW TO CONTACT *Agented submissions only.*

POCOL PRESS

Box 411, Clifton VA 20124. (703)830-5862. **Website:** www.pocolpress.com. **Contact:** J. Thomas Hetrick, editor. Estab. 1999. "Pocol Press is dedicated to producing high-quality print books and e-books from first-time, nonagented authors. However, all submissions are welcome. We're dedicated to good storytellers and to the written word, specializing in short fiction and baseball. Several of our books have been used as literary texts at universities and in book group discussions around the nation. Pocol Press does not publish children's books, romance novels, or graphic novels. Our authors are comprised of veteran writers and emerging talents." Publishes trade paperback originals. Book catalog and guidelines online.

NEEDS "We specialize in thematic short fiction collections by a single author, westerns, war stories, and baseball fiction. Expert storytellers welcome."

HOW TO CONTACT Does not accept or return unsolicited mss. Query with SASE or submit 1 sample chapter.

TERMS Pays 10-12% royalty on wholesale price. Responds in 1 month to queries; 2 months to mss.

TIPS "Our audience is aged 18 and over. Pocol Press is unique; we publish good writing and great storytelling. Write the best stories you can. Read them to you friends/peers. Note their reaction. Publishes some of the finest fiction by a small press."

THE POISONED PENCIL

Poisoned Pen Press, 6962 E. 1st Ave., Ste. 103, Scottsdale AZ 85251. (480)945-3375. **Fax:** (480)949-1707. **E-mail:** info@thepoisonedpencil.com. **E-mail:** ellen@thepoisonedpencil.com. **Website:** www.thepoisonedpencil.com. **Contact:** Ellen Larson, editor. Estab. 2012. Publishes trade paperback and electronic originals. Guidelines online.

Accepts young adult mysteries only.

NEEDS "We publish only young adult mystery novels, 45,000 to 90,000 words in length. For our purposes, a young adult book is a book with a protagonist between the ages of 13 and 18. We are looking for both traditional and cross-genre young adult mysteries. We encourage off-beat approaches and narrative choices that reflect the complexity and ambiguity of today's world. Submissions from teens are very welcome. Avoid serial killers, excessive gore, and vampires (and other heavy supernatural themes). We only consider authors who live in the US or Canada, due to practicalities of marketing promotion. Avoid coincidence in plotting. Avoid having your sleuth leap to conclusions rather than discover and deduce. Pay attention to the resonance between character and plot; between plot and theme; between theme and character. We are looking for clean style, fluid storytelling, and solid structure. Unrealistic dialogue is a real turn-off."

HOW TO CONTACT Submit proposal package including synopsis, complete ms, and cover letter.

TERMS Pays 9-15% for trade paperback; 25-35% for e-books. Pays advance of $1,000. Responds in 6 weeks to mss.

TIPS "Our audience is made up of young adults and adults who love young adult mysteries."

POISONED PEN PRESS

6962 E. 1st Ave., Ste. 103, Scottsdale AZ 85251. (480)945-3375. **Fax:** (480)949-1707. **E-mail:** submissions@poisonedpenpress.com. **Website:** www.poisonedpenpress.com. **Contact:** Robert Rosenwald, publisher; Barbara Peters, editor in chief. Estab. 1996. "Our publishing goal is to offer well-written mystery novels of crime and/or detection where the puzzle and its resolution are the main forces that move the story forward." Publishes hardcover originals, and hardcover and trade paperback reprints. Book catalog and guidelines online.

Not currently accepting submissions. Check website.

IMPRINTS The Poisoned Pencil (Young adult titles. Contact: Ellen Larson).

NEEDS Mss should generally be longer than 65,000 words and shorter than 100,000 words. Member Publishers Marketing Associations, Arizona Book Publishers Associations, Publishers Association of West. Distributes through Ingram, Baker & Taylor, Brodart. Does not want novels centered on serial killers, spousal or child abuse, drugs, or extremist groups, although we do not entirely rule such works out.

HOW TO CONTACT Accepts unsolicited mss. Electronic queries only. "Query with SASE. Submit clips, first 3 pages. We must receive both the synopsis and ms pages electronically as separate attachments to an e-mail message or as a disk or CD which we will not return."

TERMS Pays 9-15% royalty on retail price. Responds in 2-3 months to queries and proposals; 6 months to mss.

TIPS "Audience is adult readers of mystery fiction and young adult readers."

POLIS BOOKS

E-mail: info@polisbooks.com. **E-mail:** submissions@polisbooks.com. **Website:** www.polisbooks.com. Estab. 2013. "Polis Books is an independent publishing company actively seeking new and established authors for our growing list. We are actively acquiring titles in mystery, thriller, suspense, procedural, traditional crime, science fiction, fantasy, horror, supernatural, urban fantasy, romance, erotica, commercial women's fiction, commercial literary fiction, young adult and middle-grade books." Guidelines online.

HOW TO CONTACT Query with 3 sample chapters and bio via e-mail.

TERMS Offers advance against royalties. Only responds to submissions if interested

PRESS 53

560 N. Trade St., Ste. 103, Winston-Salem NC 27101. (336)770-5353. **E-mail:** kevin@press53.com. **Website:** www.press53.com. **Contact:** Kevin Morgan Watson, publisher. Estab. 2005. "Press 53 was founded in October 2005 and quickly began earning a reputation as a quality publishing house of short fiction and poetry collections." Poetry and short fiction collections only. Catalog online. Guidelines online.

NEEDS "We publish roughly 4-6 short fiction collections each year by writers who are active and earning recognition through publication and awards, plus the winner of our Press 53 Award for Short Fiction." Collections should be between 100 and 250 pages (give or take) with 70% or more of those stories previously published. Does not want novels.

HOW TO CONTACT Finds mss through contest and referrals.

TIPS "We are looking for writers who are actively involved in the writing community, writers who are submitting their work to journals, magazines and contests, and who are getting published, building readership, and earning a reputation for their work."

PRICE STERN SLOAN, INC.

Penguin Group, 375 Hudson St., New York NY 10014. (212)366-2000. **Website:** www.penguin.com. **Contact:** Francesco Sedita, president/publisher. Estab. 1963. "Price Stern Sloan publishes quirky mass market novelty series for childrens as well as licensed movie tie-in books." Price Stern Sloan only responds to submissions it's interested in publishing. Book catalog online.

NEEDS Publishes picture books and novelty/board books.

HOW TO CONTACT *Agented submissions only.*

TIPS "Price Stern Sloan publishes unique, fun titles."

PUFFIN BOOKS

Imprint of Penguin Group (USA), Inc., 375 Hudson St., New York NY 10014. (212)366-2000. **Website:** www.penguin.com. **Contact:** Eileen Bishop Kreit, publisher. "Puffin Books publishes high-end trade paperbacks and paperback reprints for preschool children, beginning and middle readers, and young adults." Publishes trade paperback originals and reprints.

HOW TO CONTACT *No unsolicited mss. Agented submissions only.*

TIPS "Our audience ranges from little children 'first books' to young adult (ages 14-16). An original idea has the best luck."

G.P. PUTNAM'S SONS HARDCOVER

Imprint of Penguin Group (USA), Inc., 375 Hudson, New York NY 10014. (212)366-2000. **Fax:** (212)366-2664. **Website:** www.penguin.com. **Contact:** Christine Ball, vice president/deputy publisher; Mark Tavani, vice president/executive editor. Publishes hardcover originals. Request book catalog through mail order department.

HOW TO CONTACT *Agented submissions only.*

TERMS Pays variable royalties on retail price. Pays varies advance.

RANDOM HOUSE PUBLISHING GROUP

Division of Random House, Inc., 1745 Broadway, New York NY 10019. (212)782-9000. **Website:** www.penguinrandomhouse.com. Estab. 1925. Random House is the world's largest English-language general trade book publisher. It includes an array of prestigious imprints that publish some of the foremost writers of our time. Publishes hardcover and paperback trade books.

IMPRINTS Ballantine Books; Bantam; Delacorte; Dell; Del Rey; Modern Library; One World; Presidio Press; Random House Trade Group; Random House Trade Paperbacks; Spectra; Spiegel & Grau; Triumph Books; Villard.

HOW TO CONTACT *Agented submissions only.*

RAZORBILL

Penguin Young Readers Group, 345 Hudson St., New York NY 10014. (212)414-3720. **E-mail:** jharriton@penguinrandomhouse.com; bschrank@penguinrandomhouse.com. **Website:** www.razorbillbooks.com. **Contact:** Jessica Almon, senior editor; Elizabeth Tingue, editor; Casey McIntyre, associate publisher; Deborah Kaplan, vice president and executive art director, Marissa Grossman; assistant editor, Tiffany Liao; associate editor. Estab. 2003. "This division of Penguin Young Readers is looking for the best and the most original of commercial contemporary fiction titles for middle-grade and young adult readers. A select quantity of nonfiction titles will also be considered."

NEEDS Middle Readers: adventure, contemporary, graphic novels, fantasy, humor, problem novels. Young adults/teens: adventure, contemporary, fantasy, graphic novels, humor, multicultural, suspense, paranormal, science fiction, dystopian, literary, romance. Average word length: middle readers—40,000; young adult—60,000.

HOW TO CONTACT Submit cover letter with up to 30 sample pages.

TERMS Offers advance against royalties. Responds in 1-3 months.

TIPS "New writers will have the best chance of acceptance and publication with original, contemporary material that boasts a distinctive voice and well-articulated world. Check out website to get a better idea of what we're looking for."

REBELIGHT PUBLISHING, INC.

23-845 Dakota St., Ste. 314, Winnipeg Manitoba R2M 5M3, Canada. **E-mail:** submit@rebelight.com. **Website:** www.rebelight.com. **Contact:** Editor. Estab. 2014. Rebelight Publishing is interested in "crack the spine, blow your mind" mss for middle-grade, young adult and new adult novels. *Only considers submissions from Canadian writers.* Publishes paperback and electronic originals. Catalog online or PDF available via e-mail request. Guidelines online.

NEEDS All genres are considered, provided they are for a middle-grade, young adult, or new adult audience. "Become familiar with our books. Study our website. Stick within the guidelines. Our tag line is 'crack the spine, blow your mind'—we are looking for well-written, powerful, fresh, fast-paced fiction. Keep us turning the pages. Give us something we just have to spread the word about."

HOW TO CONTACT Submit proposal package, including a synopsis and 3 sample chapters. Read guidelines carefully.

TERMS Pays 12-22% royalties on retail price. Does not offer an advance. Responds in 3 months to queries and mss. Submissions accepted via e-mail only.

TIPS "Review your ms for passive voice prior to submitting! (And that means get rid of it.)"

RED DEER PRESS

195 Allstate Pkwy., Markham ON L3R 4TB, Canada. (905)477-9700. **Fax:** (905)477-9179. **E-mail:** rdp@reddeerpress.com. **Website:** www.reddeerpress.com. **Contact:** Richard Dionne, publisher. Estab. 1975. Book catalog for 9 x 12 SASE.

Red Deer Press is an award-winning publisher of children's and young adult literary titles.

NEEDS Publishes young adult, adult science fiction, fantasy, and paperback originals "focusing on books by, about, or of interest to Canadians." Books: offset paper; offset printing; hardcover/perfect-bound. Average print order: 5,000. First novel print order: 2,500. Distributes titles in Canada and the US, the UK, Australia and New Zealand. Young adult (juvenile and early reader), contemporary. No romance or horror.

HOW TO CONTACT Accepts unsolicited mss. Query with SASE. No submissions on disk.

TERMS Pays 8-10% royalty. Responds to queries in 6 months.

TIPS "We're very interested in young adult and children's fiction from Canadian writers with a proven track record (either published books or widely published in established magazines or journals) and for mss with regional themes and/or a distinctive voice. We publish Canadian authors exclusively."

RED HEN PRESS

P.O. Box 40820, Pasadena CA 91114. (626)356-4760. **Fax:** (626)356-9974. **Website:** www.redhen.org. **Contact:** Mark E. Cull, publisher/executive director. Estab. 1993. "At this time, the best opportunity to be published by Red Hen is by entering one of our contests. Please find more information in our award submission guidelines." Publishes trade paperback originals. Book catalog available free. Guidelines online.

HOW TO CONTACT Query with synopsis and either 20-30 sample pages or complete ms using online submission manager.

TERMS Responds in 1-2 months.

TIPS "Audience reads poetry, literary fiction, intelligent nonfiction. If you have an agent, we may be too small since we don't pay advances. Write well. Send queries first. Be willing to help promote your own book."

REDLEAF LANE

10 Yorkton Ct., St. Paul MN 55117. (800)423-8309. **E-mail:** info@redleafpress.org. **E-mail:** acquisitions@redleafpress.org. **Website:** www.redleafpress.org. **Contact:** David Heath, director. Redleaf Lane publishes engaging, high-quality picture books for children. "Our books are unique because they take place in group-care settings and reflect developmentally appropriate practices and research-based standards." Guidelines online.

RED SAGE PUBLISHING, INC.

P.O. Box 4844, Seminole FL 33775. (727)391-3847. **E-mail:** submissions@eredsage.com. **Website:** www.eredsage.com. Estab. 1995. Publishes books of romance fiction, written for the adventurous woman. Guidelines online.

HOW TO CONTACT Read guidelines.

TERMS Pays advance.

RED TUQUE BOOKS, INC.

477 Martin St., Unit #6, Penticton BC V2A 5L2, Canada. (778)476-5750. **Fax:** (778)476-5651. **E-mail:** dave@redtuquebooks.ca. **Website:** www.redtuquebooks.ca. **Contact:** David Korinetz, executive editor. Publishes Canadian authors only, other than in the Annual Canadian Tales Anthology, which will accept stories written about Canada or Canadians by non-Canadians. Publication in the anthology is only through submissions to the Canadian Tales writing contest. See website for details.

HOW TO CONTACT Submit a query letter, 1-page synopsis, and first 5 pages only. Include total word count. Accepts ms only by mail. SASE or e-mail address for reply.

TERMS Pays 5-7% royalties on net sales. Pays $250 advance. Responds in 3-6 weeks.

TIPS "Well-plotted, character-driven stories, preferably with happy endings, will have the best chance of being accepted. Keep in mind that authors who like to begin sentences with 'and, or, and but' are less likely to be considered. Don't send anything gruesome or overly explicit; tell us a good story, but think PG."

REVELL

Division of Baker Publishing Group, 6030 E. Fulton Rd., Ada MI 49301. (616)676-9185. **Fax:** (616)676-9573. **Website:** www.bakerbooks.com. Estab. 1870. "Revell publishes to the heart (rather than to the head). For 125 years, Revell has been publishing evangelical books for the personal enrichment and spiritual growth of general Christian readers." Publishes hardcover, trade paperback and mass market paperback originals. Book catalog and ms guidelines online.

No longer accepts unsolicited mss.

RIPPLE GROVE PRESS

P.O. Box 86740, Portland OR 97286. **E-mail:** submit@ripplegrovepress.com. **Website:** www.ripplegrovepress.com. Estab. 2013. "We started Ripple Grove Press because we have a passion for well-written and beautifully illustrated children's picture books. Each story selected has been read dozens of times, then slept on, then walked away from, then talked about again and again. If the story has the same intrigue and the same interest that it had when we first read it, we move forward." Publishes hardcover originals. Catalog online. Guidelines online.

NEEDS We are looking for something unique, that hasn't been done before; an interesting story that captures a moment with a timeless feel. We are looking for picture driven stories for children ages 2-6. Please do not send early readers, middle-grade, or young adult mss. No religious or holiday themed stories. Please do not submit your story with page breaks or illustration notes. Do not submit a story with doodles or personal photographs. Do not send your "idea" for a story, send your story in ms form.

HOW TO CONTACT Submit completed mss. Accepts submissions by mail and e-mail. Please submit a cover letter including a summary of your story, the age range of the story, a brief biography of yourself, and contact information.

TERMS Authors receive between 10-12% royalty on net receipts. "Given the volume of submissions we receive we are no longer able to individually respond to each. Please allow 5 months for us to review your submission. If we are interested in your story, you can expect to hear from us within that time. If you do not hear from us after that time, we are not interested in publishing your story. It's not you, it's us! We receive thousands of submissions and only publish a few books each year. Don't give up!"

TIPS "Please read children's picture books. We create books that children and adults want to read over and over again. Our books showcase art as well as stories and tie them together to create a unique and creative product."

RIVER CITY PUBLISHING

1719 Mulberry St., Montgomery AL 36106. **E-mail:** fnorris@rivercitypublishing.com. **Website:** www.rivercitypublishing.com. **Contact:** Fran Norris, editor. Estab. 1989. Midsize independent publisher. River City publishes literary fiction, regional, short story collections. No poetry, memoir, or children's books. We also consider narrative histories, sociological accounts, and travel; however, only biographies and memoirs from noted persons will be considered. Publishes hardcover and trade paperback originals.

NEEDS No poetry, memoir, or children's books.

HOW TO CONTACT Send appropriate-sized SASE or IRC, "otherwise, the material will be recycled." Also accepts queries by e-mail. "Please include your electronic query letter as inline text and not an as attachment; we do not open unsolicited attachments of any kind." No multiple submissions. Rarely comments on rejected mss.

TERMS Responds within 9 months.

TIPS "Only send your best work after you have received outside opinions. From approximately 1,000 submissions each year, we publish no more than 8 books and few of those come from unsolicited material. Competition is fierce, so follow the guidelines exactly. First-time novelists are also encouraged to send work."

Ⓐ⊘ RIVERHEAD BOOKS

Penguin Putnam, 375 Hudson St., New York NY 10014. **Website:** www.penguin.com. **Contact:** Rebecca Saletan, vice president/editorial director.

HOW TO CONTACT *Submit through agent only. No unsolicited mss.*

Ⓐ⊘ ROARING BROOK PRESS

Macmillan Children's Publishing Group, 175 Fifth Ave., New York NY 10010. (646)307-5151. **Website:** us.macmillan.com. Estab. 2000. Roaring Brook Press is an imprint of MacMillan, a group of companies that includes Henry Holt and Farrar, Straus & Giroux. *Roaring Brook is not accepting unsolicited mss.*

NEEDS Picture books, young readers, middle readers, young adults: adventure, animal, contemporary, fantasy, history, humor, multicultural, nature/environment, poetry, religion, science fiction, sports, suspense/mystery.

HOW TO CONTACT *Not accepting unsolicited mss or queries.*

TERMS Pays authors royalty based on retail price.

TIPS "You should find a reputable agent and have him/her submit your work."

RONSDALE PRESS

3350 W. 21st Ave., Vancouver BC V6S 1G7, Canada. (604)738-4688. **Fax:** (604)731-4548. **E-mail:** ronsdale@shaw.ca. **Website:** ronsdalepress.com. **Contact:** Ronald B. Hatch (fiction, poetry, nonfiction, social commentary); Veronica Hatch (young adult novels and short stories). Estab. 1988. "Ronsdale Press is a Canadian literary publishing house that publishes 12 books each year, four of which are young adult titles. Of particular interest are books involving children exploring and discovering new aspects of Canadian history." Publishes trade paperback originals. Book catalog for #10 SASE. Guidelines online.

NEEDS Young adults: Canadian novels. Average word length: middle readers and young adults—50,000.

HOW TO CONTACT Submit complete ms.

TERMS Pays 10% royalty on retail price. Responds to queries in 2 weeks; mss in 2 months.

TIPS "Ronsdale Press is a literary publishing house, based in Vancouver, and dedicated to publishing books from across Canada, books that give Canadians new insights into themselves and their country. We aim to publish the best Canadian writers."

SADDLEBACK EDUCATIONAL PUBLISHING

3120-A Pullman St., Costa Mesa CA 92626. (888)735-2225. **E-mail:** contact@sdlback.com. **Website:** www.sdlback.com. Saddleback is always looking for fresh, new talent. "Please note that we primarily publish books for kids ages 12-18."

NEEDS "We look for diversity for our characters and content."

HOW TO CONTACT Mail typed submission along with a query letter describing the work simply and where it fits in with other titles.

Ⓐ⊘ ST. MARTIN'S PRESS, LLC

Holtzbrinck Publishers, 175 Fifth Ave., New York NY 10010. (212)674-5151. **Fax:** (212)420-9314. **Website:** www.stmartins.com. Estab. 1952. General interest publisher of both fiction and nonfiction. Publishes hardcover, trade paperback and mass market originals.

HOW TO CONTACT *Agented submissions only. No unsolicited mss.*

TERMS Pays royalty. Pays advance.

SAKURA PUBLISHING & TECHNOLOGIES

805 Lindaraxa Park North, Alhambra CA 91801. (330)360-5131. **E-mail:** skpublishing124@gmail.com. **Website:** www.sakura-publishing.com. **Contact:** Derek Vasconi, submissions coordinator. Estab. 2007. Mss that don't follow guidelines will not be considered. Sakura Publishing is a traditional, independent book publishing company that focuses on fiction, Asian culture-related books, nonfiction, and horror books. Publishes hardcover, trade paperback, mass market paperback and electronic originals and reprints. Currently accepts only the following genres: Asian fiction, Japanese fiction (in English), Nonfiction, and horror. Please do not send queries for any other genres. Book catalog available for #10 SASE. Guidelines online.

NEEDS Looking mostly for horror and anything relating to Asians, and Asian Americans, with top preference given to Japanese writers and books based in or around Japan.

HOW TO CONTACT Follow guidelines online.

TERMS Royalty payments on paperback, e-book, wholesale, and merchandise Does not pay advance. Responds in 1 week.

TIPS "Please make sure you visit our submissions page at our website and follow all instructions exactly as written. Also, Sakura Publishing has a preference for fiction/nonfiction books specializing in Asian culture."

SALINA BOOKSHELF

1120 W. University Ave., Ste. 102, Flagstaff AZ 86001. (877)527-0070. **Fax:** (928)526-0386. **Website:** www.salinabookshelf.com. Publishes trade paperback originals and reprints.

NEEDS Submissions should be in English or Navajo. "All our books relate to the Navajo language and culture."

HOW TO CONTACT Query with SASE.

TERMS Pays varying royalty. Pays advance. Responds in 3 months to queries.

SALVO PRESS

An imprint of Start Publishing, 101 Hudson St., 37th Floor, Ste. 3705, Jersey City NJ 07302. **E-mail:** info@salvopress.com. **E-mail:** submissions@start-media.com. **Website:** www.salvopress.com. Estab. 1998. Salvo Press proudly publishes mysteries, thrillers, and literary books in e-book and audiobook formats. Book catalog and ms guidelines online.

NEEDS "We are a small press specializing in mystery, suspense, espionage and thriller fiction. Our press publishes in trade paperback and most e-book formats."

HOW TO CONTACT Query by e-mail.

TERMS Pays 10% royalty. Responds in 5 minutes to 1 month to queries; 2 months to mss.

SARABANDE BOOKS, INC.

2234 Dundee Rd., Ste. 200, Louisville KY 40205. (502)458-4028. **Fax:** (502)458-4065. **E-mail:** info@sarabandebooks.org. **Website:** www.sarabandebooks.org. **Contact:** Sarah Gorham, editor in chief. Estab. 1994. "Sarabande Books was founded to publish poetry, short fiction, and creative nonfiction. We look for works of lasting literary value. Please see our titles to get an idea of our taste. Accepts submissions through contests and open submissions." Publishes trade paperback originals. Book catalog available free. Contest guidelines for #10 SASE or on website.

Charges $15 handling fee with alternative option of purchase of book from website (e-mail confirmation of sale must be included with submission).

NEEDS "We consider novels and nonfiction in a wide variety of genres. We do not consider genre fiction such as science fiction, fantasy, or horror. Our target length is 70,000-90,000 words."

HOW TO CONTACT Queries can be sent via e-mail, fax, or regular post.

TERMS Pays royalty. 10% on actual income received. Also pays in author's copies. Pays $500-1,000 advance.

TIPS "Sarabande publishes for a general literary audience. Know your market. Read-and buy-books of literature. Sponsors contests for poetry and fiction. Make sure you're not writing in a vacuum, that you've read and are conscious of contemporary literature. Have someone read your ms, checking it for ordering, coherence. Better a lean, consistently strong ms than one that is long and uneven. We like a story to have good narrative, and we like to be engaged by language."

SASQUATCH BOOKS

1904 Third Ave., Ste. 710, Seattle WA 98101. (206)467-4300. **Fax:** (206)467-4301. **E-mail:** custserv@sasquatchbooks.com. **Website:** www.sasquatchbooks.com. Estab. 1986. "Sasquatch Books publishes books for and from the Pacific Northwest, Alaska, and California is the nation's premier regional press. Sasquatch Books' publishing program is a veritable celebration of regionally written words. Undeterred by political or geographical borders, Sasquatch defines its region as the magnificent area that stretches from the Brooks Range to the Gulf of California and from the Rocky Mountains to the Pacific Ocean. Our top-selling Best Places® travel guides serve the most popular destinations and locations of the West. We also publish widely in the areas of food and wine, gardening, nature, photography, children's books, and regional history, all facets of the literature of place. With more than 200 books brimming with insider information on the West, we offer an energetic eye on the lifestyle, landscape, and worldview of our region. Considers queries and proposals from authors and agents for new projects that fit into our West Coast regional publishing program. We can evaluate query letters, proposals, and complete mss." Publishes regional hardcover and trade paperback originals. Guidelines online.

NEEDS Young readers: adventure, animal, concept, contemporary, humor, nature/environment.

TERMS Pays royalty on cover price. Pays wide range advance. Responds to queries in 3 months.

TIPS "We sell books through a range of channels in addition to the book trade. Our primary audience consists of active, literate residents of the West Coast."

SCHOLASTIC PRESS

Imprint of Scholastic, Inc., 557 Broadway, New York NY 10012. (212)343-6100. **Fax:** (212)343-4713. **Website:** www.scholastic.com. Scholastic Press publishes fresh, literary picture book fiction and nonfiction; fresh, literary nonseries or nongenre-oriented middle-grade and young adult fiction. Currently emphasizing subtly handled treatments of key relationships in children's lives; unusual approaches to commonly dry subjects, such as biography, math, history, or science. De-emphasizing fairy tales (or retellings), board books, genre, or series fiction (mystery, fantasy, etc.). Publishes hardcover originals.

NEEDS Looking for strong picture books, young chapter books, appealing middle-grade novels (ages 8-11) and interesting and well-written young adult novels. Wants fresh, exciting picture books and novels—inspiring, new talent.

HOW TO CONTACT *Agented submissions only.*

TERMS Pays royalty on retail price. Pays variable advance. Responds in 3 months to queries; 6-8 months to mss.

TIPS "Read *currently* published children's books. Revise, rewrite, rework and find your own voice, style and subject. We are looking for authors with a strong and unique voice who can tell a great story and have the ability to evoke genuine emotion. Children's publishers are becoming more selective, looking for irresistible talent and fairly broad appeal, yet still very willing to take risks, just to keep the game interesting."

SCRIBE PUBLICATIONS

18-20 Edward St., Brunswick VIC 3056, Australia. (61) (3)9388-8780. **E-mail:** info@scribepub.com.au. **Website:** www.scribepublications.com.au. **Contact:** Anna Thwaites. Estab. 1976. Scribe has been operating as a wholly independent trade-publishing house for almost 40 years. What started off in 1976 as a desire on publisher Henry Rosenbloom's part to publish 'serious nonfiction' as a one-man band has turned into a multi-award-winning company with 20 staff members in two locations — Melbourne, Australia and London, England — and a scout in New York. Scribe publishes over 65 nonfiction and fiction titles annually in Australia and about 40 in the United Kingdom. "We currently have acquiring editors working in both our Melbourne and London offices. We spend each day sifting through submissions and mss from around the world, and commissioning and editing local titles, in an uncompromising pursuit of the best books we can find, help create, and deliver to readers. We love what we do, and we hope you will, too." Guidelines online.

IMPRINTS Scribble.

HOW TO CONTACT Submit synopsis, sample chapters, CV.

TIPS "We are only able to consider unsolicited submissions if you have a demonstrated background of writing and publishing for general readers."

SCRIBNER

Imprint of Simon & Schuster Adult Publishing Group, 1230 Avenue of the Americas, 12th Floor, New York NY 10020. (212)698-7000. **E-mail:** info@simonsays.com. **Website:** www.simonsays.com. Publishes hardcover originals.

HOW TO CONTACT *Agented submissions only.*

TERMS Pays 7-15% royalty. Pays variable advance. Responds in 3 months to queries

SECOND STORY PRESS

20 Maud St., Ste. 401, Toronto ON M5V 2M5, Canada. (416)537-7850. **Fax:** (416)537-0588. **E-mail:** info@secondstorypress.ca. **Website:** www.secondstorypress.ca. "Please keep in mind that as a feminist press, we are looking for nonsexist, nonracist and nonviolent stories, as well as historical fiction, chapter books, novels and biography."

NEEDS Considers nonsexist, nonracist, and nonviolent stories, as well as historical fiction, chapter books, picture books.

SEEDLING CONTINENTAL PRESS

520 E. Bainbridge St., Elizabethtown PA 17022. (800)233-0759; **Fax:** 888-834-1303. **Website:** www.continentalpress.com. "Continental publishes educational materials for grades K-12, specializing in reading, mathematics, and test preparation materials. We are not currently accepting submissions for Seedling leveled readers or instructional materials."

NEEDS Young readers: adventure, animal, folktales, humor, multicultural, nature/environment. Does not accept texts longer than 12 pages or over 300 words. Average word length: young readers—100.

HOW TO CONTACT Submit complete ms.

TERMS Work purchased outright from authors. Responds to mss in 6 months.

TIPS "See our website. Follow writers' guidelines carefully and test your story with children and educators."

SERIOUSLY GOOD BOOKS

999 Vanderbilt Beach Rd., Naples FL 34108. **E-mail:** seriouslygoodbks@aol.com. **Website:** www.seriouslygoodbks.net. Estab. 2010. Publishes historical fiction only. Publishes trade paperback and electronic originals. Book catalog and guidelines online.

HOW TO CONTACT Query letter by e-mail. See Submissions tab on website.

TERMS Pays 15% minimum royalties (print); more on digital. Responds in 1 month to queries.

TIPS "Looking for historial fiction with substance. We seek well-researched historical fiction in the vein of Rutherfurd, Mary Renault, Maggie Anton, Robert Harris, etc. Please don't query with historical fiction mixed with other genres (romance, time travel, vampires, etc.)."

SEVEN STORIES PRESS

140 Watts St., New York NY 10013. (212)226-8760. **Fax:** (212)226-1411. **E-mail:** info@sevenstories.com. **Website:** www.sevenstories.com. **Contact:** Acquisitions. Estab. 1995. Founded in 1995 in New York City, and named for the seven authors who committed to a home with a fiercely independent spirit, Seven Stories Press publishes works of the imagination and political titles by voices of conscience. While most widely known for its books on politics, human rights, and social and economic justice, Seven Stories continues to champion literature, with a list encompassing both innovative debut novels and National Book Award–winning poetry collections, as well as prose and poetry translations from the French, Spanish, German, Swedish, Italian, Greek, Polish, Korean, Vietnamese, Russian, and Arabic. Publishes hardcover and trade paperback originals. Book catalog and ms guidelines free.

HOW TO CONTACT Submit cover letter with 2 sample chapters.

TERMS Pays 7-15% royalty on retail price. Pays advance. Responds in 1 month.

SEVERN HOUSE PUBLISHERS

Salatin House, 19 Cedar Rd., Sutton, Surrey SM2 5DA, United Kingdom. (44)(208)770-3930. **Fax:** (44) (208)770-3850. **Website:** www.severnhouse.com. Severn House is currently emphasizing suspense, romance, mystery. Large print imprint from existing authors. Publishes hardcover and trade paperback originals and reprints. Book catalog available free.

HOW TO CONTACT *Agented submissions only.*

TERMS Pays 7-15% royalty on retail price. Pays $750-5,000 advance. Responds in 3 months to proposals.

SHAMBHALA PUBLICATIONS, INC.

4720 Walnut St., Boulder CO 80304. **E-mail:** editors@shambhala.com. **Website:** www.shambhala.com. Estab. 1969. Publishes hardcover and trade paperback originals and reprints. Book catalog free. Guidelines online.

IMPRINTS Roost Books; Snow Lion.

TERMS Pays 8% royalty on retail price. Responds in 4 months.

SHIPWRECKT BOOKS PUBLISHING COMPANY LLC

309 W. Stevens Ave., Rushford MN 55971. (507)458-8190. **E-mail:** editor@shipwrecktbooks.com. **E-mail:** contact@shipwrecktbooks.com. **Website:** www.shipwrecktbooks.com. **Contact:** Tom Driscoll, managing editor. Publishes trade paperback originals, mass market paperback originals, and electronic originals. Catalog and guidelines online.

IMPRINTS Rocket Science Press (literary); Up On Big Rock Poetry Series; Lost Lake Folk Art (memoir, biography, essays, and nonfiction).

HOW TO CONTACT E-mail query first. All unsolicited mss returned unopened.

TERMS Authors receive a maximum of 35% royalties. Responds to queries within 6 months.

TIPS "Quality writing. Query first. Development and full editorial services available."

SIMON & SCHUSTER

1230 Avenue of the Americas, New York NY 10020. (212)698-7000. **Website:** www.simonandschuster.com. *Accepts agented submissions only.*

IMPRINTS Aladdin; Atheneum Books for Young Readers; Atria; Beach Lane Books; Folger Shakespeare Library; Free Press; Gallery Books; Howard Books; Little Simon; Margaret K. McElderry Books; Pocket; Scribner; Simon & Schuster; Simon & Schuster Books for Young Readers; Simon Pulse; Simon Spotlight; Threshold; Touchstone; Paula Wiseman Books.

SIMON & SCHUSTER BOOKS FOR YOUNG READERS

Imprint of Simon & Schuster Children's Publishing, 1230 Avenue of the Americas, New York NY 10020. (212)698-7000. **Fax:** (212)698-2796. **Website:** www.simonsayskids.com. "Simon and Schuster Books For Young Readers is the Flagship imprint of the S&S Children's Division. We are committed to publishing a wide range of contemporary, commercial, award-winning fiction and nonfiction that spans every age of children's publishing. BFYR is constantly looking to the future, supporting our foundation authors and franchises, but always with an eye for breaking new ground with every publication. We publish high-quality fiction and nonfiction for a variety of age groups and a variety of markets. Above all, we strive to publish books that we are passionate about." *No unsolicited mss.* All unsolicited mss returned unopened. Publishes hardcover originals. Guidelines online.

HOW TO CONTACT *Agented submissions only.*

TERMS Pays variable royalty on retail price.

TIPS "We're looking for picture books centered on a strong, fully-developed protagonist who grows or changes during the course of the story; young adult novels that are challenging and psychologically complex; also imaginative and humorous middle-grade fiction. And we want nonfiction that is as engaging as fiction. Our imprint's slogan is 'Reading You'll Remember.' We aim to publish books that are fresh, accessible and family-oriented; we want them to have an impact on the reader."

SIMPLY READ BOOKS

501-5525 W. Blvd., Vancouver BC V6M 3W6, Canada. **E-mail:** go@simplyreadbooks.com. **Website:** www.simplyreadbooks.com. Simply Read Books is current seeking mss in picture books, early readers, early chapter books, middle-grade fiction, and graphic novels.

HOW TO CONTACT Query or submit complete ms.

SKINNER HOUSE BOOKS

The Unitarian Universalist Association, 24 Farnsworth St., Boston MA 02210. (617)742-2100, ext. 603. **Fax:** (617)948-6466. **E-mail:** bookproposals@uua.org. **Website:** www.uua.org/publications/skinnerhouse. **Contact:** Betsy Martin. Estab. 1975. "We publish titles in Unitarian Universalist faith, liberal religion, history, biography, worship, and issues of social justice. Most of our children's titles are intended for religious education or worship use. They reflect Unitarian Universalist values. We also publish inspirational titles of poetic prose and meditations. Writers should know that Unitarian Universalism is a liberal religious denomination committed to progressive ideals. Currently emphasizing social justice concerns." Publishes trade paperback originals and reprints. Book catalog for 6×9 SAE with 3 first-class stamps. Guidelines online.

NEEDS Only publishes fiction for children's titles for religious instruction.

HOW TO CONTACT Query.

TERMS Responds to queries in 1 month.

TIPS "From outside our denomination, we are interested in mss that will be of help or interest to liberal churches, Sunday School classes, parents, ministers, and volunteers. Inspirational/spiritual and children's titles must reflect liberal Unitarian Universalist values."

SKY PONY PRESS

307 W. 36th St., 11th Floor, New York NY 10018. (212)643-6816. **Fax:** (212)643-6819. **Website:** skyponypress.com. Estab. 2011. Sky Pony Press is the children's book imprint of Skyhorse Publishing. "Following in the footsteps of our parent company, our goal is to provide books for readers with a wide variety of interests." Guidelines online.

NEEDS "We will consider picture books, early readers, midgrade novels, novelties, and informational books for all ages."

HOW TO CONTACT Submit ms or proposal.

SLEEPING BEAR PRESS

2395 South Huron Parkway #200, Ann Arbor MI 48104. (800)487-2323. **Fax:** (734)794-0004. **E-mail:** submissions@sleepingbearpress.com. **Website:** www.sleepingbearpress.com. **Contact:** Manuscript Submissions. Estab. 1998. Book catalog available via e-mail.

NEEDS Picture books: adventure, animal, concept, folktales, history, multicultural, nature/environment, religion, sports. Young readers: adventure, animal, concept, folktales, history, humor, multicultural, nature/environment, religion, sports. Average word length: picture books—1,800.

HOW TO CONTACT Accepts unsolicited queries three times per year. See website for details. Query with sample of work (up to 15 pages) and SASE. Please address packages to Manuscript Submissions.

SMALL BEER PRESS

150 Pleasant St., #306, Easthampton MA 01027. (413)203-1636. **Fax:** (413)203-1636. **E-mail:** info@smallbeerpress.com. **Website:** www.smallbeerpress.com. Estab. 2000. Small Beer Press also publishes the zine *Lady Churchill's Rosebud Wristlet*. "SBP's books have recently received the Tiptree and Crawford Awards."

HOW TO CONTACT Does not accept unsolicited novel or short story collection mss. Send queries with first 10-20 pages and SASE.

TIPS "Please be familiar with our books first to avoid wasting your time and ours, thank you. E-mail queries will be deleted. Really."

SMITH AND KRAUS PUBLISHERS, INC.

177 Lyme Rd., Hanover NH 03755. (603)643-6431. **E-mail:** editor@smithandkraus.com. **Website:** smithandkraus.com. Estab. 1990. Publishes hardcover and trade paperback originals. Book catalog available free.

NEEDS Does not return submissions.

HOW TO CONTACT Query with SASE.

TERMS Pays 7% royalty on retail price. Pays $500-2,000 advance. Responds in 1 month to queries; 2 months to proposals; 4 months to mss.

SOFT SKULL PRESS INC.

Counterpoint, 2650 Ninth St., Ste. 318, Berkeley CA 94710. (510)704-0230. **Fax:** (510)704-0268. **E-mail:** info@counterpointpress.com. **Website:** www.softskull.com. "Here at Soft Skull we love books that are new, fun, smart, revelatory, quirky, groundbreaking, cage-rattling and/or/otherwise unusual." Publishes hardcover and trade paperback originals. Book catalog and guidelines online.

NEEDS Does not consider poetry.

HOW TO CONTACT Soft Skull Press no longer accepts digital submissions. Send a cover letter describing your project in detail and a completed ms. For graphic novels, send a minimum of five fully inked pages of art, along with a synopsis of your storyline. "Please do not send original material, as it will not be returned."

TERMS Pays 7-10% royalty. Average advance: $100-15,000. Responds in 2 months to proposals; 3 months to mss.

TIPS "See our website for updated submission guidelines."

SOHO PRESS, INC.

853 Broadway, New York NY 10003. (212)260-1900. **E-mail:** soho@sohopress.com. **Website:** www.sohopress.com. **Contact:** Bronwen Hruska, publisher; Mark Doten, senior editor. Estab. 1986. Soho Press publishes primarily fiction, as well as some narrative literary nonfiction and mysteries set abroad. No electronic submissions, only queries by e-mail. Publishes hardcover and trade paperback originals; trade paperback reprints. Guidelines online.

NEEDS Adventure, ethnic, feminist, historical, literary, mainstream/contemporary, mystery (police procedural), suspense, multicultural.

HOW TO CONTACT Submit 3 sample chapters and cover letter with synopsis, author bio, SASE. *No e-mailed submissions.*

TERMS Pays 10-15% royalty on retail price (varies under certain circumstances). Responds in 3 months.

TIPS "Soho Press publishes discerning authors for discriminating readers, finding the strongest possible writers and publishing them. Before submitting, look at our website for an idea of the types of books we publish, and read our submission guidelines."

SOURCEBOOKS CASABLANCA

Sourcebooks, Inc., 232 Madison Ave., Ste. 1100, New York NY 10016. **E-mail:** romance@sourcebooks.com. **Website:** www.sourcebooks.com. **Contact:** Deb Werksman (deb.werksman@sourcebooks.com). "Our romance imprint, Sourcebooks Casablanca, publishes single title romance in all subgenres." Guidelines online.

NEEDS "Our editorial criteria call for: a heroine the reader can relate to, a hero she can fall in love with, a world gets created that the reader can escape into, there's a hook that we can sell within 2-3 sentences, and the author is out to build a career with us."

TERMS Responds in 2-3 months.

TIPS "We are actively acquiring single-title and single-title series romance fiction (90,000-100,000 words) for our Casablanca imprint. We are looking for strong writers who are excited about marketing their books and building their community of readers, and whose books have something fresh to offer in the genre of romance."

SOURCEBOOKS FIRE

1935 Brookdale Rd., Ste. 139, Naperville IL 60563. (630)961-3900. **Fax:** (630)961-2168. **E-mail:** submissions@sourcebooks.com. **Website:** www.sourcebooks.com. "We're actively acquiring knockout books for our young adult imprint. We are particularly looking for strong writers who are excited about promoting and building their community of readers, and whose books have something fresh to offer the ever-growing young adult audience. We are not accepting any unsolicited or unagented mss at this time. Unfortunately, our staff can no longer handle the large volume of mss that we receive on a daily basis. We will continue to consider agented mss." See website for details.

HOW TO CONTACT Query with the full ms attached in Word doc.

SOURCEBOOKS LANDMARK

Sourcebooks, Inc., 232 Madison Ave., Ste. 1100, New York NY 10016. **E-mail:** editorialsubmissions@sourcebooks.com. **Website:** www.sourcebooks.com. "Our fiction imprint, Sourcebooks Landmark, publishes a variety of commercial fiction, including specialties in historical fiction and Austenalia. We are interested first and foremost in books that have a story to tell."

NEEDS "We are actively acquiring contemporary, book club, and historical fiction for our Landmark imprint. We are looking for strong writers who are excited about marketing their books and building their community of readers."

HOW TO CONTACT Submit synopsis and full ms preferred. Receipt of e-mail submissions acknowledged within 3 weeks of e-mail.

TERMS Responds in 2-3 months.

SPENCER HILL PRESS

P.O. Box 243, Marlborough CT 06447. (860)207-2206. **E-mail:** submissions@spencerhillpress.com. **Website:** www.spencerhillpress.com. **Contact:** Jennifer Carson. Spencer Hill Press is an independent publishing house specializing in science fiction, urban fantasy, and paranormal romance for young adult readers. "Our books have that 'I couldn't put it down!' quality." Guidelines online.

NEEDS "We are interested in young adult, new adult, and middle-grade science fiction, psych-fi, paranormal, or urban fantasy, particularly those with a strong and interesting voice."

HOW TO CONTACT Check website for open submission periods.

STAR BRIGHT BOOKS

13 Landsdowne St., Cambridge MA 02139. (617)354-1300. **Fax:** (617)354-1399. **E-mail:** info@starbrightbooks.com. **Website:** www.starbrightbooks.com. Star Bright Books does accept unsolicited mss and art submissions. "We welcome submissions for picture books and longer works, both fiction and nonfiction." Also beginner readers and chapter books. Query first. Catalog available.

TERMS Pays advance. Responds in several months.

STERLING PUBLISHING CO., INC.

1166 Avenue of the Americas, 17th Floor, New York NY 10036. (212)532-7160. **Fax:** (212)981-0508. **Website:** www.sterlingpublishing.com. "Sterling publishes highly illustrated, accessible, hands-on, practical books for adults and children. Our mission is to publish high-quality books that educate, entertain, and enrich the lives of our readers." Publishes hardcover and paperback originals and reprints. Catalog online. Guidelines online.

NEEDS Publishes fiction for children.

HOW TO CONTACT Submit to attention of "Children's Book Editor."

TERMS Pays royalty or work purchased outright. Offers advances (average amount: $2,000).

TIPS "We are primarily a nonfiction activities-based publisher. We have a picture book list, but we do not publish chapter books or novels. Our list is not trend-driven. We focus on titles that will backlist well. "

STONE ARCH BOOKS

1710 Roe Crest Rd., North Mankato MN 56003. **E-mail:** author.sub@capstonepub.com. **Website:** www.stonearchbooks.com. Catalog online.

NEEDS Imprint of Capstone Publishers.Young readers, middle readers, young adults: adventure, contemporary, fantasy, humor, light humor, mystery, science fiction, sports, suspense. Average word length: young readers—1,000-3,000; middle readers and early young adults—5,000-10,000.

HOW TO CONTACT Submit outline/synopsis and 3 sample chapters. Electronic submissions preferred. Full guidelines available on website.

TERMS Work purchased outright from authors.

TIPS "A high-interest topic or activity is one that a young person would spend their free time on without adult direction or suggestion."

STONE BRIDGE PRESS

P.O. Box 8208, Berkeley CA 94707. **E-mail:** sbp@stonebridge.com. **Website:** www.stonebridge.com. **Contact:** Peter Goodman, publisher. Estab. 1989. "Independent press focusing on books about Japan and Asia in English (business, language, culture, literature, animation)." Publishes hardcover and trade paperback originals. Books: 60-70 lb. offset paper; web and sheet paper; perfect bound; some illustrations. Distributes titles through Consortium. Promotes titles through Internet announcements, special-interest magazines and niche tie-ins to associations. Available for download from company website. Ms guidelines online.

NEEDS Experimental, gay/lesbian, literary, Asia-themed. "Primarily looking at material relating to Asia, especially Japan and China. "

HOW TO CONTACT Does not accept unsolicited mss. Accepts queries by e -mail.

TERMS Pays royalty on wholesale price. Responds to queries in 4 months; mss in 8 months.

TIPS "Fiction translations only for the time being. No poetry. Looking also for graphic novels, not manga or serializations."

STONESLIDE BOOKS

Stoneslide Media LLC, P.O. Box 8331, New Haven CT 06530. **E-mail:** editors@stoneslidecorrective.com. **E-mail:** submissions@stoneslidecorrective.com. **Website:** www.stoneslidecorrective.com. **Contact:** Jonathan Weisberg, editor; Christopher Wachlin, editor. Estab. 2012. "We like novels with strong character development and narrative thrust, brought out with writing that's clear and expressive." Publishes trade paperback and electronic originals. Book catalog and guidelines online.

NEEDS "We will look at any genre. The important factor for us is that the story use plot, characters, emotions, and other elements of storytelling to think and move the mind forward."

HOW TO CONTACT Submit proposal package via online submission form including: synopsis and 3 sample chapters.

TERMS Pays 20-80% royalty. Responds in 1-2 months.

TIPS "Read the Stoneslide Corrective to see if your work fits with our approach."

SUBITO PRESS

University of Colorado at Boulder, Dept. of English, 226 UCB, Boulder CO 80309-0226. **E-mail:** subitopressucb@gmail.com. **Website:** www.subitopress.org. Subito Press is a nonprofit publisher of literary works. Each year Subito publishes one work of fiction and one work of poetry through its contest. Publishes trade paperback originals. Guidelines online.

HOW TO CONTACT Submit complete ms to contest.

TIPS "We publish 2 books of innovative writing a year through our poetry and fiction contests. All entries are also considered for publication with the press."

SUNBURY PRESS, INC.

105 S Market St., Mechanicsburg PA 17055. **E-mail:** info@sunburypress.com. **E-mail:** proposals@sunburypress.com. **Website:** www.sunburypress.com. Estab. 2004. Sunbury Press, Inc. is a publisher of trade paperback, hardcover and digital books featuring established and emerging authors in many fiction and nonfiction categories. Sunbury's books are printed in the USA and sold through leading booksellers worldwide. "Please use our online submission form." Publishes trade paperback and hardcover originals and reprints; electronic originals and reprints. Catalog and guidelines online.

NEEDS "We are especially seeking climate change / dystopian fiction and books of regional interest."

TERMS Pays 10% royalty on wholesale price. Responds in 3 months.

TIPS "Our books appeal to very diverse audiences. We are building our list in many categories, focusing on many demographics. We are not like traditional publishers—we are digitally adept and very creative. Don't be surprised if we move quicker than you are accustomed to!"

SUNSTONE PRESS

Box 2321, Santa Fe NM 87504. (800)243-5644. **Website:** www.sunstonepress.com. **Contact:** Submissions Editor. Sunstone's original focus was on nonfiction subjects that preserved and highlighted the richness of the American Southwest but it has expanded its view over the years to include mainstream themes and categories—both nonfiction and fiction—that have a more general appeal. Guidelines online.

HOW TO CONTACT Query with 1 sample chapter.

SWAN ISLE PRESS

P.O. Box 408790, Chicago IL 60640. (773)728-3780. **E-mail:** info@swanislepress.com. **Website:** www.swanislepress.com. Estab. 1999. *"We do not accept unsolicited mss."* Publishes hardcover and trade paperback originals. Book catalog online. Guidelines online.

HOW TO CONTACT Query with SASE.

TERMS Pays 7-10% royalty on wholesale price. Responds in 6-12 months.

SWEET CHERRY PUBLISHING

Unit E, Vulcan Business Complex, Vulcan Rd., Leicester Leicestershire LE5 3EB, United Kingdom. **E-mail:** info@sweetcherrypublishing.com. **E-mail:** submissions@sweetcherrypublishing.com. **Website:** www.sweetcherrypublishing.com. Estab. 2011. Sweet Cherry Publishing publishes fiction for children between the ages of 0 and 16. "We specialize in sets and series: our aim is to give our readers the opportunity to revisit their favorite characters again and again, and to create stories that will stand the test of time. If you have written an original series with strong themes and characters, we would like to hear from you." Guidelines online.

NEEDS No erotica.

HOW TO CONTACT Submit a cover letter and a synopsis with 3 sample chapters via post or e-mail. "Please note that we strongly prefer e-mail submissions."

TERMS Offers a one-time fee for work that is accepted.

TIPS "We strongly prefer e-mail submissions over postal submissions. If your work is accepted, Sweet Cherry may consider commissioning you for future series."

TAFELBERG PUBLISHERS

Imprint of NB Publishers, P.O. Box 879, Cape Town 8000, South Africa. (27)(21)406-3033. **Fax:** (27) (21)406-3812. **E-mail:** kristin@nb.co.za. **Website:** www.tafelberg.com. **Contact:** Kristin Paremoer. General publisher best known for Afrikaans fiction, authoritative political works, children's/youth literature, and a variety of illustrated and nonillustrated nonfiction.

NEEDS Picture books, young readers: animal, anthology, contemporary, fantasy, folktales, hi-lo, humor, multicultural, nature/environment, scient fiction, special needs. Middle readers, young adults: animal (middle reader only), contemporary, fantasy, hi-lo, humor, multicultural, nature/environment, problem novels, science fiction, special needs, sports, suspense/mystery. Average word length: picture books—1,500-7,500; young readers—25,000; middle readers—15,000; young adults—40,000.

HOW TO CONTACT Submit complete ms.

TERMS Pays authors royalty of 15-18% based on wholesale price. Responds to queries in 2 weeks; mss in 6 months.

TIPS "Writers: Story needs to have a South African or African style. Illustrators: I'd like to look, but the chances of getting commissioned are slim. The market is small and difficult. Do not expect huge advances. Editorial staff attended or plans to attend the following conferences: IBBY, Frankfurt, SCBWI Bologna."

TANTOR MEDIA

6 Business Park Rd., Old Saybrook CT 06475. (860)395-1155. **Fax:** (860)395-1154. **E-mail:** rightsemail@tantor.com. **Website:** www.tantor.com. **Contact:** Ron Formica, director of acquisitions. Estab. 2001. Tantor Media, a division of Recorded Books, is a leading audiobook publisher, producing more than 100 new titles every month. Publishes audiobooks. Catalog online.

HOW TO CONTACT Query with SASE, or submit proposal package including synopsis and 3 sample chapters.

TERMS Pays 5-15% royalty on wholesale price. Responds in 2 months.

TEXAS TECH UNIVERSITY PRESS

1120 Main St., Second Floor, Box 41037, Lubbock TX 79415. (806)742-2982. **Fax:** (806)742-2979. **E-mail:** ttup@ttu.edu. **Website:** www.ttupress.org. Estab. 1971. Texas Tech University Press, the book publishing office of the university since 1971 and an AAUP member since 1986, publishes nonfiction titles in the areas of natural history and the natural sciences; 18th century and Joseph Conrad studies; studies of modern Southeast Asia, particularly the Vietnam War; costume and textile history; Latin American literature and culture; and all aspects of the Great Plains and the American West, especially history, biography, memoir, sports history, and travel. In addition, the Press publishes several scholarly journals, acclaimed series for young readers, an annual invited poetry collection, and literary fiction of Texas and the West. Guidelines online.

NEEDS Fiction rooted in the American West and Southwest, Jewish literature, Latin American and Latino fiction (in translation or English).

THISTLEDOWN PRESS LTD.

410 2nd Ave., Saskatoon SK S7K 2C3, Canada. (306)244-1722. **Fax:** (306)244-1762. **E-mail:** editorial@thistledownpress.com. **Website:** www.thistledownpress.com. **Contact:** Allan Forrie, publisher. "Thistledown originates books by Canadian authors only, although we have co-published titles by authors outside Canada. We do not publish children's picture books." Book catalog on website.

NEEDS Young adults: adventure, anthology, contemporary, fantasy, humor, poetry, romance, science fiction, suspense/mystery, short stories. Average word length: young adults—40,000.

HOW TO CONTACT Submit outline/synopsis and sample chapters. *Does not accept mss.* Do not query by e-mail. "Please note: we are not accepting middle years (ages 8-12) nor children's mss at this time." See Submission Guidelines on Website.

TERMS Pays authors royalty of 10-12% based on net dollar sales. Pays illustrators and photographers by the project (range: $250-750). Responds to queries in 6 months.

TIPS "Send cover letter including publishing history and SASE."

THUNDERSTONE BOOKS

6575 Horse Dr., Las Vegas NV 89131. **E-mail:** info@thunderstonebooks.com. **Website:** www.thunderstonebooks.com. **Contact:** Rachel Noorda, editorial director. Estab. 2014. "At ThunderStone Books, we aim to publish children's books that have an educational aspect. We are not looking for curriculum for learning certain subjects, but rather stories that encourage learning for children, whether that be learning about a new language/culture or learning more about science and math in a fun, fictional format. We want to help children to gain a love for other languages and subjects so that they are curious about the world around them. We are currently accepting fiction and nonfiction submissions. Picture books without accompanying illustration will not be accepted." Publishes hardcover, trade paperback, mass market paperback, and electronic originals. Catalog available for SASE. Guidelines available.

NEEDS Interested in multicultural stories with an emphasis on authentic culture and language (these may include mythology).

HOW TO CONTACT "If you think your book is right for us, send a query letter with a word attachment of the first 50 pages to info@thunderstonebooks.com. If it is a picture book or chapter book for young readers that is shorter than 50 pages send the entire ms."

TERMS Pays 5-15% royalties on retail price. Pays $300-1,000 advance. Responds in 3 months.

TIGHTROPE BOOKS

#207-2 College St., Toronto ON M5G 1K3, Canada. (416)928-6666. **E-mail:** tightropeasst@gmail.com. **Website:** www.tightropebooks.com. **Contact:** Jim Nason, publisher. Estab. 2005. Publishes trade paperback originals. Catalog and guidelines online.

Accepting submissions for literary fiction, nonfiction and poetry from Canadian citizens and permanent Canadian residents only.

TERMS Pays 5-15% royalty on retail price. Pays advance of $200-300. Responds if interested.

TIPS "Audience is urban, literary, educated, unconventional."

TIN HOUSE BOOKS

2617 NW Thurman St., Portland OR 97210. (503)473-8663. **Fax:** (503)473-8957. **E-mail:** meg@tinhouse.com. **Website:** www.tinhouse.com. **Contact:** Meg Storey, editor; Tony Perez, editor; Masie Cochran, editor. "We are a small independent publisher dedicated to nurturing new, promising talent as well as showcasing the work of established writers." Distributes/promotes titles through W. W. Norton. Publishes hardcover originals, paperback originals, paperback reprints. Guidelines online.

HOW TO CONTACT *Agented mss only.* "We no longer read unsolicited submissions by authors with no representation. We will continue to accept submissions from agents."

TERMS Responds to queries in 2-3 weeks; mss in 2-3 months.

TITAN PRESS

PMB 17897, Encino CA 91416. **E-mail:** titan91416@yahoo.com. **Website:** https://www.facebook.com/RVClef. **Contact:** Romana V. Clef, editor. Estab. 1981. Little literary publisher. Publishes hardcover and paperback originals.

HOW TO CONTACT Does not accept unsolicited mss. Query with SASE. Include brief bio, list of publishing credits.

TERMS Pays 20-40% royalty. Responds to queries in 3 months.

TIPS "Look, act, sound, and *be* professional."

TOR BOOKS

Tom Doherty Associates, 175 Fifth Ave., New York NY 10010. **Website:** www.tor-forge.com. Tor Books is the "world's largest publisher of science fiction and fantasy, with strong category publishing in historical fiction, mystery, western/Americana, thriller, young adult." Book catalog available. Guidelines online.

HOW TO CONTACT Submit first 3 chapters, 3-10 page synopsis, dated cover letter, SASE.

TERMS Pays author royalty. Pays illustrators by the project.

TORQUERE PRESS LLC

P.O. Box 37, Waldo AR 71770. **E-mail:** editor@torquerepress.com. **E-mail:** submissions@torquerepress.com. **Website:** www.torquerepress.com. **Contact:** Kristi Boulware, submissions editor (homoerotica, suspense, gay/lesbian). Estab. 2015. "We are a gay and lesbian press focusing on romance and genres of romance. We particularly like paranormal and western romance." Publishes trade paperback originals and electronic originals and reprints. Book catalog online. Guidelines online.

NEEDS All categories gay and lesbian themed.

HOW TO CONTACT Submit proposal package, 3 sample chapters, clips.

TERMS Pays 8-40% royalty. Pays $35-75 for anthology stories. Does not pay advance. Responds in 1 month to queries and proposals; 2-4 months to mss.

TIPS "Our audience is primarily people looking for a familiar romance setting featuring gay or lesbian protagonists. Please read guidelines carefully and familiarize yourself with our lines."

TORREY HOUSE PRESS, LLC

2806 Melony Dr., Salt Lake City UT 84124. **E-mail:** anne@torreyhouse.com. **Website:** torreyhouse.com. **Contact:** Anne Terashima. Estab. 2010. Torrey House Press is an independent nonprofit publisher promoting environmental conservation through literature. Publishes hardcover, trade paperback, and electronic originals. Catalog online. Guidelines online.

NEEDS "Torrey House Press publishes literary fiction and creative nonfiction about the world environment and the American West."

HOW TO CONTACT Submit proposal package including: synopsis, complete ms, bio.

TERMS Pays 5-15% royalty on retail price. Responds in 3 months.

TIPS "Include writing experience (none okay)."

✪ TOUCHWOOD EDITIONS

The Heritage Group, 103-1075 Pendergast St., Victoria BC V8V 0A1, Canada. (250)360-0829. **Fax:** (250)386-0829. **E-mail:** edit@touchwoodeditions.com. **Website:** www.touchwoodeditions.com. **Contact:** Renée Layberry, Editor. Publishes trade paperback, originals and reprints. Book catalog and guidelines online.

HOW TO CONTACT Submit bio/CV, marketing plan, TOC, outline, word count.

TERMS Pays 15% royalty on net price. Responds in 6 months to queries.

TIPS "Our area of interest is western Canada. We would like more creative nonfiction and fiction from First Nations authors, and welcome authors who write about notable individuals in Canada's history. Please note we do not publish poetry."

✪ TRADEWIND BOOKS

202-1807 Maritime Mews, Granville Island, Vancouver BC V6H 3W7, Canada. (604)662-4405. **Website:** www.tradewindbooks.com. "Tradewind Books publishes juvenile picture books and young adult novels. Requires that submissions include evidence that author has read at least 3 titles published by Tradewind Books." Publishes hardcover and trade paperback originals. Book catalog and ms guidelines online.

NEEDS Average word length: 900 words.

HOW TO CONTACT Send complete ms for picture books. *Young adult novels by Canadian authors only. Chapter books by U.S. authors considered.* For chapter books/middle-grade fiction, submit the first 3 chapters, a chapter outline, and plot summary.

TERMS Pays 7% royalty on retail price. Pays variable advance. Responds to mss in 2 months.

TRIANGLE SQUARE

Seven Stories Press, 140 Watts St., New York NY 10013. (212)226-8760. **Fax:** (212)226-1411. **E-mail:** info@sevenstories.com. **Website:** www.sevenstories.com/trianglesquare/. Triangle Square is a children's and young adult imprint of Seven Story Press.

HOW TO CONTACT Send a cover letter with 2 sample chapters and SASE. Send c/o Acquisitions.

TRISTAN PUBLISHING

2355 Louisiana Ave. N, Golden Valley MN 55427. (763)545-1383. **Fax:** (763)545-1387. **E-mail:** info@tristanpublishing.com; manuscripts@tristanpublishing.com. **Website:** www.tristanpublishing.com. **Contact:** Brett Waldman, publisher. Estab. 2002. Publishes hardcover originals. Catalog and guidelines online.

HOW TO CONTACT Query with SASE; submit completed mss.

TERMS Pays royalty on wholesale or retail price; outright purchase. Responds in 3 months.

TIPS "Our audience is adults and children."

TU BOOKS

Lee & Low Books, 95 Madison Ave., Ste. #1205, New York NY 10016. **Website:** www.leeandlow.com/imprints/3. **Contact:** Stacy Whitman, Publisher. Estab. 2010. The Tu imprint spans many genres: science fiction, fantasy, mystery, contemporary, and more. "We don't believe in labels or limits, just great stories. Join us at the crossroads where fantasy and real life collide. You'll be glad you did." Guidelines online. Electronic submissions can be submitted here (only): https://tubooks.submittable.com/submit.

NEEDS "At Tu Books, an imprint of Lee & Low Books, our focus is on well-told, exciting, adventurous fantasy, science fiction, and mystery novels starring people of color. We also selectively publish realism that explores the contemporary and historical experiences of people of color. We look for fantasy set in worlds inspired by non-Western folklore or culture, contemporary mysteries and fantasy set all over the world starring people of color, and science fiction that centers the possibilities for people of color in the future. We welcome intersectional narratives that feature LGBTQIA and disabled POC as heroes in their own stories. We are looking specifically for stories for both middle-grade (ages 8-12) and young adult (ages 12-18) readers. Occasionally a ms might fall between those two categories; if your ms does, let us know. We are not looking for picture books, chapter books, or short stories at this time. Please do not send submissions in these categories. (See the Lee & Low Books guidelines for books for younger young readers.)"

HOW TO CONTACT Only submissions sent through Submittable or regular post will be considered. "We cannot accept submissions through e-mail or fax. Mss should be accompanied by a cover letter that includes a brief biography of the author, including publishing history. The letter should also state if the ms is a simultaneous or an exclusive submission. Include a synopsis and the first 3 chapters of the novel. Include full contact information on the cover letter and the first page of the ms."

TERMS Pays advance. Responds only if interested.

TUMBLEHOME LEARNING

P.O. Box 71386, Boston MA 02117. **E-mail:** info@tumblehomelearning.com. **E-mail:** submissions@tumblehomelearning.com. **Website:** www.tumblehomelearning.com. **Contact:** Pendred Noyce, editor. Estab. 2011. Tumblehome Learning helps kids imagine themselves as young scientists or engineeers and encourages them to experience science through adventure and discovery. "We do this with exciting mystery and adventure tales as well as experiments carefully designed to engage students from ages 8 and up." Publishes hardcover, trade paperback, and electronic originals. Catalog available online. Guideliens available on request for SASE.

NEEDS "All our fiction has science at its heart. This can include using science to solve a mystery (see *The Walking Fish* by Rachelle Burk or *Something Stinks!* by Gail Hedrick), realistic science fiction, books in our Galactic Academy of Science series, science-based adventure tales, and the occasional picture book with a science theme, such as appreciation of the stars and constellations in *Elizabeth's Constellation Quilt* by Olivia Fu. A graphic novel about science would also be welcome."

HOW TO CONTACT Submit completed ms electronically.

TERMS Pays authors 8-12% royalties on retail price. Pays $500 advance. Responds in 1 month to queries and proposals, and 2 months to mss.

TIPS "Please don't submit to us if your book is not about science. We don't accept generic books about animals or books with glaring scientific errors in the first chapter. That said, the book should be fun to read and the science content can be subtle. We work closely with authors, including first-time authors, to edit and improve their books. As a small publisher, the greatest benefit we can offer is this friendly and respectful partnership with authors."

TUPELO PRESS

P.O. Box 1767, North Adams MA 01247. (413)664-9611. **E-mail:** publisher@tupelopress.org. **Website:** www.tupelopress.org. **Contact:** Jeffrey Levine, publish/editor in chief; Jim Schley, managing editor. Estab. 2001. "We're an independent nonprofit literary press. We accept book-length poetry, poetry collections (48+ pages), short story collections, novellas, literary nonfiction/memoirs and up to 80 pages of a novel." Guidelines online.

NEEDS "For Novels—submit no more than 100 pages along with a summary of the entire book. If we're interested we'll ask you to send the rest. We accept very few works of prose (1 or 2 per year)."

HOW TO CONTACT Submit complete ms. **Charges a $45 reading fee.**

TURNSTONE PRESS

Artspace Building, 206-100 Arthur St., Winnipeg MB R3B 1H3, Canada. (204)947-1555. **Fax:** (204)942-1555. **Website:** www.turnstonepress.com. **Contact:** Submissions Assistant. Estab. 1976. "Turnstone Press is a literary publisher, not a general publisher, and therefore we are only interested in literary fiction, literary nonfiction—including literary criticism—and poetry. We do publish literary mysteries, thrillers, and noir under our Ravenstone imprint. We publish only Canadian authors or landed immigrants, we strive to publish a significant number of new writers, to publish in a variety of genres, and to have 50% of each year's list be Manitoba writers and/or books with Manitoba content." Guidelines online.

HOW TO CONTACT "Samples must be 40 to 60 pages, typed/printed in a minimum 12 point serif typeface such as Times, Book Antiqua, or Garamond."

TERMS Responds in 4-7 months.

TIPS "As a Canadian literary press, we have a mandate to publish Canadian writers only. Do some homework before submitting works to make sure your subject matter/genre/writing style falls within the publishers area of interest."

TWILIGHT TIMES BOOKS

P.O. Box 3340, Kingsport TN 37664. **E-mail:** publisher@twilighttimesbooks.com. **Website:** www.twilighttimesbooks.com. **Contact:** Andy M. Scott, managing editor. Estab. 1999. "We publish compelling literary fiction by authors with a distinctive voice." Published 5 debut authors within the last year. Averages 120 total titles; 15 fiction titles/year. Member: AAP, PAS, SPAN, SLF. Guidelines online.

HOW TO CONTACT Accepts unsolicited mss. Do not send complete mss. Queries via e-mail only. Include estimated word count, brief bio, list of publishing credits, marketing plan.

TERMS Pays 8-15% royalty. Responds in 4 weeks to queries; 2 months to mss.

TIPS "The only requirement for consideration at Twilight Times Books is that your novel must be entertaining and professionally written."

TWO DOLLAR RADIO

Website: www.twodollarradio.com. **Contact:** Eric Obenauf, editorial director. Estab. 2005. Two Dollar Radio is a boutique family-run press, publishing bold works of literary merit, each book, individually and collectively, providing a sonic progression that "we believe to be too loud to ignore." Targets readers who admire ambition and creativity. Range of print runs: 2,000-7,500 copies.

HOW TO CONTACT Submit entire, completed ms with a brief cover letter, via Submittable. No previously published work. No proposals. No excerpts. There is a $2 reading fee per submission. Accepts submissions every other month (January, March, May, July, September, November).

TERMS Advance: $500-$1,000.

TIPS "We want writers who show an authority over language and the world that is being created, from the very first sentence on."

Ⓐ⊘ TYNDALE HOUSE PUBLISHERS, INC.

351 Executive Dr., Carol Stream IL 60188. (800)323-9400. **Fax:** (800)684-0247. **Website:** www.tyndale.com. Estab. 1962. "Tyndale House publishes practical, user-friendly Christian books for the home and family." Publishes hardcover and trade paperback originals and mass paperback reprints. Guidelines online.

NEEDS "Christian truths must be woven into the story organically. No short story collections. Youth books: character building stories with Christian perspective. Especially interested in ages 10-14. We primarily publish Christian historical romances, with occasional contemporary, suspense, or standalones."

HOW TO CONTACT *Agented submissions only. No unsolicited mss.*

TERMS Pays negotiable royalty. Pays negotiable advance.

TIPS "All accepted mss will appeal to Evangelical Christian children and parents."

⊘ TYRUS BOOKS

F+W Media, 1213 N. Sherman Ave., #306, Madison WI 53704. (508)427-7100. **Fax:** (508)427-6790. **Website:** tyrusbooks.com. "We publish crime and literary fiction. We believe in the life changing power of the written word."

HOW TO CONTACT Submissions currently closed; check website for updates.

UNBRIDLED BOOKS

8201 E. Highway WW, Columbia MO 65201. **E-mail:** michalsong@unbridledbooks.com. **Website:** unbridledbooks.com. **Contact:** Greg Michalson. Estab. 2004. "Unbridled Books is a premier publisher of works of rich literary quality that appeal to a broad audience."

HOW TO CONTACT Please query first by e-mail. "Due to the heavy volume of submissions, we regret that at this time we are not able to consider uninvited mss."

TIPS "We try to read each ms that arrives, so please be patient."

UNIVERSITY OF ALASKA PRESS

P.O. Box 756240, Fairbanks AK 99775-6240. (907)474-5831 or (888)252-6657. **Fax:** (907)474-5502. **E-mail:** amy.simpson@alaska.edu. **Website:** www.uaf.edu/uapress. **Contact:** Acquisitions Editor. Estab. 1967. "The mission of the University of Alaska Press is to encourage, publish, and disseminate works of scholarship that will enhance the store of knowledge about Alaska and the North Pacific Rim, with a special emphasis on the circumpolar regions." Publishes hardcover originals, trade paperback originals and reprints. Book catalog available free. Guidelines online.

NEEDS Alaska literary series with Peggy Shumaker as series editor. Publishes 1-3 works of fiction/year.

HOW TO CONTACT Submit proposal.

TERMS Responds in 2 months to queries.

TIPS "Writers have the best chance with scholarly nonfiction relating to Alaska, the circumpolar regions and North Pacific Rim. Our audience is made up of scholars, historians, students, libraries, universities, individuals, and the general Alaskan public."

UNIVERSITY OF GEORGIA PRESS

Main Library, Third Floor, 320 S. Jackson St., Athens GA 30602. (706)369-6130. **Fax:** (706)369-6131. **Website:** www.ugapress.org. **Contact:** Mick Gusinde-Duffy, assistant director for acquisitions and editor in chief; Walter Biggins, senior acquisitions editor; Pat Allen, acquisitions editor; Beth Snead, assistant acquisitions editor. Estab. 1938. University of Georgia Press is a midsized press that publishes fiction only through the Flannery O'Connor Award for Short Fiction competition. Publishes hardcover originals, trade paperback originals, and reprints. Book catalog and guidelines online.

NEEDS Short story collections published in Flannery O'Connor Award Competition.

TERMS Pays 7-10% royalty on net receipts. Pays rare, varying advance. Responds in 2 months to queries.

TIPS "Please visit our website to view our book catalogs and for all ms submission guidelines."

UNIVERSITY OF IOWA PRESS

100 Kuhl House, 119 W. Park Rd., Iowa City IA 52242. (319)335-2000. **Fax:** (319)335-2055. **E-mail:** james-mccoy@uiowa.edu; elisabeth-chretien@uiowa.edu; cath-campbell@uiowa.edu. **Website:** www.uiowapress.org. **Contact:** James McCoy, director (short fiction, poetry, general trade); Elisabeth Chretien, acquisitions editor (literary criticism, literary and general nonfiction, military and veterans' studies); Catherine Cocks, acquisitions editor (book arts, fan studies, food studies, Midwestern history and culture, theater history and culture). Estab. 1969. The University of Iowa Press publishes both trade and academic work in a variety of fields. Publishes hardcover and paperback originals. Book catalog available free. Guidelines online.

NEEDS Currently publishes the Iowa Short Fiction Award selections. "We do not accept any fiction submissions outside of the Iowa Short Fiction Award. See www.uiowapress.org for contest details."

UNIVERSITY OF MICHIGAN PRESS

839 Greene St., Ann Arbor MI 48106. (734)764-4388. **Fax:** (734)615-1540. **Website:** www.press.umich.edu. **Contact:** Mary Francis, editorial director. "In partnership with our authors and series editors, we publish in a wide range of humanities and social sciences disciplines." Guidelines online.

NEEDS In addition to the annual Michigan Literary Fiction Awards, this publishes literary fiction linked to the Great Lakes region.

HOW TO CONTACT Submit cover letter and first 30 pages.

UNIVERSITY OF NORTH TEXAS PRESS

1155 Union Circle, #311336, Denton TX 76203. (940)565-2142. **Fax:** (940)565-4590. **E-mail:** bonnie.stufflebeam@unt.edu. **Website:** untpress.unt.edu. **Contact:** Ronald Chrisman, director; Karen De Vinney, assistant director; Amy Pierce, administrative assistant; Bonnie Stufflebeam, Marketing Manager. Estab. 1987. "We are dedicated to producing the highest quality scholarly, academic, and general interest books. We are committed to serving all peoples by publishing stories of their cultures and experiences that have been overlooked. Currently emphasizing military history, Texas history, music, Mexican-American studies." Publishes hardcover and trade paperback originals and reprints. Book catalog for 8 ½×11 SASE. Guidelines online.

NEEDS "The only fiction we publish is the winner of the Katherine Anne Porter Prize in Short Fiction, an annual, national competition with a $1,000 prize, and publication of the winning ms each Fall."

TERMS Responds in 1 month to queries.

TIPS "We publish series called War and the Southwest; Texas Folklore Society Publications; the Western Life Series; Practical Guide Series; Al-Filo: Mexican-American studies; North Texas Crime and Criminal Justice; Katherine Anne Porter Prize in Short Fiction; and the North Texas Lives of Musicians Series."

UNIVERSITY OF TAMPA PRESS

University of Tampa, 401 W. Kennedy Blvd., Tampa FL 33606. (813)253-6266. **Fax:** (813)258-7593. **E-mail:** utpress@ut.edu. **Website:** www.ut.edu/tampapress. **Contact:** Richard Mathews, editor. Estab. 1952. "We are a small university press publishing a limited number of titles each year, primarily in the areas of local and regional history and printing history." Publishes hardcover originals and reprints; trade paperback originals and reprints. Book catalog online. "We do not accept unsolicited book mss except for poetry mss submitted through the annual Tampa Review Prize for Poetry."

TERMS Does not pay advance. Responds in 3-4 months to queries.

UNIVERSITY OF WISCONSIN PRESS

1930 Monroe St., 3rd Floor, Madison WI 53711. (608)263-1110. **Fax:** (608)263-1132. **E-mail:** gcwalker@wisc.edu. **E-mail:** kadushin@wisc.edu. **Website:** uwpress.wisc.edu. **Contact:** Raphael Kadushin, senior acquisitions editor; Gwen Walker, acquisitions editor. Estab. 1937. Publishes hardcoveroriginals, paperback originals, and paperback reprints. Guidelines online.

HOW TO CONTACT Query with SASE or submit outline, 1-2 sample chapter(s), synopsis.

TERMS Pays royalty. Responds in 2 weeks to queries; 8 weeks to mss. Rarely comments on rejected mss.

TIPS "Make sure the query letter and sample text are well-written, and read guidelines carefully to make sure we accept the genre you are submitting."

USBORNE PUBLISHING

83-85 Saffron Hill, London En EC1N 8RT, United Kingdom. (44)207430-2800. **Fax:** (44)207430-1562. **E-mail:** mail@usborne.co.uk. **Website:** www.usborne.com. "Usborne Publishing is a multiple-award-winning, worldwide children's publishing company publishing almost every type of children's book for every age from baby to young adult."

NEEDS Young readers, middle readers: adventure, contemporary, fantasy, history, humor, multicultural, nature/environment, science fiction, suspense/mystery, strong concept-based or character-led series. Average word length: young readers—5,000-10,000; middle readers—25,000-50,000; young adult—50,000-100,000.

HOW TO CONTACT *Agented submissions only.*

TERMS Pays authors royalty.

TIPS "Do not send any original work and, sorry, but we cannot guarantee a reply."

VÉHICULE PRESS

P.O.B. 42094 BP Roy, Montreal QC H2W 2T3, Canada. (514)844-6073. **Fax:** (514)844-7543. **E-mail:** sd@vehiculepress.com. **E-mail:** admin@vehiculepress.com. **Website:** www.vehiculepress.com. **Contact:** Simon Dardick, nonfiction; Carmine Starnino, poetry; Dimitri Nasrallah, fiction. Estab. 1973. "Montreal's Véhicule Press has published the best of Canadian and Quebec literature-fiction, poetry, essays, translations, and social history." Publishes trade paperback originals by Canadian authors mostly. Book catalog for 9 x 12 SAE with IRCs.

IMPRINTS Signal Editions (poetry); Esplanade Editions (fiction).

NEEDS No romance or formula writing.

HOW TO CONTACT Query with SASE.

TERMS Pays 10-15% royalty on retail price. Pays $200-500 advance. Responds in 4 months to queries.

TIPS "Quality in almost any style is acceptable. We believe in the editing process."

VERTIGO

DC Universe, Vertigo-DC Comics, 1700 Broadway, New York NY 10019. **Website:** www.vertigocomics.com. At this time, DC Entertainment does not accept unsolicited artwork or writing submissions.

VIKING

Imprint of Penguin Group (USA), Inc., 375 Hudson St., New York NY 10014. (212)366-2000. **Website:** www.penguin.com. Estab. 1925. Viking publishes a mix of academic and popular fiction and nonfiction. Publishes hardcover and originals.

HOW TO CONTACT *Agented submissions only.*

TERMS Pays 10-15% royalty on retail price.

VILLARD BOOKS

Penguin Random House, 1745 Broadway, New York NY 10019. (212)572-2600. **Website:** www.penguinrandomhouse.com. Estab. 1983. "Villard Books is the publisher of savvy and sometimes quirky, best-selling hardcovers and trade paperbacks."

NEEDS Commercial fiction.

HOW TO CONTACT *Agented submissions only.*

TERMS Pays negotiable royalty. Pays negotiable advance.

VINTAGE ANCHOR PUBLISHING

Penguin Random House, 1745 Broadway, New York NY 10019. **Website:** www.penguinrandomhouse.com.

HOW TO CONTACT *Agented submissions only.*

TERMS Pays 4-8% royalty on retail price. Average advance: $2,500 and up.

VIVISPHERE PUBLISHING

675 Dutchess Turnpike, Poughkeepsie NY 12603. (845)463-1100, ext. 314. **Fax:** (845)463-0018. **E-mail:** cs@vivisphere.com. **Website:** www.vivisphere.com. **Contact:** Submissions. Estab. 1995. Vivisphere Publishing is now considering new submissions from any genre as follows: game of bridge (cards), nonfiction, history, military, new age, fiction, feminist/gay/lesbian, horror, contemporary, self-help, science fiction and cookbooks. Publishes trade paperback originals and reprints and e-books. Book catalog and ms guidelines online.

"Cookbooks should have a particular slant or appeal to a certain niche. Also publish out-of-print books."

HOW TO CONTACT Query with SASE.

TERMS Pays royalty. Responds in 6-24 months.

VIZ MEDIA LLC

P.O. Box 77010, San Francisco CA 94107. (415)546-7073. **Website:** www.viz.com. "VIZ Media, LLC is one of the most comprehensive and innovative companies in the field of manga (graphic novel) publishing, animation and entertainment licensing of Japanese content. Owned by three of Japan's largest creators and licensors of manga and animation, Shueisha Inc., Shogakukan Inc., and Shogakukan-Shueisha Productions, Co., Ltd., VIZ Media is a leader in the publishing and distribution of Japanese manga for English speaking audiences in North America, the United Kingdom, Ireland, and South Africa and is a global ex-Asia licensor of Japanese manga and animation. The company offers an integrated product line including magazines such as *Shonen Jump* and *Shojo Beat*, graphic novels, and DVDs, and develops, markets, licenses, and distributes animated entertainment for audiences and consumers of all ages."

HOW TO CONTACT "At the present, all of the manga that appears in our magazines come directly from manga that has been serialized and published in Japan."

WASHINGTON WRITERS' PUBLISHING HOUSE

P.O. Box 15271, Washington DC 20003. **E-mail:** wwphpress@gmail.com. **Website:** www.washingtonwriters.org. Estab. 1975. Guidelines online.

NEEDS Washington Writers' Publishing House considers book-length mss for publication by fiction writers living within 75 driving miles of the U.S. Capitol, Baltimore area included, through competition only. Mss may include previously published stories and excerpts. "Author should indicate where they heard about WWPH."

HOW TO CONTACT Submit an electronic copy by e-mail (use PDF, .doc, or rich text format) or 2 hard copies by snail mail of a short story collection or novel (no more than 350 pages, double or 1-1/2 spaced; author's name should not appear on any ms pages). Include separate page of publication acknowledgments plus 2 cover sheets: one with ms title, poet's name, address, telephone number, and e-mail address, the other with ms title only. Include SASE for results only; mss will not be returned (will be recycled).

TERMS Offers $1,000 and 50 copies of published book plus additional copies for publicity use.

WATERBROOK MULTNOMAH PUBLISHING GROUP

Penguin Random House, 12265 Oracle Blvd., Ste. 200, Colorado Springs CO 80921. (719)590-4999. **Fax:** (719)590-8977. **E-mail:** info@waterbrookmultnomah.com. **Website:** www.waterbrookmultnomah.com. Estab. 1996. Publishes hardcover and trade paperback originals. Book catalog online.

HOW TO CONTACT *Agented submissions only.*

TERMS Pays royalty. Responds in 2-3 months.

WHITAKER HOUSE

1030 Hunt Valley Circle, New Kensington PA 15068. **E-mail:** publisher@whitakerhouse.com. **Website:** www.whitakerhouse.com. **Contact:** Editorial Department. Estab. 1970. Publishes hardcover, trade paperback, and mass market originals. Book catalog online. Guidelines online.

NEEDS All fiction must have a Christian perspective.

HOW TO CONTACT Query with SASE.

TERMS Pays 5-15% royalty on wholesale price. Responds in 3 months.

TIPS "Audience includes those seeking uplifting and inspirational fiction and nonfiction."

WHITECAP BOOKS, LTD.

210 - 314 W. Cordova St., Vancouver BC V6B 1 E8, Canada. (604)681-6181. **Fax:** (905)477-9179. **E-mail:** steph@whitecap.ca. **Website:** www.whitecap.ca. "Whitecap Books is a general trade publisher with a focus on food and wine titles. Although we are interested in reviewing unsolicited ms submissions, please note that we only accept submissions that meet the needs of our current publishing program. Please see some of most recent releases to get an idea of the kinds of titles we are interested in." Publishes hardcover and trade paperback originals. Catalog and guidelines online.

NEEDS No children's picture books or adult fiction.

HOW TO CONTACT See guidelines.

TERMS Pays royalty. Pays negotiated advance. Responds in 2-3 months to proposals.

TIPS "We want well-written, well-researched material that presents a fresh approach to a particular topic."

WHITE MANE KIDS

73 W. Burd St., P.O. Box 708, Shippensburg PA 17257. (717)532-2237. **Fax:** (717)532-6110. **E-mail:** marketing@whitemane.com. **Website:** www.whitemane.com. **Contact:** Harold Collier, acquisitions editor. Estab. 1987. Book catalog and writer's guidelines available for SASE.

IMPRINTS White Mane Books, Burd Street Press, White Mane Kids, Ragged Edge Press.

NEEDS Middle readers, young adults: history (primarily American Civil War). Average word length: middle readers—30,000. Does not publish picture books.

HOW TO CONTACT Query.

TERMS Pays authors royalty of 7-10%. Pays illustrators and photographers by the project. Responds to queries in 1 month, mss in 6-9 months.

TIPS "Make your work historically accurate. We are interested in historically accurate fiction for middle and young adult readers. We do *not* publish picture books. Our primary focus is the American Civil War and some America Revolution topics."

WILD CHILD PUBLISHING

P.O. Box 4897, Culver City CA 90231. (310) 721-4461. **E-mail:** admin@wildchildpublishing.com. **Website:** www.wildchildpublishing.com. Estab. 1999. "We are known for working with newer/unpublished authors and editing to the standards of NYC publishers." Book catalogs on website.

NEEDS Multiple anthologies planned.

HOW TO CONTACT Query with outline/synopsis and 1 sample chapter. Accepts queries by e-mail only. Include estimated word count, brief bio. Often critiques/comments on rejected mss.

TERMS Pays royalties 10-40%. Responds in 1 month to queries and mss.

TIPS "Read our submission guidelines thoroughly. Send in entertaining, well-written stories. Be easy to work with and upbeat."

WILLIAM MORROW

HarperCollins, 195 Broadway, New York NY 10007. (212)207-7000. **Fax:** (212)207-7145. **Website:** www.harpercollins.com. Estab. 1926. "William Morrow publishes a wide range of titles that receive much recognition and prestige—a most selective house." Book catalog available free.

NEEDS Publishes adult fiction. Morrow accepts only the highest quality submissions in adult fiction. *No unsolicited mss or proposals.*

HOW TO CONTACT *Agented submissions only.*

TERMS Pays standard royalty on retail price. Pays varying advance.

WOODBINE HOUSE

6510 Bells Mill Rd., Bethesda MD 20817. (301)897-3570. **Fax:** (301)897-5838. **E-mail:** info@woodbinehouse.com. **Website:** www.woodbinehouse.com. **Contact:** Acquisitions Editor. Estab. 1985. Woodbine House publishes books for or about individuals with disabilities to help those individuals and their families live fulfilling and satisfying lives in their homes, schools, and communities. Publishes trade paperback originals. Guidelines online.

NEEDS Receptive to stories re: developmental and intellectual disabilities, e.g., autism and cerebral palsy.

HOW TO CONTACT Submit complete ms with SASE.

TERMS Pays 10-12% royalty. Responds in 3 months to queries.

TIPS "Do not send us a proposal on the basis of this description. Examine our catalog or website and a couple of our books to make sure you are on the right track. Put some thought into how your book could be marketed (aside from in bookstores). Keep cover letters concise and to the point; if it's a subject that interests us, we'll ask to see more."

WORLD WEAVER PRESS

Alpena Michigan 49707. **E-mail:** submissions@worldweaverpress.com. **Website:** www.worldweaverpress.com. **Contact:** WWP Editors. Estab. 2012. World Weaver Press publishes digital and print editions of speculative fiction at various lengths for adult, young adult, and new adult audiences. We believe in great storytelling. Catalog online. Guidelines online.

IMPRINTS **Red Moon Romance**, publishing sweet to erotic romances. Hot romance, it's what we do. Information at redmoonromance.com.

NEEDS "We believe that publishing speculative fiction isn't just printing words on the page — it's the act of weaving brand new worlds. Seeking speculative fiction in many varieties: protagonists who have strength, not fainting spells; intriguing worlds with well-developed settings; characters that are to die for (we'd rather find ourselves in love than just in lust)." Full list of interests on website. Does not want giant bugs, ghosts, post-apocalyptic and/or dystopia, angels, zombies, magical realism, surrealism, middle-grade (MG) or younger.

HOW TO CONTACT Query letter with first 5,000 words in body of e-mail. Queries accepted only during February and September annually, unless agented.

TERMS Average royalty rate of 39% net on all editions. No advance. Responds to query letters within 3 weeks. Responses to mss requests take longer.

TIPS "Use your letter to pitch us the story, not talk about its themes or inception."

O YELLOW SHOE FICTION SERIES

P.O. Box 25053, Baton Rouge LA 70894. **Website:** www.lsu.edu/lsupress. **Contact:** Michael Griffith, editor. Estab. 2004.

"Looking first and foremost for literary excellence, especially good mss that have fallen through the cracks at the big commercial presses. I'll cast a wide net."

HOW TO CONTACT Does not accept unsolicited mss. Accepts queries by mail, Attn: James W. Long.

TERMS Pays royalty. Offers advance.

YMAA PUBLICATION CENTER

P.O. Box 480, Wolfeboro NH 03894. (603)569-7988. **Fax:** (603)569-1889. **Website:** ymaa.com. **Contact:** David Ripianzi, director. Estab. 1982. YMAA publishes books on Chinese Chi Kung (Qigong), Taijiquan, (Tai Chi) and Asian martial arts. We are expanding our focus to include books on healing, wellness, meditation and subjects related to Asian culture and Asian medicine. Publishes trade paperback originals and reprints. Publishes 6-8 DVD titles/year. Book catalog online. Guidelines available free.

NEEDS "We are seeking mss that bring the venerated tradition of true Asian martial arts to readers. Your novel length ms should be a thrilling story that conveys insights into true martial techniques and philosophies."

TERMS Responds in 3 months to proposals.

TIPS "If you are submitting health-related material, please refer to an Asian tradition. Learn about author publicity options as your participation is mandatory."

ZEBRA BOOKS

Kensington, 119 W. 40th St., New York NY 10018. (212)407-1500. **E-mail:** esogah@kensingtonbooks.com. **Website:** www.kensingtonbooks.com. **Contact:** Esi Sogah, senior editor. Zebra Books is dedicated to women's fiction, which includes, but is not limited to romance. Publishes hardcover originals, trade paperback and mass market paperback originals and reprints. Book catalog online.

HOW TO CONTACT Query.

ZUMAYA PUBLICATIONS, LLC

3209 S. Interstate 35, Austin TX 78741. (512)537-3145. **Fax:** (512)276-6745. **E-mail:** business@zumayapublishing.com. **E-mail:** acquisitions@zumayapublications.com. **Website:** www.zumayapublications.com. **Contact:** Rie Sheridan Rose, acquisitions editor. Estab. 1999. Zumaya Publications is a digitally-based micropress publishing mainly in on-demand trade paperback and e-book formats. "We currently offer approximately 190 fiction titles in the mystery, SF/F, historical, romance, LGBTQ, horror, and occult genres in adult, young adult, and middle reader categories. In 2016, we plan to officially launch our graphic and illustrated novel imprint, Zumaya Fabled Ink. We publish approximately 10-15 new titles annually, at least five of which are from new authors. We do not publish erotica or graphic erotic romance at this time. We accept only electronic queries; all others will be discarded unread. A working knowledge of computers and relevant software is a necessity, as our production process is completely digital." Publishes trade paperback and electronic originals and reprints. Guidelines online.

IMPRINTS Zumaya Arcane (New Age, inspirational fiction & nonfiction), Zumaya Boundless (GLBTQ); Zumaya Embraces (romance/women's fiction); Zumaya Enigma (mystery/suspense/thriller); Zumaya Thresholds (young adult/middle-grade); Zumaya Otherworlds (SF/F/H), Zumaya Yesterdays (memoirs, historical fiction, fiction, western fiction); Zumaya Fabled Ink (graphic and illustrated novels).

NEEDS "We are open to all genres, particularly GLBT and young adult/middle-grade, historical and western, New Age/inspirational (no overtly Christian materials, please), noncategory romance, thrillers. We encourage people to review what we've already published so as to avoid sending us more of the same, at least, insofar as the plot is concerned. While we're always looking for good mysteries, especially cozies, mysteries with historical settings, and police procedurals, we want original concepts rather than slightly altered versions of what we've already published. We do not publish erotica or graphically erotic romance at this time." Does not want erotica, graphically erotic romance, experimental, literary (unless it fits into one of our established imprints).

HOW TO CONTACT A copy of our rules of submission is posted on our website and can be downloaded. They are rules rather than guidelines and should be read carefully before submitting. It will save everyone time and frustration.

TERMS Pay 20% of net on paperbacks, net defined as cover price less printing and other associated costs; 50% of net on all e-books. Does not pay advance. Responds in 3 months to queries and proposals; 6 months to mss.

TIPS "We're catering to readers who may have loved last year's best seller but not enough to want to read 10 more just like it. Have something different. If it does not fit standard pigeonholes, that's a plus. On the other hand, it has to have an audience. And if you're not prepared to work with us on promotion and marketing, particularly via social media, it would be better to look elsewhere."

CONTESTS & AWARDS

In addition to honors and, quite often, cash prizes, contests and awards programs offer writers the opportunity to be judged on the basis of quality alone, without the outside factors that sometimes influence publishing decisions. New writers who win contests may be published for the first time, while more experienced writers may gain public recognition for an entire body of work.

Listed here are contests for almost every type of fiction writing. Some focus on form, such as short stories, novels, or novellas, while others feature writing on particular themes or topics. Still others are prestigious prizes or awards for work that must be nominated.

SELECTING AND SUBMITTING TO A CONTEST

Use the same care in submitting to contests as you would sending your manuscript to a publication or book publisher. Deadlines are very important, and, where possible, we've included this information. For some contests, deadlines were only approximate at our press deadline, so be sure to write, call, or look online for complete information.

Follow the rules to the letter. If, for instance, contest rules require your name on a cover sheet only, you will be disqualified if you ignore this and put your name on every page. Find out how many copies to send. If you don't send the correct amount, by the time you are contacted to send more, it may be past the submission deadline. An increasing number of contests invite writers to query by e-mail, and many post contest information on their websites. Check listings for e-mail and website addresses.

One note of caution: Beware of contests that charge entry fees that are disproportionate to the amount of the prize. Contests offering a $10 prize and charging $7 in entry fees are a waste of your time and money.

24-HOUR SHORT STORY CONTEST

5726 Cortez Rd. W., #349, Bradenton FL 34210. 305-768-0261. **Fax:** 305-768-0261. **E-mail:** writersweekly@writersweekly.com. **Website:** www.writersweekly.com/misc/contest.php. **Contact:** Angela Hoy. Popular quarterly contest in which registered entrants receive a topic at start time (usually noon CST) and have 24 hours to write and submit a story on that topic. All submissions must be returned via e-mail. Each contest is limited to 500 people. Upon entry, entrant will receive guidelines and details on competition, including submission process. Deadline: Quarterly—see website for dates. Prize: 1st Place: $300; 2nd Place: $250; 3rd Place: $200. There are also 20 honorable mentions and 60 door prizes (randomly drawn from all participants). The top 3 winners' entries are posted on writersweekly.com (nonexclusive electronic rights only) and receive a Freelance Income Kit. Writers retain all rights to their work. See website for full details on prizes. Costs: $5. Judged by Angela Hoy (publisher of writersweekly.com and booklocker.com).

AEON AWARD

Albedo One/Aeon Press, Aeon Award, Albedo One, 2 Post Road, Lusk, Dublin , Ireland. +353 1 8730177. **E-mail:** fraslaw@yahoo.co.uk. **Website:** www.albedo1.com. **Contact:** Frank Ludlow, event coordinator. Estab. 2004. Prestigious fiction writing competition for short stories in any speculative fiction genre, such as fantasy, science fiction, horror, or anything in-between or unclassifiable. Deadline: November 30. Contest begins January 1. Prize: Grand Prize: €1,000; 2nd Prize: €200; and 3rd Prize: €100. The top three stories are guaranteed publication in *Albedo One*. Costs: €7.50. Judged by Ian Watson, Eileen Gunn, Todd McCaffrey, and Michael Carroll.

AESTHETICA ART PRIZE

Aesthetica Magazine, P.O. Box 371, York YO23 1WL, United Kingdom. **E-mail:** info@aestheticamagazine.com; artprize@aestheticamagazine.com. **Website:** www.aestheticamagazine.com. The Aesthetica Art Prize is a celebration of excellence in art from across the world and offers artists the opportunity to showcase their work to wider audiences and further their involvement in the international art world. There are 4 categories: Photograpic & Digital Art, Three Dimensional Design & Sculpture, Painting & Drawing, Video Installation & Performance. See guidelines at www.aestheticamagazine.com. Deadline: August 31. Prizes: £5,000 main prize courtesy of Hiscox, £1,000 Student Prize courtesy of Hiscox, group exhibition, and publication in the Aesthetica Art Prize Anthology. Entry is £15 and permits submission of 2 works in 1 category. Costs: £10 each category.

AHWA FLASH & SHORT STORY COMPETITION

AHWA (Australian Horror Writers Association), **E-mail:** ahwacomps@australianhorror.com; ahwa@australianhorror.com. **E-mail:** ctrost@hotmail.com. **Website:** www.australianhorror.com. **Contact:** Cameron Trost, competitions officer. Competition/award for short stories and flash fiction. Looking for horror stories, tales that frighten, yarns that unsettle readers in their comfortable homes. All themes in this genre will be accepted, from the well used (zombies, vampires, ghosts, etc.) to the highly original, so long as the story is professional and well written. Deadline: May 31. Prize: The authors of the winning Flash Fiction and Short Story entries will each receive paid publication in *Midnight Echo*, the magazine of the AHWA, and an engraved plaque. Costs: $5 for flash fiction, $10 for short story; free for AHWA members.

ALABAMA STATE COUNCIL ON THE ARTS INDIVIDUAL ARTIST FELLOWSHIP

201 Monroe St., Montgomery AL 36130. (334)242-4076, ext. 236. **Fax:** (334)240-3269. **E-mail:** anne.kimzey@arts.alabama.gov. **Website:** www.arts.state.al.us. **Contact:** Anne Kimzey, literature program manager. Recognizes the achievements and potential of Alabama writers. Deadline: March 1. Applications must be submitted online by eGRANT. Costs: No entry fee. Judged by independent peer panel. Winners notified by mail and announced on website in June.

MARIE ALEXANDER POETRY SERIES

English Department, 2801 S. University Ave., Little Rock AR 72204. **E-mail:** editor@mariealexanderseries.com. **Website:** mariealexanderseries.com. **Contact:** Nickole Brown. Annual contest for a collection of previously unpublished prose poems or flash fiction by a U.S. writer. Deadline: July 31. Open to submissions on July 1. Prize: $1,000, plus publication.

ALLIGATOR JUNIPER AWARD

Alligator Juniper/Prescott College, 220 Grove Ave., Prescott AZ 86301. (928)350-2012. **Fax:** (928)776-5102. **E-mail:** alligatorjuniper@prescott.edu. **Website:** www.prescott.edu/alligatorjuniper/national-contest/index.html. **Contact:** Skye Anicca, managing editor. Annual contest for unpublished fiction, creative nonfiction, and poetry. Open to all age levels. Each entrant receives a personal letter from staff regarding the status of their submission, as well as minor feedback on the piece. Deadline: October 1. Prize: $1,000, plus publication in all 3 categories. Finalists in each genre are recognized as such, published, and paid in copies. Costs: $15. Judged by the distinguished writers in each genre and Prescott College writing students enrolled in the Literary Journal Practicum course.

AMERICAN ASSOCIATION OF UNIVERSITY WOMEN AWARD IN JUVENILE LITERATURE

4610 Mail Service Center, Raleigh NC 27699-4610. (919)807-7290. **E-mail:** michael.hill@ncdcr.gov. **Website:** www.ncdcr.gov. **Contact:** Michael Hill, awards coordinator. Annual award. Book must be published during the year ending June 30. Submissions made by author, author's agent, or publisher. SASE for contest rules. Recognizes the year's best work of juvenile literature by a North Carolina resident. Deadline: July 15. Prize: Awards a cup to the winner and winner's name inscribed on a plaque displayed within the North Carolina Office of Archives and History. Judged by three-judge panel.

Competition receives 10-15 submissions per category.

THE AMERICAN GEM LITERARY FESTIVAL

FilmMakers Magazine/Write Brothers, FilmMakers Magazine (filmmakers.com), **E-mail:** info@filmmakers.com. **Website:** filmmakers.com/contests/short_story. **Contact:** Jennifer Brooks. Estab. 2004. Worldwide contest to recognize excellent short screenplays and short stories. Deadlines: Early—February 29; Regular—April 30; Late—June 30; Final—July 31. Prize: Short Script: 1st Place: $1,000. Other cash and prizes to top 5. Costs: Ranges from $19-59, based on number of pages, entry type. Full details via website.

AMERICAN LITERARY REVIEW CONTESTS

American Literary Review, P.O. Box 311307, University of North Texas, Denton TX 76203-1307. (940)565-2755. **E-mail:** americanliteraryreview@gmail.com. **Website:** www.americanliteraryreview.com. Contest to award excellence in short fiction, creative nonfiction, and poetry. Multiple entries are acceptable, but each entry must be accompanied with a reading fee. Do not put any identifying information in the file; include the author's name, title(s), address, e-mail address, and phone number in the boxes provided in the online submissions manager. Short fiction: Limit 8,000 words per work. Creative nonfiction: Limit 6,500 words per work. Deadline: October 1. Submission period begins June 1. Prize: $1,000 prize for each category, along with publication in the Spring online issue of the *American Literary Review*. Costs: $15 reading fee for 1 short story, 1 creative nonfiction entry, or up to 3 poems.

O AMERICAN MARKETS NEWSLETTER SHORT STORY COMPETITION

1974 46th Ave., San Francisco CA 94116. **E-mail:** sheila.oconnor@juno.com. Award is to give short story writers more exposure. Contest offered biannually. Open to any writer. All kinds of fiction are considered. Especially looking for women's pieces—romance, with a twist in the tale—but all will be considered. Results announced within 3 months of deadlines. Winners notified by mail if they include SASE. Deadline: June 30 and December 31. Prize: 1st Place: $300; 2nd Place: $100; 3rd Place: $50. Costs: $15 per entry; $25 for 2; $30 for 3. Judged by a panel of independent judges.

AMERICAN-SCANDINAVIAN FOUNDATION TRANSLATION PRIZE

The American-Scandinavian Foundation, 58 Park Ave., New York NY 10016. (212)779-3587. **E-mail:** grants@amscan.org; info@amscan.org. **Website:** www.amscan.org. **Contact:** Matthew Walters, director of fellowships and grants. The annual ASF translation competition is awarded for the most outstanding translations of poetry, fiction, drama, or literary prose written by a Scandinavian author born after 1800. Deadline: June 1. Prize: The Nadia Christensen Prize includes a $2,500 award, publication of an excerpt in *Scandinavian Review*, and a commemorative bronze medallion. The Leif and Inger Sjöberg Award, given to an individual whose literature translations have not previously been published, includes a $2,000 award, publication of an excerpt in *Scandinavian Review*, and a commemorative bronze medallion.

SHERWOOD ANDERSON FICTION AWARD

Mid-American Review, Dept. of English, Box WM, BGSU, Bowling Green OH 43403. (419)372-2725. **Fax:** (419)372-4642. **E-mail:** mar@bgsu.edu. **Website:** www.bgsu.edu/midamericanreview. **Contact:** Abigail

Cloud, editor in chief. Offered annually for unpublished mss (6,000-word limit). Contest is open to all writers not associated with a judge or *Mid-American Review*. Deadline: November 1. Prize: $1,000, plus publication in the spring issue of *Mid-American Review*. Four Finalists: Notation, possible publication. Costs: $10. Judged by editors and a well-known writer, i.e., Aimee Bender or Anthony Doerr.

THE SHERWOOD ANDERSON FOUNDATION FICTION AWARD

12330 Ashton Mill Terrace, Glen Allen VA 23059. **E-mail:** sherwoodandersonfoundation@gmail.com. **Website:** www.sherwoodandersonfoundation.org. **Contact:** Anna McKean, foundation president. Estab. 1988. Contest is to honor, preserve, and celebrate the memory and literary work of Sherwood Anderson, American realist for the first half of the 20th century. Annual award supports developing writers of short stories and novels. Deadline: April 1. Prize: $20,000 grant award. Costs: $100 application fee (payable to Sherwood Anderson Foundation).

ARROWHEAD REGIONAL ARTS COUNCIL INDIVIDUAL ARTIST CAREER DEVELOPMENT GRANT

Arrowhead Regional Arts Council, 600 E. Superior St., Suite 404, Duluth MN 55802. (218)722-0952 or (800)569-8134. **E-mail:** info@aracouncil.org. **Website:** www.aracouncil.org. Award is to provide financial support to regional artists wishing to take advantage of impending, concrete opportunities that will advance their work or careers. Deadline: October and April. Grant awards of up to $3,000. Candidates are reviewed by a panel of ARAC Board Members and Community Artists.

ART AFFAIR SHORT STORY AND WESTERN SHORT STORY CONTESTS

Art Affair—Contest, P.O. Box 54302, Oklahoma City OK 73154. **E-mail:** artaffair@aol.com. **Website:** www.shadetreecreations.com. Estab. 2003. The annual Art Affair Writing Contests include (General) Short Story and Western Short Story categories. Open to any writer. All short stories must be unpublished. Multiple entries accepted in both categories with separate entry fees for each. Submit original stories on any subject and time frame for general Short Story category, and submit original western stories for Western Short Story—word limit for all entries is 5,000 words. Guidelines available on website. Deadline: October 1. Prize (in both categories): 1st Place: $50; 2nd Place: $25; 3rd Place: $15. Costs: $5/per story.

Stories must be unpublished at time of entry. Entries may be mailed together.

ARTIST TRUST FELLOWSHIP AWARD

1835 12th Ave., Seattle WA 98122. (209)467-8734, ext. 11. **Fax:** (866)218-7878. **E-mail:** info@artisttrust.org. **Website:** www.artisttrust.org. **Contact:** Miguel Guillen, program manager. Fellowships award $7,500 to practicing professional artists of exceptional talent and demonstrated ability. The Fellowship is merit-based, not project-based. Recipients present a Meet the Artist Event to a community in Washington state that has little or no access to the artist and their work. Awards 14 fellowships of $7,500 and 2 residencies with $1,000 stipends at the Millay Colony. Deadline: January 13. Applications available December 3. Prize: $7,500.

ARTS & LETTERS PRIZES

Arts & Letters Journal of Contemporary Culture, Campus Box 89, GC&SU, Milledgeville GA 31061. (478)445-1289. **E-mail:** al.journal@gcsu.edu. **Website:** al.gcsu.edu. **Contact:** The Editors. Offered annually for unpublished work. Deadline: March 31. Prize: $1,000 prize for each of the 4 major genres. Fiction, poetry, and creative nonfiction winners are published in Fall or Spring issue. The prize-winning one-act play is produced at the Georgia College campus (usually in March). Costs: $20/entry (payable to GC&SU). Judged by the editors (initial screening); see website for final judges and further details about submitting work.

THE ATHENAEUM LITERARY AWARD

The Athenaeum of Philadelphia, 219 S. Sixth St., Philadelphia PA 19106-3794. (215)925-2688. **Fax:** (215)925-3755. **E-mail:** jilly@PhilaAthenaeum.org. **Website:** www.PhilaAthenaeum.org. **Contact:** Jill Lee, Librarian. Estab. 1950. The Athenaeum Literary Award was established to recognize and encourage literary achievement among authors who are bona fide residents of Philadelphia or Pennsylvania living within a radius of 30 miles of City Hall at the time their book was written or published. Any volume of general literature is eligible; technical, scientific, and juvenile books are not included. Nominated works are reviewed on the basis of their significance and importance to the general public as well as for literary excellence. Deadline: December 31.

ATLANTIC WRITING COMPETITION FOR UNPUBLISHED MANUSCRIPTS

Writers' Federation of Nova Scotia, 1113 Marginal Rd., Halifax NS B3H 4P7. (902)423-8116. **Fax:** (902)422-0881. **E-mail:** programs@writers.ns.ca. **Website:** www.writers.ns.ca. **Contact:** Robin Spittal, communications and development officer. Estab. 1975. Annual program designed to honor work by unpublished writers in all 4 Atlantic Provinces. Entry is open to writers unpublished in the category of writing they wish to enter. Prizes are presented in the fall of each year. Categories include novel, writing for children, poetry, short story, juvenile/young adult novel, creative nonfiction, and play. Judges return written comments when competition is concluded. Deadline: January 7. Prizes vary based on categories. See website for details. Costs: $35 fee for novel ($30 for WFNS members); $25 fee for all other categories ($20 for WFNS members).

AUTUMN HOUSE FICTION PRIZE

Autumn House Press, 87½ Westwood St., Pittsburgh PA 15211. **E-mail:** info@autumnhouse.org. **Website:** autumnhouse.org. Fiction submissions should be approximately 200-300 pages. All fiction subgenres (short stories, short shorts, novellas, or novels), or any combination of subgenres, are eligible. All finalists will be considered for publication. Deadline: June 30. Prize: Winners will receive book publication, $1,000 advance against royalties, and a $1,500 travel grant to participate in the Autumn House Master Authors Series in Pittsburgh. Costs: $30. Judged by William Lychack (final judge).

AUTUMN HOUSE POETRY, FICTION, AND NONFICTION PRIZES

P.O. Box 60100, Pittsburgh PA 15211. (412)381-4261. **E-mail:** gcerto@autumhouse.org; info@autumnhouse.org. **Website:** autumnhouse.org; autumnhousepress.submittable.com/submit. **Contact:** Christine Stroud, senior editor. Estab. 1998. Offers annual prize and publication of book-length ms with national promotion. Submission must be unpublished as a collection, but individual poems, stories, and essays may have been previously published elsewhere. Considers simultaneous submissions. "Autumn House is a nonprofit corporation with the mission of publishing and promoting poetry and other fine literature. We have published books by Chana Bloch, Ellery Akers, Gerald Stern, Ruth L. Schwartz, Ed Ochester, Andrea Hollander, George Bilgere, Ada Limon, and many others." Deadline: June 30. Prize: The winner (in each of 3 categories) will receive book publication, $1,000 advance against royalties, and a $1,500 travel/publicity grant to promote his or her book. Costs: $30/ms. Judged by David St. John(poetry), William Lychack (fiction), and Michael Martone (nonfiction).

AWP AWARD SERIES

Association of Writers & Writing Programs, George Mason University, 4400 University Dr., MSN 1E3, Fairfax VA 22030. **E-mail:** supriya@awpwriter.org. **Website:** www.awpwriter.org. **Contact:** Supriya Bhatnagar, director of publications. AWP sponsors the Award Series, an annual competition for the publication of excellent new book-length works. The competition is open to all authors writing in English regardless of nationality or residence, and is available to published and unpublished authors alike. Offered annually to foster new literary talent. Deadline: Postmarked between January 1 and February 28. Prize: AWP Prize for the Novel: $2,500 and publication by New Issues Press; Donald Hall Prize for Poetry: $5,500 and publication by the University of Pittsburgh Press; Grace Paley Prize in Short Fiction: $5,500 and publication by the University of Massachusetts Press; and AWP Prize for Creative Nonfiction: $2,500 and publication by the University of Georgia Press. Costs: $30 for nonmembers, $20 for members.

BALCONES FICTION PRIZE

Austin Commmunity College, Department of Creative Writing, 1212 Rio Grande St., Austin TX 78701. (512)584-5045. **E-mail:** joconne@austincc.edu. **Website:** www.austincc.edu/crw/html/balconescenter.html. **Contact:** Joe O'Connell. Awarded to the best book of literary fiction published the previous year. Books of prose may be submitted by publisher or author. Send 3e copies. Deadline: January 31. Prize: $1,500, winner is flown to Austin for a campus reading. Costs: $30 reading fee.

THE BALTIMORE REVIEW CONTESTS

The Baltimore Review, 6514 Maplewood Rd., Baltimore MD 21212. **E-mail:** editor@baltimorereview.org. **Website:** www.baltimorereview.org. **Contact:** Barbara Westwood Diehl, senior editor. Estab. 1996. Each Summer and Winter issue includes a contest theme (see submissions guidelines for theme). Prizes are awarded for 1st, 2nd, and 3rd place among all categories—poetry, short stories, and creative nonfiction.

All entries are considered for publication. Deadline: May 31 and November 30. Prize: 1st Place: $500; 2nd Place: $200; 3rd Place: $100. All entries are considered for publication. Provides a small compensation to all contributors. Costs: $10 entry fee. Judged by the editors of *The Baltimore Review* and a guest final judge.

BARD FICTION PRIZE

Bard College, P.O. Box 5000, Annandale-on-Hudson NY 12504-5000. (845)758-7087. **Fax:** (845)758-7917. **E-mail:** bfp@bard.edu. **Website:** www.bard.edu/bfp. **Contact:** Irene Zedlacher. Estab. 2001. The Bard Fiction Prize is awarded to a promising, emerging writer who is an American citizen aged 39 years or younger at the time of application. The Bard Fiction Prize is intended to encourage and support young writers of fiction to pursue their creative goals and to provide an opportunity to work in a fertile and intellectual environment. Deadline: June 15. Prize: $30,000 and appointment as writer-in-residence at Bard College for 1 semester. Judged by a committee of 5 judges (authors associated with Bard College).

MILDRED L. BATCHELDER AWARD

50 E. Huron St., Chicago IL 60611-2795. **Website:** www.ala.org/alsc/awardsgrants. Estab. 1966. The Batchelder Award is given to the most outstanding children's book originally published in a language other than English in a country other than the U.S., and subsequently translated into English for publication in the U.S. The purpose of the award, a citation to an American publisher, is to encourage international exchange of quality children's books by recognizing U.S. publishers of such books in translation. Deadline: December 31.

BELLEVUE LITERARY REVIEW GOLDENBERG PRIZE FOR FICTION

Bellevue Literary Review, NYU Dept of Medicine, 550 First Ave., OBV-A612, New York NY 10016. (212)263-3973. **E-mail:** info@blreview.org; stacy@blreview.org. **Website:** www.blreview.org. **Contact:** Stacy Bodziak, managing editor. The *BLR* prizes award outstanding writing related to themes of health, healing, illness, the mind, and the body. Annual competition/award for short stories. Receives about 200-300 entries per category. Send credit card information or make checks payable to *Bellevue Literary Review*. Guidelines available in February. Accepts inquiries by e-mail, phone, mail. Submissions open in February. Results announced in December and made available to entrants with SASE, by e-mail, on website. Winners notified by mail or e-mail. Deadline: July 1. Prize: $1,000 and publication in *The Bellevue Literary Review*. Honorable mention winners receive $250 and publication. Costs: $20, or $30 to include one-year subscription. *BLR* editors select semifinalists to be read by an independent judge who chooses the winner. Previous judges include Nathan Englander, Jane Smiley, Francine Prose, and Andre Dubus III.

O GEORGE BENNETT FELLOWSHIP

Phillips Exeter Academy, 20 Main St., Exeter NH 03833. **E-mail:** teaching_opportunities@exeter.edu. **Website:** www.exeter.edu/bennettfellowship. Annual award for fellow and family to provide time and freedom from material considerations to a person seriously contemplating or pursuing a career as a writer. Applicants should have a ms in progress which they intend to complete during the fellowship period. Ms should be fiction, nonfiction, novel, short stories, or poetry. Duties: to be in residency at the Academy for the academic year; to make oneself available informally to students interested in writing. Committee favors writers who have not yet published a book with a major publisher. Deadline: November 30. A choice will be made and all entrants notified in mid-April. Prize: Cash stipend (currently $14,933), room and board. Costs: $15 application fee. Application form and guidelines on website. Judged by committee of the English department.

BINGHAMTON UNIVERSITY JOHN GARDNER FICTION BOOK AWARD

Creative Writing Program, Binghamton University, Binghamton University, Department of English, General Literature, and Rhetoric, Library North Room 1149, P.O. Box 6000, Binghamton NY 13902-6000. (607)777-2713. **E-mail:** cwpro@binghamton.edu. **Website:** binghamton.edu/english/creative-writing. **Contact:** Maria Mazziotti Gillan, director. Estab. 2001. Contest offered annually for a novel or collection of fiction published in previous year in a press run of 500 copies or more. Each book submitted must be accompanied by an application form. Publisher may submit more than 1 book for prize consideration. Send 2 copies of each book. Guidelines available on website. Deadline: March 1. Prize: $1,000. Judged by a professional writer not on Binghamton University faculty.

JAMES TAIT BLACK MEMORIAL PRIZES

University of Edinburgh, School of Literatures, Languages, and Cultures, 50 George Square, Edinburgh EH8 9LH, Scotland. (44-13)1650-3619. **E-mail:** s.strathdee@ed.ac.uk. **Website:** www.ed.ac.uk/news/events/tait-black. Estab. 1919. Open to any writer. Entries must be previously published. Winners notified by phone via publisher. Contact department of English Literature for list of winners, or check website. Accepts inquiries by e-mail or phone. Deadline: December 1. Prize: Two prizes each of £10,000 are awarded: 1 for the best work of fiction, 1 for the best biography or work of that nature, published during the calendar year January 1-December 31. Judged by professors of English Literature with the assistance of teams of postgraduate readers.

THE BLACK RIVER CHAPBOOK COMPETITION

Black Lawrence Press, 326 Bingham St., Pittsburgh PA 15211. **E-mail:** editors@blacklawrencepress.com. **Website:** www.blacklawrence.com. **Contact:** Kit Frick, senior editor. Twice each year Black Lawrence Press will run the Black River Chapbook Competition for an unpublished chapbook of poems or short fiction, 16-36 pages in length. Spring deadline: May 31. Fall deadline: October 31. Prize: $500, publication, and 10 copies. Costs: $15. Judged by a revolving panel of judges, in addition to the Chapbook Editor and other members of the BLP editorial staff.

THE BOARDMAN TASKER PRIZE FOR MOUNTAIN LITERATURE

The Boardman Tasker Charitable Trust, 8 Bank View Rd., Darley Abbey Derby DE22 1EJ, UK. 01332 342246. **E-mail:** steve@people-matter.co.uk. **Website:** www.boardmantasker.com. **Contact:** Steve Dean. Offered annually to reward a work with a mountain theme, whether fiction, nonfiction, drama, or poetry, written in the English language (initially or in translation). Subject must be concerned with a mountain environment. Previous winners have been books on expeditions, climbing experiences, a biography of a mountaineer, novels. Guidelines available in January by e-mail or on website. Entries must be previously published. Open to any writer. The award is to honor Peter Boardman and Joe Tasker, who disappeared on Everest in 1982. Deadline: August 1. Prize: £3,000. Judged by a panel of 3 judges elected by trustees.

THE BOSTON AUTHORS CLUB BOOK AWARDS

The Boston Authors Club, 33 Brayton Rd., Brighton MA 02135. (617)783-1357. **E-mail:** alan.lawson@bc.edu. **Website:** www.bostonauthorsclub.org. **Contact:** Alan Lawson, president. Julia Ward Howe Prize offered annually in the spring for books published the previous year. Two awards are given: 1 for adult books of fiction, nonfiction, or poetry, and 1 for children's books, middle grade, and young adult novels, nonfiction, or poetry. No picture books or subsidized publishers. There must be 2 copies of each book submitted. Deadline: January 15. Prize: $1,000 in each category. Several books will also be cited with no cash awards as Finalists or Highly Recommended. Costs: $25/title.

BOSTON GLOBE-HORN BOOK AWARDS

The Boston Globe, Horn Book, Inc., 300 The Fenway, Palace Road Building, Suite P-311, Boston MA 02115. (617)278-0225. **Fax:** (617)278-6062. **E-mail:** info@hbook.com; khedeen@hbook.com. **Website:** hbook.com/bghb. **Contact:** Katrina Hedeen. Estab. 1967. Offered annually for excellence in literature for children and young adults (published June 1-May 31). Categories: picture book, fiction and poetry, nonfiction. Judges may also name up to 2 honor books in each category. Books must be published in the U.S., but may be written or illustrated by citizens of any country. *The Horn Book Magazine* publishes speeches given at awards ceremonies. Guidelines for SASE or online. Deadline: May 15. Prize: $500 and an engraved silver bowl; honor book recipients receive an engraved silver plate. Judged by a panel of 3 judges selected each year.

BOULEVARD SHORT FICTION CONTEST FOR EMERGING WRITERS

Boulevard Magazine, 6614 Clayton Rd., PMB #325, Richmond Heights MO 63117. (314)862-2643. **Website:** www.boulevardmagazine.org. **Contact:** Jessica Rogen, editor. Estab. 1985. Offered annually for unpublished short fiction to a writer who has not yet published a book of fiction, poetry, or creative nonfiction with a nationally distributed press. Holds first North American rights on anything not previously published. Open to any writer with no previous publication by a nationally known press. Guidelines for SASE or on website. Deadline: December 31. Prize: $1,500, and publication in 1 of the next year's issues.

Costs: $15 fee/story, includes one-year subscription to *Boulevard.*

THE BRIAR CLIFF REVIEW FICTION, POETRY, AND CREATIVE NONFICTION COMPETITION

The Briar Cliff Review, Briar Cliff University, 3303 Rebecca St., Sioux City IA 51104-0100. **E-mail:** tricia.currans-sheehan@briarcliff.edu (editor); jeanne.emmons@briarcliff.edu (poetry). **Website:** www.bcreview.org. **Contact:** Tricia Currans-Sheehan, editor. *The Briar Cliff Review* sponsors an annual contest offering $1,000 and publication to each 1st Prize winner in fiction, poetry, and creative nonfiction. Previous year's winner and former students of editors ineligible. Winning pieces accepted for publication on the basis of first-time rights. Considers simultaneous submissions, "but notify us immediately upon acceptance elsewhere. We guarantee a considerate reading." No mss returned. Award to reward good writers and showcase quality writing. Deadline: November 1. Prize: $1,000 and publication to each 1st Prize winner in fiction, poetry, and creative nonfiction. Costs: $20 per story/creative nonfiction piece or 3 poems. Judged by *Briar Cliff Review* editors.

THE BRIDPORT PRIZE

P.O. Box 6910, Dorset DT6 9QB, United Kingdom. **E-mail:** info@bridportprize.org.uk; kate@bridportprize.org.uk. **Website:** www.bridportprize.org.uk. **Contact:** Kate Wilson, Bridport Prize administrator. Estab. 1973. Award to promote literary excellence, discover new talent. Categories: short stories, poetry, flash fiction, first novel. Deadline: May 31 each year. Open for submissions starting November 15. Prize: £5,000; £1,000; £500; various runners-up prizes and publication of approximately 13 best stories and 13 best poems in anthology, plus 6 best flash fiction stories. 1st Prize of £1,000 for the best short short story under 250 words. £1,000 plus up to a year's mentoring for winner of Peggy Chapman-Andrews Award for a first novel. Costs: £9 for poems, £10 for short stories, £8 for flash fiction, and £20 for novels. Judged by 1 judge for short stories (in 2016, Tessa Hadley), 1 judge for poetry (in 2016, Patience Agbabi) and 1 judge for flash fiction (in 2016, Tim Stevenson). The Novel award is judged by a group comprising representatives from The Literary Consultancy, A.M. Heath Literary Agents, and (in 2016) judge Kerry Young.

BRITISH CZECH AND SLOVAK ASSOCIATION WRITING COMPETITION

24 Ferndale, Tunbridge Wells Kent TN2 3NS, England. **E-mail:** prize@bcsa.co.uk. **Website:** www.bcsa.co.uk/specials.html. Estab. 2002. Annual contest for original writing (entries should be 1,500-2,000 words) in English on the links between Britain and the Czech/Slovak Republics, or describing society in transition in the Republics since 1989. Entries can be fact or fiction. Topics can include history, politics, the sciences, economics, the arts, or literature. Deadline: June 30. Winners announced in November. Prize: 1st Place: £300; 2nd Place: £100.

THE RBC BRONWEN WALLACE AWARD FOR EMERGING WRITERS

The Writers' Trust of Canada, 460 Richmond St. W., Suite 600, Toronto ON M5C 1P1, Canada. (416)504-8222. **Fax:** (416)504-9090. **E-mail:** info@writerstrust.com. **Website:** www.writerstrust.com. **Contact:** Amanda Hopkins. Presented annually to a Canadian writer under the age of 35 who is not yet published in book form. The award, which alternates each year between poetry and short fiction, was established in memory of Bronwen Wallace. Deadline: March 7. Prize: $5,000. Two finalists receive $1,000 each.

BURNABY WRITERS' SOCIETY CONTEST

E-mail: info@bws.ca. **Website:** www.bws.ca; www.burnabywritersnews.blogspot.com. **Contact:** Contest Committee. Offered annually for unpublished work. Open to all residents of British Columbia. Categories vary from year to year. Send SASE for current rules. For complete guidelines see website or burnabywritersnews.blogspot.com. Purpose is to encourage talented writers in all genres. Deadline: May 31. Prizes: 1st Place: $200; 2nd Place: $100; 3rd Place: $50; and public reading. Costs: $5/entry, or 3 entries for $10.

THE CAINE PRIZE FOR AFRICAN WRITING

51 Southwark St., London SE1 1RU, United Kingdom. **E-mail:** info@caineprize.com. **Website:** www.caineprize.com. **Contact:** Lizzy Attree. Estab. 1999. Entries must have appeared for the first time in the 5 years prior to the closing date for submissions, which is January 31 each year. Publishers should submit 6 copies of the published original with a brief cover note (no pro forma application). "Please indicate nationality or passport held." The Caine Prize is open to writers

from anywhere in Africa for work published in English. Its focus is on the short story, reflecting the contemporary development of the African story-telling tradition. Deadline: January 31. Prize: £10,000.

CALIFORNIA BOOK AWARDS

Commonwealth Club of California, 555 Post Street, San Francisco CA 94102, USA. (415) 597-6700. **Fax:** (415)597-6729. **E-mail:** bookawards@commonwealthclub.org. **Website:** www.commonwealthclub.org/. **Contact:** Renee Miguel. Estab. 1931. Offered annually to recognize California's best writers and illuminate the wealth and diversity of California-based literature. Award is for published submissions appearing in print during the previous calendar year. Can be nominated by publisher or author. Open to California residents (or residents at time of publication). Deadline: December 22. Prize: Medals and cash prizes to be awarded at publicized event. Judged by 12-15 California professionals with a diverse range of views, backgrounds, and literary experience.

JOHN W. CAMPBELL MEMORIAL AWARD FOR BEST SCIENCE FICTION NOVEL OF THE YEAR

English Department, University of Kansas, Lawrence KS 66045. (785)864-3380. **Fax:** (785)864-1159. **E-mail:** cmckit@ku.edu. **Website:** www.sfcenter.ku.edu/campbell.htm. **Contact:** Chris McKitterick. Estab. 1973. Honors the best science fiction novel of the year. Deadline: Check website. Prize: Campbell Award trophy. Winners receive an expense-paid trip to the university to receive their award. Their names are also engraved on a permanent trophy. Judged by a jury.

✪ CANADIAN AUTHORS ASSOCIATION AWARD FOR FICTION

6 West St. N., Suite 203, Orilla ON L3X 5B8, Canada. **Website:** www.canadianauthors.org. **Contact:** Anita Purcell, executive director. Estab. 1975. Award for full-length, English language literature for adults by a Canadian author. Deadline: January 15. Prize: $1,000. Judging: Each year a trustee for each award appointed by the Canadian Authors Association selects up to 3 judges. Identities of the trustee and judges are confidential.

✪ CANADIAN AUTHORS ASSOCIATION EMERGING WRITER AWARD

6 West St. N., Suite 203, Orilla ON L3X 5B8, Canada. **Website:** www.canadianauthors.org. **Contact:** Anita Purcell, executive director. Estab. 2006. Annual award for a writer under 30 years of age deemed to show exceptional promise in the field of literary creation. Deadline: January 15. Prize: $500. Judging: Each year a trustee for each award appointed by the Canadian Authors Association selects up to 3 judges. Identities of the trustee and judges are confidential.

THE ALEXANDER CAPPON PRIZE FOR FICTION

New Letters, University of Missouri-Kansas City, *New Letters* Awards for Writers, UMKC, University House, 5101 Rockhill Rd., Kansas City MO 64110-2499. (816)235-1168. **Fax:** (816)235-2611. **E-mail:** newletters@umkc.edu. **Website:** http://www.newletters.org/writers-wanted/writing-contests. Offered annually for the best short story to discover and reward new and upcoming writers. Buys first North American serial rights. Open to any writer. Deadline: May 18. Prize: 1st Place: $1,500 and publication in a volume of *New Letters*. Costs: $20 for first entry; $15 for every entry after. If entering online, add a $5 service charge to entry fee.

CASCADE WRITING CONTEST & AWARDS

Oregon Christian Writers, 1075 Willow Lake Road N., Keizer Oregon 97303. **E-mail:** cascade@oregonchristianwriters.org. **E-mail:** cascade@oregonchristianwriters.org. **Website:** http://oregonchristianwriters.org/. **Contact:** Marilyn Rhoads and Julie McDonald Zander. The Cascade Awards are presented at the annual Oregon Christian Writers Summer Conference (held at the Red Lion on the River in Portland, Oregon, each August) attended by national editors, agents, and professional authors. The contest is open for both published and unpublished works in the following categories: contemporary fiction book, historical fiction book, speculative fiction book, nonfiction book, memoir book, young adult/middle grade fiction book, young adult/middle grade nonfiction book, children's chapter book and picture book (fiction and nonfiction), poetry, devotional, article, column, story, or blog post. Two additional special Cascade Awards are presented each year: the Trailblazer Award to a writer who has distinguished him/herself in the field of Christian writing; and a Writer of Promise Award for a writer who demonstrates unusual promise in the field of Christian writing. For a full list of categories, entry rules, and scoring elements, visit website. Annual multi-genre competition to encourage both published and emerging writers in the field of Christian writing. Deadline: March 31. Submissions period begins February 14. Prize: Award certificate and pin presented at the Cascade Awards ceremony during the Oregon Christian Writers Annual Summer Conference. Finalists are listed in the conference notebook and winners are listed online. Cascade Trophies are awarded to the recipients of the Trailblazer and Writer of Promise Awards. Costs: Book entry: $30 (OCW member), $40 (nonmember). Judged by published authors, editors, librarians, and retail book store owners and employees. Final judging by editors, agents, and published authors from the Christian publishing industry.

JAMIE CAT CALLAN HUMOR PRIZE

Category in the Soul-Making Keats Literary Competition, The Webhallow House, 1544 Sweetwood Dr., Broadmoor Village CA 94015-2029. **E-mail:** SoulKeats@mail.com. **Website:** www.soulmakingcontest.us. **Contact:** Eileen Malone. Deadline: November 30. Prize: First Place: $100; Second Place: $50; Third Place: $25. Costs: $5. Judged by Jamie Cat Callan.

KAY CATTARULLA AWARD FOR BEST SHORT STORY

Texas Institute of Letters, P.O. Box 609, Round Rock TX 78680. **E-mail:** tilsecretary@yahoo.com. **Website:** www.texasinstituteofletters.org. Offered annually for work published January 1-December 31 of previous year to recognize the best short story. The story submitted must have appeared in print for the first time to be eligible. Writers must have been born in Texas, must have lived in Texas for at least 2 consecutive years, or the subject matter of the work must be associated with Texas. See website for guidelines. Deadline: January 10. Prize: $1,000.

G. S. SHARAT CHANDRA PRIZE FOR SHORT FICTION

BkMk Press, University of Missouri-Kansas City, BkMk Press, University of Missouri-Kansas City, 5100 Rockhill Rd., Kansas City MO 64110-2499, USA. (816)235-2558. **Fax:** (816)235-2611. **E-mail:** bkmk@umkc.edu; newletters@umkc.edu. **Website:** www.umkc.edu/bkmk. **Contact:** Ben Furnish. Estab. 2002 (Chandra Prize established); 1971 (press established). Offered annually for the best book-length ms collection (unpublished) of short fiction in English by a living author. Translations are not eligible. Initial judging is done by a network of published writers. Final judging is done by a writer of national reputation. Guidelines for SASE, by e-mail, or on website. Deadline: January 15. Prize: $1,000, plus book publication by BkMk Press. Costs: $25 fee, $5 additional for online submission.

PEGGY CHAPMAN-ANDREWS FIRST NOVEL AWARD

P.O. Box 6910, Dorset DT6 9QB, United Kingdom. **E-mail:** info@bridportprize.org.uk. **Website:** www.bridportprize.org.uk. **Contact:** Kate Wilson, Prize Administrator. Estab. 1973. Award to promote literary excellence and new writers. Enter first chapters of novel, up to 8,000 words (minimum 5,000 words) plus 300 word synopsis. Deadline: May 31. Prize: 1st Place: £1,000 plus mentoring & possible publication; Runner-Up: ££500. Costs: £20. Judged by The Literary Consultancy & A.M. Heath Literary Agents.

THE CHARITON REVIEW SHORT FICTION PRIZE

Truman State University Press, 100 East Normal Ave., Kirksville MO 63501-4221. (660)785-7336. **Fax:** (660)785-4480. **E-mail:** chariton@truman.edu; tsup@truman.edu. **Website:** tsup.truman.edu. **Contact:** Barbara Smith-Mandell. Estab. 1975. An annual award for the best unpublished short fiction on any theme up to 5,000 words in English. Deadline: September 30. Prize: $500 and publication in *The Chariton Review* for the winner. Two or three finalists will also be published and receive $200 each. Costs: include a nonrefundable reading fee of $20 for each ms submitted, make check payable to Truman State University Press. The final judge will be announced after the finalists have been selected in January.

THE CITY OF VANCOUVER BOOK AWARD

Cultural Services Dept., Woodward's Heritage Building, 111 W. Hastings St., Suite 501, Vancouver BC V6B 1H4, Canada. (604) 829-2007. **Fax:** (604)871-6005. **E-mail:** marnie.rice@vancouver.ca; culture@vancouver.ca. **Website:** https://vancouver.ca/people-programs/city-of-vancouver-book-award.aspx. Estab. 1989. The annual City of Vancouver Book Award recognizes authors of excellence of any genre who contribute to the appreciation and understanding of Vancouver's history, unique character, or the achievements of its residents. The book must exhibit excellence in one or more of the following areas: content, illustration, design, format. Deadline: May 18. Prize: $3,000. Costs: $20/entry. Judged by an independent jury.

CLOUDBANK JOURNAL CONTEST

P.O. Box 610, Corvallis OR 97339. (541)752-0075. **E-mail:** michael@cloudbankbooks.com. **Website:** www.cloudbankbooks.com. **Contact:** Michael Malan. Estab. 2009. Deadline: April 30, 2016 Prize: $200 and publication, plus an extra copy of the issue in which the winning poem appears. Two contributors' copies will be sent to writers whose work appears in the magazine. Costs: $15 entry fee. Make check out to *Cloudbank*. All writers who enter the contest will receive a 2-issue subscription to *Cloudbank* magazine. Judged by Michael Malan and Peter Sears.

Submissions for contests are accepted via Submittable and by mail. Complete guidelines are available at website. Accept both poetry and flash fiction.

COLORADO BOOK AWARDS

Colorado Humanities & Center for the Book, 7935 E. Prentice Ave., Suite 450, Greenwood Village CO 80111. (303)894-7951. **Fax:** (303)864-9361. **E-mail:** lansdown@coloradohumanities.org. **Website:** www.coloradohumanities.org. **Contact:** Marnie Lansdown. Estab. 1991. An annual program that celebrates the accomplishments of Colorado's outstanding authors, editors, illustrators, and photographers. Awards are presented in at least ten categories including anthology/collection, biography, children's, creative nonfiction, fiction, history, nonfiction, pictorial, poetry, and young adult. Deadline: January 8.

COPTALES CONTEST

Sponsored by Oak Tree Press, 1700 Dairy Avenue Apt #49, Corcoran CA 93212. **E-mail:** publisher@oaktreebooks.com. **E-mail:** CT-ContestAdmin@oaktreebooks.com. **Website:** www.oaktreebooks.com. **Contact:** Billie Johnson, publisher. Open to novels and true stories that feature a law enforcement main character. Word count should range from 60,000-80,000 words. The goal of the CopTales Contest is to discover and publish new authors, or authors shifting to a new genre. This annual contest is open to writers who have not published in the mystery genre in the past three years, as well as completely unpublished authors. Deadline: September 1. Prize: Publishing contract, book published in trade paperback and e-book formats with a professionally designed, four-color cover. See website for details. Costs: $25/novel. Judged by a select panel of editors and professional crime writers.

THE CUTBANK CHAPBOOK CONTEST

CutBank Literary Magazine, *CutBank*, University of Montana, English Dept., LA 133, Missoula MT 59812. **E-mail:** editor.cutbank@gmail.com. **Website:** www.cutbankonline.org. **Contact:** Allison Linville, editor-in-chief. This competition is open to original English language mss in the genres of poetry, fiction, and creative nonfiction. While previously published stand-alone pieces or excerpts may be included in a ms, the ms as a whole must be an unpublished work. Looking for startling, compelling, and beautiful original work. "We're looking for a fresh, powerful ms. Maybe it will overtake us quietly; gracefully defy genres; satisfyingly subvert our expectations; punch us in the mouth page in and page out. We're interested in both prose and poetry—and particularly work that straddles the lines between genres." Deadline: March 31. Submissions period begins January1. Prize: $1,000 and 25 contributor copies. Costs: $20. Judged by a guest judge each year.

CWW ANNUAL WISCONSIN WRITERS AWARDS

Council for Wisconsin Writers, 6973 Heron Way, De Forest WI 53532. **E-mail:** karlahuston@gmail.com. **Website:** www.wiswriters.org. **Contact:** Geoff Gilpin, president and annual awards co-chair; Karla Huston, secretary and annual awards co-chair; Jennifer Morales, annual awards co-chair; Edward Schultz, annual awards co-chair. Estab. 1964. Offered annually for work published by Wisconsin writers during the previous calendar year. Nine awards: Major Achievement (presented in alternate years); short fiction; short nonfiction; nonfiction book; poetry book; fiction book; children's literature; Lorine Niedecker Poetry Award; Christopher Latham Sholes Award for Outstanding Service to Wisconsin Writers p(resented in alternate years); Essay Award for Young Writers. Open to Wisconsin residents. Deadline: February 1. Submissions open on November 1. Prizes: First place prizes: $500. Honorable mentions: $50. Costs: $25 nonrefundable fee.

DANA AWARDS IN THE NOVEL, SHORT FICTION, AND POETRY

200 Fosseway Dr., Greensboro NC 27445. (336)644-8028. **E-mail:** danaawards@gmail.com. **Website:**

www.danaawards.com. **Contact:** Mary Elizabeth Parker, chair. Estab. 1996. Three awards offered annually for unpublished work written in English. Works previously published online are not eligible. The Dana Awards are re-vamping. The Novel Award is now increased to $2,000, based on a new partnership with Blue Mary Books: Blue Mary has agreed to consider for possible publication not only the Novel Award winning ms, but the top 9 other Novel finalists, as well as the 30 top Novel semifinalists. The Short Fiction and Poetry Awards offer the traditional $1,000 awards each and do not offer a publishing option (currently, Blue Mary publishes only novels). See website for further updates. Purpose is monetary award for work that has not been previously published or received monetary award, but will accept work published simply for friends and family. Deadline: October 31 (postmarked). Prizes: $2,000 for the Novel Award; $1,000 each for the Short Fiction and Poetry awards awards. Costs: $30 per novel entry; $15 per short fiction entry; $15 per 5 poems.

The Dana Awards and Blue Mary Books are separate entities. Blue Mary has no part in the reading and judging of mss to determine the Novel Award and the Dana Awards does not advise Blue Mary on publishing. The Dana Awards gives its monetary award only; then, as a further courtesy, will put winner, finalists and semifinalists in touch with Blue Mary. All further agreements and contracts are solely between the authors and Blue Mary.

THE DANAHY FICTION PRIZE

Tampa Review, University of Tampa, 401 W. Kennedy Blvd., Tampa FL 33606. 813-253-6266. **E-mail:** utpress@ut.edu. **Website:** www.ut.edu/TampaReview. Estab. 2006. Annual award for the best previously unpublished short fiction. Deadline: November 30. Prize: $1,000, plus publication in *Tampa Review*. Costs: $20.

DARK OAK MYSTERY CONTEST

Oak Tree Press, 1700 Dairy Avenue, # 49, Corcoran CA 93212. (217)824-6500. **E-mail:** publisher@oaktreebooks.com. **E-mail:** DO-ContestAdmin@oaktreebooks.com. **Website:** www.oaktreebooks.com. Offered annually for an unpublished mystery ms (between 60,00-80,000 words) of any sort from police procedurals to amateur sleuth novels. Acquires first North American, audio and film rights to winning entry. Open to authors not published in the past 3 years. Deadline: September 1. Prize: Publishing Agreement, and launch of the title. Costs: $25/ms. Judged by a select panel of editors and professional mystery writers.

THE DEADLY QUILL SHORT STORY WRITING CONTEST

Deadly Quill Magazine, **E-mail:** lorne@deadlyquill.com. **E-mail:** contest@deadlyquill.com. **Website:** www.deadlyquill.com. **Contact:** Lorne McMIllan. Estab. 2015. "We are hoping to give an outlet for short stories that follow the tradition of The Twilight Zone, Alfred Hitchcock, and The Outer Limits." Deadline: August 31. Prizes: $250 first place; $200 second place; $150 third place. Plus, more prizes described online. Costs: Charges $10 entry fee. Author Edward Willett, Author Lorne McMillan, Author Colin Douglas

The stories should reach out and grab you, pull you in, and keep you in. A good ending is crucial.

DEAD OF WINTER

E-mail: editors@toasted-cheese.com. **Website:** www.toasted-cheese.com. **Contact:** Stephanie Lenz, editor. The contest is a winter-themed horror fiction contest with a new topic/theme each year. Theme and word count parameters announced October 1. Deadline: December 21. Results announced January 31. Winners notified by e-mail. List of winners on website. Prize: Amazon gift certificates and publication in *Toasted Cheese*. Also offers honorable mention. Judged by 2 *Toasted Cheese* editors who blind judge each contest. Each judge uses her own criteria to rate entries.

DELAWARE DIVISION OF THE ARTS

820 N. French St., Wilmington DE 19801. (302)577-8278. **Fax:** (302)577-6561. **E-mail:** Roxanne.stanulis@state.de.us. **Website:** www.artsdel.org. **Contact:** Roxanne Stanulis. Award to help further careers of emerging and established professional artists. For Delaware residents only. Guidelines available after May 1 on website. Accepts inquiries by e-mail, phone. Results announced in December. Winners notified by mail. Results available on website. Deadline: August 1. Prize: $10,000 for masters; $6,000 for established professionals; $3,000 for emerging professionals. Judged by out-of-state, nationally recognized professionals in each artistic discipline.

Expects to receive 25 fiction entries.

DIAGRAM/NEW MICHIGAN PRESS CHAPBOOK CONTEST

New Michigan Press, P.O. Box 210067, English, ML 424, University of Arizona, Tucson AZ 85721. **E-mail:** nmp@thediagram.com. **Website:** www.thediagram.com. **Contact:** Ander Monson, editor. Estab. 1999. The annual *DIAGRAM*/New Michigan Press Chapbook Contest offers $1,000, plus publication and author's copies, with discount on additional copies. Deadline: April 29. Prize: $1,000, plus publication. Finalist chapbooks also considered for publication. Costs: $19.

DOBIE PAISANO WRITER'S FELLOWSHIP

The Graduate School, The University of Texas at Austin, Attn: Dobie Paisano Program, 110 Inner Campus Drive Stop G0400, Austin TX 78712-0531. (512)232-3609. **Fax:** (512)471-7620. **E-mail:** gbarton@austin.utexas.edu. **Website:** www.utexas.edu/ogs/Paisano. **Contact:** Gwen Barton. Sponsored by the Graduate School at The University of Texas at Austin and the Texas Institute of Letters, the Dobie Paisano Fellowship Program provides solitude, time, and a comfortable place for Texas writers or writers who have written significantly about Texas through fiction, nonfiction, poetry, plays, or other mediums. The Dobie Paisano Ranch is a very rural and rustic setting, and applicants should read the guidelines closely to insure their ability to reside in this secluded environment. Deadline: January 15. Applications are accepted beginning December 1 and must be post-marked no later than January 15. The Ralph A. Johnston memorial Fellowship is for a period of 4 months with a stipend of $6,250 per month. It is aimed at writers who have already demonstrated some publishing and critical success. The Jesse H. Jones Writing Fellowship is for a period of approximately 6 months with a stipend of $3,000 per month. It is aimed at, but not limited to, writers who are early in their careers. Costs: Application fee: $20 for one fellowship; $30 for both fellowships.

$ THE JACK DYER FICTION PRIZE

Crab Orchard Review, Department of English, Mail Code 4503, Faner Hall 2380, Southern Illinois University Carbondale, 1000 Faner Drive, Carbondale IL 62901. (618)453-6833. **Fax:** (618)453-8224. **E-mail:** jtribble@siu.edu. **Website:** www.craborchardreview.siu.edu. **Contact:** Jon C. Tribble, managing editor. Estab. 1995 magazine/1997 fiction prize. Annual award for unpublished short fiction. Entries should consist of 1 story up to 6,000 words maximum in length. *Crab Orchard Review* acquires first North American serial rights to all submitted work. One winner and at least 2 finalists will be chosen. Deadline: April 21. Submissions period begins February 21. Prize: $2,000, publication and 1-year subscription to *Crab Orchard Review*. Finalists are offered $500 and publication. Costs: $15/entry (up to 3 entries); entrants receive copy of the 2017 Winter/Spring issue of *Crab Orchard Review*, which will include the winner and finalists of this competition ($14 value; $1 for Submittable service) sent to a U.S. postal address for your first entry and extend your subscription beyond that according to the number of entries you have. Due to the extremely high cost of International Mail and uncertainty of successful delivery, individuals entering from overseas will need to provide a United States postal address to receive a copy of the issue. Judged by editorial staff (prescreening); winner chosen by genre editor.

EATON LITERARY AGENCY'S ANNUAL AWARDS PROGRAM

Eaton Literary Agency, P.O. Box 49795, Sarasota FL 34230-6795. (941)366-6589. **Fax:** (941)365-4679. **E-mail:** eatonlit@aol.com. **Website:** www.eatonliterary.com. **Contact:** Richard Lawrence, V.P.. Offered biannually for unpublished mss. Entries must be unpublished. Open to any writer. Guidelines available for SASE, by fax, e-mail, or on website. Accepts inquiries by fax, phone, and e-mail. Results announced in April and September. Winners notified by mail. For contest results, send SASE, fax, e-mail, or visit website. Deadline: March 31 (short story); August 31 (book-length). Prize: $2,500 (book-length); $500 (short story). Judged by an independent agency in conjunction with some members of Eaton's staff.

◐ EMERGING VOICES FELLOWSHIP

PEN Center USA, P.O. Box 6037, Beverly Hills CA 90212, United States. 424 354 0582. **E-mail:** ev@penusa.org. **E-mail:** NA. **Website:** www.penusa.org. **Contact:** Libby Flores. Estab. 1996. Emerging Voices is a literary fellowship based in Los Angeles that aims to provide new writers, who lack access, with the tools they will need to launch a professional writing career. The eight-month fellowship includes the following: PROFESSIONAL MENTORSHIP: Emerging Voices mentors are carefully chosen from PEN Center USA's membership and from professional writers based in Los Angeles. The mentor-fellow relationship is expected to challenge the fellow's work and compel significant creative progress. Mentors will meet and offer written feedback on the Emerging Voices fellows' work in progress. Authors who have been mentors in the past include Ron Carlson, Harryette Mullen, Chris Abani, Jerry Stahl, Ramona Ausubel, Meghan Daum, and Sherman Alexie. CLASSES AT THE UCLA EXTENSION WRITERS' PROGRAM: Participants will attend two free courses (a 12-week writing course and a one-day workshop) at UCLA Extension, donated by the Writers' Program. AUTHOR EVENINGS: Every Monday, fellows will meet with a visiting author, editor or publisher and ask questions about craft. Fellows must read each visiting author's book in advance. Authors who have participated in the past have included Jonathan Lethem, Percival Everett, Maggie Nelson, Cynthia Bond, Aimee Bender, Jerry Stahl, Danzy Senna, and Roxane Gay. MASTER CLASSES: The Master Class is a genre-specific workshop with a professional writer and affords the fellows the opportunity to exchange feedback on their works in progress. Previous Master Class Instructors have included Diana Wagman, Alex Espinoza, and Paul Mandelbaum. VOLUNTEER PROJECT: All Emerging Voices fellows are expected to complete a 25-hour volunteer project that is relevant to the literary community. A few of the organizations that have hosted volunteers included WriteGirl, 826LA, Cedars-Sinai Hospital, and STARS – San Diego Youth Services. VOICE INSTRUCTION CLASS: The Fellowship will provide a one-day workshop with Dave Thomas, a professional voice actor. The Emerging Voices fellows will read their work in a recording studio and receive instruction on reading their work publicly. PUBLIC READINGS: Fellows will participate in three public readings in Los Angeles. STIPEND: The fellowship includes a $1,000 stipend, given in $500 increments. Participants need not be published, but the fellowship is directed toward poets and writers of fiction and creative nonfiction who have clear ideas of what they hope to accomplish through their writing. Each applicant needs to explain how they lack access creatively and/or financially. To provide new writers, who lack access, with the tools they will need to launch a professional writing career. Deadline: August. Costs: $10.

THE FAR HORIZONS AWARD FOR SHORT FICTION

The Malahat Review, University of Victoria, P.O. Box 1700, Stn CSC, Victoria BC V8W 2Y2, Canada. (250)721-8524. **Fax:** (250)472-5051. **E-mail:** malahat@uvic.ca. **E-mail:** horizons@uvic.ca. **Website:** www.malahatreview.ca. **Contact:** John Barton, editor. Open to "emerging short fiction writers from Canada, the US, and elsewhere" who have not yet published their fiction in a full-length book (48 pages or more). 2011 winner: Zoey Peterson; 2013 winner: Kerry-Lee Powell. Deadline: May 1. Prize: $1,000 CAD, publication in fall issue of *The Malahat Review* (see separate listing in Magazines/Journals). Announced in fall on website, Facebook page, and in quarterly e-newsletter, *Malahat Lite*. Costs: $25 CAD for Canadian entries, $30 USD for US entries; $45 USD from Mexico and outside North America; includes a 1-year subscription to *The Malahat Review*.

THE VIRGINIA FAULKNER AWARD FOR EXCELLENCE IN WRITING

Prairie Schooner, 123 Andrews Hall, University of Nebraska-Lincoln, Lincoln NE 68588-0334. (402)472-0911. **Fax:** (402)472-1817. **E-mail:** PrairieSchooner@unl.edu. **Website:** www.prairieschooner.unl.edu. **Contact:** Kwame Dawes. Offered annually for work published in *Prairie Schooner* in the previous year. Categories: short stories, essays, novel excerpts, and translations. Prize: $1,000. Judged by editorial board.

FINELINE COMPETITION FOR PROSE POEMS, SHORT SHORTS, AND ANYTHING IN BETWEEN

Mid-American Review, Dept. of English, Bowling Green State University, Bowling Green OH 43403. (419)372-2725. **E-mail:** mar@bgsu.edu. **Website:** www.bgsu.edu/midamericanreview. **Contact:** Abigail Cloud, editor-in-chief. Offered annually for previously unpublished submissions. Contest open to all writers not associated with current judge or *Mid-American Review*. Deadline: June 1. Prize: $1,000, plus publication in fall issue of *Mid-American Review*; 10 finalists receive notation plus possible publication. Costs: $10 for up to 3 prose poems or short shorts; all participants receive prize issue. 2015 judge: Michael Czyzniejewski.

FIRSTWRITER.COM INTERNATIONAL

SHORT STORY CONTEST

firstwriter.com, , United Kingdom. **Website:** https://www.firstwriter.com/competitions/short_story_contest/. **Contact:** J. Paul Dyson, managing editor. Accepts short stories up to 3,000 words on any subject and in any style. Deadline: April 1. The prize-money for first place is £200 (over $300). Ten special commendations will also be awarded, and all the winners will be published in firstwriter.magazine and receive a voucher that can be used to take out an annual subscription for free. Costs: $9.75 for 1 short story; $17.25 for 2; $22.50 for 3; and $30 for 5. Judged by firstwriter.magazine magazine editors.

FISH PUBLISHING FLASH FICTION COMPETITION

Durrus, Bantry, County Cork , Ireland. **E-mail:** info@fishpublishing.com. **Website:** www.fishpublishing.com. **Contact:** Clem Cairns. Estab. 2004. Annual prize awarding flash fiction. "This is an opportunity to attempt what is one of the most difficult and rewarding tasks—to create, in a tiny fragment, a completely resolved and compelling story in 300 words or less." Deadline: February 28. First Prize: $1,200. The 10 published authors will receive 5 copies of the Anthology and will be invited to read at the launch during the West Cork Literary Festival in July. Costs: $18. Judged by Nuala O'Connor.

FOREWORD'S INDIEFAB BOOK OF THE YEAR AWARDS

Foreword Magazine, 425 Boardman Ave, Traverse City MI 49684. (231)933-3699. **Fax:** (231)933-3899. **Website:** www.forewordreviews.com. **Contact:** Michele Lonoconus. Estab. 1998. Awards offered annually. In order to be eligible, books must have a current year copyright and be independently published which includes university presses, privately held presses, and self-published authors. International submissions are welcome. New editions of previously published books are eligible if significant content has been changed and the book has a new ISBN. Reissued editions in new formats are not eligible. *Foreword's*INDIEFAB Book of the Year Awards were established to bring increased attention from librarians, booksellers, and avid readers, to the literary achievements of independent publishers and their authors. Deadline: January 15th. Prize: $1,500 cash will be awarded to a Best Fiction and Best Nonfiction choice. In addition, all entries are automatically eligible to win awards for Best Cover Design, Best Packaging, and Best Coffee Table Book. Costs: We offer a $79 Early Bird entry fee for books registered before September 1st. Choose a second (or third, or fourth) category for the same book and the fee drops to $59 for each additional submission. After September 1st, the fee is $99 per entry, and $79 for additional categories. Our awards process is unique and well respected because we assemble a jury of volunteer booksellers and librarians to make the final judgment on the books and who select winners based on their experience with readers. Their decisions also take into consideration editorial excellence, professional production, originality of the narrative, author credentials relative to the subject matter, and the value the title adds to its genre.

SOEURETTE DIEHL FRASER AWARD FOR BEST TRANSLATION OF A BOOK

P.O. Box 609, Round Rock TX 78680. **E-mail:** tilsecretary@yahoo.com. **Website:** http://texasinstituteofletters.org. Offered every 2 years to recognize the best translation of a literary book into English. Translator must have been born in Texas or have lived in the state for at least 2 consecutive years at some time. Deadline: January 10. Prize: $1,000.

FREEFALL SHORT PROSE AND POETRY CONTEST

Freefall Literary Society of Calgary, 922 9th Ave. SE, Calgary AB T2G 0S4, Canada. **E-mail:** editors@freefallmagazine.ca. **Website:** www.freefallmagazine.ca. **Contact:** Ryan Stromquist, managing editor. Offered annually for unpublished work in the categories of poetry (5 poems/entry) and prose (3,000 words or less). Recognizes writers and offers publication credits in a literary magazine format. Contest rules and entry form online. Acquires first Canadian serial rights; ownership reverts to author after one-time publication. Deadline: December 31. Prize: 1st Place: $500 (CAD); 2nd Place: $250 (CAD); 3rd Place: $75; Honorable Mention: $25. All prizes include publication in the spring edition of *FreeFall Magazine*. Winners will also be invited to read at the launch of that issue, if such a launch takes place. Honorable mentions in each category will be published and may be asked to read. Travel expenses not included. Costs: $25. Judged by current guest editor for issue (who are also published authors in Canada).

THE GHOST STORY SUPERNATURAL FICTION AWARD

The Ghost Story, P.O. Box 601, Union ME 04862. **E-mail:** editor@theghoststory.com. **Website:** www.theghoststory.com. **Contact:** Paul Guernsey. Biannual contest for unpublished fiction. "Ghost stories are welcome, of course—but submissions may involve *any* paranormal or supernatural theme, as well as magic realism. What we're looking for is fine writing, fresh perspectives, and maybe a few surprises in the field of supernatural fiction." Deadline: April 30 and September 30. Winner receives $1,000 and publication in *The Ghost Story*. Honorable Mention wins $250 and publication, and Second Honorable Mention is awarded $100 and publication. Costs: $20. Judged by the editors of *The Ghost Story*.

GIVAL PRESS NOVEL AWARD

Gival Press, LLC, P.O. Box 3812, Arlington VA 22203. (703)351-0079. **E-mail:** givalpress@yahoo.com. **Website:** www.givalpress.submittable.com. **Contact:** Robert L. Giron. Offered annually for a previously unpublished original novel (not a translation). Guidelines by phone, on website, via e-mail, or by mail with SASE. Results announced late fall of same year. Winners notified by phone. Results made available to entrants with SASE, by e-mail, on website. Purpose is to award the best literary novel. Deadline: May 30. Prize: $3,000, plus publication of book with a standard contract and author's copies. Costs: $50. Final judge is announced after winner is chosen. Entries read anonymously.

O GIVAL PRESS SHORT STORY AWARD

Gival Press, P.O. Box 3812, Arlington VA 22203. (703)351-0079. **E-mail:** givalpress@yahoo.com. **Website:** www.givalpress.submittable.com. **Contact:** Robert L. Giron, publisher. Annual literary, short story contest. Entries must be unpublished. Open to anyone who writes original short stories, which are not a chapter of a novel, in English. Receives about 100-150 entries per category. Guidelines available online, via e-mail, or by mail. Results announced in the fall of the same year. Winners notified by phone. Results available with SASE, by e-mail, and on website. Recognizes the best literary short story. Deadline: August 8. Prize: $1,000 and publication on website. Costs: $25 entry fee; make checks payable to Gival Press, LLC. Judged anonymously.

GLIMMER TRAIN'S FAMILY MATTERS CONTEST

Glimmer Train, P.O. Box 80430, Portland OR 97280. (503)221-0836. **Fax:** (503)221-0837. **E-mail:** eds@glimmertrain.org. **Website:** www.glimmertrain.org. **Contact:** Susan Burmeister-Brown. Estab. 1990. This contest is now held once a year, during the months of November and December. Winners are contacted on March 1. Submit online at www.glimmertrain.org. Deadline: December 31. Prize: 1st Place: $2,500, publication in *Glimmer Train Stories*, and 10 copies of that issue; 2nd Place: $500 and consideration for publication; 3rd Place: $300 and consideration for publication. Costs: $18/story. The editors judge.

Represented in recent editions of *The Pushcart Prize, New Stories from the Midwest, The PEN/O. Henry Prize Stories, New Stories from the South, Best of the West, Best American Mystery Stories*, and *Best American Short Stories Anthologies*.

GLIMMER TRAIN'S FICTION OPEN

Glimmer Train, Inc., Glimmer Train Press, Inc., P.O. Box 80430, Portland OR 97280. (503)221-0836. **Fax:** (503)221-0837. **E-mail:** eds@glimmertrain.org. **Website:** www.glimmertrain.org. **Contact:** Susan Burmeister-Brown. Estab. 1990. Submissions to this category generally range from 3,000-8,000 words, but up to 20,000 is fine. Held twice a year: March 1 - April 30 and July 1 - August 31. Submit online at www.glimmertrain.org. Winners will be called 2 months after the close of the contest. Deadline: April 30 and August 31. Prize: 1st Place: $3,000, publication in *Glimmer Train Stories*, and 10 copies of that issue; 2nd Place: $1,000 and consideration for publication; 3rd Place: $600 and consideration for publication. Costs: $22/story. Judged by the editors.

Represented in recent editions of *The Pushcart Prize, New Stories from the Midwest, The PEN/O. Henry Prize Stories, New Stories from the South, Best of the West, Best American Mystery Stories*, and *Best American Short Stories Anthologies*.

GLIMMER TRAIN'S SHORT-STORY AWARD FOR NEW WRITERS

Glimmer Train Press, Inc., P.O. Box 80430, Portland OR 97280. (503)221-0836. **Fax:** (503)221-0837. **E-mail:** eds@glimmertrain.org. **Website:** www.glimmertrain.org. **Contact:** Susan Burmeister-Brown. Estab. 1990. Offered for any writer whose fiction hasn't appeared in a nationally distributed print publication with a circulation over 5,000. Submissions to this category generally range from 1,500–5,000 words, but up to 12,000 is fine. Held three times a year: January 1–February 29, May 1–June 30, September 1–October 31. Submit online at www.glimmertrain.org. Winners will be called 2 months after the close of the contest. Deadline: February 29, June 30, and October 31. Prize: 1st Place: $2,500, publication in *Glimmer Train Stories*, and 10 copies of that issue; 2nd Place: $500 and consideration for publication; 3rd Place: $300 and consideration for publication. Costs: $18/story.

Represented in recent editions of *The Pushcart Prize, New Stories from the Midwest, The PEN/O. Henry Prize Stories, New Stories from the South, Best of the West, Best American Mystery Stories,* and *Best American Short Stories Anthologies*. Pays over $50,000 every year to writers. The prize was increased in 2016.

GLIMMER TRAIN'S VERY SHORT FICTION CONTEST

Glimmer Train Press, Inc., P.O. Box 80430, Portland OR 97280. (503)221-0836. **Fax:** (503)221-0837. **E-mail:** eds@glimmertrain.org. **Website:** www.glimmertrain.org. **Contact:** Susan Burmeister-Brown. Estab. 1990. Offered to encourage the art of the very short story. Word count: 3,000 maximum. Held twice a year: March 1–April 30 and July 1–August 31. Submit online at www.glimmertrain.org. Results announced 2 months after the close of the contest. To encourage the art of the very short story. Deadline: April 30 and August 31. Prize: 1st Place: $2,000, publication in *Glimmer Train Stories*, and 10 copies of that issue; 2nd Place: $500 and consideration for publication; 3rd Place: $300 and consideration for publication. Costs: $16 fee/story. Judged by the editors.

Represented in recent editions of *The Pushcart Prize, New Stories from the Midwest, The PEN/O. Henry Prize Stories, New Stories from the South, Best of the West, Best American Mystery Stories,* and *Best American Short Stories Anthologies*. The prize was just increased in 2016.

GOVERNOR GENERAL'S LITERARY AWARDS

Canada Council for the Arts, 150 Elgin St., P.O. Box 1047, Ottawa ON K1P 5V8, Canada. 1-800-263-5588, ext. 5573. **Website:** www.canadacouncil.ca. Estab. 1937. The Canada Council for the Arts provides a wide range of grants and services to professional Canadian artists and art organizations in dance, media arts, music, theatre, writing, publishing, and the visual arts. The Governor General's Literary Awards are given annually for the best English-language and French-language work in each of 7 categories, including fiction, non-fiction, poetry, drama, children's literature (text), children's literature (illustrated books), and translation. Deadline: Depends on the book's publication date. See website for details. Prize: Each GG winner receives $25,000. Non-winning finalists receive $1,000. Publishers of the winning titles receive a $3,000 grant for promotional purposes. Evaluated by fellow authors, translators, and illustrators. For each category, a jury makes the final selection.

THE GOVER PRIZE

Best New Writing, P.O. Box 11, Titusville NJ 08530. **Fax:** (609)968-1718. **E-mail:** submissions@bestnewwriting.com. **Website:** www.bestnewwriting.com/BNWgover.html. **Contact:** Christopher Klim, senior editor. The Gover Prize, named after groundbreaking author Robert Gover, awards an annual prize and publication in *Best New Writing* for the best short fiction and creative nonfiction. Deadline: January 10. Open to submissions on September 15. Prize: $250 grand prize; publication in *Best New Writing* for finalists (approximately 12), holds 6-month world exclusive rights. Costs: $5. Judged by *Best New Writing* editorial staff.

GREAT LAKES COLLEGES ASSOCIATION NEW WRITERS AWARD

The Great Lakes Colleges Association, 535 W. William, Suite 301, Ann Arbor MI 48103. (734)661-2350. **Fax:** (734)661-2349. **E-mail:** wegner@glca.org. **Website:** www.glca.org. **Contact:** Gregory R. Wegner, Director of Program Development. Estab. 1970. The Great Lakes Colleges Association (GLCA) is a consortium of 13 independent liberal arts colleges in Ohio, Michigan, Indiana, and Pennsylvania. Deadline: July 25. Prize: Honorarium of at least $500 for winning writers who are invited to give a reading at a member college campus. Each award winner receives invitations from several of the 13 colleges of the GLCA to visit campus. At these campus events an author will give readings, meet students and faculty, and occasionally lead discussions or classes. In addition to an honorarium for each campus visit, travel costs to colleges are paid by

GLCA and its member colleges. Judged by professors of literature and writers in residence at GLCA colleges.

Annual award for a first published volume of poetry, fiction, and creative nonfiction.

GUGGENHEIM FELLOWSHIPS

John Simon Guggenheim Memorial Foundation, 90 Park Ave., New York NY 10016. (212)687-4470. **E-mail:** fellowships@gf.org. **Website:** www.gf.org. Estab. 1925. Often characterized as "midcareer" awards, Guggenheim Fellowships are intended for men and women who have already demonstrated exceptional capacity for productive scholarship or exceptional creative ability in the arts. Fellowships are awarded through two annual competitions: one open to citizens and permanent residents of the United States and Canada, and the other open to citizens and permanent residents of Latin America and the Caribbean. Candidates must apply to the Guggenheim Foundation in order to be considered in either of these competitions. The Foundation receives between 3,500 and 4,000 applications each year. Although no one who applies is guaranteed success in the competition, there is no prescreening: all applications are reviewed. Approximately 200 Fellowships are awarded each year. Deadline: September 15.

LYNDALL HADOW/DONALD STUART SHORT STORY COMPETITION

Fellowship of Australian Writers (WA), P.O. Box 6180, Swanbourne WA 6910, Australia. (61)(8)9384-4771. **Fax:** (61)(8)9384-4854. **E-mail:** fellowshipaustralianwriterswa@gmail.com. **Website:** www.fawwa.org. Annual contest for unpublished short stories (maximum 3,000 words). Reserves the right to publish entries in a FAWWA publication or on website. Guidelines online or for SASE. Deadline: June 1. Submissions period begins April 1. Prize: 1st Place: $400; 2nd Place: $100; Highly Commended (2): $50. Costs: $10/story (maximum of 3).

HAMMETT PRIZE

International Association of Crime Writers, North American Branch, 243 Fifth Avenue, #537, New York NY 10016. **E-mail:** mfrisque@igc.org. **Website:** www.crimewritersna.org.. **Contact:** Mary A. Frisque, executive director, North American Branch. Award for crime novels, story collections, nonfiction by one author. "Our reading committee seeks suggestions from publishers and they also ask the membership for recommendations." Nominations announced in January; winners announced in fall. Winners notified by e-mail or mail and recognized at awards ceremony. For contest results, send SASE or e-mail. Award established to honor a work of literary excellence in the field of crime writing by a US or Canadian author. Deadline: December 15. Prize: Trophy. Judged by a committee of members of the organization. The committee chooses 5 nominated books, which are then sent to 3 outside judges for a final selection. Judges are outside the crime writing field.

WILDA HEARNE FLASH FICTION CONTEST

Big Muddy: A Journal of the Mississippi River Valley, WHFF Contest, Southeast Missouri State University Press, One University Plaza, MS 2650, Cape Girardeau MO 63701. (573) 651-2044. **E-mail:** sswartwout@semo.edu. **Website:** www.semopress.com. **Contact:** Susan Swartwout, publisher. Annual competition for flash fiction, held by Southeast Missouri State University Press. Deadline: October 1. Prize: $500 and publication in *Big Muddy: A Journal of the Mississippi River Valley*. Costs: $15. Semi-finalists will be chosen by a team of published writers. The final ms will be chosen by Susan Swartwout, publisher of the Southeast Missouri State University Press.

DRUE HEINZ LITERATURE PRIZE

University of Pittsburgh Press, 7500 Thomas Blvd., Pittsburgh PA 15260. **Fax:** (412)383-2466. **E-mail:** info@upress.pitt.edu. **Website:** www.upress.pitt.edu. Estab. 1981. Offered annually to writers who have published a book-length collection of fiction or a minimum of 3 short stories or novellas in commercial magazines or literary journals of national distribution. Does not return mss. Deadline: June 30. Open to submissions on May 1. Prize: $15,000. Judged by anonymous nationally known writers such as Robert Penn Warren, Joyce Carol Oates, and Margaret Atwood.

LORIAN HEMINGWAY SHORT STORY COMPETITION

Hemingway Days Festival, P.O. Box 2011 c/o Cynthia. D. Higgs: Key West Editorial, Key West FL 33045. **E-mail:** shortstorykeywest@hushmail.com. **Website:** www.shortstorycompetition.com. **Contact:** Eva Eliot, editorial assistant. Estab. 1981. Offered annually for unpublished short stories up to 3,500 words. Guidelines available via mail, e-mail, or online. Award to encourage literary excellence and the efforts of writers whose voices have yet to be heard. Deadline: May

15. Prizes: 1st Place: $1,500, plus publication of his or her winning story in *Cutthroat: A Journal of the Arts*; 2nd-3rd Place: $500; honorable mentions will also be awarded. Costs: $15/story postmarked by May 1; $20/ story postmarked by May 15. Judged by a panel of writers, editors, and literary scholars selected by author Lorian Hemingway. (Lorian Hemingway is the competition's final judge.)

O HIGHLIGHTS FOR CHILDREN FICTION CONTEST

803 Church St., Honesdale PA 18431-1824. (570)253-1080. **Fax:** (570)251-7847. **E-mail:** eds@highlightscorp.com. **Website:** www.highlights.com. **Contact:** Christine French Cully, editor-in-chief. Stimulates interest in writing for children and rewards and recognizes excellence. Deadline: January 31. Submission period begins January 1. Prize: Three prizes of $1,000 or tuition for any Highlights Foundation Founders Workshop.

TONY HILLERMAN PRIZE

Wordharvest, 1063 Willow Way, Santa Fe NM 87507. (505)471-1565. **E-mail:** wordharvest@wordharvest.com. **Website:** www.wordharvest.com. **Contact:** Anne Hillerman and Jean Schaumberg, co-organizers. Estab. 2006. Awarded annually, and sponsored by St. Martin's Press, for the best first mystery set in the Southwest. Murder or another serious crime or crimes must be at the heart of the story, with the emphasis on the solution rather than the details of the crime. Honors the contributions made by Tony Hillerman to the art and craft of the mystery. Deadline: June 1. Prize: $10,000 advance and publication by St. Martin's Press. Nominees will be selected by judges chosen by the editorial staff of St. Martin's Press, with the assistance of independent judges selected by organizers of the Tony Hillerman Writers Conference (Wordharvest), and the winner will be chosen by St. Martin's editors.

THE HODDER FELLOWSHIP

Lewis Center for the Arts, 185 Nassau St., Princeton NJ 08544. (609)258-6926. **E-mail:** ysabelg@princeton.edu. **Website:** arts.princeton.edu. **Contact:** Ysabel Gonzalez, fellowships assistant. The Hodder Fellowship will be given to writers of exceptional promise to pursue independent projects at Princeton University during the current academic year. Typically the fellows are poets, playwrights, novelists, creative nonfiction writers and translators who have published one highly acclaimed work and are undertaking a significant new project that might not be possible without the "studious leisure" afforded by the fellowship. Deadline: October 1. Open to applications in July. Prize: $75,000 stipend.

ERIC HOFFER AWARD

Hopewell Publications, LLC, P.O. Box 11, Titusville NJ 08560-0011. **Fax:** (609)964-1718. **E-mail:** info@hopepubs.com. **Website:** www.hofferaward.com. **Contact:** Christopher Klim, chair. Annual contest for previously published books. Recognizes excellence in independent publishing in many unique categories: Art (titles capture the experience, execution, or demonstration of the arts); Poetry (all styles); General Fiction (nongenre-specific fiction); Commercial Fiction (genre-specific fiction); Children (titles for young children); Young Adult (titles aimed at the juvenile and teen markets); Culture (titles demonstrating the human or world experience); Memoir (titles relating to personal experience); Business (titles with application to today's business environment and emerging trends); Reference (titles from traditional and emerging reference areas); Home (titles with practical applications to home or home-related issues, including family); Health (titles promoting physical, mental, and emotional well-being); Self-help (titles involving new and emerging topics in self-help); Spiritual (titles involving the mind and spirit, including relgion); Legacy (titles over 2 years of age that hold particular relevance to any subject matter or form). Open to any writer of published work within the last 2 years, including categores for older books. This contest recognizes excellence in independent publishing in many unique categories. Also awards the Montaigne Medal for most though-provoking book, the Da Vinci Eye for best cover, and the First Horizon Award for best new authors. Results published in the US Review of Books. Deadline: January 21. 1st place: $2,000. Costs: Charges $55.

THE JULIA WARD HOWE/BOSTON AUTHORS AWARD

The Boston Authors Club, The Boston Authors Club, 36 Sunhill Lane, Newton Center MA 02459. **E-mail:** bostonauthors@aol.com;. **Website:** www.bostonauthorsclub.org. **Contact:** Alan Lawson. Estab. 1900. This annual award honors Julia Ward Howe and her literary friends who founded the Boston Authors Club in 1900. It also honors the membership over 110 years, consisting of novelists, biographers, historians, governors, senators, philosophers, poets, playwrights, and other luminaries. There are 2 categories: trade books and books for young readers (beginning with chapter books through young adult books). Deadline: January 15. Prize: $1,000. Costs: $25/title. Judged by the members.

HENRY HOYNS & POE/FAULKNER FELLOWSHIPS

Creative Writing Program, 219 Bryan Hall, P.O. Box 400121, University of Virginia, Charlottesville VA 22904-4121. (434)924-6675. **Fax:** (434)924-1478. **E-mail:** creativewriting@virginia.edu. **Website:** creativewriting.virginia.edu. **Contact:** Jeb Livingood, associate director. Two-year MFA program in poetry and fiction; all students receive fellowships and teaching stipends that total $18,000 in both years of study. Sample poems/prose required with application. Deadline: December 15.

CAROL OTIS HURST CHILDREN'S BOOK PRIZE

Westfield Athenaeum, 6 Elm St., Westfield MA 01085. (413)568-7833. **Fax:** (413)568-0988. **Website:** www.westath.org. **Contact:** Pamela Weingart. Estab. 2007. The Carol Otis Hurst Children's Book Prize honors outstanding works of fiction and nonfiction, including biography and memoir, written for children and young adults through the age of eighteen that exemplify the highest standards of research, analysis, and authorship in their portrayal of the New England Experience. The prize will be presented annually to an author whose book treats the region's history as broadly conceived to encompass one or more of the following elements: political experience, social development, fine and performing artistic expression, domestic life and arts, transportation and communication, changing technology, military experience at home and abroad, schooling, business and manufacturing, workers and the labor movement, agriculture and its transformation, racial and ethnic diversity, religious life and institutions, immigration and adjustment, sports at all levels, and the evolution of popular entertainment. The public presentation of the prize will be accompanied by a reading and/or talk by the recipient at a mutually agreed upon time during the spring immediately following the publication year. Deadline: December 31. Prize: $500.

INDIANA REVIEW ½ K PRIZE

Indiana Review, Ballantine Hall 465, 1020 E. Kirkwood Ave., Indiana University, Bloomington IN 47405-7103. (812)855-3439. **Fax:** (812)855-9535. **E-mail:** inreview@indiana.edu. **Website:** http://indianareview.org. **Contact:** Katie Moulton, consulting editor. Offered annually for unpublished work. Maximum story/poem length is 500 words. Guidelines available in March for SASE, by phone, e-mail, on website, or in publication. Deadline: August 15. Submission period begins July 1. Prize: $1,000, plus publication, contributor's copies, and a year's subscription to *Indiana Review*. Costs: $20 fee for no more than 3 pieces; includes a 1-year subscription.

INK & INSIGHTS WRITING CONTEST

Critique My Novel, 2408 W. 8th, Amarillo TX 79106. **E-mail:** contest@InkandInsights.com. **Website:** http://InkandInsights.com. **Contact:** Catherine York, contest administrator. Ink & Insights is a writing contest geared toward strengthening the skills of independent writers by focusing on feedback. Each entry is assigned four judges who specialize in the genre of the ms. They read, score, and comment on specific aspects of the segment. The top three mss in the Master and Nonfiction categories move on to the Agent Round and receive a guaranteed read and feedback from a panel of agents. Deadline: April 30 (regular entry), June 30 (late entry). Prize: Prizes vary depending on category. Every novel receives personal feedback from 4 judges. Costs: Early bird entry: $35; Regular entry: $40; Late entry: $45. Judges listed on website, including the agents who will be helping choose the top winners this year.

INTERNATIONAL READING ASSOCIATION CHILDREN'S AND YOUNG ADULT'S BOOK AWARDS

P.O. Box 8139, 800 Barksdale Rd., Newark DE 19714-8139. (302)731-1600, ext. 221. **E-mail:** kbaughman@reading.org. **E-mail:** committees@reading.org. **Website:** www.reading.org. **Contact:** Kathy Baughman. The IRA Children's and Young Adults Book Awards are intended for newly published authors who show unusual promise in the children's and young adults' book field. Awards are given for fiction and nonfiction in each of three categories: primary, intermediate, and young adult. Books from all countries and published in English for the first time during the previous calendar year will be considered. Deadline: January 15. Prize: $1,000.

THE IOWA REVIEW AWARD IN POETRY, FICTION, AND NONFICTION

308 EPB, University of Iowa, Iowa City IA 52242. **E-mail:** iowa-review@uiowa.edu. **Website:** www.iowareview.org. *The Iowa Review* Award in Poetry, Fiction, and Nonfiction presents $1,500 to each winner in each genre and $750 to runners-up. Winners and runners-up published in *The Iowa Review*. Deadline: January 31. Submission period begins January 1. Costs: $20. Make checks payable to *The Iowa Review*. Enclose additional $10 (optional) for year-long subscription. Judged by Brenda Shaughnessy, Kelly Link, and Eula Biss in 2016.

THE IOWA SHORT FICTION AWARD & JOHN SIMMONS SHORT FICTION AWARD

Iowa Writers' Workshop, 507 N. Clinton St., 102 Dey House, Iowa City IA 52242-1000. **Website:** www.uiowapress.org. **Contact:** James McCoy, director. Annual award to give exposure to promising writers who have not yet published a book of prose. Open to any writer. Current University of Iowa students are not eligible. No application forms are necessary. Announcement of winners made early in year following competition. Winners notified by phone. No application forms are necessary. Do not send original ms. Include SASE for return of ms. Deadline: September 30. Submission period begins August 1. Prize: Publication by University of Iowa Press. Judged by senior Iowa Writers' Workshop members who screen mss; published fiction author of note makes final selections.

IRA SHORT STORY AWARD

International Reading Association, International Reading Association, 800 Barksdale Rd., PO Box 8139, Newark DE 19714-8139. (302)731-1600. **Fax:** (302)731-1057. **E-mail:** committees@reading.org. **Website:** www.reading.org. Offered to reward author of an original short story published for the first time in a periodical for children. (Periodicals should generally be aimed at readers around age 12.) Write for guidelines or download from website. Award is non-monetary. Deadline: November 15.

TILIA KLEBENOV JACOBS RELIGIOUS ESSAY PRIZE CATEGORY

Soul Making Keats Literary Competition, The Webhallow House, 1544 Sweetwood Dr., Broadmoor Village CA 94015-2029. **E-mail:** SoulKeats@mail.com. **Website:** www.soulmakingcontest.us. **Contact:** Eileen Malone. Estab. 2012. Call for thoughtful writings of up to 3,000 words. "No preaching, no proselytizing." Open annually to any writer. Deadline: November 30. Prize: 1st Place: $100; 2nd Place: $50; 3rd Place: $25. Costs: $5.

JAPAN-U.S. FRIENDSHIP COMMISSION PRIZE FOR THE TRANSLATION OF JAPANESE LITERATURE

Japanese Literary Translation Prize, Donald Keene Center of Japanese Culture, Columbia University, 507 Kent Hall

1140 Amsterdam Ave., New York NY 10027, USA. **Website:** http://www.keenecenter.org/. **Contact:** Yoshiko Niiya, Program Coordinator. Estab. 1979. The Donald Keene Center of Japanese Culture at Columbia University annually awards Japan-U.S. Friendship Commission Prizes for the Translation of Japanese Literature. A prize is given for the best translation of a modern work or a classical work, or the prize is divided between equally distinguished translations. Deadline: June 1. Prize: $6,000.

Translations must be book-length Japanese literary works: novels, collections of short stories, manga, literary essays, memoirs, drama, or poetry. Works may be unpublished mss, works in press, or books published during the two years prior to the prize year.

JESSE H. JONES AWARD FOR BEST WORK OF FICTION

P.O. Box 609, Round Rock TX 78680. **E-mail:** tilsecretary@yahoo.com. **Website:** http://texasinstituteofletters.org. Offered annually by Texas Institute of Letters for work published January 1-December 31 of year before award is given to recognize the writer of the best book of fiction entered in the competition. Writers must have been born in Texas, have lived in the state for at least 2 consecutive years at some time, or the subject matter of the work should be associated with the state. Deadline: January 10. Prize: $6,000.

JAMES JONES FIRST NOVEL FELLOWSHIP

Wilkes University, Creative Writing Department, Wilkes University, 84 West South Street, Wilkes-Barre PA 18766. (570)408-4547. **Fax:** (570)408-3333. **E-mail:** jamesjonesfirstnovel@wilkes.edu. **Website:** www.wilkes.edu/. Offered annually for unpublished novels and novellas (must be works-in-progress). This competition is open to all American writers who have not previously published novels. The award is intended to honor the spirit of unblinking honesty, determination, and insight into modern culture exemplified by the late James Jones. Deadline: March 15. Submission period begins October 1. Prize: $10,000; 2 runners-up get $1,000 honorarium. Costs: $30.

JUNIPER PRIZE FOR FICTION

University of Massachusetts Press, East Experiment Station, 671 North Pleasant St., Amherst MA 01003. (413)545-2217. **Fax:** (413)545-1226. **E-mail:** info@umpress.umass.edu; kfisk@umpress.umass.edu. **E-mail:** fiction@umpress.umass.edu. **Website:** www.umass.edu/umpress. **Contact:** Karen Fisk, competition coordinator. Estab. 2004. Award to honor and publish outstanding works of literary fiction. Deadline: September 30. Submissions period begins August 1. Winners announced online in April on the press website. Prize: $1,000 cash and publication. Costs: $25.

THE LAWRENCE FOUNDATION AWARD

Prairie Schooner, 123 Andrews Hall, University of Nebraska-Lincoln, Lincoln NE 68588-0334. (402)472-0911. **Fax:** (402)472-9771. **E-mail:** prairieschooner@unl.edu. **Website:** www.prairieschooner.unl.edu. Offered annually for the best short story published in Prairie Schooner in the previous year. Only work published in *Prairie Schooner* in the previous year is considered. Work is nominated by editorial staff. Results announced in the Spring issue. Winners notified by mail in February or March. Prize: $1,000. Judged by editorial staff of *Praire Schooner.*

LAWRENCE FOUNDATION PRIZE

Michigan Quarterly Review, 0576 Rackham Bldg., 915 E. Washington Street, Ann Arbor MI 48109-1070. (734)764-9265. **E-mail:** mqr@umich.edu. **Website:** www.michiganquarterlyreview.com. **Contact:** Vicki Lawrence, managing editor. Estab. 1978. This annual prize is awarded by the *Michigan Quarterly Review* editorial board to the author of the best short story published in *MQR* that year. The prize is sponsored by University of Michigan alumnus and fiction writer Leonard S. Bernstein, a trustee of the Lawrence Foundation of New York. Approximately 20 short stories are published in *MQR* each year. Prize: $1,000. Judged by editorial board.

THE STEPHEN LEACOCK MEMORIAL MEDAL FOR HUMOUR

149 Peter St. N., Orillia ON L3V 4Z4, Canada. (705)326-9286. **E-mail:** bettewalkerca@gmail.com. **Website:** www.leacock.ca. **Contact:** Bette Walker, award committee, Stephen Leacock Associates. The Leacock Associates awards the prestigious Leacock Medal for the best book of literary humor written by a Canadian and published in the current year. The winning author also receives a cash prize of $15,000 thanks to the generous support of the TD Financial Group. 2 runners-up are each awarded a cash prize of $1,500. Entry fee: $200. Deadline: December 31.

LEAGUE OF UTAH WRITERS CONTEST

The League of Utah Writers, The League of Utah Writers, P.O. Box 64, Lewiston UT 84320. (435)755-7609. **E-mail:** luwcontest@gmail.com; luwriters@gmail.com. **Website:** www.luwriters.org. Open to any writer, the LUW Contest provides authors an opportunity to get their work read and critiqued. Multiple categories are offered; see website for details. Entries must be the original and unpublished work of the author. Winners are announced at the Annual Writers Round-Up in September. Those not present will be notified by e-mail. Deadline: June 15. Submissions period begins March 15. Prize: Cash prizes are awarded. Judged by professional authors and editors from outside the League.

LES FIGUES PRESS NOS BOOK CONTEST

P.O. Box 7736, Los Angeles CA 90007. (323)734-4732. **E-mail:** info@lesfigues.com. **Website:** www.lesfigues.com. **Contact:** Teresa Carmody, director. Les Figues Press creates aesthetic conversations between writers/artists and readers, especially those interested in innovative/experimental/avant-garde work. The Press intends in the most premeditated fashion to champion the trinity of Beauty, Belief, and Bawdry. Deadline: September 15. Prize: $1,000, plus publication by Les Figues Press. Each entry receives LFP book. Costs: $25.

LET'S WRITE LITERARY CONTEST

The Gulf Coast Writers Association, P.O. Box 4808, Biloxi MS 39535. **E-mail:** writerpllevin@gmail.com. **Website:** www.gcwriters.org. **Contact:** Philip Levin. The Gulf Coast Writers Association sponsors this nationally recognized contest, which accepts unpublished poems and short stories from authors all around the US. This is an annual event which has been held for over 26 years. Deadline: July 31. 1st Prize: $100; 2nd Prize: $60; 3rd Prize: $25. Costs: Charges $8 for prose, $8 for 3 poems.

FENIA AND YAAKOV LEVIANT MEMORIAL PRIZE IN YIDDISH STUDIES

Modern Language Association of America, 85 Broad Street, suite 500, New York NY 10004-2434. (646)576-5141. **Fax:** (646)458-0030. **E-mail:** awards@mla.org. **Website:** www.mla.org. **Contact:** Coordinator of book prizes. Offered in even-numbered years for an outstanding English translation of a Yiddish literary work or the publication of a scholarly work. Cultural studies, critical biographies, or edited works in the field of Yiddish folklore or linguistic studies are eligible to compete. See website for details on which they are accepting. Deadline: May 1. Prize: A cash prize, and a certificate, to be presented at the Modern Language Association's annual convention in January.

LITERAL LATTÉ FICTION AWARD

Literal Latté, 200 E. 10th St., Suite 240, New York NY 10003. (212)260-5532. **E-mail:** litlatte@aol.com. **E-mail:** Link to submittable on www.literal-latte.com. **Website:** www.literal-latte.com. **Contact:** Edward Estlin, contributing editor. Estab. 1994. Award to provide talented writers with 3 essential tools for continued success: money, publication, and recognition. Offered annually for unpublished fiction (maximum 20,000 words). Guidelines online. Open to any writer. Deadline: January 15. Prize: 1st Place: $1,000 and publication in *Literal Latté*; 2nd Place: $300; 3rd Place: $200; also up to 7 honorable mentions. All winners published in *Literal Latté*. Costs: $10 per story; $15 for two.

LITERAL LATTE SHORT SHORTS CONTEST

Literal Latté, 200 E. 10th St., Suite 240, New York NY 10003. (212)260-5532. **E-mail:** litlatte@aol.com. **E-mail:** Link to submittable on www.literal-latte.com. **Website:** www.literal-latte.com. **Contact:** Jenine Gordon Bockman, editor. Estab. 1994. Annual contest. Send unpublished shorts, 2,000 words max. All styles welcome. Name, address, phone number, e-mail address (optional) on cover page only. Include SASE or e-mail address for reply. All entries considered for publication. Deadline: June 30. Prize: $500. Costs: $10 for up to three shorts. Judged by the editors.

THE HUGH J. LUKE AWARD

Prairie Schooner, 123 Andrews Hall, University of Nebraska-Lincoln, Lincoln NE 68588-0334. (402)472-0911. **Fax:** (402)472-1817. **E-mail:** prairieschooner@unl.edu. **Website:** www.prairieschooner.unl.edu. **Contact:** Kwame Dawes. Offered annually for work published in *Prairie Schooner* in the previous year. Results announced in the Spring issue. Winners notified by mail in February or March. Prize: $250. Judged by editorial staff of *Prairie Schooner*.

THE MARY MACKEY SHORT STORY PRIZE CATEGORY

Soul-Making Keats Literary Competition, The Webhallow House, 1544 Sweetwood Dr., Broadmoor Village CA 94015. **E-mail:** SoulKeats@mail.com. **Website:** www.soulmakingcontest.us. **Contact:** Eileen Malone. Open annually to any writer. Deadline: November 30. Prize: Cash prizes. Costs: $5/entry (make checks payable to NLAPW).

THE MALAHAT REVIEW NOVELLA PRIZE

The Malahat Review, University of Victoria, P.O. Box 1700 STN CSC, Victoria BC V8W 2Y2, Canada. (250)721-8524. **E-mail:** malahat@uvic.ca. **E-mail:** novella@uvic.ca. **Website:** malahatreview.ca. **Contact:** John Barton, editor. Held in alternate years with the Long Poem Prize. Offered to promote unpublished novellas. Obtains first world rights. After publication rights revert to the author. Open to any writer. Deadline: February 1 (even years). Prize: $1,500 CAD and one year's subscription. Winner published in summer issue of *The Malahat Review* and announced on website, Facebook page, and in quarterly e-newsletter, *Malahat Lite*. Costs: $35 CAD for Canadian entrants; $40 US for American entrants; $45 US for entrants from elsewhere (includes a 1-year subscription to *Malahat*). $15 CAD from anywhere for each additional entry after the first. Judges for the 2016 Novella Prize are Mark Anthony Jarman, Stephen Marche, and Joan Thomas. Their bios are on our website.

THE MAN BOOKER PRIZE

Four Colman Getty PR, 20 St Thomas Street, London SE1 9BF, United Kingdom. (44)(207)697 4200. **Website:** www.themanbookerprize.com. **Contact:** Four Colman Getty PR. Estab. 1968. Books are only accepted through UK publishers. However, publication outside the UK does not disqualify a book once it is published in the UK. Open to any full-length novel (published October 1-September 30). No novellas, collections of short stories, translations, or self-published books. Open to citizens of the Commonwealth or Republic of Ireland. Deadline: July. Prize: £50,000. Judges appointed by the Booker Prize Management Committee.

MANITOBA BOOK AWARDS

c/o Manitoba Writers' Guild, 218-100 Arthur St., Winnipeg MB R3B 1H3, Canada. (204)944-8013. **E-mail:** events@mbwriter.mb.ca. **Website:** www.manitobabookawards.com. **Contact:** Anita Daher. Offered annually: The McNally Robinson Book of Year Award (adult); The McNally Robinson Book for Young People Awards (8 and under and 9 and older); The John Hirsch Award for Most Promising Manitoba Writer; The Mary Scorer Award for Best Book by a Manitoba Publisher; The Carol Shields Winnipeg Book Award; The Eileen McTavish Sykes Award for Best First Book; The Margaret Laurence Award for Fiction; The Alexander Kennedy Isbister Award for Nonfiction; The Manuela Dias Book Design of the Year Award; The Best Illustrated Book of the Year Award; the biennial Le Prix Littéraire Rue-Deschambault; The Beatrice Mosionier Aboriginal Writer of the Year Award; and The Chris Johnson Award for Best Play by a Manitoba Playwright. Deadline: October 31 and December 31. See website for specific details on book eligibility at deadlines. Prize: Several prizes up to $5,000 (Canadian).

MARSH AWARD FOR CHILDREN'S LITERATURE IN TRANSLATION

The English-Speaking Union, Dartmouth House, 37 Charles St., London En W1J 5ED, United Kingdom. 020 7529 1590. **E-mail:** emma.coffey@esu.org. **Website:** www.marshcristiantrust.org; www.esu.org. **Contact:** Emma Coffey, education officer. Estab. 1996. The Marsh Award for Children's Literature in Translation, awarded biennially, was founded to celebrate the best translation of a children's book from a foreign language into English and published in the UK. It aims to spotlight the high quality and diversity of translated fiction for young readers. The Award is administered by the ESU on behalf of the Marsh Christian Trust.

MARY MCCARTHY PRIZE IN SHORT FICTION

Sarabande Books, 2234 Dundee Rd., Suite 200, Louisville KY 40205. (502)458-4028. **Fax:** (502)458-4065. **E-mail:** info@sarabandebooks.org. **Website:** www.sarabandebooks.org. **Contact:** Sarah Gorham, Editor-in-Chief. Annual competition to honor a collection of short stories, novellas, or a short novel. Deadline: April 30. Submission period begins March 15. Prize: $2,000 and publication (standard royalty contract). Costs: $28.

THE MCGINNIS-RITCHIE MEMORIAL AWARD

Southwest Review, Southern Methodist University, P.O. Box 750374, Dallas TX 75275-0374. (214)768-1037. **Fax:** (214)768-1408. **E-mail:** swr@mail.smu.edu. **Website:** www.smu.edu/southwestreview. **Contact:** Jennifer Cranfill, senior editor. The McGinnis-Ritchie Memorial Award is given annually to the best works of fiction and nonfiction that appeared in the magazine in the previous year. Mss are submitted for publication, not for the prizes themselves. Guidelines for SASE or online. Prize: $500. Judged by Jennifer Cranfill and Willard Spiegelman.

MARJORIE GRABER MCINNIS SHORT STORY AWARD

ACT Writers Centre, Gorman House Arts Centre, Ainslie Ave., Braddon ACT 2612, Australia. (61)(2)6262-9191. **Fax:** (61)(2)6262-9191. **E-mail:** admin@actwriters.org.au. **Website:** www.actwriters.org.au. Open theme for a short story with 1,500-3,000 words. Guidelines available on website. Open only to unpublished emerging writers residing within the ACT or region. Deadline: September 18. Submissions period begins in early September. Prize: $600 and publication. Five runners-up receive book prizes. All winners may be published in the ACT Writers Centre newsletter and on the ACT Writers Centre website. Costs: $7.50 for nonmembers; $5 for members.

MCKNIGHT ARTIST FELLOWSHIPS FOR WRITERS, LOFT AWARD(S) IN CHILDREN'S LITERATURE/CREATIVE PROSE/POETRY

The Loft Literary Center, 1011 Washington Ave. S., Suite 200, Open Book, Minneapolis MN 55415. (612)215-2575. **Fax:** (612)215-2576. **E-mail:** loft@loft.org. **Website:** www.loft.org. **Contact:** Bao Phi. "The Loft administers the McKnight Artists Fellowships for Writers. Five $25,000 awards are presented annually to accomplished Minnesota writers and spoken word artists. Four awards alternate annually between creative prose (fiction and creative nonfiction) and poetry/spoken word. The fifth award is presented in children's literature and alternates annually for writing for ages 8 and under and writing for children older than 8." The awards provide the writers the opportunity to focus on their craft for the course of the fellowship year. Prize: $25,000.

MEMPHIS MAGAZINE FICTION CONTEST

Memphis Magazine, co-sponsored by booksellers of Laurelwood and Burke's Book Store, Fiction Contest, c/o *Memphis* magazine, P.O. Box 1738, Memphis TN 38101. (901)521-9000, ext. 451. **Fax:** (901)521-0129. **E-mail:** sadler@memphismagazine.com. **Website:** www.memphismagazine.com. **Contact:** Marilyn Sadler. Annual award for authors of short fiction living within 150 miles of Memphis. Deadline: February 15. Prize: $1,000 grand prize, along with being published in the annual Cultural Issue; two honorable-mention awards of $500 each will be given if the quality of entries warrants. Costs: $10/story.

DAVID NATHAN MEYERSON PRIZE FOR FICTION

Southwest Review, Southern Methodist University, P.O. Box 750374, Dallas TX 75275-0374. (214)768-1037. **Fax:** (214)768-1408. **E-mail:** swr@smu.edu. **Website:** www.smu.edu/southwestreview. **Contact:** Jennifer Cranfill, senior editor. Annual award given to a writer who has not published a first book of fiction, either a novel or collection of stories. All contest entrants will receive a copy of the issue in which the winning piece appears. Deadline: May 1 (postmarked). Prize: $1,000 and publication in the *Southwest Review*. Costs: $25/story.

MILKWEED NATIONAL FICTION PRIZE

1011 Washington Ave. S., Suite 300, Minneapolis MN 55415. (612)332-3192. **Fax:** (612)215-2550. **E-mail:** editor@milkweed.org. **Website:** www.milkweed.org. **Contact:** Patrick Thoman, editor and program manager. Annual award for unpublished works. Mss should be one of the following: a novel, a collection of short stories, one or more novellas, or a combination of short stories and one or more novellas. Deadline: Rolling submissions. Check website for details of when they're accepting mss. Prize: Publication by Milkweed Editions and a cash advance of $5,000 against royalties, agreed upon in the contractual arrangement negotiated at the time of acceptance. Judged by the editors.

MILKWEED PRIZE FOR CHILDREN'S LITERATURE

Milkweed Editions, 1011 Washington Ave. S., Suite 300, Minneapolis MN 55415. (612)332-3192. **Fax:** (612)215-2550. **E-mail:** editor@milkweed.org. **Website:** www.milkweed.org. Milkweed Editions will award the Milkweed Prize for Children's Literature to the best mss for young readers that Milkweed accepts for publication during the calendar year by a writer not previously published by Milkweed. All mss for young readers submitted for publication by Milkweed are automatically entered into the competition. Recognizes an outstanding literary novel for readers ages 8-13 and encourage writers to turn their attention to readers in this age group. Prize: $10,000 cash prize in addition to a publishing contract negotiated at the time of acceptance. Judged by the editors of Milkweed Editions.

MINNESOTA BOOK AWARDS

325 Cedar Street, Suite 555, St. Paul MN 55101. (651)222-3242. **Fax:** (651)222-1988. **E-mail:** mnbookawards@thefriends.org; friends@thefriends.org; info@thefriends.org. **Website:** www.mnbookawards.org. Estab. 1988. A year-round program celebrating and honoring Minnesota's best books, culminating in an annual awards ceremony. Recognizes and honors achievement by members of Minnesota's book and book arts community. Deadline: Nomination should be submitted by 5:00 p.m. on the first Friday in December.

MISSISSIPPI REVIEW PRIZE

Mississippi Review, 118 College Dr., #5144, Hattiesburg MS 39406-0001. (601)266-4321. **Fax:** (601)266-5757. **E-mail:** msreview@usm.edu. **Website:** www.mississippireview.com. Annual contest starting August 1 and running until January 1. Winners and finalists will make up next spring's print issue of the national literary magazine *Mississippi Review*. Each entrant will receive a copy of the prize issue. Deadline: January 1. Prize: $1,000 in fiction and poetry. Costs: $15 mail submission; $16 online submission. Judged by Andrew Malan Milward in fiction, and Angela Ball in poetry.

MONTANA PRIZE IN FICTION

Cutbank Literary Magazine, *CutBank*, University of Montana, English Dept., LA 133, Missoula MT 59812.

E-mail: editor.cutbank@gmail.com. **Website:** www.cutbankonline.org. **Contact:** Allison Linville, editor-in-chief. The Montana Prize in Fiction seeks to highlight work that showcases an authentic voice, a boldness of form, and a rejection of functional fixedness. Deadline: January 15. Submissions period begins November 9. Prize: $500 and featured in the magazine. Costs: $20. Judged by a guest judge each year.

JENNY MCKEAN MOORE VISITING WRITER

English Department, George Washington University, Rome Hall, 801 22nd St. NW, Suite 760, Washington DC 20052. (202)994-6180. **Fax:** (202)994-7915. **E-mail:** tvmallon@gwu.edu. **Website:** http://columbian.gwu.edu/departmentsprograms/english/creativewriting/activitiesevents. **Contact:** Lisa Page, Acting Director of Creative Writing. The position is filled annually, bringing a visiting writer to The George Washington University. During each semester the Writer teaches 1 creative-writing course at the university as well as a community workshop. Seeks someone specializing in a different genre each year—fiction, poetry, creative nonfiction. Annual stipend between $50,000 and $60,000, plus reduced-rent townhouse on campus (not guaranteed). Application Deadline: December 3. Annual stipend varies, depending on endowment performance; most recently, stipend was $58,000, plus reduced-rent townhouse (not guaranteed).

THE HOWARD FRANK MOSHER SHORT FICTION PRIZE

Vermont College, 36 College St., Montpelier VT 05602. (802)828-8517. **E-mail:** hungermtn@vcfa.edu. **Website:** www.hungermtn.org. **Contact:** Samantha Kolber, managing editor. Estab. 2002. The Howard Frank Mosher Short Fiction Prize is an annual contest for short fiction. Deadline: March 1 Prize: One first place winner receives $1,000 and publication. Two honorable mentions receive $100 each, and are considered for publication. Costs: $20. Judged by Janet Burroway in 2016 and Caitlyn Horrocks in 2017.

NATIONAL BOOK AWARDS

The National Book Foundation, 90 Broad St., Suite 604, New York NY 10004. (212)685-0261. **E-mail:** nationalbook@nationalbook.org; agall@nationalbook.org. **Website:** www.nationalbook.org. **Contact:** Amy Gall. The National Book Foundation and the National Book Awards celebrate the best of American literature, expand its audience, and enhance the cultural value of great writing in America. The contest offers prizes in 4 categories: fiction, nonfiction, poetry, and young people's literature. Books should be published between December 1 and November 30 of the past year. Deadline: Submit entry form, payment, and a copy of the book by July 1. Prize: $10,000 in each category. Finalists will each receive a prize of $1,000. Costs: $135/title. Judged by a category specific panel of 5 judges for each category.

NATIONAL OUTDOOR BOOK AWARDS

921 S. 8th Ave., Stop 8128, Pocatello ID 83209. (208)282-3912. **E-mail:** wattron@isu.edu. **Website:** www.noba-web.org. **Contact:** Ron Watters. Nine categories: History/biography, outdoor literature, instructional texts, outdoor adventure guides, nature guides, children's books, design/artistic merit, natural history literature, and nature and the environment. Additionally, a special award, the Outdoor Classic Award, is given annually to books which, over a period of time, have proven to be exceptionally valuable works in the outdoor field. Application forms and eligibility requirements are available online. Applications for the Awards program become available in early June. Deadline: August 25. Prize: Winning books are promoted nationally and are entitled to display the National Outdoor Book Award (NOBA) medallion. Costs: $75.

NATIONAL READERS' CHOICE AWARDS

Oklahoma Romance Writers of America (OKRWA), **E-mail:** nrca@okrwa.com. **Website:** www.okrwa.com. **Contact:** Kathy L Wheeler. Estab. 1990. "To provide writers of romance fiction with a competition where their published novels are judged by readers." See the website for categories and descriptions. Additional award for best first book. All entries must have an original copyright date during the current contest year. Entries will be accepted from authors, editors, publishers, agents, readers, whoever wants to fill out the entry form, pay the fee, and supply the books. No limit to the number of entries, but each title may be entered only in one category. Open to any writer published by an RWA approved non-vanity/non-subsidy press. For guidelines, send e-mail or visit website. Deadline: December 1st. Prize: Plaques and finalist certificates awarded at the awards banquet hosted at the Annual National Romance Writers Convention.

Costs: $30 per entry, plus $5 for Best First Book Category. Judged by readers.

O NATIONAL WRITERS ASSOCIATION NOVEL WRITING CONTEST

The National Writers Association, 10940 S. Parker Rd. #508, Parker CO 80134. (303)841-0246. **E-mail:** natlwritersassn@hotmail.com. **Website:** www.nationalwriters.com. **Contact:** Sandy Whelchel, director. Open to any genre or category. Contest begins December 1. Open to any writer. Annual contest to help develop creative skills, to recognize and reward outstanding ability, and to increase the opportunity for the marketing and subsequent publication of novel mss. Deadline: April 1. Prize: 1st Place: $500; 2nd Place: $250; 3rd Place: $150. Costs: $35. Judged by editors and agents.

NATIONAL WRITERS ASSOCIATION SHORT STORY CONTEST

10940 S. Parker Rd., #508, Parker CO 80134. (303)841-0246. **E-mail:** natlwritersassn@hotmail.com. **Website:** www.nationalwriters.com. Estab. 1971. The purpose of the National Writers Assn. Short Story Contest is to encourage the development of creative skills, recognize and reward outstanding ability in the area of short story writing. Prize: 1st Prize: $250; 2nd Prize: $100; 3rd Prize: $50; 4th-10th places will receive a book. 1st-3rd place winners may be asked to grant one-time rights for publication in *Authorship* magazine. Honorable Mentions receive a certificate. Costs: $15. Judging will be based on originality, marketability, research, and reader interest. Copies of the judges evaluation sheets will be sent to entrants furnishing an SASE with their entry.

THE NELLIGAN PRIZE FOR SHORT FICTION

Colorado Review/Center for Literary Publishing, Colorado State University, 9105 Campus Delivery, Dept. of English, Colorado State University, Ft. Collins CO 80523-9105. (970)491-5449. **E-mail:** creview@colostate.edu. **Website:** http://nelliganprize.colostate.edu. **Contact:** Stephanie G'Schwind, editor. Annual competition/award for short stories. Receives approximately 900 stories. All entries are read blind by Colorado Review's editorial staff. Ten-to-fifteen entries are selected to be sent on to a final, outside judge. Stories must be unpublished and between 10 and 50 pages. "The Nelligan Prize for Short Fiction was established in memory of Liza Nelligan, a writer, editor, and friend of many in Colorado State University's English Department, where she received her master's degree in literature in 1992. By giving an award to the author of an outstanding short story each year, we hope to honor Liza Nelligan's life, her passion for writing, and her love of fiction." Deadline: March 14. Prize: $2,000 and publication of story in *Colorado Review*. Costs: $15, send credit card information or make checks payable to Colorado Review; payment also accepted via our online submission manager link from website. Judged by a different writer each year.

THE NEUTRINO SHORT-SHORT CONTEST

Passages North, Dept. of English, Northern Michigan University, 1401 Presque Isle Ave., Marquette MI 49855. (906)227-1203. **Fax:** (906)227-1096. **E-mail:** passages@nmu.edu. **Website:** www.passagesnorth.com. **Contact:** Jennifer Howard. Offered every 2 years to publish new voices in literary fiction, nonfiction, hybrid-essays and prose poems (maximum 1,000 words). Guidelines available for SASE or online. Deadline: April 15. Submission period begins February 15. Prize: $1,000, and publication for the winner; 2 honorable mentions also published; all entrants receive a copy of *Passages North*. Costs: $15 for up to 3 pieces. Judged by Lindsay Hunter in 2016.

NEW ENGLAND BOOK AWARDS

1955 Massachusetts Ave., #2, Cambridge MA 02140. (617)547-3642. **Fax:** (617)547-3759. **E-mail:** nan@neba.org. **Website:** http://www.newenglandbooks.org/BookAwards. **Contact:** Nan Sorenson, administrative coordinator. Estab. 1990. Annual award. Previously published submissions only. Submissions made by New England booksellers; publishers. Submit written nominations only; actual books should not be sent. Member bookstores receive materials to display winners' books. Award is given to a specific title, fiction, non-fiction, children's. The titles must be either about New England, set in New England or by an author residing in the New England. The titles must be hardcover, paperback original or reissue that was published between September 1 and August 31. Entries must be still in print and available. Deadline: June 10. Prize: Winners will receive $250 for literacy to a charity of their choice. Judged by NEIBA membership.

O *NEW LETTERS* LITERARY AWARDS

New Letters, University of Missouri-Kansas City, 5101 Rockhill Rd., Kansas City MO 64110-2499, USA. (816)235-1168. **Fax:** (816)235-2611. **Website:**

http://www.newletters.org/writers-wanted/writing-contests. Estab. 1986. Award has 3 categories (fiction, poetry, and creative nonfiction) with 1 winner in each. Offered annually for previously unpublished work. For guidelines, send an SASE to *New Letters*, or visit http://www.newletters.org/writers-wanted/writing-contests. Deadline: May 18. Prize: 1st place: $1,500, plus publication. Costs: $20 for first entry, $15 for every entry after; add an extra $5 service charge if entering online. Judged by regional writers of prominence and experience. Final judging by someone of national repute. Previous judges include Maxine Kumin, Albert Goldbarth, Charles Simic, and Janet Burroway.

NEW MILLENNIUM AWARDS FOR FICTION, POETRY, AND NONFICTION

New Millennium Writings, 4021 Garden Dr., Knoxville TN 37918. (865)254-4880. **Website:** www.newmillenniumwritings.org. **Contact:** Alexis Williams, Editor and Publisher. Estab. 1996. No restrictions as to style, content or number of submissions. Previously published pieces acceptable if online or under 5,000 print circulation. Simultaneous and multiple submissions welcome. Deadline: Postmarked on or before January 31 for the Winter Awards and July 31 for the Summer Awards. Prize: $1,000 for Best Poem; $1,000 for Best Fiction; $1,000 for Best Nonfiction; $1,000 for Best Short-Short Fiction. Costs: $20.

NEW SOUTH WRITING CONTEST

English Department, Georgia State University, P.O. Box 3970, Atlanta GA 30302-3970. **E-mail:** newsouth@gsu.edu. **Website:** newsouthjournal.com/contest. **Contact:** Stephanie Devine, editor-in-chief. Offered annually to publish the most promising work of up-and-coming writers of poetry (up to 3 poems) and fiction (9,000 word limit). Rights revert to writer upon publication. Guidelines online. Deadline: April 15. Prize: 1st Place: $1,000 in each category; 2nd Place: $250; and publication to winners. Costs: $15. Judged by Anya Silver in poetry and Matthew Salesses in prose.

NORTH CAROLINA ARTS COUNCIL REGIONAL ARTIST PROJECT GRANTS

North Carolina Arts Council, Dept. of Cultural Resources, MSC #4632, Raleigh NC 27699-4634. (919)807-6512. **Fax:** (919)807-6532. **E-mail:** david.potorti@ncdcr.gov. **Website:** www.ncarts.org. **Contact:** David Potorti, literature director. See website for contact information for the local arts councils that distribute these grants. Deadline: Late summer/early fall. Prize: $500-3,000 awarded to writers to pursue projects that further their artistic development.

NORTH CAROLINA WRITERS' FELLOWSHIPS

North Carolina Arts Council, North Carolina Arts Council, Writers' Fellowships, Department of Cultural Resources, Raleigh NC 27699-4632. (919)807-6512. **Fax:** (919)807-6532. **E-mail:** david.potorti@ncdcr.gov. **Website:** www.ncarts.org. **Contact:** David Potorti, literature and theater director. The North Carolina Arts Council offers grants in two categories to writers, spoken-word artists, playwrights, and screenwriters: fellowships (every other year) and residency grants (every year). Offered every even year to support writers of fiction, poetry, literary nonfiction, literary translation, and spoken word. See website for guidelines and other eligibility requirements. Deadline: November 1. Prize: $10,000 grant. Reviewed by a panel of literature professionals (writers and editors).

NORTHERN CALIFORNIA BOOK AWARDS

Northern California Book Reviewers Association, c/o Poetry Flash, 1450 Fourth St. #4, Berkeley CA 94710. (510)525-5476. **E-mail:** ncbr@poetryflash.org; editor@poetryflash.org. **Website:** www.poetryflash.org. **Contact:** Joyce Jenkins, executive director. Estab. 1981. Annual Northern California Book Award for outstanding book in literature, open to books published in the current calendar year by Northern California authors. NCBR presents annual awards to Bay Area (northern California) authors annually in fiction, nonfiction, poetry and children's literature. Encourages writers and stimulates interest in books and reading. Deadline: December 28. Prize: $100 honorarium and award certificate. Judging by voting members of the Northern California Book Reviewers.

SEAN O'FAOLAIN SHORT STORY COMPETITION

The Munster Literature Centre, Frank O'Connor House, 84 Douglas Street, Cork , Ireland. +353-0214319255. **E-mail:** munsterlit@eircom.net. **Website:** www.munsterlit.ie. **Contact:** Patrick Cotter, artistic director. Purpose is to reward writers of outstanding short stories. Deadline: July 31. Prize: 1st prize €2,000; 2nd prize €500. Four runners-up prizes of €100 (approx $146). All six stories to be published in *Southword Literary Journal*. First-Prize Winner offered week's residency in Anam Cara Artist's Retreat in Ireland. Costs: $20.

FRANK O'CONNOR AWARD FOR SHORT FICTION

descant, Texas Christian University's literary journal, TCU Box 298300, Fort Worth TX 76129. (817)257-5907. **Fax:** (817)257-6239. **E-mail:** descant@tcu.edu. **Website:** www.descant.tcu.edu. **Contact:** Matthew Pitt, editor. Offered annually for an outstanding story accepted for publication in the current edition of the journal. Publication retains copyright but will transfer it to the author upon request. Deadline: September 1 - March 31. Prize: $500.

OHIOANA BOOK AWARDS

Ohioana Library Association, 274 E. First Ave., Suite 300, Columbus OH 43201-3673. (614)466-3831. **Fax:** (614)728-6974. **E-mail:** ohioana@ohioana.org. **Website:** www.ohioana.org. **Contact:** David Weaver, executive director. Estab. 1942. Offered annually to bring national attention to Ohio authors and their books, published in the last year. (Books can only be considered once.) Categories: Fiction, nonfiction, juvenile, poetry, and books about Ohio or an Ohioan. Deadline: December 31. Prize: $1,000 cash prize, certificate, and glass sculpture. Judged by a jury selected by librarians, book reviewers, writers and other knowledgeable people.

OHIOANA WALTER RUMSEY MARVIN GRANT

Ohioana Library Association, 274 E. First Ave., Suite 300, Columbus OH 43201. (614)466-3831. **Fax:** (614)728-6974. **E-mail:** ohioana@ohioana.org. **Website:** www.ohioana.org. **Contact:** David Weaver, executive director. Award to encourage young, unpublished writers 30 years of age or younger. Competition for short stories or novels in progress. Deadline: January 31 Prize: $1,000.

OKLAHOMA BOOK AWARDS

200 NE 18th St., Oklahoma City OK 73105. (405)521-2502. **Fax:** (405)525-7804. **E-mail:** connie.armstrong@libraries.ok.gov. **Website:** www.odl.state.ok.us/ocb. **Contact:** Connie Armstrong, executive director. Estab. 1989. This award honors Oklahoma writers and books about Oklahoma. Awards are presented to best books in fiction, nonfiction, children's, design and illustration, and poetry books about Oklahoma or books written by an author who was born, is living or has lived in Oklahoma. SASE for award rules and entry forms. Winner will be announced at banquet in Oklahoma City. The Arrell Gibson Lifetime Achievement Award is also presented each year for a body of work. Deadline: January 10. Prize: Awards a medal. Costs: $25. Judging by a panel of 5 people for each category, generally a librarian, a working writer in the genre, booksellers, editors, etc.

ON THE PREMISES CONTEST

On The Premises, LLC, 4323 Gingham Court, Alexandria VA 22310. **E-mail:** questions@onthepremises.com. **Website:** www.onthepremises.com. **Contact:** Tarl Kudrick or Bethany Granger, co-publishers. *On the Premises* aims to promote newer and/or relatively unknown writers who can write creative, compelling stories told in effective, uncluttered, and evocative prose. Each contest challenges writers to produce a great story based on a broad premise that the editors supply as part of the contest. Deadline: Short story contests held twice a year; smaller mini-contests held four times a year; check website for exact dates. Prize: 1st Prize: $220; 2nd Prize: $160; 3rd Prize: $120; Honorable Mentions receive $60. All prize winners are published in *On the Premises* magazine in HTML and PDF format. Costs: There are no fees for entering our contests. Judged by a panel of judges with professional editing and writing experience.

OPEN SEASON AWARDS

The Malahat Review, University of Victoria, P.O. Box 1700, Stn CSC, Victoria BC V8V 2Y2, Canada. (250)721-8524. **Fax:** (250)472-5051. **E-mail:** malahat@uvic.ca. **Website:** www.malahatreview.ca. **Contact:** John Barton, editor. The Open Season Awards accepts entries of poetry, fiction, and creative nonfiction. Winners published in spring issue of *Malahat Review* announced in winter on website, facebook page, and in quarterly e-newsletter, *Malahat lite*. Deadline: November 1. Prize: $1,000 CAD and publication in *The Malahat Review* in each category. Costs: $35 CAD for Canadian entries; $40 USD for US entries ($45 USD for entries from Mexico and outside North America). $15 for each additional entry. Includes a 1-year subscription to *The Malahat Review*.

OREGON BOOK AWARDS

925 SW Washington St., Portland OR 97205. (503)227-2583. **Fax:** (503)241-4256. **E-mail:** la@literary-arts.org. **Website:** www.literary-arts.org. **Contact:** Susan Denning, director of programs and events. The annual Oregon Book Awards celebrate Oregon authors

in the areas of poetry, fiction, nonfiction, drama and young readers' literature published between August 1 and July 31 of the previous calendar year. Awards are available for every category. See website for details. Deadline: August 29. Prize: Grant of $2,500. (Grant money could vary.) Judged by writers who are selected from outside Oregon for their expertise in a genre. Past judges include Mark Doty, Colson Whitehead and Kim Barnes.

● OREGON LITERARY FELLOWSHIPS

925 S.W. Washington, Portland OR 97205. (503)227-2583. **E-mail:** susan@literary-arts.org. **Website:** www.literary-arts.org. **Contact:** Susan Moore, Director of programs and events. Oregon Literary Fellowships are intended to help Oregon writers initiate, develop, or complete literary projects in poetry, fiction, literary nonfiction, drama, and young readers literature. Writers in the early stages of their career are encouraged to apply. The awards are merit-based. Deadline: Last Friday in June. Prize: $3,000 minimum award, for approximately 8 writers and 2 publishers. Judged by out-of-state writers

$ KENNETH PATCHEN AWARD FOR THE INNOVATIVE NOVEL

Eckhard Gerdes Publishing, 1110 Varsity Blvd., Apt. 221, DeKalb IL 60115. **E-mail:** egerdes@experimentalfiction.com. **Website:** www.experimentalfiction.com. **Contact:** Eckhard Gerdes. This award will honor the most innovative novel submitted during the previous calendar year. Kenneth Patchen is celebrated for being among the greatest innovators of American fiction, incorporating strategies of concretism, asemic writing, digression, and verbal juxtaposition into his writing long before such strategies were popularized during the height of American postmodernist experimentation in the 1970s. Deadline: All submissions must be postmarked between January 1 and July 31. Prize: $1,000 and 20 complimentary copies. Costs: $25 entry fee. Judged by novelist Dominic Ward.

THE PATERSON FICTION PRIZE

The Poetry Center at Passaic Community College, One College Blvd., Paterson NJ 07505. (973)684-6555. **Fax:** (973)523-6085. **E-mail:** mgillan@pccc.edu. **Website:** www.pccc.edu/poetry. **Contact:** Maria Mazziotti Gillan, executive director. Offered annually for a novel or collection of short fiction published the previous calendar year. For more information, visit the website or send SASE. Deadline: April 1. Prize: $1,000.

O JUDITH SIEGEL PEARSON AWARD

Judith Siegel Pearson Award, c/o Department of English, Wayne State University, Attn: Royanne Smith, 5057 Woodward Ave, Ste. 9408, Detroit MI 48202. **E-mail:** fm8146@wayne.edu. **Website:** https://wsu-writingawards.submittable.com/submit. **Contact:** Donovan Hohn. Offers an annual award for the best creative or scholarly work on a subject concerning women. The type of work accepted rotates each year: drama in 2016, poetry in 2017; nonfiction in 2018; fiction in 2019. Open to all interested writers and scholars. Only submit the appropriate genre in each year. Deadline: February 22. Prize: $500. Judged by members of the writing faculty of the Wayne State University English Department.

PEN CENTER USA LITERARY AWARDS

PEN Center USA, P.O. Box 6037, Beverly Hills CA 90212. (323)424-4939. **E-mail:** awards@penusa.org. **E-mail:** awards@penusa.org. **Website:** www.penusa.org. Offered for work published or produced in the previous calendar year. Open to writers living west of the Mississippi River. Award categories: fiction, poetry, research nonfiction, creative nonfiction, translation, children's/young adult, graphic literature, drama, screenplay, teleplay, journalism. Deadline for book categories: 4 copies must be postmarked by December 31. Deadline for non-book categories: 4 copies must be postmarked by February 28. Prize: $1,000. Costs: $35 entry fee per submission.

PEN/FAULKNER AWARDS FOR FICTION

PEN/Faulkner Foundation, 201 E. Capitol St. SE, Washington DC 20003. (202)898-9063. **E-mail:** awards@penfaulkner.org. **Website:** www.penfaulkner.org. **Contact:** Emma Snyder, executive director. Offered annually for best book-length work of fiction by an American citizen published in a calendar year. Deadline: October 31. Prize: $15,000 (one Winner); $5,000 (4 Finalists).

PENGUIN RANDOM HOUSE CREATIVE WRITING AWARDS

One Scholarship Way, P.O. Box 297, St. Peter MN 56082. (212)782-9348. **Fax:** (212)782-5157. **E-mail:** creativewriting@penguinrandomhouse.com. **Website:** www.penguinrandomhouse.com/creativewriting. **Contact:** Melanie Fallon Hauska, director. Offered annually for unpublished work to NYC public high school seniors. 72 awards given in literary and nonliterary categories. Four categories: poetry, fiction/drama, personal essay, and graphic novel. Applicants must be seniors (under age 21) at a New York high school. No college essays or class assignments will be accepted. Deadline: February 5 for all categories. Graphic Novel extended deadline: March 1st. Prize: Awards range from $500-10,000. The program usually awards just under $100,000 in scholarships.

PHOEBE WINTER FICTION CONTEST

Phoebe, MSN 2D6, George Mason University, 4400 University Dr., Fairfax VA 22030. (703)993-2915. **E-mail:** phoebe@gmu.edu. **Website:** www.gmu.edu/pubs/phoebe. Offered annually for an unpublished story (25 pages maximum). Guidelines online or for SASE. First serial rights if work is accepted for publication. Purpose is to recognize new and exciting fiction. Deadline: March 21. Prize: $500 and publication in the Spring online issue. Costs: $10. Judged by a recognized fiction writer, hired by *Phoebe* (changes each year). For 2016, the fiction judge will be Joshua Ferris.

THE PINCH LITERARY AWARDS

Literary Awards, The Pinch, Department of English, The University of Memphis, Memphis TN 38152-6176. (901)678-4591. **E-mail:** editor@thepinchjournal.com. **Website:** www.thepinchjournal.com. Offered annually for unpublished short stories of 5,000 words maximum or up to three poems. Guidelines on website. Cost: $20, which is put toward one issue of *The Pinch*. Deadline: March 15. Prize: 1st place Fiction: $1,500 and publication; 1st place Poetry: $1,000 and publication. Offered annually for unpublished short stories and prose of up to 5,000 words and 1-3 poems. Deadline: March 15. Open to submissions on December 15. Prizes: $1,000 for 1st place in each category. Costs: $20 for initial entry, $10 each for subsequent entries.

PNWA LITERARY CONTEST

Pacifc Northwest Writers Association, PMB 2717, 1420 NW Gilman Blvd., Suite 2, Issaquah WA 98027. (452)673-2665. **Fax:** (452)961-0768. **E-mail:** pnwa@pnwa.org. **Website:** www.pnwa.org. Annual literary contest with 12 different categories. See website for details and specific guidelines. Each entry receives 2 critiques. Winners announced at the PNWA Summer Conference, held annually in mid-July. Deadline: February 20. Prize: 1st Place: $600; 2nd Place: $300; 3rd Place: $100. Costs: $35 for PNWA members; $50 for non-members. Judged by an agent or editor attending the conference.

O POCKETS FICTION-WRITING CONTEST

P.O. Box 340004, Nashville TN 37203-0004. (615)340-7333. **Fax:** (615)340-7267. **E-mail:** pockets@upperroom.org. **Website:** www.pockets.upperroom.org. **Contact:** Lynn W. Gilliam, senior editor. Designed for 6- to 12-year-olds, *Pockets* magazine offers wholesome devotional readings that teach about God's love and presence in life. The content includes fiction, scripture stories, puzzles and games, poems, recipes, colorful pictures, activities, and scripture readings. Freelance submissions of stories, poems, recipes, puzzles and games, and activities are welcome. The primary purpose of *Pockets* is to help children grow in their relationship with God and to claim the good news of the gospel of Jesus Christ by applying it to their daily lives. *Pockets* espouses respect for all human beings and for God's creation. It regards a child's faith journey as an integral part of all of life and sees prayer as undergirding that journey. Deadline: August 15. Submission period begins March 15. Prize: $500 and publication in magazine.

EDGAR ALLAN POE AWARD

1140 Broadway, Suite 1507, New York NY 10001. (212)888-8171. **E-mail:** mwa@mysterywriters.org. **Website:** www.mysterywriters.org. Estab. 1945. Mystery Writers of America is the leading association for professional crime writers in the United States. Members of MWA include most major writers of crime fiction and nonfiction, as well as screenwriters, dramatists, editors, publishers, and other professionals in the field. Purpose of the award: Honor authors of distinguished works in the mystery field. Previously published submissions only. Submissions should be made by the publisher. Work must be published/produced the year of the contest. Deadline: November 30. Prize: Awards ceramic bust of "Edgar" for winner; certificates for all nominees. Judged by active status members of Mystery Writers of America (writers).

THE KATHERINE ANNE PORTER PRIZE FOR FICTION

Nimrod International Journal, The University of Tulsa, 800 S. Tucker Dr., Tulsa OK 74104. (918)631-3080. **Fax:** (918)631-3033. **E-mail:** nimrod@utulsa.edu. **Website:** www.utulsa.edu/nimrod. **Contact:** Eilis O'Neal. Deadline: April 30. Prizes: 1st Place: $2,000 and publication; 2nd Place: $1,000 and publication. Costs: $20, includes a 1-year subscription (2 issues) to *Nimrod*; make checks payable to *Nimrod*. Judged by the *Nimrod* editors, who select the finalists and a recognized author, who selects the winners.

PRAIRIE SCHOONER BOOK PRIZE

Prairie Schooner and the University of Nebraska Press, Prairie Schooner Prize Series, 123 Andrews Hall, Lincoln NE 68588-0334. (402)472-0911. **E-mail:** PS-BookPrize@unl.edu. **Website:** prairieschooner.unl.edu. **Contact:** Kwame Dawes, editor. Annual competition/award for story collections. Deadline: March 15. Prize: $3,000 and publication through the University of Nebraska Press. Costs: $25.

PRESS 53 AWARD FOR SHORT FICTION

Press 53, 560 N. Trade St., Suite 193, Winston-Salem NC 27101. (336)770-5353. **E-mail:** kevin@press53.com. **Website:** www.press53.com. **Contact:** Kevin Morgan Watson, Publisher. Estab. 2014. Awarded to an outstanding, unpublished collection of short stories. Deadline: December 31. Submission period begins September 1. Finalists announced March 1. Winner announced no later than May 1. Publication in October. Prize: Publication of winning short story collection, $1,000 cash advance, 1/4-page color ad in *Poets & Writers* magazine, plus 10 copies of the book. Costs: $30 via Submittable. Judged by Press 53 publisher Kevin Morgan Watson.

PRIME NUMBER MAGAZINE AWARDS

Press 53, 560 N. Trade St., Suite 103, Winston-Salem NC 27101. (336)770-5353. **Fax:** N/A. **E-mail:** kevin@press53.com. **Website:** www.press53.com. **Contact:** Kevin Morgan Watson, Publisher. Awards $1,000 in poetry and short fiction. Deadline: April 15. Submission period begins January 1. Finalists announced June 1. Winner announced on August 1. Prize: $1,000 cash. All winners receive publication in Prime Number Magazine online. Costs: $15 via submittable. Judged by industry professionals to be named when the contest begins.

PRISM INTERNATIONAL ANNUAL SHORT FICTION, POETRY, AND CREATIVE NONFICTION CONTESTS

PRISM International, Creative Writing Program, UBC, Buch. E462, 1866 Main Mall, Vancouver BC V6T 1Z1, Canada. **E-mail:** promotions@prismmagazine.ca. **Website:** www.prismmagazine.ca. **Contact:** Claire Matthews. Estab. 1959. Offered annually for unpublished work to award the best in contemporary fiction, poetry, drama, translation, and nonfiction. Works of translation are eligible. Guidelines are available on website. Acquires first North American serial rights upon publication, and limited web rights for pieces selected for website. Open to any writer except students and faculty in the Creative Writing Department at UBC, or people who have taken a creative writing course at UBC within 2 years of the contest deadline. Entry includes subscription. Deadlines: Creative Nonfiction: November 20; Fiction and Poetry: January 15. Prize: All grand prizes are $1,500, $600 for first runner up, and $400 for second runner up. Winners are published. Costs: $35 Canadian entries, $40 US entries, and $45 International entries; $5 each additional entry. Entries accepted via Submittable at http://prisminternational.submittable.com/submit or by mail.

PRISM INTERNATIONAL ANNUAL SHORT FICTION CONTEST

Creative Writing Program, UBC, Buch. E462 - 1866 Main Mall, Vancouver BC V6T 1Z1, Canada. (604)822-2514. **Fax:** (604)822-3616. **Website:** http://prismmagazine.ca/contests. **Contact:** Clara Kumagai, executive editor, promotions. Offered annually for unpublished work to award the best in contemporary fiction. Works of translation are eligible. Guidelines by SASE, by e-mail, or on website. Acquires first North American serial rights upon publication, and rights to publish online for promotional or archival purposes. Open to any writer except students and faculty in the Creative Writing Department at UBC, or people who have taken a creative writing course at UBC with the 2 years prior to the contest deadline. Deadline: February 1. Prize: 1st Place: $1,500; 1st Runner-up: $600; 2nd Runner-up: $400; winner is published. Costs: $35 CAD entries; $40 US entries; $45 international entires; $5 each additional entry (outside Canada, pay US currency); includes subscription.

PURPLE DRAGONFLY BOOK AWARDS

4696 W. Tyson St., Chandler AZ 85226-2903. (480)940-8182. **Fax:** (480)940-8787. **E-mail:** cristy@fivestarpublications.com; fivestarpublications@gmail.com. **Website:** www.purpledragonflybookawards.com; www.fivestarpublications.com; www.fivestarbookawards.com. **Contact:** Cristy Bertini, contest coordinator. The Purple Dragonfly Book Awards are designed with children in mind. Awards are divided into 43 distinct subject categories, ranging from books on the environment and cooking to sports and family issues. The Purple Dragonfly Book Awards are geared toward stories that appeal to children of all ages. Deadline: May 1. Prize: Grand Prize winner will receive a $300 cash prize, 100 foil award seals (more can be ordered for an extra charge), 1 hour of marketing consultation from Five Star Publications, and $100 worth of Five Star Publications' titles, as well as publicity on Five Star Publications' websites and inclusion in a winners' news release sent to a comprehensive list of media outlets. The Grand Prize winner will also be placed in the Five Star Dragonfly Book Awards virtual bookstore with a thumbnail of the book's cover, price, 1-sentence description and link to Amazon.com for purchasing purposes, if applicable. 1st Place: All first-place winners of categories will be put into a drawing for a $100 prize. In addition, each first-place winner in each category receives a certificate commemorating their accomplishment, 25 foil award seals (more can be ordered for an extra charge) and mention on Five Star Publications' websites. Judged by industry experts with specific knowledge about the categories over which they preside.

PUSHCART PRIZE

Pushcart Press, P.O. Box 380, Wainscott NY 11975. (631)324-9300. **Website:** www.pushcartprize.com. **Contact:** Bill Henderson. Estab. 1976. Published every year since 1976, The Pushcart Prize - Best of the Small Presses series "is the most honored literary project in America. Hundreds of presses and thousands of writers of short stories, poetry and essays have been represented in the pages of our annual collections." Little magazine and small book press editors (print or online) may make up to six nominations from their year's publicatoins by the deadline. The nominations may be any combination of poetry, short fiction, essays or literary whatnot. Editors may nominate self-contained portions of books — for instance, a chapter from a novel. Deadline: December 1.

THOMAS H. RADDALL ATLANTIC FICTION AWARD

Writers' Federation of Nova Scotia, 1113 Marginal Rd., Halifax NS B3H 4P7, Canada. (902)423-8116. **Fax:** (902)422-0881. **E-mail:** director@writers.ns.ca. **Website:** www.writers.ns.ca. **Contact:** Nate Crawford, executive director. Estab. 1990. The Thomas Head Raddall Atlantic Fiction Award is awarded for a novel or a book of short fiction by a full-time resident of Atlantic Canada. Deadline: First Friday in December. Prize: Valued at $25,000 for winning title.

DAVID RAFFELOCK AWARD FOR PUBLISHING EXCELLENCE

National Writers Association, 10940 S. Parker Rd., #508, Parker CO 80134. (303)841-0246. **E-mail:** natlwritersassn@hotmail.com. **Website:** www.nationalwriters.com. **Contact:** Sandy Whelchel. Contest is offered annually for books published the previous year. Published works only. Open to any writer. Guidelines for SASE, by e-mail, or on website. Winners will be notified by mail or phone. List of winners available for SASE or visit website. Purpose is to assist published authors in marketing their works and to reward outstanding published works. Deadline: May 15. Prize: Publicity tour, including airfare, valued at $5,000. Costs: $100.

THE RED HOUSE CHILDREN'S BOOK AWARD

Red House Children's Book Award, 123 Frederick Road, Cheam, Sutton, Surrey SM1 2HT, United Kingdom. **E-mail:** info@rhcba.co.uk. **Website:** www.redhousechildrensbookaward.co.uk. **Contact:** Sinead Kromer, national coordinator. Estab. 1980. The Red House Children's Book Award is the only national book award that is entirely voted for by children. A shortlist is drawn up from children's nominations and any child can then vote for the winner of the three categories: Books for Younger Children, Books for Younger Readers and Books for Older Readers. The book with the most votes is then crowned the winner of the Red House Children's Book Award. Deadline: December 31.

RHODE ISLAND ARTIST FELLOWSHIPS AND INDIVIDUAL PROJECT GRANTS

Rhode Island State Council on the Arts, State of Rhode Island, One Capitol Hill, 3rd Floor, Providence RI 02908. (401)222-3880. **Fax:** (401)222-3018. **E-mail:** Cristina.DiChiera@arts.ri.gov. **Website:** www.arts.ri.gov. **Contact:** Cristina DiChiera, director of individual artist programs. Annual fellowship competition is based upon panel review of poetry, fiction, and playwriting/screenwriting mss. Project grants provide funds for community-based arts projects. Rhode Island artists who have lived in the state for at least 12 consecutive months may apply without a nonprofit sponsor. Applicants for all RSCA grant and award programs must be at least 18 years old and not currently enrolled in an arts-related degree program. Online application and guidelines can be found at www.arts.ri.gov/grants/guidelines/. Deadline: April 1 and October 1. Fellowship awards: $5,000 and $1,000. Grants range from $500-5,000, with an average of around $1,500. Judged by a rotating panel of artists.

THE ROGERS WRITERS' TRUST FICTION PRIZE

The Writers' Trust of Canada, 460 Richmond St. W., Suite 600, Toronto ON M5V 1Y1, Canada. (416)504-8222. **Fax:** (416)504-9090. **E-mail:** info@writerstrust.com. **Website:** www.writerstrust.com. **Contact:** Amanda Hopkins. Awarded annually to the best novel or short story collection published within the previous year. Presented at the Writers' Trust Awards event held in Toronto each fall. Open to Canadian citizens and permanent residents only. Deadline: July 27. Prize: $25,000 and $2,500 to 4 finalists.

LOIS ROTH AWARD

Modern Language Association, 85 Broad Street, suite 500, New York NY 10004-2434. (646)576-5141. **Fax:** (646)458-0030. **E-mail:** awards@mla.org. **Website:** www.mla.org. Offered in odd-numbered years for an outstanding translation into English of a book-length literary work. Translators need not be members of the MLA. Deadline: April 1. Prize: A cash award and a certificate to be presented at the Modern Language Association's annual convention in January.

ROYAL DRAGONFLY BOOK AWARDS

Five Star Publications, Inc., 4696 W. Tyson St., Chandler AZ 85226. (480)940-8182. **Fax:** (480)940-8787. **E-mail:** cristy@fivestarpublications.com; fivestarpublications@gmail.com. **E-mail:** cristy@fivestarpublications.com. **Website:** www.fivestarpublications.com; www.fivestarbookawards.com; www.royaldragonflybookawards.com. **Contact:** Cristy Bertini. Offered annually for any previously published work to honor authors for writing excellence of all types of literature—fiction and nonfiction—in 62 categories, appealing to a wide range of ages and comprehensive list of genres. Open to any title published in English. Entry forms are downloadable at www.royaldragonflybookawards.com. Deadline: October 1. Prize: Grand Prize winner receives $300, while another entrant will be the lucky winner of a $100 drawing. All first-place winners receive foil award seals and are included in a publicity campaign announcing winners. All first- and second-place winners and honorable mentions receive certificates. Costs: $60 for one title in one category, $50 per title when multiple books are entered or $50 per category when one book is entered in multiple categories; all entry fees are per title, per category.

ERNEST SANDEEN PRIZE IN POETRY AND THE RICHARD SULLIVAN PRIZE IN SHORT FICTION

University of Notre Dame, Dept. of English, 356 O'Shaughnessy Hall, Notre Dame IN 46556-5639. (574)631-7526. **Fax:** (574)631-4795. **E-mail:** creativewriting@nd.edu. **Website:** http://english.nd.edu/creative-writing/publications/sandeen-sullivan-prizes. **Contact:** Director of Creative Writing. Estab. 1994. The Sandeen & Sullivan Prizes in Poetry and Short Fiction is awarded to the author who has published at least one volume of short fiction or one volume of poetry. Awarded biannually, but judged quadrennially. Submissions Period: May 1 - September 1. Prize: $1,000, a $500 award and a $500 advance against royalties from the Notre Dame Press. Costs: $15.

SASKATCHEWAN BOOK AWARDS

315-1102 Eighth Ave., Regina SK S4R 1C9, Canada. (306)569-1585. **E-mail:** director@bookawards.sk.ca. **Website:** www.bookawards.sk.ca. **Contact:** Courtney Bates-Hardy, Administrative Director. Estab. 1993. Saskatchewan Book Awards celebrates, promotes, and rewards Saskatchewan authors and publishers worthy of recognition through 14 awards, granted on an annual or semiannual basis. Awards: Fiction, Nonfiction, Poetry, Scholarly, First Book, *Prix du Livre Français*, Regina, Saskatoon, Aboriginal Peoples' Writing, Aboriginal Peoples' Publishing, Publishing in Education, Publishing, Children's Literature/Young Adult Literature, Book of the Year. Deadline: Early November. Prize: $2,000 (CAD) for all awards except Book of the Year, which is $3,000 (CAD). Costs: Costs $50 per award entered. Juries are made up of writing and publishing professionals from outside of Saskatchewan.

Saskatchewan Book Awards is the only provincially focused book award program in Saskatchewan and a principal ambassador for Saskatchewan's literary community. Its solid reputation for celebrating artistic excellence in style is recognized nationally.

THE SATURDAY EVENING POST GREAT AMERICAN FICTION CONTEST

The Saturday Evening Post Society, 1100 Waterway Blvd., Indianapolis IN 46202. **E-mail:** fictioncontest@saturdayeveningpost.com. **Website:** www.saturdayeveningpost.com/fiction-contest. "In its nearly 3 centuries of publication, *The Saturday Evening Post* has included fiction by a who's who of American authors, including F. Scott Fitzgerald, William Faulkner, Kurt Vonnegut, Ray Bradbury, Louis L'Amour, Sinclair Lewis, Jack London, and Edgar Allan Poe. The *Post*'s fiction has not just entertained us; it has played a vital role in defining who we are as Americans. In launching this contest, we are seeking America's next great, unpublished voices." Deadline: July 1. The winning story will receive $500 and publication in the magazine and online. Five runners-up will be published online and receive $100 each. Costs: $10.

ALDO AND JEANNE SCAGLIONE PRIZE FOR A TRANSLATION OF A LITERARY WORK

Modern Language Association, 85 Broad Street, suite 500, New York NY 10004-2434. (646)576-5141. **Fax:** (646)458-0030. **E-mail:** awards@mla.org. **Website:** www.mla.org. **Contact:** Coordinator of Book Prizes. Offered in even-numbered years for an outstanding translation into English of a book-length literary work. Deadline: April 1. Prize: A cash award and a certificate to be presented at the Modern Language Association's annual convention in January.

O THE SCARS EDITOR'S CHOICE AWARDS

E-mail: editor@scars.tv. **Website:** http://scars.tv. **Contact:** Janet Kuypers, editor/publisher (whom all reading fee checks need to be made out to). Award to showcase good writing in an annual book. Prize: Publication of story/essay and 1 copy of the book. Costs: $19/short story and $15/poem.

THE MONA SCHREIBER PRIZE FOR HUMOROUS FICTION & NONFICTION

3940 Laurel Canyon Blvd., #566, Studio City CA 91604. **E-mail:** brad.schreiber@att.net. **Website:** www.bradschreiber.com. **Contact:** Brad Schreiber. Estab. 2000. The purpose of the contest is to award the most creative humor writing, in any form less than 750 words, in either fiction or nonfiction, including but not limited to stories, articles, essays, speeches, shopping lists, diary entries, and anything else writers dream up. Complete rules and previous winning entries on website. Deadline: December 1. Prize: 1st Place: $500; 2nd Place: $250; 3rd Place: $100. Costs: $5 fee/entry (checks payable to Mona Schreiber Prize). Foreign entries may include US currency. Judged by Brad Schreiber, author, journalist, consultant, and instructor.

JOANNA CATHERINE SCOTT NOVEL EXCERPT PRIZE CATEGORY

Soul-Making Keats Literary Competition Category, The Webhallow House, 1544 Sweetwood Dr., Broadmoor Village CA 94015-2029. **E-mail:** soulkeats@mail.com. **Website:** www.soulmakingcontest.us. **Contact:** Eileen Malone. Open annually to any writer. Deadline: November 30. Prize: 1st Place: $100; 2nd Place: $50; 3rd Place: $25. Costs: $5/entry (make checks payable to NLAPW).

SCREAMINMAMAS MAGICAL FICTION CONTEST

1911 Cleveland St., Hollywood FL 33020. **E-mail:** screaminmamas@gmail.com. **Website:** www.screaminmamas.com/contests. **Contact:** Darlene Pistocchi, editor/managing director. This contest celebrates moms and the magical spirit of the holidays. If you had an opportunity to be anything you wanted to be, what would you be? Transport yourself! Become that character and write a short story around that character. Can be any genre. Length: 800-3,000 words. Open only to moms. Deadline: June 30. Prize: complementary subscription to magazine, plus publication.

SCREAMINMAMAS VALENTINE'S DAY CONTEST

1911 Cleveland St., Hollywood FL 33020. **E-mail:** screaminmamas@gmail.com. **Website:** www.screaminmamas.com/contests. **Contact:** Darlene Pistocchi, editor/managing director. "Looking for light romantic comedy. Can be historical or contemporary—something to lift the spirits and celebrate the gift of innocent romance that might be found in the everyday life of a busy mom." Length: 800-2,000 words. Open only to moms. Deadline: June 30. Prize: Publication, complementary print copy. Costs: $5.

SCRIPTAPALOOZA TELEVISION WRITING COMPETITION

(310)801-5366. **E-mail:** info@scriptapalooza.com. **Website:** www.scriptapaloozatv.com. Estab. 1999. Biannual competition accepting entries in 4 categories: Reality shows, sitcoms, original pilots, and 1-hour dramas. There are more than 30 producers, agents, and managers reading the winning scripts. Two past winners won Emmys because of Scriptapalooza and 1 past entrant now writes for Comedy Central. Winners announced February 15 and August 30. For contest results, visit website. Deadline: October 15 and April 15. Prize: 1st Place: $500; 2nd Place: $200; 3rd Place: $100 (in each category); production company consideration. Costs: $45; accepts PayPal credit card only. All the judging is done by over 25 producers.

SKIPPING STONES HONOR (BOOK) AWARDS

P.O. Box 3939, Eugene OR 97403, USA. (541)342-4956. **Fax:** (541)342-4956. **E-mail:** editor@skippingstones.org. **Website:** www.skippingstones.org. **Contact:** Arun N. Toké. Estab. 1994. *Skipping Stones* is a well respected, multicultural literary magazine now in its 28th year. Annual award to promote multicultural and/or nature awareness through creative writings for children and teens and their educators. Seeks authentic, exceptional, child/youth friendly books that promote intercultural, international, intergenerational harmony, or understanding through creative ways. Deadline: February 29. Prize: Honor certificates; gold seals; reviews; press release/publicity. Costs: $50. Judged by a multicultural committee of teachers, librarians, parents, students and editors.

SKIPPING STONES YOUTH AWARDS

P.O. Box 3939, Eugene OR 97403-0939. (541)342-4956. **Fax:** (541)342-4956. **E-mail:** editor@skippingstones.org. **Website:** www.skippingstones.org. **Contact:** Arun N. Toké. Annual awards to promote creativity as well as multicultural and nature awareness in youth. Deadline: June 25. Prize: Publication in the autumn issue of *Skipping Stones*, honor certificate, subscription to magazine, plus 5 multicultural and/or nature books. Costs: $5/entry. Make checks payable to Skipping Stones. Judged by editors and reviewers at *Skipping Stones* magazine.

THE BERNICE SLOTE AWARD

Prairie Schooner, 123 Andrews Hall, PO Box 880334, Lincoln NE 68588-0334. (402)472-0911. **Fax:** (402)472-1817. **E-mail:** PrairieSchooner@unl.edu. **Website:** www.prairieschooner.unl.edu. **Contact:** Kwame Dawes. Offered annually for the best work by a beginning writer published in *Prairie Schooner* in the previous year. Celebrates the best and finest writing that they have published for the year. Prize: $500. Judged by editorial staff of *Prairie Schooner*.

BYRON CALDWELL SMITH BOOK AWARD

The University of Kansas, Hall Center for the Humanities, 900 Sunnyside Ave., Lawrence KS 66045. (785)864-4798. **E-mail:** vbailey@ku.edu. **Website:** www.hallcenter.ku.edu. **Contact:** Victor Bailey, director. Offered in odd years. To qualify, applicants must live or be employed in Kansas and have written an outstanding book published within the previous 2 calendar years. Translations are eligible. Guidelines for SASE or online. Deadline: March 1. Prize: $1,500.

JEFFREY E. SMITH EDITORS' PRIZE IN FICTION, ESSAY AND POETRY

The Missouri Review, 357 McReynolds Hall, UMC, Columbia MO 65211. (573)882-4474. **Fax:** (573)884-4671. **E-mail:** contest_question@moreview.com. **Website:** www.missourireview.com. **Contact:** Editor. Offered annually for unpublished work in 3 categories: fiction, essay, and poetry. Guidelines online or for SASE. Deadline: October 15. Prize: $5,000 and publication for each category winner. Costs: $20, includes a 1-year print or digital subscription.

KAY SNOW WRITING CONTEST

Willamette Writers, Willamette Writers, 2108 Buck St., West Linn OR 97068. (503)305-6729. **Fax:** (503)344-6174. **E-mail:** reg@willamettewriters.com. **Website:** www.willamettewriters.com. Willamette Writers is the largest writers' organization in Oregon and one of the largest writers' organizations in the United States. It is a non-profit, tax-exempt Oregon corporation led by volunteers. Elected officials and directors administer an active program of monthly meetings, special seminars, workshops, and an annual writing conference. Continuing with established programs and starting new ones is only made possible by strong volunteer support. The purpose of this annual writing contest, named in honor of Willamette Writer's founder, Kay Snow, is to help writers reach professional goals in writing in a broad array of categories and to encourage student writers. Deadline: April 23. Submission deadline begins January 15. Prize: One first prize of $300, one second place prize of $150, and a third place prize of $50 per winning entry in each of the six categories. Student first prize is $50, $20 for second place, $10 for third. Costs: $10-$15, no fee for student entries (grades 1-12).

SOCIETY OF MIDLAND AUTHORS AWARD

Society of Midland Authors, Society of Midland Authors, P.O. Box 10419, Chicago IL 60610-0419. **E-mail:**

marlenetbrill@comcast.net. **Website:** www.midlandauthors.com. **Contact:** Marlene Targ Brill, awards chair. Since 1957, the Society has presented annual awards for the best books written by Midwestern authors. The Society of Midland Authors (SMA) Award is presented to one title in each of six categories: adult nonfiction, adult fiction, adult biography and memoir, children's nonfiction, children's fiction, and poetry. Books and entry forms must be mailed to the 3 judges in each category; for a list of judges and the entry form, visit the website. Do not mail books to the society's P.O. box. The fee can be sent to the SMA P.P. box or paid via Paypal. Deadline: January 7. Prize: $500 and a plaque that is awarded at the SMA banquet in May in Chicago. Honorary winners receive a plaque. Costs: $10 entry fee.

THE ST. LAWRENCE BOOK AWARD

Black Lawrence Press, **E-mail:** editors@blacklawrencepress.com. **Website:** www.blacklawrencepress.com. "Black Lawrence Press is an independent publisher of contemporary poetry, fiction, and creative nonfiction. We also publish the occasional translation from German. Founded in 2004, Black Lawrence became an imprint of Dzanc Books in 2008. In January 2014, we spread our wings and became an independent company in the state of New York. Our books are distributed nationally through Small Press Distribution to Amazon, Barnes & Noble, and various brick and mortar retailers. We also make our titles available through our website and at various conferences and book fairs. Through our annual contests and open reading periods, we seek innovative, electrifying, and thoroughly intoxicating mss that ensnare themselves in our hearts and minds and won't let go." Each year Black Lawrence Press awards The St. Lawrence Book Award for an unpublished first collection of poems or short stories. The St. Lawrence Book Award is open to any writer who has not yet published a full-length collection of short stories or poems. The winner of this contest will receive book publication, a $1,000 cash award, and ten copies of the book. Prizes are awarded on publication. Deadline: August 31. Prize: Publication and $1000. Judged by the Black Lawrence Press editors.

STONY BROOK SHORT FICTION PRIZE

Stony Brook Southampton, 239 Montauk Highway, Southampton NY 11968. **Website:** www.stonybrook.edu/fictionprize. Deadline: March 15. Prize: $1,000.

STORYSOUTH MILLION WRITERS AWARD

E-mail: terry@storysouth.com. **Website:** www.storysouth.com. **Contact:** Terry Kennedy, editor. Estab. 2003. Annual award to honor and promote the best fiction published in online literary journals and magazines during the previous year. Most literary prizes for short fiction have traditionally ignored web-published fiction. This award aims to show that world-class fiction is being published online and to promote to the larger reading and literary community. Deadline: August 15. Nominations of stories begins on March 15. Prize: Prize amounts subject to donation. Check website for details.

SUBTERRAIN MAGAZINE'S ANNUAL LITERARY AWARDS COMPETITION: THE LUSH SUBTERRAIN MAGAZINE'S ANNUAL LUSH TRIUMPHANT LITERARY AWARDS COMPETITION

P.O. Box 3008 MPO, Vancouver BC V6B 3X5, Canada. (604)876-8710. **Fax:** (604)879-2667. **E-mail:** subter@portal.ca. **Website:** www.subterrain.ca. Estab. Magazine est. 1988; Lush Triumphant est. 2002. Entrants may submit as many entries in as many categories as they like. Fiction: Max of 3,000 words. Poetry: A suite of 5 related poems (max of 15 pages). Creative Nonfiction (based on fact, adorned with fiction): Max of 4,000 words. Deadline: May 15. Prize: Winners in each category will receive $1,000 cash (plus payment for publication) and publication in the Winter issue. First runner-up in each category will be published in the Spring issue of *subTerrain.* Costs: $27.50/entry includes a 1-year subscription to *subTerrain.*

SYDNEY TAYLOR MANUSCRIPT COMPETITION

Association of Jewish Libraries, Sydney Taylor Manuscript Award Competition, 204 Park St., Montclair NJ 07042-2903. **E-mail:** stmacajl@aol.com. **Website:** www.jewishlibraries.org/main/Awards/SydneyTaylorManuscriptAward.aspx. **Contact:** Aileen Grossberg. Estab. 1985. This competition is for unpublished writers of fiction. Material should be for readers ages 8-13, with universal appeal that will serve to deepen the understanding of Judaism for all children, revealing positive aspects of Jewish life. To encourage new fiction of Jewish interest for readers ages 8-13. Deadline: September 30. Prize: $1,000. Judging by qualified judges from within the Association of Jewish Libraries.

THE TEXAS INSTITUTE OF LETTERS LITERARY AWARDS

E-mail: Betwx@aol.com. **Website:** www.texasinstituteofletters.org. Estab. 1936. The Texas Institute of Letters gives annual awards for books by Texas authors and writers who have produced books about Texas, including Best Books of Poetry, Fiction, and Nonfiction. Awards are also given for best Short Story, Magazine or Newspaper Article, Essay, and best Books for Children and Young Adults. Work submitted must have been published in the year stipulated, and entries may be made by authors or by their publishers. Complete guidelines and award information is available on the Texas Institute of Letters website.

O THREE CHEERS AND A TIGER

E-mail: editors@toasted-cheese.com. **Website:** www.toasted-cheese.com. **Contact:** Stephanie Lenz, editor. Contestants are to write a short story (following a specific theme) within 48 hours. Contests are held first weekend in spring (mystery) and first weekend in fall (science fiction/fantasy). Word limit announced at the start of the contest. Contest-specific information is announced 48 hours before the contest submission deadline. Results announced in April and October. Winners notified by e-mail. List of winners on website. Prize: Amazon gift certificates and publication. Blind-judged by 2 *Toasted Cheese* editors. Each judge uses his or her own criteria to choose entries.

THE THURBER PRIZE FOR AMERICAN HUMOR

77 Jefferson Ave., Columbus OH 43215. **Website:** www.thurberhouse.org. This award recognizes the art of humor writing. Deadline: April. Prize: $5,000 for the finalist, non-cash prizes awarded to two runners-up. Judged by well-known members of the national arts community.

TIMELESS LOVE/ROMANCE CONTEST

Sponsored by Oak Tree Press, 1700 Diary Avenue, #49, Corcoran CA 93217. **E-mail:** tl-contestadmin@oaktreebooks.com. **Website:** www.oaktreebooks.com. Annual contest for unpublished authors or authors shifting to a new genre. Accepts novels of all romance genres, from sweet to supernatural. Guidelines and entry forms are available for SASE. Deadline: July 31. Prize: Publication in both paper and e-book editions. Costs: $25. Judged by publishing industry professionals who prescreen entries; publisher makes final selection.

O TOM HOWARD/JOHN H. REID FICTION & ESSAY CONTEST

Winning Writers, 351 Pleasant Street, PMB 222, Northampton MA 01060-3961, USA. (866)946-9748. **Fax:** (413)280-0539. **E-mail:** adam@winningwriters.com. **Website:** www.winningwriters.com. **Contact:** Adam Cohen, President. Estab. 1993. Since 2001, Winning Writers has provided expert literary contest information to the public. We sponsor four contests. One of the "101 Best Websites for Writers" (*Writer's Digest*). Deadline: April 30. Prizes: Two 1st prizes of $1,500 will be awarded, plus 10 honorable mentions of $100 each. Top 12 entries published online. Costs: $18. Judged by Arthur Powers, assisted by Lauren Singer.

This contest is in its 24th year. Open to all writers. Submit any type of short story or essay. Both published and unpublished works are welcome. If you win a prize, we will request nonexclusive rights to publish your submission online, in e-mail newsletters, in e-books, and in press releases.

TORONTO BOOK AWARDS

City of Toronto c/o Toronto Arts & Culture, Cultural Partnerships, City Hall, 9E, 100 Queen St. W., Toronto ON M5H 2N2, Canada. **E-mail:** shan@toronto.ca. **Website:** www.toronto.ca/book_awards. Estab. 1974. The Toronto Book Awards honor authors of books of literary or artistic merit that are evocative of Toronto. Deadline: April 30. Prize: Each finalist receives $1,000 and the winning author receives the remaining prize money ($14,000 total in prize money available).

STEVEN TURNER AWARD FOR BEST FIRST WORK OF FICTION

6335 W. Northwest Hwy., #618, Dallas TX 75225. **Website:** www.texasinstituteofletters.org. Offered annually for work published January 1-December 31 for the best first book of fiction. Deadline: normally first week in January; see website for specific date. Prize: $1,000.

WAASNODE SHORT FICTION PRIZE

Passages North, Department of English, Northern Michigan University, 1401 Presque Isle Ave., Marquette MI 49855. (906)227-1203. **Fax:** (906)227-1096. **E-mail:** passages@nmu.edu. **Website:** www.passagesnorth.com. **Contact:** Jennifer Howard. Offered every 2 years to publish new voices in literary fiction (maximum 10,000 words). Guidelines for SASE or online. Submissions accepted online. Deadline: April 15.

Submission period begins February 15. Prize: $1,000 and publication for winner; 2 honorable mentions are also published; all entrants receive a copy of *Passages North*. Costs: $15 reading fee/story, make checks payable to Northern Michigan University. Judged by Tiphanie Yanique in 2016.

WABASH PRIZE FOR FICTION

Sycamore Review, Department of English, 500 Oval Dr., Purdue University, West Lafayette IN 47907. **E-mail:** sycamore@purdue.edu; sycamorefiction@purdue.edu. **Website:** www.sycamorereview.com/contest/. **Contact:** Kara Krewer, editor-in-chief. Annual contest for unpublished fiction. Deadline: November 15. Prize: $1,000 and publication. Costs: $20 reading fee; $5 for each additional story.

THE WASHINGTON WRITERS' PUBLISHING HOUSE FICTION PRIZE

Washington Writers' Publishing House, P.O. Box 15271, Washington DC 20003. **E-mail:** wwphpress@gmail.com. **Website:** www.washingtonwriters.org. Fiction writers living within 75 miles of the Capitol are invited to submit a ms of either a novel or a collection of short stories (no more than 350 pages, double-spaced). Deadline: November 15. Submission period begins July 1. Prize: $1,000 and 50 copies of the book. Costs: $25 reading fee.

THE ROBERT WATSON LITERARY PRIZE IN FICTION AND POETRY

The Robert Watson Literary Prizes, *The Greensboro Review*, MFA Writing Program, 3302 MHRA Building, Greensboro NC 27402-6170. (336)334-5459. **E-mail:** jlclark@uncg.edu. **Website:** www.greensbororeview.org. **Contact:** Jim Clark, editor. Offered annually for fiction (up to 25 double-spaced pages) and poetry (up to 10 pages). Entries must be unpublished. Open to any writer. Deadline: September 15. Prize: $1,000 each for best short story and poem. Costs: $14. Judged by editors of *The Greensboro Review*.

WESTERN AUSTRALIAN PREMIER'S BOOK AWARDS

State Library of Western Australia, Perth Cultural Centre, 25 Francis St., Perth WA 6000, Australia. (61)(8)9427-3151. **E-mail:** premiersbookawards@slwa.wa.gov.au. **Website:** pba.slwa.wa.gov.au. **Contact:** Karen de San Miguel. Estab. 1982. Annual competition for Australian citizens or permanent residents of Australia, or writers whose work has Australia as its primary focus. Categories: children's books, digital narrative, fiction, nonfiction, poetry, scripts, writing for young adults, West Australian history, and Western Australian emerging writers. Deadline: January 31. Prize: Awards $25,000 for Premier's Prize; awards $15,000 each for the Children's Books, Digital Narrative, Fiction, and Nonfiction categories; awards $10,000 each for the Poetry, Scripts, Western Australian History, Western Australian Emerging Writers, and Writing for Young Adults; awards $5,000 for People's Choice Award.

WESTERN HERITAGE AWARDS

National Cowboy & Western Heritage Museum, 1700 NE 63rd St., Oklahoma City OK 73111-7997. (405)478-2250. **Fax:** (405)478-4714. **Website:** www.nationalcowboymuseum.org. **Contact:** Jessica Limestall. Estab. 1961. The National Cowboy & Western Heritage Museum Western Heritage Awards were established to honor and encourage the legacy of those whose works in literature, music, film, and television reflect the significant stories of the American West. Accepted categories for literary entries: western novel, nonfiction book, art book, photography book, juvenile book, magazine article, or poetry book. The WHA are presented annually to encourage the accurate and artistic telling of great stories of the West through 16 categories of western literature, television, film and music; including fiction, nonfiction, children's books and poetry. See website for details and category definitions. Deadline: November 30. Prize: Awards a Wrangler bronze sculpture designed by famed western artist, John Free. Costs: $50. Judged by a panel of judges selected each year with distinction in various fields of western art and heritage.

WESTERN WRITERS OF AMERICA

271CR 219, Encampment WY 82325. (307)329-8942. **Fax:** (307)327-5465 (call first). **E-mail:** wwa.moulton@gmail.com. **Website:** www.westernwriters.org. **Contact:** Candy Moulton, executive director. Estab. 1953. Seventeen Spur Award categories in various aspects of the American West. The nonprofit Western Writers of America has promoted and honored the best in Western literature with the annual Spur Awards, selected by panels of judges. Awards, for material published last year, are given for works whose inspirations, image and literary excellence best represent the reality and spirit of the American West. Costs: No fee.

WESTMORELAND POETRY & SHORT STORY CONTEST

Westmoreland Arts & Heritage Festival, 252 Twin Lakes Road, Latrobe PA 15650-9415. (724)834-7474. **Fax:** (724)850-7474. **E-mail:** info@artsandheritage.com. **Website:** www.artsandheritage.com. **Contact:** Diane Shrader. Offered annually for unpublished work. Two categories: Poem and Short Story. Short story entries no longer than 4,000 words. Family-oriented festival and contest. Deadline: February 16. Prizes: Award: $200; 1st Place: $125; 2nd Place: $100; 3rd Place: $75. Costs: $10/story or for 2 poems; both categories may be entered for $20.

WILLA LITERARY AWARD

Women Writing the West, 8547 East Arapaho Rd., #J-541, Greenwood Village CO 80112-1436. **E-mail:** Anneschroederauthor@gmail.com. **Website:** www.womenwritingthewest.org. **Contact:** Anne Schroeder. The WILLA Literary Award honors the year's best in published literature featuring women's or girls' stories set in the West. Women Writing the West (WWW), a nonprofit association of writers and other professionals writing and promoting the Women's West, underwrites and presents the nationally recognized award annually (for work published between January 1 and December 31). The award is named in honor of Pulitzer Prize winner Willa Cather, one of the country's foremost novelists. The award is given in 7 categories: historical fiction, contemporary fiction, original softcover fiction, creative nonfiction, scholarly nonfiction, poetry, and children's/young adult fiction/nonfiction. Entry forms available on the website. Deadline: November 1–February 1. Prize: $100 and a trophy. Finalist receives a plaque. Both receive digital and sticker award emblems for book covers. Notice of Winning and Finalist titles mailed to more than 4,000 booksellers, libraries, and others. Award announcement is in early August, and awards are presented to the winners and finalists at the annual WWW Fall Conference. Costs: $50. Judged by professional librarians not affiliated with WWW.

TENNESSEE WILLIAMS/NEW ORLEANS LITERARY FESTIVAL CONTESTS

Tennessee Williams/New Orleans Literary Festival, 938 Lafayette St., Suite 514, New Orleans LA 70113. (504)581-1144. **E-mail:** info@tennesseewilliams.net. **Website:** www.tennesseewilliams.net/contests. **Contact:** Paul J. Willis. Annual contests for: Unpublished One Act, Unpublished Short Fiction, and Unpublished Poem. "Our competitions provide playwrights an opportunity to see their work fully produced before a large audience during one of the largest literary festivals in the nation, and for the festival to showcase the undiscovered talents of poetry and fiction writers." Deadline: November 1 (One Act); November 15 (Poetry); December 1 (Fiction). Prize: One Act: $1,500, staged read at the next festival, full production at the festival the following year, VIP All-Access Festival pass for two years ($1,000 value), and publication in Bayou. Poetry: $1,500, public reading at next festival, publication in Louisiana Cultural Vistas Magazine. Fiction: $1,500, public reading at next festival, publication in Louisiana Literature. Costs: $25 entry fee for One Act and Fiction submissions; $20 entry fee for Poetry submissions. Judged by an anonymous expert panel for One Act contest. Judged by special guest judges, who change every year, for fiction and poetry.

See website for full details.

O WISCONSIN INSTITUTE FOR CREATIVE WRITING FELLOWSHIP

6195B H.C. White Hall, 600 N. Park St., Madison WI 53706. **E-mail:** rfkuka@wisc.edu. **Website:** creativewriting.wisc.edu/fellowships.html. **Contact:** Sean Bishop, graduate coordinator. Estab. 1986. Fellowship provides time, space and an intellectual community for writers working on first books. Receives approximately 300 applicants a year for each genre. Judged by English Department faculty and current fellows. Candidates can have up to one published book in the genre for which they are applying. Open to any writer with either an M.F.A. or Ph.D. in creative writing. Please enclose a SASE for notification of results. Results announced on website by May 1. Deadline: Last day of February. Open to submissions on December 15. Prize: $30,000 for a 9-month appointment. Costs: $45, payable to the Dept. of English; see website for payment instructions.

THOMAS WOLFE PRIZE AND LECTURE

North Carolina Writers' Network, Thomas Wolfe Fiction Prize, Great Smokies Writing Program, Attn: Nancy Williams, CPO #1860, UNC, Asheville NC 28805. **Website:** englishcomplit.unc.edu/wolfe. Estab. 1999. The Thomas Wolfe Fiction Prize honors internationally celebrated North Carolina novelist Thomas Wolfe. The prize is administered by Tommy Hays and the Great Smokies Writing Program at the

University of North Carolina at Asheville. Deadline: January 30. Submissions period begins December 1. Prize: $1,000 and potential publication in *The Thomas Wolfe Review*. Costs: $15 fee for members of the NC Writers' Network, $25 for non-members.

TOBIAS WOLFF AWARD FOR FICTION

Bellingham Review, Mail Stop 9053, Western Washington University, Bellingham WA 98225. (360)650-4863. **E-mail:** bellingham.review@wwu.edu. **Website:** www.bhreview.org. **Contact:** Susanne Paola Antonetta, editor-in-chief; Louis McLaughlin, managing editor. Offered annually for unpublished work. Guidelines available on website; online submissions only. Categories: novel exceprts and short stories. Deadline: March 15. Submissions period begins December 1. Prize: $1,000, plus publication and subscription. Costs: $20 entry fee for 1st entry; $10 for each additional entry.

WORLD FANTASY AWARDS

P.O. Box 43, Mukilteo WA 98275. **E-mail:** sfexecsec@gmail.com. **Website:** www.worldfantasy.org. **Contact:** Peter Dennis Pautz, president. Offered annually for previously published work in several categories, including life achievement, novel, novella, short story, anthology, collection, artist, special award-pro and special award-nonpro. Works are recommended by attendees of current and previous 2 years' conventions and a panel of judges. Awards to recognize excellence in fantasy literature worldwide. Deadline: June 1. Prize: Trophy. Judged by panel.

WORLD'S BEST SHORT-SHORT STORY CONTEST, NARRATIVE NONFICTION CONTEST & SOUTHEAST REVIEW POETRY CONTEST

The Southeast Review, Florida State University, English Department, Tallahassee FL 32306. **E-mail:** southeastreview@gmail.com. **Website:** www.southeastreview.org. **Contact:** Erin Hoover, editor. Estab. 1979. Annual award for unpublished short-short stories (500 words or less), poetry, and narrative nonfiction (6,000 words or less). Visit website for details. Deadline: March 15. Prize: $500 per category. Winners and finalists will be published in *The Southeast Review*. Costs: $16 reading fee for up to 3 stories or poems, or 1 narrative essay.

WOW! WOMEN ON WRITING QUARTERLY FLASH FICTION CONTEST

WOW! Women on Writing, P.O. Box 41104, Long Beach CA 90853. **E-mail:** contestinfo@wow-womenonwriting.com. **Website:** www.wow-womenonwriting.com/contest.php. **Contact:** Angela Mackintosh, editor. Contest offered quarterly. "We are open to all themes and genres, although we do encourage writers to take a close look at our literary agent guest judge for the season if you are serious about winning." Deadline: August 31, November 30, February 28, May 31. Prize: 1st place: $350 cash prize, $25 Amazon gift certificate, story published on WOW! Women On Writing, interview on blog; 2nd place: $250 cash prize, $25 Amazon gift certificate, story published on WOW! Women On Writing, interview on blog; 3rd place: $150 cash prize, $25 Amazon gift certificate, story published on WOW! Women On Writing, interview on blog; 7 runners up: $25 Amazon gift certificate, story published on WOW! Women on Writing, interview on blog; 10 honorable mentions: $20 gift certificate from Amazon, story title and name published on WOW!Women On Writing. Costs: $10. Judged by a different guest every season, who is either a literary agent, acquiring editor or publisher.

WRITER'S DIGEST ANNUAL WRITING COMPETITION

Writer's Digest, a publication of F+W Media, Inc., 10151 Carver Rd., Suite 200, Cincinnati OH 45242. (715)445-4612, ext. 13430. **E-mail:** writing-competition@fwmedia.com. **Website:** www.writersdigest.com. Writing contest with 10 categories: Inspirational Writing (spiritual/religious, maximum 2,500 words); Memoir/Personal Essay (maximum 2,000 words); Magazine Feature Article (maximum 2,000 words); Short Story (genre, maximum 4,000 words); Short Story (mainstream/literary, maximum 4,000 words); Rhyming Poetry (maximum 32 lines); Nonrhyming Poetry (maximum 32 lines); Stage Play (first 15 pages and 1-page synopsis); TV/Movie Script (first 15 pages and 1-page synopsis). Entries must be original, in English, unpublished/unproduced (except for Magazine Feature Articles), and not accepted by another publisher/producer at the time of submission. *Writer's Digest* retains one-time publication rights to the winning entries in each category. Deadline: May (early bird); June. Grand Prize: $3,000 and a trip to the Writer's Digest Conference to meet with editors and agents; 1st Place: $1,000 and $100 of Writer's Digest Books; 2nd Place: $500 and $100 of Writer's Digest Books; 3rd Place: $250 and $100 of Writer's Digest Books; 4th Place: $100 and $50 of *Writer's Digest* Books. Costs: $15/first poetry entry; $10/additional poem. All other entries are $25/first ms; $20/additional ms.

WRITER'S DIGEST POPULAR FICTION AWARDS

Writer's Digest , 10151 Carver Road, Suite #200, Blue Ash OH 45242. (715)445-4612 ext 13430. **E-mail:** WritersDigestWritingCompetition@fwmedia.com. **Website:** www.writersdigest.com. **Contact:** Nicole Howard, contest administrator. Annual competition/award for short stories. Categories include romance, crime, science fiction, thriller, horror, and young adult. Length: 4,000 words or fewer. Top Award Winners will be notified by mail by December 31. Winners will be listed in the May/June issue of Writer's Digest, and on writersdigest.com after the issue is published. Early-Bird Deadline: September 16; Final Deadline: October 15. Prizes: Grand Prize: $2,500, a trip to the *Writer's Digest* Conference, $100 off a purchase at writersdigest.com, and the latest edition of *Novel & Short Story Writer's Market*; 1st Place (one for each of 6 categories): $500 cash, $100 off a purchase at writersdigest.com, and the latest edition of *Novel & Short Story Writer's Market*; Honorable Mentions (4 in each of 6 categories): will receive promotion at writersdigest.com and the latest edition of *Novel & Short Story Writer's Market*. Costs: $20 (by September 16); $25 (by October 15).

WRITER'S DIGEST SELF-PUBLISHED BOOK AWARDS

Writer's Digest, 10151 Carver Road, Suite #200, Blue Ash OH 45242. (715)445-4612, ext. 13430. **E-mail:** WritersDigestSelfPublishingCompetition@fwmedia.com. **Website:** www.writersdigest.com. **Contact:** Nicole Howard. Estab. 1992. Contest open to all English-language, self-published books for which the authors have paid the full cost of publication, or the cost of printing has been paid for by a grant or as part of a prize. Categories include: Mainstream/Literary Fiction, Genre Fiction, Nonfiction, Inspirational (spiritual/new age), Life Stories (biographies/autobiographies/family histories/memoirs), Children's Books, Reference Books (directories/encyclopedias/guide books), Poetry, and Middle-Grade/Young Adult Books. Judges reserve the right to re-categorize entries. Judges reserve the right to withhold prizes in any category. All winners will be notified in October. Early bird deadline: April 1; Deadline: May 2. Prizes: Grand Prize: $8,000, a trip to the Writer's Digest Conference, promotion in *Writer's Digest*, 10 copies of the book will be sent to major review houses, and a guaranteed review in *Midwest Book Review*; 1st Place (9 winners): $1,000 and promotion in *Writer's Digest*; Honorable Mentions: $50 worth of Writer's Digest Books and promotion on writersdigest.com. All entrants will receive a brief commentary from one of the judges. Costs: $99; $75/additional entry.

WRITER'S DIGEST SELF-PUBLISHED E-BOOK AWARDS

Writer's Digest, 10151 Carver Road, Suite #200, Blue Ash OH 45242. (715)445-4612, ext. 13430. **E-mail:** WritersDigestSelfPublishingCompetition@fwmedia.com. **Website:** www.writersdigest.com. **Contact:** Nicole Howard. Estab. 2013. Contest open to all English-language, self-published e-books for which the authors have paid the full cost of publication, or the cost of publication has been paid for by a grant or as part of a prize. Categories include: Mainstream/Literary Fiction, Genre Fiction, Nonfiction (includes reference books), Inspirational (spiritual/new age), Life Stories (biographies/autobiographies/family histories/memoirs), Children's Books, Poetry, and Middle-Grade/Young Adult Books. Judges reserve the right to re-categorize entries. Judges reserve the right to withhold prizes in any category. All winners will be notified by December 31. Early bird deadline: August 1; Deadline: September 19. Prizes: Grand Prize: $3,000, promotion in *Writer's Digest*, a full 250-word (minimum) editorial review, $200 worth of Writer's Digest Books, and more; 1st Place (9 winners): $1,000 and promotion in *Writer's Digest*; Honorable Mentions: $50 worth of Writer's Digest Books and promotion on writersdigest.com. All entrants will receive a brief commentary from one of the judges. Costs: $99; $75/additional entry.

WRITER'S DIGEST SHORT SHORT STORY COMPETITION

Writer's Digest, 10151 Carver Road, Suite 200, Blue Ash OH 45242. (715)445-4612; ext. 13430. **E-mail:** WritersDigestShortShortStoryCompetition@fwmedia.com. **Website:** www.writersdigest.com. **Contact:** Nicole Howard. Looking for fiction that's bold, brilliant, and brief. Send your best in 1,500 words or fewer. All entries must be original, unpublished, and not submitted elsewhere at the time of submission. *Writer's Digest* reserves one-time publication rights to the 1st-25th winning entries. Winners will be notified by Feb. 28. Early bird deadline: November 17. Final deadline: December 15. Prize: 1st Place: $3,000 and a trip to the Writer's Digest Conference; 2nd Place: $1,500; 3rd Place: $500; 4th-10th Place: $100; 11th-25th Place: $50 gift certificate for writersdigestshop.com. Costs: $25.

WRITERS-EDITORS NETWORK INTERNATIONAL WRITING COMPETITION

CNW Publishing, P.O. Box A, North Stratford NH 03590-0167. **E-mail:** contestentry@writers-editors.com. **E-mail:** info@writers-editors.com. **Website:** www.writers-editors.com. **Contact:** Dana K. Cassell, executive director. Annual award to recognize publishable talent. New categories and awards for 2016: Nonfiction (unpublished or self-published; may be an article, blog post, essay/opinion piece, column, nonfiction book chapter, children's article or book chapter); fiction (unpublished or self-published; may be a short story, novel chapter, Young Adult [YA] or children's story or book chapter); poetry (unpublished or self-published; may be traditional or free verse poetry or children's verse). Guidelines available online. Deadline: March 15. Prize: 1st Place: $150 plus one year Writers-Editors membership; 2nd Place: $100; 3rd Place: $75. All winners and Honorable Mentions will receive certificates as warranted. Most Promising entry in each category will receive a free critique by a contest judge. Costs: $10 (active or new WEN/FFWA members) or $20 (nonmembers) for each fiction or nonfiction entry; $3 (members) or $5 (nonmembers) for each poem; or $10 for 5 poems (members), $10 for 3 poems (nonmembers). Judged by editors, librarians, and writers.

WRITERS' GUILD OF ALBERTA AWARDS

Writers' Guild of Alberta, Percy Page Centre, 11759 Groat Rd., Edmonton AB T5M 3K6, Canada. (780)422-8174. **Fax:** (780)422-2663. **E-mail:** mail@writersguild.ca. **Website:** writersguild.ca. **Contact:** Executive Director. Offers the following awards: Wilfrid Eggleston Award for Nonfiction; Georges Bugnet Award for Fiction; Howard O'Hagan Award for Short Story; Stephan G. Stephansson Award for Poetry; R. Ross Annett Award for Children's Literature; Gwen Pharis Ringwood Award for Drama; Jon Whyte Memorial Essay Award; James H. Gray Award for Short Nonfiction. Deadline: December 31. Prize: Winning authors receive $1,500; short piece prize winners receive $700.

WRITERS' LEAGUE OF TEXAS BOOK AWARDS

Writers' League of Texas, 611 S. Congress Ave., Suite 200A-3, Austin TX 78704. (512)499-8914. **Fax:** (512)499-0441. **E-mail:** sara@writersleague.org. **E-mail:** sara@writersleague.org. **Website:** www.writersleague.org. Open to Texas authors of books published the previous year. Authors are required to show proof of Texas residency (current or past), but are not required to be members of the Writers' League of Texas. Deadline: Open to submissions from October 1 to January 15. Prize: $1,000 and a commemorative award. Costs: $60/title; $40 for WLT members.

LAMAR YORK PRIZE FOR FICTION AND NONFICTION CONTEST

The Chattahoochee Review, Georgia Perimeter College, 2101 Womack Rd., Dunwoody GA 30338-4497. (770)274-5479. **E-mail:** gpccr@gpc.edu. **Website:** thechattahoocheereview.gpc.edu. **Contact:** Anna Schachner, Editor. Offered annually for unpublished creative nonfiction and nonscholarly essays and fiction up to 5,000 words. *The Chattahoochee Review* buys first rights only for winning essay/ms for the purpose of publication in the summer issue. Deadline: January 31. Submission period begins October 1. Prize: 2 prizes of $1,000 each, plus publication. Costs: $15 fee/entry; subscription included in fee. Judged by the editorial staff of *The Chattahoochee Review.*

ZOETROPE SHORT STORY CONTEST

Zoetrope: All Story, Zoetrope: All-Story, Attn: Fiction Editor, 916 Kearny St., San Francisco CA 94133. (415)788-7500. **E-mail:** contests@all-story.com. **Website:** www.all-story.com. Annual short fiction contest. Considers submissions of short stories and one-act plays no longer than 7,000 words. Excerpts from larger works, screenplays, treatments, and poetry will be returned unread. Deadline: October 1. Submissions period begins July 1. Prizes: 1st place: $1,000 and publication on website; 2nd place: $500; 3rd place: $250. Costs: $20.

ZONE 3 FICTION AWARD

Zone 3, Austin Peay State University, P.O. Box 4565, Clarksville TN 37044. (931)221-7031. **Fax:** (931)221-7149. **E-mail:** wallacess@apsu.edu. **Website:** www.apsu.edu/zone3/contests. **Contact:** Susan Wallace, Managing Editor. Annual contest for unpublished fiction. Open to any fiction writer. Deadline: April 1. Prize: $250 and publication.

CONFERENCES & WORKSHOPS

Why are conferences so popular? Writers and conference directors alike tell us it's because writing can be such a lonely business—at conferences writers have the opportunity to meet (and commiserate) with fellow writers, as well as meet and network with publishers, editors, and agents. Conferences and workshops provide some of the best opportunities for writers to make publishing contacts and pick up valuable information on the business, as well as the craft, of writing.

The bulk of the listings in this section are for conferences. Most conferences last from one day to one week and offer a combination of workshop-type writing sessions, panel discussions, and a variety of guest speakers. Topics may include all aspects of writing from fiction to poetry to scriptwriting, or they may focus on a specific type of writing, such as those conferences sponsored by the Romance Writers of America (RWA) for writers of romance or by the Society of Children's Book Writers and Illustrators (SCBWI) for writers of children's books.

Workshops, however, tend to run longer—usually one to two weeks. Designed to operate like writing classes, most require writers to be prepared to work on and discuss their fiction while attending. An important benefit of workshops is the opportunity they provide writers for an intensive critique of their work, often by professional writing teachers and established writers.

Each of the listings here includes information on the specific focus of an event as well as planned panels, guest speakers, and workshop topics. It is important to note, however, some conference directors were still in the planning stages for 2017 when we contacted them. If it was not possible to include 2017 dates, fees, or topics, we provided the most up-to-date information available so you can get an idea of what to expect. For the most current information, it's best to check the conference website or send a self-addressed, stamped envelope to the director in question about three months before the date(s) listed.

FINDING A CONFERENCE

Many writers try to make it to at least one conference a year, but cost and location count as much as subject matter or other considerations when determining which conference to attend. There are conferences in almost every state and province, and even some in Europe open to North Americans.

To make it easier for you to find a conference close to home—or to find one in an exotic locale to fit into your vacation plans—we've divided this section into geographic regions. The conferences appear in alphabetical order under the appropriate regional heading.

Note that conferences appear under the regional heading according to where they will be held, which is sometimes different from the address given as the place to register or send for information. The regions are as follows:

LEARNING AND NETWORKING

Besides learning from workshop leaders and panelists in formal sessions, writers at conferences also benefit from conversations with other attendees. Writers on all levels enjoy sharing insights. A conversation over lunch can reveal a new market for your work or let you know which editors are most receptive to the work of new writers. You can find out about recent editor changes and about specific agents. A casual chat could lead to a new contact or resource in your area.

Many editors and agents make visiting conferences a part of their regular search for new writers. A cover letter or query that starts with "I met you at the Green Mountain Writers Conference," or "I found your talk on your company's new romance line at the Moonlight and Magnolias Writers Conference most interesting ..." may give you a small leg up on the competition.

While a few writers have been successful in selling their manuscripts at a conference, the availability of editors and agents does not usually mean these folks will have the time to read your novel or six best short stories (unless, of course, you've scheduled an individual meeting with them in advance). While editors and agents are glad to meet writers and discuss work in general terms, usually they don't have the time (or energy) to give an extensive critique during a conference. In other words, use the conference as a way to make a first, brief contact.

SELECTING A CONFERENCE

Besides the obvious considerations of time, place, and cost, choose your conference based on your writing goals. If, for example, your goal is to improve the quality of your writing, it will be more helpful to choose a hands-on craft workshop rather than a conference offering a series of panels on marketing and promotion. If, on the other hand, you are a science fiction novelist who would like to meet your fans, try one of the many science fiction conferences or "cons" held throughout the country and the world.

Look for panelists and workshop instructors whose work you admire and who seem to be writing in your general area. Check for specific panels or discussions of topics relevant to what you are writing now. Think about the size—would you feel more comfortable with a small workshop of eight people or a large group of one hundred or more attendees?

If your funds are limited, start by looking for conferences close to home, but you may want to explore those that offer contests with cash prizes—and a chance to recoup your expenses. A few conferences and workshops also offer scholarships, but the competition is stiff and writers interested in these should seek out the requirements early. Finally, students may want to look for conferences and workshops that offer college credit. You will find these options included in the listings here. Again, check the conference website or send a self-addressed, stamped envelope for the most current details.

MULTIPLE U.S. LOCATIONS

ARTIST-IN-RESIDENCE NATIONAL PARKS

ME **E-mail:** Acadia_Information@nps.gov. **Website:** www.nps.gov/subjects/arts/air.htm. **Contact:** Artist-In-Residence Coordinator. Thirty-seven National Parks offer residency programs open to two-dimensional visual artists, photographers, sculptors, performers, writers, composers, video/filmmakers, and others.

ADDITIONAL INFORMATION See website for individual park and contact information.

WRITER'S DIGEST CONFERENCES

F+W Media, Inc., 10151 Carver Rd., Suite 200, Blue Ash OH 45242. (877)436-7764 (option 2). **E-mail:** writersdigestconference@fwmedia.com. **E-mail:** phil.sexton@fwmedia.com. **Website:** www.writersdigest-conference.com. **Contact:** Taylor Sferra. Estab. 1995.

COSTS Cost varies by location and year. There are typically different pricing options for those who wish attend the pitch slam and those who just want to attend the conference education.

ACCOMMODATIONS A block of rooms at the event hotel are reserved for guests. See the travel page on the website for more information.

NORTHEAST

⊙ BREAD LOAF ORION ENVIRONMENTAL WRITERS' CONFERENCE

Middlebury College, Middlebury VT 05753. (802)443-5286. **Fax:** (802)443-2087. **E-mail:** blwc@middlebury.edu. **Website:** www.middlebury.edu/bread-loaf-conferences/BLOrion. Estab. 2014.

ACCOMMODATIONS Mountain campus of Middlebury College in Vermont.

ADDITIONAL INFORMATION The event is designed to hone the skills of people interested in producing literary writing about the environment and the natural world. The conference is co-sponsored by the Bread Loaf Writers' Conference, Orion magazine, and Middlebury College's Environmental Studies Program.

BREAD LOAF WRITERS' CONFERENCE

Middlebury College, Middlebury College, Middlebury VT 05753. (802)443-5286. **Fax:** (802)443-2087. **E-mail:** blwc@middlebury.edu. **Website:** www.middlebury.edu/bread-loaf-conferences/bl_writers. Estab. 1926.

ACCOMMODATIONS Bread Loaf Campus in Ripton, Vermont.

ADDITIONAL INFORMATION 2016 Conference Dates: August 10-20. Location: Bread Loaf campus of Middlebury College in Vermont. Average attendance: 230. The application deadline for the 2016 event is March 1, 2015; there is $15 application fee.

CAPE COD WRITERS CENTER ANNUAL CONFERENCE

P.O. Box 408, Osterville MA 02655. **E-mail:** writers@capecodwriterscenter.org. **Website:** www.capecod-writerscenter.org. **Contact:** Nancy Rubin Stuart, executive director.

COSTS Costs vary, depending on the number of courses selected.

ACCOMMODATIONS Held at Resort and Conference Center of Hyannis, Hyannis, MA.

CHILDREN'S LITERATURE CONFERENCE

239 Montauk Hwy, Southampton NY 11968-6700. (631)632-5030. **Fax:** (631)632-2578. **Website:** www.stonybrook.edu/writers. **Contact:** Adrienne Unger, administrative coordinator. 239 Montauk Hwy., Southampton, NY 11968-6700. (631)632-5030. **Fax:** (631)632-2578. **E-mail:** southamptonwriters@notes.cc.sunysb.edu. **Website:** www.stonybrook.edu/writers. Annual conference held in July. "The seaside campus of Stony Brook Southampton is located in the heart of the Hamptons, a renowned resort area only 70 miles from New York City. During free time, participants can draw on inspiration from the Atlantic beaches or explore the charming seaside towns." Faculty have included Richard Peck, Tor Seidler, Cindy Kane, Gahan Wilson James McMullan, and Mitchell Kriegman. Among the guest presenters currently scheduled are author/illustrator Jules Feiffer, children's literature historian Leonard Marcus, marketing guru Susan Raab, best-selling author and illustrator team Kate and Jim McMullan, and children's literature specialist Connie Rockman.

COSTS Fees vary. 2016 fees will be available online.

ACCOMMODATIONS On-campus housing, doubles and small singles with shared baths, is modest but comfortable. Housing assignment is by lottery. Supplies list of lodging alternatives.

ADDITIONAL INFORMATION "Applicants must complete an application and submit a writing sample of original, unpublished work. See Web for details. Accepts inquiries by e-mail, phone, and fax."

GOTHAM WRITERS' WORKSHOP

WritingClasses.com, 555 Eighth Ave., Suite 1402, New York NY 10018. (212)974-8377. **Fax:** (212)307-6325. **Website:** www.writingclasses.com. Estab. 1993.

ADDITIONAL INFORMATION See the website for courses and pricing and instructors.

GREEN MOUNTAIN WRITERS CONFERENCE

47 Hazel St., Rutland VT 05701. (802)236-6133. **E-mail:** ydaley@sbcglobal.net. **E-mail:** yvonnedaley@me.com. **Website:** vermontwriters.com. **Contact:** Yvonne Daley, director. Estab. 1998.

COSTS $575 before April 15; $625 before May 15; $650 before June 1. Partial scholarships are available

ACCOMMODATIONS Dramatically reduced rates at The Mountain Top Inn and Resort for attendees. Close to other area hotels, B&Bs in Rutland County, Vermont.

ADDITIONAL INFORMATION Participants' mss can be read and commented on at a cost. Sponsors contests. Conference publishes a literary magazine featuring work of participants. Brochures available on website or e-mail. "We offer the opportunity to learn from some of the nation's best writers at a small, supportive conference in a lakeside setting that allows one-to-one feedback. Participants often continue to correspond and share work after conferences."

IWWG SPRING BIG APPLE CONFERENCE

International Women's Writing Guild, NY. 917-720-6959. **E-mail:** iwwgquestions@gmail.com. **Website:** www.iwwg.wildapricot.org/events.

Writing workshops; author panel discussing publishing trends; book fair; agent panel and one-on-one pitch sessions.

JOURNEY INTO THE IMAGINATION: A FIVE-DAY WRITING RETREAT

995 Chapman Rd., Yorktown NY 10598. (914)962-4432. **E-mail:** emily@emilyhanlon.com. **Website:** www.thefictionwritersjourney.com/pendle-hill-spring-writers-retreat.html. **Contact:** Emily Hanlon. Estab. 2004.

COSTS 2014: 5 nights—$1350 for a double room. $1450 for a single room. All rooms are private with shared bath.

ADDITIONAL INFORMATION For brochure, visit website.

KINDLING WORDS EAST

VT. **Website:** www.kindlingwords.org.

THE MACDOWELL COLONY

100 High St., Peterborough NH 03458. (603)924-3886. **Fax:** (603)924-9142. **E-mail:** admissions@macdowellcolony.org. **Website:** www.macdowellcolony.org. Estab. 1907.

COSTS Travel reimbursement and stipends are available for participants of the residency, based on need. There are no residency fees.

MUSE AND THE MARKETPLACE

Grub Street, 162 Boylston St., 5th Floor, Boston MA 02116. (617)695-0075. **E-mail:** info@grubstreet.org. **Website:** museandthemarketplace.com.

The Muse and the Marketplace is a three-day literary conference designed to give aspiring writers a better understanding about the craft of writing fiction and nonfiction, to prepare them for the changing world of publishing and promotion, and to create opportunities for meaningful networking. On all three days, prominent and nationally-recognized established and emerging authors lead sessions on the craft of writing— the "muse" side of things— while editors, literary agents, publicists and other industry professionals lead sessions on the business side— the "marketplace."

ACCOMMODATIONS Boston Park Plaza Hotel.

ODYSSEY FANTASY WRITING WORKSHOP

P.O. Box 75, Mont Vernon NH 03057. (603)673-6234. **E-mail:** jcavelos@sff.net. **Website:** www.odyssey-workshop.org. **Contact:** Jeanne Cavelos. Estab. 1996.

COSTS In 2016: $2,025 tuition, $850 housing (double room), $1,700 housing (single room), $40 application fee, $600 food (approximate), $700 optional processing fee to receive college credit.

ADDITIONAL INFORMATION Students must apply and include a writing sample. Application deadline: April 8. Students' works are critiqued throughout the 6 weeks. Workshop information available in October. For brochure/guidelines, send SASE, e-mail, visit website, or call. Accepts inquiries by SASE, e-mail, phone.

RT BOOKLOVERS CONVENTION

81 Willoughby Street, Suite 701, Brooklyn NY 11201. **E-mail:** Tere@rtconvention.com. **Website:** rtconvention.com. **Contact:** Tere Michaels.

COSTS $489 normal registration; $425 for industry professionals (agents, editors). Special discounted rate for readers, $449. Many other pricing options available. See website.

ACCOMMODATIONS Rooms available at the 2016 convention hotel: Rio Hotel & Casino.

THE SOUTHAMPTON WRITERS CONFERENCE

Stony Brook Southampton MFA in Creative Writing Program, 239 Montauk Highway, Southampton NY 11968. (631)632-5007. **E-mail:** christian.mclean@stonybrook.edu. **Website:** www.stonybrook.edu/southampton/mfa/summer/cwl_home.html. **Contact:** Christian McLean. Estab. 1976.

COSTS 12-day Master Class: $975 (does not include afternoon faculty-led workshop). 5-day workshop only: $1,395. 5-day workshop + residency: $1,995 (12 days total). 12-day workshop: $1,995. 12-day residency: $975.

ACCOMMODATIONS Participants can stay on campus in air-conditioned dorms. Shared room: $35 per night (5-day conference: $140). Shared room with linen: $42 per night (5-day conference: $168). Single room: $40.55 per night (5-day conference: $162.20). Single room with linen: $47.50 per night (5-day conference: $190).

THRILLERFEST

P.O. Box 311, Eureka CA 95502. **E-mail:** infocentral@thrillerwriters.org. **Website:** www.thrillerfest.com. **Contact:** Kimberley Howe, executive director. Estab. 2006.

COSTS Price will vary from $475-1,199, depending on which events are selected. Various package deals are available offering savings, and early-bird pricing is offered beginning September of each year.

ACCOMMODATIONS Grand Hyatt in Manhattan.

UNICORN WRITERS CONFERENCE

P.O. Box 176, Redding CT 06876. (203)938-7405. **E-mail:** unicornwritersconference@gmail.com. **Website:** www.unicornwritersconference.com. **Contact:** Jan L. Kardys, Chairman. Estab. 2010.

The 40 pages for manuscript reviews are read in advance by your selected agents/editors but follow the submission guidelines on the website. Check the Genre Chart for each agent and editor before you make your selection.

COSTS $325 includes all workshops (5 every hour to select on the day of the conference) which includes all workshops, gift bag, and three meals. Additional cost for manuscript reviews: $60.

ACCOMMODATIONS Held at Reid Castle, Purchase, NY. Directions available on event website.

ADDITIONAL INFORMATION The first self published authors will be featured on the website and the bookstore will sell their books at the event.

VERMONT STUDIO CENTER

P.O. Box 613, 80 Pearl Street, Johnson VT 05656. (802)635-2727. **Fax:** (802)635-2730. **E-mail:** info@vermontstudiocenter.org. **Website:** www.vermontstudiocenter.org. **Contact:** Gary Clark, Writing Program Director. Estab. 1984. P.O. Box 613, Johnson VT 05656. (802)635-2727. **Fax:** (802)635-2730. **E-mail:** info@vermontstudiocenter.org. **Website:** www.vermontstudiocenter.org. **Contact:** Gary Clark, writing program director. Estab. 1984. Ongoing residencies. Conference duration: From 2-12 weeks. Average attendance: 55 writers and visual artists/month. "The Vermont Studio Center is an international creative community located in Johnson, Vermont, and serving more than 600 American and international artists and writers each year (50 per month). A Studio Center Residency features secluded, uninterrupted writing time, the companionship of dedicated and talented peers, and access to a roster of two distinguished Visiting Writers each month. All VSC Residents receive three meals a day, private, comfortable housing and the company of an international community of painters, sculptors, poets, printmakers and writers. Writers attending residencies at the Studio Center may work on whatever they choose—no matter what month of the year they attend." Visiting writers have included Ron Carlson, Donald Revell, Jane Hirshfield, Rosanna Warren, Chris Abani, Bob Shacochis, Tony Hoagland, and Alice Notley.

ACCOMMODATIONS "The cost of a 4-week residency is $3,950. Generous fellowship and grant assistance available. "Accommodations available on site. "Residents live in single rooms in ten modest, comfortable houses adjacent to the Red Mill Building. Rooms are simply furnished and have shared baths. Complete linen service is provided. The Studio Center is unable to accommodate guests at meals, overnight guests, spouses, children or pets."

ADDITIONAL INFORMATION Fellowships application deadlines are February 15, June 15 and October 1. Writers encouraged to visit website for more information. May also e-mail, call, fax.

WESLEYAN WRITERS CONFERENCE

Wesleyan University, 294 High St., Room 207, Middletown CT 06459. (860)685-3604. **Fax:** (860)685-2441. **E-mail:** agreene@wesleyan.edu. **Website:** www.wesleyan.edu/writing/conference. Estab. 1956.

ACCOMMODATIONS Meals are provided on campus. Lodging is available on campus or in town.

ADDITIONAL INFORMATION Ms critiques are available, but not required.

WRITERS OMI AT LEDIG HOUSE

55 Fifth Ave., 15th Floor, New York NY 10003. (212)206-6114. **E-mail:** writers@artomi.org. **Website:** www.artomi.org.

ACCOMMODATIONS Residents provide their own transportation. Offers overnight accommodations.

ADDITIONAL INFORMATION "Agents and editors from the New York publishing community are invited for dinner and discussion. Bicycles, a swimming pool, and nearby tennis court are available for use."

YADDO

The Corporation of Yaddo Residencies, P.O. Box 395, 312 Union Ave., Saratoga Springs NY 12866-0395. (518)584-0746. **Fax:** (518)584-1312. **E-mail:** chwait@yaddo.org. **Website:** www.yaddo.org. **Contact:** Candace Wait, program director. Estab. 1900. Two seasons: large season is May-August; small season is October-May (stays from 2 weeks to 2 months; average stay is 5 weeks). Accepts 230 artists/year. Accommodates approximately 35 artists in large season. Those qualified for invitations to Yaddo are highly qualified writers, visual artists (including photographers), composers, choreographers, performance artists and film and video artists who are working at the professional level in their fields. Artists who wish to work collaboratively are encouraged to apply. An abiding principle at Yaddo is that applications for residencies are judged on the quality of the artists' work and professional promise. Site includes four small lakes, a rose garden, woodland, swimming pool, tennis courts. Yaddo's non-refundable application fee is $30, to which is added a fee for media uploads ranging from $5-10 depending on the discipline. Application fees must be paid by credit card. Two letters of recommendation are requested. Applications are considered by the Admissions Committee and invitations are issued by March 15 (deadline: January 1) and October 1 (deadline: August 1). Information available on website.

COSTS No fee is charged; residency includes room, board and studio space. Limited travel expenses are available to artists accepted for residencies at Yaddo.

ACCOMMODATIONS No stipends are offered.

MIDATLANTIC

ALGONKIAN NOVEL WORKSHOPS

2020 Pennsylvania Ave. NW, Suite 443, Washington DC 20006. **E-mail:** info@algonkianconferences.com. **Website:** algonkianconferences.com/index.htm.

ASSOCIATION OF WRITERS & WRITING PROGRAMS ANNUAL CONFERENCE

Association of Writers & Writing Programs, George Mason University, 4400 University Drive, MSN 1E3, Fairfax VA 22030-4444. (703)993-4317. **Fax:** (703)993-4302. **E-mail:** conference@awpwriter.org; events@awpwriter.org. **Website:** www.awpwriter.org/awp_conference. Estab. 1992.

ADDITIONAL INFORMATION Upcoming conference: Washington, D.C. (February 8-11, 2017).

BALTIMORE COMIC-CON

Baltimore Convention Center, 1 West Pratt St., Baltimore MD 21201. (410)526-7410. **E-mail:** general@baltimorecomiccon.com. **Website:** www.baltimorecomiccon.com. **Contact:** Marc Nathan. Estab. 1999.

COSTS General Admission, VIP, Celebrity, and Harvey Awards tickets are available at baltimorecomiccon.com/tickets.

ACCOMMODATIONS Does not offer overnight accommodations. Provides list of area hotels and lodging options offering associated discounts.

ADDITIONAL INFORMATION For brochure, visit website.

BALTIMORE WRITERS' CONFERENCE

English Department, Liberal Arts Bldg., Towson University, 8000 York Rd., Towson MD 21252. (410)704-3695. **E-mail:** prwr@towson.edu. **Website:** baltimorewritersconference.org. Estab. 1994.

This conference has sold out in the past.

CONFERENCES & WORKSHOPS

ACCOMMODATIONS Hotels are close by, if required.

ADDITIONAL INFORMATION Writers may register through the BWA website. Send inquiries via e-mail.

BAY TO OCEAN WRITERS CONFERENCE

P.O. Box 1773, Easton MD 21601. 410-482-6337. **E-mail:** info@baytoocean.com. **Website:** www.baytoocean.com. Estab. 1998.

COSTS Adults $115, students $55. A paid manuscript review is also available – details on website. Includes continental breakfast and networking lunch.

ADDITIONAL INFORMATION Registration is on website. Pre-registration is required; no registration at door. Conference usually sells out one month in advance. Conference is for all levels of writers.

CONFLUENCE

P.O. Box 3681, Pittsburgh PA 15230-3681. **Website:** parsec-sff.org/confluence. (412)344-0456. **E-mail:** confluence@parsec-sff.org. Estab. 1996. Confluence is about programming that lets fans of science fiction and fantasy hear about the views and visions of some of the leading authors, editors, and critics in the genre. Annual. Conference. Site: Doubletree by Hilton Cranberry Pittsburgh.

HIGHLIGHTS FOUNDATION FOUNDERS WORKSHOPS

814 Court St., Honesdale PA 18431. (570)253-1122. **Fax:** (570)253-0179. **E-mail:** klbrown@highlightsfoundation.org. **E-mail:** jo.lloy@highlightsfoundation.org. **Website:** highlightsfoundation.org. **Contact:** Kent L. Brown, Jr. Estab. 2000.

COSTS Prices vary based on workshop. Check website for details.

ACCOMMODATIONS Coordinates pickup at local airport. Offers overnight accommodations. Participants stay in guest cabins on the wooded grounds surrounding Highlights Founders' home adjacent to the house/conference center.

ADDITIONAL INFORMATION Some workshops require pre-workshop assignment. Brochure available for SASE, by e-mail, on website, by phone, by fax. Accepts inquiries by phone, fax, e-mail, SASE. Editors attend conference. "Applications will be reviewed and accepted on a first-come, first-served basis, applicants must demonstrate specific experience in writing area of workshop they are applying for—writing samples are required for many of the workshops."

MONTROSE CHRISTIAN WRITERS' CONFERENCE

218 Locust St., Montrose PA 18801. (570)278-1001 or (800)598-5030. **Fax:** (570)278-3061. **E-mail:** mbc@montrosebible.org. **Website:** montrosebible.org. Estab. 1990.

COSTS Tuition is $180.

ACCOMMODATIONS Will meet planes in Binghamton, NY and Scranton, PA. On-site accommodations: room and board $340-475/conference, including food (2015 rates). RV court available.

ADDITIONAL INFORMATION "Writers can send work ahead of time and have it critiqued for a small fee." The attendees are usually church related. The writing has a Christian emphasis. Conference information available in April. For brochure, visit website, e-mail or call. Accepts inquiries by phone or e-mail.

JENNY MCKEAN MOORE COMMUNITY WORKSHOPS

English Department, George Washington University, 801 22nd St. NW, Rome Hall, Suite 760, Washington DC 20052. (202)994-6180. **Fax:** (202)994-6637. **E-mail:** lpageinc@gwu.edu. **Website:** www.gwu.edu/~english/creative_jennymckeanmoore.html. **Contact:** Lisa Page, director of creative writing. Estab. 1976.

ADDITIONAL INFORMATION Admission is competitive and by decided by the quality of a submitted ms.

NEW JERSEY ROMANCE WRITERS PUT YOUR HEART IN A BOOK CONFERENCE

P.O. Box 513, Plainsboro NJ 08536. **Website:** www.njromancewriters.org/conference.html. Estab. 1984.

WILLIAM PATERSON UNIVERSITY SPRING WRITER'S CONFERENCE

English Department, Atrium 232, 300 Pompton Rd., Wayne NJ 07470. (973)720-3067. **Fax:** (973)720-2189. **E-mail:** liut@wpunj.edu. **Website:** wpunj.edu/cohss/departments/english/writers-conference.

COSTS $22-65.

PHILADELPHIA WRITERS' CONFERENCE

P.O. Box 7171, Elkins Park PA 19027-0171. (215) 619-7422. **E-mail:** info@pwcwriters.org. **E-mail:** info@pwcwriters.org. **Website:** pwcwriters.org. Estab. 1949.

"A three-day conference that offers from 14 workshops, usually four seminars, several 'manuscript rap' sessions, a Friday Roundtable Forum Buffet with speaker, and the Saturday Annual Awards Banquet with speaker. The 150 to 200 conferees may submit manuscripts in advance for criticism by the workshop leaders, and are eligible to submit entries in about a dozen contest categories. Cash prizes and certificates are given to first and second place winners, plus full tuition for the following year's conference to first place winners."

ACCOMMODATIONS Wyndham Hotel (formerly the Holiday Inn), Independence Mall, Fourth and Arch Streets, Philadelphia, PA 19106-2170. Hotel offers discount for early registration.

ADDITIONAL INFORMATION Accepts inquiries by e-mail. Agents and editors attend the conference. Many questions are answered online.

SCBWI—NEW JERSEY; ANNUAL SUMMER CONFERENCE

SCBWI-New Jersey: Society of Children's Book Writers & Illustrators, New Jersey NJ **Website:** newjersey.scbwi.org. **Contact:** Leeza Hernandez, regional advisor.

MIDSOUTH

AMERICAN CHRISTIAN WRITERS CONFERENCES

P.O. Box 110390, Nashville TN 37222-0390. (800)219-7483, (800)21-WRITE. **E-mail:** ACWriters@aol.com. **Website:** www.ACWriters.com. **Contact:** Reg Forder, director. Estab. 1981.

COSTS Costs vary based on conference. Prices also depend on whether it is a conference or a mentoring retreat.

ACCOMMODATIONS Special rates are available at the host hotel (usually a major chain like Holiday Inn).

ADDITIONAL INFORMATION E-mail or call for conference brochures

BLUE RIDGE CHRISTIAN "AUTUMN IN THE MOUNTAINS" NOVELISTS RETREAT

NC. (800)588-7222. **E-mail:** ylehman@bellsouth.net. **Website:** ridgecrestconferencecenter.org/event/blueridgemountainchristianwritersconference#.Vo_pJTZWKf4. **Contact:** Yvonne Lehman, director. Estab. 2007.

COSTS Registration: $325. To register: 1-800-588-7222.

CELEBRATION OF SOUTHERN LITERATURE

Southern Lit Alliance, 3069 S. Broad St., Ste. 2, Chattanooga TN 37408-3056. (423)267-1218. **Fax:** (866)483-6831. **E-mail:** srobinson@southernlitalliance.org. **Website:** www.southernlitalliance.org. **Contact:** Susan Robinson.

This event happens every other year in odd-numbered years.

CHRISTOPHER NEWPORT UNIVERSITY WRITERS' CONFERENCE & WRITING CONTEST

(757)269-4368. **E-mail:** eleanor.taylor@cnu.edu. **Website:** writers.cnu.edu. Estab. 1981.

ACCOMMODATIONS Provides list of area hotels.

HAMPTON ROADS WRITERS CONFERENCE

P.O. Box 56228, Virginia Beach VA 23456. **E-mail:** hrwriters@cox.net. **Website:** hamptonroadswriters.org.

COSTS Costs vary. There are discounts for members, for early bird registration, for students and more.

HIGHLAND SUMMER CONFERENCE

Box 7014, Radford University, Radford VA 24142-7014. **E-mail:** tburriss@radford.edu; rbderrick@radford.edu. **Website:** tinyurl.com/q8z8ej9. **Contact:** Dr. Theresa Burriss, Ruth Derrick. Estab. 1978.

JAMES RIVER WRITERS CONFERENCE

2319 East Broad St., Richmond VA 23223. (804)433-3790. **Fax:** (804)291-1466. **E-mail:** info@jamesriverwriters.com; fallconference@jamesriverwriters.com. **Website:** www.jamesriverwriters.com. Estab. 2003.

COSTS Check website for updated pricing.

KILLER NASHVILLE

P.O. Box 680759, Franklin TN 37068-0686. (615)599-4032. **E-mail:** contact@killernashville.com. **Website:** www.killernashville.com. Estab. 2006.

COSTS Costs are $128-210 for basic registration. Add-on costs available for other items.

ADDITIONAL INFORMATION Additional information about registration is provided online.

NORTH CAROLINA WRITERS' NETWORK FALL CONFERENCE

P.O. Box 21591, Winston-Salem NC 27120. (336)293-8844. **E-mail:** mail@ncwriters.org. **Website:** www.ncwriters.org. Estab. 1985.

COSTS Approximately $250 (includes 4 meals).

ACCOMMODATIONS Special rates are usually available at the conference hotel, but conferees must make their own reservations.

ADDITIONAL INFORMATION Available at www.ncwriters.org.

SOUTH CAROLINA WRITERS WORKSHOP

4840 Forest Drive, Suite 6B: PMB 189, Columbia SC 29206. **E-mail:** scwwliaison@gmail.com; scww2013@gmail.com. **Website:** www.myscww.org. Estab. 1991.

WILDACRES WRITERS WORKSHOP

233 S. Elm St., Greensboro NC 27401. (336)255-8210. **E-mail:** judihill@aol.com. **Website:** www.wildacres-writers.com. **Contact:** Judi Hill, Director. Estab. 1985.

COSTS The current price is $830. Check the website for more info.

ADDITIONAL INFORMATION Include a 1-page writing sample with your registration. See the website for information.

WRITE ON THE RIVER

8941 Kelsey Lane, Knoxville TN 37922. **E-mail:** bob@bobmayer.org. **Website:** www.bobmayer.org. **Contact:** Bob Mayer. Estab. 2002.

COSTS Varies; depends on venue. Please see website for any updates.

ADDITIONAL INFORMATION Limited to 4 participants, and focused on their novel and marketability.

THE WRITERS' WORKSHOP

387 Beaucatcher Rd., Asheville NC 28805. (828)254-8111. **E-mail:** writersw@gmail.com. **Website:** www.twwoa.org. Estab. 1984.

COSTS Cost varies. Financial assistance available to low-income writers. Information on overnight accommodations is made available.

ADDITIONAL INFORMATION We also sponsor Annual Contests in Poetry, Literary Fiction, Memoirs, and Essay. For guidelines: www.twwoa.org.

SOUTHEAST

ALABAMA WRITERS' CONCLAVE

Website: www.alabamawritersconclave.org. **Contact:** Sue Walker, president. Estab. 1923.

COSTS Previous fees for the conference have been $150 (member)/$175 (nonmember), includes 2 meals. Critique fee $25 (member)/$30 (nonmember). Membership $25.

ADDITIONAL INFORMATION "We have major speakers and faculty members who conduct intensive, energetic workshops. Our annual writing contest guidelines and all other information is available at www.alabamawritersconclave.org."

ARKANSAS WRITERS' CONFERENCE

1815 Columbia, Conway AR 72034. (501) 833-2756. **E-mail:** breannaconel@yahoo.com. **Website:** www.arkansaswritersconference.org.

ATLANTA WRITERS CONFERENCE

Atlanta Writers Club, Westin Atlanta Airport Hotel, 4736 Best Rd., Atlanta GA 30337, USA. **E-mail:** awconference@gmail.com. **E-mail:** gjweinstein@yahoo.com. **Website:** www.atlantawritersconference.com. **Contact:** George Weinstein. Estab. 2008.

COSTS Manuscript Critique are $160 each (maximum of two spots/waitlists—no charge for waitlists unless there's a cancellation that opens a spot for you). Pitch on Saturday is $60 each (maximum of two spots/waitlists—no charge for waitlists unless there's a cancellation that opens a spot for you). Query Letter Critique on Friday is $60 (you may register for only one spot). Other workshops and panels may also cost extra—check the website. The Conference Package "All Activities" option (which includes two manuscript critiques, two pitches, and one of each remaining activity): $560.

ACCOMMODATIONS Westin Airport Atlanta Hotel

ADDITIONAL INFORMATION There is a free shuttle that runs between the airport and the hotel.

ATLANTIC CENTER FOR THE ARTS

1414 Art Center Ave, New Smyrna Beach FL 32618. **Website:** atlanticcenterforthearts.org. 1414 Art Center Ave, New Smyrna Beach FL 32618. (386)427-6975. **E-mail:** shiggins@atlanticcenterforthearts.com. **Website:** atlanticcenterforthearts.org. **Contact:** program department. Three week long residency offered several times a year. "Associates selected will get one-on-one experience with a Master Artist. The Master Artist selects Associate Residents from the applications."

ACCOMMODATIONS "Van transportation is provided from ACA two days per week at regularly scheduled times to the shopping center and art supply stores. Many artists do bring their own vehicles and car-pooling may be an option. ACA does provide van transportation to outreaches, when possible. Master Artists are supplied with a car. Bikes are available at ACA." Offers overnight accommodations.

DRAGON CON

P.O. Box 16459, Atlanta GA 30321. **Website:** www.dragoncon.org. P.O. Box 16459, Atlanta GA 30321. (404)669-0773. **E-mail:** dragoncon@dragoncon.org. **Website:** www.dragoncon.org. Annual. Labor Day Weekend, September 2-5, 2016. "Dragon*Con is the largest multimedia, popular culture convention focusing on science fiction and fantasy, gaming, comics, literature, art, music, and film in the US."

FLORIDA CHRISTIAN WRITERS CONFERENCE

Word Weavers International, Inc., 530 Lake Kathryn Circle, Casselberry FL 32707. (386)295-3902. **E-mail:** FloridaCWC@aol.com. **Website:** floridacwc.net. **Contact:** Eva Marie Everson & Mark T. Hancock. Estab. 1988.

COSTS Ranges: daily rate $275 (in advance, includes lunch and dinner; specify days); full conference $1,495 (attendee and participating spouse/family member in same room).

ACCOMMODATIONS Private rooms and double-occupancy.

FLORIDA ROMANCE WRIITERS FUN IN THE SUN CONFERENCE

Florida Romance Writers, P.O. Box 550562, Fort Lauderdale FL 33355. **E-mail:** frwfuninthesun@yahoo.com. **Website:** frwfuninthesunmain.blogspot.com. Estab. 1986.

KACHEMAK BAY WRITERS' CONFERENCE

Kenai Peninsula College - Kachemak Bay Campus, 533 East Pioneer Ave., Homer AK 99603. (907)235-7743. **E-mail:** iyconf@uaa.alaska.edu. **Website:** writersconf.kpc.alaska.edu.

Previous keynote speakers have included Dave Barry, Amy Tan, Jeffrey Eugenides, and Anne Lamott.

COSTS See the website. Some scholarships available.

ACCOMMODATIONS Homer is 225 miles south of Anchorage, Alaska on the southern tip of the Kenai Peninsula and the shores of Kachemak Bay. There are multiple hotels in the area.

MONTEVALLO LITERARY FESTIVAL

Comer Hall, Station 6420, University of Montevallo, Montevallo AL 35115. (205)665-6420. **Fax:** (205) 665-6420. **E-mail:** murphyj@montevallo.edu. **Website:** www.montevallo.edu/arts-sciences/college-of-arts-sciences/departments/english-foreign-languages/student-organizations/montevallo-literary-festival/. **Contact:** Dr. Jim Murphy, director. Estab. 2003.

MOONLIGHT AND MAGNOLIAS WRITER'S CONFERENCE

Georgia Romance Writers, 3741 Casteel Park Dr., Marietta GA 30064. **Website:** www.georgiaromancewriters.org/mm-conference. Estab. 1982.

OZARK CREATIVE WRITERS, INC. CONFERENCE

P.O. Box 9076, Fayetteville AR 72703. **E-mail:** ozarkcreativewriters1@gmail.com. **Website:** www.ozarkcreativewriters.org.

A full list of sessions and speakers is online. The conference usually has agents and/or editors in attendance to meet with writers.

SLEUTHFEST

MWA Florida Chapter, FL. **E-mail:** Sleuthfestinfo@yahoo.com. **Website:** sleuthfest.com.

ACCOMMODATIONS Doubletree by Hilton in Deerfield Beach

SOUTHEASTERN WRITERS ASSOCIATION—ANNUAL WRITERS WORKSHOP

E-mail: purple@southeasternwriters.org. **Website:** www.southeasternwriters.org. Estab. 1975.

Instruction offered for novel writing, nonfiction, young adult, commercial writing, screenwriting, marketing/social media. Agent in residence/Publisher in residence.

COSTS Cost of workshop: $445 for 4 days, or lower prices for daily tuition. (See website for tuition pricing.)

ACCOMMODATIONS Lodging at Epworth and throughout St. Simons Island. Visit website for more information.

WRITERS IN PARADISE

Eckerd College, 4200 54th Ave. S., St. Petersburg FL 33711. (727)864-7994. **Fax:** (727)864-7575. **E-mail:** wip@eckerd.edu. **Website:** writersinparadise.eckerd.edu. Estab. 2005.

ADDITIONAL INFORMATION Application (December deadline) materials are required of all attendees.

MIDWEST

ANTIOCH WRITERS' WORKSHOP

c/o Antioch University Midwest, 900 Dayton St., Yellow Springs OH 45387. (937)769-1803. **E-mail:** info@antiochwritersworkshop.com. **Website:** www.antiochwritersworkshop.com. **Contact:** Sharon Short, director. Estab. 1986.

ACCOMMODATIONS Accommodations are available at local hotels and bed and breakfasts.

ADDITIONAL INFORMATION The easiest way to contact this event is through the online website contact form.

BACKSPACE AGENT-AUTHOR SEMINAR

P.O. Box 454, Washington MI 48094-0454. (732)267-6449. **Fax:** (586)532-9652. **E-mail:** chrisg@bksp.org. **E-mail:** karendionne@bksp.org. **Website:** www.backspacewritersconference.com. **Contact:** Karen Dionne. Estab. 2006.

COSTS Each workshop is $225. Attendance limited to 10. You can register for as many conferences as you wish.

BOOKS-IN-PROGRESS CONFERENCE

Carnegie Center for Literacy and Learning, 251 West Second Street, Lexington KY 40507. (859)254-4175. **E-mail:** lwhitaker@carnegiecenterlex.org. **Website:** carnegiecenterlex.org. **Contact:** Laura Whitaker. Estab. 2010.

Note: Personal meetings with faculty (agents and editors) are only available to full conference participants. Limited slots available. Please choose only 1 agent; only one pitching session per participant.

ACCOMMODATIONS Several area hotels are nearby.

CAPON SPRINGS WRITERS' WORKSHOP

2836 Westbrook Dr., Cincinnati OH 45211-7617. (513)481-9884. **E-mail:** whbeckman@gmail.com. **Website:** wendyonwriting.com. Estab. 2000.

COSTS Check close to Fall 2016.

ACCOMMODATIONS Facility has swimming, hiking, fishing, tennis, badminton, volleyball, basketball, ping pong, etc. A 9-hole golf course is available for an additional fee.

ADDITIONAL INFORMATION Brochures available for SASE. Inquire via e-mail.

CHICAGO WRITERS CONFERENCE

E-mail: mare@chicagowritersconference.org. **Website:** chicagowritersconference.org. **Contact:** Mare Swallow. Estab. 2011.

DETROIT WORKING WRITERS ANNUAL WRITERS CONFERENCE

Detroit Working Writers, Box 82395, Rochester MI 48308. **E-mail:** conference@detworkingwriters.org. **Website:** dww-writers-conference.org. Estab. 1961.

COSTS Costs vary, depending on early bird registration and membership status within the organization.

FESTIVAL OF FAITH AND WRITING

Department of English, Calvin College, 1795 Knollcrest Circle SE, Grand Rapids MI 49546. (616)526-6770. **E-mail:** ffw@calvin.edu. **Website:** festival.calvin.edu. Estab. 1990.

COSTS Consult festival website.

ACCOMMODATIONS Shuttles are available to and from local hotels. Shuttles are also available for overflow parking lots. A list of hotels with special rates for conference attendees is available on the festival website. High school and college students can arrange on-campus lodging by e-mail.

INDIANA UNIVERSITY WRITERS' CONFERENCE

464 Ballantine Hall, 1020 E. Kirkwood Ave., Bloomington IN 47405-7103. (812)855-1877. **Fax:** (812)855-9535. **E-mail:** writecon@indiana.edu. **Website:** www.indiana.edu/~writecon. Estab. 1940.

ACCOMMODATIONS Information on accommodations available on website.

ADDITIONAL INFORMATION Connect on Twitter at @iuwritecon.

KENTUCKY WOMEN WRITERS CONFERENCE

University of Kentucky College of Arts & Sciences, 232 E. Maxwell St., Lexington KY 40506. (859)257-2874. **E-mail:** kentuckywomenwriters@gmail.com. **Website:** kentuckywomenwriters.org. **Contact:** Julie Wrinn, director. Estab. 1979.

COSTS 2015 prices are $200 for general admission and a workshop and $125 for admission with no workshop. Check website for 2016 pricing.

ADDITIONAL INFORMATION Sponsors prizes in poetry ($200), fiction ($200), nonfiction ($200), playwriting ($500), and spoken word ($500). Winners also invited to read during the conference. Pre-registration opens May 1.

KENTUCKY WRITERS CONFERENCE

Southern Kentucky Book Fest, Knicely Conference Center, 2355 Nashville Road, Bowling Green KY 42101. (270)745-4502. **E-mail:** sara.volpi@wku.edu]. **Website:** www.sokybookfest.org/KYWritersConf. **Contact:** Sara Volpi.

Since the event is free, interested attendees are asked to register in advance. information on how to do so is on the website.

KENYON REVIEW WRITERS WORKSHOP

Kenyon Review, Kenyon College, Gambier OH 43022. (740) 427-5196. **Fax:** (740) 427-5417. **E-mail:** kenyonreview@kenyon.edu; writers@kenyonreview.org. **Website:** www.kenyonreview.org. **Contact:** Anna Duke Reach, director. Estab. 1990. T

COSTS Fiction, Literary Nonfiction, Poetry, Nature Writing: $2,295. Novel: $2,995. Art of Text: $1,595. Teachers: $1,495. All rates includes tuition, room and board.

ACCOMMODATIONS The workshop operates a shuttle to and from Gambier and the airport in Columbus, Ohio. Offers overnight accommodations. Participants are housed in Kenyon College student housing. The cost is covered in the tuition.

ADDITIONAL INFORMATION Application includes a writing sample. Admission decisions are made on a rolling basis. Workshop information is available online at www.kenyonreview.org/workshops in November. For brochure send e-mail, visit website, call, or fax. Accepts inquiries by SASE, e-mail, phone, fax.

MAGNA CUM MURDER

Magna Cum Murder Crime Writing Festival, The E.B. and Bertha C. Ball Center, Ball State University, Muncie IN 47306. (765)285-8975. **Fax:** (765)747-9566. **E-mail:** magnacummurder@yahoo.com; kennisonk@aol.com. **Website:** www.magnacummurder.com. Estab. 1994.

COSTS Check website for updates.

MIDWEST WRITERS WORKSHOP

Ball State University, Department of English, Muncie IN 47306. (765)282-1055. **E-mail:** midwestwriters@yahoo.com. **Website:** www.midwestwriters.org. **Contact:** Jama Kehoe Bigger, director.

COSTS $155-400. Most meals included.

ADDITIONAL INFORMATION Offers scholarships. See website for more information. Keep in touch with the MWW at facebook.com/MidwestWriters and twitter.com/MidwestWriters.

OHIO KENTUCKY INDIANA CHILDREN'S LITERATURE CONFERENCE

Northern Kentucky University, 405 Steely Library, Highland Heights KY 41099. (859)572-6620. **Fax:** (859)572-5390. **E-mail:** smithjen@nku.edu. **Website:** oki.nku.edu. **Contact:** Jennifer Smith.

COSTS $85; includes registration/attendance at all workshop sessions, continental breakfast, lunch, author/illustrator signings. Manuscript critiques are available for an additional cost. E-mail or call for more information.

SPACE (SMALL PRESS AND ALTERNATIVE COMICS EXPO)

Back Porch Comics, P.O. Box 20550, Columbus OH 43220. **E-mail:** bpc13@earthlink.net. **Website:** www.backporchcomics.com/space.htm.

COSTS Admission: Free!

ADDITIONAL INFORMATION For brochure, visit website. Editors participate in conference.

WESTERN RESERVE WRITERS & FREELANCE CONFERENCE

7700 Clocktower Dr., Kirtland OH 44094. (440)525-7812. **E-mail:** deencr@aol.com. **Website:** www.deannaadams.com. **Contact:** Deanna Adams, director/conference coordinator. Estab. 1983.

COSTS Previous costs for Fall all-day conference includes lunch: $105.

ADDITIONAL INFORMATION Brochures for the conferences are available by January (for spring conference) and July (for fall). Also accepts inquiries by e-mail and phone. Check Deanna Adams' website for all updates. Editors always attend the conferences. Private editing consultations are available, as well.

WOMEN WRITERS WINTER RETREAT

Steele Mansion Bed and Breakfast, 348 Mentor Ave., Painesville OH 44077. (440)463-4633. **E-mail:** deencr@aol.com. **Website:** www.deannaadams.com. Estab. 2007.

COSTS Single room: $395; shared room: $295 (includes complete weekend package, with B&B stay in this historic mansion, breakfast and workshops); weekend commute: $165; Saturday only: $135.

ADDITIONAL INFORMATION Brochures for the writers retreat are available by December. Accepts inquiries and reservations by e-mail or phone. See Deanna's website for additional information and updates.

WRITE-TO-PUBLISH CONFERENCE

WordPro Communication Services, 9118 W. Elmwood Dr., Suite 1G, Niles IL 60714-5820. (847)296-3964. **Fax:** (847)296-0754. **E-mail:** lin@writetopublish.com. **Website:** www.writetopublish.com. **Contact:** Lin Johnson, director. Estab. 1971.

COSTS Call or e-mail for more information.

ACCOMMODATIONS Call or e-mail for more information

ADDITIONAL INFORMATION Conference information available in January. For details, visit website, or e-mail brochure@writetopublish.com. Accepts inquiries by e-mail, fax, phone.

NORTH CENTRAL

GREAT LAKES WRITERS FESTIVAL

Lakeland College, P.O. Box 359, Sheboygan WI 53082-0359. **E-mail:** elderk@lakeland.edu. **Website:** www.greatlakeswritersfestival.org. Estab. 1991.

COSTS Free and open to the public. Participants may purchase meals and must arrange for their own lodging.

ACCOMMODATIONS Does not offer overnight accommodations. Provides list of area hotels or lodging options.

ADDITIONAL INFORMATION All participants who would like to have their writing considered as an object for discussion during the festival workshops should submit it to Karl Elder electronically by October 15. Participants may submit material for workshops in 1 genre only (poetry, fiction, or creative nonfiction). Sponsors contest. Contest entries must contain the writer's name and address on a separate title page, typed, and be submitted as clear, hard copy on Friday at the festival registration table. Entries may be in each of 3 genres per participant, yet only 1 poem, 1 story, and/or 1nonfiction piece may be entered. There are 2 categories—high school students on 1 hand, all others on the other—of cash awards for first place in each of the 3 genres. The judges reserve the right to decline to award a prize in 1 or more of the genres. Judges will be the editorial staff of *Seems* (a.k.a. Word of Mouth Books), excluding the festival coordinator, Karl Elder. Information available in September. For brochure, visit website.

GREEN LAKE CHRISTIAN WRITERS CONFERENCE

W2511 State Road 23, Green Lake Conference Center, Green Lake WI 54941-9599. (920)294-3323. **E-mail:** program@glcc.org. **E-mail:** janet.p.white@gmail.com. **Website:** glcc.org. **Contact:** Janet White, Conference Director. Estab. 1948.

COSTS Check website for updated pricing.

ACCOMMODATIONS Hotels, lodges and all meeting rooms are a/c. Affordable rates, excellent meals.

ADDITIONAL INFORMATION Brochure and scholarship info from website or contact Jan White (920-294-7327). To register, call 920-294-3323.

INTERNATIONAL MUSIC CAMP CREATIVE WRITING WORKSHOP

111 11th Ave. SW, Minot ND 58701. (701)838-8472. **Fax:** (701)838-1351. **E-mail:** info@internationalmusiccamp.com. **Website:** www.internationalmusiccamp.com. **Contact:** Christine Baumann and Tim Baumann, camp directors. Estab. 1956.

COSTS Fees vary based on activities. Check website for full details.

ACCOMMODATIONS Airline and depot shuttles are available upon request. Housing is included in the fee.

ADDITIONAL INFORMATION Conference information is available on the website. Welcomes questions via e-mail.

IOWA SUMMER WRITING FESTIVAL

The University of Iowa, C215 Seashore Hall, University of Iowa, Iowa City IA 52242. (319)335-4160. **Fax:** (319)335-4743. **E-mail:** iswfestival@uiowa.edu. **Website:** www.iowasummerwritingfestival.org. Estab. 1987.

ACCOMMODATIONS Accommodations available at area hotels. Information on overnight accommodations available by phone or on website.

ADDITIONAL INFORMATION Brochures are available in February. Inquire via e-mail or on website.

UNIVERSITY OF WISCONSIN AT MADISON WRITERS INSTITUTE

21 N. Park St., Madison WI 53715-1218. (608)265-3972. **E-mail:** laurie.scheer@wisc.edu. **Website:** https://uwwritersinstitute.wisc.edu/. Estab. 1990.

COSTS $125-260, depending on discounts and if you attend one day or multiple days.

UW-MADISON WRITERS' INSTITUTE

21 North Park St., Room 7312, Madison WI 53715. (608)265-3972. **Fax:** (608)265-2475. **E-mail:** laurie.scheer@wisc.edu. **Website:** www.uwwritersinstitute.org. **Contact:** Laurie Scheer. Estab. 1989.

COSTS $180-330; includes materials, breaks.

ACCOMMODATIONS Provides a list of area hotels or lodging options.

ADDITIONAL INFORMATION Sponsors contest.

WISCONSIN BOOK FESTIVAL

Madison Public Library, 201 W. Mifflin St., Madison WI 53703. (608)266-6300. **E-mail:** bookfest@mplfoundation.org. **Website:** www.wisconsinbookfestival.org. Estab. 2002.

COSTS All festival events are free.

WISCONSIN WRITERS ASSOCIATION

9708 Idell Ave., Sparta WI 54656. (608)269-8541. **E-mail:** execdir@wiwrite.org. **Website:** www.wiwrite.org. **Contact:** Laurel Bragstad, executive director. Estab. 1948. **E-mail:** registration@wrwa.net. **Website:** www.wrwa.net. **Contact:** Nate Scholze, Fall Conference Coordinator; Roxanne Aehl, Spring Conference Coordinator. Estab. 1948. Annual. Conferences held in May and September "are dedicated to self-improvement through speakers, workshops and presentations. Topics and speakers vary with each event." Average attendance: 100-150. "We honor all genres of writing. Fall conference is a two-day event featuring the Jade Ring Banquet and awards for six genre categories. Spring conference is a one-day event."

COSTS $80-$100.

ACCOMMODATIONS Rooms available at the host conference center through the Wisconsin Writers Association.

SOUTH CENTRAL

ASPEN SUMMER WORDS LITERARY FESTIVAL & WRITING RETREAT

Aspen Words, 110 E. Hallam St., #116, Aspen CO 81611. (970)925-3122. **Fax:** (970)925-5700. **E-mail:** aspenwords@aspeninstitute.org. **Website:** www.aspenwords.org. **Contact:** Caroline Tory, programs coordinator. Estab. 1976.

AUSTIN FILM FESTIVAL & CONFERENCE

1801 Salina St., Suite 210, Austin TX 78702. (512)478-4795; (800)310-FEST. **Fax:** (512)478-6205. **Website:** www.austinfilmfestival.com. **Contact:** Conference director. Estab. 1994.

COSTS Austin Film Festival offers 4 badge levels for entry into the October festival, which also features access to the conference, depending on the Badge level. Go online for offers, and to view the different options with available with each badge.

CRESTED BUTTE WRITERS CONFERENCE

P.O. Box 1361, Crested Butte CO 81224. **E-mail:** coordinator@conf.crestedbuttewriters.org. **Website:** www.crestedbuttewriters.org/conf.php. **Contact:** Barbara Crawford or Theresa Rizzo, co-coordinators. Estab. 2006.

COSTS Previous prices: $330 nonmembers; $300 members; $297 Early Bird; The Sandy Writing Contest Finalist $280; and groups of 5 or more $280.

ACCOMMODATIONS The conference has been held at The Elevation Hotel, located at the Crested Butte Mountain Resort at the base of the ski mountain. The quaint historic town lies nestled in a stunning mountain valley 3 short miles from the resort area of Mt. Crested Butte. A free bus runs frequently between the 2 towns. The closest airport is 30 miles away, in Gunnison. The conference website lists 3 lodging options besides rooms at the event facility. All condos, motels, and hotel options offer special conference rates. No special travel arrangements are made through the conference; however, information for car rental from Gunnison airport or the Alpine Express shuttle is listed on the online conference FAQ page.

ADDITIONAL INFORMATION "Our conference workshops address a wide variety of writing craft and business. Our most popular workshop is Our First Pages Readings—with a twist. Agents and editors read opening pages volunteered by attendees-with a few best selling authors' openings mixed in. Think the A/E can identify the bestsellers? Not so much. Each year one of our attendees has been mistaken for a best-seller and obviously garnered requests from some on the panel. Writers may request additional information by e-mail."

EAST TEXAS CHRISTIAN WRITERS CONFERENCE

The School of Humanities, Dr. Jerry L. Summers, Dean, Scarborough Hall, East Texas Baptist University, 1 Tiger Dr., Marshall TX 75670. (903)923-2083. **E-mail:** ehoyer@etbu.edu; contest@etbu.edu. **Website:** www.etbu.edu/about/news/east-texas-christian-writers-conference. **Contact:** Elizabeth Hoyer, humanities secretary. Estab. 2002.

ACCOMMODATIONS Visit website for a list of local hotels offering a discounted rate.

THE GLEN WORKSHOP

Image, 1160 Camino Cruz Blanca, Santa Fe NM 87505. (206)281-2988. **Fax:** (206)281-2335. **E-mail:** glenworkshop@imagejournal.org. **Website:** glenworkshop.com. Estab. 1995. 3307 Third Ave. W. Seattle, WA 98119. (206)281-2988; (206)281-2335. **E-mail:** glenworkshop@imagejournal.org; jmullins@imagejournal.org. **Website:** www.imagejournal.org/glen. Registration for the 2010 Glen Workshop is open until the deadline of June 1. Some workshops are already full, so consider registering soon to ensure a place in your workshop of choice. Writing classes. Art classes. A seminar on arts and aesthetics. A retreat option. The Glen Workshop combines an intensive learning experience with a lively festival of the arts. It takes place in the stark, dramatic beauty of the Sangre de Cristo mountains and within easy reach of the rich cultural, artistic, and spiritual traditions of northern New Mexico. Estab. 1991. Annual. Held first full week in August. 2010: August 1-8, Santa Fe, NM. Theme: Creativity from the Margins: Art as Witness. Conference duration: 1 week. Average attendance: 150-200. Workshop focuses on "fiction, poetry, spiritual writing, songwriting, playwriting, painting, drawing, and mixed media. Run by Image, a literary journal with a religious focus. The Glen welcomes writers who practice or grapple with religious faith." Site: features "presentations and readings by the faculty." Faculty has included Lauren F. Winner (spiritual writing), B.H. Fairchild and Marilyn Nelson (poetry), Mark St. Germain (playwriting), and Over the Rhine (songwriting).

COSTS See costs online. A limited number of partial scholarships are available.

ACCOMMODATIONS Offers dorm rooms, dorm suites, and apartments.

ADDITIONAL INFORMATION Like *Image*, the Glen is grounded in a Christian perspective, but its tone is informal and hospitable to all spiritual wayfarers. Depending on the teacher, participants may need to submit workshop material prior to arrival (usually 10-25 pages).

TONY HILLERMAN WRITERS CONFERENCE

1063 Willow Way, Santa Fe NM 87505. (505)471-1565. **E-mail:** wordharvest@wordharvest.com. **Website:** www.wordharvest.com. **Contact:** Anne Hillerman and Jean Schaumberg, co-founders. Estab. 2004.

COSTS Check website for current pricing.

ACCOMMODATIONS Hilton Santa Fe Historic Plaza.

KINDLING WORDS WEST

Lake Travis TX. **Website:** www.kindlingwords.org. Kindling Words is open only to authors, illustrators and editors working with a traditional children's book publisher.

MISSOURI WRITERS' GUILD CONFERENCE

St. Louis MO **E-mail:** mwgconferenceinfo@gmail.com. **Website:** www.missouriwritersguild.org. **Contact:** Tricia Sanders, vice president/conference chairman.

ADDITIONAL INFORMATION The primary contact individual changes every year, because the conference chair changes every year. See the website for contact info.

NATIONAL WRITERS ASSOCIATION FOUNDATION CONFERENCE

10940 S. Parker Rd., #508, Parker CO 80138. (303)841-0246. **E-mail:** natlwritersassn@hotmail.com. **Website:** www.nationalwriters.com. **Contact:** Sandy Whelchel, executive director. Estab. 1926.

ADDITIONAL INFORMATION Awards for previous contests will be presented at the conference. Brochures/guidelines are online, or send an SASE.

NETWO WRITERS CONFERENCE

Northeast Texas Writers Organization, P.O. Box 411, Winfield TX 75493. (469)867-2624 or Paul at (903)573-6084. **E-mail:** jimcallan@winnsboro.com. **Website:** www.netwo.org. Estab. 1987.

COSTS $90 for members before February 29th, and $100 after. $112.50 for non-members before February 29th, and $125 after.

ACCOMMODATIONS Online, we have posted information on lodging - motels and hotels.The conference is held at the Titus County Civic Center in Mt. Pleasant, Texas.

ADDITIONAL INFORMATION Conference is cosponsored by the Texas Commission on the Arts. See website for current updates.

THE NEW LETTERS WEEKEND WRITERS CONFERENCE

University of Missouri-Kansas City, 5101 Rockhill Rd., Kansas City MO 64110-2499. (816)235-1168. **Fax:** (816)235-2611. **E-mail:** newletters@umkc.edu. **Website:** newletters.org/writers-wanted/nl-weekend-writing-conference. **Contact:** Robert Stewart, director. Estab. 1970s (as The Longboat Key Writers Conference).

COSTS Participants may choose to attend as a noncredit student or they may attend for 1 hour of college credit from the University of Missouri-Kansas City. Conference registration includes Friday evening reception and keynote speaker, Saturday and Sunday continental breakfast and lunch.

ACCOMMODATIONS Registrants are responsible for their own transportation, but information on area accommodations is available.

ADDITIONAL INFORMATION Those registering for college credit are required to submit a ms in advance. Ms reading and critique are included in the credit fee. Those attending the conference for noncredit also have the option of having their ms critiqued for an additional fee. Brochures are available for a SASE after March. Accepts inquiries by e-mail and fax.

NIMROD ANNUAL WRITERS' WORKSHOP

800 S. Tucker Dr., Tulsa OK 74104. (918)631-3080. **E-mail:** nimrod@utulsa.edu. **Website:** www.utulsa.edu/nimrod. **Contact:** Eilis O'Neal, editor-in-chief. Estab. 1978.

COSTS Approximately $60. Lunch provided. Scholarships available for students.

ADDITIONAL INFORMATION *Nimrod International Journal* sponsors literary awards: The Katherine Anne Porter Prize for fiction and The Pablo Neruda Prize for poetry. Poetry and fiction prizes: $2,000 each and publication (top prize); $1,000 each and publication (other winners). Deadline: must be postmarked no later than April 30.

NORTHERN COLORADO WRITERS CONFERENCE

2107 Thunderstone Court, Fort Collins CO 80525. (970)556-0908. **E-mail:** kerrie@northerncoloradowriters.com. **Website:** www.northerncoloradowriters.com. Estab. 2006.

COSTS $250-550+, depending on what package the attendee selects, whether you're a member or nonmember, and whether you're renewing your NCW membership.

ACCOMMODATIONS The 2016 conference is hosted at the Fort Collins Marriot, where rooms are available at a special rate.

PENNWRITERS CONFERENCE

5706 Sonoma Ridge, Missouri City TX 77459. **E-mail:** conferenceco@pennwriters.org; info@pennwriters.org. **Website:** pennwriters.org/conference. Estab. 1987.

As the official writing organization of Pennsylvania, Pennwriters has 8 different areas that have smaller writing groups that meet. Each of these areas sometimes has their own, smaller event during the year in addition to the annual writing conference.

ACCOMMODATIONS Costs vary. Pennwriters members in good standing get a slightly reduced rate.

ADDITIONAL INFORMATION Sponsors contest. Published authors judge fiction in various categories. Agent/editor appointments are available on a first-come, first serve basis.

PIKES PEAK WRITERS CONFERENCE

Pikes Peak Writers, P.O. Box 64273, Colorado Springs CO 80962. (719)244-6220. **Website:** www.pikespeakwriters.com/ppwc/. Estab. 1993.

COSTS $395-465 (includes all 7 meals).

ACCOMMODATIONS Marriott Colorado Springs holds a block of rooms at a special rate for attendees until late March.

ADDITIONAL INFORMATION Readings with critiques are available on Friday afternoon. Registration forms are online; brochures are available in January. Send inquiries via e-mail.

ROMANCE WRITERS OF AMERICA NATIONAL CONFERENCE

14615 Benfer Road, Houston TX 77069. (832)717-5200. **Fax:** (832)717-5201. **E-mail:** info@rwa.org. **Website:** www.rwa.org/conference. Estab. 1981.

COSTS $450-675 depending on your membership status as well as when you register.

ADDITIONAL INFORMATION Annual RTA awards are presented for romance authors. Annual

Golden Heart awards are presented for unpublished writers. Numerous literary agents are in attendance to meet with writers and hear book pitches.

SCIENCE FICTION WRITERS WORKSHOP

English Department/University of Kansas, Wesoce Hall, 1445 Jayhawk Blvd., Room 3001, Lawrence KS 66045-7590. (785)864-2508. **E-mail:** cmckit@ku.edu. **Website:** www.sfcenter.ku.edu/sfworkshop.htm. Estab. 1985.

COSTS $600, exclusive of meals and housing.

ACCOMMODATIONS Housing information is available. Several airport shuttle services offer reasonable transportation from the Kansas City International Airport to Lawrence.

ADDITIONAL INFORMATION Admission to the workshop is by submission of an acceptable story, usually by May. Two additional stories are submitted by the middle of June. These 3 stories are distributed to other participants for critiquing and are the basis for the first week of the workshop. One story is rewritten for the second week, when students also work with guest authors. See website for guidelines. This workshop is intended for writers who have just started to sell their work or need that extra bit of understanding or skill to become a published writer.

SEWANEE WRITERS' CONFERENCE

735 University Ave., 119 Gailor Hall, Stamler Center, Sewanee TN 37383-1000. (931)598-1654. **E-mail:** swc@sewanee.edu. **Website:** www.sewaneewriters.org. **Contact:** Adam Latham. Estab. 1990.

COSTS $1,100 for tuition and $800 for room, board, and activity costs.

ACCOMMODATIONS Participants are housed in single rooms in university dormitories. Bathrooms are shared by small groups.

STEAMBOAT SPRINGS WRITERS GROUP

P.O. Box 774284, Steamboat Springs CO 80477. (970)879-8079. **E-mail:** susan@steamboatwriters.com. **Website:** www.steamboatwriters.com. **Contact:** Susan de Wardt, director. Estab. 1982.

COSTS $60 before May 15, $75 after. Fee covers all seminars and luncheon.

ACCOMMODATIONS Lodging available at Steamboat Resorts.

ADDITIONAL INFORMATION Optional dinner and activities during evening preceding conference. Accepts inquiries by e-mail, phone, mail.

SUMMER WRITING PROGRAM

Naropa University, 2130 Arapahoe Ave., Boulder CO 80302. (303)245-4862. **Fax:** (303)546-5287. **E-mail:** swpr@naropa.edu. **Website:** www.naropa.edu/swp. **Contact:** Kyle Pivarnik, special projects manager. Estab. 1974.

ADDITIONAL INFORMATION Writers can elect to take the Summer Writing Program for noncredit, graduate, or undergraduate credit. The registration procedure varies, so consider whether or not you'll be taking the SWP for academic credit. All participants can elect to take any combination of the first, second, third, and/or fourth weeks. To request a catalog of upcoming program or to find additional information, visit naropa.edu/swp. Naropa University also welcomes participants with disabilities.

TAOS SUMMER WRITERS' CONFERENCE

Department of English Language and Literature, MSC 03 2170, 1 University of New Mexico, Albuquerque NM 87131-0001. **E-mail:** swarner@unm.edu. **Website:** taosconf.unm.edu. **Contact:** Sharon Oard Warner. Estab. 1999.

COSTS Week-long workshop registration $700, weekend workshop registration $400, master classes between $1,350 and $1,625, publishing consultations are $175.

WRITERS' LEAGUE OF TEXAS AGENTS & EDITORS CONFERENCE

Writers' League of Texas, 611 S. Congress Ave., Suite 200 A-3, Austin TX 78704. (512)499-8914. **E-mail:** conference@writersleague.org. **E-mail:** jennifer@writersleague.org. **Website:** www.writersleague.org. **Contact:** Jennifer Ziegler, Program Director. Estab. 1982.

The 2016 Writers' League of Texas Agents & Editors Conference will be held just steps from the shores of beautiful Lady Bird Lake in downtown Austin, Texas. The weekend-long event offers panels and presentations on the craft of writing and the business of publishing with editors and agents representing many genres and categories (both adult and YA, fiction and nonfiction) as well as genre specific meetings and networking opportunities. Writers also have the option to meet one-on-one with an agent or editor. Call, e-mail, or visit the website for more information.

COSTS Registration opens December 1, 2015 for members only at the early bird rate of $349. After January 5, 2016: $389 members / $449 nonmembers. After April 6, 2016: $429 members / $489 nonmembers. After June 5, 2016: $469 members / $509 nonmembers.

ADDITIONAL INFORMATION 2016 dates: June 24-26. Contests and awards programs are offered separately. Brochures are available upon request.

WRITING FOR THE SOUL

Jerry B. Jenkins Christian Writers Guild, P.O. Box 88288, Black Forest CO 80908. (866)495-7551. **Fax:** (719)494-1299. **E-mail:** Jerry@JerryJenkins.com. **Website:** www.Jerry-Jenkins.com.

THE HELENE WURLITZER FOUNDATION

P.O. Box 1891, Taos NM 87571. (575)758-2413. **Fax:** (575)758-2559. **E-mail:** hwf@taosnet.com. **Website:** www.wurlitzerfoundation.org. **Contact:** Michael A. Knight, executive director. Estab. 1954. Residence duration: 10-12 weeks.

ACCOMMODATIONS "Provides individual housing in fully furnished studio/houses (casitas), rent and utility free. Artists are responsible for transportation to and from Taos, their meals, and materials for their work. Bicycles are provided upon request."

WEST

ALTERNATIVE PRESS EXPO (APE)

Comic-Con International, P.O. Box 128458, San Diego CA 92112-8458. (619)491-2475. **Fax:** (619)414-1022. **E-mail:** cci-info@comic-con.org. **Website:** www.alternativepressexpo.com. **Contact:** Eddie Ibrahim, director of programming.

AWP ANNUAL CONFERENCE AND BOOKFAIR

MS 1E3, George Mason Univ., Fairfax VA 22030. (703)993-4317. **E-mail:** conference@awpwriter.org. **Website:** www.awpwriter.org/awp_conference/overview. Estab. 1967.

COSTS Early registration fees: $40 student; $140 AWP member; $160 nonmember.

ACCOMMODATIONS Provides airline discounts and rental-car discounts.

ADDITIONAL INFORMATION AWP Annual Conference & Bookfair, Los Angeles, CA 2016. Annual. Conference duration: 4 days. AWP holds its Annual Conference in a different region of North America in order to celebrate the outstanding authors, teachers, writing programs, literary centers, and small press publishers of that region. The Annual Conference typically features 350 presentations: readings, lectures, panel discussions, and forums plus hundreds of book signings, receptions, dances, and informal gatherings. The conference attracts more than 8,000 attendees and more than 500 publishers. All genres are represented. "We will offer 175 panels on everything from writing to teaching to critical analysis." In 2009, Art Spiegelman was the keynote speaker. Others readers were Charles Baxter, Isaiah Sheffer, Z.Z. Packer, Nareem Murr, Marilynne Robinson; 2008: John Irving, Joyce Carol Oates, among others.

BLOCKBUSTER PLOT INTENSIVE WRITING WORKSHOPS (SANTA CRUZ)

Santa Cruz CA. **E-mail:** contact@blockbusterplots.com. **Website:** www.blockbusterplots.com. **Contact:** Martha Alderson (also known as the Plot Whisperer), instructor. Estab. 2000.

COSTS Costs vary based on the time frame of the retreat/workshop.

ACCOMMODATIONS Updated website provides list of area hotels and lodging options.

ADDITIONAL INFORMATION Accepts inquiries by e-mail.

CALIFORNIA CRIME WRITERS CONFERENCE

E-mail: sistersincrimela@gmail.com. **Website:** www.ccwconference.org. Estab. 1995. Co-sponsored by Sisters in Crime/Los Angeles and the Southern California Chapter of Mystery Writers of America.

ADDITIONAL INFORMATION Conference information is available at www.ccwconference.org.

CLARION SCIENCE FICTION AND FANTASY WRITERS' WORKSHOP

UC San Diego, 9500 Gilman Dr., #0410, La Jolla CA 92093-0410. (858)534-2115. **E-mail:** clarion@ucsd.edu. **Website:** clarion.ucsd.edu. **Contact:** Program coordinator. Estab. 1968.

COSTS The fees for 2016 (tuition, room and board) are approximately $4,957. Application fee is $50 before February 15, 2016, and $65 after. Scholarships are available.

ACCOMMODATIONS Participants make their own travel arrangements to and from the campus. Campus residency is required. Participants are housed in semi-private accommodations (private bedroom, shared bathroom) in student apartments. The room and board fee includes 3 meals a day at a campus dining facility. Room and board are included in the workshop fee.

ADDITIONAL INFORMATION "Workshop participants are selected on the basis of their potential for highly successful writing careers. Applications are judged by a review panel composed of the workshop instructors. Applicants submit an application ($50 fee) and 2 complete short stories, each between 2,500 words and 6,000 words in length. The application deadline (typically, March 1) is posted on the Clarion website." Information available in September. For additional information, visit website.

INTERNATIONAL COMIC-CON

Comic-Con International, P.O. Box 128458, San Diego CA 92112-8458. (619)491-2475. **Fax:** (619)414-1022. **E-mail:** cci-info@comic-con.org. **Website:** www.comic-con.org/cci. **Contact:** Gary Sassaman, director of print/publications. Annual. Conference duration: 4 days. Average attendance: 104,000. "The comics industry's largest expo, hosting writers, artists, editors, agents, publishers, buyers and sellers of comics and graphic novels." Site: San Diego Convention Center. "Nearly 300 programming events, including panels, seminars and previews, on the world of comics, movies, television, animation, art, and much more." Legendary comics creator Neal Adams was a special guest for 2010, plus a diverse line up of special guests. We're also, of course, featuring Golden and Silver Age creators, sf/fantasy writers and artists, and longtime Comic-Con friends. Previous special guests included Ray Bradbury, Forrest J. Ackerman, Sergio Aragones, John Romita Sr., J. Michael Straczynski, Daniel Clowes, George Perez.

COSTS Prices vary. Check website for full costs.

ACCOMMODATIONS Does not offer overnight accommodations. Provides list of area hotels or lodging options. Special conference hotel and airfare discounts available. See website for details.

ADDITIONAL INFORMATION For brochure, visit website. Agents and editors participate in conference.

LAS VEGAS WRITERS CONFERENCE

Henderson Writers' Group, PO Box 92032, Henderson NV 89009. (702)564-2488; or, toll-free, (866)869-7842. **E-mail:** lasvegaswritersconference@gmail.com. **Website:** www.lasvegaswritersconference.com.

COSTS Costs vary depending on the package. See the website. There are early bird rates as well as deep discounts for Clark County high school students.

ADDITIONAL INFORMATION Sponsors contest. Agents and editors participate in conference.

LEAGUE OF UTAH WRITERS' ANNUAL WRITER'S CONFERENCE

Dianne Hardy, League of Utah Writers, 420 W. 750 N., Logan UT 84321. **E-mail:** Luwriters@gmail.com. **Website:** www.luwriters.org/index.html. **Contact:** Tim Keller.

⊙ MOUNT HERMON CHRISTIAN WRITERS CONFERENCE

PO Box 413, Mount Hermon CA 95041. **E-mail:** info@mounthermon.org. **Website:** writers.mounthermon.org. Estab. 1970.

NAPA VALLEY WRITERS' CONFERENCE

Napa Valley College, 1088 College Ave., St. Helena CA 94574. (707)967-2900. **E-mail:** writecon@napavalley.edu. **Website:** www.napawritersconference.org. **Contact:** Andrea Bewick, managing director. Estab. 1981.

On Twitter as @napawriters and on Facebook as facebook.com/napawriters.

COSTS $975; $25 application fee.

PACIFIC COAST CHILDREN'S WRITERS WHOLE-NOVEL WORKSHOP: FOR ADULTS AND TEENS

P.O. Box 244, Aptos CA 95001. **Website:** www.childrenswritersworkshop.com. Estab. 2003.

PIMA WRITERS' WORKSHOP

Pima College, 2202 W. Anklam Rd., Tucson AZ 85709. (520)206-6084. **Fax:** (520)206-6020. **E-mail:** mfiles@pima.edu. **Website:** https://www.pima.edu/press-room/news-releases/2015/201505-writers-workshop.html. **Contact:** Meg Files, director.

SAN DIEGO STATE UNIVERSITY WRITERS' CONFERENCE

SDSU College of Extended Studies, 5250 Campanile Dr., San Diego State University, San Diego CA 92182-1920. (619)594-3946. **Fax:** (619)594-8566. **E-mail:** sdsuwritersconference@mail.sdsu.edu. **Website:** ces.sdsu.edu/writers. Estab. 1984.

COSTS Approximately $495-549. Extra costs for consultations.

ACCOMMODATIONS Attendees must make their own travel arrangements. A conference rate for attendees is available at the event hotel (Marriott Mission Valley Hotel).

SAN FRANCISCO WRITERS CONFERENCE

1029 Jones St., San Francisco CA 94109. (415)673-0939. **E-mail:** Barbara@sfwriters.org; Sfwriterscon@aol.com. **Website:** sfwriters.org. **Contact:** Barbara Santos, marketing director. Estab. 2003.

COSTS Check the website for pricing on later dates. Pricing starts at $725 (as of the 2016 event) depending on when you signed up and early bird registration, etc.

ACCOMMODATIONS The Intercontinental Mark Hopkins Hotel is a historic landmark at the top of Nob Hill in San Francisco. The hotel is located so that everyone arriving at the Oakland or San Francisco airport can take BART to either the Embarcadero or Powell Street exits, then walk or take a cable car or taxi directly to the hotel.

ADDITIONAL INFORMATION "Present yourself in a professional manner and the contacts you will make will be invaluable to your writing career. Fliers, details and registration information are online."

SANTA BARBARA WRITERS CONFERENCE

27 W. Anapamu St., Suite 305, Santa Barbara CA 93101. (805)568-1516. **E-mail:** info@sbwriters.com. **Website:** www.sbwriters.com. Estab. 1972.

COSTS Early conference registration is $575, and regular registration is $650.

ACCOMMODATIONS Hyatt Santa Barbara.

ADDITIONAL INFORMATION Register online or contact for brochure and registration forms.

SCBWI—CENTRAL-COASTAL CALIFORNIA FALL CONFERENCE

P.O. Box 1500, Simi Valley CA 93062-1500, USA. **E-mail:** cencal@scbwi.org. **Website:** cencal.scbwi.org. **Contact:** Mary Ann Fraser, regional advisor. Estab. 1971.

SCBWI WINTER CONFERENCE ON WRITING AND ILLUSTRATING FOR CHILDREN

8271 Beverly Blvd., Los Angeles CA 90048. (323)782-1010. **Fax:** (323)782-1892. **E-mail:** scbwi@scbwi.org. **Website:** www.scbwi.org. **Contact:** Stephen Mooser. Estab. 2000.

COSTS See website for current cost and conference information

ADDITIONAL INFORMATION SCBWI also holds an annual summer conference in August in Los Angeles.

COMMUNITY OF WRITERS AT SQUAW VALLEY

Community of Writers at Squaw Valley, P.O. Box 1416, Nevada City CA 95959-1416, USA. (530)470-8440. **E-mail:** info@communityofwriters.org. **Website:** www.communityofwriters.org. **Contact:** Brett Hall Jones, Executive Director. Estab. 1969.

Annual conference held in July. Conference duration: 7 days. Average attendance: 124. "Writers workshops in fiction, nonfiction, and memoir assist talented writers by exploring the art and craft as well as the business of writing." Offerings include daily morning workshops led by writer-teachers, editors, or agents of the staff, limited to 12-13 participants; seminars; panel discussions of editing and publishing; craft colloquies; lectures; and staff readings. Past themes and panels included "Personal History in Fiction, Narrative Structure, Promise and Premise: Recognizing Subject"; "The Nation of Narrative Prose: Telling the Truth in Memoir and Personal Essay"; and "Anatomy of a Short Story." The workshops are held in a ski lodge at the foot of a ski area. Literary agent speakers have recently included Michael Carlisle, Susan Golomb, Joy Harris, Mary Evans, B.J. Robbins, Janet Silver, and Peter Steinberg. Agents will be speaking and available for meetings with attendees. Agents and editors attend/participate in conferences.

COSTS Tuition is $1,075, which includes 6 dinners. Limited financial aid is available.

ACCOMMODATIONS The Community of Writers rents houses and condominiums in the Valley for participants to live in during the week of the conference. Single room (1 participant): $700/week. Double room (twin beds, room shared by conference participant of the same sex): $465/week. Multiple room (bunk beds, room shared with 2 or more participants of the same sex): $295/week. All rooms subject to availability; early requests are recommended. Can arrange airport shuttle pick-ups for a fee.

ADDITIONAL INFORMATION https://communityofwriters.org/workshops/writers-workshops/

TMCC WRITERS' CONFERENCE

Truckee Meadows Community College, 7000 Dandini Blvd., Reno NV 89512. (775)673-7111. **E-mail:** wdce@tmcc.edu. **Website:** wdce.tmcc.edu. Estab. 1991.

ACCOMMODATIONS Contact the conference manager to learn about accommodation discounts.

ADDITIONAL INFORMATION "The conference is open to all writers, regardless of their level of experience. Brochures are available online and mailed in January. Send inquiries via e-mail."

UCLA EXTENSION WRITERS' PROGRAM

10995 Le Conte Ave., #440, Los Angeles CA 90024. (310)825-9415 or (800)388-UCLA. **Fax:** (310)206-7382. **E-mail:** writers@uclaextension.edu. **Website:** www.uclaextension.org/writers. Estab. 1891. 10995 Le Conte Avenue, #440, Los Angeles CA 90024-2883. (310)825-9971 or (818)784-7006. UCLA. **Fax:** (310)206-7382. **E-mail:** writers@UCLAextension.edu. **Website:** www.uclaextension.edu/writers. **Contact:** Cindy Lieberman, program manager. Courses held year-round with one-day or intensive weekend workshops to 12-week courses. Writers Studio held in February. 9-month master classes are also offered every fall. "The diverse offerings span introductory seminars to professional novel and script completion workshops. The annual Writers Studio and a number of 1-, 2- and 4-day intensive workshops are popular with out-of-town students due to their specific focus and the chance to work with industry professionals. The most comprehensive and diverse continuing education writing program in the country, offering over 550 courses a year, including screenwriting, fiction, writing for the youth market, poetry, nonfiction, playwriting and publishing. Adult learners in the UCLA Extension Writers' Program study with professional screenwriters, fiction writers, playwrights, poets and nonfiction writers, who bring practical experience, theoretical knowledge and a wide variety of teaching styles and philosophies to their classes." Site: Courses are offered in Los Angeles on the UCLA campus, in the 1010 Westwood Center in Westwood Village, at the Figueroa Courtyard in downtown Los Angeles, as well as online.

COSTS Depends on length of the course.

ACCOMMODATIONS Students make their own arrangements. Out-of-town students are encouraged to take online courses.

ADDITIONAL INFORMATION Some advanced-level classes have ms submittal requirements; see the UCLA Extension catalog or see website.

WRITE ON THE SOUND

City of Edmonds Arts Commission, Frances Anderson Center, 700 Main St., Edmonds WA 98020. (425)771-0228. **E-mail:** wots@edmondswa.gov. **Website:** www.writeonthesound.com. Estab. 1985.

COSTS See website for complete information.

ADDITIONAL INFORMATION Schedule posted on website mid-June. Registration open by late July.

WRITERS@WORK WRITING RETREAT

P.O. Box 711191, Salt Lake City UT 84171-1191. (801)996-3313. **E-mail:** jennifer@writersatwork.org. **Website:** www.writersatwork.org. Estab. 1985.

There are several pricing levels for this event, depending on lodging and if the attendee wants a private consultation.

COSTS $650-1,000, based on housing type and consultations.

ACCOMMODATIONS Onsite housing available. Additional lodging information is on the website.

WRITERS STUDIO AT UCLA EXTENSION

1010 Westwood Blvd., Los Angeles CA 90024. (310)825-9415. **E-mail:** writers@uclaextension.edu. **Website:** writers.uclaextension.edu/programs-services/writers-studio/. **Contact:** Katy Flaherty. Estab. 1997.

ADDITIONAL INFORMATION For more information, call or e-mail.

WRITERS WEEKEND AT THE BEACH

P.O. Box 877, Ocean Park WA 98640. (360)665-4367. **E-mail:** director@opretreat.org. **Website:** www.opretreat.org/event/writers-weekend-at-the-beach/. **Contact:** Brandon Scheer; Tracie Heskett. Estab. 1992.

COSTS $200 for full registration before Feb. 15 and $215 after Feb. 15.

ACCOMMODATIONS Offers on-site overnight lodging.

WRITING AND ILLUSTRATING FOR YOUNG READERS CONFERENCE

1480 East 9400 South, Sandy UT 84093. **E-mail:** staff@wifyr.com. **Website:** www.wifyr.com. Estab. 2000. BYU, conferences and workshops, 348 HCEB, BYU, Provo UT 84602-1532. (801)422-2568. **Fax:** (801)422-0745. **E-mail:** cw348@byu.edu. **Website:** wifyr.byu.

edu. **Contact:** Conferences & Workshops. Estab. 2000. Annual. 5-day workshop held in June of each year. The workshop is designed for people who want to write or illustrate for children or teenagers. Participants focus on a single market during daily four-hour morning writing workshops led by published authors or illustrators. Afternoon workshop sessions include a mingle with the authors, editors and agents. Workshop focuses on fiction for young readers: picture books, book-length fiction, fantasy/science fiction, nonfiction, mystery, illustration and general writing. Site: Conference Center at Brigham Young University in the foothills of the Wasatch Mountain range.

Guidelines and registration are on the website.

COSTS Costs available online.

ACCOMMODATIONS A block of rooms are available at the Best Western Cotton Tree Inn in Sandy, UT at a discounted rate. This rate is good as long as there are available rooms.

ADDITIONAL INFORMATION There is an online form to contact this event.

NORTHWEST

ALASKA WRITERS CONFERENCE

Alaska Writers Guild, PO Box 670014, Chugiak AK 99567. **E-mail:** alaskawritersguild.awg@gmail.com. **Website:** alaskawritersguild.com.

Ms critiques available. Note also that the AWG has many events and meetings each year, not just the annual conference.

CENTRUM'S PORT TOWNSEND WRITERS' CONFERENCE

P.O. Box 1158, Port Townsend WA 98368-0958. (360)385-3102. **E-mail:** info@centrum.org. **Website:** centrum.org/the-port-townsend-writers-conference/. **Contact:** Jordan Hartt, director of programs. Estab. 1974. P.O. Box 1158, Port Townsend, WA 98368-0958. (360)385-3102. FaxL (360)385-2470. **E-mail:** info@centrum.org; jhartt@centrum.com. **Website:** www.centrum.org. Estab. 1974. Annual. Conference held mid-July. 2011: July 17-24. Average attendance: 180. Conference to promote poetry, fiction, creative nonfiction "featuring many of the nation's leading writers." Two different workshop options: "New Works" and "Works-in-Progress." Site: The conference is held at Fort Worden State Park on the Strait of Juan de Fuca. "The site is a Victorian-era military fort with miles of beaches, wooded trails and recreation facilities. The park is within the limits of Port Townsend, a historic seaport and arts community, approximately 80 miles northwest of Seattle, on the Olympic Peninsula." Guest speakers participate in addition to full-time faculty.

COSTS Tuition for the Conference is $200-$700. Room and board options range from $250 to $700. Admission to afternoon workshops ranges from $200-$300. Register online at website.

ACCOMMODATIONS "Modest room and board facilities on site." Also list of hotels/motels/inns/bed & breakfasts/private rentals available.

ADDITIONAL INFORMATION Brochures/guidelines available for SASE or on website. "The conference focus is on the craft of writing and the writing life, not on marketing."

CLARION WEST WRITERS WORKSHOP

P.O. Box 31264, Seattle WA 98103-1264. (206)322-9083. **E-mail:** info@clarionwest.org. **Website:** www.clarionwest.org. **Contact:** Nelle Graham, Workshop Director.

COSTS $3,800 (for tuition, housing, most meals). Limited scholarships are available based on financial need.

ACCOMMODATIONS Workshop tuition, dormitory housing and most meals: $3,800. Students stay on-site in workshop housing at one of the University of Washington's sorority houses. "Students write their own stories every week while preparing critiques of all the other students' work for classroom sessions. This gives participants a more focused, professional approach to their writing. The core of the workshop remains speculative fiction, and short stories (not novels) are the focus." Conference information available in Fall. For brochure/guidelines send SASE, visit website, e-mail or call. Accepts inquiries by e-mail, phone, SASE. Limited scholarships are available, based on financial need. Students must submit 20-30 pages of ms with 4-page biography and $50 fee ($30 if received prior to February 10) for applications sent by mail or e-mail to qualify for admission.

ADDITIONAL INFORMATION This is a critique-based workshop. Students are encouraged to write a story every week; the critique of student material produced at the workshop forms the principal activity of the workshop. Students and instructors critique mss as a group. Visit the website for updates and complete details.

⊕ EMERALD CITY COMICON

800 Convention Place, Washington State Convention Center, Seattle WA 98037. (425)744-2767. **Fax:** (425)675-0737. **E-mail:** info@emeraldcitycomicon.com; george@emeraldcitycomicon.com. **Website:** www.emeraldcitycomicon.com. **Contact:** George Demonakos, operations director. Estab. 2002. Site: 800 Convention Place, Washington State Convention Center, Seattle, WA 98037. Emerald City Comicon, 3333 184th St. SW., Suite GLynnwood, WA 98037. (425)744-2767. **Fax:** (425)675-0737. **E-mail:** info@emeraldcitycomicon.com; george@emeraldcitycomicon.com. **Website:** www.emeraldcitycomicon.com. Estab. 2002. Annual. 10th Annual ECCC: March 30 - April 1, 2012.| "The premiere comic book convention of the Pacific Northwest. Includes comic creators and media guests, various creative and publishing panels, exhibitors, dealers and much more." Guests include Jim Cheung, Cully Hamner, Steve McNiven, Yanick Paquette, Pete Woods and many more.

COSTS Prices vary based on day.

ACCOMMODATIONS Offers overnight accommodations. Discounted rate at Roosevelt Hotel, Crowne Plaza and Red Lion in Seattle.

ADDITIONAL INFORMATION For information, visit website. Editors participate in conference.

HEDGEBROOK

PO Box 1231, Freeland WA 98249-9911. (360)321-4786. **Fax:** (360)321-2171. **Website:** www.hedgebrook.org. **Contact:** Vito Zingarelli, residency director. Estab. 1988.

This residency program takes applications 6 months in advance. For example, you can apply for a 2015 residency in June 2014.

ADDITIONAL INFORMATION Go online for more information.

IDAHO WRITERS LEAGUE WRITERS' CONFERENCE

601 W. 75 S., Blackfoot ID 83221-6153. (208)684-4200. **Website:** www.idahowritersleague.org. Estab. 1940.

COSTS Pricing varies. Check website for more information.

JACKSON HOLE WRITERS CONFERENCE

PO Box 1974, Jackson WY 83001. (307)413-3332. **E-mail:** connie@blackhen.com. **Website:** jacksonholewritersconference.com. Estab. 1991.

ADDITIONAL INFORMATION Held at the Center for the Arts in Jackson, Wyoming and online.

NORWESCON

100 Andover Park W. PMB 150-165, Tukwila WA 98188-2828. (425)243-4692. **E-mail:** info@norwescon.org. **Website:** www.norwescon.org. Estab. 1978.

ACCOMMODATIONS Conference is held at the Doubletree Hotel Seattle Airport.

OREGON CHRISTIAN WRITERS SUMMER CONFERENCE

Red Lion Hotel on the River, 909 N. Hayden Island Dr., Portland OR 97217-8118. **E-mail:** summerconf@oregonchristianwriters.org. **Website:** www.oregonchristianwriters.org. **Contact:** Lindy Jacobs, OCW Summer Conference Director. Estab. 1989.

COSTS $525 for OCW members, $560 for nonmembers. Registration fee includes all classes, workshops, and 2 lunches and 3 dinners. Lodging additional. Full-time registered registrants may also pre-submit three proposals for review by an editor (or agent) through the conference, plus sign up for a half-hour mentoring appointment with an author.

ACCOMMODATIONS Conference is held at the Red Lion on the River Hotel. Conferees wishing to stay at the hotel must make a reservation through the hotel. A block of rooms has been reserved at the hotel at a special rate for conferees and held until mid-July. The hotel reservation link will be posted on the website in late spring. Shuttle bus transportation will be provided by the hotel for conferees from Portland Airport (PDX) to the hotel, which is 20 minutes away.

ADDITIONAL INFORMATION Conference details will be posted online beginning in January. All conferees are welcome to attend the Cascade Awards ceremony, which takes place Wednesday evening during the conference. For more information about the Cascade Writing Contest, please check the website.

OUTDOOR WRITERS ASSOCIATION OF AMERICA ANNUAL CONFERENCE

615 Oak St., Suite 201, Missoula MT 59801. (406)728-7434. **E-mail:** info@owaa.org. **Website:** owaa.org. **Contact:** Jessica Seitz, conference and membership coordinator.

COSTS Registration is $225 until May 13 for members and $249 after May 13. For nonmembers, early bird pricing is $425 and $449 after May 13. Single day rates are also available.

PNWA SUMMER WRITERS CONFERENCE

317 NW Gilman Blvd., Suite 8, Issaquah WA 98027. (425)673-2665. **E-mail:** pnwa@pnwa.org. **Website:** www.pnwa.org. Estab. 1955.

SITKA CENTER FOR ART AND ECOLOGY

56605 Sitka Dr., Otis OR 97368. (541)994-5485. **Fax:** (541)994-8024. **E-mail:** info@sitkacenter.org. **Website:** www.sitkacenter.org. **Contact:** Caroline Brooks, program manager. Estab. 1970.

COSTS Workshops are generally $25-505; they do not include meals or lodging.

ACCOMMODATIONS Does not offer overnight accommodations. Provides a list of area hotels or lodging options.

ADDITIONAL INFORMATION Brochure available in February of each year; request a copy by e-mail or phone, or visit website for listing. Accepts inquiries in-person or by e-mail, phone, fax.

SOUTH COAST WRITERS CONFERENCE

Southwestern Oregon Community College, P.O. Box 590, 29392 Ellensburg Ave., Gold Beach OR 97444. (541)247-2741. **Fax:** (541)247-6247. **E-mail:** scwc@socc.edu. **Website:** www.socc.edu/scwriters. **Contact:** Karim Shumaker. Estab. 1996.

COSTS Friday conference cost is $55.00, Saturday conference cost is $60 before January 31, and $70 after. Lunch is $12.00 and available for purchase in advance.

ACCOMMODATIONS List of local motels that offer discounts to conference participants is available on request.

ADDITIONAL INFORMATION See website for cost and additional details.

TIN HOUSE SUMMER WRITERS' WORKSHOP

TIN HOUSE, 2601 NW Thurman Street, Portland OR 97210. (503)219-0622. **Fax:** (503)222-1154. **E-mail:** lance@tinhouse.com. **Website:** www.tinhouse.com/blog/workshop. **Contact:** Lance Cleland. Estab. 2003.

"Including scholarship applications, we average around 1,000 applications per summer. Our acceptance rate last year was 34 percent. Applications are rolling. Other than for scholarships, there is no firm deadline for applying, though we do tend to start filling up in early May. The average turnaround time for applications is six weeks."

COSTS Cost: $40 application fee; $1,100 for tuition; $650 for room & board; $750-$1,000 mentorships; $300 Audit; scholarships available.

ACCOMMODATIONS The Tin House Summer Writers' Workshop is held at Reed College, located on 100 acres of rolling lawns, winding lanes, and magnificent old trees in the southeast area of Portland, Oregon, just minutes from downtown and twelve miles from the airport.

ADDITIONAL INFORMATION Attendees must apply; all information available online.

WILLAMETTE WRITERS CONFERENCE

2108 Buck St., West Linn OR 97068. (503)305-6729. **Fax:** (503)344-6174. **Website:** willamettewriters.com/wwcon/. Estab. 1981.

An extensive list literary agents and editors, plus Hollywood film managers, agents and producers, will be on hand to listen to pitches.

COSTS Pricing schedule available online.

ACCOMMODATIONS If necessary, arrangements can be made on an individual basis through the conference hotel. Special rates may be available. 2015 location is the Lloyd Center DoubleTree Hotel.

ADDITIONAL INFORMATION Brochure/guidelines are available for a catalog-sized SASE.

CANADA

BOOMING GROUND MENTORSHIP PROGRAM & MANUSCRIPT EVALUATION SERVICE

Buch E-462, 1866 Main Mall, UBC, Vancouver BC V6T 1Z1, Canada. **Fax:** (604)648-8848. **E-mail:** contact@boomingground.com. **Website:** www.boomingground.com.

SAGE HILL WRITING EXPERIENCE

Box 1731, Saskatoon SK S7K 3S1, Canada. (306)652-7395. **E-mail:** sage.hill@sasktel.net; info.sagehill@sasktel.net. **Website:** sagehillwriting.ca.

ACCOMMODATIONS Located at Lumsden, 45 kilometers outside Regina.

ADDITIONAL INFORMATION See the website for pricing and courses.

SASKATCHEWAN FESTIVAL OF WORDS

217 Main St. N., Moose Jaw SK S6J 0W1, Canada. **Website:** www.festivalofwords.com. Estab. 1997.

ACCOMMODATIONS Information available at www.templegardens.sk.ca, campgrounds, and bed and breakfast establishments. Complete information about festival presenters, events, costs, and schedule also available on website.

THE SCHOOL FOR WRITERS FALL WORKSHOP

The Humber School for Writers, Humber Institute of Technology & Advanced Learning, 3199 Lake Shore Blvd. W., Toronto ON M8V 1K8, Canada. (416)675-6622 extension 3449. **E-mail:** antanas.sileika@humber.ca; hilary.higgins@humber.ca. **Website:** www.humber.ca/scapa/programs/school-writers.

COSTS $850 (in 2015). Some scholarships are available.

ADDITIONAL INFORMATION Accepts inquiries by e-mail, phone, and fax.

INTERNATIONAL

ABROAD WRITERS CONFERENCES

17363 Sutter Creek Rd., Sutter Creek CA 95685 (209)296-4052. **E-mail:** abroadwriters@yahoo.com; nancy@abroadwritersconference.com. **Website:** abroadwritersconference.com.

See the complete schedule online. Recent events include Italy, Spain, and England in 2014-2015.

COSTS See website for pricing details.

ADDITIONAL INFORMATION Agents participate in conference. Application is online at website.

ART WORKSHOPS IN GUATEMALA

4758 Lyndale Ave. S., Minneapolis MN 55419-5304. (612)825-0747. **E-mail:** info@artguat.org. **Website:** www.artguat.org. **Contact:** Liza Fourre, director. Estab. 1995.

COSTS See website. includes tuition, lodging, breakfast, ground transportation.

ACCOMMODATIONS All transportation and accommodations included in price of conference.

ADDITIONAL INFORMATION Conference information available now. For brochure/guidelines visit website, e-mail or call. Accepts inquiries by e-mail, phone.

BREAD LOAF IN SICILY WRITERS' CONFERENCE

Middlebury College, Middlebury VT 05753. (802)443-5286. **Fax:** (802)443-2087. **E-mail:** blwc@middlebury.edu. **Website:** www.middlebury.edu/bread-loaf-conferences/blSicily. Estab. 2011.

COSTS The fee (contributor, $2,930) includes the conference program, transfer to and from Palermo Airport, six nights of lodging, three meals daily (except for Wednesday), wine reception at the readings, and an excursion to the ancient ruins of Segesta. The charge for an additional person is $1,750. There is a $15 application fee an a $300 deposit.

ACCOMMODATIONS Accommodations are single rooms with private bath. Breakfast and lunch are served at the hotel and dinner is available at select Erice restaurants. A double room is possible for those who would like to be accompanied by a spouse or significant other.

ADDITIONAL INFORMATION "Application Period: November 1, 2015-March 15, 2016. Rolling admissions. Space is limited."

BYRON BAY WRITERS FESTIVAL

Northern Rivers Writers' Centre, P.O. Box 1846, 69 Johnson St., Byron Bay NSW 2481, Australia. 040755-2441. **E-mail:** jeni@nrwc.org.au. **Website:** www.byronbaywritersfestival.com. **Contact:** Jeni Caffin, director. Estab. 1997.

COSTS See costs online under Tickets. Early bird, NRWC members and students, kids.

INTERNATIONAL WOMEN'S FICTION FESTIVAL

Via Cappuccini 8E, Matera 75100, Italy. (39)0835-312044. **Fax:** (39)0835-312093. **E-mail:** e.jennings@womensfictionfestival.com. **Website:** www.womensfictionfestival.com. **Contact:** Elizabeth Jennings. Estab. 2004.

COSTS Registration costs vary. Check website for full details.

ACCOMMODATIONS Le Monacelle, a restored 17th century convent. Conference travel agency will find reasonably priced accommodation. A paid shuttle is available from the Bari Airport to the hotel in Matera.

SALT CAY WRITERS RETREAT

Salt Cay , Bahamas. (732)267-6449. **E-mail:** admin@saltcaywritersretreat.com. **Website:** www.saltcaywritersretreat.com. **Contact:** Karen Dionne and Christopher Graham.

Individualized instruction from bestselling authors, top editors, and literary agents; dolphin swim; built-in scheduled writing time; evening gatherings with student and author readings; closing festivities including authentic Bahamian feast. All sleeping rooms at the retreat hotel are suites; free or deeply discounted activities for families, including water park, water bikes, kayaks, dolphin and sea lion encounters, snorkeling, scuba-diving, and much more. Complimentary guest access to Atlantis Resort & Casino.

COSTS $2,450 through May 1; $2,950 after.

ACCOMMODATIONS Comfort Suites, Paradise Island, Nassau, Bahamas.

THE UNIVERSITY OF WINCHESTER WRITERS' FESTIVAL

University of Winchester, Winchester Hampshire WA S022 4NR, United Kingdom. 44(0)1962-827238. **E-mail:** judith.heneghan@winchester.ac.uk. **Website:** www.writersfestival.co.uk.

WRITE IT OUT

P.O. Box 704, Sarasota FL 34230-0704. (941)359-3824. **E-mail:** rmillerwio@aol.com. **Website:** www.writeitout.com. **Contact:** Ronni Miller, director. Estab. 1997.

COSTS Costs vary by workshop.

ADDITIONAL INFORMATION "Critiques on work are given at the workshops." Conference information available year round. For brochures/guidelines e-mail, call, or visit website. Accepts inquiries by phone, e-mail. Workshops have "small groups, option to spend time writing and not attend classes, with personal appointments with instructors."

PUBLISHERS & THEIR IMPRINTS

The publishing world is in constant transition. With all the buying, selling, reorganizing, consolidating, and dissolving, it's hard to keep publishers and their imprints straight. To help make sense of these changes, here's a breakdown of major publishers (and their divisions)—who owns whom and which imprints are under each company umbrella. Keep in mind that this information changes frequently. The website of each publisher is provided to help you keep an eye on this ever-evolving business.

HACHETTE BOOK GROUP

www.hachettebookgroup.com

GRAND CENTRAL PUBLISHING

Forever
Forever Yours
Grand Central Life & Style
Twelve

HACHETTE AUDIO

HACHETTE BOOKS

HACHETTE NASHVILLE

Center Street
FaithWords
Jericho Books

LITTLE, BROWN AND COMPANY

- Back Bay Books
- Lee Boudreaux Books
- Mulholland Books

LITTLE, BROWN AND COMPANY BOOKS FOR YOUNG READERS

- LB Kids
- Poppy

ORBIT

- Redhook
- Yen Press

HARPERCOLLINS

www.harpercollins.com

ADULT

- Amistad
- Anthony Bourdain Books
- Avon
- Avon Impulse
- Avon Inspire
- Avon Red
- Bourbon Street Books
- Broadside Books
- Dey Street
- Ecco Books
- Harper Books
- Harper Business
- Harper Design
- Harper Luxe
- Harper Paperbacks
- Harper Perennial
- Harper Voyager
- Harper Wave
- HarperAudio
- HarperCollins 360

HarperElixir
HarperOne
William Morrow
William Morrow Paperbacks
Witness

CHILDREN'S

Amistad
Balzer + Bray
Greenwillow Books
HarperAudio
HarperCollins Children's Books
HarperFestival
HarperTeen
HarperTeen Impulse
Katherine Tegen Books
Walden Pond Press

CHRISTIAN PUBLISHING

Bible Gateway
Blink
Editorial Vida
FaithGateway
Grupo Nelson
Nelson Books
Olive Tree
Thomas Nelson
Tommy Nelson
W Publishing Group
WestBow Press
Zonderkidz
Zondervan
Zondervan Academic

HARLEQUIN

Carina Press
Harlequin Books
Harlequin TEEN

HQN Books
Kimani Press
Love Inspired
MIRA Books
Worldwide Mystery

HARPERCOLLINS AUSTRALIA

HARPERCOLLINS CANADA

Collins
Harper Avenue
Harper Perennial
Harper Weekend
HarperCollins Canada
Patrick Crean Editions

HARPERCOLLINS NEW ZEALAND

HARPER INDIA

HARPERCOLLINS UK

4th Estate
Avon
Carina
Collins
Harper Audio
Harper Voyager
Harper360
HarperCollins Children's Books
HarperFiction
HarperImpulse
HarperNonFiction
Mills & Boon
MIRA
MIRA Ink
The Borough Press
Times Books
William Collins

MACMILLAN PUBLISHERS

us.macmillan.com

DISTRIBUTED PUBLISHERS

Bloomsbury USA and Walker & Company
The College Board
Drawn and Quarterly
Entangled Publishing
Graywolf Press
Guinness World Records
Media Lab Books
Page Street Publishing Co.
Papercutz
Rodale

FARRAR, STRAUS AND GIROUX

Books for Young Readers
Hill and Wang
Faber and Faber Inc.
North Point Press

FIRST SECOND

FLATIRON BOOKS

HENRY HOLT & CO.

Henry Holt Books for Young Readers
Holt Paperbacks
Metropolitan Books
Times Books

MACMILLAN AUDIO

MACMILLAN CHILDREN'S

Farrar, Straus & Giroux for Young Readers
Feiwel & Friends
Henry Holt Books for Young Readers
Imprint
Kingfisher
Priddy Books
Roaring Brook Press

Square Fish
Tor Children's

PICADOR

QUICK AND DIRTY TIPS

ST. MARTIN'S PRESS

Griffin
Let's Go
Minotaur Books
St. Martin's Press Paperbacks
Thomas Dunne Books
Truman Talley Books

TOR/FORGE

Starscape
Tor Teen Books

PENGUIN RANDOM HOUSE

www.penguinrandomhouse.com

CROWN PUBLISHING GROUP

Amphoto Books
Broadway Books
Clarkson Potter
Convergent Books
Crown
Crown Archetype
Crown Business
Crown Forum
Harmony Books
Hogarth
Image Books
Pam Krauss Books
Ten Speed Press
Three Rivers Press
Tim Duggan Books
WaterBrook Multnomah
Watson-Guptill

KNOPF DOUBLEDAY PUBLISHING GROUP

Alfred A. Knopf
Anchor Books
Doubleday
Everyman's Library
Nan A. Talese
Pantheon
Schocken Books
Vintage Books

PENGUIN

Avery
Berkley/NAL
Blue Rider Press
Celebra
DAW
Dial Books for Young Readers
Dutton
Dutton Children's Books
Firebird
Frederick Warne
G.P. Putnam's Sons
G.P. Putnam's Sons Books for Young Readers
Grosset & Dunlap
InterMix
Kathy Dawson Books
Nancy Paulsen Books
Penguin Audio
Penguin
Penguin Young Readers
Penguin Press
Perigee
Philomel
Plume
Portfolio
Price Stern Sloan
Puffin
Razorbill
Riverhead

Speak
TarcherPerigee
Viking Books
Viking Children's Books

PENGUIN RANDOM HOUSE PUBLISHING GROUP

Ballantine Books
Bantam
Delacorte
Dell
Del Rey/Manga
Del Rey/Lucas Books
The Dial Press
The Modern Library
One World
Presidio Press
Penguin Random House Trade Group
Penguin Random House Trade Paperbacks
Spectra
Spiegel & Grau
Triumph Books
Villard Books

PENGUIN RANDOM HOUSE CHILDREN'S BOOKS

Kids@Random (RH Children's Books)
Golden Books
Princeton Review
Sylvan Learning

RH DIGITAL PUBLISHING GROUP

Books on Tape
Fodor's Travel
Living Language
Listening Library
Penguin Random House Audio
RH Large Print

RH INTERNATIONAL

Penguin Random House Mondadori (Argentina)
Penguin Random House Australia

Penguin Random House of Canada
Penguin Random House Mondadori (Chile)
Penguin Random House Mondadori (Colombia)
Verlagsgruppe Penguin Random House
Penguin Random House India
Transworld Ireland
Penguin Random House Mondadori (Mexico)
Penguin Random House New Zealand
Penguin Random House Struik (South Africa)
Penguin Random House Mondadori (Spain)
The Penguin Random House Group (UK)
Penguin Random House Mondadori (Uruguay)
Penguin Random House Mondadori (Venezuela)

SIMON & SCHUSTER

www.simonandschuster.com

SIMON & SCHUSTER ADULT PUBLISHING

Atria
Emily Bestler Books
Enliven
Folger Shakespeare Library
Free Press
Gallery
Howard
Jeter Publishing
North Star Way
Pocket
Pocket Star
Scout Press
Scribner
Simon & Schuster
Threshold
Touchstone

SIMON & SCHUSTER CHILDREN'S PUBLISHING

Aladdin
Atheneum

Simon & Schuster Books for Young Readers
Beach Lane Books
Little Simon
Margaret K. McElderry
Paula Wiseman Books
Saga Press
Salaam Reads
Simon Pulse
Simon Spotlight

SIMON & SCHUSTER AUDIO PUBLISHING

Pimsleur
Simon & Schuster Audio

SIMON & SCHUSTER INTERNATIONAL

Simon & Schuster Australia
Simon & Schuster Canada
Simon & Schuster UK

GLOSSARY

ADVANCE. Payment by a publisher to an author prior to the publication of a book, to be deducted from the author's future royalties.

ADVENTURE STORY. A genre of fiction in which action is the key element, overshadowing characters, theme, and setting. The conflict in an adventure story is often man against nature. A secondary plot that reinforces this kind of conflict is sometimes included.

ALL RIGHTS. The rights contracted to a publisher permitting a manuscript's use anywhere and in any form, including movie and book club sales, without additional payment to the writer.

AMATEUR SLEUTH. The character in a mystery, usually the protagonist, who does the detection but is not a professional private investigator or police detective.

ANTHOLOGY. A collection of selected writings by various authors.

ASSOCIATION OF AUTHORS' REPRESENTATIVES (AAR). An organization for literary agents committed to maintaining excellence in literary representation.

AUCTION. Publishers sometimes bid against each other for the acquisition of a manuscript that has excellent sales prospects.

BACKLIST. A publisher's books not published during the current season but still in print.

BIOGRAPHICAL NOVEL. A life story documented in history and transformed into fiction through the insight and imagination of the writer. This type of novel melds the elements of biographical research and historical truth into the framework of a novel, complete with dialogue, drama, and mood. A biographical novel resembles historical fiction, save for one aspect: Characters in a historical novel may be fabricated and then placed into an authentic setting; characters in a biographical novel have actually lived.

BOOK PRODUCER/PACKAGER. An organization that may develop a book for a publisher based upon the publisher's idea or may plan all elements of a book, from its initial concept to writing and marketing strategies, and then sell the package to a book publisher and/or movie producer.

CLIFFHANGER. Fictional event in which the reader is left in suspense at the end of a chapter or episode, so that interest in the story's outcome will be sustained.

CLIP. Sample, usually from a newspaper or magazine, of a writer's published work.

CLOAK-AND-DAGGER. A melodramatic, romantic type of fiction dealing with espionage and intrigue.

COMMERCIAL. Publishers whose concern is salability, profit, and success with a large readership.

CONTEMPORARY. Material dealing with popular current trends, themes, or topics.

CONTRIBUTOR'S COPY. Copy of an issue of a magazine or published book sent to an author whose work is included.

CO-PUBLISHING. An arrangement in which the author and publisher share costs and profits.

COPYEDITING. Editing a manuscript for writing style, grammar, punctuation and factual accuracy.

COPYRIGHT. The legal right to exclusive publication, sale, or distribution of a literary work.

COVER LETTER. A brief letter sent with a complete manuscript submitted to an editor.

"COZY" (OR "TEACUP") MYSTERY. Mystery usually set in a small British town, in a bygone era, featuring a somewhat genteel, intellectual protagonist.

ELECTRONIC RIGHTS. The right to publish material electronically, either in book or short story form.

ELECTRONIC SUBMISSION. A submission of material by e-mail or on computer disk.

ETHNIC FICTION. Stories whose central characters are black, Native American, Italian-American, Jewish, Appalachian, or members of some other specific cultural group.

EXPERIMENTAL FICTION. Fiction that is innovative in subject matter and style; avant-garde, non-formulaic, usually literary material.

EXPOSITION. The portion of the story line, usually the beginning, where background information about character and setting is related.

E-ZINE. A magazine that is published electronically.

FAIR USE. A provision in the copyright law that says short passages from copyrighted material may be used without infringing on the owner's rights.

FANTASY (TRADITIONAL). Fantasy with an emphasis on magic, using characters with the ability to practice magic, such as wizards, witches, dragons, elves, and unicorns.

FANZINE. A noncommercial, small-circulation magazine usually dealing with fantasy, horror or science-fiction literature and art.

FIRST NORTH AMERICAN SERIAL RIGHTS. The right to publish material in a periodical before it appears in book form, for the first time, in the United States or Canada.

FLASH FICTION. *See* short short stories.

GALLEY PROOF. The first typeset version of a manuscript that has not yet been divided into pages.

GENRE. A formulaic type of fiction such as romance, western, or horror.

GOTHIC. This type of category fiction dates back to the late eighteenth and early nineteenth centuries. Contemporary gothic novels are characterized by atmospheric, historical settings and feature young, beautiful women who win the favor of handsome, brooding heroes—simultaneously dealing successfully with some life-threatening menace, either natural or supernatural. Gothics rely on mystery, peril, romantic relationships, and a sense of foreboding for their strong, emotional effect on the reader. A classic early gothic novel is Emily Brontë's *Wuthering Heights*.

GRAPHIC NOVEL. A book (original or adapted) that takes the form of a long comic strip or heavily illustrated story of forty pages or more, produced in paperback. Though called a novel, these can also be works of nonfiction.

HARD-BOILED DETECTIVE NOVEL. Mystery novel featuring a private eye or police detective as the protagonist; usually involves a murder. The emphasis is on the details of the crime, and the tough, unsentimental protagonist usually takes a matter-of-fact attitude toward violence.

HARD SCIENCE FICTION. Science fiction with an emphasis on science and technology.

HIGH FANTASY. Fantasy with a medieval setting and a heavy emphasis on chivalry and the quest.

HISTORICAL FICTION. A fictional story set in a recognizable period of history. As well as telling the stories of ordinary people's lives, historical fiction may involve political or social events of the time.

HORROR. Howard Phillips (H.P.) Lovecraft, generally acknowledged to be the master of the horror tale in the twentieth century and the most important American writer of this genre since Edgar Allan Poe, distinguishes horror literature from fiction based entirely on physical fear and the merely gruesome. It is that atmosphere—the creation of a particular sensation or emotional level—that, according to Lovecraft, is the most important element in the creation of horror literature. Contemporary writers enjoying considerable success in horror fiction include Stephen King, Robert Bloch, Peter Straub, and Dean Koontz.

HYPERTEXT FICTION. A fictional form, read electronically, which incorporates traditional elements of storytelling with a nonlinear plot line, in which the reader determines the direction of the story by opting for one of many author-supplied links.

IMPRINT. Name applied to a publisher's specific line (e.g., Owl, an imprint of Henry Holt).

INTERACTIVE FICTION. Fiction in book or computer-software format where the reader determines the path the story will take by choosing from several alternatives at the end of each chapter or episode.

INTERNATIONAL REPLY COUPON (IRC). A form purchased at a post office and enclosed with a letter or manuscript to an international publisher, to cover return postage costs.

JUVENILES, WRITING FOR. This includes works intended for an audience usually between the ages of two and eighteen. Categories of children's books are usually divided in this way: (1) picture books and storybooks (ages two to eight); (2) young readers or easy-to-read books (ages five to eight); (3) middle readers or middle grade (ages nine to eleven); (4) young adult books (ages twelve and up).

LIBEL. Written or printed words that defame, malign, or damagingly misrepresent a living person.

LITERARY AGENT. A person who acts for an author in finding a publisher or arranging contract terms on a literary project.

LITERARY FICTION. The general category of fiction that employs more sophisticated technique, driven as much or more by character evolution than action in the plot.

MAINSTREAM FICTION. Fiction that appeals to a more general reading audience, versus literary or genre fiction. Mainstream is more plot-driven than literary fiction and less formulaic than genre fiction.

MALICE DOMESTIC NOVEL. A mystery featuring a murder among family members, such as the murder of a spouse or a parent.

MANUSCRIPT. The author's unpublished copy of a work, usually typewritten, used as the basis for typesetting.

MASS MARKET PAPERBACK. Softcover book on a popular subject, usually around 4" × 7", directed to a general audience and sold in drugstores and groceries as well as in bookstores.

MIDDLE READER. Also called *middle grade.* Juvenile fiction for readers aged nine to eleven.

MS(S). Abbreviation for *manuscript(s).*

MULTIPLE SUBMISSION. Submission of more than one short story at a time to the same editor. Do not make a multiple submission unless requested.

MYSTERY. A form of narration in which one or more elements remain unknown or unexplained until the end of the story. The modern mystery story contains elements of the mainstream novel: a convincing account of a character's struggle with various physical and psychological obstacles in an effort to achieve his goal, good characterization, and sound motivation.

NARRATION. The account of events in a story's plot as related by the speaker or the voice of the author.

NARRATOR. The person who tells the story, either someone involved in the action or the voice of the writer.

NEW AGE. A term including categories such as astrology, psychic phenomena, spiritual healing, UFOs, mysticism, and other aspects of the occult.

NOIR. A style of mystery involving hard-boiled detectives and bleak settings.

NOM DE PLUME. French for "pen name"; a pseudonym.

NONFICTION NOVEL. A work in which real events and people are written [about] in novel form, but are not camouflaged, as they are in the roman à clef. In the nonfiction novel, reality is presented imaginatively; the writer imposes a novelistic structure on the actual events, keying sections of narrative around moments that are seen (in retrospect) as symbolic. In this way, he creates a coherence that the actual story might not have had. *The Executioner's Song,* by Norman Mailer, and *In Cold Blood,* by Truman Capote, are notable examples of the nonfiction novel.

NOVELLA (ALSO NOVELETTE). A short novel or long story, approximately 20,000–50,000 words.

#10 ENVELOPE. 4" × 9½" envelope, used for queries and other business letters.

OFFPRINT. Copy of a story taken from a magazine before it is bound.

ONETIME RIGHTS. Permission to publish a story in periodical or book form one time only.

OUTLINE. A summary of a book's contents, often in the form of chapter headings with a few sentences outlining the action of the story under each one; sometimes part of a book proposal.

OVER THE TRANSOM. A phrase referring to unsolicited manuscripts, or those that come in "over the transom."

PAYMENT ON ACCEPTANCE. Payment from the magazine or publishing house as soon as the decision to print a manuscript is made.

PAYMENT ON PUBLICATION. Payment from the publisher after a manuscript is printed.

PEN NAME. A pseudonym used to conceal a writer's real name.

PERIODICAL. A magazine or journal published at regular intervals.

PLOT. The carefully devised series of events through which the characters progress in a work of fiction.

POPULAR FICTION. Generally, a synonym for category or genre fiction; i.e., fiction intended to appeal to audiences for certain kinds of novels. Popular, or category, fiction is defined as such primarily for the convenience of publishers, editors, reviewers, and booksellers who must identify novels of different areas of interest for potential readers.

PRINT ON DEMAND (POD). Novels produced digitally one at a time, as ordered. Self-publishing through print on demand technology typically involves some fees for the author. Some authors use POD to create a manuscript in book form to send to prospective traditional publishers.

PROOFREADING. Close reading and correction of a manuscript's typographical errors.

PROOFS. A typeset version of a manuscript used for correcting errors and making changes, often a photocopy of the galleys.

PROPOSAL. An offer to write a specific work, usually consisting of an outline of the work and one or two completed chapters.

PROTAGONIST. The principal or leading character in a literary work.

PSYCHOLOGICAL NOVEL. A narrative that emphasizes the mental and emotional aspects of its characters, focusing on motivations and mental activities rather than on exterior events. The psychological novelist is less concerned about relating what happened than about exploring why it happened. The term is most often used to describe twentieth-century works that employ techniques such as interior monologue and stream of consciousness. Two examples of contemporary psychological novels are Judith Guest's *Ordinary People* and Mary Gordon's *The Company of Women*.

PUBLIC DOMAIN. Material that either was never copyrighted or whose copyright term has expired.

PULP MAGAZINE. A periodical printed on inexpensive paper, usually containing lurid, sensational stories or articles.

QUERY. A letter written to an editor to elicit interest in a story the writer wants to submit.

READER. A person hired by a publisher to read unsolicited manuscripts.

READING FEE. An arbitrary amount of money charged by some agents and publishers to read a submitted manuscript.

REGENCY ROMANCE. A subgenre of romance, usually set in England between 1811 and 1820.

REMAINDERS. Leftover copies of an out-of-print book, sold by the publisher at a reduced price.

REPORTING TIME. The number of weeks or months it takes an editor to report back on an author's query or manuscript.

REPRINT RIGHTS. Permission to print an already published work whose rights have been sold to another magazine or book publisher.

ROMAN À CLEF. French "novel with a key." A novel that represents actual living or historical characters and events in fictionalized form.

ROMANCE NOVEL. A type of category fiction in which the love relationship between a man and a woman pervades the plot. The story is often told from the viewpoint of the heroine, who meets a man (the hero), falls in love with him, encounters a conflict that hinders their relationship, then resolves the conflict. Romance is the overriding element in this kind of story: The couple's relationship determines the plot and tone of the book.

ROYALTIES. A percentage of the retail price paid to an author for each copy of the book that is sold.

SAE. Self-addressed envelope.

SASE. Self-addressed stamped envelope.

SCIENCE FICTION (VS. FANTASY). It is generally accepted that, to be science fiction, a story must have elements of science in either the conflict or setting (usually both). Fantasy, on the other hand, rarely utilizes science, relying instead on magic, mythological and neomythological beings, and devices and outright invention for conflict and setting.

SECOND SERIAL (REPRINT) RIGHTS. Permission for the reprinting of a work in another periodical after its first publication in book or magazine form.

SELF-PUBLISHING. In this arrangement, the author keeps all income derived from the book, but he pays for its manufacturing, production, and marketing.

SERIAL RIGHTS. The rights given by an author to a publisher to print a piece in one or more periodicals.

SERIALIZED NOVEL. A book-length work of fiction published in sequential issues of a periodical.

SETTING. The environment and time period during which the action of a story takes place.

SHORT SHORT STORY. A condensed piece of fiction, usually under 1,000 words.

SIMULTANEOUS SUBMISSION. The practice of sending copies of the same manuscript to several editors or publishers at the same time. Some editors refuse to consider such submissions.

SLANT. A story's particular approach or style, designed to appeal to the readers of a specific magazine.

SLICE OF LIFE. A presentation of characters in a seemingly mundane situation that offers the reader a flash of illumination about the characters or their situation.

SLUSH PILE. A stack of unsolicited manuscripts in the editorial offices of a publisher.

SOCIAL FICTION. Fiction written with the purpose of bringing positive changes in society.

SOFT/SOCIOLOGICAL SCIENCE FICTION. Science fiction with an emphasis on society and culture versus scientific accuracy.

SPACE OPERA. Epic science fiction with an emphasis on good guys versus bad guys.

SPECULATION (OR SPEC). An editor's agreement to look at an author's manuscript with no promise to purchase.

SPECULATIVE FICTION (SPECFIC). The all-inclusive term for science fiction, fantasy, and horror.

SUBSIDIARY. An incorporated branch of a company or conglomerate (e.g., Alfred Knopf, Inc., a subsidiary of Random House, Inc.).

SUBSIDIARY RIGHTS. All rights other than book publishing rights included in a book contract, such as paperback, book club, and movie rights.

SUBSIDY PUBLISHER. A book publisher who charges the author for the cost of typesetting, printing, and promoting a book. Also called a *vanity publisher*.

SUBTERFICIAL FICTION. Innovative, challenging, nonconventional fiction in which what seems to be happening is the result of things not so easily perceived.

SUSPENSE. A genre of fiction where the plot's primary function is to build a feeling of anticipation and fear in the reader over its possible outcome.

SYNOPSIS. A brief summary of a story, novel or play. As part of a book proposal, it is a comprehensive summary condensed in a page or page and a half.

TABLOID. Publication printed on paper about half the size of a regular newspaper page (e.g., the *National Enquirer*).

TEARSHEET. Page from a magazine containing a published story.

THEME. The dominant or central idea in a literary work; its message, moral, or main thread.

THRILLER. A novel intended to arouse feelings of excitement or suspense. Works in this genre are highly sensational, usually focusing on illegal activities, international espionage, sex, and violence. A thriller is often a detective story in which the forces of good are pitted against the forces of evil in a kill-or-be-killed situation.

TRADE PAPERBACK. A softbound volume, usually around 5" × 8", published and designed for the general public, available mainly in bookstores.

UNSOLICITED MANUSCRIPT. A story or novel manuscript that an editor did not specifically ask to see.

URBAN FANTASY. Fantasy that takes magical characters, such as elves, fairies, vampires, or wizards, and places them in modern-day settings, often in the inner city.

VANITY PUBLISHER. See subsidy publisher.

VIEWPOINT. The position or attitude of the first- or third-person narrator or multiple narrators, which determines how a story's action is seen and evaluated.

WESTERN. Genre with a setting in the West, usually between 1860 and 1890, with a formula plot about cowboys or other aspects of frontier life.

WHODUNIT. Genre dealing with murder, suspense, and the detection of criminals.

WORK-FOR-HIRE. Work that another party commissions you to do, generally for a flat fee. The creator does not own the copyright and therefore cannot sell any rights.

YOUNG ADULT (YA). The general classification of books written for readers twelve and up.

ZINE. A small, noncommercial magazine, often one- or two-person operations run from the home of the publisher/editor. Themes tend to be specialized, personal, experimental, and often controversial.

GENRE GLOSSARY

Definitions of Fiction Subcategories

The following were provided courtesy of The Extended Novel Writing Workshop, created by the staff of Writers Online Workshops (www.writersonlineworkshops.com).

MYSTERY SUBCATEGORIES

The major mystery subcategories are listed below, each followed by a brief description and the names of representative authors, so you can sample each type of work. Note that we have loosely classified "suspense/thriller" as a mystery category. While these stories do not necessarily follow a traditional "whodunit" plot pattern, they share many elements with other mystery categories.

AMATEUR DETECTIVE. As the name implies, the detective is not a professional detective (private or otherwise), but is almost always a professional something. This professional association routinely involves the protagonist in criminal cases (in a support capacity), gives him or her a special advantage in a specific case, or provides the contacts and skills necessary to solve a particular crime. (Jonathan Kellerman, Patricia Cornwell, Jan Burke)

CLASSIC MYSTERY (WHODUNIT). A crime (almost always a murder) is solved. The detective is the viewpoint character; the reader never knows any more or less about the crime than the detective, and all the clues to solving the crime are available to the reader.

COURTROOM DRAMA. The action takes place primarily in the courtroom; protagonist is generally a defense attorney out to prove the innocence of his or her client by finding the real culprit.

COZY. A special class of the amateur detective category that frequently features a female protagonist. (Agatha Christie's Miss Marple stories are the classic example.) There is less onstage violence than in other categories, and the plot is often wrapped up in a final scene where the detective identifies the murderer and explains how the crime was solved. In contemporary stories, the protagonist can be anyone from a chronically curious housewife to a mystery-buff clergyman to a college professor, but he or she is usually quirky, even eccentric. (Susan Isaacs, Andrew Greeley, Lillian Jackson Braun)

ESPIONAGE. The international spy novel is less popular since the end of the Cold War, but stories can still revolve around political intrigue in unstable regions. (John le Carré, Ken Follett)

HEISTS AND CAPERS. The crime itself is the focus. Its planning and execution are seen in detail, and the participants are fully drawn characters that may even be portrayed sympathetically. One character is the obvious leader of the group (the "brains"); the other members are often brought together by the leader specifically for this job and may or may not have a previous association. In a heist, no matter how clever or daring the characters are, they are still portrayed as criminals, and the expectation is that they will be caught and punished (but not always). A caper is more lighthearted, even comedic. The participants may have a noble goal (something other than personal gain) and often get away with the crime. (Eric Ambler, Tony Kenrick, Leslie Hollander)

HISTORICAL. May be any category or subcategory of mystery, but with an emphasis on setting, the details of which must be diligently researched. But beyond the historical details (which must never overshadow the story), the plot develops along the lines of its contemporary counterpart. (Candace Robb, Caleb Carr, Anne Perry)

JUVENILE/YOUNG ADULT. Written for the 8–12 age group (middle grade) or the 12 and up age group (young adult), the crime in these stories may or may not be murder, but it is serious. The protagonist is a kid (or group of kids) in the same age range as the targeted reader. There is no graphic violence depicted, but the stories are scary and the villains are realistic. (Mary Downing Hahn, Wendy Corsi Staub, Cameron Dokey, Norma Fox Mazer)

MEDICAL THRILLER. The plot can involve a legitimate medical threat (such as the outbreak of a virulent plague) or the illegal or immoral use of medical technology. In the former scenario, the protagonist is likely to be the doctor (or team) who identifies the virus and procures the antidote; in the latter he or she could be a patient (or the relative of a victim) who uncovers the plot and brings down the villain. (Robin Cook, Michael Palmer, Michael Crichton, Stanley Pottinger)

POLICE PROCEDURALS. The most realistic category, these stories require the most meticulous research. A police procedural may have more than one protagonist since cops rarely work alone. Conflict between partners, or between the detective and his or her superiors, is a common theme. But cops are portrayed positively as a group, even though there may be a couple of bad or ineffective law enforcement characters for contrast and conflict. Jurisdictional disputes are still popular sources of conflict as well. (Lawrence Treat, Joseph Wambaugh, Ridley Pearson, Julie Smith)

PRIVATE DETECTIVE. When described as "hard-boiled," this category takes a tough stance. Violence is more prominent, characters are darker, the detective—while almost always licensed by the state—operates on the fringes of the law, and there is often open resentment between the detective and law enforcement. More "enlightened" male detectives and a crop of contemporary females have brought about new trends in this category. (For female P.I.s: Sue Grafton, Sara Paretsky; for male P.I.s: John D. MacDonald, Lawrence Sanders)

SUSPENSE/THRILLER. Where a classic mystery is always a whodunit, a suspense/thriller novel may deal more with the intricacies of the crime, what motivated it, and how the villain (whose identity may be revealed to the reader early on) is caught and brought to justice. Novels in this category frequently employ multiple points of view and have broader scopes than more traditional murder mysteries. The crime may not even involve murder—it may be a threat to global economy or regional ecology; it may be technology run amok or abused at the hands of an unscrupulous scientist; it may involve innocent citizens victimized for personal or corporate gain. Its perpetrators are kidnappers, stalkers, serial killers, rapists, pedophiles, computer hackers, or just about anyone with an evil intention and the means to carry it out. The protagonist may be a private detective or law enforcement official, but is just as likely to be a doctor, lawyer, military officer, or other individual in a unique position to identify the villain and bring him or her to justice. (James Patterson, John J. Nance)

TECHNO-THRILLER. These are replacing the traditional espionage novel and feature technology as an integral part of not just the setting but the plot as well.

WOMAN IN JEOPARDY. A murder or other crime may be committed, but the focus is on the woman (and/or her children) currently at risk, her struggle to understand the nature of the danger, and her eventual victory over her tormentor. The protagonist makes up for her lack of physical prowess with intellect or special skills and solves the problem on her own or with the help of her family (but she runs the show). Closely related to this category is romantic suspense. But, while the heroine in a romantic suspense is certainly a "woman in jeopardy,"' the mystery or suspense element is subordinate to the romance. (Mary Higgins Clark, Mary Stewart, Jessica Mann)

ROMANCE SUBCATEGORIES

These categories and subcategories of romance fiction have been culled from the *Romance Writer's Sourcebook* (Writer's Digest Books) and Phyllis Taylor Pianka's *How to Write Romances* (Writer's Digest Books). We've arranged the "major" categories below, with the subcategories beneath them, each followed by a brief description and the names of authors who write in each category, so you can sample representative works.

CATEGORY OR SERIES. These are published in "lines" by individual publishing houses (such as Harlequin); each line has its own requirements as to word length, story content, and amount of sex. (Debbie Macomber, Nora Roberts, Glenda Sanders)

CHRISTIAN. With an inspirational Christian message centering on the spiritual dynamic of the romantic relationship and faith in God as the foundation for that relationship; sensuality is played down. (Janelle Burnham, Ann Bell, Linda Chaikin, Catherine Palmer, Dee Henderson, Lisa Tawn Bergen)

GLITZ. So called because they feature generally wealthy characters with high-powered positions in careers that are considered glamorous—high finance, modeling/acting, publishing, fashion—and are set in exciting or exotic (often metropolitan) locales, such as Monte Carlo, Hollywood, London, or New York. (Jackie Collins, Judith Krantz)

HISTORICAL. Can cover just about any historical (or even prehistorical) period. Setting in the historical is especially significant, and details must be thoroughly researched and accurately presented. For a sampling of a variety of historical styles, try Laura Kinsell (*Flowers from the Storm*), Mary Jo Putney (*The Rake and the Reformer*), and Judy Cuevas (*Bliss*). Some currently popular periods/themes in historicals are:

- **GOTHIC:** Historical with a strong element of suspense and a feeling of supernatural events, although these events frequently have a natural explanation. Setting plays an important role in establishing a dark, moody, suspenseful atmosphere. (Phyllis Whitney, Victoria Holt)
- **HISTORICAL FANTASY:** With traditional fantasy elements of magic and magical beings, frequently set in a medieval society. (Amanda Glass, Jayne Ann Krentz, Kathleen Morgan, Jessica Bryan, Taylor Quinn Evans, Carla Simpson, Karyn Monk)
- **EARLY AMERICAN:** Usually Revolution to Civil War, set in New England or the South, but "frontier" stories set in the American West are quite popular as well. (Robin Lee Hatcher, Ann Maxwell, Heather Graham)

- **NATIVE AMERICAN:** Where one or both of the characters are Native Americans; the conflict between cultures is a popular theme. (Carol Finch, Elizabeth Grayson, Karen Kay, Kathleen Harrington, Genell Dellim, Candace McCarthy)
- **REGENCY:** Set in England during the Regency period from 1811 to 1820. (Carol Finch, Elizabeth Elliott, Georgette Heyer, Joan Johnston, Lynn Collum)

MULTICULTURAL. Most currently feature African-American or Hispanic couples, but editors are looking for other ethnic stories as well. Multiculturals can be contemporary or historical and fall into any subcategory. (Rochelle Alers, Monica Jackson, Bette Ford, Sandra Kitt, Brenda Jackson)

PARANORMAL. Containing elements of the supernatural or science fiction/fantasy. There are numerous subcategories (many stories combine elements of more than one) including:

- **TIME TRAVEL:** One or more of the characters travels to another time—usually the past—to find love. (Jude Deveraux, Linda Lael Miller, Diana Gabaldon, Constance O'Day-Flannery)
- **SCIENCE FICTION/FUTURISTIC:** S/F elements are used for the story's setting: imaginary worlds, parallel universes, Earth in the near or distant future. (Marilyn Campbell, Jayne Ann Krentz, J.D. Robb [Nora Roberts], Anne Avery)
- **CONTEMPORARY FANTASY:** From modern ghost and vampire stories to "New Age" themes such as extraterrestrials and reincarnation. (Linda Lael Miller, Anne Stuart, Antoinette Stockenberg, Christine Feehan)

ROMANTIC COMEDY. Has a fairly strong comic premise and/or a comic perspective in the author's voice or the voices of the characters (especially the heroine). (Jennifer Crusie, Susan Elizabeth Phillips)

ROMANTIC SUSPENSE. With a mystery or psychological thriller subplot in addition to the romance plot. (Mary Stewart, Barbara Michaels, Tami Hoag, Nora Roberts, Linda Howard, Catherine Coulter)

SINGLE TITLE. Longer contemporaries that do not necessarily conform to the requirements of a specific romance line and therefore feature more complex plots and nontraditional characters. (Mary Ruth Myers, Nora Roberts, Kathleen Gilles Seidel, Kathleen Korbel)

YOUNG ADULT (YA). Focus is on first love with very little, if any, sex. These can have bittersweet endings, as opposed to the traditional romance happy ending, since first loves are often lost loves. (YA historical: Nancy Covert Smith, Louise Vernon; YA contemporary: Kathryn Makris)

SCIENCE FICTION SUBCATEGORIES

Peter Heck, in his article "Doors to Other Worlds: Trends in Science Fiction and Fantasy," which appears in the 1996 edition of *Science Fiction and Fantasy Writer's Sourcebook* (Writer's Digest Books), identifies some science fiction trends that have distinct enough characteristics to be defined as categories. These distinctions are frequently the result of marketing decisions as much as literary ones, so understanding them is important in deciding where your novel idea belongs. We've supplied a brief description and the names of authors who write in each category. In those instances where the author writes in more than one category, we've included titles of appropriate representative works.

ALTERNATE HISTORY. Fantasy, sometimes with science fiction elements, that changes the accepted account of actual historical events or people to suggest an alternate view of history. (Ted Mooney, *Traffic and Laughter*; Ward Moore, *Bring the Jubilee*; Philip K. Dick, *The Man in the High Castle*)

CYBERPUNK. Characters in these stories are tough outsiders in a high-tech, generally near-future society where computers have produced major changes in the way society functions. (William Gibson, Bruce Sterling, Pat Cadigan, Wilhelmina Baird)

HARD SCIENCE FICTION. Based on the logical extrapolation of real science to the future. In these stories the scientific background (setting) may be as, or more, important than the characters. (Larry Niven)

MILITARY SCIENCE FICTION. Stories about war that feature traditional military organization and tactics extrapolated into the future. (Jerry Pournelle, David Drake, Elizabeth Moon)

NEW AGE. A category of speculative fiction that deals with subjects such as astrology, psychic phenomena, spiritual healing, UFOs, mysticism, and other aspects of the occult. (Walter Mosley, *Blue Light*; Neil Gaiman)

SCIENCE FANTASY. Blend of traditional fantasy elements with scientific or pseudoscientific support (genetic engineering, for example, to "explain" a traditional fantasy creature like the dragon). These stories are traditionally more character driven than hard science fiction. (Anne McCaffrey, Mercedes Lackey, Marion Zimmer Bradley)

SCIENCE FICTION MYSTERY. A cross-genre blending that can either be a more-or-less traditional science fiction story with a mystery as a key plot element, or a more-or-less traditional whodunit with science fiction elements. (Philip K. Dick, Lynn S. Hightower)

SCIENCE FICTION ROMANCE. Another genre blend that may be a romance with science fiction elements (in which case it is more accurately placed as a subcategory within the romance genre) or a science fiction story with a strong romantic subplot. (Anne McCaffrey, Melanie Rawn, Kate Elliott)

SOCIAL SCIENCE FICTION. The focus is on how the characters react to their environments. This category includes social satire. (George Orwell's *1984* is a classic example.) (Margaret Atwood, *The Handmaid's Tale*; Ursula K. Le Guin, *The Left Hand of Darkness*; Marge Piercy, *Woman on the Edge of Time*)

SPACE OPERA. From the term "horse opera," describing a traditional good-guys-versus-bad-guys western, these stories put the emphasis on sweeping action and larger-than-life characters. The focus on action makes these stories especially appealing for film treatment. (The Star Wars series is one of the best examples; also Samuel R. Delany.)

STEAMPUNK. A specific type of alternate-history science fiction set in Victorian England in which characters have access to 20th-century technology. (William Gibson; Bruce Sterling, *The Difference Engine*)

YOUNG ADULT. Any subcategory of science fiction geared to a YA audience (12–18), but these are usually shorter novels with characters in the central roles who are the same age as (or slightly older than) the targeted reader. (Jane Yolen, Andre Norton)

FANTASY SUBCATEGORIES

Before we take a look at the individual fantasy categories, it should be noted that, for purposes of these supplements, we've treated fantasy as a genre distinct from science fiction. While these two are closely related, there are significant enough differences to warrant their separation for study purposes. We have included here those science fiction categories that have strong fantasy elements, or that have a significant amount of crossover (these categories appear in both the science fiction and the fantasy supplements), but "pure" science fiction categories are not included below. If you're not sure whether your novel is fantasy or science fiction, consider this definition by Orson Scott Card in *How to Write Science Fiction and Fantasy* (Writer's Digest Books): "Here's a good, simple, semi-accurate rule of thumb: If the story is set in a universe that follows the same rules as ours, it's science fiction. If it's set in a universe that doesn't follow our rules, it's fantasy. Or in other words, science fiction is about what could be but isn't; fantasy is about what couldn't be."

But even Card admits this rule is only "semi-accurate." He goes on to say that the real boundary between science fiction and fantasy is defined by how the impossible is achieved: "If you have people do some magic, impossible thing [like time travel] by stroking a talisman or praying to a tree, it's fantasy; if they do the same thing by pressing a button or climbing inside a machine, it's science fiction."

Peter Heck, in his article "Doors to Other Worlds: Trends in Science Fiction and Fantasy," which appears in the 1996 edition of the *Science Fiction and Fantasy Writer's Sourcebook* (Writer's Digest Books), does note some trends that have distinct enough characteristics to be defined as separate categories. These categories are frequently the result of marketing decisions as much as literary ones, so understanding them is important in deciding where your novel idea belongs. We've supplied a brief description and the names of authors who write in each category, so you can sample representative works.

ARTHURIAN. Reworking of the legend of King Arthur and the Knights of the Round Table. (T.H. White, *The Once and Future King*; Marion Zimmer Bradley, *The Mists of Avalon*)

CONTEMPORARY (ALSO CALLED "URBAN") FANTASY. Traditional fantasy elements (such as elves and magic) are incorporated into an otherwise recognizable modern setting. (Emma Bull, *War for the Oaks*; Mercedes Lackey, *The SERRAted Edge*; Terry Brooks, the Word & Void series)

DARK FANTASY. Closely related to horror but generally not as graphic. Characters in these stories are the "darker" fantasy types: vampires, witches, werewolves, demons, etc. (Anne Rice; Clive Barker, *Weaveworld*, *Imajica*; Fred Chappell)

FANTASTIC ALTERNATE HISTORY. Set in an alternate historical period (in which magic would not have been a common belief) where magic works, these stories frequently feature actual historical figures. (Orson Scott Card, *Alvin Maker*)

GAME-RELATED FANTASY. Plots and characters are similar to high fantasy, but are based on a particular role-playing game. (Dungeons and Dragons; Magic: The Gathering; World of Warcraft)

HEROIC FANTASY. The fantasy equivalent to military science fiction, these are stories of war and its heroes and heroines. (Robert E. Howard, the Conan the Barbarian series; Elizabeth Moon, *Deed of Paksenarrion*; Michael Moorcock, the Elric series)

HIGH FANTASY. Emphasis is on the fate of an entire race or nation, threatened by an ultimate evil. J.R.R. Tolkien's Lord of the Rings trilogy is a classic example. (Terry Brooks, David Eddings, Margaret Weis, Tracy Hickman)

HISTORICAL FANTASY. The setting can be almost any era in which the belief in magic was strong; these are essentially historical novels where magic is a key element of the plot and/or setting. (Susan Schwartz, *Silk Roads and Shadows*; Margaret Ball, *No Earthly Sunne*; Tim Powers, *The Anubis Gates*)

JUVENILE/YOUNG ADULT. Can be any type of fantasy, but geared to a juvenile (8–12) or YA audience (12–18); these are shorter novels with younger characters in central roles. (J.K. Rowling, Christopher Paolini, C.S. Lewis)

SCIENCE FANTASY. A blend of traditional fantasy elements with scientific or pseudoscientific support (genetic engineering, for example, to "explain" a traditional fantasy creature like the dragon). These stories are traditionally more character driven than hard science fiction. (Anne McCaffrey, Mercedes Lackey, Marion Zimmer Bradley)

HORROR SUBCATEGORIES

Subcategories in horror are less well defined than in other genres and are frequently the result of marketing decisions as much as literary ones. But being familiar with the terms used to describe different horror styles can be important in understanding how your own novel might be best presented to an agent or editor. What follows is a brief description of the most commonly used terms, along with names of authors and, where necessary, representative works.

DARK FANTASY. Sometimes used as a euphemistic term for horror in general, but also refers to a specific type of fantasy, usually less graphic than other horror subcategories, that features more "traditional" supernatural or mythical beings (vampires, werewolves, zombies, etc.) in either contemporary or historical settings. (Contemporary: Stephen King, *Salem's Lot*; Thomas Tessier, *The Nightwalker.* Historical: Brian Stableford, *The Empire of Fear* and *Werewolves of London*)

HAUNTINGS. "Classic" stories of ghosts, poltergeists, and spiritual possessions. The level of violence portrayed varies, but many writers in this category exploit the reader's natural fear of the unknown by hinting at the horror and letting the reader's imagination supply the details. (Peter Straub, *Ghost Story*; Richard Matheson, *Hell House*)

JUVENILE/YOUNG ADULT. Can be any horror style, but with a protagonist who is the same age as, or slightly older than, the targeted reader. Stories for middle grades (8–12 years old) are scary, with monsters and violent acts that might best be described as "gross," but stories for young adults (12–18) may be more graphic. (R.L. Stine, Christopher Pike, Carol Gorman)

PSYCHOLOGICAL HORROR. Features a human monster with horrific, but not necessarily supernatural, aspects. (Thomas Harris, *The Silence of the Lambs, Hannibal*; Dean Koontz, *Whispers*)

SPLATTERPUNK. Very graphic depiction of violence—often gratuitous—popularized in the 1980s, especially in film. (*Friday the 13th, Halloween, Nightmare on Elm Street*, etc.)

SUPERNATURAL/OCCULT. Similar to the dark fantasy, but may be more graphic in its depiction of violence. Stories feature satanic worship, demonic possession, or ultimate evil incarnate in an entity or supernatural being that may or may not have its roots in traditional mythology or folklore. (Ramsey Campbell; Robert McCammon; Ira Levin, *Rosemary's Baby*; William Peter Blatty, *The Exorcist*; Stephen King, *Pet Sematary*)

TECHNOLOGICAL HORROR. "Monsters" in these stories are the result of science run amok or technology turned to purposes of evil. (Dean Koontz, *Watchers*; Michael Crichton, *Jurassic Park*)

PROFESSIONAL ORGANIZATIONS

AGENTS' ORGANIZATIONS

ASSOCIATION OF AUTHORS' AGENTS (AAA) Curtis Brown, Haymarket House, 28-29 Haymarket, London SW1Y 4SP. (020)7393-4420. E-mail: wiseoffice@curtisbrown.co.uk. Website: www.agentsassoc.co.uk.

ASSOCIATION OF AUTHORS' REPRESENTATIVES (AAR) 302A West 12th Street, #122, New York, NY 10014. E-mail: administrator@aaronline.org. Website: aaronline.org.

ASSOCIATION OF TALENT AGENTS (ATA) 9255 Sunset Blvd., Suite 930, Los Angeles, CA 90069. (310)274-0628. Fax: (310)274-5063. E-mail: rnoval@agentassociation.com. Website: www.agentassociation.com.

WRITERS' ORGANIZATIONS

ACADEMY OF AMERICAN POETS 75 Maiden Lane, Suite 901, New York, NY 10038. (212)274-0343. Fax: (212)274-9427. E-mail: academy@poets.org. Website: www.poets.org.

AMERICAN CRIME WRITERS LEAGUE (ACWL) E-mail: info@acwl.org. Website: www.acwl.org.

AMERICAN MEDICAL WRITERS ASSOCIATION (AMWA) 30 West Gude Drive, Suite 525, Rockville, MD 20850-4347. (240)238-0940. Fax: (301)294-9006. E-mail: amwa@amwa.org. Website: www.amwa.org.

AMERICAN SCREENWRITERS ASSOCIATION (ASA) E-mail: info@americanscreenwriters.com. Website: www.americanscreenwriters.com.

AMERICAN TRANSLATORS ASSOCIATION (ATA) 225 Reinekers Lane, Suite 590, Alexandria, VA 22314. (703)683-6100. Fax: (703)683-6122. E-mail: ata@atanet.org. Website: www.atanet.org.

EDUCATION WRITERS ASSOCIATION (EWA) 3516 Connecticut Avenue NW, Washington, DC 20008. (202)452-9830. Website: www.ewa.org.

THE ASSOCIATION OF GARDEN COMMUNICATORS (GWA) 355 Lexington Avenue, 15th Floor, New York, NY 10017. (212)297-2198. Fax: (212)297-2149. E-mail: info@gardenwriters.org. Website: www.gardenwriters.org.

HORROR WRITERS ASSOCIATION (HWA) P.O. Box 56687, Sherman Oaks, CA 91413. (818)220-3965. E-mail: hwa@horror.org. Website: www.horror.org.

THE INTERNATIONAL WOMEN'S WRITING GUILD (IWWG) 274 Madison Avenue, Suite 1202, New York, NY 10016. (917)720-6959. E-mail: iwwgquestions@gmail.com Website: iwwg.wildapricot.com.

MYSTERY WRITERS OF AMERICA (MWA) 1140 Broadway, Suite 1507, New York, NY 10001. (212)888-8171. Fax: (212)888-8107. Website: www.mysterywriters.org.

NATIONAL ASSOCIATION OF SCIENCE WRITERS (NASW) P.O. Box 7905, Berkeley, CA 94707. (510)647-9500. E-mail: editor@nasw.org. Website: www.nasw.org.

ORGANIZATION OF BLACK SCREENWRITERS (OBS) 3010 Wilshire Boulevard, #269, Los Angeles, CA 90010. (323)735-2050. Website: www.obswriter.com.

OUTDOOR WRITERS ASSOCIATION OF AMERICA (OWAA) 615 Oak Street, Suite 201, Missoula, MT 59801. (406)728-7434. E-mail: info@owaa.org. Website: www.owaa.org.

POETRY SOCIETY OF AMERICA (PSA) 15 Gramercy Park, New York, NY 10003. (212)254-9628. Website: www.poetrysociety.org.

POETS & WRITERS 90 Broad St., Suite 2100, New York, NY 10004. (212)226-3586. Fax: (212)226-3963. Website: www.pw.org.

ROMANCE WRITERS OF AMERICA (RWA) 14615 Benfer Road, Houston, TX 77069. (832)717-5200. E-mail: info@rwa.org. Website: www.rwa.org.

SCIENCE FICTION AND FANTASY WRITERS OF AMERICA (SFWA) P.O. Box 3238, Enfield, CT 06083-3238. Website: www.sfwa.org.

SOCIETY OF AMERICAN BUSINESS EDITORS AND WRITERS (SABEW) Walter Cronkite School of Journalism and Mass Communication, Arizona State University, 555 North Central Avenue, Suite 406E, Phoenix, AZ 85004-1248 (602)496-7862. Fax: (602)496-7041. E-mail: sabew@sabew.org. Website: www.sabew.org.

SOCIETY OF AMERICAN TRAVEL WRITERS (SATW) 1 Parkview Plaza, Suite 800, Oakbrook Terrace, IL 60181. (312)420-6846. E-mail: info@satw.org. Website: www.satw.org.

SOCIETY OF CHILDREN'S BOOK WRITERS & ILLUSTRATORS (SCBWI) 4727 Wilshire Boulevard, Suite 301, Los Angeles, CA 10010. (323)782-1010. E-mail: scbwi@scbwi.org. Website: www.scbwi.org.

WESTERN WRITERS OF AMERICA (WWA) E-mail: wwa.moulton@gmail.com. Website: www.westernwriters.org.

INDUSTRY ORGANIZATIONS

AMERICAN BOOKSELLERS ASSOCIATION (ABA) 333 Westchester Avenue, Suite S202, White Plains, NY 10604. (914)406-7500. Fax: (914)417-4013. E-mail: info@bookweb.org. Website: www.bookweb.org.

AMERICAN SOCIETY OF JOURNALISTS & AUTHORS (ASJA) 355 Lexington Avenue, 15th Floor, New York, NY 10017-6603. (212)997-0947. Website: www.asja.org.

ASSOCIATION FOR WOMEN IN COMMUNICATIONS (AWC) 1717 East Republic Road, Suite A, Springfield, MO 65804. (417)886-8606. Fax: (417)886-3685. E-mail: info@womcom.org. Website: www.womcom.org.

ASSOCIATION OF AMERICAN PUBLISHERS (AAP) 71 Fifth Avenue, Second Floor, New York NY 10003. (212)255-0200. Fax: (212)255-7007. Or: 455 Massachusetts Avenue NW, Suite 700, Washington, DC 20001. (202)347-3375. Fax: (202)347-3690. Website: publishers.org.

ASSOCIATION OF WRITERS & WRITING PROGRAMS (AWP) George Mason University, 4400 University Drive, MSN 1E3, Fairfax, VA 22030. (703)993-4301. Fax: (703)993-4302. E-mail: awp@awpwriter.org. Website: www.awpwriter.org.

THE AUTHORS GUILD, INC. 31 East 32nd Street, Seventh Floor, New York, NY 10016. (212)563-5904. Fax: (212)564-5363. E-mail: staff@authorsguild.org. Website: www.authorsguild.org.

CANADIAN AUTHORS ASSOCIATION (CAA) 6 West Street North, Suite 203, Orilla, ON L3V 5B8 Canada. (705)325-3926. E-mail: admin@canadianauthors.org. Website: www.canadianauthors.org.

CHRISTIAN BOOKSELLERS ASSOCIATION (CBA) 1365 Garden of the Gods Road, Suite 105, Colorado Springs, CO 80907. (800)252-1950. Fax: (719)272-3510. E-mail: info@cbaonline.org. Website: cbaonline.org.

THE DRAMATISTS GUILD OF AMERICA 1501 Broadway, Suite 701, New York, NY 10036. (212)398-9366. Fax: (212)944-0420. Website: www.dramatistsguild.com.

NATIONAL LEAGUE OF AMERICAN PEN WOMEN (NLAPW) Pen Arts Building, 1300 17th St. NW, Washington DC 20036-1973. (202)785-1997. Fax: (202)452-6868. E-mail: contact@nlapw.org. Website: www.nlapw.org.

NATIONAL WRITERS ASSOCIATION (NWA) 10940 South Parker Road, #508, Parker, CO 80134. (303)841-0246. E-mail: natlwritersassn@hotmail.com. Website: www.nationalwriters.com

NATIONAL WRITERS UNION (NWU) 256 West 38th Street, Suite 703, New York, NY 10018. (212)254-0279. Fax: (212)254-0673. E-mail: nwu@nwu.org. Website: www.nwu.org.

PEN AMERICAN CENTER 588 Broadway, New York, NY 10012. (212)334-1660. E-mail: info@pen.org. Website: www.pen.org.

THE PLAYWRIGHTS GUILD OF CANADA (PGC) 401 Richmond Street West, Suite 350, Toronto, ON M5V 3A8 Canada. (416)703-0201. Fax: (416)703-0059. E-mail: info@playwrightsguild.ca. Website: www.playwrightsguild.ca.

VOLUNTEER LAWYERS FOR THE ARTS (VLA) 1 East 53rd Street, New York, NY 10022. (212)319-2787, ext.1. E-mail: vlany@vlany.org. Website: www.vlany.org.

WOMEN IN FILM (WIF) 6100 Wilshire Boulevard, Suite 710, Los Angeles, CA 90048. (323)935-2211. Fax: (323)935-2212. E-mail: info@wif.org. Website: www.wif.org.

WOMEN'S NATIONAL BOOK ASSOCIATION (WNBA) P.O. Box 237, FDR Station, New York NY 10150. (212)208-4629. Fax: (212)208-4629. E-mail: info@wnba-books.org. Website: www.wnba-books.org.

WRITERS GUILD OF ALBERTA (WGA) Main Floor, Percy Page Centre, 11759 Groat Road NW, Edmonton AB T5M 3K6 Canada. (780)422-8174. Fax: (780)422-2663 (Attn: Writer's Guild of Alberta). E-mail: mail@writersguild.ca. Website: writersguild.ab.ca.

WRITERS GUILD OF AMERICA, EAST (WGA) 250 Hudson Street, Suite 700, New York, NY 10013. (212)767-7800. Fax: (212)582-1909. E-mail: gbynoe@wgaeast.org. Website: www.wgaeast.org.

WRITERS GUILD OF AMERICA, WEST (WGA) 7000 West Third Street, Los Angeles, CA 90048. (323)951-4000. Fax: (323)782-4800. Website: www.wga.org.

WRITERS UNION OF CANADA (TWUC) 600-460 Richmond Street West, Toronto, ON MSV 1Y1 Canada. (416)703-8982. Fax: (416)504-9090. E-mail: info@writersunion.ca. Website: www.writersunion.ca.

LITERARY AGENTS SPECIALTIES INDEX

ACTION

ADVENTURE

COMIC BOOKS

COMMERCIAL

CONTEMPORARY ISSUES

CRIME

DETECTIVE

EROTICA

ETHNIC

EXPERIMENTAL

FAMILY SAGA

FANTASY

FEMINIST

FRONTIER

GAY

GLITZ

HISTORICAL

HORROR

HUMOR

INSPIRATIONAL

JUVENILE

LESBIAN

LITERARY

MAINSTREAM

MIDDLE-GRADE

MILITARY

MYSTERY

NEW ADULT

NEW AGE

OCCULT

PARANORMAL

PICTURE BOOKS

POLICE

PSYCHIC

REGIONAL

RELIGIOUS

ROMANCE

SATIRE

SCIENCE FICTION

SHORT STORY COLLECTIONS

SPIRITUAL

SPORTS

SUPERNATURAL

SUSPENSE

THRILLER

TRANSLATION

URBAN FANTASY

WAR

WESTERNS

WOMEN'S

YOUNG ADULT

CATEGORY INDEX

BOOK PUBLISHERS

ADVENTURE

CHILDREN'S/JUVENILE

COMICS/GRAPHIC NOVELS

EROTICA

ETHNIC/MULTICULTURAL

EXPERIMENTAL

FANTASY

FEMINIST

GAY

HISTORICAL

HORROR

HUMOR/SATIRE

LESBIAN

LITERARY

MAINSTREAM

MILITARY/WAR

MYSTERY/SUSPENSE

NEW AGE

REGIONAL

RELIGIOUS

ROMANCE

SCIENCE FICTION

SHORT STORY COLLECTIONS

THRILLER/ESPIONAGE

TRANSLATIONS

WESTERN

YOUNG ADULT/TEEN

MAGAZINES

ADVENTURE

CHILDREN'S/JUVENILE

COMICS/GRAPHIC NOVELS

EROTICA

ETHNIC/MULTICULTURAL

EXPERIMENTAL

FANTASY

FEMINIST

GAY

HISTORICAL

HORROR

HUMOR/SATIRE

LESBIAN

LITERARY

MAINSTREAM

MILITARY/WAR

MYSTERY/SUSPENSE

NEW AGE

PSYCHIC/SUPERNATURAL

REGIONAL

RELIGIOUS

SCIENCE FICTION

THRILLER/ESPIONAGE

TRANSLATIONS

WESTERN

YOUNG ADULT/TEEN

GENERAL INDEX

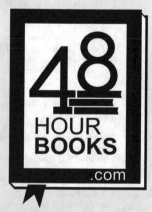